Slaybr / 2013

THE MERGER DELUSION

The Merger Delusion

How Swallowing Its Suburbs Made
an Even Bigger Mess of Montreal

PETER F. TRENT

McGill-Queen's University Press
Montreal & Kingston • London • Ithaca

ISBN 978-0-7735-3932-7

Legal deposit first quarter 2012
Bibliothèque nationale du Québec

Printed in Canada on acid-free paper that is 100% ancient forest free
(100% post-consumer recycled), processed chlorine free

McGill-Queen's University Press acknowledges the support of the
Canada Council for the Arts for our publishing program. We also
acknowledge the financial support of the Government of Canada
through the Canada Book Fund for our publishing activities.

Library and Archives Canada Cataloguing in Publication
Trent, Peter (Peter F.)

   The merger delusion : how swallowing its suburbs made an even
bigger mess of Montreal / Peter F. Trent.

Includes bibliographical references and index.
ISBN 978-0-7735-3932-7

   1. Annexation (Municipal government) – Québec (Province) –
Montréal. 2. Montréal (Québec) – Politics and government. I. Title.

JS1761.3.A6A56 2012 320.8'590971428 C2011-905202-4

Typeset by Jay Tee Graphics Ltd. in 10.5/13 Sabon

For Kathryn

Contents

Preface

When future historians reflect on the history of Montreal in the twenty-first century, they will very likely conclude that the most damaging assault suffered by the metropolis was at the hands of the Parti Québécois government, which, at the turn of the century, threw itself, eyes closed, into the forced mergers of Quebec cities. Just as the metropolis was gradually becoming a major city that was both cosmopolitan and tolerant, this governmental intrusion, unwanted by Montrealers, constituted a fifty-year step backward to the era when Boulevard Saint-Laurent was the border between the anglophone and francophone communities. This action furthermore resulted in shaky management and a financial cost much higher than anticipated.

It is that story that Peter Trent, mayor of Westmount, relates here – blow by blow – with an abundance of information, a vividness in the description of numerous events (and people), and a frenetic flow of polemics, questions, and arguments – all of it coated with a particular sense of humour to which, I suspect, only anglophones know the secret.

What are the fundamental reasons for this lamentable failure? In a nutshell: the essence of a culture cannot be reduced to the expression of a distinct language. As shown by the tensions felt in the rare Western cities formed by two or more cultures – such as Prague and Trieste in the late nineteenth century, or Brussels and Barcelona today – complex urban agglomerations, ever in precarious balance, cannot be blindly treated as cities with a homogenous culture.

Thus, this book reveals the cultural traits particular, respectively, to francophones and anglophones that changed the course of this tragedy. In the case of francophones, a quest for grandeur, inherited from a monarchic mother nation and exacerbated by their minority status, leads them too often to adhere to concepts without properly weighing the implications. Mayor Drapeau was a prime example, notably when he declared that the 1976 Olympics could no more have a deficit than a man could have a baby. Yet the Olympic Stadium itself is still in the process of becoming the most expensive stadium in human history! One Island One City ... such was Mayor Drapeau's dream, which Mayor Bourque reignited without fully recognizing the potential for its nasty consequences.

The municipal mergers decreed by Ontario Premier Mike Harris became a source of inspiration for the politicians sitting in Quebec City, supported in this regard by most editorialists from the francophone press. As for the Parti Québécois, in addition to seeing in the "One Island One City" concept a strategy for fiscal equity, it seized the opportunity – finally! – to "contain" that Babylon of anglophones and ethnic groups, dreaming that the big city would naturally emerge speaking French, as the law would now apply uniformly to everyone.

And yet this project of forced mergers on the Island of Montreal was criticized by most of the province's academics and researchers. Could it be possible, as thought Duplessis in his day, that these intellectuals were all wrong at the same time? Without presuming that they have a monopoly on lucid thinking, it might behoove us to recognize that, having access to studies and experiences ranging beyond the narrow confines of local issues, they might have fewer blinders.

The culture of Quebecers with Anglo-Saxon roots also cannot be reduced to a distinct language. It, too, possesses characteristic traits: pragmatism, respect of rights, and a strong feeling of belonging to one's local community are only a few examples. How could Quebec politicians wish to rip the Island of Montreal's anglophones from their local communities? What kind of worldview, dogmatism, or ignorance could have led them to that goal?

The result was a memorable fight between David and Goliath: in this instance, David being personified by the mettlesome Mayor Peter Trent, determined to have his group's culture be respected. By dint of various studies, cases brought before the Superior Court, and an unshakeable determination, Westmount and most of Montreal's anglophone communities eventually regained their autonomy. But in the process, did the metropolis not lose its innocence?

Jean-Claude Marsan

Foreword

Peter Trent's book is certainly timely, as the events he describes remain upsetting for many people living in the metropolitan regions of Quebec, especially in Montreal and Quebec City.

The cities on the Island of Montreal did not want to be absorbed. They were forced into that position by the PQ government. Montreal Mayor Gérald Tremblay endorsed the government actions. Amalgamation was done for purely political reasons, among which was to curry the favour of the municipal unions, notably those of the City of Montreal.

Quebec's unions demonstrated their power, and the government not only flinched but gave in, at a huge cost to the citizens of its two largest cities. The unions established even bigger labour monopolies, to the long-term detriment of Quebec's productivity and competitiveness. One person in four employed in Quebec now works for one government or another and receives $100 per week more in pay than the average non-labour union member in the province, plus far better fringe benefits and pensions. The government has created a dangerous situation by allowing union power to increase beyond even the excessive level existing before amalgamation.

The Liberals went into the provincial 2003 election with a promise to allow the former municipalities to vote to de-amalgamate. However, once returned to power, the Liberals by no means re-established the status quo ante for those former cities that mustered enough votes to get out. As well as making the conditions of leaving amalgamation extremely tough – far tougher than in any normal election or referendum – the Liberals forced those municipalities that left to shoulder a heavy burden of debt and revenue. Westmount, for example, went into amalgamation with a debt one-quarter the amount it was stuck with when it voted to leave.

The argument that amalgamation would reduce costs turned out to be absolutely wrong. Instead it raised costs and taxes, especially for the suburban entities. And Quebec was already one of the highest taxed jurisdictions in Canada and North America.

Peter Trent led the opposition in Montreal against the betrayal of democracy that was forced mergers. When Westmount demerged from Montreal, it did it with 92 per cent voting in favour of doing so. Again, Peter Trent was the spark plug.

His book describes in detail how all this happened. It is a courageous book by a man who has never lacked courage in fighting for fairness and honest government. He demonstrated these qualities as mayor of Westmount from 1991 to 2001, and his return by acclamation in 2009 underlines Westmount's admiration.

Stephen A. Jarislowsky

Acknowledgments

I give deep thanks to my sisters Ruth and Josie; to Philip Cercone of McGill-Queen's University Press, who gave his indefectible support to, and enthusiasm for, the project; to Marc Collin, who translated the work into French with great élan; to Maureen Garvie, who edited the manuscript so deftly; to Richard Gervais, for all his counsel; to Stephen Jarislowsky, my favourite curmudgeon and an unwavering straight-shooter; to Lawrence Poitras, who vetted chapter 16; to Anne Renaud, my dedicated executive assistant; to Bruce St. Louis, my former city manager whose loyalty gave me courage; to Andrew Sancton, who did much more than review someone who was not his peer; and to Denis Vaugeois of Les éditions du Septentrion, whose professionalism and passion ensured a remarkable French edition of this work. I also thank Henry Aubin, Claude Bédard, Geneviève Beullac, Peter Blaikie, Caroline Breslaw, Jacques Chagnon, François Des Rosiers, Joseph Doré, Peter Duffield, Dennis Dwyer, Jean Fortier, Julia Gersovitz, André Gervais, Jonathan Goldbloom, Julius Grey, Nicholas Hoare, Philip Johnston, David Laidley, Roger D. Landry, Marc Laperrière, Dominique Leduc, Pierre Lortie, Cynthia Lulham, Karin Marks, Jean-Claude Marsan, Jane Martin, Andrew Molson, Reed Scowen, Laureen Sweeney, and Christine Tindall. I also owe thanks to some who will never see this book: Sally Aitkin, Phillip Aspinall, May Cutler, Douglass McDougall, Stuart Robertson, Don Wedge, and James Wright. And, lastly, I cannot describe how much I am indebted to my wife, Kathryn Stephenson, without whom there would be neither book nor happiness in my life.

Dramatis Personae

Jacques Parizeau (PQ)	Premier of Quebec, September 1994–January 1996
Lucien Bouchard (PQ)	Premier of Quebec, January 1996–March 2001
Bernard Landry (PQ)	Premier of Quebec, March 2001–April 2003
Jean Charest (L)	Premier of Quebec, as of April 2003
Claude Ryan (L)	Minister of Municipal Affairs, 1990–94
Guy Chevrette (PQ)	Minister of Municipal Affairs, 1994–96
Rémy Trudel (PQ)	Minister of Municipal Affairs, 1996–98
Louise Harel (PQ)	Minister of Municipal Affairs and the Métropole, 1999–2002
André Boisclair (PQ)	Minister of Municipal Affairs and the Métropole, 2002–03
Jean-Marc Fournier (L)	Minister of Municipal Affairs, 2003–05
Nathalie Normandeau (L)	Minister of Municipal Affairs, 2005–09
Laurent Lessard (L)	Minister of Municipal Affairs, 2009–
Serge Ménard (PQ)	Minister of the Métropole, 1996–97
Robert Perreault (PQ)	Minister of the Métropole, 1997–98
Jean Doré	Mayor of Montreal, 1986–94
Pierre Bourque	Mayor of Montreal, 1994–2001
Gérald Tremblay	Mayor of Montreal, 2002–

Vera Danyluk   Chair of the Executive Committee,
                           Montreal Urban Community,
                           1994–2001

Georges Bossé   Mayor of Verdun, 1993–2001; presi-
                           dent of the Union of Montreal Island
                           Suburban Municipalities, 1998–2001

Yves Ryan   Mayor of Montreal North, 1963–2001

Peter Trent   Mayor of Westmount, 1991–2001,
                           2009– ; president of the Union
                           of Montreal Island Suburban
                           Municipalities,* 1994–98

Frank Zampino   Mayor of Saint-Leonard, 1990–2001,
                           chair of Executive Committee, City of
                           Montreal, 2002–08

* Formerly the Conference of Montreal Suburban Mayors

Peter Trent is elected by acclamation as mayor of Westmount for the first time, with outgoing Mayor May Cutler's evident support, a support that continued unabated throughout the merger and demerger years. (*Montreal Gazette*, October 1991. Photo credit: Allen McInnis)

December 2000. Peter Trent addresses 70,000 Montreal suburbanites rallying against forced mergers. (Courtesy of the author)

December 2000. News conference after the mega-rally. From the left: Peter Trent, Georges Bossé, and Marc Vaillancourt. (Courtesy of the author)

70,000 suburbanites voice their anger. (*Montreal Gazette*, 11 December 2000. Photo credit: John Mahoney)

Judgment day. Peter Trent at a news conference directly following the Superior Court loss on Thursday, 28 June 2001. (*Globe and Mail*, May 2004. Photo credit: Ryan Remiorz)

Last-ditch plea to Bouchard. Quebec Premier Lucien Bouchard, centre, and municipal affairs minister Louise Harel, left, meet with the coalition of mayors against the merger legislation. The mayors in the back from left to right: Peter Trent (Westmount); Ralph Mercier (Charlesbourg); Andrée Boucher (Sainte-Foy); and Jacques Langlois (Beauport). Not shown: Luis Miranda (Anjou) and Guy Boissy (Saint-Lambert). (*La Presse*, December 2000. Photo credit: Jacques Boissinot/Canadian Press)

Debate with Vera Danyluk, Peter Trent, and Pierre Bourque. (*Montreal Gazette*, September 1999. Photo credit: John Mahoney)

The work of the Montreal Transition Committee, whose job it was to put into effect the legislated merger of all the Montreal Island Cities, did not meet with universal approval – or cooperation. (*Westmount Examiner*, 17 May 2001. Cartoon credit: Ferg Gadzala)

Louise Harel and Louis Bernard. (*La Presse*, 3 March 2000. Photo credit: Michel Gravel)

Jean-Marc Fournier and Montreal Mayor Gérald Tremblay. (*La Presse*, 29 April 2003. Photo credit: Pierre McCann)

The majesty of the law. The legal battle to stop Bill 170. From the right: Lawyers Guy Bertrand, Gérald Tremblay, Jean Marois, and Jacques Richard. (*Le Devoir*, 20 February 2001. Photo credit: Jacques Nadeau)

Peter Trent in front of Westmount City Hall. (*La Presse*, 17 June 2003. Photo credit: Robert Mailloux)

Trent is very uncomfortable with lawyer Guy Bertand's histrionics in court. (*La Presse*, 24 May 2001. Cartoon credit: Pascal Elie)

Mayor Pierre Bourque does not quite deliver on his commitment to collect 100,000 legitimate signatures in support of One Island One City. (*Montreal Gazette*, April 2001. Cartoon credit: Aislin)

Westmount celebrates St Jean Baptiste Day for the first time in history. Trent impersonates the first mayor of Westmount, Eustache Prud'homme. (*Le Devoir*, 25 June 1999. Photo credit: Jacques Nadeau)

Gérald Tremblay and Peter Trent, just before their televised debate in English. (*Le Devoir*, 7 June 2004. Photo credit: Jacques Nadeau)

Peter Trent hugs Westmount Councillor Cynthia Lulham with a smiling Karin Marks following a positive Westmount vote for demerger. 23 June 2004. (Photo credit: Martin C. Barry)

Former foes come together in their opposition to the Quebec Transport Department's plan to rehabilitate Montreal highways, a plan that ignored public transit. Left to right: Richard Bergeron (leader, Project Montreal); Louise Harel (leader, Vision Montreal); Gérald Tremblay (mayor of Montreal); Peter Trent (mayor of Westmount). (*Le Devoir*, 23 April 2010. Photo credit: Jacques Nadeau)

INTRODUCTION

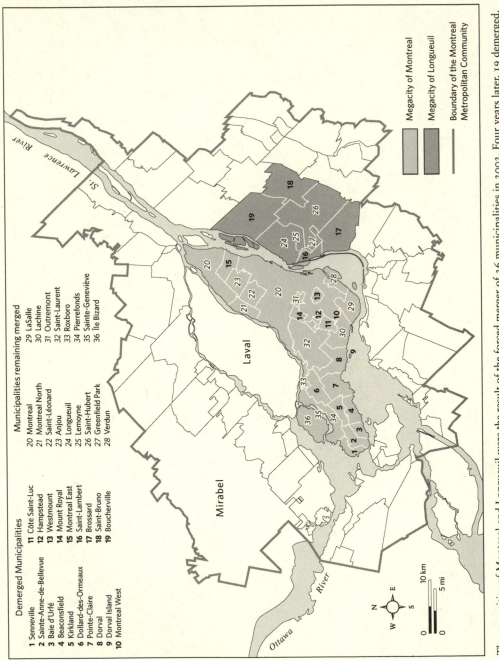

The megacities of Montreal and Longueuil were the result of the forced merger of 36 municipalities in 2002. Four years later, 19 demerged.

Demerged Municipalities

1 Senneville
2 Sainte-Anne-de-Bellevue
3 Baie d'Urfé
4 Beaconsfield
5 Kirkland
6 Dollard-des-Ormeaux
7 Pointe-Claire
8 Dorval
9 Dorval Island
10 Montreal West
11 Côte Saint-Luc
12 Hampstead
13 Westmount
14 Mount Royal
15 Montreal East
16 Saint-Lambert
17 Brossard
18 Saint-Bruno
19 Boucherville

Municipalities remaining merged

20 Montreal
21 Montreal North
22 Saint-Léonard
23 Anjou
24 Longueuil
25 Lemoyne
26 Saint-Hubert
27 Greenfield Park
28 Verdun
29 LaSalle
30 Lachine
31 Outremont
32 Saint-Laurent
33 Roxboro
34 Pierrefonds
35 Sainte-Geneviève
36 Île Bizard

Megacity of Montreal

Megacity of Longueuil

Boundary of the Montreal
Metropolitan Community

1

Synopsis: The Cult of Giantism

Rien n'est plus fermement cru que nous n'en sachions le moins. (Nothing is so firmly believed as that which we least know.)

Michel de Montaigne, 1580

It is unfortunate, considering that enthusiasm moves the world, that so few enthusiasts can be trusted to speak the truth.

Arthur James Balfour, 1891

Politicians' logic: We must do something. This is something. Therefore we must do it.

Yes, Prime Minister, BBC, 1987

On 20 December 2000 at 2:15 AM, inside the Second Empire majesty of the National Assembly in Quebec City, a law was adopted that put Quebec's municipalities through a cataclysm of change, the worst such upheaval in their 150 years of existence. This is the story of what happened before and after that law was rammed through against the public's will. My chronicle is part history, part opinion, and part memoir.

Biographer Lytton Strachey described how the historian "will row out over that great ocean of material, and lower down into it, here and there, a little bucket, which will bring up to the light of day some characteristic specimen, from those far depths, to be examined with a careful curiosity." Some may find both my bucket and body of water rather small. But a microscope can expose a world as engrossing as that uncovered by a telescope. And, indeed, this book is not just about the City of Westmount, my Camelot lost and mostly regained. Nor is it just about the formation, the reformation, and the counter-reformation of the City of Montreal. Nor is it just about Quebec, an enchanted world so full of contradictions and quirks that even Jonathan Swift could not have dreamed it up. My story is also about how politics is played, how governments impose decisions, and how bad ideas take root.

That fateful December morning, the Quebec National Assembly imposed municipal mergers* throughout the province, mergers that were to come into effect a year later. Then, 1 January 2006, some of those same mergers were rather messily undone. For five years, successive provincial governments made 212 municipalities dance the merger and de-merger gavotte.[1] When the music stopped, only thirty of them had regained their freedom.[2]

Three people were responsible for this wholesale obliteration of municipalities: Pierre Bourque, Louise Harel, and Lucien Bouchard. In my least charitable thoughts, I think that the mayor of Montreal in the 1990s, the otherworldly Pierre Bourque, was caught up in his own sense of grandeur in trying to deliver what his idol, Mayor Jean Drapeau, had failed to create in the 1960s: one city covering the whole Island of Montreal. In that same sour frame of mind I think that Louise Harel, the provincial minister responsible for putting through the forced mergers and, notably, One Island One City, wanted to do something monumental, all the while settling old grievances against the "privileged" suburban cities. Lucien Bouchard, the saturnine provincial premier, was fed up with the carping of truculent and fractious municipalities and just wanted them to go away. That his political party, the Parti Québécois (PQ) had no electoral mandate to do so, and that his government had never formally consulted the population, did not seem to bother him.

ANNEX, EH?

In my most charitable mood, I think all three were caught up in a bizarrely Canadian zeitgeist that caused politicians to think that imposing megacities or forcibly merging towns was fair and efficient and would help put their province on the world map. In the latter half of the 1990s, the governments of Nova Scotia, Ontario, and then Quebec embraced mass municipal mergers as a panacea for

---

* Outside Quebec, municipal mergers are usually referred to as amalgamations. However, the *de jure* merger of Montreal in 2002 was, de facto, an annexation. Merger or amalgamation suggests voluntary joining. Annexation suggests forcible incorporation, instigated by the larger unit.

their urban ills. Lemming logic prevailed. Ten years and ten billion wasted dollars later, they should all feel a little silly.[3]

There was no such similar movement in the United States, where the last municipal merger as Canadians know them took place one hundred years before. And that one was voluntary. The United States did, however, while Eastern Canada was busily merging municipalities, undergo a kind of merger mania in the private sector. Corporate mergers from 1998 to 2001 have been estimated to have destroyed some $134 billion of shareholder wealth.[4] The ill-defined vogue words "synergy" and "critical mass" were on everyone's lips ten years ago, eagerly pressed into service as amalgamationist cant, whether to sell dodgy corporate mergers in New York or unneeded municipal mergers in Ontario and Quebec.

Quebecers were repeatedly told that municipal mergers were a worldwide trend, and we had to climb on board or miss the bus. Yet even in Europe the postwar merger binge was over by the mid-1970s, and it had only affected some countries. France, Greece, and Italy did not touch their municipalities.[5] The keenest European amalgamationist – Britain – had, on average, created cities that were five times as large as those in Sweden, its nearest competitor in the consolidation stakes. Perhaps not coincidentally, Britain today experiences the lowest local election turnout of any country in Europe – by a long chalk.[6]

MASS DELUSION OR THE BANDWAGON EFFECT

This is also a book about mass delusion, a delusion that affected not just the Canadian political class but also the public at large. I wanted to subtitle this book *Extraordinary Popular Delusions and the Madness of Crowds*, but that title had been taken long ago for one of my favourite books, written in 1841 by Charles Mackay. In his foreword to the 1932 edition, Bernard Baruch quoted an unnamed contemporary: "Have you ever seen, in some wood, on a sunny quiet day, a cloud of flying midges – thousands of them – hovering, apparently motionless, in a sunbeam? ... Yes? ... Did you ever see the whole flight – each mite apparently preserving its distance from all others – suddenly move, say three feet, to one side or the other? Well, *what made them do that?* A breeze? I said a *quiet* day. But try to recall – did you ever see them move directly back again in the same unison? Well, what made them do *that?* Great human mass movements are slower of inception but much more effective."[7] Mackay's book goes on to describe how philosophical fads and fascinations cause humans to change course suddenly and together, just like those midges.

Fashion fads have run the gamut from codpieces to baseball caps; political fads are driven by the same thirst for change. Government is a millpond of repetitive actions, easily disturbed by eddies and currents from any passing vogue. And in a world where people have readily believed, without a shred of evidence, in feng shui, astrology, herbal remedies, and Nortel stock at $120, it is not surprising that the popular belief that bigger cities cost less to run could have taken hold. Belief lodges in one's brain with so much less effort and examination than anything entering through the process of rational thinking. And, closer to home, it was easy to believe that the Montreal Island suburbs were living off the City of Montreal. It didn't help that the spokesperson for the suburbs was Peter Trent, the mayor of Westmount, a place that's the certified symbol of anglophone money in Quebec.

TORONTO AND MONTREAL: A TALE OF TWO MEGACITIES

Far from being the result of many years' analysis, both the Toronto and the Montreal megacities came as bolts from the blue. The respective provincial governments had no electoral mandate for them. No report had recommended either megacity. Both in Ontario and in Quebec, it was the lack of metropolitan governance that had long been the focus of concern, overshadowing any velleities of having the central city accrete its suburbs.[8] Most arguments hurriedly wheeled out in support of the megacities had the distinct odour of *ex post facto* rationalizations. Toronto and Montreal were frog-marched down the path to megapolitan status by their provincial governments, who were chivvied on by their respective media and Boards of Trade. The one major difference is that, in the case of Toronto the central city was against the merger, whereas in Montreal the central city mayor was actually the instigator of the whole idea.

We were caught up in a merger maelstrom whose virtues were considered self-evident.

That two ideologically antipodal governments could arrive at the same municipal merger policy is, on the face of it, surprising.[9] But the Progressive Conservatives in Ontario under Mike Harris, whom few accused of being overly intellectually sophisticated, saw mergers as a way to *reduce* government. As Professor Andrew Sancton has cleverly put it, "That there should be confusion between *less* government and *fewer* governments is a shameful commentary on our political, if not our general, literacy."[10] The far more statist PQ government in Quebec suffered from no such confusion. It generally saw government as a good thing, and bigger municipal government was, ipso facto, better; a big state government was imposing big local governments. For Harris, the creation of mega-Toronto was strictly an exercise in efficiency, not one of societal tub-thumping, fiscal equity, or social engineering.

The PQ, a left-leaning political party created to take Quebec out of Canada, a party justifiably proud of Quebec's cultural and political creativity, found it necessary to import holus-bolus the makeshift merger program of a right-wing federalist Ontario party for another reason: to maintain status in a long-standing intercity rivalry.

FISCAL EQUITY: THE MAIN REASON TO MERGE

The supreme irony of the Montreal merger had to do with the loudest rallying cry of those in favour of mergers: "fiscal equity," a state of affairs imperatively sought after for the Island of Montreal.[11] "Fiscal equity" was shorthand for "everybody should pay the same property tax rate." It was unfair, went the argument, that the City of Montreal had a much higher tax rate than all its Island neighbours. I discovered while doing my research for this book that before the merger Montreal incorrectly reported its tax rate; in actuality, its residential rate for years was barely 13 per cent above those of the suburbs. This is why, once the megacity of Montreal had been created through merger, the tax rate for residents of the former City of Montreal scarcely dipped. Those who "benefited" from a more uniform tax rate were the former Island suburbs. And they didn't want the merger in the first place.

So, the merger brought more uniform tax rates.[12] What about tax bills? Before the megacity, each municipality on the Island of Montreal paid for pooled *regional* costs (police, mass transit) in proportion to their real-estate wealth. Once merged, *local* costs (recreation, streets) too were now pooled. Because the former City of Montreal was not a "poor" municipality, thanks to its huge commercial sector, this meant that the "richer" former suburbs would eventually wind up subsidizing the local costs of the "poorer" former suburbs. Montreal's tax burden did not really change. All this came as no surprise – to some. Well before the megacity was imposed, both the City of Montreal and the provincial government had worked it out that Montreal would get no tax relief by merging. Since the main justification for the merger was to "help" Montreal by getting the Island suburbs to contribute taxes, one is forced to conclude the entire exercise was a colossal waste of time and money. In fact, it was a fraud.

Aside from rampant urban sprawl, what needed fixing in Quebec's municipal world was not boundaries or tax rates but the arcane, decrepit, and capricious municipal tax system itself, which, along with years of editorials and politicians' polemics, had convinced just about everybody that the Island suburbs were insouciantly sponging off the City of Montreal, when in fact that was just not true, as we will see in detail in chapter 9. The off-Island suburbs were, however, sponging off the whole Island of Montreal for regional services.

This municipal tax system, based on a rough and rare guesstimate of a property's value, created far more fiscal inequities among taxpayers than any variation in tax rates did among municipalities. But not a whisper was heard about reforming *that*. And was it not inconsistent (to be generous) for the PQ to be so worked up about supposed property tax unfairness that they turned the whole municipal world upside down and put it back together in lumps, while the gross unfairness, universally acknowledged, that municipal employees earned 30 per cent more than their provincial counterparts did not bestir them to do anything?[13] "It was a municipal problem," we were told – we, who were almost as naked and powerless in front of the unions as we were in front of the provincial government.

Although most of us fighting the mergers had a massive emotional stake in our cause, it would be a mistake to think our political opponents were motivated, as were the civil servants, by purely administrative considerations. In the PQ government's campaign for province-wide mergers, there was a crusading element of social justice. For Premier Bouchard, personally, mergers had a strong resonance: fiscal equity was anything but a dry economic concept for him. Bouchard, in common with us all, was emotionally driven by things experienced while growing up. He grew up in the Saguenay municipality of Jonquière, next door to two fiscally spoilt company towns,

Arvida,[14] founded by the Aluminium Company of Canada in 1926, and Kénogami, founded by the paper company Price Brothers Limited in 1912, carved out of a piece of Jonquière. Said Bouchard, "I was raised in Jonquière, in a working-class area. There were just cabins there because everybody worked in Arvida or Kénogami ... The bosses had nice houses with flowerbeds watered by the city. They didn't pay taxes because they were the only ones who benefited from the property taxes paid by the factory."[15] Bouchard continued, "Jonquière had the smells, the hydrocarbons. We had none of the advantages. Jonquière was the poor town."[16] Jonquière (and Bouchard, no doubt) had the last laugh, though, when it annexed both Arvida and Kénogami in 1976. Mind you, it in turn disappeared, folded into the new megacity of Saguenay by Bouchard's own merger law. In this manner, then, ancient but keenly felt resentments have now been dealt with, buried under successive layers of municipality.

Bouchard, a complex man, and fundamentally a democrat, fretted about the forced nature of the mergers, at one time admitting to his local paper that "a forced marriage never works."

ELIMINATED CITIES, NOT PROBLEMS

In addition to fiscal equity, three lesser reasons were given for mergers in the Montreal Metropolitan Region: to contain urban sprawl, to achieve economies of scale, and to reduce political "fragmentation." The Montreal megacity has failed on all three counts. First, urban sprawl: we were told that mergers would help "solidify" the Island of Montreal and act as a brake on the flight to the exurbs. It has turned out that most of the region's population growth has taken place in the very off-Island suburbs that were generally spared mergers because of their political clout.[17] The population of the Island of Montreal did not really budge from 2003 to 2008; in fact, the net loss to off-Island suburbs fractionally grew.[18] As I write this, the population of the metropolitan region outside the Island of Montreal has grown to the point that, for the first time, it is equal to that of the Island itself. Like ink on blotting paper (or gasoline film on a puddle), Montreal's exurbia continues its uncontrolled, centrifugal sprawl.

Secondly, *ab urbe condita*, the megacity increased its spending by three times the rate of inflation: I calculate that the megacity will eventually cost us over $4 billion. No one should be surprised. There was a merger poster child directly to the north of Montreal: per capita, the City of Laval (merged in 1965) cost nearly one-third more to run and amassed twice the debt of its unmerged cousins on the south shore. In fact, the government's own studies before the merger predicted that the cost of running the Montreal megacity would rise by $100 million or $200 million a year for payroll alone.[19] Yet Premier Bouchard was promising *savings* of the same order of magnitude.

As for political fragmentation, there has been no attempt to reduce the welter of government structures that makes regional planning impossible. The province has always taken a sedimentary approach to structures, forever adding, rarely taking away. There are still five administrative regions, fourteen counties, and twenty transport commissions in the Montreal Metropolitan Region. The overarching mistake that Quebec made was in merging municipalities, not government structures. There were and are far more government agencies, boards, commissions, corporations, councils, and counties cluttering up the Montreal Metropolitan Region than cities and towns. The motto of the Quebec government could be "salvation through structures."[20]

Quebec's obsession with the number of municipalities blinded it to the real problems such as this "structuritis," urban sprawl, Montreal's execrable administration, or union muscle. Take pay packets: Montreal police demanded – and got – wage parity with police in Toronto,[21] where the average resident earned 30 per cent more than in Montreal. This was just one of the reasons why employees of the City of Montreal made 40 per cent more than the rest of the Quebec public sector. It was just one of the problems that should have been addressed, but politicians were too lily-livered to take it on. This is nothing new. Rather than dealing with Montreal's congenital mismanagement, indebtedness, and corruption by breaking it up into more manageable cities, Quebec has always done the reverse and rewarded Montreal by encouraging or legislating annexations, whether in 1910, the 1960s, or 2000.

Not known as a megacity sceptic at the time of the mergers, the *La Presse* columnist and legally trained cynic Yves Boisvert had to admit by June 2007 that the megacity was an "enormous fiasco. What was running well runs less well. What was running badly runs just as badly."[22] Even when it came to fiscal equity, he was not sure it was achieved, but it did not need that "shambles" to do it. Salaries were equalized by going upwards, as were the costs. And if services were better, it was a well-kept secret. Certainly, the mayor of Montreal did not seem to have more clout in Quebec. "At least there is one thing that we accomplished," he quoted Louise Harel as saying, "now the cities that did not have subsidized housing pay for those that do have it. I'm proud of that." Harel, or course, neglected to mention that the Montreal Metropolitan Community took over that job. It was not necessary to merge to get it done.

CHICKEN LITTLE COMES TO TOWN

We were repeatedly told, "Something has to be done. Now." This Chicken Little approach to municipal reform had not much to recommend it. Creating a bunch of megacities did not solve anything – it covered up rather than getting rid of problems. Yes, the exurbs around Montreal Island did not pay their share. Yes, there were too many government structures. But the Montreal sky was not falling. It was a manufactured crisis. Most if not all of these problems are still with us, yet no one at this moment is calling for municipal reform. We are all just catching our breath after the municipal "reforms" that were put into effect on January 2002.

The merger-demerger fiasco made some matters even worse. Today, the citizen of the megacity of Montreal is catered to by *six* layers of government, depending on the problem: the borough council, the city council, the agglomeration council, the Montreal Metropolitan Community, the provincial government, or the federal government.[23]

A subset of the "political fragmentation" argument was that we had to merge the suburbs with Montreal because there were simply too many of them. This was begging the question. These cities, a unique heritage of municipal corporations, many of them erected over a hundred years ago, were to be cleared away like so much bric-a-brac in a 1990s update of urban renewal. In Europe and North America, the average "central city" is anywhere from 20 per cent to 30 per cent of the size of its urban region. Montreal, before mergers, had 30 per cent of the population of its region; it was already big. After the merger this proportion grew to 50 per cent.

THE TYRANNY OF THE RURALITY

That the City of Montreal and the Montreal Metropolitan Region are no longer the responsibility of a dedicated department but today fall under the minister of "Municipal Affairs and *the Regions*" says volumes about the way Quebec treats its only urban region of international importance, an area that cranks out 54 per cent of the province's GDP. Municipalities are so much under the foot of Quebec that it even imposes its own system of government on a local scale. Yesterday's eighty member Montreal Urban Community and today's sixty-five member megacity council:[24] these are assemblies modelled after Quebec's National Assembly. But massive parliamentary assemblies don't work as a way to run urban municipalities. Of course, Quebec doesn't know: none of its ministers of municipal affairs has ever run one.[25]

Quebec has always suffered from what I call the tyranny of the rurality. Rural ridings have greater electoral clout than urban ridings. Yet the rural ridings get the money that the economic engine of the province throws off: the old whine about the regions providing the natural resources that are gobbled up by urban manufacturing is pathetically out of date in a services-dominated economy. What about the social conditions in the regions? Isn't it only right that the government help out rural Quebec? Not really. The rate of welfare cases[26] is higher on the Island of Montreal than in any other region in Quebec, and only the Gaspé has a higher unemployment rate.[27]

It is also a fact of Quebec life that provincial elections are won or lost outside the Island of Montreal. Any attempt to create a meaningful Montreal Metropolitan Region has been thwarted by the off-Island suburbs' refusal to contribute, and by the political pusillanimity of both the Liberal Party* and the Parti Québécois to force them to do so for fear of losing those same ridings. The electorate only wields real power in swing ridings, not in ridings that always vote one way.[28]

The best illustration of the tyranny of the rurality in Quebec can be found in the swarm of rural towns and hamlets, most of them living off government aid. In 1999, *two-thirds* of all Quebec municipalities had a population of less than 1,600 people. *One-half* of their total revenues came from government handouts. They were home to only 11 per cent of Quebec's population.[29] These small municipalities should have been slowly weaned off government life support,

---

* Of the three main political parties in Quebec today, the Liberal Party and the Parti Québécois (the PQ or *péquistes*) have alternated as the governing party since 1970.

and if that led to a few of them merging, it would not have been the end of the world – although it is far from certain that would have been the result. This bizarre rural condition represented the only need or justification for government action. As it turned out, the tiny municipalities were little affected by mergers. During the decade leading up to Harel's mass mergers of 2002, municipalities with a population of less than one thousand consistently made up 44 per cent of all Quebec municipalities; even four years after, they *still* made up 44 per cent of the total, yet were home to only 275,000 Quebecers. On the other hand, over one-half of the 3,400,000 Quebecers who had chosen to live in medium-sized municipalities[30] woke up on 1 January 2002 to find them gone: these people had been made the unwilling citizens of one of the new megacities imposed all over Quebec.

We were told that mergers were necessary to reduce Quebec's vast number of municipalities – vast, that is, when compared with Ontario's. Yet at the end of all the municipal bloodletting, Quebec still had four times the number of municipalities per capita than did Ontario,[31] mainly because Quebec wiped out fifty of its bigger municipalities rather than getting rid of five hundred of its small ones: not the most efficient way to go about it. If you find your jar of coins too heavy, you get rid of the mountain of pennies, not a molehill of dimes. But that is almost beside the point: Quebec's unhealthy fixation on the number of municipalities was driven by bureaucratic neatness, not logic. France and the United States have many more municipalities per capita than does Quebec, and they seem to muddle along all right.

We were then told that urban mergers were needed to "reinforce" agglomerations. One would think that improved infrastructure, mass transit, financing, and control of urban sprawl – not the simplistic act of congealing cities – would have done an admirable job of reinforcing Quebec's agglomerations. One reinforces concrete with steel bars, plastics with fibres, and glass with wire mesh: reinforcing is done judiciously at stress points using exogenous materials. One doesn't just force a mass to coalesce into one homogenous lump.

ENCLAVE AVOIDANCE

And what about the Montreal merger itself? Of the many media champions of Island mergers, one of the most eloquent was Lysiane

Gagnon, the redoubtable and intelligent *La Presse* journalist, whom I quote extensively in this book. Gagnon argued that the former City of Montreal was shorn of its natural élites, such as the "enclaves" of Westmount, Outremont, and the Town of Mount Royal. She theorized that the low calibre of Montreal politicians could be explained by this alleged handicap, a handicap that led to a "parade of mediocre or megalomaniac mayors." When the law creating the megacity was about to be adopted, Gagnon was over the moon: "Utopia can sometimes become reality," she wrote. "From the death of those little cities that occupy the natural territory of Montreal, leeching off the central city to which they owe everything, will be born a real metropolis ... In ten years, Montreal will be unrecognizable. The quality of politicians will inevitably be improved."[32]

The Montreal megacity captured the enclave of Outremont. As well as coming from this newly annexed "élite" enclave, Gérald Tremblay, who became the first mayor of the megacity, had élite credentials en masse: lawyer, Harvard MBA, former cabinet minister. In spite of all that éliteness, it would be hard to argue during his first two terms that he was – how shall I put this? – less mediocre than his predecessors.[33] I must say, though, we saw a completely new and chastened Tremblay going into his third term. However, I am not sure if anyone can run such a bureaucratic monster. The problem is not fundamentally with the captain: it's the ruddy ship.

A LINGUISTIC SPLIT?

And how can one talk about Montreal Island mergers without bringing up the omnipresent Quebec bête noire of language? It was really only when the battle to fight the merger was raging that the PQ discovered yet another reason to impose One Island One City. It became not just a matter of fiscal equity, controlling urban sprawl, reducing political fragmentation, and saving money; it emerged that the megacity, through social engineering so dear to the hearts of some PQ luminaries, would also bring about something else: the integration of non-francophones. It would allow French to solvate heretofore immiscible linguistic liquids. In the words of former premier Bernard Landry, One Island One City would bring about "tremendous socio-economic and cultural integration."[34] He went so far as to call it (with typical Landrian understatement) "the most beautiful attempt of intercultural integration in history."[35]

In the anglophone community, many had been muttering that language was the real motivation behind mergers from the outset.[36] I said at the time that the disappearance of anglophone cities was a "felicitous by-product" for the PQ but not the main goal of the mergers, which, after all, were province wide. I often said that there were ten reasons to be against the mergers. and language was number eleven. That being said, on the Island of Montreal, the mergers affected the two language groups very differently: two out of three anglophones had their municipality taken away, whereas only one out of three francophones went though the same loss.[37]

If one looks at that statistic in reverse, it means that two-thirds of francophones who lived on the Island happened to live in the former City of Montreal. Montrealers were always much more favourable to the megacity, even when only half of them wanted it. This geographic imbalance goes a long way to explain the supposed linguistic *clivage* that existed during the merger and demerger debates. But that was not all. For anglophones, the municipal level of government was the only level they felt reflected them or over which they had some control. Anglos did not see themselves in the provincial government apparatus, which is completely francophone – as is the City of Montreal, for that matter.

To my chagrin, I was forced to use the language card when I led the legal battle against mergers: it was the only legal hook possible. There was something else that helped to give the impression the whole matter was a "French/English thing": all major francophone Montreal newspapers were solidly behind One Island One City, whereas the sole English daily* came out against it. In the English media, the merged cities were called "megacities." In the French media, especially after the law was passed, we got such positive appellations as *le nouveau Montréal*, *le nouveau Longueuil*, *la nouvelle ville*, or *le grand Montréal*.

Linguistic tensions were cranked up even tighter during the demergers. Eight out of the ten wealthiest cities in Quebec demerged,[38]

---

* In coming out against mergers, the *Montreal Gazette* was bucking a Canadian journalistic trend. For reasons that escape me, the four Toronto dailies came out in favour of the Toronto megacity in the late 1990s in spite of widespread public opposition. Even that was nothing new: back in the 1950s, all the major daily newspapers in Toronto campaigned for outright amalgamation rather than the creation of Metro Toronto, a body widely regarded as the first modern example of a federation of cities.

and most of them were majority anglophone. While personal income should have nothing to do with municipal organization, the fact that rich anglos voted to "quit" Montreal did not help my cause and soon turned me into a pariah among certain francophones, especially in the media. Demerger was seen as a rejection not just of Montreal but of the whole of Quebec. While most Quebecers – of all linguistic persuasions – were against forced mergers, a year or so after their creation some francophones saw it as bad form, almost antisocial, to want to break up the *grande ville*.[39] There was, in other words, a certain amount of rallying round the municipal flag, once it was run up the flagpole. Such solidarity runs deep: it is one of the reasons Quebec has managed to keep its francophone uniqueness alive against overwhelming odds.

AND THE *WAY* IT WAS DONE?

The boundaries of municipalities, no less than the boundaries of provinces and countries, should not be imposed. Municipalities were created by their citizens. If they pay their own way, they should be free to flourish – or to die by their citizens' hands. Indeed, forced mergers were always the exception, not the rule, in Quebec. During most of the twentieth century in the province, there was only one other period when mergers had been forced, and that was between 1965 and 1982, during which some twenty different laws imposing mergers were adopted – all but one enacted by Liberal governments. These mergers affected, all told, around a million people. December 2000, however, was the first time in Quebec's history that wholesale, wide-ranging mergers were imposed by just *one* piece of legislation, a single bill that affected 3.1 million people. And that was not all. An earlier piece of legislation[40] had empowered the cabinet, not the legislature, to decree many other mergers; another 1.2 million citizens saw their municipalities disappear as a consequence. The government fired a machine gun, not a rifle, at the municipal world. And when Louise Harel tried to invoke "urgency" as the justification for such extreme measures, few swallowed it. There was no *force majeure* to excuse the scope of the mergers, the sweeping powers given to the government, nor, indeed, the lack of consultation.

   Even though many thought mergers were a Good Thing, there still was much anger over them simply because they were imposed. This anger arose out of both the surprise and helplessness people felt about not being able to vote on the matter. Bizarrely, Louise Harel, most of whose mergers ran contrary to the public's will, began ruminating in 2002 about the citizen's role in running government: "Up until now, the only form of citizen protest is found in the streets ... this is not normal: we have to re-invent the way citizens are represented. That they feel they have a say in things ... we have to reflect profoundly on what could become participatory democracy, as opposed to our current representative democracy."[41]

In waging war against the mergers and then for the demergers, we were up against more than just the francophone media, the Quebec government, and the City of Montreal. All the labour unions and, finally, the Board of Trade came out against us. But the largest group of all, the population of the Island of Montreal, was on our side. From May 1999, when Bourque announced his One Island One City campaign, public support on the Island for his grand plan never went above 50 per cent; in fact, it began a slow decline. Support levelled off at about 35 per cent in the second half of 2001 to the end of 2002, a year after the merger. To refer to the mergers as "imposed" is indubitably the correct term.

(The demerger referendums, on the other hand, allowed citizens to right a wrong. Before the 2006 Quebec demergers, the only demerger[42] – albeit rural – that occurred just about anywhere in the world happened in Quebec in 1980, under the watch of Premier René Lévesque, a democrat and the spiritual father of the PQ, who said at the time, "We have moved heaven and earth to respond to the popular will, as shown by a referendum."[43])

The PQ paid the price for forcing mergers on Quebecers when it lost the 2003 election to the Liberals. Nearly six years after the forced mergers, PQ leader Pauline Marois gave her *mea culpa*. In November 2008, she admitted that the electorate was still angry with her party for imposing the mergers and for not getting an electoral mandate for them. She also admitted that the economies that Bouchard guaranteed would flow from mergers never materialized.[44]

The PQ never expected such a backlash to their blithe overhaul of the municipal world, and they certainly never expected local resentment to have such a long half-life. Likewise, the demerger fiasco was also not easily forgotten. In April 2010, Léger Marketing conducted a poll[45] asking Quebecers after seven years of Liberal rule, "What was the most significant event of the Charest era?" Naturally, the most recent (the provincial budget) gained top place. The next matter related to ongoing allegations of corruption in the construction industry, after which came the interminable struggle to build a

French superhospital. The fourth choice was the implementation of demergers, a debate that had finished *six years* before.

Most Quebecers had not realized that, in Canada, the freedom to live in a municipality of one's choice had definitively (and long ago) been given over to the province. Citizens thought they owned their municipality. They thought it could not be expropriated. If there were a problem with "fiscal equity," then deal with it fiscally and write a cheque, they said: you don't have to wipe out my municipality. In my view, for Quebec to go against the popular will by imposing mergers, the existing situation had to be both demonstrably and grossly unjust, and, moreover, the remedy had to be of proven efficacy. Neither was the case.

Any search for the causes of the mass municipal mergers of 2002 must begin in the warren of offices that houses the Department of Municipal Affairs in Quebec City. Like architects designing houses they will probably never live in, these mandarins are responsible for writing the laws that decree how municipal and regional bodies operate. They also whisper policy positions in politicians' ears. It was a truism for Quebec bureaucrats that the plethora of towns all over the province was a bad state of affairs. It was an obsession with them. While it was less clearly expressed, they also disliked – and distrusted – the patchwork of cities that made up the Island of Montreal. It upset their sense of neatness, offended their bureaucratic aesthetic. Merger fever waxed and then waned over the whole of the twentieth century in the bosom of Montreal politicians, but government bureaucrats never ceased needling their elected bosses about reducing the number of municipalities.

Government civil servants started to focus even more on Montreal in the 1990s when it became clearer and clearer that the City of Montreal was grossly mismanaged and that its free-spending chickens were coming home to roost. Because of the huge deficits of its operations, pension funds, and strange beasts called "paramunicipals," Montreal owed some $4.4 billion, an amount equal to 7 per cent of the entire provincial debt. Employing a typically bureaucratic mindset, one solution to the debt problem was merger with Island suburbs with their comparatively low debt – in other words, sweep Montreal's problems under a bigger rug.*

---

* There was an old precedent for this "dilute the problem" strategy. In October 1969, helpless in the face of a City of Montreal police strike that had led to uncontrolled looting

Ultimately, then, it was the Quebec bureaucrats in Municipal Affairs who promoted mergers and, naturally, made mergers happen. Over the years, parliaments have given over massive powers to the state apparatus. The danger today comes not so much from a totalitarian state as from bureaucracies, bureaucracies made omniscient and omnipotent by the computer. Complexity is the bureaucrat's friend. Most ministers, let alone backbenchers, have no clue as to what is really going on in government. Today's elected official, more likely than not, is a professional politician owing allegiance not to voters but to the party. He or she is acutely aware of the need to draw a salary, as, once elected, bridges are burnt, and a safe return to private life is far from assured.

Because provincial and federal politicians are the least trusted of any professions in our society, citizens felt that they were had when their municipality was taken away. Poll after poll has shown that local politicians – at least those representing the smaller cities – are far more respected and trusted than provincial politicians. Yet local politicians were treated as *roitelets* (kinglets) and reactionaries by the media, as parochial throwbacks only wanting to hold onto their little patch of ground. One editorialist called those mayors who saw nothing wrong with the status quo as "vaguely Palaeolithic."

Time and again the polls also showed that people were not necessarily against mergers; in fact, as I have suggested, the popular canard had it that mergers would lead to economies of scale. But the same polls emphatically showed that all citizens believed that each merger must be preceded by some sort of referendum.

As things heated up, the merger question had nothing to do with what was best for local government but what was best for provincial politicians. Since municipal boundaries often shared provincial electoral district boundaries, the merger battle was directly and immediately transferred to specific provincial seats. In spite of high-tech weaponry such as polling and TV ads, politics today is still very much of a ground war. In 1999, decisions were being made about mergers based on whether the PQ "owned" the electoral district or not. On the Island of Montreal, it was almost caricatural: all

of a mile of Ste-Catherine Street and the death of a provincial police officer, Quebec's panicked solution was to merge Island police forces and impose the Montreal Urban Community to help fund the pay settlement with the police. While such regional cost-sharing was overdue, a shotgun marriage was not the best way to go about it.

twenty-six municipalities threatened with disappearance happened to be in Liberal ridings, except for one very small one. The PQ knew they would never win most of these ridings, so if the Liberal voters' ox was being gored, that was just fine. On the other hand, the whole north shore was PQ territory: few mergers happened there. The south shore was more evenly divided: it was brave of the PQ to merge municipalities there. In the event, they paid the price in the next election. That today's municipal landscape was the result of partisan politics is something all Quebecers should be ashamed of. And I can't help but ask: if they were so convinced that mergers were beneficial, why did the PQ largely reserve them for their political enemies?

In essence, the public was lied to. They were told that mergers would save money and would redirect suburban tax revenue to Montreal. They were told that mergers were a world-wide trend and had been always imposed in Quebec. None of those things was true.

ALTOGETHER NOW

Not content with merging municipalities, Louise Harel also decided to merge the date of Quebec municipal elections. Since at least 1916, these elections were held at four-year intervals starting with the year of each municipality's founding. This way, elections, which were held the same day in November, were spread over a four-year cycle with roughly one-quarter of the municipalities having an election in any given year. For the first time, starting November 2005, all municipalities all over Quebec had an election on the same date. Supposedly, this bunching would increase voter turnout. Unsurprisingly, it had the opposite effect: only 45 per cent of electors showed up at the municipal polls that year, down from the usual average of 53 per cent. For smaller, unmerged municipalities, merging election dates meant that bigger cities squeezed them out in media coverage during elections. And the newly merged municipalities suffered an even greater drop in turnout, because, as the Municipal Affairs Department well knew, the larger the municipality, the lower the election turnout.[46] The worst example was the case of the Montreal megacity, where voter turnout plummeted from 49 per cent in 2001 to 35 per cent in 2005.[47] When Louise Harel herself decided to run for the mayoralty of the Montreal megacity in 2009, she was hoist with her own petard. Even though, owing to a hot three-way race, the turnout edged up a bit to 39 per cent, Harel blamed her defeat on the poor participation rate.[48]

WHY SHOULD THE 1990S COUNT?

While some may feel I have devoted too much space in this book to the eight-year period before the mergers, I've done this for four reasons.

First, the municipal problems that preoccupied us in the early 1990s – urban sprawl, freeloading off-Island cities, the lack of a regional spirit, overpaid municipal employees, the endemic mismanagement of the City of Montreal – are still with us today. Actually, many of them were amplified by the mergers.*

Secondly, there was, from 1992 onwards, a mood of expectation of change that suffused the whole region, thanks to the Pichette Task Force going about its work and Municipal Affairs Minister Claude Ryan's musings about mergers. This expectation, felt and then fed by the mayors, the department, and the media, became almost irresistibly self-fulfilling; it eventually led to Harel's fatuous statement that "the status quo is not an option" and, quickly thereafter, to mergers. And I was as guilty as anyone with all my pronouncements on the need to rationalize structures and to create a metropolitan coordinating body. The only one who saw the danger was the mayor of Montreal North and brother of Claude, Yves Ryan. But there was nothing we could do: had we not participated with his brother in all that early soul-searching, something would have probably been imposed much sooner.

Thirdly, in 1997 the partitionist movement was at its height. The partitionists, who were mostly anglophones, wanted municipalities loyal to Canada to remain Canadian in the event of the separation of Quebec. This idea sent shivers down the spines of many francophones, particularly the separatist PQ, and made the latter receptive to the idea of submerging into the megacity all the West Island municipalities that could otherwise have served as a base for territorial partition.

---

* One illustration may suffice. The title of the fellow in charge of supervising Montreal's 2007 statistical yearbook is "the Divisional Head of the Strategic and Tactical Operations Group of the Land-use Planning Administration of the Department of Patrimonial and Territorial Development."

Fourthly, the 1990s were the "downloading" years. When a higher government dumped costs into the laps of lower government, it became known as downloading. Repetitive acts of downloading by the province in the seven-year period of 1992 to 1998 amounting to over $1.1 billion a year* (nearly 20 per cent of property tax revenues) created a state of war between municipalities and Quebec. The downloading also created bitter divisions within the municipal world itself. As the war worsened and divisions deepened, it became easier for Quebec to reach for radical solutions to put an end to the obstreperous little cities and their incessant whining. In a climate of mistrust and mutual dislike, the one with the power uses the power.

Why all the downloading? From Claude Ryan onwards, it was an article of faith with successive governments that Quebec was under-using property taxes when compared to Ontario. This belief fuelled Ryan's merciless cuts and those of his replacement, Rémy Trudel. Even today Quebec is convinced of this "truth," conveniently ignoring two facts. First, Ontario municipalities taxed their commercial sectors much more than Quebec cities did. This meant the Quebec residential sector was more heavily hit by property taxes than government statistics would suggest. Second, people in Ontario were richer. In 1999 the median net worth of Ontario families was 67 per cent higher than that of Quebec families.[49] Now, property taxes are – wrongly – used and sometimes regarded as a wealth tax. Still, as a proportion of their wealth, Quebecers pay much more in property taxes than Ontarians.

And Quebec municipalities did not pass on all this downloading to the taxpayer. Debt is the accretion of years of such tax bill pusillanimity: municipal and school debt in Quebec is – by far – the highest in Canada.[50]

BOUCHARD WAS THE KEY

Even though Pierre Bourque, the mayor of Montreal, announced his One Island One City campaign publicly in May 1999, I would trace the birth of the idea of mass mergers in Quebec to March 1997. It came about as a confluence of a number of events. Bourque made

* This does not include a $600 million increase in school property taxes.

his pilgrimage to PQ Premier Lucien Bouchard in Quebec City with
five other "central-city" mayors that month, demanding forced mergers, principally in the name of fiscal equity. Meanwhile, the minister of the regions, Guy Chevrette, wanted to scrap the Metropolitan
Development Commission, which was a dog that could not hunt, yet
would have, in many people's minds, obviated the "need" for mergers. March was also the month Chevrette went public with the need
for fiscal equity on the Island of Montreal, a cry that Harel picked
up later.

But what transformed mergers from idea to, finally, a reality was
the re-election of Bouchard as premier in late 1998 and his naming
of Harel as minister of municipal affairs. It took the close collusion
of Bouchard and Harel to make mergers happen. In contrast with
the klutziness with which the PQ had implemented health and education "reforms," the team of Bouchard and Harel exhibited the political stick-handling needed to impose the municipal "reform." Harel
(and her predecessor, Rémy Trudel) can be credited with the brilliant strategy of dividing municipal Quebec into warring factions –
urban against rural, central cities against suburbs. No sooner a scab
formed over wounded provincial-municipal relations than Quebec
ripped it off. However, had Bouchard not taken over the whole merger file in his last year, it was unlikely that Harel could have pushed
it through alone. It is a monument to Bouchard's political skill and
powerful personality that it did happen.

Unlike his predecessor, PQ Premier Jacques Parizeau, who had
long ago taken a position against municipal mergers, Bouchard was
bound by no such convictions, nor by the PQ 1994 election platform that prohibited forced mergers. Harel's plan seemed harmless
enough to him at the beginning. And Bouchard was out of the picture well before the forced mergers of 2002 would lead to the PQ
losing the next election in 2003: he announced he was quitting only
three weeks after the forced merger legislation was adopted.

It always struck me as passing strange that one of the most eloquent voices against mergers belonged to Parizeau: "There always
was an appetite in government administrations for mergers – for the
government's convenience, not the citizen's. Governments are always
in favour of mergers. It's more convenient for the minister of municipal affairs to deal with 200 municipalities rather than 1,400. It is
useless to seek to justify mergers by saying they are for the citizen's
advantage. The citizen is devilishly suspicious when he sees mergers

that bring increased costs per person." Said Parizeau, "We are wasting our time and our money" in discussing forced mergers. Considering that Quebec has complete power when it comes to municipal mergers, he warned the government, "To have the power and to have the judgment to exercise it, that's not the same thing."[51]

THE MUC "DIDN'T WORK"

In selling his dream of One Island One City to Bouchard and Harel, Bourque had an incognizant accomplice: Vera Danyluk, the energetic, articulate, and charming chair of the executive committee of the Montreal Urban Community (the MUC), a body that delivered Island-wide services – the main service being police protection. Danyluk became an unwitting catalyst for forced mergers when the MUC began to be seen as a wasp's nest of squabbling mayors. Frustrated in her role as a mediator between the MUC's two "shareholders" (the City of Montreal and the suburban cities), Danyluk felt that the existing municipal structures on the Island simply were not working: something had to be done. For her, that something was turning the MUC into a level of government, and she mounted an indefatigable campaign to do just that, invoking the term "One Island One Metropolis" and supporting three separate provincial government reports that, *inter alia*, recommended forced mergers – although she herself was in favour of voluntary mergers. Since the provincial government, on its part, did not want two levels of government (the MUC and Montreal) on the Island, the simpler expedient of folding everything into one big municipality became a very attractive solution.

MAYOR CULPA: POLITICAL ETHICS AND THE DEMERGER PLEDGE

Some may feel that I have been a bit harsh at times on megacity Mayor Gérald Tremblay. While I have been judgmental, my comments have not been gratuitous. If there is one message I would like to deliver with this book, it has to do with the need to hack away at the public's deep distrust of politicians and the cynicism toward politics in general. Politicians should be held to a very high standard – not in their peccadilloes, in their personal life, or even in their propensity for little white lies, but in their solemn public commitments.

While Tremblay is a fundamentally honest, intelligent, and hard-working man who believes passionately in the megacity, I have difficulty with something he did – and he knows it. He reneged on the one promise that got him elected in 2001: that, while he would try to build a megacity that everyone would love, he would not stand in the way of Montreal demergers if ever the Liberals got elected and honoured their pledge to allow them.[52]

The 2001 municipal election had only two serious contenders for the mayoralty of the megacity: Gérald Tremblay and Pierre Bourque. Since the latter was the "father" of the megacity, voters who were against it were forced to vote for Tremblay. Moreover, there was a direct correlation between the popularity of demerger and the popularity of Tremblay. Had he openly admitted in 2001 that he would fight demergers with every weapon he had, including lobbying to delay them for two years and pushing for a minimum turnout rate in demerger referenda,[53] his almost soviet-like voting support in the West Island would have evaporated; as a consequence, he would have not been elected mayor of the megacity of Montreal.[54]

Now, politicians should be able to change their minds on just about any issue, but not on a key commitment. And not only did Tremblay promise not to interfere with demergers but he surrounded himself with ex-mayors who openly favoured demerger and for whom his non-interference promise had got them on side. In changing his position, he no doubt felt the end justified the means, but that kind of ratiocination leads to precisely why politicians are in such bad odour: they believe (encouraged by their aides) that they are doing absolutely the right thing and pardon themselves for any ethical skating they have to do to get it done. Tremblay would have been a strange mayor if he did not defend his megacity – but that was the bed of ambiguity he made for himself. He was not alone in this bed, however. Two former suburban mayors, originally vehemently pro-demerger, had made a conversion on the road to the megacity executive committee.

Liberal leader Jean Charest came close to committing a similar lapse to Tremblay's. Charest's party won the 2003 Quebec election owing to its demerger pledge. While not reneging on this pledge, Charest did allow it to be quite denatured. Come to think of it, both he and Tremblay each had clear electoral mandates to permit – not to encourage, mind you – unimpeded and full demergers. Instead, they colluded to make demergers as difficult, unattractive, and incomplete as possible. The difference was that Tremblay did everything in his power to stop demergers, and Charest at least had the decency to put through a law that made them, on paper, achievable. However, by subjecting the referendums to novel and unusual conditions, Charest managed to put a lid on the number of demergers. Had normal referendum rules applied, one million citizens instead of only 440,000 would have got their municipality back.

RULE BY CHANGE

"To change is human. It's always threatening. But, at the same time, if we don't overcome this fear of change, we do not progress."[55] Thus spake Louise Harel. In modern societies it is an article of faith that change inevitably leads to progress, and progress inevitably leads to our betterment. The world's environmental mess should tell us this cult of change can be very dangerous. Certainly, government-driven change is often plain wrong, or at best useless. This is because government initiatives (as opposed to reacting to an unexpected problem) are often inspired by the politician's credo, *mutatio gratia mutationis*: change for the sake of change.

Cabinet ministers become dervishes the minute they are given their portfolios: they know their days are numbered and that a transfer, demotion, or change of government is just around the corner. They have to make their mark, and quickly. They usually know nothing about their department, so they call in their deputy minister and plead for a project that will make a big enough change that the result will be noticeable by their leader and the media. Nothing is more dangerous than a politician who has to *do* something. This is how we wind up with a kainotocracy, or rule by change. As Thomas Jefferson wrote, "I am not a friend to a very energetic government. It is always oppressive." I sometimes think that governing consists of getting rid of problems by replacing them with new ones. The existing system is always inferior to the ideal system, up until the moment the ideal system is implemented.

For a freshly nominated minister of municipal affairs, there is not much to shake up within his or her department; besides, bureaucrats will wax enthusiastic about change for others, not for themselves. So what does the deputy minister tell the boss, the minister, to do? Why, reduce the number of municipalities. I am sure that ministers of municipal affairs discuss with their predecessors how many municipalities they still have in the same way businesspeople compare golf scores.

Reducing the number of municipalities, though, is a kind of negative change; building megacities sounds more constructive. In this way, Harel could be seen to be *creating* something, and something that, for Montreal, would not antagonize the exurban swing ridings north of Montreal and something that the PQ strongholds on the Island would applaud. Not for the first time in history, good public policy was sacrificed to political expediency. The problems of the region, such as fiscal inequality between the Island and the rest of the region and urban sprawl (costing the province in highway, school, and hospital construction) were not eased by One Island One City. But the megacity did address the perception of the "squabbling mayors" and the non-existent "fiscal enclaves."

STATE OWNERSHIP AND MONOPOLIES

The merger saga raises deeper questions about government. I do not see myself as particularly right wing, but I do harbour a wariness of big government, a wariness grown keener by the merger experience. If you think that governments at all levels should have a watertight monopoly on providing a fixed bundle of services without any input by you, the consumer, as to what they should be and how they should be provided; if you think that this monopoly should be uniquely funded based on your assumed ability to pay or your relative wealth, then you will not agree with a number of ideas I put forward here. If, however, you think that certain local services – if not a few provincial and federal services – should be provided based on what you are looking for and not on what the government thinks you want, and that you should pay for at least *some* of those services based on your consumption of them, then you will be at ease with fiscal policies advocated in this book.

Why do we give governments – or, more precisely, why do governments arrogate – a monopoly on providing their services? The role of government to redistribute income can be easily divorced from the role of government to provide certain services. Yes, justice, defence, personal protection – these sorts of services – have to be provided by governments alone. But why should provincial governments have a self-assigned monopoly on electric power distribution, for example? Or alcohol sales? A century ago, these things and many others were provided by the private sector. The reasons for their nationalization a half-century ago may no longer be valid. Other than assuring equal access, which governments can build into a privately run system, what is the justification for some of these monopolies? Because they are the only sector left that's still highly unionized, governments are also walled off from competition, thanks to union contracts that make their monopolies even more impregnable. Unions, it must not be forgotten, are self-appointed monopolies in their own right.

During the merger battle, Madame Harel and the media forever referred to the "sterile" competition among municipalities.[56] One never heard of complaints of "sterile" competition among private-sector companies vying for customers. Why are governments so averse to monopolies in the private sector, yet find their own monopolies completely necessary? The thought of bank monopolies or even oligopolies has kept Ottawa mandarins awake at night, yet Ottawa has had a monopoly on mail delivery for 150 years. Up until mass municipal mergers – a kind of nationalization of cities – municipal consumers at least had a choice of a specific bundle of services they could consume, simply by moving to a specific municipality. Should not consumers have a choice of municipality as well as a choice of house? By what right did Quebec remove from a resident of, say, the suburb of Anjou, access to a particular mix of services that Anjou provided? In the name of efficiency? Surely not. In the name of fiscal equity? That is what was invoked but not what happened. In reality, citizen choice was removed because that is what governments do: they monopolize.

One advantage of a federalist system is that citizens can choose to live in whatever province or state that provides the type of services and style of life they want. In a much more evident and efficient way, a variety of municipalities offers residents a choice of services (and costs). Yet in terms of services, the megacity of Montreal closed down well-established boutiques and replaced them with a Soviet-era department store.

The fundamental difference I had with both the francophone editorialists and the PQ party – who were almost universal in their support for mergers – was our differing conceptions of just what was "government." For the pro-merger camp, all governments, local, regional, or provincial, should provide equal services to all. Government was government. The anti-merger camp, explicitly or implicitly, felt that *local* government was intrinsically different from the "higher" forms of government. Local government was a service-delivery vehicle. It was permissible, even desirable, to have a variety of municipalities, each providing different quality and quantity of services, depending on how much a taxpayer was willing to pay. We all felt that regional services (basic police services and public transit, for example) should be uniform; but if local citizens were prepared to pay for it, why should not a given municipality provide a certain service another municipality might decide not to provide? Where was the harm? Unfortunately this rather simple, possibly resolvable difference was clouded over by the fiscal equity issue: the pro-mergerites were convinced that the Montreal Island suburban cities were not paying their fair share.

In the 1980s I taught a university course in marketing. The "modern marketing concept" is the doctrine that services and products should be designed and sold based on the consumer's needs, not those of the supplier. Since cities are in the service delivery business, the same principle should apply. But the megacity was all about rearrangement at the top. "Building the new city," no matter how often Tremblay repeated it, did not resonate with taxpayers, being for them an abstract, glittery new thing for the political and journalistic class to play with.

GENTLY TO HEAR, KINDLY TO JUDGE, OUR PLAY

Before starting our story, we need to describe the setting. The next chapter paints a portrait of cultural and linguistic Quebec, an admittedly personal portrait that might be useful in understanding how the mergers came about. Then we visit Westmount to illustrate why, in municipalities both like and unlike Westmount, Quebec citizens fought so hard to preserve the municipality they loved. "Westmount" is also synecdochic shorthand for "privileged anglo," and it was elementary grist to the merger mill, serving itself up for many in the pro-merger faction as a heaven-sent example of why mergers were necessary.

The whole merger-demerger saga has much to teach us about the unique nature of Quebec government, politics, and people. I hope, though, that the lessons to be drawn about mergers are not exclusive to Quebec. "Truth is the daughter of time," said Aulus Gellius somewhat hopefully in the second century. Whether ten years is enough time for me to squeeze out some truth from the bewildering actions of 2001, only further time will tell. However, if this book can make policy-makers think twice about resorting to widespread amalgamations at some future date, it will have served its purpose.

2

Language: Quebec's Necessary Obsession

Montreal. It is above all an inconsolable city – it weeps still for that clash of distant powers that, two centuries ago, first tossed it from empire to empire, culture to culture.

Jan Morris, *City to City*

I was born in England in 1946, on my mother's birthday. My mother was a teacher and a committed socialist. My father was a builder whose enthusiasm for socialism was, on the whole, easily contained. They decided to move to Canada for two reasons: there would be less likelihood of an atomic war there (my mother's reason), and it was a place to get a better job (my father's reason). Besides, while the bomb damage and food rationing had finally gone, London was still grim and grey – and town planners were going to raze our neighbourhood.[1]

The Trent family arrived in Toronto in the mid-1950s. We really did not see ourselves as immigrants. Canada in those days was almost an extension of Britain, just another room in the same house. The governor-general looked like someone who had just marched out of St James's Palace and probably had; envelopes from Ottawa were franked On Her Majesty's Service; and we sang "God Save the Queen" at school every morning and in cinemas at the end of the film. I learned to sing "The Maple Leaf Forever" and lustily belted out "In days of yore, from Britain's shore, / Wolfe, the dauntless hero came." That's something you don't hear these days.

So the Trents fairly easily settled in, but my sisters and I thought the move was a mistake. Rather than a crumbling old Regency house in London with a semi-circular drive, half-dozen fireplaces, sprawling garden, and cricket pitch, we were stuck in a postwar bungalow with a garage covered in tarpaper in a town called Swansea, where my father was at one point elected councillor – up until Swansea was merged with Toronto in 1967. The town's volunteer fire brigade was summoned by means of an air-raid siren, the sound making my parents blanch, thinking of those far-off nights during the London Blitz.

I left home at seventeen to go to university. Four years later I was working for the Canadian subsidiary of Rohm and Haas, a large American chemical firm. I became a bit of a specialist in the chemistry of surface-active agents used in the manufacture of things like detergents. Although based in Toronto, I was sent to the company's Montreal office four times during the Expo year of 1967. Accompanied by an anglophone sales representative, I was asked to use my newly acquired expertise in advising the company's Montreal customers. Neither of us spoke French, and it was considered quite normal in those days for us to visit manufacturing plants around Montreal, speaking English to owners, plant managers, and chemists who were, by and large, francophone.

The next year I was promoted to a job in another department of Rohm and Haas that made various polymers used in paints, coatings, and plastics. It meant moving permanently to Montreal, which, for a twenty-two-year-old, was close to bachelor nirvana. The golden glow of Expo still lit up the city. When I pointed out that I spoke no French – in spite of (or because of) five years of high-school French – my boss said that it was not necessary. After four months' training at the company's research laboratories in Philadelphia, where I learned such things as the glass transition temperature of polyisobutylmethacrylate, I moved to Montreal in 1968. I was smitten, but I did what many newcomers to Quebec did then: got an apartment in a hulking great building, this one pretentiously called Sutton Square in western Notre Dame de Grâce (NDG), where seldom was heard a francophone word. Even more than today, francophones lived in east-end Montreal, anglophones in the west.

Over the next three years, I travelled all over Quebec. I was involved in research trials in paper mills in places like Port Neuf, Grand-Mère, La Tuque, and Lac Saint-Jean. I visited rubber factories in the Eastern Townships. I talked paint formulations with chemists in Montreal, Quebec City, and Shawinigan. And I never spoke a word of French. In 1972, I left Rohm and Haas, a year after founding a company with a francophone, Raymond Charlebois. As well as sinking just about all my small inheritance in the firm – my parents had died in 1968 – I decided it was high time I learned French. Sessions at Language Power Systems did very little, but working with our sole and unilingual employee finally made me shakily bilingual.

Raymond and I created a partnership that would last eighteen years. We invented a polymer composite material used in construction and engineering applications, which we patented in dozens of countries. (I was not the first inventor in my family; my mother's brother, Dr William Percival, who helped develop stereo and television in the 1930s and radar during the war, was awarded 120 patents over fifty years.)

Our original "plant" was a garage on Montcalm Street in east-end Montreal (the next street over was called Wolfe). We then moved to a proper factory in Montreal North in 1972 and afterwards to Saint-Leonard. By then I was living in another apartment building, a vertical concrete lump in NDG called L'Escale West. (There was, significantly, no L'Escale East.) Linguistically, I lived in two hermetically sealed worlds. I drove daily to east Montreal using that soul-destroying elevated blight that serves as Montreal's spine: the Metropolitan Boulevard. Never a car lover, I got rid of my car in 1977 and I haven't owned one since. When we moved to the old Atlas Asbestos plant at Hochelaga and L'Assomption in 1979, the metro was quicker anyway.

In all the fifteen years I worked in the east end of Montreal, I never once encountered a hint of discrimination as an anglophone. In fact, I was warmly welcomed by all francophones I met, even if regarded as a bit of a curiosity. On the other hand, when our company left the east end in 1987, after building a 50,000 square-foot factory on thirteen acres in the West Island, our employees – nearly all French – could rarely get served in French in the local restaurants. The reality of the two solitudes sunk home.

Over the eighteen years I spent as an entrepreneur, I managed to raise about $50 million in equity for our company, the money coming mostly from British or American multinationals, including Shell Oil. Never was there any sign of hesitation on their part to invest in a company that operated in French, well before the law required it. While potential investors were only bemused by the language spoken, I did have to allay their fears about the threat of Quebec independence.

FRANCOPHOBIA BEGAT ANGLOPHOBIA

So, in the quarter-century I spent in Quebec before I became mayor, I never ran into any form of anglophobia. Francophobia – or, in reality, disdain for the French – was another matter. In the 1960s at least, it was not hard to find. Here was the big difference with Britain, where the educated class felt that the ability to speak French was a necessity for anyone claiming to be cultivated; indeed, my mother was proud of flaunting her singsong French. When I first came to Quebec, the older generation of wealthy anglophones felt that French was the language of the working class, or worse, the domestic staff. It was no feather in their social cap to be able to speak it. Naturally, they went on about the execrable quality of French spoken here, as if that made their unilingualism acceptable. This francophobia is now only alive in the minds of older *péquistes*, who use it as part of their mythology of blame. Thus francophobia begat anglophobia.

Forty years ago, it was rare to hear of a francophone company president. In 1971, only 13 per cent of boards of directors had a majority of francophones[2] and 83 per cent of managers were English.[3] Was this scarcity of francophones in business a self-inflicted wound caused by their traditional education and religion?[4] Or were francophones simply shut out by a contemptuous English élite? That debate will always rage in Quebec. The fact remains that the paucity of francophones in business until the 1980s created fertile ground for anglophobia among the French chattering classes. With reason: in 1961 unilingual English-speakers earned almost twice as much as unilingual French-speakers.[5] Anglophones and foreign investors owned the vast majority of industries. Even when francophones ran something, English was the lingua franca. My partner, Raymond Charlebois, used to work for a company that was actually run by francophones, yet operated with the name the Standard Paper Box Company. I always thought that Raymond's nationalistic leanings were reinforced when he participated in meetings of a few dozen francophones and one anglophone, conducted entirely in English.

Back in 1962, Donald Gordon, the president of Canadian National Railways (CN), was asked at parliamentary hearings why none of his seventeen vice-presidents was French. After all, CN was based in Montreal. He replied to the effect that "We can't find any competent French-Canadians." The Student Union of the Université de Montréal responded to this crashingly insensitive remark with a massive demonstration outside CN's Queen Elizabeth Hotel – so-named in another bout of anglophone insensitivity. The Student Union president and organizer of the rally was none other than the future committed sovereignist and premier of Quebec, Bernard Landry.[6]

Another source of anglophobia among the French élite came, in my view, from a surprising quarter: the Canadian military, which unknowingly created leaders of the independence movement. The military were good at recruiting, in that sense. Take Serge Ménard: after he was named minister of the métropole by the PQ government in January 1996,* I had quite a few dealings with him. I always rather liked Ménard, as he was quite genuine, and, for a politician, quite diffident. When uncomfortable, he tended to twitch and get red in the face. He never gave the impression of being very sure of himself. One morning found us in the Ritz-Carlton restaurant for breakfast. His bodyguard sat at a nearby table. Ménard had just spilled his coffee all over his lap and was a bit flustered. By way of making small talk, he asked me, "Do you know why I became a member of the PQ?"

"No, Serge. Tell me."

"Well, when I was seventeen, I joined the naval reserve" – I just knew what was to come next – "and they made fun of my accent in English." He didn't have to say that the Canadian Navy was run entirely in English then. That was *sous-entendu*.

Like a disappointed parent, I said to him, "But that was forty years ago, Serge. The Canadian military in Quebec is now run in French. I'm an honorary colonel, so I know what I'm talking about. The bad old days are gone. The French have won, Serge."

"Whatever," he said. "The damage is done."

The same thing marked Bernard Landry. When Landry was speaking, as premier, to the Cree grand chief in 2002, he told how, when he was a young lieutenant in the Canadian Army, his colonel "ordered" him to speak English. He refused.[7] In Alan Hustak's 2003 obituary of Pierre Bourgault, the separatist firebrand, one reads, "He joined the Canadian Army in 1952 and became an artillery officer posted to Manitoba. It was that experience that led to his becoming a separatist. 'In the army, French Canadians studied in English, were commanded in English, and were despised in English,' he said."[8]

So in the 1960s and even 1970s, francophones had to be bilingual, but anglophones did not. My first marriage was to a franco-

---

* He created quite a shockwave among the PQ establishment when he said that perhaps language protection legislation was no longer necessary, in that French was no longer in danger in Montreal (*Le Devoir*, 31 January 1996).

phone who spoke perfect English and happened to be a supporter of the PQ. Because I had become so sympathetic to the way the French were treated, even I voted PQ in 1973. (When I recounted this ten years later to Don MacCallum, mayor of Westmount at the time, he nearly spat out the scotch he was drinking.) I slowly came to realize that the PQ could have a doctrinaire, interventionist, and even undemocratic side. I also developed a stronger attachment to Canada. And, most importantly, the lot of French Canadians started to improve by leaps and bounds in the 1980s.

Although I experienced no anti-English sentiment personally in my early years in Quebec, it was not surprising to me that the linguistically oppressed majority would want to assert itself. In the 1960s, sadly, some chose the violent route. The Front de Libération du Quebec (FLQ) was born. Their attacks were aimed at the English and at perceived British symbols. Around 3 AM one May morning in 1963, five bombs exploded out of twelve that were placed in as many mailboxes in Westmount; another went off later that day while Sergeant-Major Walter Leja of the 3rd Field Engineer Regiment in Westmount was dismantling it. Leja lost an arm and was paralyzed on his right side for life. He could only say a few words at a time. In 1965, FLQ terrorists Pierre Vallières and Charles Gagnon tried to blow up Westmount City Hall; thanks to two-foot-thick stone walls, the bomb caused only minor damage. In 1968, Vallières wrote *White Niggers of America*. In 1970, more FLQ bombs exploded in Westmount. And, later that year in Montreal, James Cross, the British trade commissioner, was kidnapped, and Liberal minister Pierre Laporte was murdered. The year before, a big demonstration (that included Louise Harel) demanded that McGill University become French. Later, French-Canadians also began asserting themselves pacifically through legislation, addressing the problem of immigrants who gravitated to English rather than French, because, when you are talking about the survival of a language and culture, numbers matter.[9]

INDIVIDUALISM VERSUS COLLECTIVISM

While the defence of French is an important backdrop to my story, Quebec cultural differences are also germane. Anglophones and francophones have different ways of looking at the world; English often seems to be the mirror image of French. The spines on French books have titles reading from bottom to top: in English, they go from top to bottom. French books have the table of contents at the end. Acronyms in French are often the precise reverse of English: SUV becomes VUS, UN becomes NU, PIN becomes NIP, NATO becomes OTAN, and so forth. The translation of "take French leave" is "*filer à l'anglaise,*" a French letter is "*capote anglaise,*" and a French seam is "*couture anglaise.*"

This looking-glass symmetry continues in a more serious vein when one compares the French approach to the state with the English. The former tends to be top down, the latter bottom up. The English are concerned about individual and minority rights; the French feel it makes sense for the majority, the *collectivité*, to rule. Even though it is North American in its consumer habits, and even though it was abandoned by the French some 250 years ago, Quebec still is imbued with a good dollop of French republican thinking (individual rights are irrevocably given over to the government to express the general will and collectivist rights) rather than American thinking (individual rights are sacred and, while they can be sometimes delegated to the government, they are only on loan). The homogenous nature of French Quebec society and the trust in government through *solidarité* that it engenders also explain the earlier paternalistic and later statist nature of Quebec politics.[10]

In France, both law and language are standardized and codified to form a pure, untouchable whole. French vocabulary and grammar have been standardized since 1635 by L'Académie française; French law was codified by *la coutume de Paris* in 1510 and then by *le Code Napoléon* in 1804. In Quebec, language is only indirectly standardized through French influence; but Quebec law, originally based on *la coutume de Paris*, was re-codified by the civil code of Lower Canada in 1866 and then the Quebec civil code of 1994. Prescriptive law is inflexible and uniform, qualities that are both its glory and its drawback. The uniformity of codification had its echo in the imposed structures of the municipal mergers. Yes, mergers occurred in common law regimes such as Ontario, but they were sold on economic, not structural, grounds.

Colloquial and familiar short forms in Quebec French often end in "o": *frigo, resto, écolo, McDo, négo.* You even get things like *collabo, proprio, parano, edito.* So intellectuals in Quebec have been given a warm, fuzzy name: *intello. Intellos* are as influential in Quebec as they are uninfluential in the rest of Canada. For example, there is no equivalent newspaper to *Le Devoir* in English Canada. To start off with, *Le Devoir* is visually spare, elegant, and non-sensationalist. Its editors have no qualms about printing op-ed pieces running to thousands of words – mostly written by *intellos*. The key thing is that this newspaper is read not just by *intellos* but by politicians. Did I mention that it is also sovereignist? *Le Devoir* reinforces the message that, to be an *intello* in Quebec, one should really be a sovereignist.

Quebec intellectuals command a degree of follower-ship, respect, and political influence unheard of in anglophone circles. Unfortunately, this intellectual élite do not always exhibit the practicality of the rest of Quebec's society. They were quite taken with the *idea* of creating one monolithic municipality of Montreal; the nuts and bolts of how it was to operate were less important.

Certainly the average francophone, unlike many belonging to the intellectual class, was upset by the forced nature of the mergers. However, once mergers happened, there was a typical rally-round-the-flag attitude that took over. Out of solidarity, many francophones – especially the élite – got behind the megacity and were upset to see their anglophone co-citizens still resisting this fait accompli. It was bad form. The collectivity had made a decision that all were supposed to support. The fact that demerger sentiment in Outremont was nearly non-existent had less to do with the lack of local political leadership than with the francophone desire to close ranks and move on. The contrast with Westmount could not have been more evident. Once again, the French élite, as well as being quite happy to integrate into a new city that had been declared officially French, exhibited the francophone trait of accepting a decision made by the collectivity – the government.

The citizens of Westmount, still incensed by the brutal nature with which the megacity had been imposed and the trampling of what they saw as their right to live in a municipality of their choice, were warmly receptive to the demerger call. Undoubtedly there was an added reason: their identity. And it was not just a question of preserving their "English municipalities" (in reality, "bilingual municipalities") but of preserving the one level of government where they felt at home. Anglos don't trust Quebec City, especially when the PQ is in charge. Francophones, not unnaturally, feel at one with a legislature and bureaucracy that operates exclusively in French. They trust the provincial government as a faithful reflection of them.

Francophones are very un-American in this regard: Americans are loyal to their country, not to their government. And Quebec has a lot of government: compared to Ontario, for example, it has 12 per cent more public-sector workers per capita.[11]

This francophone desire to create solidarity reached its purest expression whenever PQ governments called for commissions, "*chantiers*" or "socio-economic summits," where all were supposed to arrive at a societal consensus on the major issues of the day. Something deep in the Quebec collective psyche seemed to well up, calling for this kind of group decision-making. It is based on the notion that, if you get a bunch of people under one roof with a problem to solve, they'll eventually come up with a solution – not perhaps the best solution, but one that most can live with. It's a bit like an intellectual barn-raising or quilting bee. A key characteristic of this summitry *à la québécoise* is the mixing together of elected and non-elected. Throw in union leaders, academics, businesspeople, and social activists – all are supposed to agree spontaneously through the miracle of *concertation*. The collective desideratum is a *projet de societé* – a plan for society. While just about all societies try to obtain consensus, French Quebec goes a step beyond. If consensus can't be managed, then a decision is applied. All are supposed to accept it and get on with their lives. With Anglo-Saxons, rancour sets in, and issues are rarely put to bed.

Seen in this light, the fact that Quebec has the most unionized workforce in North America starts to become understandable. Overall unionization rate in Quebec is 40 per cent (82 per cent in the public sector and 25 per cent in the private sector). The rest of Canada is 31 per cent. Only 13 per cent of the US workforce is unionized (and a miniscule 7 per cent of its private sector[12]). Unique in North America, not only are Quebec's union leaders regularly interviewed by the media on a wide range of matters but the power of the labour unions is so strong that the construction industry is shut down for two weeks' summer vacation.[13] Given Quebec's brutal winters, this is the height of the construction season. Quebec is so comfortable with its unions that in 1983 it set up the FTQ Solidarity Fund, run by the FTQ union with a tax-sheltered status: investors buying its shares get an income-tax break.

The Quebec government is not afraid to legislate. It dictated how many people can work in a grocery store on weekends. Other laws dictated that margarine cannot be coloured like butter and that all apartment leases had to come due on 30 June. Even maple syrup (Quebec produces 80 per cent of the world's supply) is marketed through a monopoly. In the Montreal region, while not a law, all car dealerships are closed on weekends. Citizens put up with all this restraint of consumer freedom without a whimper. Social engineering also can take precedence over freedom of choice: since 1981, women are prohibited from changing their maiden name on marrying. So when the Quebec authorities said, "For your benefit, we are going to wipe out your municipality," it was very much part of a meddlesome tradition.

Had French Quebecers not had this highly developed sense of solidarity, though, I am convinced that their language and culture would not have survived.

THE NATIONALIZATION OF QUEBEC

Quebec has slowly become nomenclaturally nationalized over the years. The Provincial Bank became the National Bank. St Jean Baptiste Day was rebaptized la Fête nationale in 1978. Victoria Day (after becoming la Fête de Dollard), was declared National Patriots' Day in 2002. In 2006, even Charest's government came out with programs such as the Politique nationale de la ruralité. What are called provincial parks in the rest of Canada are called national parks in Quebec.

Vexillologically, Quebec also asserts its nationality. Back in 1967 the provincial government under the Liberal Jean Lesage decreed that the Quebec flag must be flown on all public buildings in the position of honour: on the viewer's left or in the centre of a group of three flags. Naturally, this flew in the face of international protocol, which requires that the national flag must take precedence. The mayor of Montreal of the time, Jean Drapeau, flouted the Quebec decree. To this day, Montreal City Hall stubbornly continues Drapeau's practice, while some of its own boroughs fly the Quebec flag in the position of honour.[14]

Quebecers are happy to allow their government monopolies on (or control over) electricity, agriculture, construction, health services, liquor sales, and vehicle insurance. The Quebec government has in the past also nationalized or taken a position in certain industries: airlines, mining, steel, forestry, petroleum, and asbestos (yes, asbestos). In 1977 the newly elected PQ government decided to nationalize (in effect, expropriate) the asbestos industry. They created the Société nationale de l'amiante (SNA), a Crown corporation wholly owned by the province. From General Dynamics, the SNA first acquired control, then all of Asbestos Corporation. The SNA then bought Atlas Asbestos and Bell Asbestos Mines from Turner and Newall of England, who owned the majority shares in my own company at the time. Generally, these foreign corporations played the Quebec government for all they were worth and were delighted to dump their holdings, especially as the toxicity of asbestos was becoming more and more an actionable matter.

ANGLO REALITY TODAY

The reality of Quebec politics today is that there is little recognition of the English, and any of their positive contributions have been mostly written out of Quebec's history. The English are not really a force in Quebec anymore. Just examine the demographics: the number of mother-tongue anglophones has plummeted from 13.8 per cent of the Quebec population in 1951 to 8.2 per cent in 2006. Mind you, the francophone population also dropped, but much less steeply, going from 82.5 per cent in 1951 to 79.6 per cent in 2006.

The decline and fall of the once-powerful – and societally corrosive – anglo hegemony is nowhere more obvious than its evaporated political clout. Take Alliance Quebec: this organization, created in 1982 and funded by Ottawa, was supposed to promote and protect English rights in Quebec. Headed up in the past by true leaders such as Reed Scowen, Peter Blaikie, Alex Paterson, and Eric Maldoff, all the anglo community seemed to be able to muster as president in February 2004 was Darryl Grey, who blew in from Halifax under a cloud in 1998 (after blowing into Halifax from Atlanta under a cloud in 1990).[15] And to reinforce the old anglo stereotype, Grey was resolutely unilingual. By 2003, Alliance Quebec could boast only 1,554 members.[16] By June 2005 it was being sued for unpaid rent. The Reverend Grey could not comment, being in Los Angeles attending a meeting of the Moonies.[17] Today, Alliance Quebec no longer exists.

Then there was the Equality Party. A protest party born out of anglo frustration with the Liberals' mishandling of the law regarding the language of signs, the Equality Party had a brief moment of very relative glory when it elected four members in 1989. The lack of anglo political power was never more obvious. The French had the

PQ; the best the anglo community could produce was this fractious Lilliputian party, comprised of a ragtag quartet of Robert Libman in his first foray into politics, the larger-than-life Gordon Atkinson, the portly, intelligent Neil Cameron, and the unpredictable gadfly Richard Holden, who represented Westmount. Delivering a final coup de grace to anglo pride, Holden later decamped to the PQ. Reed Scowen, sage commentator of the Quebec scene, feels that today there is simply no leader of the English community.[18]

Soon after becoming the head of a PQ government in 1996, Lucien Bouchard decided to make overtures to the English community, addressing some four hundred anglos at the Centaur Theatre. I said at the time that I thought he decided to talk to us while it was still possible to *find* four hundred anglos in Quebec. Some "angryphones" accused those of us who attended of fraternizing with the enemy. I didn't see things in those terms: Bouchard was not "the enemy." He represented what a good number of Quebecers thought. Were he the enemy, so were millions of people with whom anglos shared this province.

As a measure of how unimportant anglos had become in Quebec, the Centaur event was revealing. Rather than expecting to have their favour curried, anglophones were chuffed that Bouchard would bother. In the event, nothing came of this one-time attempt of rapprochement.

Owing to the massive pluralities the Liberals pile up in anglo ridings, anglos are underrepresented in the Quebec National Assembly. This phenomenon is exacerbated by the tyranny of rurality in Quebec. Because the rural ridings are less populous than the urban (and coincidentally contain few anglos), rural Quebec has a substantial edge in the National Assembly when compared to, say, the region of Montreal. Combining the effect of the "wasted" Liberal pluralities and this rural bias, the anglophone voter has far less political clout than the francophone voter. After the March 2007 election, Charest named only one anglo to his cabinet: twenty-nine-year-old Yolande James. *La Presse* columnist Lysiane Gagnon commented: "For the first time in the history of the Liberals, the cabinet does not include any credible anglophone representative, yet there used to be generally two or three – and a seat was always reserved for the Jewish community."[19]

It was not just in the political arena that anglos were a spent force. Perhaps significantly, the legal proceedings against the municipal merger law, Bill 170, were conducted exclusively in French, even though they (unfortunately) revolved around preserving the anglo sense of identity. Not a word of English sullied the court case for days on end. Mind you, precious few anglophone lawyers pleaded our case; that too was intentional. In common with today's Quebec anglo, we were anxious to show how well integrated we were. Bilingualism used to mean it was francophones who spoke English to anglophones; today it means most anglophones feel obliged to speak French to francophones. For example, whenever the Union of Montreal Island Suburban Municipalities had a meeting, they did so entirely in French, even though half the mayors were English. This happened even when I presided. Naturally, all MUC meetings were conducted exclusively in French.

For further evidence of the anglo demise, *circumspice*: the Blue Bonnets Racetrack became the Hippodrome, Burnside and Western avenues became de Maisonneuve. Craig Street became St-Jacques. Dorchester became René-Lévesque – except in Westmount. When leaving a black-tie dinner some years ago, I was accosted by a former minister of cultural affairs in René Lévesque's government, Clément Richard, who nearly grabbed my wing collar demanding why Westmount had the impudence to continue to refuse to change Dorchester's name. I calmly replied I didn't believe in erasing history, which got him even angrier. The people putting on their coats around us stared in disbelief. In October 1996 another proposal for a street name change came up: the executive committee of the City of Montreal formally requested the Toponymy Commission to change the name of Sherbrooke Street to rue Bourassa.[20] I went ballistic. It did not happen.

WESTMOUNT DOES ITS BIT

In common with many anglos, I supported language laws protecting French – even though, of necessity, these laws affect English speakers disproportionately, or at least differently. French language and culture are indeed threatened in Quebec, and any and all reasonable limitations on English are understandable. However, the various language laws' application can be a bureaucratic burlesque. There used to be four bodies charged with the protection and promotion of French: the Commission de toponymie (to assure "proper" place names), the Conseil de la langue française, the Office de la langue française (OLF), and the Commission de protection de la langue française. One way or another, the City of Westmount dealt with all four.

A constant stream of civil servants armed with copies of a few laws and copious photographic evidence of our most blatant infractions came calling at Westmount City Hall, as we were an "institution providing services to persons, a majority of whom speak a language other than French." These people making their appointed rounds were to "negotiate Westmount's francization program." In 1985 we were gently scolded by a M. Quesnel of the Service de la promotion du français of the OLF, who told us in conspiratorial tones that he had overheard a switchboard operator answering incoming calls with the word "Westmount" followed by – gasp! – "a unilingual English greeting," the nature of which his delicate sensibilities prevented him from revealing. He helpfully suggested "Bonjour, good morning," which was readily agreed on. Then, of course, there was the question of stop signs, those ubiquitous symbols of linguistic impurity, those octagonal red flags to the *independantiste* bulls. Bilingual signs (STOP/ARRêT) were not acceptable: we would have to replace our three hundred signs with ARRêT, at a cost of some $40,000. In my most reasonable and persuasive tones, I told him that, after all, the imperative *stop* has been a perfectly good French word since 1792, so our only solecism was that our signs contained a redundant word. "Is redundancy illegal?" I asked, puckishly.

"*Stop* may be a French word," he allowed, "but we cannot have what appear to be bilingual stop signs."

"But we are designated a bilingual city," I protested.

"Ah," he said, "but these are traffic signs. All traffic signs in Quebec must be in French, or be in pictograms."

"But," I said, "STOP signs are used in France, for God's sake."

"This is Quebec," he said – not one of his finest arguments.

In desperation, I said, "But *arrêt* is a noun. What you need is an imperative. A verb."

"We just apply the law," he said. Which said it all.

Much later, in 1993, Quebec relented on the stop sign issue. You could have ARRêT, you could have STOP. But you couldn't have both. We still had to pull out all the stops that cohabitated.

Street signs were also problematic. Westmount, quite cleverly, we thought, had quietly over time removed the generic "street," "road," "crescent," and so forth from its signs to come to some sort of a reasonable accommodation with regard to the language laws. We were left with what we thought were inoffensive, if Englishy, proper names. This policy, explained the ever-helpful M. Quesnel, was unlawful. We had to show the French generic. We were told to expect a visit from the Commission de toponymie. Sure enough, in due course, a civil servant from this august body produced himself, having thoughtfully prepared a comprehensive list of all our street names and precisely how they should be rendered into French. There were many pitfalls, though. For instance, if "Church Hill" were two words, the sign must say "Chemin de la côte de l'église." However, if this little street honoured Winston, it should become "Avenue Churchill." Likewise, the residents of Braeside Place would have to do their bit to establish the French face of Quebec. Their letterheads would henceforth read "Impasse Braeside." But it was not so simple. A bit more research was necessary. If by chance this street had been named after Braeside, Australia, then it became "Impasse de Braeside." Assuming it was named after a palace, "Avenue de Kensington" was likewise permissible. And the name Belmont Crescent could not be replaced by "Croissant Belmont" on the ground that the street was not a half-circle. Another name must be found.

It was on such matters that the fate of the French language in Quebec depended.

By July 1999, after fourteen years of desultory negotiations, we reached a historic compromise. The Belmont issue was resolved with "Chemin du Belmont Crescent." That was a piece of brilliance. However, "Avenue de Kensington" remained. The *de* was de rigueur. In a broad gesture of magnanimity, we were at liberty to spell Belvedere without accents, since we had argued it was a place name, not a place to admire the view. The Académie française would have been proud.

THE TWO FRENCH QUEBECS

When this brand of otherworldly Cartesian logic was equally and resolutely applied to the "problem" of the smorgasbord of municipalities cluttering up the Island of Montreal, is it any wonder the provincial francophone bureaucracy militated in favour of One Island One City? Bureaucrats the world over value neatness and have a slavish respect for first principles. But in Quebec and in France, they enjoy a sympathetic and receptive ear from the politicians, many of whom were trained the same way. The tension that exists in anglo societies between the bureaucrats and the elected officials is almost non-existent in Quebec. They share – and are taught to share – the same problem-solving approach.

The pragmatic French-Canadians are found in business. They have no use for bureaucrats or their companions-in-arms, Quebec politicians. Indeed, there are two Quebecs, each led by its own élite: the political élite and the business élite. The former élite has as its spiritual forebears the French nobles and clergy who ruled New France. Their approach is top down, deductive, *dirigiste*. The second élite, whose adaptability and resilience are like that of the *coureurs du bois* and the farmers eking out a living in a hostile climate, are down to earth, inductive, and persuaded by common sense (*le gros bon sens*). The founders of Cascades, Bombardier, Jean Coutu, and Maax seem to have descended from the men who tilled the land, trapped the furs, and swatted the blackflies.

Today, francophones have pretty much taken over the Quebec business world, but not quite. There are twenty-two Canadian billionaires, and eight of them are Quebecers, but of that eight, only three (Paul Desmarais, Guy Laliberté, and Jean Coutu) are francophone.[21] So the process takes a while. Certainly, for lesser economic mortals, francophone incomes are coming alongside anglophone incomes, even though the proportion of francophones with a university degree is much lower. Because of some very wealthy anglophones, the average anglophone income is still much higher than francophone, but the median income is close.[22] (When Paul Demarais walks in a room, the average wealth of the occupants zooms up; the median wealth stays the same.)

QUEBEC FEARS A LANGUAGE, NOT A PEOPLE

Everything in Quebec is viewed through the prism of language, or, more broadly, the sociological labels afforded by language. For example, the fact that francophones and anglophones have separate hospitals and schools inevitably leads to headlines – usually in the French media – comparing the two. "Montreal hospitals: The anglos better than the francos?" is a typical front-page headline.[23] It should be pointed out that "anglo" hospitals are required to offer complete services in French; in fact, one-third of their clientele is French-speaking.

Every newspaper poll in Quebec is routinely broken down into francophones and anglophones – more frequently than even between males and females. And the subject of language provides endless grist to the media mill. According to a 2005 *La Presse* poll,[24] 40 per cent of francophones (and 49 per cent of *péquistes*) would not be favourable to an anglophone premier – but only 9 per cent say they would be unfavourable to a black as premier. That Quebecers have no compunction about admitting such a bias tempts one to interpret this as proof of how mainstream anglophobia has become.

But is this really anglophobia? Is it not just evidence of a concern that an anglo premier would not be a good standard-bearer for the French face and fact of Quebec? Indeed, had this fictitious premier-cum-straw-man spoken impeccable French, I think the poll would have shown a much different result. In trying to understand the attitude of francophones in Quebec toward English speakers, one must make a distinction between anglophobia (antipathy toward the English) and what one might whimsically call anglolinguaphobia (antipathy toward the English language). Dislike of English-speaking people is fuelled by a certain jaundiced view of history: the Conquest of New France (when one European country won a battle against another), or the previous dominance of the majority by a minority. It is atavistic and recriminative. Fear of the English language, on the other hand, is fuelled by a fear of losing French.[25] It is protective and, to a good extent, defensible, or at least understandable.[26] The PQ has been particularly adept at welding these two, quite distinct fears together.

That bilingualism can contribute to the de-francophonization of Quebec is also a thesis that is very much alive. A recent book by Christian Dufour, *Quebecers and English: The Return of the Sheep*,[27] has an image of a sheep on the front cover bleating "I'm baaa-lingual." Dufour writes that, for a francophone Quebecer, to regard being bilingual as something essential or even very desirable is an example of the "atavism of the conquered." I am not taking issue with his thesis, just pointing out how such convictions coloured the question of mergers on the Island of Montreal. For some francophone language militants, English remains the language of the conquerors "rather than the tool allowing Quebecers to conquer the world," as editorialist André Pratte wrote in another context.[28]

While most French Quebecers are, almost of necessity, somewhat ethnocentric, they are far from being racist.[29] And, in spite of some politically driven anglophobia, they are very open to others, including the English. Jim Corcoran, Normand Brathwaite, Judi Richards, Nanette Workman: these are examples of a number of anglophones who have become *vedettes* (stars) in Quebec. Commercial services such as the Kane and Fetterly Funeral Home, heavily advertised on French radio, prove that francophones are even prepared to die in English, at least in an English-run funeral home. Indeed, the CBC's French version, Radio Canada (both TV and radio), is not anglophobic. I have, however run into a streak of anglophobia promoted by the lowbrow TV and radio stations (not unlike the equivalent pronouncements of the ineffable Don Cherry in English); since, unlike the rest of Canada, most programming is "made in Quebec," these attitudes are easy to pass along.

During a Just for Laughs festival held the summer of 2005 and later broadcast on television, a comedian, François Morency, and the notorious filmmaker Pierre Falardeau, put on a skit.[30] Morency said, "Last week we planted an anglo. Let's see how it's doing." A dummy was buried head-first in a bucket of earth. Falardeau proceeded to water it so as to not "dry up his anglo." Pretty tame stuff – if it were fifty years ago. Replace the word "anglo" with "Jew," or "Frenchman," and one sees how acceptable it is even today to make fun of the anglo minority. To be fair, this little skit drew an excoriating editorial from André Pratte of *La Presse*.

A sure sign of our comeuppance, we English have taken to making fun of ourselves. For reasons lost in the mists of history, the French call the English *têtes carrés*, "squareheads." So when the Bowser and Blue comedy duo decided to mount an all-anglo event at the 1997 Just for Laughs festival, they called it Woodstock for Squareheads. We all wore four-sided brown paper bags over our heads. The audience was subjected to fifty anglo celebrities singing, "We are here to stay, and we are *têtes carrés* and we are proud to say, that *we're here*." The bathos of anglo decline was never more in evidence, but at least we had fun. The highlight of the event was the separatist passionara (and perfectly bilingual) Josée Legault doing a deft take-off on the queen offering her sovereign services to an independent Quebec.

Something that should have been on Just for Laughs was a comment by no less than the former premier of Quebec, Bernard Landry – but he was being serious. Asked what he thought about the privatization of the provincial liquor board, the SAQ, Landry came to its defence. He rhapsodized about all the SAQ had done. For example, it had educated Quebecers about the charms of wine, which helped them get closer to their Western European roots and away from the Anglo-Saxon traditions of drinking "hard stuff."[31] I did not make this up. He also opined that the SAQ was like Hydro-Québec, offering the same product at the same price anywhere in Quebec. This was "an essential Quebec characteristic of solidarity, in that we get the same choice in Montreal as in Rouyn-Noranda."[32]

CRYING WOLFE

Anglophobia among diehard sovereignists got a shot in the arm when the last referendum on sovereignty was lost because of the anglos. They were the spoilers. For a small portion of the French intellectual and political class, anglos have always been spoilers: even today one hears references to "the Conquest" as if General Wolfe beat General Montcalm in 1959 rather than 1759. In a Canada where nobody under sixty can sing "The Maple Leaf Forever," let alone remember lyrics that glorify Wolfe's victory, the Conquest pops up in French Quebec to ensure a language debate has a good dose of emotion.

The Plains of Abraham, where Wolfe beat Montcalm in a short battle, is treated as a sort of consecrated ground by those who wish to keep the old grudges going. In July 2008, when three PQ members signed a petition denouncing ex-Beatle Paul McCartney's plans to give a concert on the Plains of Abraham to celebrate the four hundredth anniversary of Quebec City, PQ leader Pauline Marois eventually had to distance herself from their position when it became an international embarrassment. Even for her, the idea that it was disrespectful for an English entertainer to sing in the same place the French lost a battle to the English 250 years ago, and that it would "bring back painful memories of our Conquest," was a bit of a stretch. Then, in February 2009, a planned re-enactment in August of the battle of the Plains of Abraham was cancelled following threats of violence from some sovereignists. In September that year, a hundred or so artists and PQ luminaries read 130 Québécois literary excerpts while standing on the Plains – which was fine, except that the organizers decided to include the reading of the 1970 FLQ manifesto.

So it is not too surprising that, when we had to play the language card to try to win our legal case, Louise Harel talked about the "foul stench of colonialism." It just came naturally. By keeping such resentment alive, some in the PQ hoped it would help to win the next referendum.

REFERENDUM

The chance of yet another referendum on sovereignty loomed over Quebec like a threatening storm in the late 1990s. Every puff of wind created by a poll was measured, the entrails of every political failure were examined, all in name of referendum augury. The municipal mergers, of course, did not escape the referendum soothsayers. The merger debate was not devoid of its ironies. One can understand the PQ wanting to integrate the English into a (now legally declared) francophone Montreal, since as undigested anglos they would never vote the right way in any referendum on sovereignty; but how does one explain the position of the federalist *La Presse*, for example: it was in favour of integrating anglos into the megacity, yet would have recoiled in horror at the thought of the French being forced to integrate into the Canadian whole.

RESIDUAL ANGLO UNILINGUALISM

Today, a greater proportion of Quebec anglophones can speak French than francophones can speak English. However, this was decidedly not true one or two generations ago, when the typical anglo was imprisoned in unilingualism. The West Island of Montreal in those days resembled a piece of Ontario that somehow had drifted east. Thus it was not surprising to have a number of West Island mayors who in the 1990s still spoke no French. These mayors were invariably in their sixties and seventies, living reminders of the way things had been.

Malcolm Knox, one of the great Pointe-Claire mayors, spoke no French. He understood it, though. He would sit on the executive of the mass transit board and absorb everything that went on, but when he opened his mouth, out came English. In 1994, he was very hurt when the suburb's time came to choose a chairman for the board, and I had to tell him gently that his lack of French meant he was out. He said that his family had been in Quebec for many generations and he was as much a Quebecer as the next person. Under this bluster, he knew it would have been politically impossible for us to name him. Mac, as he was called, was a big man, a proud navy man, and ran Pointe-Claire like a tight ship.

Every Beaconsfield mayor I knew was unilingual, from Patricia Rustad to Roy Kemp to Anne Myles. Until the imposition of the megacity in January 2002, Myles had been the mayor of Baie d'Urfé for eighteen years. You don't mess with Myles, a tiny woman with a tremulous voice and piercing blue eyes. If there were a female equivalent to avuncular, she would be it. In October 2003 she ran for Beaconsfield borough chairperson (and, perforce, megacity councillor) in a by-election. Mayor Gérald Tremblay was beside himself that she was running; if she won, he would lose his majority on council. In desperation he attacked her unilingualism. "Mrs Myles does not speak a word of French. It seems to me, out of respect for the citizens, the least one could ask of an elected official ... is that he or she can speak French."[33] Given that Beaconsfield was around 25 per cent French, Tremblay was not wrong. And it's one thing to be mayor of the little town of Baie d'Urfé, another to be a city councillor for a megacity that operates entirely in French. However, Myles was quick to point out that her lack of French was no impediment when Tremblay was wooing her to become a member of his party in 2001. Once again, Tremblay was caught in a contradiction. And he looked like a bully, taking on a seventy-six-year old woman. If the electors – who appreciated Myles's steadfastness on the merger question – wanted to vote in someone who spoke Swahili, it was their privilege.

In the event, Myles won 69 per cent of the vote. Next thing you know, the ultra-nationalist Gilles Rhéaume filed a complaint with the Office de la langue française because she spoke no French. A few weeks later, the secretary-treasurer of CUPE, a union that represented 80 per cent of the municipal employees in Quebec, waded into the larger debate, saying that Premier Charest, with his demerger project, only wanted "to please the Rhodesians on the Island of Montreal."[34] Things got nasty. In late October 2003, seven members of a self-described "militia," the Movement de liberation nationale de Québec – including, bizarrely, an ex-city councillor from Otterburn Park – were arrested for spray-painting the Baie d'Urfé town hall.[35] Their handiwork included things like "Une île une ville française," "Fuck Canada," "Fusion Montréal," "Canadians go home," and "FLQ." Three primitive explosive devices were found. The president of the Movement de liberation nationale de Québec, Raymond

Villeneuve, approved of these actions "against the enemies of the Quebec people."[36] The seven were given suspended sentences.

A week later, it was time to hear from ex-mayor Pierre Bourque, who was languishing as leader of the opposition on the megacity council. "Today, it's the anglophone community that is in power. They run the [mega]city. They don't want to give too much to downtown. They are still suspicious of Montreal,"[37] he said. That remark, politically incorrect really only in the literal sense, set off a firestorm of protest – among anglophones, of course.

Only an infinitesimal fraction of francophones become splenetic revanchists who try to make the news on a slow day. Just about all non-political francophones, particularly younger ones, are simply insecure about their language's survival and have no brief against the English. André Pratte, *La Presse* editor and writer, quotes in *Aux pays des merveilles* a 2004 PQ workshop that commented that "the depiction of a Quebec economically exploited and culturally dominated by the 'English' seems quaint for someone born in 1990."[38]

A FRENCH QUEBEC AND AN ENGLISH CANADA

At the height of the anti-merger fight in 1999 I felt it time to send a message that Westmount was anti-merger but not anti-French. Following up on a suggestion from a francophone Westmounter, I decided that Westmount should celebrate Saint Jean Baptiste Day for the first time ever. It got massive media coverage in French. The visiting mayor from Rimouski, our twin city, and Phillipe Cantin, writing in *La Presse*, both expressed their approval by calling it a "masterstroke." Once again, this sort of reaction was proof of the iconic power of the brand-name "Westmount" among francophones, especially when conjoined with that other brand-name, Saint Jean Baptiste, patron saint of Quebec. But this was not a stunt: I felt it was a necessary statement, although I admit the timing was somewhat opportunistic. Dressed as Westmount's first mayor, Eustache Prud'homme (fortunately, he was French), I lit the traditional Saint Jean bonfire. In spite of the approval of most Westmounters, my initiative was not universally applauded. The next day, little signs appeared: "Westmount Council: Quislings personified."

The Lachine Canal was built in the 1800s to skirt the rapids that made the St Lawrence River unnavigable, and along its banks rose the multi-storey Victorian industrial buildings in the dull brick now so beloved of loft-dwellers. When this canal was reopened, there was a concern that power boats would churn up toxic industrial sediments that had lain on the canal floor for years. Likewise, my reluctant but necessary decision in 2001 to plead the language argument in court to fight mergers stirred up a sludge of anglophobia. It still had not settled by the time of the demerger referendums in 2004, when things got even worse – grist to the mill for some PQ politicians, who publicly wrung their hands over the *clivage linguistique*.

So the merger and demerger mess actually increased both francophobia *and* anglophobia in Montreal. Rather than getting more English to assimilate into French Montreal, the merger created even more distrust of the French political élite among the English. On the other hand, the demerger created a strong anti-English reaction from the French. Why were most of the demerging municipalities English? Why were they rejecting the French majority? Why did they wish to retreat to their enclaves? The answer that came naturally to the French élites was that the English, as always, want to live in rich and splendid isolation. This insular interpretation ignored the fact that all of the demerging municipalities on the south shore were French-speaking.

And the sovereignty question in Quebec is never far from the surface. The French, of all stripes, were once again reminded that, in the same way the English did not want to embrace the "new city" concept, they were even colder to the "new country" project.

For many older anglophones, in the space of a generation Quebec went from being "our place" to "their place." If this were truly necessary in order to preserve French in Quebec, then it was worth it, but it is sad. There is hope, though. The next generation of anglophones has a deep attachment to Quebec, and their francophone equivalents no longer need to nurse old grievances to make them proud of Quebec. Still, we are a long way from the palmy days of Expo 67, when some dreamed a psychedelic dream of a bilingual Canada – before multiculturalism, two referenda on independence, and Canada's rejection of Quebec as a distinct society gave us a French Quebec and an English Canada.

3

Westmount Then and Now

To love the little platoon we belong to in society is the first principle (the germ as it were) of public affections. It is the first link in the series by which we proceed towards a love to our country and to mankind.

Edmund Burke, 1790

Like an old calliope starting up, the military band starts to wheeze out the old hymn. Raggedly, some voices emerge from the motley of local dignitaries. "O God our help in ages past," they intone, glancing at the program for the words. "Our hope for years to come." The rest stare at the granite plinth of the cenotaph. Above us a bronze angel points heavenward to a marching bronze soldier, putteed in the Great War manner. Inscribed on the plinth is "Their name liveth for evermore."

We have made a stately progress to the cenotaph from the crenellated tower of Westmount's neo-Tudor City Hall, accompanied by a gaggle of uniforms, mostly the green of the Canadian Forces. There are a few RCMP officers in scarlet tunics, yellow-striped breeches, and brown leather boots and belts. The Mountie flash contrasts with the dark blue of the Westmount public security force. At my first Remembrance Day ceremony twenty-five years ago, there was a retired army officer resplendent in khaki, Sam Browne belt, and spit-and-polished brown boots.

We are standing on sisal matting considerately laid down on the cold wet November grass. The area around us is called Garden Point. I am wearing the mayor's gold chain of office, worn not like a clunky necklace but draped equidistantly over front and back like a latter-day Sir Thomas More.

The band finishes. Since traffic has been stopped on Sherbrooke Street, silence wraps around us. We become part of a shared memory stretching back in time. To 1918. To 1945. Flags snap sharply in the wind like rifle shots. The grey granite monument broods over the dead, their names slowly eroding on stone tablets. One by one, the wreaths are laid. The old veterans stumble a bit but salute smartly after setting down a little ring of green leaves and plastic poppies. At each corner of the cenotaph, four young soldiers wearing combats stand stock-still with rifles reversed.

The ceremony, organized by the Royal Montreal Regiment, begins with "O Canada" and ends with the singing of "God Save the Queen." Out of the corner of my eye, I try to see whether Lucienne Robillard, the federal cabinet minister representing Westmount in Ottawa, manages to mouth the words to the royal anthem. Usually, Jacques Chagnon, the provincial representative, gamely sings along. "God Save the Queen" are not words that easily escape the lips of francophones in Quebec.

To the south of us are buff-coloured Jacobethan-style apartment houses and a huge gothic church. To the north is a short terrace of red brick townhouses with bow windows. Behind us is Selwyn House School and the ivy-covered City Hall. If one glances up to Westmount's summit, the windows of big stone houses wink back as the bare tree branches move. Except for the pavement, we could be on a village green in one of the Home Counties of England.

The hymns and prayers finished, it's time for the march-past. The three military units with armouries in Westmount exercise their respective Freedoms of the City with "drums beating, colours flying, and bayonets fixed." After a few hundred soldiers come the cadets, some invariably out of step. Bringing up the rear, a knot of West-mount Scouts and Guides sheepishly salute. The ceremony is over for another year, the only reminder being an assortment of plastic wreaths in various degrees of wholeness, scattered about the ceno-taph. It is the mid-1990s, but it could have been a decade before or after.

The word "cenotaph" means "empty tomb." In some ways, we are not just remembering the war dead. We are also remembering the Westmount of long ago. The ceremony, which never fails to move me, is a tableau of what Westmount was, not what it is.

But the media don't want to know: the Westmount of old makes for good copy; actually, it makes for copy that writes itself. God is in his heaven, the queen in her palace. Westmounters are clipping cou-pons and taking tea: this was and is the cliché retailed by the media of a Westmount of hill-dwelling Anglo-Saxon plutocrats. Oh, and they live in fully staffed mansions. Is this my city? Let me take you by the hand and lead you through the streets of Westmount – of yesterday and today.

WESTMOUNT FROM ABOVE AND BELOW

Westmount is roughly an oblong, measuring a bit more north-south than east-west. (*Caveat lector*: when Montrealers use the word "north," it means what they choose it to mean. What they call "north," compasses will tell you is almost west.) Westmount is trisected east-west by two streets: Sherbrooke and, higher up, The Boulevard. This trisection creates Lower Westmount (below Sherbrooke), Middle Westmount (between Sherbrooke and The Boulevard), and Upper Westmount (above The Boulevard) – or, if you like, the flat, the slope, and the summit. Westmount measures about two kilometres east-west and a maximum of 2.5 kilometres north-south, for a total area of four square kilometres. Westmounters of old would have used English measure (or Imperial, for even better measure): their municipality would be one thousand acres.

The top of the summit, at 201 metres above sea level,* makes a minuscule mountain, but it is Westmount's own. On the sunny slopes, protected from the rude north wind, Westmount enjoys a balmy microclimate. Below ground, things get complicated. On clearing away the overburden of geological flotsam and jetsam left from the last Ice Age (stuff called glacial till), one usually finds limestone bedrock – that is, until one gets closer to the southern edge of the municipality, which sits at about 40 metres above sea level, dropping to 20 metres at the southeastern tip. Most of Lower Westmount is a "beach terrace" created by the receding waters of the extinct Champlain Sea. While sounding romantic, this ex-seaside location can be a problem. Large trees, which drink as much as a thousand litres of water a day, tend to shrink the clay layer that is up to ten metres deep, sometimes causing settlement problems in old houses. Other houses on the flat are built over drained swamps or on filled ravines of small streams that once trickled down Westmount's little mountain, exiting in a gully called The Glen in the

---

* Montreal's Mount Royal is 233 metres above sea level.

south-west part of the municipality. This bit of geological history, fascinating as it might be, generally does not find its way into real-estate agents' patter.

At the southern border of Westmount is a concrete gash called the Ville-Marie Expressway. It acts as a kind of a raised traffic sewer to sluice away the cars and trucks that, before 1972, went directly though Westmount. The increasing reliance of Montrealers on the eternal combustion engine means that today we are almost back to where we started. Traffic is the bugbear of all Westmounters. Those living next to the expressway desperately demand a noise barrier, but most Westmounters "on the flat" don't really hear it. However, the twenty-four hour thrum of traffic of the Ville-Marie and Decarie expressways travels unimpeded up the mountain. You see the St Lawrence River from the slope or the summit, but you also hear cars and trucks. The noise refracts around houses to become an uninvited guest. In the middle of Summit Woods, the untouched forest is brutally and unremittingly violated by traffic sound wafting in on all sides.

WESTMOUNT: THE PRODUCT OF A DIVORCE[1]

It wasn't always like that. Had you entered Westmount 135 years ago from Sherbrooke Street, you would not have got far before arriving at the tollgate at Greene Avenue. This tollgate led to the only east-west passage through Westmount: the Côte St Antoine Road, originally an Indian trail, which for generations of Westmounters was called "the Coat Road."

Westmount was "erected" in 1874 as the Village of Notre Dame de Grâce. Then five thousand acres, the municipality was five times larger than it is today, sprawling over an area that included today's Notre Dame de Grâce and Côte Saint-Luc. It did not take long before the municipality's first mayor, Eustache Prud'homme, managed to have the major part secede and call itself Notre Dame de Grâce *West*, leaving a rump called Notre Dame de Grâce (full stop). This latter name was changed to Côte St Antoine in 1879, and, finally, to Westmount in 1895. Why was Notre Dame de Grâce split up? Most speculation suggests that it was on educational and linguistic grounds, the western part being more francophone and agricultural.[2] Thus Westmount, so often the target of annexation, started out as the product of secession.

By 1891, Westmount had about three thousand residents. This number increased when Sherbrooke Street was built in 1893 from Greene Avenue to the western limits and a railway station appeared in 1896. But it was the municipality's contract with the Montreal Street Railway to provide electric tram service that really kick-started Westmount's growth. Tram service was inaugurated on Sherbrooke Street in 1894, eight years after the tollgates at the entrances to Westmount were dismantled. By 1901, Westmount had nearly nine thousand residents, with two-thirds of today's mileage of streets already built. By 1911, with a population of 14,579, Westmount was the sixth-largest municipality in Quebec.[3]

WHY DECAMP TO WESTMOUNT?

Did those who settled in this new suburb desert the City of Montreal in order to avoid high taxes, grime, and noise? Yes. Did Montreal anglophones in those days settle in Westmount to be with their own kind? Most likely. If one asks the same two questions of the francophones who desert Montreal in droves one hundred years later to settle in Laval, Saint-Bruno, or Boisbriand, one gets the same answers. The desire to be comfortable and in control in one's environment, especially before acquiring property and putting down roots, is universal. If to fulfil this desire means commuting, so be it. In that sense, the Westmounters who took the tram to downtown Montreal in 1910 were no different from the Bouchervillois creeping toward Montreal Island in their cars every morning in 2010.

But though both escaped from and commuted to Montreal, there is a remarkable difference in behaviour between the suburbanite of old and of today. The first thing on the minds of the home-buyers who contributed to the explosive growth of Westmount from 1891 to 1911 was to build a community. In that twenty-year period when its population increased nearly fivefold, Westmount taxpayers built some dozen schools and churches, a public library, a community hall, parks, a lawn-bowling green, even a golf club. Except for the golf course, all of this built infrastructure is still with us and still admirably serves as its community armature.

In today's anarchic sprawling suburbs, each bungalow surrounded by a green moat of grass, residents do not invest the time, energy, or money to build much of a community infrastructure. Their family is their community; let the government build what's needed, they say. This car-induced exurban entropy leads to isolation. The tramway-induced density of Westmount, with its many attached houses, naturally led to interaction, calling for community involvement and investment. Five thousand people per square kilometre now live in Westmount, around ten times the density found in suburbs outside the Island of Montreal. This close community helps explain Westmount's ferocity in battling annexation, whether in 1910, 1960, or 2000.

THE APPREHENDED ANNEXATION OF 1910

The first battle was in 1910. At that time Montreal looked particularly unappetizing to Westmounters. Judge Cannon had just made public the results of his investigation that concluded that Montreal was riddled with corruption, favouritism, and patronage. He was convinced that at least eight aldermen (including a future mayor, Médéric Martin) were guilty of such practices.[4] Westmount fought annexation, "not because of the possibility of increased taxes, but against the spread of decadent morals," the council minutes read. Although this disavowal of fiscal concerns must be taken with a grain of salt, it was the power to legislate *private* rectitude that contributed to the uniqueness of Westmount in their eyes, and therefore to its resistance to annexation. "Intoxicating liquors" were prohibited, the Sabbath was strictly observed, cinemas were banned, and Westmount even restricted the kind of dancing at Victoria Hall. Fed up with Westmount's banning of golf on Sunday, members of the Westmount Golf Club had packed up and moved to Beaconsfield (or at least that's what the Beaconsfield Golf Club claims).

If the Westmount of old was prim, it was also somewhat inbred. W.H. Trenholme, who was mayor in 1909–10, had a cousin who was the wife of J.K. Ward, mayor from 1875 to 1883. W.H. was married to the sister of George Hogg, the mayor who served from 1927 to 1932. Hogg was also W.H.'s partner in the Guaranteed Pure Milk Company.

Now, it turns out that W.H.'s uncle, T.A. Trenholme,[5] who founded Elmhurst Dairies, was the last mayor of Notre Dame de Grâce (today, usually called NDG). In 1910, W.H. fought annexation tooth and nail, while T.A. actually spearheaded NDG's annexation with Montreal. At that point Westmount was a prosperous municipality of 14,500, while NDG, population 4,000, was deeply in debt.[6] Not unreasonably, Montreal wanted to swallow Westmount as a consolation for having to absorb such debt-ridden municipalities as NDG.[7]

But Montreal did all right in the end: by 1931, NDG had a population of 47,000 and was probably a nice little source of tax revenue. Today it boasts a population of 70,000 – 70 per cent of whom are tenants – and is lost in a massive Montreal borough with the poly-hyphenated name of Côte-des-Neiges–Notre-Dame-de-Grâce, weighing in with a total population of 170,000.

NDG's annexation* in 1910 without the approval of its taxpayers preyed on the minds of Westmounters at the time. A 1909 cartoon depicted Westmount as an innocent maiden, warding off her pursuer, the fat villain Montreal. Another cartoon in 1910, in the *Montreal Star*, entitled "As it appears to Westmount," pictured Westmount as a gent grabbed about the neck by a fat mugger called Montreal who holds the pistol marked "annexation" in his other hand. The mugger says, "Hand over your tax money now!" The victim asks, "What for?" Exclaims the mugger, "What for! To spend for myself, of course. I need the money!" The *Montreal Herald* pictured a Montreal cat stalking a Westmount mouse and speculated that annexation "would introduce thirst-quenching establishments within the Sacred Precincts."

FOR KING AND COUNTRY

But Westmount's allergy to annexation in 1910 was not just a question of money. Westmount was indeed special. As well as being priggish, Westmounters were also staunchly royalist, as evidenced by Victoria Hall, Victoria Avenue, and Prince Albert Avenue. The monarch's Canadian governors were honoured in street names: Metcalfe, Clandeboye, Carleton, Sydenham, Lansdowne, Bruce, Argyle, and Aberdeen. King's School was opened in 1896, to be equisexually followed by Queen's three years later. The city crest between 1895 and 1908 had a huge crown on its top.

In World War I, Westmount heeded the mother country's call. The 58th Westmount Rifles was organized in 1914 as a regiment

---

* This annexation was the final step in Montreal's slow encirclement of Westmount. Through no action of its own, Westmount was henceforth condemned to bear the sobriquet "enclave," although why this state of affairs is problematical in Montrealers' minds, I never understood. They remind me of the drunk, who, on feeling his way around a lamppost, says, "It's no use. I'm walled in."

five hundred strong; two hundred went overseas. Another 150 men made up the 21st Westmount Field Artillery, and there was the Westmount Squadron of the 13th Scottish Light Dragoons. But it was the Royal Montreal Regiment that became Westmount's regiment: on returning after four years of fighting and nearly 1,200 dead, the RMR merged with the 58th Westmount Rifles, and Westmount provided the land for probably the only municipally funded armoury in Canada. In 1925 the RMR settled in.

Westmount gave Mayor John Jenkins two months' leave of absence in 1937 to represent the city at the coronation of King George VI. When the king and queen visited Westmount in 1939, Murray Park was renamed King George Park, a name that today only the City of Westmount obstinately insists on using: Westmounters still call it Murray Park. (To add to the confusion, newcomers and real-estate agents erroneously call it Murray Hill Park.)

In World War II, Westmount commissioned a warship (HMCS *Westmount*), and an air force squadron was eventually named after her – the 401 City of Westmount Squadron – the only Canadian squadron to fight in the Battle of Britain. Westmount was the first municipality in Canada to have a lawful coat of arms, granted by the Lord Lyon King of Arms in Edinburgh, and as such holds "a special place in the story of the development of Canadian heraldry."[8]

When Queen Elizabeth and Prince Philip visited Westmount in 1959, they were presented with a silver maple syrup jug. Ever since, City Hall has sent the queen a shipment of maple syrup with which some obliging Buck House maid can refill her jug. As mayor, I would get a letter from the Master of the Household, embossed with a mulberry-coloured royal coat of arms and "Buckingham Palace" at the top, saying "I am commanded by Her Majesty to write and thank you and the people of Westmount for the very generous shipment of Maple Syrup which has arrived at Buckingham Palace ..." But in addressing me, the Master of the Household dropped a bit of a royal clanger. The letter would start "Mr Mayor," or even, "Mayor." *O tempora, O mores*! Westmount had always insisted on addressing its mayor as "Your Worship."[9]

A MUNICIPALITY OF FIRSTS

So the municipality of Westmount has always been rather traditional, yet its smallness and independence encouraged creativity in the same way that innovation in business is mostly found in small companies. Westmount built the first tax-supported public library in Quebec in 1899 and the first power plant in North America to burn garbage for electricity in 1906. By 1911, it had spent over $600,000 (about $12 million today) in acquiring land for parks, and by 1931 had more park acreage per capita than any other municipality in Quebec.[10]

A mayor of Westmount co-founded the Federation of Canadian Municipalities. Westmount was the first municipality in Canada to institute the city-manager system of government in 1913. Starting in 1906, it scrutinized all exterior architectural designs before issuing building permits, the first Canadian municipality to do so.

SETTING ARCHITECTURAL STANDARDS

The static riot of Westmount housing styles beggars description. At least one fieldstone farmhouse remains that is 273 years old. A few clapboard country-style houses from a later era are dotted around the city. A number of Greek Revival and Georgian-style cut stone villas and British garrison houses from the 1840s and 1850s also still remain. The late Westmount architect Richard Bolton idiosyncratically classed the wave of romantic architecture that came next as "Gothic Revival, Tudor Revival, Castellated, Dutch Gable, Rhine Castle, Carpentered Gothic, Flamboyant, and Eclectic." One suspects the latter two categories were superfluous. Most of the development in Upper Westmount of free-standing houses that typifies Westmount in the popular imagination came in the 1920s and 1930s. We got Scottish Baronial, Neo-Quebec, and lots of stone houses in what I call Cotswold Twee.

The City of Westmount always was concerned about its built environment. As Walter van Nus wrote in *Montreal Metropolis, 1880–1930*:

> Westmount set the pace, as its competitors often copied Westmount's latest upgraded construction standards soon after they had been adopted by "Canada's model city." Westmount's extraordinarily detailed and highly technical building bylaws of 1909 and 1911 set a new benchmark for Island suburbs. By 1911, Westmount had banned new wooden buildings and even those of plank frames and brick veneer (the NDG standard) ...

Imposing strict building standards seemed to pay. In the long run, these bylaws helped preserve Westmount's architectural heritage. More immediately, they encouraged imitation by other towns keen to repeat Westmount's success. In 1910, Outremont plagiarized Westmount's 1909 building bylaw ...

When the new municipality of Hampstead established its building bylaw in 1921, it simply adopted the entire Westmount building code. The mayor of Montreal West was merely more candid than the heads of other affluent suburbs when he declared in 1912 that his town "had established Westmount as its ideal and was copying her example in many methods of civic improvement."

Zoning laws were another tool of exclusivity. Here, too, Westmount led the way. In 1897, the town reserved its entire upper portion (north and along Montrose Avenue) for detached or semi-detached single-family homes ...

When in June 1928 Westmount restricted its most prestigious area (north of The Boulevard) to detached houses (henceforth excluding semi-detached ones), Outremont followed four months later with the same restriction for its finest streets ...

Once again, Westmount set the regional precedent. Its Architectural Commission, established in 1916, consisted of the mayor, the city manager, the city engineer (*ex officio*), and four local architects named by the city council. The Commission's task was to approve the plans and specifications of every new building, statue, arch, fountain, and even fence before construction could start.[11]

THE BLOSSOMING OF UPPER WESTMOUNT

Westmount generally filled up from the bottom. In 1911, with well over three thousand houses in Lower or Middle Westmount, there were perhaps just a few dozen houses in Upper Westmount. Westmount was resolutely middle class. The Montreal rich still lived in the élite Square Mile district downtown, but in the 1920s, a number of big houses in Upper Westmount were built by some who could never have made it in that suffocating club. As Donald MacKay recounts in *The Square Mile: Merchant Princes of Montreal*, "The *arrivistes*, however, were now building out in Westmount. Noah Timmins, who developed the Hollinger Mine, one of the richest gold mines in northern Ontario, built a house there at Belvedere Place. After Samuel Bronfman opened his distillery in Montreal in 1925, the Bronfmans lived in Westmount rather than the Square Mile ... Square Milers continued to regard it as outside the pale, socially as well as geographically."[12] (Later, even the Square Mile, crushed by both the changing times and the pressure of Montreal's development, started to send rich refugees to Westmount.)

Noah Timmins spent $1 million to build his neo-Tudor mansion on the summit in 1929, about $12 million in today's money. In 1962, this house, probably the largest in Westmount, was ignominiously divided in two by slicing a 23-foot gap right through the billiard and trophy room and part (part!) of the dining room to make two houses that would sell in the $100,000 bracket,[13] or $1.4 million for the pair in today's money – thereby proving that dealing in such real estate is a mug's game. The larger of the two houses, the residence of the late Jacques Francoeur, was sold in 2006 for $5.6 million, the second-highest price ever seen in Westmount. The other half sold for $5.3 million in 2007. So the original house undivided would today have finally fetched what it cost, but it took seventy-five years to do it.

THE TRAVAILS OF LOWER WESTMOUNT

Before the Ville-Marie expressway was built, the biggest danger to Lower Westmount was, sadly, the City of Westmount itself. After the City of Montreal created Dorchester Boulevard as an east-west artery in the mid-1950s, Westmount, in the early 1960s, likewise knocked down some seventy grand old houses to widen Westmount's Dorchester Street and make an undignified curved highway-like western end. Expropriation and demolition costs alone were over $1 million, or about $8 million today, not to mention the tax revenue lost. Where graceful houses stood, serial parking lots have appeared here and there like scurf, forming a long forlorn swath of asphalt and concrete. That area still looks bombed out fifty years later.

Professor Bland, hired by the City of Westmount in 1960, recommended in his master plan that great hunks of Lower Westmount should be expropriated for large-scale development. The "valley concept" emerged: where Westmount met Montreal on its southeast and southwest flanks, high-rises should be built to "rise up" to Montreal's zoning. The 1967 Sunderland report was even worse: it recommended redeveloping the entire ninety acres south of St Catherine Street by planting a series of twenty- to thirty-storey behemoths.

The scariest plan of all was that commissioned by Canadian Pacific for the Glen Yard in the southwest in the late 1960s: Arthur Erickson helped produce a ninety-page proposal that involved housing twenty thousand people in a sixty-acre site straddling Westmount and Montreal. Heights would reach sixty storeys: fifteen storeys higher than Montreal's Place Ville Marie. The plan called for eighty-six elevators.

So being independent of Montreal did not prevent Westmount from being caught up in the expansionist hysteria of the 1960s. By 2000, planners said back then, the Montreal Metropolitan Region would have a population of seven million.[14] A place had to be found where all these people – and their cars – could go. "Urban renewal" or "redevelopment" was our only salvation. Out with the Victorian gingerbread, in with Le Corbusier point towers and windswept plazas.

Some of this stuff did actually get built: the hurly-burly mishmash of Alexis Nihon Plaza towers, the brooding dark shapes of Westmount Square designed by Mies van der Rohe, unceremoniously plunked down like an alien among two-storey housing, wiping out another seventy houses in the process. The International Style had its drawbacks: how was van der Rohe to know that his acres of beautiful white travertine paving would be pulverized by Montreal winters?

In 1963, Westmount zoned the whole residential enclave below Dorchester as a business district. Thank God grassroot groups have a long history in Westmount: the Lower Westmount Citizens' Committee, after chivvying city council into easing this "urban renewal" zoning in the area and into building Stayner Park, helped restore that area and made it into the residential mini-community it is today. In 1971 the committee won a Governor-General's Award for its efforts.

The story of the closure of de Maisonneuve, a street running east-west just below Sherbrooke, shows how another small group, led by one determined citizen, cajoled a relatively reluctant city council to do something that improved the quality of life of hundreds of citizens. In 1966, Westmount had taken a quiet residential street called Western and turned it into a new traffic artery called de Maisonneuve Boulevard. It was Dorchester Boulevard all over again:

because Montreal was creating an artery, so went the thinking of the time, so must Westmount. I remember shortly after coming to Montreal in 1968, and before becoming carless forever in 1977, barrelling down de Maisonneuve through Westmount Park in my Firebird. Most people drove at double the speed limit. Twelve thousand cars a day were using it. Then, in 1972, the east-west Ville-Marie expressway opened, and a local resident, John Udy, came up with the brilliant idea of closing de Maisonneuve at Westmount Park.[15] Eventually Westmount got around to landscaping the crumbling pavement and thereby increasing the size of the park. That delightful Lower Westmount area now is back to its quiet pre-arterial days. Such a thing could never have happened had Westmount not had its own city council.

Lower Westmount, and particularly its southern areas, had originally developed sympathetically and symbiotically around the railway over a hundred years ago. The Ville-Marie raised expressway, while paradoxically saving all of Lower Westmount from serving as a throughway for outsiders to get downtown like some giant pinball machine, threatened to become a community-killer on a smaller scale. Etymologically, concrete means to "grow together": it generally has the opposite effect. The Ville-Marie amputated any roads in its way, asserting itself visually and aurally in the southernmost sectors. In the southeast sector alone, at least a hundred Westmount houses were razed to make way for the expressway, including the imposing Hallowell House, built in 1806.

ANNEXATION REDUX

In 1960, Montreal proposed the annexation of all Island municipalities over a period of years. Westmount, in a letter to citizens that could have been written forty years later, vehemently denied "that annexation will lead to the solution of the metropolitan problems of the Island of Montreal." Westmount City Council, after hiring a Quebec City lawyer "in connection with various private bills being submitted to the Legislature by the City of Montreal,"[16] wrote to Liberal Premier Jean Lesage expressing its "strong opposition." The letter did say, in a surprisingly non-parochial way, "The preservation of independence in no way precludes the development of truly metropolitan projects and services and sharing their costs ... Examples of this are traffic interchanges such as the one under construction at Pine and Park Avenues and that are needed for the new Champlain Bridge. Such projects are of advantage to all residents of the Island and therefore the independent municipalities should be required to pay the cost."[17] Especially for 1961, this was pretty radical stuff coming from Westmount, proof that its later "I'm all right, Jack" image of an uncaring and parasitical enclave was unfounded.

THE WAY CAMELOT WAS RUN

This demesne, this Camelot, this bejewelled isle
Rises from the noxious and plebeian vapours
Of engirdling Montreal, whose pestilential water
Is Westmount required to purchase at ruinous price.
Centred in this happy Island, a castle
Is found, with battlements strong and lofty tower,
Which local vassals clepe their City Hall,
Bedecked with ivy in Summer, at Yuletide
Bespangled with magick faerie lights.

The mock-Tudor City Hall of Westmount has more than once inspired people (like me, above) to refer to Westmount as Camelot. At one time, Westmount was the dreaming suburb of Quebec fable, whose only problems revolved around how many dogs you could own, or whether the yearly shipment of maple syrup to the queen should be cut back, or what to do about people not wearing white while lawn bowling. No member of council was remunerated: the job was strictly volunteer. There were a few perks: aldermen's wives received weekly flowers from the greenhouse. All city council debates were conducted behind closed doors, with nothing publicly reported, "because we feel that the dignity of the city might be lessened by the publishing of controversial statements of various councillors," as A.W.D. Swan, the secretary-treasurer of the City of Westmount, primly offered up in 1957. Swan may have captured the soporific nature of city council up until the 1970s, but things began to change.

Until then, the Westmount Municipal Association, founded in 1908, actually controlled the City of Westmount. The WMA put forward candidates for mayor and council, and these candidates almost invariably were elected by acclamation. In the 1950s the WMA, not city council, had eight or nine committees such as the Education and

Library Committee, the Traffic Committee, the Recreation Committee, and (biggest and most important) the Membership Committee.
To get on the executive of the WMA, you had to fill in a form, giving details about yourself, including your university degree and your
religion. All WMA presidents from 1918 to at least the 1960s were
WASPs (White Anglo-Saxon Protestants), excepting three francophones. Of the fifty people on committees in 1956, only four had
names that were not clearly WASP. Even as late as the 1983 elections,
the WMA, while much reduced in clout, still "endorsed" candidates. I
was one of them. Today, the WMA is just a citizens' association.

THE TRANSITION YEARS

Donald MacCallum, mayor from 1975 to 1983, ran Westmount
as it had always been run: everything was decided in camera. The
staff was pretty much wall-to-wall old-stock anglophone. There
was one departure from tradition: MacCallum, being retired, was a
full-time mayor. Most, if not all, mayors before him ran Westmount
like board chairmen: MacCallum, a former senior army officer and
engineer, was more like a CEO. He did a good, conscientious job, but
in a style that was already outdated. Westmount had changed: it was
no longer WASP, royalist, and comfortable with being run by an old
boys' club. As a vice-president of the WMA in 1982, I named myself
MacCallum's "shadow": we had a number of liquid lunches at the
University Club, whither he was driven by a city chauffeur.

Times were changing. Citizens began demanding more access to
information. Westmount is an urban village where the local paper
is important. In its heyday, the *Westmount Examiner* ensured that
no morsel of Westmount life went unexamined. It was our Hansard.
The "Who's Doing What?" column in 1982 told you, *inter alia*, that
Brian Gallery at 627 Belmont was installing four plumbing fixtures
for $1,000. You want to know who bought or sold houses in the
month of December in 1982? The highest price was paid by a future
prime minister: 51 Belvedere Circle was sold by James W. Burns to
Sheila Cowan (Martin) for $575,000 (its assessment was $396,800
and the average house price that month was $154,172). The "Where
Were They Going?" column reported on the weekly exploits of the
fire engines. We were informed, for example, that on 23 December
1982, at 12:14 PM, an alarm was activated by an electric saw at 464
Wood Avenue. On 2 January 1983, at 3:20 PM, a TV antenna was

hanging from the roof at 57 Arlington Avenue, and on 3 January at 2:16 PM, a child with a split lip was taken to the Montreal Children's' Hospital after sliding in King George Park.

Suddenly, in the spring of 1983, chief reporter Laureen Sweeney was barred from the fire hall offices and could not get details to write her "Where Were They Going?" column. John Sancton, the *Examiner*'s editor and publisher, thundered from his press pulpit that the ban was a disgrace. Though the Quebec Press Council called upon MacCallum to let Sweeney "accomplish her work freely," he adamantly refused. It became a minor Canadian *cause célèbre*. MacCallum handled the whole thing badly, probably the reason he did not run again. It typified the complete lack of public access, a subject that dominated council meetings, with accusations the city was being run "as a banana republic." At least in one case, criticism was rewarded with a harassing series of home inspections.

MacCallum was a gentleman of the old school and looked the part, with pure white hair, eyebrows, and moustache. And he rather liked his tipple. It was as if he was personally making up for all those abstemious folk who ran Westmount in years gone by. His wet approach was in contrast to the style of the next mayor, Brian Gallery, who drank only milk before council meetings. MacCallum didn't like Gallery, finding him too political and outspoken. He even got me to scout out some descendant of George Hogg's to get him to run for mayor against Gallery, although this never materialized. In spite of my lack of experience, he would have preferred even me running for mayor. But I had a company to run, and I was only thirty-seven.

Gallery was elected in November 1983 in what was probably only the second contested mayoral election in Westmount's history. A buddy of, and bagman for, Prime Minister Brian Mulroney, he shared Mulroney's wonderful old-time blarney. Gallery was warm and engaging and brought out the best in his aldermanic team. However, where MacCallum had been active in the Montreal Urban Community, Gallery wanted nothing to do with anything going on outside Westmount. And he thought that city staff could do no wrong. But he loved being mayor and did the job well.

What MacCallum never quite realized was that the council chamber was becoming a stage upon which the tensions of the time were played out as Westmount evolved. Gallery understood this. A place of conflict *and* resolution: people wanted to let off steam, and sometimes it was the only place they could go. Parking, dogs, the library, and zoning were often the purported reason citizens came to council, but they were also there because they wanted to connect. After the election of the PQ in 1976 and the first sovereignty referendum in 1980, anglophones felt vulnerable as a community. As alliances formed in the council chamber, comfort in a cold world was gained.

Then came May Cutler, who wanted to open up the city operations even more. When I refused to change the zoning on Sherbrooke Street to permit her to operate her publishing company from her house, she decided to run for mayor of Westmount in the 1987 election. She beat Gallery, to her, Westmount's, and particularly Gallery's surprise. He was inconsolable. But Cutler, in spite of her style, was a necessary agent of change. If MacCallum was establishment and Gallery became establishment, Cutler was anti-establishment. She had three degrees, an Irish cop for a father, and a chip on her shoulder that could make a Sumo wrestler tremble. She had no patience for pretence – she measured out her life not with coffee spoons but brass buckets. So we went from old boys to a new girl, the first female mayor of Westmount. The trouble was, most of her councillors (the term "aldermen" falling victim to gender sensitivities) were second-termers from the Gallery years and couldn't stand her.

Cutler, while a successful publisher, knew nothing about how a municipality was run. Uncovering errors, incompetence, and even a cheque scam, she was convinced Westmount was run inefficiently and corruptly. So what did she do? Early in 1989, she suspended the city manager for "exceeding his authority" and, for good measure, relieved Councillor Tingley (today a judge) of his commissionership of administration. She flounced out of City Hall and set up mayoral headquarters in her home. She then held a rally at Victoria Hall, where some seven hundred people showed up. Slowly, things quietened down, and Cutler and her councillors established a shaky truce.

I – thankfully – had not run in the 1987 election, but when a councillor stepped down in the fall of 1989, Cutler called me while I was in England and asked me to run again as councillor and to run for mayor in 1991. I said, "May, I supported Gallery and publicly asked you to resign!"

"I don't care," she snapped, "We need you." So, calling our new relationship a *mariage de raison*, I got back on council, becoming the commissioner of finance. It wasn't long before Laureen Sweeney, the intrepid *Examiner* reporter, discovered the city had not billed some $300,000 in business taxes. "Aha!" said Cutler. "See, I told you there was lots of hanky-panky going on in the administration." I replied, "Nonsense. This is just a balls-up. You worry about the hanky-panky, and I'll tighten up the administration." She put all the tax files in a bank vault while she, a former reporter, sleuthed around. She found nothing.

May Cutler had always been my indefectible supporter. She was judgmental, but not "grudgemental." And she was brutally honest. At the boozy farewell party held for her, she said to me a bit wistfully, "Peter, you know something? People respect me, but they don't like me." I gave her a hug.

MY PHYSICAL FIXATION

My political career began in 1981 with yellow marks on the sidewalk outside my house. I soon learned their meaning; ours was to be one of the last Westmount streets to have its cast-iron fourteen-foot, Washington-style street lamps yanked out to be replaced with thirty-foot, highway-style "cobra-heads," a replacement program started in the 1950s to improve illumination. I got my neighbours together to protest, halted the work, and wrote a report that showed how, with more frequent placement of reproduction Washingtonians with a modern light source, the illumination would be fine. Now whenever a street is reconstructed, out come the highway lights and in come Washingtonians. This little story is typical of how most municipal candidates are created: if you don't like the way things are done, you get involved.

As a city councillor from 1983 to 1987, I was responsible for the architectural and planning commission, which met inside the crenellated tower of City Hall. Some applicants for building permits, I am sure, thought it was an ivory tower. Next door was a huge scale model of Westmount and above us the whirring mechanism that ran the six-foot exterior clock, our own Tiny Ben. Such is the feebleness of some modern architecture that when Dimitri Dimakopoulas came to the tower to present his design for rebuilding one of the Alexis Nihon Plaza high-rises gutted by fire, we told him his proposed square building was too bland and invasive. He asked me, what did I suggest? I half-jokingly suggested he cut the four corners to make an octagonal building. Which is precisely what he did.

Being the unenthusiastic legatee of the 1960s orgy of high-rise commercial zoning, I cut back permissible heights and commercial uses in Lower Westmount. Some council members feared erosion of our tax base; I feared erosion of our low-rise residential charm. Besides, nearly half of all new tax revenues went to the Montreal Urban Community, not to Westmount: yet it was Westmounters who had to put up with the traffic, wind, and shadow created by high-rises.

THE VIRTUE OF SMALLNESS

One of my most satisfying bits of work was launching a heritage study of all Westmount buildings. Ultimately, Westmount put into place probably the most comprehensive measures in Quebec to preserve historical architecture. (Any other province would celebrate Westmount's bountiful collection of heritage houses. It should be – and is not – a source of regional pride that three-quarters of owned dwellings in Westmount are over sixty-five years old, and half are over ninety years old – the highest proportions of any other municipality or borough in Montreal. The entire West Island has about one thousand houses built before 1921. Westmount alone has 2,400.[18])

And Westmount tries to build new to last as long as the old. When overseeing the rewrite of our building code in 1987, I insisted we keep the provision, possibly unique in Canada, that exterior walls of houses be solid masonry that can resist fire for two hours. We were the first municipality in Quebec to require all new houses be sprinklered.

Westmount's firsts were not confined to the built environment: during my term as mayor, we were among the first municipalities in Quebec to pass laws controlling pesticides and smoking. And we were the only municipality in Quebec to adopt a pay-as-you-go policy for major expenditures that virtually eliminated debt. I was particularly proud of that and saddened to see what happened to my handiwork after the merger.

If one were to draw up a list of municipal innovations of the City of Montreal, it would be a bit of a strain – certainly if the list had to be proportional to its size. The point of all this chest-thumping is that such innovations come from small, locally controlled municipalities that are reactive to their citizens. To be fair, Westmount is usually blessed with city councillors of calibre, drawn from a municipality with a high proportion of professionals. But Westmount's smallness and sense of community also play a role in getting good people to run. These were the kind of people who should have been on Montreal's council, but it was far too big, far less rewarding, and required far too much time.

THE LIBRARY RENEWAL PROJECT

Perhaps the best illustration of why Westmount fought so hard against its incorporation into Montreal is the story of the expansion and restoration of the Westmount Public Library. This mid-1990s project[19] could never have happened had Westmount been just a megacity borough. The library is Westmount's most used and loved facility ever since it was built in 1899. You mess with it at your peril, especially with such a building heavy with nostalgia. After years of neglect and spoliation, though, we had to reset and polish this jewel in Westmount's crown. Polishing requires friction, but the result made all the friction worthwhile.

From the outset we wanted the project to be partially financed by the citizens. Again, this was perhaps another first in Quebec and another example of what a small municipality can do. While big donations came from foundations and wealthy benefactors, the community fundraising guaranteed citizens' ownership in the project. They held rummage, garage, plant, and book sales. They had street and coffee parties, auctions, house and garden tours, barbeques, and car washes. Many Westmount schoolchildren contributed. To be fair, few other municipalities could have called on the likes of David Culver, the former chairman of Alcan, to head up the fundraising. He agreed to do it on one condition: if I promised to bring in the project on time and on budget, he promised to get the donations.

To use tax money wisely, you almost have to treat it as if it were your own. Public money is squandered when no one is accountable, when buildings go up without passion and care, when elected officials are too removed. The idea of a megacity mayor being able to be involved at the level of one building is preposterous.[20] And was a larger vision sacrificed by such attention to detail? No. I, like many suburban mayors, was very involved in regional matters too.

The formal opening of the refurbished, expanded library was held just ten days after the province-wide sovereignty referendum in October 1995. I said, "As Westmounters emerge shell-shocked from this divisive question, we're asking another one: 'Is there a future for us in Quebec?' Look around you. This is Westmount's answer."

VICTORIA HALL

Four years later we had finished restoring Victoria Hall, another of those great architectural legacies that help knit Westmounters together. First built in 1898 as a red-brick companion to the library, it burned down in 1924. Opened anew in 1925 (by Lord and Lady Byng, of course), it served as the social hub of Westmount. In its heyday, stars such as Giselle McKenzie, Norma Shearer (a Westmounter), Fay Wray, and Oscar Peterson performed there. Today, the lords, ladies, and stars are long gone, but, as well as concerts and plays, this cavernous space is used for rallies, Rotary Club meetings, meet-the-candidate nights, public information meetings, exercise classes, local art exhibits, and *vins d'honneur* that welcome new residents, honour deceased ones, or open the semi-annual flower shows.

But what sets Victoria Hall apart from other civic centres are those particularly Westmount events, events that just would not happen in an annexed Westmount. There's the Quarter Century Club: the annual nostalgic get-together and feast thanking all Westmount employees and pensioners for their years of service to Westmount. Then came the Junior Firefighters, an idea born in Westmount in 1969: kids who have learned all about fire prevention graduate in front of adoring parents. Then come the sports "banquets," where Vic Hall is inundated with hundreds of kids and as many proud parents and volunteers. The kids get hot dogs (cooked by volunteers and served by city council members) and come up on stage to be awarded all sorts of sports prizes. At these events, overwhelmingly, participants are part of average, mortgage-ridden two-income families trying to do the best for their kids, along with a number of single parents and seniors getting by on pensions. No, most are not poor, and some are even comfortably off, but few are as flush as the media would have us believe.

WOULD THE REAL WESTMOUNT IDENTIFY ITSELF?

Now is the time to explode three myths about Westmount: all Westmounters live in mansions, all are Anglo-Saxon, and all are rich.

Myth no. 1: All Westmounters live in mansions on the summit

Everyone in Quebec just knows that Westmount's cosseted residents all inhabit huge mansions that dapple the mountain's sun-kissed summit. Whenever Westmount is in the news, the TV cameras invariably pan to a few big houses up there. Yet only 10 per cent of Westmount's population lives on the summit. Being mostly detached, their houses do, however, take up one-quarter of Westmount's land.

Not only do most Westmounters not live on the summit but only 12 per cent of Westmount dwellings are detached houses. Another 30 per cent are attached, usually brick, with a flat roof,[21] and perhaps 3,000 to 4,000 square feet of land. The average house size runs to eight or nine rooms, spacious, but quite comparable to most houses going up today and hardly the stuff of River Oaks in Houston, Beacon Hill in Boston, or Rosedale in Toronto. The rest of Westmount dwellings, 58 per cent of them, are apartments, condominiums, or duplexes. Once they are added to the calculations, the average Westmount dwelling sports 6.3 rooms – half a room more than the average in the rest of Quebec. Even up in what some wags call the "nosebleed" section of Westmount, the summit, the average number of rooms per house is only ten.

Fully half of all Westmounters live in Lower Westmount below Sherbrooke Street. Less than one-quarter of these people live in houses; the rest live in apartments or condominiums. And those who do live in houses, especially in the south-east and south-west parts of Lower Westmount, have had to put up with foundation settlement, redevelopment master plans, and, in 1972, the final depredation of a main highway bunged in next door.

Such is the legacy of Westmount's 1960s up-zoning that, today, one-quarter of *all* the dwellings in Lower Westmount were built in the 1960s – most of them apartments.

Nearly half of Lower Westmount households are people living alone, many of them elderly. There are over one hundred public housing units in Westmount. Hardly the Westmount of song and story.

Myth no. 2: All Westmounters are Anglo-Saxon

When it is not being used once a year for Remembrance Day, the Westmount cenotaph serves as a gathering place, an unofficial schoolyard for francophone students from the École internationale next door. They clamber all over the dais and sit on its low granite walls. One wall bears the names of the nearly 200 Westmount men who died in World War I. Two other walls were subtly and sadly added for the 258 World War II dead. Even the latter list is made up of Anglo-Saxon names nineteen times out of twenty. Most of the remainder are French. The proportions reflect the Westmount of the early 1940s, and the Westmount that lives on in the minds of those outside its borders.

Things slowly changed after the war. The 1951 Census listed 74 per cent of Westmounters as "mother-tongue" English, and 19 per cent "mother-tongue" French. In 1956 there were 6,732 "heads of families" in Westmount: 4,024 Protestant, 783 Roman Catholic (French), 1,031 Roman Catholic (English), 738 Jewish, and 156 "Neutral."[22] Those were the days when your religion determined where your school taxes went.

Westmount has always had a solid, if small, Jewish component, going back to 1840 when Moses Judah Hays built four fieldstone houses on Côte St Antoine Road. In 1911, Temple Emanu-el was built in Westmount and in 1922, the Shaar Hashomayim Synagogue.* The singer and poet Leonard Cohen was born in Westmount. His grandfather and father were Westmounters; his father served in Westmount's Royal Montreal Regiment in World War I.

Over the years a few media commentators managed to capture the changing Westmount and avoid the wall-to-wall WASP stereotype. Back in 1977, Robert Stewart, writing in *The Canadian* magazine ("Adieu Westmount: Montreal's Crown Colony Faces le Nouveau Québec"), noted that only two out of thirty-one householders on Summit Circle had British names, and that Westmount was home to seventeen judges: three Jewish, eight French, and six "of British stock." Still, Westmount was 60 per cent British in 1977, Stewart said. Writing in *Saturday Night* in 1981 ("Above All, Westmount"), Ron Graham quoted Mayor Donald MacCallum: "We do know that there are a lot a foreigners here who weren't here before, particularly up on top." And I can just hear him saying such a thing.

---

* In 1911 the most populous ethnic group on Montreal Island, after the French and British, were Jewish (Paul-André Linteau, *Histoire de Montréale depuis la Confédération*).

What is Westmount today? Starting in 1996, it became impossible to track the ethnic makeup of Westmounters (and all Canadians, for that matter). Statistics Canada's increasingly delicate sensibilities required that, ethnically, we would be henceforth self-appointed; that is, we are who we say we are.[23] The question of ethnic origin is now open-ended: no more selecting from a list of ethnicities. So now some people tell Statistics Canada their ethnic origin is "Canadian," or even "Québécois." We do know, in 2006, that 22 per cent of Westmounters claimed French as their mother tongue, up from 19 per cent in 2001 – exactly the same percentage as in 1951. My guess is that Westmount today is 23 per cent Anglo-Saxon, 22 per cent francophone, 30 per cent Jewish, and 25 per cent "other." Therefore, in less than sixty years, Westmount has gone from being three-quarters Anglo-Saxon to one-quarter. Yet even today we are usually portrayed as 100 per cent Anglo-Saxon.

I was always tempted to blame the Parti Québécois for keeping alive this anachronistic imperialistic Anglo-Saxon bugaboo, but that is not really fair. They are far from being alone. Take, for example, the *Toronto Star*, Canada's highest-circulation daily newspaper. I was embarrassed each time they interviewed me for one of their multi-page articles in colour, although I probably was to blame for egging them on, giving them exactly the WASPY show they wanted. The *Star*'s 1994 effort, entitled "Westmount Keeps a Stiff Upper Lip," went on to say, "Westmount Mayor Peter Trent, like the prosperous anglophone enclave he rules over, is a throwback to the halcyon days of the British empire." They even managed to find someone to opine, "Westmount is still a place where tea and crumpets, and lawn bowling are big recreations." In 2001, at least the *Star* got Graham Fraser to write something, but even then the headline went, "Montreal's Famed English Bastion of Wealth and Power Is Fighting for Its Life." For another big article in 2003, after taking dozens of standard photos, the *Star* photographer persuaded me to climb a ladder in order to get a head-and-torso shot level with the top of the mayor's lampposts, emblazoned with the city's crest. Given the precariousness of my perch, I could only manage an unconvincing smile that made me look positively cretinous. Dressed for my role in a regimental tie, blue-striped shirt, and brass-buttoned blazer, I came across as the perfect upper-class twit, which is precisely the look they were after. Naturally, that was the picture they ran, taking up half a page in full colour. The text reinforced this image, describing me as "speaking in a WASPish tone that bespeaks good breeding, a stiff upper lip and all the other attributes of empire." It seems the *Toronto Star* has an incorrigible hang-up on stiff upper lips and empire.

G.K. Chesterton called tradition "the democracy of the dead. Tradition refuses to submit to the small and arrogant oligarchy of those who merely happen to be walking about." Many Westmounters also used to think it only proper to allow those who went before them to have some say in how things should be run. Now those who went before us are not the same as we. Many traditions are dying. But no one will miss the Britocentric, class-ridden, royalist, moralistic Westmount of years gone by. The days are long gone when people could tut-tut about a neighbour being a shopkeeper, or *Country Life* ceasing to run full-page photos of British brides-to-be wearing pearls. The queen's maple syrup and the mayor's chain of office are charming but harmless hangovers from the palmy days of Royal Westmount.

But the British cult of not displaying wealth is a trait that does bear reviving in some quarters. In the place of Westmount matrons of old, it is not unknown to run across gum-chewing vulgariannes braying into their mobile phones in accents more Beverly Hills than Belgravia. The solid high-street shops that used to populate Greene Avenue – Tweedy clothes, Smithers shoes, and Ohman's the jeweller – are today replaced by glitzy specialty shops. Westmount houses are now put up for sale described in terms such as "fully loaded." Of the few new houses that are going up in Upper Westmount, most are gigantic affairs stuffed into little leftover lots, like Cinderella's sisters shoving their big feet into tiny slippers. These houses, a few looking like Norman chateaux built of peanut brittle, are often swathed in stone balustrades and adorned with precast pillars. I once wrote a bit of doggerel about this New Westmount:

The summit fills up with new money,
Their thirst for display they can't quench,
Arrivistes, parvenus, nouveaux riches:
It sounds so much nicer in French.

From the heights of our hill they look down,
With their vistas both winter and summer,
The only way up there, it seems,
Is by Range Rover, Audi, or Hummer.

They socially climbed our mountain,
Which now is just slightly old hat,
As over the years, with no fuss,
Old money moved to the flat.

The two syllables "West" and "mount" signify little outside Canada – perhaps together they create the image of just another rather unimaginatively named leafy suburban community. In the rest of Canada, the word exudes a vague odour of wealth, and, thanks to the media, Britishness. But in Quebec, the word "Westmount" exercises even today an almost iconic power, freighted with images of anglo influence and prestige, encapsulating centuries of French resentment against the English, feelings that were essential in fuelling the separatist movement. The spiritual father-figure of this movement, René Lévesque, would utter Keith Spicer's phrase "Westmount Rhodesians" through clenched teeth. All "liberation" movements need some group to blame, and the English minority in Quebec was that group – and what better place than Westmount to provide the symbol of the archetypal rich anglo so dear to some of the francophone political élite.

Yes, the French were exploited and treated dismissively by the English in days past. You couldn't be understood in French while buying goods in many shops right up until the 1970s. Westmount was once populated by unilingual anglophones who worshipped things British. But no longer. In my battle for the freedom of Westmount, the ghost of long-gone English power was hovering over the field. The cruel irony of the merger saga developed when, to save our city, I had to breathe life into this ghost: more on that later. But today, on the summit of Westmount, one-quarter of the residents are francophone.

Myth no. 3: All Westmounters are rich

The French media persist in portraying Westmounters as filthy rich. In 1993, when Nathalie Petrowski of *La Presse* visited Summit Circle in Upper Westmount, it was because she "needed to see wealth displayed in all its cruel splendour. Needed to know that it was still possible to squander money. I was not disappointed,"[24] she said. "There are at least four garage doors per house." (Actually, they averaged one and a half.) She went on to talk about "maids in white uniforms." (I have never seen such a thing anywhere in Westmount.) And the houses? "The Westmount rich are the most under-evaluated on earth."

The perennial media sport of caricaturing Westmount was fodder to those in favour of mergers. Odile Tremblay, in *Le Devoir* of 6 April 2002, wrote this about the Westmount library being open to all Montrealers and not just Westmounters, following the merger: "The venerable Westmount library is 102 years old, with its beautiful park and its rich collection of volumes. For the chic residents of Westmount, to go and read newspapers, books, and magazines there is like going down to take 5 o'clock tea at the Ritz or to see a première of the Montreal Opera. It is an old cultural tradition that dates back to a British past. One has to admit in wealthy neighbourhoods, traditions seem better rooted than elsewhere, no doubt owing to the many rich and leisured who keep them going. Well-off Westmount, with its slate roofs, its trees, its Bentleys, and its turrets, is a protected milieu; a calm and exquisite *de luxe* enclave whether for a manor, or for a library."

If one tosses aside the caricatures, one finds Westmount's least-known feature is its most attractive: its heterogeneity. Our image notwithstanding, some Westmounters are plain poor: 19 per cent of Lower Westmounters (and 14 per cent of all Westmounters) live below the low-income cut-off. Most of the others are middle class. However, a light sprinkling of gold dust from a few hundred Westmounters who are hyper-rich gooses up the average. But, when data are skewed like this, "average" numbers are meaningless. If a seventy-two year old enters a bus carrying ten six-year-olds, the average age of the passengers doubles, but the *median* age is unchanged. This is why, when there are huge variations such as incomes in Westmount, median income is the better way to measure relative wealth.[25] The owners of Power Corporation, Molson Coors, Bombardier, and such others do live in Westmount, and we are happy for them and to have them, but their fabulous wealth does not make the rest of us one cent richer. If Westmount is the preferred habitat for such exotic species to put down roots and flourish, in spite of being a distinct minority among the more garden-variety bourgeois types, then it is a boon for all Quebec.

Even including the very rich, the old rich, and the nouveau rich, the median household income in Westmount in the year 2005 was $79,466, whereas the median household income in the rest of

Quebec was $46,419, or nearly 60 per cent of what Westmount-
ers made. *After income tax*, Quebecers pulled in fully two-thirds of
what Westmounters made, either as a household or as an individual.[26] No one will be taking up a collection for Westmounters, but
they are not as rich as they are portrayed.

Even though most Westmounters are not Croesus rich, they *are*
house rich. Above Sherbrooke Street, the price of a typical house is
equal to around nine times the median yearly household income in
that area, after tax. For the entire Montreal Metropolitan Region,
house prices run at around six times after-tax income. Westmount
homeowners have a big stake in their houses: this is why their community and how well it is run is of great importance to them. They
look to City Hall to protect their investment.

THE WESTMOUNT I KNOW

People have chosen to settle in Westmount because they liked what
they saw and proceeded to make it their own. Communities don't
rise up out of nowhere, and if it took a bunch of abstemious royalist
WASPs to create Westmount over one hundred years ago, so what?
Who they were does not negate the value of what they created – a
value that other groups have come to appreciate. The smattering of
Westmounters who live on the summit or who are very rich would
get the services they want whether they were part of Montreal or
not. It is the members of the middle class who principally populate
Westmount and who fought annexation in 1910, 1960, and 2000.
Not because they lived in mansions, not because they were Anglo-
Saxon, not because they were rich: it was because Westmount is a
delightful place in which to live and it deserved to survive.

THE STORY

4

Political Eunuchs and Fiscal Footmen

O, it is excellent to have a giant's strength, but it is tyrannous to use it like a giant.

William Shakespeare, *Julius Caesar*, 1604

Canadians, when their minds turn to such matters, think there are three levels of government in Canada. There are, in reality, only two. The municipal "level of government" is a wholly owned subsidiary of its respective provincial government. Most voters are unaware that our city councils are populated by the eunuchs of Canadian politics. Only when municipalities get wiped out – whenever the province feels like "consolidating" municipalities – does it dawn on Canadians that their province owns their municipalities and therefore can make them disappear at will.

Yet municipalities have as much democratic legitimacy as provinces. While provinces are fixed and arbitrary straight-line divisions drawn by nineteenth-century surveyors, municipalities are organic, evolving, spatially relevant entities that reflect their residents' needs more faithfully than provinces can ever do. Many Canadian city councils are also free of the shackles of the party system. But they get no respect. What the media call "bickering" at city hall is referred to as "debate" in the legislative assembly.

What has passed for municipal policy in Canada for the last half-century has amounted to little more than outbreaks of a naïve belief that wholesale amalgamation will solve our urban ills. Rather, these sporadic bouts of amalgamation fever have simply swept our municipalities' problems under a bigger rug. It is much safer to merge municipalities than it is to give them the power they need. And even when not under threat of their own disappearance, Canadian municipalities are still doomed by the country's constitution to be in thrall to their provincial masters. When 80 per cent of Canada's population was rural and cities were little more than comfortable trading posts, that probably made sense; today, in spite of the vast majority of citizens who live in cities, we are still organized as we were back in 1867. In fact, in Quebec, the "regions" have more clout in the National Assembly than the urban centres; their vote is worth twice as much in extreme cases.* I call this the tyranny of the rurality.

It is nothing short of scandalous to treat the most important demographic structures that emerged in the twentieth century as a simple extension of the province's apparatus, or worse, as a bunch of immature children. In Quebec, whenever a municipality borrows money, changes a speed limit, or adopts an urban plan, the province has to approve it. Quebec also jealously guards its fiscal power over municipalities, using them as piggybanks to be shaken, or even broken, when needed. Quebec has trouble keeping its hands off the municipalities' main source of revenue, property taxes – all the while refusing to give them access to any other source. Today, Quebec's municipalities are pitifully dependent on property taxes, which have no relationship to one's consumption of services and only an assumed relationship to one's ability to pay. Property taxes are a holdover from the days when only rich people owned property.

We have to pry loose our municipalities from the iron grasp of the provinces and let them flourish. This process starts with getting average citizens to realize just how much their municipality is under the thumb of their province.† I hope this book helps to do that.

THE FIRST THREE HUNDRED YEARS

The precariousness of municipal structures in Canada has a long history. Canada's first mayor, with the splendid name of Jean-Baptiste Le Gardeur, sieur de Repentigny, was elected in Quebec City in 1663, along with two aldermen. Their jobs lasted thirty-six days, just long enough for them to look around and realize that, with a

---

* At least three rural ridings, such as in the Gaspé, have less than half as many voters as some dozen urban ridings in the Montreal region.

† The classic illustration of this was cited in the 1986 Parizeau Report: Longueuil, a city of 126,000, had to wait to get the Quebec Department of the Environment to approve the installation of a drinking fountain in a city park.

population of three hundred living in only sixty houses, and with no local services, a municipal council was unneeded – a wonderful example indeed of voluntary dis-election. Ten years later, municipal hope springing eternal, three new aldermen were elected; this time their positions lasted four years. Any further attempt at setting up municipalities had to wait until after the British Conquest of 1759, even though Quebec City had grown by then to over eight thousand souls. This allergy to local government can be blamed squarely on Louis XIV. The Sun King, while having to tolerate the ancient municipal institutions back home, refused to allow them in New France. Anything that smacked of popular rule in remote colonies was seen as a threat to France's rather shaky exercise of authority at such a distance. By default, many municipal responsibilities at the time devolved onto the parishes and therefore came under the control of the church. The number of parishes grew to 113 by the end of the French Regime.

While Upper Canada (today, Ontario) – partially prompted by the influx of loyalists accustomed to local government – got around to appointing a few local officials, little happened in Lower Canada (today, Quebec). Montreal and Quebec City finally got municipal councils in 1831, only to see these charters expire in 1836. And during those five years, all resolutions of the city council had to be approved by the Court of King's Bench. Finally, a year after Lord Durham deplored the total lack of municipal institutions (and local taxes) in his 1839 report on Lower Canada, something was done about it. Over the next fifteen years, various forms of local government were tried – including temporarily giving municipalities responsibility for schools – and the whole thing came together in 1855 with a law that created Quebec's municipal structures more or less as we know them today.

In 1855, Lower Canada bristled with five hundred municipalities: six cities, twenty-nine villages, sixty-one counties, 112 townships, and 277 parishes (both Catholic and Protestant). Note the rather strange transformation of parishes into actual municipalities. While politic at the time – the British found it convenient to respect the established structures under the former French Regime – this decision eventually led to a cluttering-up of the Quebec municipal world. Over time, the number of municipalities became artificially inflated through overlapping: both villages and the parishes that surrounded them were municipalities. At that time, Quebec was quite rural: the total population in 1855 was about one million, only 15 per cent of whom lived in urban areas, and no one seemed to mind this plethora of municipal structures.[1]

When the Fathers of Confederation were sitting around the table in their paternal way, deciding on how the power pie would be sliced up between the provinces and the federal government, they kept what was considered in 1867 to be the important things for the central government. The feds got defence, foreign affairs, transport, fisheries, money and banking, immigration, and criminal law. The provinces got what were then considered the unimportant things like education and health care and, almost as an afterthought, municipalities. In Quebec, schools and hospitals were mostly run by the church anyway, and, as we saw, half the municipalities were parishes. Today, of course, the tables have turned, and more is spent provincially on health and education than all federal program spending put together. And who can deny the crucial importance of urban municipalities in today's world?

In a unitary state such as Britain, municipalities are automatically the responsibility of the central government; however, when creating a federation, it was only logical for states (or provinces) to be responsible for institutions that are eminently territorial in nature. So the municipalities became the "creatures" of Canada's provincial governments: "creatures" in the etymological sense of being their "creation." A more appropriate definition of "creature" can be found in the dictionary: "owing status to, and obsequiously subservient to, another" or even "an instrument or puppet." Provinces in Canada, then, have life-or-death powers over municipalities. Interestingly, in that great federation to the south with its long and proud tradition of local government, municipalities have the right to exist, even if they are the responsibility of individual states.

For nearly a century after Confederation, this absolute power to wipe out municipalities remained pretty much dormant. In fact, for Quebec, this period was the golden age of municipal growth. For fifty of those years, until the Department of Municipal Affairs was created at the request of some mayors in 1918, there was even no bureaucracy to "rationalize" such growth, and no provincial politicians busy skimming off the municipalities' revenues. By the turn of the century in 1901, Quebec boasted over a thousand municipalities, including 53 cities, 136 villages, and 439 parishes. The total population at the time was only 1.7 million. In fact, 1901 represents the high-water mark when calculating the number of municipalities per person in Quebec. This ratio has steadily diminished ever since. By 1951, while there were 1,700 municipalities – including 163 cities, 330 villages, and 559 parishes – the province's population had reached four million people. Two residents out of three now lived in an urban agglomeration. Even during this period of explosive growth, however, it was clear who was boss. Premier Maurice Duplessis, who reigned in the 1940s and 1950s, was fond of saying, "the municipalities are the daughters of the province."

In the 1960s the Quebec government started to flex its constitutional muscles, and real meddling in municipal matters began. Quebec adopted an often confrontational, sometimes contemptuous attitude towards local politicians that continues to this day. In politics, eventually one begins to disdain those over whom one has power. On and off over the last forty years, if Quebec was not busy wiping out municipal sources of revenue, it was wiping out the municipalities themselves. With the constitutional gun held to each municipality's temple, Quebec was demanding "Your money!" or "Your life!" Let's start with money.

A RICH BANQUET OF TAXES

Up until the 1960s, municipalities in Quebec had always enjoyed a certain fiscal freedom. For example, in the early 1940s, the City of Montreal availed itself of a rich banquet of taxes. While property taxes made up half of its revenues, Montreal managed to tax water, amusements, utilities, telephones ($3 a year), radios ($2 a year), cars ($5 a year), and even insurance premiums. Most interestingly, a municipal income tax – which piggybacked on the federal one – was also in force from 1935 to 1942. And Montreal had pioneered the use of sales taxes in 1935, five years before the introduction of the Quebec provincial sales tax.

In fact, since 1944 a number of municipalities in Quebec had the right to their own sales tax in their territory – up to a maximum of 2 per cent of the sale amount. As well as reducing the dependency on property taxes, municipal sales taxes made a lot of sense: an increase in economic activity in a given municipality generates an increase in revenue. In over half of US states, municipalities levy sales taxes.[2] And sales taxes are paid by everyone, not just property owners: as a way to fund municipal services provided to persons as opposed to property, sales taxes are fairer. And, finally, sales tax revenues are much higher in the urban areas than elsewhere.

In the 1960s, the reaction of Quebec to all this fiscal diversity mirrored its reaction to the municipalities' spatial diversity; that is, it abhorred such a potpourri and championed the principle of uniformity. So, in 1965, the province stepped in and expropriated all municipal sales taxes. As the government typically does in these circumstances, it eased the pain by giving "compensation." In government-speak, "compensation" means "money to stop complaining." Usually, after a decent enough interval, the government will suddenly seem to awaken to the fact it is "subsidizing" municipalities and proceed to wipe out whatever is left of this "compensation." In this case, Quebec was uncharacteristically generous: the compensation for eliminating municipal sales tax in 1965 became grants equivalent to a one-quarter share of the 8 per cent provincial sales tax, and these grants lasted nearly fifteen years.

THE FISCAL REFORM OF 1980

Then, in the late 1970s, came one shining municipal moment. In spite of the province's plenipotentiary powers over its municipalities, the lord of the manor actually sat down with his tenants across the province and treated them as equals.* Thus was born Quebec's municipal Magna Carta – or at least the closest the municipalities would ever get to such a thing. It was called Fiscal Reform, and it was adopted as a law in late December 1979 that came into effect January 1980. This reform was also remarkable considering the time allowed for consultation: eighteen months elapsed from the day the government made its proposals to the day the government adopted the law. Quebec even staged a joint committee two years later to see how things worked out.[3] It was a rare model of provincial-municipal cooperation.

Representing the municipalities in the discussions that led to the reform was the mayor of Sherbrooke and president of the Union of Quebec Municipalities, a man with the delightfully Gallo-Hibernian name of Jacques O'Bready. Jacques Parizeau, a future premier, was

---

* The school boards were not consulted and were treated in the usual doormat fashion.

minister of finance at the time. Unusually for most "reforms" in Quebec, both sides agreed on a number of basic principles that are still quoted – but not adhered to – by the Department of Municipal Affairs today. For example, all agreed that local taxation must be autonomous, accountable, and simple to understand and to administer. Crucially important were the principles of neutrality and equity. *This meant that every municipal taxpayer should contribute to municipal costs based on the benefit he or she received. The redistribution of wealth was not the job of municipalities.*[4] Furthermore, the government agreed that any sloughing off of its responsibilities onto the municipalities (later to be dubbed "downloading") would be accompanied by an equivalent transfer of a new revenue source (*champ fiscal*).

In the name of one of these principles – autonomy – the sales tax grants were eliminated. The government said in 1979, "You municipalities should not be dependent on government grants anymore. Tell you what: we'll get rid of the grants, but, on the other hand, we'll eliminate – well, we'll sort of eliminate – school property taxes, thereby allowing you to use the property tax room so created. You should be even-Steven. And, just think: you'll be 95 per cent financially autonomous." The problem was, those grants were there as compensation for expropriating the municipal sales tax in the first place. If the government wanted the municipalities to be so autonomous, all they had to do was to give back the right to levy a municipal sales tax that Quebec had arrogated for itself in 1965. Instead, municipalities got their straitjacket of property taxes tightened up a few more notches.

In spite of the heady spirit of Fiscal Reform, the municipalities still got shafted. By grabbing the one-quarter of sales tax revenue that previously was given over to the local level, the provincial government gave itself the gift that kept on giving. While overall government revenues grew by a factor of three between 1981 and 2006, sales tax revenues grew fivefold.[5]

Neither the federal nor the provincial government pays property taxes on any of their buildings, whether schools, universities, hospitals, or office buildings. Because it is beneath them to pay taxes to a lower order of government, governments pay municipalities what it pleases them to call "in lieu of taxes." These payments (no surprise) are usually a fraction of property taxes as levied on the common taxpayer. Now, in a fit of guilt, or perhaps to make the municipalities swallow the loss of the sales tax grants, the minister of municipal affairs, during the tabling of the Fiscal Reform law, solemnly promised that within five years Quebec would be paying "in lieu of taxes" equivalent to what everybody else paid; and this would apply to *all* their properties, including schools.

In fact, none of the promises of Fiscal Reform was honoured over the long haul. The province sneaked back into the school tax field; it never really paid full taxes on its buildings, even cutting the amount paid for schools by half ten years later; and its municipal policies never respected the principle of taxation according to benefit received. For the last twenty-five years, Quebec has been saying one thing and doing the opposite. To this day, provincial politicians, bureaucrats, and government publications repeat the principles of Fiscal Reform like a mantra. They insist that municipal taxes should be based on consumption, yet whenever they chunter on about "fiscal fairness," they have in mind uniform tax rates, which, as we shall see later, are equivalent to a wealth tax, not a consumption tax.

THE SCHOOL PROPERTY TAX: A FISCAL RELIC REVIVED

Following Fiscal Reform, Quebec kept its foot in the school tax door, supposedly to allow school boards a way to pay for "local, non-essential" school costs. The school boards, with the government's approval, began to use the school property tax instead to fund their deficits. In dollar terms, the school tax, which was $1 per $100 of property value throughout Quebec in 1979, was supposed to drop to next to nothing with Fiscal Reform. The absolute maximum was set at 25 cents. But there was another, much stricter cap: revenue from school property taxes could not be greater than 6 per cent of Quebec's total spending on schools.

School property taxes are a poster child for why property taxes make no sense. Even if a case can possibly be made that property values have something remotely to do with some municipal services rendered, property values have absolutely nothing to do with educational services received. You might as well pay for health services by imposing a hospital property tax. School property taxes are simply a general tax on assumed wealth. Some suggest we have this wealth tax on property because homeowners don't pay capital gains tax when they sell their house.[6] Of course, that doesn't justify the huge property tax revenues flowing from commercial sectors that are also forced to fund schools. And the federal government doesn't levy any such tax. The only answer you'll get from Quebec as to why it has a school tax on property is "that's what Ontario does."

Back in the days before school busing, when kids actually walked to school, there was some connection between property taxes and schools: schools were an integral part of the community and run by that community through the local school board. This, of course, led to the gross unfairness of better schools in wealthier communities. Today, most people would agree that the government should pay for schools to ensure equal funding.

There is, however, one way in which school taxes can be easily justified: to combat urban sprawl. If people want to locate in the exurbs, in order, precisely, to *save* on property taxes, or to have their bungalow surrounded by lots of green, they should pay the cost of this decision. The construction costs of any new school built off the Island of Montreal – along with the cost of closing schools on-Island – should be funded by off-Island property taxes. Right now these costs are covered by Quebec's general revenues. To be logical, should we not also charge exurbanites for new hospitals and – most importantly – new highways and bridges?

A few decades ago, when the school property tax bill could be as large as the municipal tax bill, at least taxpayers could complain to their school board. Now, what's left of the school property tax is rightly seen as being a provincial tax, and people just live with it. They don't hold the school boards accountable for it. If municipal politicians are the eunuchs of Quebec politics, the school commissioners are its indentured servants. While municipalities can get a 50 per cent turnout in elections, most urban school boards are delirious if they get 10 per cent.[7] Few members of the public or even the Quebec National Assembly really give a damn about them. They are wards of the state. School boards in the 1930s were run with 86 per cent of their own revenues;[8] today, they get less than 10 per cent, if one excludes the government-imposed property tax. Municipalities, on the other hand, have control over about 95 per cent of their revenues.

It is perhaps instructive to note that the number of school boards in Quebec was slashed, through merger, from 2,000 at the start of the 1950s to 158 in 1998 and to 72 today.[9] These 72 boards and their 1,300 elected commissioners oversee 2,744 schools. This consolidation has been almost universally hailed as progress and served as

inspiration for the attempt at a similar radical pruning of municipalities. Since this mass merger of school boards was accompanied by
an equivalent reduction in power, I am not sure progress was made.
Certainly, the model of each community running its own school
board – or, in effect, a board for each school – has been trashed for
massive boards with massive bureaucracies under the thumb of a
central provincial bureaucracy.

PROPERTY-TAX REVOLTS IN THE EARLY 1980S

The upshot of Fiscal Reform was that the municipalities gave up
their share of a tax that increased with economic activity (the sales
tax) in order to get saddled with even more of a tax that was based
on property values. The early 1980s gave everyone an idea of just
how capricious such a tax can be, when homeowners across the
Island of Montreal suffered massive tax increases. Municipal taxes in
Westmount, for example, nearly doubled from 1980 to 1983. There
was a giant rally at the Montreal Forum in April 1982, and Howard Jarvis of Proposition 13 fame* was brought in from California by a group called Taxe$ Action. As a director of the Westmount
Municipal Association, I helped in the organizing of local protests:
eight hundred Westmount taxpayers filled Victoria Hall in February
that year. From the audience, local gadfly Allen Nutik intoned in his
trademark style, "The revolution, if it is going to come, has got to
start in this room. Tonight." Our own call-to-arms was only slightly
less bellicose: we delivered pamphlets headlined, "We're fed up and
we won't take it any more." Well, we were, and we did.

When tax increases continued in 1983, I decided that understanding the problem was more important than railing against it, so I
spent months researching why these sickening leaps in our tax bills
were happening. I presented the results of my study at a much more
restrained public meeting in February 1983 with Mayor MacCallum
and the head of the Montreal Urban Community, Pierre Des Marais
II, as speakers. It was my maiden municipal speech. I maintained

---

* Proposition 13, passed by California voters in 1978, limits property taxes to 1 per
cent of the purchase price of one's house and caps assessment increases to 2 per cent a
year until the house is sold. Moreover, any new property taxes require a two-thirds vote
by state and local legislatures (*The Economist*, 5 November 2005).

that, firstly, the tax increases came about owing to a hugely disproportionate increase in house values when compared to other classes
of property,[10] shifting the tax burden to the homeowner. The average
Westmount homeowner was by then paying six times the amount
of property tax as the average apartment dweller, yet consuming
roughly the same level of services.[11] (Rent control artificially lowers
the values of apartment buildings, and thereby lowers their property
taxes.) Secondly, house *assessments* were rising while house *prices*
were falling, as there was a long lag between the time when houses
sold and when they were assessed. So houses were temporarily over-
assessed. The third element of the tax increases had to do with runaway Montreal Urban Community spending on regional services
such as mass transit and police.

A few months before the tax meeting, Mayor MacCallum and I
had met with Jacques Léonard, the Parti Québécois minister of municipal affairs. I wish I could have filmed the two of them together: the
elderly patrician-looking WASP speaking a workmanlike French with
a long-haired "separatist." Léonard was quite deferential and open.
"In my view," I pompously told Léonard, "the only solution to the
problem is to allow municipalities to charge different tax rates for
different classes of property" in order to soften such roller-coaster
changes in home values. Léonard confided to us that the only reason
Quebec was reluctant to do such a thing was the concern that small,
rural municipalities would misuse such power. Once again, Quebec
municipal policy hamstrung the cities because of Quebec's rurality.
Léonard was, however, not opposed to what we called an "occupancy tax," a code word at the time for a poll tax.[12]

Property values are moving targets that would make for a hit-
or-miss exercise even if an army of assessors were crawling over
our houses every year. And this elusive target has no relationship
with services consumed. So much for taxing according to the benefit received, which was the principle of Fiscal Reform. When taxes
doubled, did Westmounters get double the number or quality of services all of a sudden? Of course not.

1990: THE DECADE OF DOWNLOADING BEGINS

Now we move ahead to 1990. Since Fiscal Reform, school taxes on
the Island of Montreal had slowly and quietly dropped from about
14 cents to 7 cents for each $100 of assessment. Then the time bomb

went off. In the spring of 1990, the Liberals, with Claude Ryan as minister of education, cut school grants throughout Quebec by $320 million. This meant that school taxes would have to jump to $584 million to make up the difference. Small problem: since the government gave about $5 billion a year to school boards, this meant nearly 12 per cent of school spending would be financed through property taxes – a complete violation of Fiscal Reform. What to do? Why, the government simply scrapped the 6 per cent cap, and, while they were at it, raised the maximum rate to 35 cents from 25 cents. I was reminded of a quote: "Promises only bind those who believe them."[13]

On the Island of Montreal, school taxes more than doubled: the rate went from 7 cents to 15 cents, yet still far below its cap of 35 cents. The City of Westmount signalled its disapproval by refusing to participate in the government's beautification competition, which it had won the previous year. The shock in Quebec City must have been immeasurable. Mount Royal decided to lower its flag to half-staff. Westmount prudently refused a citizen's suggestion to fly our municipal flag upside down "as a sign of distress." The mayor of Dorval, Peter Yeomans, never at a loss for a hyperbole nor a gory metaphor, said, "We're at war now and there is going to be blood on the floor."

Another surprise awaited. Buried within the Liberal's budget speech of April 1990 lurked a passing reference to the government's intention to wipe out operating grants for public transit, shifting it onto property taxpayers, using the excuse that Quebecers paid lower property taxes than "neighbouring provinces." Both this slashing of school grants and the later elimination of public transit grants had entered the Canadian municipal lexicon as "downloading" almost at the same time this term was being used in computerese to mean "transfer to a smaller unit." "Downloading" (the French use the more graphic *délestage*, or "un-ballasting") involves, in its narrowest definition, the imposition by the province of new responsibilities on local governments without transferring the means to pay for them. A broader definition (which I am using) includes the cutting of provincial subsidies for certain municipal responsibilities that were once thought inappropriate to fund through municipal revenues. In effect, it meant that services that were once funded through income or sales taxes were now to be funded through the good old property tax. Of course, downloading is in direct violation of one of the principles of the 1980 Fiscal Reform, but who cares about principles when you have absolute power?

In December 1990 the government acted. Claude Ryan, who had become minister of municipal affairs in October, gave the municipalities the details of the downloading alluded to in the April budget. By then I was back on Westmount City Council, this time as commissioner of finance. As always, Ryan was as prepared as the municipalities were unprepared. With interminable details and justifications laid out in a two-hundred-page document, "Towards a New Balance"[14] released in December 1990, Ryan shocked the municipal world with a list totalling $478 million of permanent costs to be unceremoniously dumped onto Quebec's municipalities. Supposedly, this downloading was necessary to "improve Quebec's financial health" when federal transfer payments failed to keep up with inflation.

In a breathtaking demonstration of ignorance as to how municipal finances work, "Towards a New Balance" argued that, since real-estate assessments had climbed faster than property taxes, that there was therefore "room" for a higher property tax load. Further bolstering this specious argument of under-taxation, Ryan reiterated the government line that the property tax load was much higher in Ontario. (The Montreal Police Brotherhood always used a similar technique: they would argue that their salaries were not on a par with policemen in Toronto, ignoring the fact that the average Torontonian made over 30 per cent more than the average Montrealer.)[15] Yes, because of school taxes, total property taxes were higher in Ontario, but it was only a decade before that Quebec, with great fanfare, had essentially got rid of the school tax. Now they were arguing the school tax load was not high enough. And, what was not really revealed was that Ontario municipalities taxed the commercial sector much more than did Quebec. The commercial sector in Ontario paid 37 per cent of all property taxes (municipal *and* school), compared to 23 per cent in Quebec.[16] The upshot of all this was that, after the Ryan Reform, the average Quebec residential taxpayer paid 20 per cent more in property taxes than would be the case in Ontario.[17]

The Ryan Reform ruthlessly cut all operating subsidies for mass transit in Quebec, from $295 million a year down to zero.[18] Alone in North America, the "higher" level of government in Quebec would henceforth not help fund the operating costs of public transit. Why?

It seems that passengers were getting a bit of a free ride: by 1990, they were paying only one-third of the costs of public transit, down from one-half in 1976. But mass transit fares are, in most modern societies, not considered a simple municipal service. As Fiscal Reform stated, redistribution of income is up to provincial and federal levels of government, especially when it comes to discounted fares for students and the elderly. By 1995, Quebec municipalities were contributing over three times as much per capita to mass transit costs as Ontario municipalities.[19]

But the Ryan Reform, like the Trudel Reform that was to follow it, did attempt to deal with the traditional financial mollycoddling of the rural towns and villages. Up until then, towns with a population below 5,000 and without a police force got *free* local police services from the provincial police force, the Sûreté du Québec. An amazing 92 per cent of Quebec municipalities used the SQ for such services.[20] The Ryan Reform only asked them to pay one-half this cost. Likewise, 32,000 of the 40,000 kilometres of local roads all over rural Quebec were maintained *free* by the government. Ryan's original proposal only wanted the towns and villages to contribute one-quarter of this cost. By the time it became law, this was reduced to one-eighth. As usual, rural Quebec kept most of its privileges. So a metro user (or, what was more likely, the urban property taxpayer) had to pay more for public transit, but all over rural Quebec transport by car was subsidized.

The frustration with dealing with the prickly and financially parasitical rural towns surfaced in another way. Buried in "Towards a New Balance" was the now familiar lament that two-thirds of Quebec municipalities had a population of less than two thousand. You could almost see the hand-wringing as the authors revealed shamefacedly that Quebec had double the number of municipalities as Ontario, with only two-thirds its population. With the ever-increasing responsibilities devolving on Quebec's municipalities, this "fragmentation" had become a "stumbling block" for the delivery of quality, up-to-date services. This bare assertion had absolutely no supporting evidence, yet has been repeated like a mantra ever since. Surely the best judges of "quality services" should be the citizen-taxpayers, who seem to have been totally left out of any ruminations on the part of the minister of municipal affairs. Naturally, mergers were proffered as a solution to such "problems," but "the government wanted to avoid as *much as possible* authoritarian solutions" [my emphasis]. It started to become clear, even at this date, that it was easier for the minister of municipal affairs to recommend mergers than it was simply to get the rural municipalities weaned off government aid.

The municipal world reacted to Ryan's proposed reform with an explosion. Calling it "the dossier of the century," the Union of Quebec Municipalities (the UMQ) went on the warpath. They were joined there by the Parti Québécois. Parizeau, now opposition leader, denounced the cuts as "villainous,"[21] saying he would scrap the whole law. (The PQ, interestingly and cynically enough, never did restore any of Ryan's cuts. In fact, as we shall see, they dumped an additional and identical amount on the municipalities' heads. It was strange that a left-of-centre party did not at least restore the subsidies to mass transit.)

After a bitter battle, little over six months after being sprung on an unsuspecting public the Ryan Reform became law. The original bill of $478 million was reduced, by arduous political attrition, and with the introduction of a $30 fee for each car registration in urban areas, to $379 million. The municipalities generally found this money by jacking up commercial taxes and collecting more of the gimmicky "welcome tax," a tax on property transfers that became mandatory under the Ryan Reform.

Trying to piece together the true cost of this reform amid a welter of confusing government statistics cost me many hours of detective work. My most revealing guide was an internal 1992 government report that did a complete post-mortem on the Ryan Reform.[22] But governments have short and selective memories. Today, in a breathtaking distortion of the effect of these swingeing cuts, the government maintains this reform only cost the municipalities $97 million,[23] not $379 million.

The tyranny of the rurality worked its rough magic on the Ryan Reform. The 1992 report concluded that one-half of its "budgetary shock" was borne by the Island of Montreal alone. Businesses on the Island paid most, the rest being picked up by an unsuspecting federal government, which got dinged with a $47 million yearly tax bill when the old business tax – which it did not pay – was cleverly replaced by Ryan's surtax.

Overall, Ryan had exacerbated Montreal's already poor financial health, which became one of the reasons invoked later for creating the megacity. His $190 million hit to the Island is equivalent to $270 million a year in today's dollars. Another perverse effect of Ryan's savage cut was the determined effort by local politicians during the rest of the 1990s to cut municipal funding for mass transit on the Island of Montreal. By the end of the decade, these counterbalancing cuts had whittled down the Island's mass transit contribution to the point of "restoring" one-half of Ryan's original cuts, once inflation was taken into account.

THE PICHETTE REPORT IS SILENT ON MERGERS

Claude Ryan was not your garden-variety politician. Honest to the core and proud of his profession, he was a perfectionist. Physically, the kindest thing you could say about Ryan is that he was a *beau laid*, with a chiselled, sallow face, lopsided smile, and small eyes. His nose wanted to grow in a number of directions, finally settling on downward. He spoke softly, almost mumbling. He always came prepared and scribbled things down in a little ten-cent notepad, a hangover from his journalistic days. His trademark was a subtle little joke that slipped out unannounced. Following the delivery of some bon mot, a quiet staccato cackle served as a sort of homemade laugh track. Ryan often quoted Latin. My six years of Latin didn't always get me through his Latinate brambles. He was incisive, in control, and not to be messed with. Having my share of run-ins with his brother Yves, the mayor of Montreal North, I can say that the Ryan clan respected those who stood up to them. Both Ryans lived simply; they were ascetic, almost priest-like. Yet Yves, at least, used to love a good party; in that way, he played Rabelais to his brother's Descartes. They both were wonderfully articulate. And inflexible.

We were not freed yet from the deeds of Claude Ryan: far from it. After twice demanding (successfully), "Your money!" from Montreal area municipalities, his next request was, "Your life!" Four months after I was elected mayor of Westmount in November 1991, he convinced the Quebec cabinet of the need for a task force to study the problems of the Montreal region.[24] The product of those deliberations became known as the Pichette Report. In his memo to the cabinet,[25] Ryan made it clear that he felt that "urban sprawl stirs up an obvious competition among municipalities; which, without an overall vision, feeds a spiralling increase in public spending." He went on to say, "The region's fragmentation makes nearly impossible a fair sharing of the tax load. Municipal boundaries become permeable fiscal frontiers. The City of Montreal has to provide a much higher level of service as a central city." All these assertions were offered as self-evident truths. Then out came the old standby: let's exploit Quebec/Ontario urban envy: "Our region has 102 municipalities"* he wrote. "The Toronto region has 31." The Pichette group was instructed to make recommendations on the "number and size" of political structures.

When news of this cabinet decision leaked out in March 1992, I said that Westmount would work both publicly and behind the scenes to "pull out all the stops" to prevent the extinction of our municipality. Shortly thereafter, I hired my friend and public relations specialist Richard Gervais to help us influence Ryan, saying I did not want to leave Westmount's future in the hands of the Conference of Montreal Suburban Mayors, whom I called "a bunch of sleepyheads."

During the ensuing year, Ryan made all sorts of cryptic comments about mergers. Saying he had "no choice" but try to cut back the number of municipalities, he called the job "delicate but unavoidable." At first he scrupulously refused to comment on whether he might eventually force mergers, or whether he thought One Island One City would be too big.[26] He began to emphasize that all of Quebec, not just the Montreal region, had too many municipalities. In a speech[27] given to the UMRCQ – the "other" municipal union, today restyled the FQM, whose clientele was the rural towns and hamlets of Quebec – he went on again about Quebec having 1,450 municipalities, 1,000 of which had a population of less than 2,000. While he held out the possibility, longer term, of "more restricting" measures, "until the next election," he said candidly, "we will stick with a policy of voluntary mergers."

The interim report of the Pichette Task Force was published in January 1993. Claude Pichette, its chairman, stopped short of recommending mergers, although he did not rule out even forced mergers.[28]

Then, in March 1993, Claude Ryan showed up at the Four Seasons Hotel, an exposed-aggregate-clad hulk on Sherbrooke Street close to

---

* A pro-merger shibboleth: 80 per cent of the region's population lived in thirty-seven cities – Laval, the cities making up the Island of Montreal, and the immediate south shore cities.

the Ritz-Carlton Hotel (in both proximity and, surprisingly, price).
Ryan was there to deliver the opening speech[29] for the annual meeting of the Conference of Montreal Suburban Mayors. "I am happy
to find myself among you as a son of the region of Montreal ...
where I was born in 1925, for the information of you in the media"
(a short cackle). "I have spent two-thirds of my life in the City of
Montreal, and, even when I spent the other one-third in Montreal
North or Outremont, I always considered myself, first and foremost,
a Montrealer. I still do." He proceeded to give us the two main reasons why he created the Pichette Task Force: "Firstly, during the public hearings on Bill 145 [Ryan's Reform] in the spring of 1991, the
City of Montreal told us about the problems that their politicians
were up against. It was a real cry of alarm. They demanded a public
inquiry into the future of Montreal. Secondly, Daniel Johnson, who
was the minister responsible for Greater Montreal in the cabinet,
had produced an economic development plan for Greater Montreal
in December 1991 that intentionally did not deal with municipal
matters." The Pichette Report was to complete Johnson's work by
doing precisely that, all the while "ensuring that the metropolis of
Quebec would not be abandoned to its fate."

While Ryan did not wish, publicly, to tell the Pichette Task Force
what to conclude, he proceeded as delicately as only he could manage to do precisely that:

> You would think that the only mandate of this group was to
> propose a new superstructure that would oversee all the existing
> structures, a superstructure from which, by magic, a uni-
> fied vision of the region would emerge. But the main thrust of
> Pichette's mandate concerned the next level down. For example,
> one major concern, which was skimmed over by Pichette's
> progress report, had to do with the size and form of existing
> municipalities. Now, these days, and in all fields, there is a notice-
> able movement in favour of mergers. We cannot avoid asking
> ourselves about the legitimacy of the existing distribution of
> cites in the region, particularly on the Island of Montreal. In
> the eyes of many commentators, having 29 municipalities of
> hugely varying sizes cannot lead to any sort of rational plan-
> ning. Instead of examining the number of cities, we have, up until
> now, left them alone – which is infinitely easier – and we have

simply stuck superstructures on top of them, structures to which we have given many different functions. Now, I have nothing against such superstructures as the Montreal Urban Community or the counties,* but once in a while, we have to ask ourselves a question.

Here it came: "What is the minimum size we should give our cities in order that they can take on most efficiently and economically the many and costly services that their citizens want?" Ryan slowly looked around at all the mayors, making sure we got his point. "I know, and I am perfectly aware, that this is a difficult question. But it is in the mandate that the government gave to the task force, and I would hope that this question will also be raised by the groups that will make presentations to it, especially by the cities you represent. And I hope this question will receive a response that will meet the minimum requirements of logic and realism. Now, in saying that, I am not dictating any particular solution to the task force. I do not wish to meddle at all in their affairs. Not at all." There it was: we, the Montreal Island mayors, should recommend to the Pichette Task Force the minimum size of municipality that should exist on the Island of Montreal. We should decide which of our municipalities should disappear.

The rest of Ryan's speech was anti-climactic but relevant to his message: "On a related matter: I am aware of the bitter memories you have of the questionable leadership of the City of Montreal, and of the financial load dumped on the region and on Quebec by the City of Montreal acting alone. And if I weren't aware of these memories, the mayor of Montreal North has reminded me of them recently. But Montreal was the motor that created prosperity for, and the development of, the larger society around her. This role requires a certain size and could not have been taken on by a bunch of small cities acting independently and in competition with one another."

At this same annual meeting, we also heard from Gérald Tremblay,[30] at that time minister of industry, trade, and technology in Premier Bourassa's cabinet. Nobody in the room had any idea we were

---

* For simplicity, I refer to Quebec's "Regional County Municipalities" as counties.

listening to the man who would become the first mayor of the Montreal megacity. Tremblay's address contrasted with Ryan's closely reasoned speech. "I have always said the economic development strategy of Quebec was an evolutionary and dynamic strategy,[31] so it is in that sense that you will realize that it has evolved and it is still very dynamic." Clearly infatuated with an idea that started with Michael Porter of the Harvard Business School, Tremblay presented "industrial clusters" as the nostrum for our economic ills. He even suggested creating "municipal clusters." During his speech I played my version of what today is called "buzzword bingo." Each time I heard Tremblay say a vogue word, I wrote down "Bingo." In the space of twenty minutes he invoked the word "challenge" twenty times and "industrial clusters" seventeen times; "added value," "strategy," "interdependence," and "synergy" were good for over five mentions each. And when he wasn't offering up clichés such as "the most important assets of a corporation are its human resources," he got cryptic: "non-quality cost Quebec $28 billion" and "40 per cent of our houses from now until the year 2000 will be 'intelligent houses.'" The Gérald Tremblay of today has not changed; his predilection for academic cant unfortunately still can sterilize a fertile and retentive intellect.

Interestingly, the other Quebec minister at our general meeting was Daniel Johnson. In the fall of 1993, Tremblay had mounted a campaign against Johnson for the leadership of the party but had inexplicably pulled out at the last minute, much to the irritation of Claude Ryan, who had backed Tremblay. It still rankled when I mentioned Tremblay's name to Ryan during a visit to his apartment nearly ten years later. In the event, Johnson won the party leadership without any opposition in December 1993, and replaced Robert Bourassa as premier a month later. Johnson is a quiet, thoughtful man who exudes decency. He was palpably relieved to leave politics in May 1998.

A THIRTY-YEAR OBSESSION WITH MERGERS

Ryan announced something that affected the whole Quebec municipal field during his address to the annual meeting of the Montreal suburban mayors in March 1993: he unveiled a plan to encourage voluntary mergers across Quebec. His main target[32] was the 375 villages that coexisted with parishes: 187 municipalities could be got rid of right there.* Ryan announced there would be an increase in government incentives favouring municipal mergers. They were no longer called mergers, or *"fusions,"* but went by the user-friendly name of *"regroupements,"* a term that the Department of Municipal Affairs, relying on its not insignificant command of newspeak, was convinced would convey "the idea of reinforcement by union." Ryan was quick to point out that while he was a fan of mergers, he was still talking about voluntary mergers.

By plumping for voluntary mergers, Ryan was following in the footsteps of many of his predecessors. As far back as the 1960s, Quebec had begun to be obsessed with reducing the number of municipalities – in spite of the constant drop since 1901 in the number of structures per person, or, if you like, a steady increase in the number of residents per municipality. In 1964 the Liberal minister of municipal affairs, Pierre Laporte,† had clamoured for a housecleaning of Quebec's municipal structures: urban agglomerations had spread beyond the boundaries delimited by the patchwork of villages, parishes, and cities that made them up. In 1965 the Liberals passed a bill promoting voluntary mergers. Actually, their idea of "voluntary" was to empower municipal councils to put their municipality to death without necessarily consulting the electors. Pierre Laporte said the goal of this bill was to reduce the number of municipalities from sixteen hundred to nine hundred. In the event, over the next six years, the number dropped by only fifty-two.[33]

The Liberals were then replaced by the Union Nationale party in 1966. Since their electoral base was rural, the UN soft-pedalled any attempt to reduce the number of rural municipalities. But this meant they did as they liked with the urban agglomerations, and so, in December 1969, they imposed urban or regional communities on Montreal, Quebec, and the Outaouais – where half of Quebec's population lived and where nearly three-quarters of municipal spending took place. Robert Lussier, the Union Nationale's minister of municipal affairs, did say his government was against merging

---

* Just one illustration as to the need for rural mergers in Quebec: Compton City Hall in the Eastern Townships was home to three mayors. Each mayor had his own office and his own six-member council. One mayor ran Compton, one ran Compton Station, and one ran the Township of Compton. Total population thus governed: 2,850.

† Pierre Laporte was tragically and inexplicably murdered by the Front du Libération du Québec in 1970.

all the Montreal Island municipalities at that time because it would
"go against the wishes of an important part of the population and
would misjudge the real meaning and raison d'être of local municipalities."[34] The Liberals were back in power in 1971 when their
minister of municipal affairs, Maurice Tessier, passed yet another
bill promoting voluntary mergers; this time, however, they required
a referendum. Following 1971, the total number of municipalities
dropped by 114.[35] There was yet another try in 1989, with a paltry drop of sixteen. So Ryan's list in 1993 was the Liberals' fourth
attempt to encourage voluntary mergers.

What was the position on mergers of the Parti Québécois, which
came on the Quebec scene in 1968? Well, the PQ's credo that blessed
forced municipal mergers can be traced back to at least 1971. No
less a man than René Lévesque, the PQ's founder, had laid it all out in
his inimitable polysyllabic style in a 1971 article in Pointe de Mire.[36]
He inveighed against the "implausible jungle of antiquated municipalities" about which the Liberal government was doing nothing,
out of "this crazy respect for the pseudo-independence of old municipal entities ... 1600 municipalities, and 1100 of them with less than
1500 citizens! Three-quarters of these caricatures of local governments ... don't even amount to a fifth of Quebec's population." Then
he rounded on the Union Nationale party and their creation of the
Montreal Urban Community, "a new inter-city administrative level
that is content to gather together municipal 'entities' that are politically untouchable, taking great care not to allow even one to disappear." Just in case the reader missed his point, he referred to these
new "monster" urban communities as "the anarchic pullulation of
squabbling and jealous" municipalities.

Then Lévesque really got into his stride on mergers. "Generally
speaking, it's been a question of free will. Since 1965, we even had a
law virtuously calling for 'voluntary mergers.' If I am not mistaken,
this law delivered a sum total of twenty-two of these agreed mar-
riages! Even if one adds the unions forced at legislative gunpoint
such as those of Laval (fourteen municipalities) or Bécancour (ten
municipalities), after five years one arrives at the staggering total
of sixty-two mergers: at that pace, it would take a bit more than a
century to complete this slapdash process." Lévesque went on to say
that it was essential to merge as soon as possible some four hundred to five hundred municipalities: "Our regions, riddled with these
local entities that punctuate them like so many little ghettos, struggle

along in complete stagnation, losing their vital forces, chasing away the youth." One can almost hear "La Marseillaise" playing as he wrote this. What was stopping the elimination of this terrible sociological affliction? "The one and only barrier is the incurable weakness of political guts. It's very simple: [the politicians] are afraid.* Afraid of municipal councils that are outdated, but full of 'weighty' voters." Interestingly, this dire need to impose mergers on a grand scale had seemingly evaporated by the time Lévesque became premier five years later.

Lévesque's invective notwithstanding, the Liberals did force a number of mergers in their time. In a slick little brochure[37] put out by the Department of Municipal Affairs in 1993, the glories of mass mergers were laid out in loving detail, appending a list of some five hundred municipalities that had laid down their lives over a thirty-year period in order that two hundred new and bigger municipalities could rise and see the light of day. This brochure piously said that the support of the citizens was essential to a successful merger, yet this list of battle honours contained some municipalities that were forcibly merged. Over the period, the government approved mergers involving some 2,500,000 citizens. Since a lot of the voluntary mergers involved small towns and villages, 90 per cent were voluntary, but the 10 per cent that were forced represented nearly half of the populations involved,[38] as it was often the larger municipalities that were forced to merge.

So, at least in the sticks, carrots did the job without sticks. All told, the Liberals' voluntary merger incentives, along with a general law allowing voluntary annexation, resulted in the merger of 387 municipalities from 1961 to 1990.[39] Had Quebec just continued simply to pay a rich bounty for merging, the "problem" of too many small municipalities in Quebec would have ultimately resolved itself through the painless expedient of waiting. And it was the small villages and hamlets that were, at that time, the cause of all the hand-wringing on the part of the ministers and the media.

---

* The PQ had long forgotten this call to arms thirty years later when its government baulked at merging the Montreal north shore towns and villages, owing to a strong PQ base.

RYAN: MERGERS AHEAD, VOLUNTARY OR NOT

The province's main union of municipalities, the Union of Quebec Municipalities (UMQ), faced with Ryan's relentless crusade for mergers, started to wobble on the issue. Back in 1986 when the UMQ got the former minister of finance (and future premier) Jacques Parizeau to head a commission to write a three-hundred-page tome costing $700,000 on the Quebec municipal situation,[40] Parizeau made no bones about his contempt for mergers, voluntary or forced: "There is little justification in attempting to reduce the number of municipalities," he said. In 1993 and 1994, however, two successive UMQ presidents[41] came out in favour of mergers – voluntary, of course.

When Pichette's final report was made public in December 1993, and no mergers were immediately recommended, we, the suburban mayors, hailed it as a victory for our vision of things. Ryan being the epitome of inscrutability, it was hard to read his reaction. He later told me he was very disappointed that Pichette did not come out in favour of mergers and just dealt with structures. Certainly, Ryan's message, as his reign as minister of municipal affairs came near its close in May 1994, was that "the pace of mergers must accelerate. If not, the government will eventually be sorely tempted to resort to measures more likely to procure the desired results."[42] The latter formulation was Ryanspeak for forced mergers. He went on to say that dozens of studies were underway, all designed to analyze the advantages of mergers. In another speech later that month,[43] he pointed out that $60 million was already set aside to encourage mergers, and if more were necessary, so be it: "Whatever colour the next government happens to be, the political will to reduce the number of municipalities will be there," allowing that the government could impose mergers in certain cases, such as those municipalities organized as both parishes and villages. And then, unknowingly echoing what René Lévesque wrote twenty-three years before, he said, "We will not wait for the holding of 350 referendums, making us wait until the end of the next century."

Ryan's thoughts were picked up by Agnès Gruda in *La Presse* in May 1994.[44] Her editorial was a harbinger of *La Presse* editorials that would follow a few years later, all lauding municipal mergers in general and Island mergers in particular, and all using pretty much the same arguments. Gruda looked with a jealous eye to Ontario, where 150 municipalities were "wiped off the map" to arrive at half the number Quebec had, with two million more people. Calling for mergers in the name of "efficiency and equity," Gruda was happy with the pruning of the rural scene but said the real payoff would happen with wholesale mergers in urban areas. This was where the effects of "balkanization" were apparently the most costly, and where they created "social segregation." Why have the City of Outremont right in the middle of Montreal? The residents of these "city-enclaves," she asserted, often commute downtown and don't pay for services.* The message that *La Presse* and all the supporters of mergers repeated like a drumbeat from here on in ad nauseam was that mergers would lead to a uniform tax rate and hence fiscal fairness.

The game was not yet afoot, but could easily be stirred.

---

* Another shibboleth. The lion's share of Montreal taxes was and is paid not by the residents but by the commercial sector where these commuters work.

5

Metropolitan Montreal: Suffocated by Structures

The nearest approach to immortality on earth is a government bureau.
James F. Byrnes, *Speaking Frankly*, 1947

Reorganizing the civil service is like drawing a knife through a bowl of marbles.
Sir Humphrey Appleby in *Yes, Minister*, BBC, 1980s

It was a cold winter's night in February 1994. Among the sprays of flowers and a collection of rented glasses and silverware, we were sitting on rented bentwood chairs at a long table in the low-ceilinged basement of my house. A fire burned in the fireplace. I had invited twenty mayors to fête Vera Danyluk, who, with some prodding on my part, had quit her job as mayor of the Town of Mount Royal and president of the Montreal suburban mayors to become the chair of the executive committee of the Montreal Urban Community. We had great hopes, as she had consistently questioned the way the MUC was run and voted against its year-after-year budget increases that were well above the rate of inflation. In 1992, she had even supported a petition[1] calling for municipalities to have the option of withdrawal from the MUC because of its profligate spending, lecturing the *Montreal Gazette* that this spending "makes opting out of the MUC a sobering alternative, not a 'sterile fantasy' as suggested in your editorial."[2] While I could not go that far, Vera and I were close ideological soul-mates: she shared my view that the MUC was far too cumbersome and must become a simple provider of regional services, reversing its tendency to become a level of government in its own right. And that was the official position of all of us mayors.

In January I had become the president of the suburban mayors myself. A few days before that, with great misgivings, I had refused to pursue a likely offer to become the president and publisher of the *Gazette*. I had told the head-hunter that, had I accepted the position, it would have been opportunistic: I would have let down my electors, my council, my mayors ... and Vera. Looking back, I realize I was pretty naïve.

So, in spite of a nagging feeling that I should have pursued the *Gazette* offer further, I still was happy at that evening's dinner, looking forward to helping Vera slim down the MUC, and working on creating a sense of region for metropolitan Montreal. As we all toasted Vera in the candlelight, there was a sense of comradeship, accomplishment, and shared purpose. Montreal could no longer use the MUC as an extension of its own bureaucracy – and treasury. We had finally got our own person in there. We were the masters of our own little universe. As it happened, though, things didn't work out so swimmingly. Nor did that evening: the chimney blocked and smothered our happy little group with smoke.

THE MUC

My personal battle against MUC spending had begun in early 1991, when I was Westmount's commissioner of finance and decided to do, on my own, a financial analysis of the MUC. I discovered that MUC administration costs had increased five times faster than all other costs over the previous fifteen years. I sent the results of my work to the MUC for comment. The MUC treasurer, a chartered accountant, claimed that I was wrong and everything was fine, but I subsequently discovered he had made a major mistake in his fifteen-page rebuttal. Mayor May Cutler and I got a letter of apology.

The MUC was a structure set up to run regional services such as police and wastewater treatment across the Island of Montreal. Public transit was the responsibility of yet another body. The MUC Council, which met every two months, was sovereign, but given its unwieldy size – it was made up of all the mayors on the Island, plus all the city councillors from Montreal (eighty all told) – everything was really decided behind closed doors by the executive committee and eventually rubber-stamped publicly by the council. The executive committee itself was made up of the chairs and vice-chairs of five public commissions* – Administration, Planning, Economic Development, Environment, and Public Security. Thrown in for good measure on the executive committee were the chair and vice-chair of the MUC Council. There were therefore thirteen members of the executive committee: six from Montreal, six from the suburbs, and a supposedly neutral chair who alternated between being from Montreal and from the suburbs, and who was now Vera Danyluk.

In December 1993, a few months before the party for Danyluk, I had a public row with the MUC executive committee that probably led to my getting elected president of the suburban mayors, a group that was starting to get fed up with the executive committee's high-handedness. Back in October 1992, the MUC Council had approved (I was one of the few against) a new "police map" that reduced the number of police stations across the Island from twenty-four regular stations to fourteen superstations. The goal was to "improve services and save money" by, in effect, merging police stations – not the last time we would hear such a pro-merger argument. These mergers would have meant the closure of Westmount's police station and its replacement by a mini-station – a two-man sentry-box.

For the next fourteen months, I had fought this decision with everything I had. I commissioned a study by a leading criminologist. I called a public meeting of five hundred Westmounters at Victoria Hall for them to tell the police chief and the Public Security Commission chairman (and an executive committee vice-chairman), Peter Yeomans, the salesman behind the idea, what they thought of it. I floated the idea of a "community station" that would be half-way between a mini-station and a superstation.† I got nowhere, even with a five-page letter I had written to the executive committee saying, "We need a radical change in the way the MUC makes decisions. They should not be based on remote-control administrative shuffles made without consultation, but on the needs of your clients and

---

* The commissions themselves did not, publicly, decide or debate anything of substance, and so the media stayed away in droves. These commissions (equivalent to standing committees) were set up ten years prior as a sop to those who were clamouring for more transparency in the workings of the MUC. Commission meetings were staged, proforma sideshows that didn't come cheap. Besides, by 1997, 86 of their 102 meetings that year were behind closed doors. So much for transparency.

† In the event, this was precisely what the MUC police finally implemented in January 1997, under the leadership of the new police chief, Jacques Duchesneau.

shareholders. Anachronistic aberrations such as police superstations and administrative centralization would cause private firms to go bankrupt." Mayor Yeomans characterized my manoeuvring to stop the closing of our station as "scandalous."

I managed to get an eleventh-hour reprieve in December 1993 by using the double-majority rule in the MUC Council, whereby the majority of both the Conference of Montreal Suburban Mayors and the City of Montreal had to vote in favour for any motion to pass. The council was asked to approve the merger of Montreal's downtown Station 25 with Westmount's and locate it in a new building in Montreal. Two-thirds of suburban mayors joined me in voting against the idea, much to the consternation of the Montreal councillors, who were justifiably worried about the delay in closing their clapped-out Station 25, and much to the fury of the executive committee, who saw this as a public affront to their judgment. After some name-calling, tempers flared. A recess was called. The two groups closeted separately, and Michel Hamelin, the outgoing chairman of the executive committee, served as a go-between. He formulated a new motion that kept our station in Westmount. It passed unanimously. Watching this drama from up in the gods in the visitors' gallery was Jacques Duchesneau, who was to become the new police chief.

THE MUC: A GOVERNMENT OR SERVICE CO-OP?

This contretemps did not exactly endear me to the way the MUC operated. Louis Roquet, the MUC's savvy general manager at the time, was fond of saying that Montreal and the Island suburbs had to decide what the MUC actually was. Was it a level of government or was it simply a public corporation to deliver services? It was an important question. If the MUC had been a true level of government – which would mean that Montreal Island citizens would be supporting four levels *in toto* – then at least the chairman of its executive committee should have been directly elected, and the MUC should have had direct taxation powers rather that being funded by its member municipalities. But that was not all. As a level of government, it was geographically too small. Even back when the MUC was created in December 1969, the Montreal Metropolitan Region included Laval and the south shore. One would have been hard pressed even then to make a case for creating a regional government restricted just to the Island.

I felt very strongly that the MUC should *not* be a level of government and be seen as a service-delivery organization owned by its shareholders and clients, Montreal and the Island suburbs. This was the view given in our brief, delivered by Vera Danyluk to the Pichette Task Force. As it turned out, the final Pichette Report recommended precisely that, and that similar intermunicipal service agencies be set up for areas outside the Island of Montreal. This would mean the elimination of the twelve counties surrounding the Island, each with its own mayor-cum-prefect. Unfortunately, this recommendation alone meant the report would die a-borning, given the power these counties had, as they served as an eternal electoral battleground between the Liberals and the Parti Québécois.

REGIONS, COUNTIES, COMMISSIONS

By the time the Pichette Report came out, it was plain to everyone except the mayors of the towns and villages surrounding the Island that, because of the insidious effect of urban sprawl, the metropolitan region had by then encompassed a far larger area than Montreal Island, Laval, and the immediate south shore. Something had to be set up to orchestrate the players in the metropolitan region. So the Pichette Report recommended the creation of a Montreal Metropolitan Council comprised of twenty-one elected officials from all over the region – something else the north shore mayors were also dead against. This light regional structure would have been responsible for things like planning, air quality, wastewater, mass transit, and international business and tourism promotion. While a similar – if toothless – structure was eventually created in the year 2000, it was overshadowed by the waste of billions of dollars and ten years in an unplanned nightmarish adventure with imposed mergers and botched demergers of the region's municipalities.

The day after I became the president of the suburban mayors in January 1994, I had a lunch at Montreal City Hall with Jean Doré, the mayor of Montreal, Roger Ferland, the mayor of Longueuil, and Gilles Vaillancourt, the mayor of Laval. Doré was very enthusiastic about the Pichette Report, as I was. Vaillancourt, after initially praising it, was starting to pan it. He represented all the mayors of the north shore and felt their heat. Ferland was in favour, generously saying that the south shore should help pay for the advantages of being next to Montreal. But, aside from Boucherville, he was alone with this progressive view in the south shore. It became clear that the report would be scuttled by the ferocious opposition of the north and most of the south shores, whose mayors did not wish to be dragged into the Montreal Metropolitan Region by paying their share of its costs.

While the Pichette Task Force did not make a huge issue of it for fear of offending its provincial masters who commissioned their report, the biggest barrier to creating a coordinated Montreal Region was – and still is today – the provincial government itself. Seen through government eyes, there is no Montreal Metropolitan Region. It does not exist. Instead, there are five government "regions," only two of which are wholly within the urban fabric: the Island of Montreal (prosaically known as Region 06) and Laval. The rest of the Montreal Metropolitan Region is lost in little orphan tips of three vast government regions: Montérégie, Lanaudière, and Laurentides. Why is this a problem? Well, all government services – health, education, transport, economic development, tourism, labour – are funnelled through these huge, mostly rural regions, which sprawl over some 45,000 square kilometres, or nearly one hundred times the area of the Island of Montreal. And each region has a cabinet minister responsible for it. So Longueuil finds itself controlled by the Montérégie region,[3] Repentigny by the Lanaudière region, and Mirabel by the Laurentides region. Once again the rural tails are wagging the urban dog, and those tails are being pulled in at least three different directions. The bizarre thing is, before 1988 the Montreal Metropolitan Region *was* a single administrative region. Why Quebec decided to carve up this region like postwar Berlin is anyone's guess. The result (or the cause) was, once again, the hegemony of the hinterlands.

In 1994 the Montreal Metropolitan Region sagged under the weight of twelve counties (each with its own prefect) spread out among five administrative regions, five Regional Development Councils (one for each "region"), five tourist promotion boards, and, for good measure, twenty transport commissions. Today things are pretty much the same. This cat's cradle of imposed government structures is still the biggest impediment to the idea of metropolitan Montreal. I was fond of saying then that there were more government structures in the region than municipalities. Rather than wiping out the latter, Quebec should have at least started with eliminating the former. To invoke "regional fragmentation" as the rationale behind mergers was a hypocrisy that only the government could get away with. The fragmentation created by all these structures made regional planning impossible, whether it involved public and vehicular transport, water treatment plants, green-space protection, or controlling urban sprawl. Paradoxically, the areas that had the greatest number of towns also had the most counties and other structural paraphernalia. As it turned out, these were the very towns that escaped getting merged.

According to the 1991 Census of the Montreal Metropolitan Region, the towns surrounding the urban core (which consisted of Laval, the Island of Montreal, and the south shore) had only 20 per cent of the region's population, yet accounted for two-thirds of the number of municipalities – and nearly three-quarters of the region's counties. Most of them remain unmerged, and they still sprawl over as many counties. Yet it was these municipalities that were the beneficiaries of most of the population growth in the entire region since 1991. If mergers were supposed to contain urban sprawl, they hit the wrong target: 80 per cent of the mergers took place on the Island of Montreal and the south shore. If mergers were supposed to reduce "fragmentation," they again missed the target. The number of counties, administrative regions, and transport commissions remains the same.

RYAN'S METROPOLITAN ROUND TABLE

While Claude Ryan will be, municipally, remembered for his brutal downloading, and possibly for reviving the old remedy of mergers, he should also be remembered as the man who got things moving to try to create a sense of region in the Montreal area. The many briefs submitted to the Pichette Task Force (which, after all, was his idea) certainly stirred up the regional actors, and got the media into thinking regionally. Stoically accepting that the authors of the final Pichette Report in December 1993 had refused to grasp the nettle of mergers, Ryan tried to make the best of what he considered to be a bad job. In March 1994, he would create the Montreal Metropolitan Round Table (Table de concertation de Montréal métropolitain). Ryan probably sensed it was to be his swan song as minister of municipal affairs and, indeed, as a politician. While the round table was supposed to last a year, there was only time for four meetings, the last one being in August, as the provincial election of 12

September 1994 resulted in the Liberals being booted out, and so Ryan's initiative was flushed away in the Parti Québécois tide.

Nobody remembers this round table today, but it was significant: the first time ever that any sort of a structure comprising local elected officials[4] had been created by the government, albeit temporarily, to guide the development of the Montreal Metropolitan Region. It was the progenitor of a later, stillborn structure, the Montreal Metropolitan Development Commission and, finally, the Montreal Metropolitan Community. The latter structure is now permanent, although ineffective.

Ryan's round table was charged with coming up with a regional economic development plan, attempting to come to grips with urban sprawl, and, generally, advising the government as to how the Pichette Report should be implemented. It was impossibly ambitious. During one meeting I became increasingly frustrated by the smug attitude of the off-Island mayors and prefects and their trashing of the Pichette Report. I told them,

> We in North America have always based our economic planning on a model of continuous growth of our population. It's easy to manage constant growth. Unlike Europe, we have never had to manage an economy based on static populations. This will soon change. You, however, living in the periphery around Montreal Island, are still experiencing the old kind of rapid economic growth because of your ever-increasing population, much of which originates from the Island or from other parts of Quebec. During all this, Montreal Island has had to manage a decreasing population. Between 1980 and 1990, we closed thirty-one schools. You built eleven new ones.[5] This has to stop. While the Island has managed to offset some of its population loss by immigration, this just adds problems of integration and of the newcomers' acceptance of Quebec society's values, problems that you people living off-Island do not simply have.[6]

This was music to the ears of Jean Doré, who said, "If we add up all your planning documents together, you have earmarked some *500 square kilometres* – an area as big as the whole Island of Montreal – to be put aside for new development. This would lead to unmanageable dispersion in the current context of no overall growth."[7]

Doré was a fairly short, powerfully built man with a radio announcer's voice. Because he talked a lot, the media called him "motor-mouth," but he always came prepared and well briefed: it may have been his legal training. He was as polite and pleasant as Léa Cousineau, the chairwoman of Montreal's executive committee, was acerbic and tough. Both had a sense of humour, though. Before one press conference we gave together, they said, "Peter, it's time to get our teeth dried." (This was a reference to the dry mouth experienced by most politicians before or during a speech, explaining the gaggle of water bottles and glasses that seem to surround politicians like a claque.) A real family man, Doré drove his child from his condo in a converted greystone nunnery to the École internationale in Westmount every day before going on to Montreal City Hall.

Doré did not push for the idea of One Island One City, the slogan of the mayor he beat in 1986. He said to the Pichette Task Force that the importance of regional coordination was more important than mergers themselves.[8] I formed such a good relationship with Doré that I felt like a traitor when I agreed to meet the man who was preparing to run against him in that November's election: Pierre Bourque. Through Marc Vaillancourt, the general manager of the Conference of Montreal Suburban Mayors, Bourque's people had requested a lunch with me. We met, appropriately, at Chez Pierre in Old Montreal, and I was not impressed. I felt Bourque would be more suited to starting a spiritualist movement.

THE REGIONAL DEVELOPMENT COUNCILS

Yet another structure came into being in 1994: the Regional Development Council for the Island of Montreal (RDCIM). Each of the sixteen administrative regions[9] of Quebec had its own Regional Development Council. Most had been created in 1969; there was even a province-wide organization to coordinate them. We on the Island were the last to set up such a council, as we were never very interested in such time-wasting structures. After all, we had the MUC. My more mercenary colleagues' interest only perked up in 1992 when the Liberals decided to give every Regional Development Council $3 million of government money to play with each year. No matter how small or large, every region got the same amount. The Island of Montreal, with 1.8 million people, got the same as the Lower Saint-Laurent, with 200,000 people. The Liberals were, as always, trying to boost their popularity in rural Quebec, the stronghold of the PQ. And once again, the way Quebec is divided up by administrative regions reinforced the false notion that the Island of Montreal was itself the entire Montreal region. Indeed, the mission of the council was to boost the *attractivité* of the Island and to "stimulate its economic, social, and cultural development."

Naturally, such a grandiloquent mandate called for an equally impressive slate of local heavyweights. The RDCIM was run by a council of fifty-two members: twenty-six municipal and provincial elected officials and twenty-six "socio-economic partners" such as businesspeople, union officials, community and arts groups, tourist board representatives, school commissioners, university rectors, and health specialists. People from the Board of Trade were sitting next to presidents of union centrals. A more heterogeneous and factious group could not be imagined. To top it all off, and to further the charade of solidarity, once a year there was a general assembly of 167 people: fifty-six municipal politicians, thirty-three provincial representatives, twenty-seven from the business sector, twenty-seven from the unions, and so forth. "It's like an Estates-General," I publicly sniffed. Even for the first, much-ballyhooed general assembly in October 1994, only 104 bothered to show up.[10] By 1996 the quorum for both the council and the general assembly had to be discreetly reduced to one-third. By 2001 there was a total capitulation to pragmatism: the general assembly was cut down to fifty-two people and the council to fifteen. That it took seven years to do something so patently obvious gives one a measure of the survival instincts of Quebec government structures.

Of the rather paltry manna the RDCIM distributed in its first five years, barely 10 per cent went for grants to small businesses – and only to fifty of them. (Why those particular firms out of the nearly fifty thousand businesses on the Island were singled out for largesse, I never knew. And how so few needles in such a huge haystack could possibly make a difference, I also never knew.) An equal amount went to the arts: the RDCIM funded dance festivals and theatre groups – even though the MUC had an arts council to do just that. But over half of the $23 million the RDCIM handed out in that period[11] went to groups involved in the "social economy" that were, for example, fighting poverty by "social insertion of people who are in a situation of exclusion." As always happens when somewhat ersatz idealism and government money meet, some members active in the RDCIM made it their honey pot. "If you fund my pet project, I'll vote to have yours funded" was pretty much the way they worked things.[12]

Power got concentrated. With such a huge council, one had to resort to an executive committee of fifteen, who, in turn, had to have a permanent director-general. By 1996 they had a staff of nineteen costing $1.3 million a year:[13] the RDCIM then only got about $3.3 million a year from the government, an amount that was later jacked up. Most municipal politicians saw the imposition of this structure as a huge waste of time. The deliberative mountain laboured and always brought forth a financial mouse. I was also very uncomfortable about non-elected people, unaccountable to the electorate, sharing in the decision on how tax dollars should be spent.

During the long RDCIM meetings I had to attend as its reluctant vice-president, I mused about the fate of provincial taxpayers' money. Every dollar would have been first filtered through the Quebec bureaucracy – most likely the Department of Employment and Solidarity or the Department of Regional Development – and, somewhat reduced by that trip, have found itself in the eager hands of the RDCIM. Their overheads would then eat up another chunk of it. After yet more was siphoned off to contribute to the millions of dollars for all the forums, studies, consultations, and "socio-economic summits" the RDCIM sponsored, much of what little was left would then go to pay the co-coordinator, "activist," or consultant who ran the community group whose job it was to distribute the few dimes that were left to train or feed the poor, the unemployed, or the immigrant.

As well as doling out money, the RDCIM was also required to produce soviet-like five-year plans for the development of the Island. The first plan, for 1995–2000, ran to 350 pages with all its reports and annexes. I am sure that nobody outside the RDCIM ever read a word of this mountain of paper. Actually, the diagnostic was well done, but the action plan was typically platitudinous. It duly produced another plan five years later. Today the RDCIM is still with us, having changed its name to the Regional Conference of Montreal Elected Officials (CRÉ in French), boasting 150 members.[14] CRÉs replaced all the Regional Development Councils in Quebec, but now a majority of each council is made up of elected officials.

To be fair to the RDCIM, in spite of its insular mandate, it did try to help in the creation of the Montreal Metropolitan Region – or, in its jargon, *mobiliser les partenaires* and *développer la solidarité métropolitaine*. But this just added to the cacophony of advice that the government got from all sides. Because the ownership of the RDCIM was so diffuse and loosey-goosey, its advice was too.

THE MAYORS' ROUND TABLE AND YEARLY SYMPOSIA

The mayor of Laval, Gilles Vaillancourt, had and continues to have a reputation for being a wily, sphinx-like politician. Ruling from his vast insular domain of Île Jésus, and elected term after term with massive majorities, he is a political fixture whom nobody can dislodge. He loves politics the way actors adore the stage or courtesans love to love. A portly man, he could not be accused of being handsome, but he has that optimistic, offhand charm that French Quebecers can possess in abundance. Negotiating, strategizing, holding forth in a group, he is in his element. To me, Vaillancourt was always funny, warm, and engaging. But he scared the hell out of many other politicians, something that gave him immense secret pleasure. Rumour has it that when he started off in politics, he was too shy even to give a speech. When I got to know him, he was the most articulate of an admittedly inarticulate bunch.

Vaillancourt and I got along well.[15] We rarely agreed, though. He was afraid that the Pichette Report would trim his power and lead to regional cost sharing. I was hoping for just such a thing. He was afraid all the talk of region was just a bailout for the City of Montreal. He was not totally wrong, but he never wanted to understand that unless Montreal was financially healthy, the whole region suffered. He pooh-poohed urban sprawl as not being a serious problem. And he was against any permanent regional structure, especially if it meant Laval would lose its unique status as a city, a county, and an administrative region for the Government of Quebec.[16] In other words, he was against just about everything the Pichette Report recommended. But we could at least discuss such things. And, at that point at least, Vaillancourt said he was against *forced* mergers but saw mergers as a great simplifying tool. After all, that's how his dear Laval was created. Our friendship developed further when we decided to fly to Georgia in September 1994 for a week-long course in regional leadership given by the Atlanta Regional Commission along with some fifty movers and shakers from the Atlanta region: business people, state legislators, academics, civil servants, professionals, and mayors. We learned a lot about regional cooperation that was not based on the heavy-handed, top-down Quebec model.

Back in 1992, Vaillancourt had come up with the idea of a yearly symposium of Mayors of Greater Montreal. It took place first in November 1993 and subsequently in 1994, 1995, and 1996. Out of these symposia came a thing called the Prefects' and Mayors' Round Table of Greater Montreal, which met quite regularly and yet died a quiet death in February 1997. I put a lot of time and energy into both, but nothing really came of them, as they were purely voluntary, ad hoc structures. If Claude Ryan could not get the north and south shore mayors to contribute to building up the region, these gabfests had little hope of success. I sometimes wondered whether Vaillancourt knew this all along and got involved in such activities as they gave the impression that something was being done regionally, and therefore government intervention would be seen as unnecessary. The round table at least served as a sounding board for a succession of ministers once the PQ was elected in September 1994.

For the second symposium in November 1994, Vaillancourt and I were co-chairs. Vaillancourt got very upset when he heard me say to the media that the MUC should be dismantled and turned into the service-delivery agency that the Pichette Report had recommended. I said the MUC's Economic Expansion Office should itself expand and cover the whole region – an idea that became a huge bone of contention with Vera Danyluk a few years later. I also said that the three transport boards (serving Montreal Island, Laval and the south shore) should be merged, which equally did not find favour with Vaillancourt.[17] At that point, Pierre Bourque, who had replaced Jean Doré as mayor of Montreal, was far from being in disagreement. My public sortie on the MUC earned me two long epistolary rants from Yves Ryan, the mayor of Montreal North and brother of Claude. He accused me of being "neo-regionalist" and of chumming up with the City of Montreal. The last accusation was an unpardonable sin in Ryan's book, as he harboured a deep loathing for Montreal.

THERE WERE THIRTY-ONE CENTRAL CITIES IN QUEBEC

After the Parti Québécois electoral victory in September 1994, Guy Chevrette became the minister of municipal affairs. The trivialization of Montreal's role as the only real metropolis in Quebec reached the apogee of absurdity when Chevrette released a report in December 1994 of (yet another) round table whose job it was to worry about the "central city" problem. Chevrette's Department of Municipal Affairs had drawn up a list of thirty-one "urban agglomerations[18] of more than 10,000 residents," leaving one to speculate as to how many of them could possibly have *fewer* than 10,000 citizens. (Actually, in 1997 the scales fell from my cynical eyes, thanks to a letter from Jacques Brisebois, on whom was bestowed the impressive title "the mayor of the City of Mont-Laurier and the spokesman for central cities with fewer than 10,000 citizens," who informed me there were around fifty of them.) The careful municipal classification in Quebec would have done Linnaeus proud.

That Lachute (population 11,730) and Cowansville (population 12,500) could be considered as "urban agglomerations" in the same way as Montreal is a measure of Quebec's rural obsession and is in line with its concomitant refusal to treat Montreal as a distinct, unique entity in the province. The Montreal Metropolitan Region then had a population of 3.1 million; the next closest was Quebec at 0.6 million, with size rapidly diminishing thereafter. This report on central cities dragged out the now-familiar heavy artillery against the "multiplicity" of local administrations, the overabundance of elected officials, and, naturally, "fiscal inequalities." Since "the fragmented territory hurts the development of urban agglomerations, mergers would be an advantageous solution for the future," it proclaimed, without any proof worthy of that name.

In spite of the risibility of the idea of lumping Montreal in with Lachute and Cowansville, the central-city idea stayed around. A number of years later, when Quebec went on another downloading spree, it softened the impact for the six larger central cities. About the same time, Bourque had cottoned on to the idea that, by associating his large city with five much smaller central ones, his clout in Quebec increased considerably, a revealing Quebec paradox. When he pushed for urban mergers, it was that gang of six, not Bourque alone, who pushed for them. So it was that places deep in rural Quebec like Trois-Rivières, Sherbrooke, and Chicoutimi enjoyed a disproportionate power by being Bourque's sidekicks. The real prize for Bourque was that Jean-Paul L'Allier, the mayor of Quebec City, came with this band of brothers. L'Allier gave a much-needed aura of class and intelligence that Bourque could never muster, not to mention the clear advantage of being a known and fervent sovereignist and PQ supporter.

THE METROPOLITAN TRANSPORT AGENCY (THE AMT)

At the end of March 1995 the minister of transport, Jacques Léonard, announced the creation of the Metropolitan Transport Agency – the AMT in French. The AMT, which would coordinate regional mass transit and run suburban trains, replaced another structure called the CMTC, created five years earlier, which in turn had replaced something called the COTREM, which had replaced the CTRM, which had replaced the BAREM, which had replaced another CTRM. Quebec's fecundity for structural invention knew no bounds. We were at first teased with the possibility of a choice of three different modi operandi for this brave new structure: it could be run by existing local politicians (as was the CMTC), run by a whole new level of elected officials, or run by government commissars.

Naturally, a round table had to be created to help Léonard in his decision. So a transport round table of thirty-six people was duly set up, eighteen from the municipal sector. By the time it met, Léonard had already decided that the AMT would be run by government appointees only. Just before our second meeting in the middle of June, a bill was presented to the National Assembly to that effect. So much for consultation – and so much for decentralization. The day before Léonard presented his bill, the government had approved Chevrette's Green Paper, *Décentralisation: Un choix de société*, a document that preached the virtues of transferring powers to regional and local authorities in an independent Quebec, and, to a much more limited extent, even under the current constitutional system. Yet it was decided the AMT would be run by a board of people hand-picked by the government. In other words, the AMT would be a form of government trusteeship. As I said rather diplomatically at the time, "The government talks of decentralization and at the same time takes control – that's paradoxical. And that's a nice word for it."[19]

If commuters living outside the Island of Montreal could not be convinced to switch to public transit, we were told, some four new bridges would have had to be built, at a cost of $2 billion.[20] Another of the tasks of the AMT was to get off-Island users of the metro to help contribute to it, since they represented 20 per cent of metro riders, as indeed they do today. They also had to be dragged, kicking and screaming, to pay for their share of the suburban trains. Essentially, the AMT got (and still gets) its money from a $30 car-registration fee and 1.5 cents per litre of gasoline sold in its territory, along with ticket revenues and a small contribution from municipalities.[21]

In October 1995, the Prefects' and Mayors' Round Table of Greater Montreal, shaking itself into action, and after six months' work, made a counterproposal that upped the car fee to $55 and gave local officials a majority of the seats of the AMT. Léonard rejected it out of hand, even though the counterproposal came from politicians representing 88 per cent of the region's population. (Predictably, Mirabel and five other counties did not go along with it.) By the time the law was adopted in December 1995, Mirabel, home of the world's second-largest airport in land area, was excluded from the territory of the AMT on the ground that less than half its commuters worked outside Mirabel.[22] So not only was Mirabel free of any municipal contribution but Mirabelois were liberated from the $30 car-registration fee and the 1.5-cent gas tax.

MONTREAL INTERNATIONAL

Pierre Bourque was an atheist but was driven by something very spiritual, hence his love of the Orient. His rather otherworldly mien allowed people around him to forgive the sudden way he would spurt out an idea, like Athena springing fully armed from the head of Zeus. Many of his flashes were ill thought out, and, while they resided comfortably in his own brain, often struck the outside world as being impractical. But there were exceptions. His idea to upgrade and exploit the waterways around the Island – Montréal bleu – was bang on. Likewise, his idea, no doubt germinating during meetings with his private sector advisory committee (the so-called "committee of the wise men") to create a public-private organization to promote Montreal internationally, was brilliant.

Montreal International would include the whole Montreal Metropolitan Region, reduce the number of structures already involved with international promotion, and incorporate the private sector along with all three levels of government. Unfortunately, it started off on the wrong foot. Typically, Bourque had failed to sell his partners on the idea before setting things in motion. His style was to come down from his own mountain with tablets proclaiming that the merits of the idea were patent: why go into details? He always adopted a pained, puzzled look when people questioned his "flashes." Bourque marched to his own drum – often out of step. If Montreal International was Bourque's brainchild, Jean-Jacques Bourgeault, senior executive vice-president of Air Canada, helped in the delivery. But it was Guy Coulombe, Quebec's "Mr Fix-It," who tended to the infant and ensured it survived. Coulombe had been cooling his heels running the Montreal Centre for International Conferences after a varied and impressive career as head of the Sûreté du Québec, president of Consolidated Bathurst, and, before that, CEO of Hydro-Quebec. He was paid $90,000 from February to October 1996 for his work as Montreal International's coordinator. Coulombe was a gruff bear of a man with no polish and an "out-of-my-way" approach to getting things done. After finishing his restaurant breakfast, he would stub out his cigarette in what remained of his eggs. But he could be surprisingly gentle and persuasive when the situation called for it.

Jean de Grandpré, the rather patrician former chairman of Bell Canada, agreed to chair the interim board of Montreal International. He and I were on the selection committee to find a president. Jacques Girard was hired for the position in January 1997 at a salary of $200,000 a year. At the time he was chairman of Domtar, former president of Quebecor, and former deputy minister of education. A friend of the Bouchard government (Domtar was controlled by the provincial government), he had come out for the Yes in the last referendum. It was thought that a nice political and linguistic balance was achieved when Francis Fox, an ex-Liberal federal cabinet minister and president of Rogers-Cantel, agreed to take over as chairman. The supremely confident and outgoing Girard contrasted with the intense, diffident Fox. The board of directors read like a Who's Who of corporate Montreal and included André Bérard, president of the National Bank, and André Caillé, president of Hydro-Quebec.

With this gang of heavy hitters, by October 1996 Montreal International managed to collect about $5 million from the private sector and another $5 million from the public sector as a nest egg. Companies with over $2.5 billion in sales were asked for $250,000; from $1 billion to $2.5 billion, $200,000; and so on. It was like a bigtime charity drive. Many companies coughed up. Still, something like 80 per cent of all its financing came from the federal, provincial, and municipal governments. Yet the chairman and president/general manager, and the majority of its board of twenty-five, came from the private sector. By the next year, Montreal International was costing about $5 million a year to operate.[23] Today, it costs about $10 million a year.

In spite of – or because of – its private-sector bias, I think the idea still makes sense, even if they spent quite lavishly. Was, or is, Montreal International worth the money? I'll leave that up to others to answer. But it was one of the few out of a plethora of organizations that operated for the whole Montreal Metropolitan Region that combined all levels of government and that remains an interesting experiment in public-private cooperation – all thanks to Pierre Bourque.

I sat on the board until February 1998, when I was no longer president of the suburban mayors.

THE METROPOLITAN DEVELOPMENT COMMISSION

In January 1996, Serge Ménard became the minister for the métropole. The latter word was confusing, as the media employed "metropolis" when referring to the City of Montreal alone. After all, etymologically it means "mother city," and in French or English is usually defined as "chief city." Now "metropolis" was being used to refer to the entire Montreal Metropolitan Region. The nonce-term "city-region," used by the authors of the Pichette Report, was by then consigned to the dustbin, a fate soon to be shared by the term "metropolis" used regionally.

In Quebec, the word "development" has a totemic value: it finds itself incorporated into the names of many structures and titles. It was not surprising, then, that the structure the newly minted minister Ménard was to bring into this world would be called the Metropolitan Development Commission, not to be confused with the Regional Development Councils, or the Local Development Councils, or the Community Economic Development Corporations, or the Regional Development Cooperatives, or the Community Futures Development Corporations, or the Cultural Enterprise Development Corporations – most of which are still very much with us today.

In 1993, the Quebec Government's Secrétariat aux affaires régionales estimated that, on the Island of Montreal alone, there were 136 organizations employing 862 people, promoting business development – from industrial commissioners, to boards of trade, to government structures. On top of that, there were thirty-one organizations (such as Innovatech and the Fonds regional de solidarité) that were offering financial support.[24] If one wanted to make a rough guess as to what was being spent to run these things, a figure of $50 million a year would be easily defensible just for the Island of Montreal. And that does not include the money being handed over to the companies in the form of aid. Jobs were certainly being created – government jobs.

If there is one word more potent in Quebec nomenclature than "development," it is "region," a term guaranteed to add a kind of emotive afterburner to any name. Hence, the term "regional development" is a sure-fire winner. In June 1996, on the rickety stage formed by the multiplicity of regional structures, the theatre of the absurd started to mount its performances. Ménard was supposedly responsible for the Montreal Metropolitan Region, but as we have seen, it in turn was broken up into five administrative regions, each reporting to a different cabinet minister. Topping it all off was an über-minister in the form of Guy Chevrette, responsible, among his many other duties, for the development of *all* the regions.

But, by the order-in-council decree of January 1996, Ménard was responsible for "promoting the development of the Montreal Metropolitan Region." Clearly he did not report to Chevrette, as they were both *ministres d'état*. It was not long before they got in a tussle. Specifically, Ménard wanted to boost the amount given to the Regional Development Council for the Island of Montreal because of the huge population it served. But the RDCIM did not report to Ménard,[25] but to Chevrette, in spite of its name. "No way!" said Chevrette to the request for more funding. Each region in Quebec must be treated the same, regardless of population. "We have to stop talking of so many dollars per head," he said, without explaining why.[26] Once again, the hinterland beat out the urban.

On being named minister, Ménard talked about the need to get rid of structures, but he was less and less insistent as time went on.

DECENTRALIZATION

As far as I could make out, there were three qualifications for membership in the PQ inner circle in the 1980s and 1990s. First, you must believe in the independence of Quebec; second, you must be a product of the labour movement; and third, you must smoke. A number of times, I was seated at dinner next to Guy Chevrette, an incurable sovereignist, unionist, and smoker. The haze around him made an apt metaphor for the philosophical barrier between us, so I had to work at keeping the conversation going and my gorge from rising. I like smoked food, but not particularly food flavoured with Player's Light. Chevrette in 1995 was the PQ house leader and minister of both regional development and municipal affairs. He was a squat, scrappy bullfrog of a man who would have made a great leader of the Montreal blue-collar workers. Though far from stupid, he was inflexible and imbued with that particularly PQ brand of hatred for what they saw as the élite. Chevrette was the PQ's point man on decentralization. In common with most things in Quebec, a simple word can hide a lot.

Decentralization is supposed to mean "the transfer of power from a central to a local authority." Before the PQ got into power in 1994, it simply meant the sloughing off of certain responsibilities from the provincial to the regional or municipal level. (If no new source of financing came with it, it was called downloading.) But for the PQ, decentralization became part of the Grand Plan leading up to the referendum of 30 October 1995. When Quebec became a sovereign country with a whole bunch of new powers, the government would be hard pressed to manage alone. It would *have* to push down powers to municipalities – or so went the PQ argument. Otherwise, according to Jacques Parizeau, Quebec would have become the most centralized country around. One problem, aside from the obvious one that Quebec had not yet separated, was that decentralization meant that costs would substantially increase. That's because municipalities pay their employees 30 per cent more than does the province.

During the 1994 election campaign, premier-to-be Parizeau went from village to village announcing the end of the Jacobin state. "Our Father which art in Quebec" is finished, he declared.[27] When he formed his cabinet, he gave Chevrette a charge worthy of Sir Gawain. "Today," he said, "I place on your shoulders the mission, which, along with the sovereignty plan, constitutes the most important task of our new team. As minister of state for regional development and minister of municipal affairs ... you shall see to it that the regionalization of the levers of power happens rapidly, efficiently, and tidily. You are, M. Chevrette, the enemy number one of the wall-to-wall approach."[28] Cue the trumpet voluntary.

Chevrette's decentralization bible, all hundred pages of it, was published as a Green Paper in June 1995 with the title *Décentralisation: Un choix de société* by the Government of Quebec under his imprimatur.[29] The tone of the book was quickly set with a remark concerning the "disastrous" nature of the existing constitutional situation and the "incapacity of the federal system to recognize constitutionally Quebec's distinctiveness." It then went on to bewail the number of Quebec municipalities and, interestingly, the "multiplicity" of government structures.

With a jealous eye, its unknown authors looked at how Sweden, Denmark, Germany, and the United Kingdom had radically reduced the number of their municipalities between 1951 and 1980. They glossed over the fact that France and many others had not done likewise. Readers had to, pencil in hand, work out for themselves the average size of municipality from the statistics in this document. It turned out that Quebec's municipalities were far from being the smallest even then. France came in at an average municipal population of 1,550, Greece at 2,000, Switzerland at 2,150, Austria at 3,350, and Spain at 4,800. Germany and Quebec were tied at 5,000. Then came Italy at 7,060, the United States at 7,250,[30] Ontario at 13,400, Belgium at 17,000, Denmark at 18,700, the Netherlands at 22,800 and Sweden at 29,400. The U.K. took the prize at 141,000.[31]

In *Décentralisation: Un choix de société*, one can read that when "Quebec is freed from the constraints of federalism," Quebec's central government will control (among other things) defence, the promotion of French, railroads, the national police, the postal service and telecommunications, and monetary policy. This new "unitary state," with its budget some 66 per cent bigger than the current province of Quebec, would have no choice but to decentralize massively. (Without sovereignty, the reader is warned, there would be only minor decentralization.) "Most of the municipalities, owing to their small populations and limited resources, might well find themselves unable to assume certain powers" that require a critical mass of population. They would not be able to handle all the new decentralized responsibilities such as the "distribution of passports and identity cards," unemployment insurance, and prisons. The only solution would be mergers. So, the message to municipal Quebec went, all this low-hanging fruit could be theirs if they mustered the courage to merge – and to vote for sovereignty in the next referendum.

The PQ strategy of the period before and after the referendum was cunning; *de jure* independence would be less painless if the planning to manage the new country of Quebec were already done and a few trappings were in place. Under the guise of decentralization and regionalization, the sixteen administrative regions of Quebec were to be strengthened, to become simulacra of the sixteen "provinces" that would make up a sovereign Quebec. The architect behind this Quiet Regionalization remained Guy Chevrette. Poor Serge Ménard was swimming weakly upstream against this regionalization trend. The two concepts – regionalization and metropolization – could not co-exist, as the former treated the sixteen Quebec regions as being equal, and the latter regarded the Montreal Metropolitan Region as unique, indivisible, and the true economic guts of Quebec. As well as the imposition of the Montreal Metropolitan Development Commission that was to be layered over a surfeit of existing structures, there was to be a new series of equivalent and competing government structures reflecting Chevrette's regionalization policy. These two ministers together were trying to achieve the bureaucratic equivalent of two parallel universes: Franz Kafka meets Lewis Carroll.

Of course, instead of actually delegating power, Quebec tended to hang on to it. Government-imposed structures, especially those imposed by doctrinaire, meddling ideologues, are unnatural, unwanted, and unremovable.

LOCAL DEVELOPMENT CENTRES AND LOCAL EMPLOYMENT CENTRES

So, in spite of a farrago of existing structures, Guy Chevrette figured there weren't enough to his liking. Inspired by the Summit on the Economy and Employment held in late 1996, along with his government's policy of decentralization, he decided to create well over one hundred Local Development Centres across Quebec, ten just for the Island suburbs of Montreal.[32] Today, there are 120 CLDs across Quebec and about twenty-two in the Montreal Metropolitan Region. CLDs are Regional Development Councils in miniature. They are run with the same kind of heterogeneous leadership, with at least one board member coming from each of the business, labour, municipal, cooperative, community, health, and educational sectors. Their role is supposed to be a *guichet unique,* a funnel for all government programs directed at small business and the social economy, permitting a kind of one-stop shopping. Their policies, however, are pretty much dictated by Quebec.

At least Montreal's Board of Trade got it right. Its president said, "These CLDs are an aberration for the metropolis. There are already at least fifty structures in the region dedicated to economic development."[33] Claude Picher, writing in *La Presse,* raised Chevrette's ire with his article "The Comedy of the CLDs."[34] Today, the CLDs, all together, sport fifteen hundred employees and give out around $30 to $50 million a year to various enterprises, or less than $0.5 million per CLD. It's like trying to irrigate a wheat field with a watering can, a leaky one at that.

Why did Chevrette do this? He maintained he was actually *reducing* the number of structures dispensing local development, which – he said – numbered seven hundred across Quebec at that point, eating up $175 million a year just to run them.[35] It is beyond the scope of this book and the wit of its author to ascertain whether most of these structures have, in fact, since been eliminated with the advent of CLDs. I remain in doubt.[36] What many people missed is that the imposition of the CLDs was yet another form of downloading, as the municipal level was forced to contribute to them.

Not content with lumbering the region (and all Quebec) with CLDs, Chevrette also created the Local Employment Centres, the CLEs. Today, there are 150 of these things scattered all over Quebec, with around thirty-seven in the Montreal Metropolitan Region. With great pomp, hailing "the triumph of common sense," Chevrette announced both the CLDs and the CLEs in a white paper released 30 April 1997.[37] This is when it was announced that Serge Ménard, as minister of the metropolis, would have the pleasure of being responsible for the CLDs in the Montreal region and their implantation, along with the Regional Development Council for the Island of Montreal.

In his white paper Chevrette deplored the fact there were fourteen hundred municipalities in Quebec, with two-thirds of them having less than two thousand citizens, and only forty-nine with more than 25,000. "For the government, this fragmentation of the municipal reality" made it very difficult to have them handle the CLDs. So he gave them to the counties and to the urban communities – all ninety-nine of them.

SUMMARY

Thanks to the superimposition of structures with the CLDs at the base, we are now blessed with an administrative carving-up that would do proud a whole country – which was, of course, Chevrette's whole idea. The trouble is, it is appropriate for a country the size of India. The development of Quebec must certainly be very important, since there are four levels of structures to ensure that it happens. Just think: the minister of the regions (or the possessor of whatever title is in vogue today) sets the "national" agenda for economic development, the (stillborn) Metropolitan Development Commission (today, the Montreal Metropolitan Community) plans economic development for Greater Montreal, the Regional Development Council (today, the Regional Conference of Montreal Elected Officials) does the Island of Montreal, and the Local Development Centres worry about local economic development. The appalling thing is that matters are no better today: only the names have changed.

Ten years ago there were ten different varieties of government-imposed structures cluttering up the Montreal Metropolitan Region,[38] half of them invented in 1994, 1995, or 1996; they too all remain with us. This surfeit of structures still suffocates the region with no hope in sight of rationalization.[39] All that was (and is) needed are three structures: something to coordinate metropolitan activities, something to run metropolitan mass transit, and something to run Montreal Island shared services.

The government's penchant for a cat's cradle of structures is not by any means limited to the Montreal Metropolitan Region. In the Saguenay region,[40] there were sixty municipalities, four counties, eleven school commissions, five tourist agencies, and so on, all to serve a population of 300,000.

In Quebec, the arteries of government have become clogged with nodular deposits of useless structures, a disease for which there appears no immediate relief. This is because, as with arteriosclerosis, there is little or no awareness of a problem even existing. Between 1992 and 2002, owing to wholesale municipal mergers, the Montreal Metropolitan Region lost about forty municipalities. During the same period, there was an addition of at least forty government-imposed structures. This is what Quebec called progress. Why was the merger of municipalities so necessary but not the merger of structures?

At least there aren't any government round tables today. The government still manages to go round in circles without them.

6

Merger Plans, the MUC, and a Metropolitan Miscarriage

Mountains appear more lofty the nearer they are approached, but great men resemble them not in this particular.

Lady Marguerite Blessington (1789–1849)

Mountains will go into labour and a ridiculous mouse will be born.

Horace, ca. 8 BC

On 5 January 1996, in huddled bunches, some eighty guests arrived at our house out of the icy Montreal winter. They rubbed shoulders in a small oak-panelled vestibule. Women (hired by the caterer) dressed in incongruous Japanese costumes carefully put each slushy boot of each guest in a white plastic bag, writing a name on it in black marker and whisking bags and coats upstairs via the back stairs. The guests, now unimpeded but still cold, moved to the hall and took wine from waiters. Hovering in the background, making delicate, last-minute adjustments to the decorations, was the caterer, George Alevisatos, a hulking ex-footballer who himself never wore a winter coat.

The guests, while not the pillars of Westmount society, might have been the pilasters. From outside Westmount came four principal actors in my personal drama that would unfold over the next five years: Vera Danyluk, from the Montreal Urban Community; Montreal Mayor Pierre Bourque; the director-general of the Conference of Montreal Suburban Mayors, Marc Vaillancourt; and his twenty-three-year-old daughter, Claudia. Unknown to themselves or to me at the time, these four would radically change the direction of my public and private life.

The hall floor was tiled in large black and white squares. I had always wanted to stage a chess game on it with people as chess pieces. It never happened. The house was built in 1910 by William Rutherford, the sixteenth mayor of Westmount and a lumber merchant. A later owner, the director of the Museum of Fine Arts, painted over Rutherford's oak panelling in the hall to better set off his paintings; subsequent stripping and revarnishing left a smeared, dull surface. The hall opened up via two sets of glazed pocket doors into the Adam-y living room to the west and the faux-Tudor dining room to the east.

With smug self-congratulation, I had decided to celebrate my fiftieth birthday with this party. Two months prior, I had been re-elected mayor of Westmount by acclamation. I remained president of the Montreal Suburban Mayors and vice-chairman of the Montreal Urban Community. A mixture of naïveté and hubris attached itself to me in my expansive fin-de-demi-siècle mood. Dinner was followed by a series of maudlin toasts, as people's tongues, ties, and inhibitions loosened. I remember singing and playing the guitar while Bourque swayed and clapped off-beat. After duly cutting my birthday cake, I don't remember much.

Twelve months later my marriage had been mercy-killed and the Canadian municipal merger movement was already underway with the creation – on April Fool's Day 1996 – of mega-Halifax.[1] The Toronto megacity was announced in November 1996. And, by December, Serge Ménard's alternative to merger, a toothless talk-shop covering the Montreal Metropolitan Region, was thoroughly panned by politicians and the media alike. The merger steamroller was by then gathering speed.

GUY CHEVRETTE SETS THE TONE

Barely two months before my birthday, the Parti Québécois had suffered a wrenching loss in the sovereignty referendum – the loss of their country-to-be by a 1 per cent margin. Crushed and angry, Parizeau resigned as premier the day after. Lucien Bouchard took over and the PQ got going on what the PQ does when it isn't beating the drum for sovereignty – messing about with government structures. Just as Mao Tse-tung kept the flame alive in China by constantly fomenting internal revolutions, the PQ went about channelling its energies to prepare for the next referendum and victory. If you don't get to own your own home, at least you can rearrange furniture in anticipation of home ownership.

In the waning weeks of his term as municipal affairs minister, Guy Chevrette began to sound more and more like Claude Ryan when he was giving his swan song. "The pace of mergers must accelerate. If not, the government will eventually be sorely tempted to resort to measures more likely to procure the desired results,"[2] said Ryan in May 1994. "The government must, sooner or later, thump its fist on the table and proceed unilaterally with legislation,"[3] said Chevrette in December 1995, typically using more direct language than his more subtle predecessor. Chevrette had already put together a map of desirable mergers across Quebec. The goal was to merge "at least 800 municipalities out of the 1,412 that exist."[4] His frustration was almost palpable when he wrote, "the present government was not elected with the mandate to force mergers."[5] In fact, the PQ program for the 1994 election specifically excluded "coercive measures" for mergers.[6]

All of this sabre-rattling was directed at Quebec's plethora of rural hamlets. But, as a parting shot late in January 1996, a few days before Bouchard officially became the new premier, the shortly-to-be ex-minister of municipal affairs could not resist stating publicly that Montreal Island amalgamations were a desirable thing. "One can easily get extraordinary economies of scale,"[7] said Chevrette, brushing aside, probably unknowingly, all the academic literature that supported the opposite view. Chevrette was a former labour leader, a breed that, like politicians, rarely lets facts undermine dogma.

Bouchard formed his first cabinet on 29 January 1996. Bernard Landry was vice-premier and minister of finance, Guy Chevrette minister for the regions, Serge Ménard minister for the métropole, André Boisclair responsible for immigration and cultural communities, and Rémy Trudel minister of municipal affairs.

As long as Parizeau was premier, there had been no chance of forced mergers, as he had taken the position since 1986, and repeated it on a number of occasions, that mergers were for bureaucratic convenience and led to no economies of scale. Once his mind was made up, Parizeau was not the sort to change direction. Bouchard had never taken such a stance.

MINISTER OF THE MÉTROPOLE

The two-page document had "Government of Quebec" at the top, followed by "Order-in-Council number 125–96," and the date, 29

January 1996. "It is ordered," it began, "that the minister of state for the métropole has the mandate to promote the development of the Montreal Metropolitan Region." The minister was to do this with "the constant preoccupation of simplifying the existing structures" and "ensuring the coherence of government actions in the territory." His principal mission was to figure out how to create the Montreal Metropolitan Development Commission. With such high-flown bureaucratese was launched Quebec's first attempt to rationalize the government structures in the Montreal Metropolitan Region and to give it a permanent regional coordinating body. Serge Ménard, a former criminal lawyer and probably the most popular star in the cabinet of Premier Parizeau, had no background at all for his new job. More importantly, he had precious little political experience: elected for the first time slightly over two years before, he had put in only sixteen months as a cabinet minister: someone with two years' political experience was being given the trickiest job going in Quebec. Ménard was no match for the likes of Chevrette and Bernard Landry – and they were on his team.

Yet Ménard swanned onto his new stage with far more enthusiasm than caution. In a scattershot interview[8] just after his appointment and on emerging from an hour-long meeting with Montreal Mayor Pierre Bourque, he proclaimed that he now understood the problems of the Montreal Metropolitan Region. He wanted to address the prickly question of "fiscal inequity" between Montreal and the suburbs, taking as read that such a thing existed. He wanted to look into imposing one commercial tax rate, saying, "I think it is ridiculous that municipalities fight among themselves to attract industries." Then, almost without missing a beat, he said, "Yes, 102 municipalities, that's far too many. The Pichette Report offers an interesting approach without forcing mergers." He did say that pooling of services à la Pichette could lead naturally to mergers "with citizen approval." He also decried the number of government structures: "Now, that was exactly the goal of my nomination. We never wanted to do any housecleaning and we went and accumulated structures one on top of each other." Even throwing a bone to the English, he said, "Those who could not accept the French character of Montreal have gone, and those who remain appreciate it ... we have to re-evaluate whether French is in danger any longer in Montreal."

Ménard's giddy frankness rubbed off on Bourque, who excitedly chimed in that it was "evident" the number of municipalities on the

Island of Montreal must be reduced.[9] He later assured me that he was misquoted and that he was talking about off-Island suburbs. My doubts about Bourque started to set in.

The next day, the astute representative for Westmount–Saint-Louis, Jacques Chagnon, pointed out that while Ménard had a seat on every cabinet committee, he did not sit on the all-important Treasury Board, which holds the government's purse-strings.[10] He also said that Ménard was a minister without portfolio and therefore did not run a government department and could not veto any others. He would be competing with Guy Chevrette, for example, for money.

While I, as head of the Montreal Island suburban mayors, lauded Ménard's appointment, it did not take long for the off-Island mayors to react. In a news conference, prefects representing nine counties and seventy municipalities surrounding the Island of Montreal raked both Bourque and Ménard over the coals because of their desire to boost "Montreal the king" and promote "fiscal sprawl." They were particularly incensed by Ménard's musings about resurrecting the Pichette Report and imposing one commercial tax rate, and by his eminently logical suggestion that Mirabel Airport be closed.

Hubert Meilleur, the irascible mayor of Mirabel and one-time Bloc Québécois candidate, said, "If the minister tries to penalize suburbanites, tries to take the shirts off our backs – you saw the Mohawk revolution at Oka. Well, there will be a suburban revolution."[11] Later he said, "The problem with Montreal is on the Island of Montreal, with the MUC. There are too many cities that are badly run and there are, in any case, too many of them."[12] On the radio, he opined that Westmount, specifically, should disappear, proselytizing the virtues of One Island One City. So one of the first people to disinter Montreal Mayor Drapeau's 1960s slogan was the mayor of Mirabel, a "city" that took up as much territory as the whole Island of Montreal but with 1 per cent of its population.

At least Meilleur was consistent in his desire for splendid isolation. In order to avoid the small gas tax that helped fund regional public transit, he had succeeded in pulling Mirabel out from the Metropolitan Transport Agency. One irony clearly escaped him, however, when he complained about the moving of flights from Mirabel to Dorval: he was the one who got the second-largest airport in the world excluded from the transport agency's transport plan.

Such was the evanescence of Ménard's nostrums that, one month later, he had dropped the idea of uniform commercial tax rates. He started talking about his main goal: his commission would be mostly consultative, would be made up of a majority of elected people, and would administer some kind of regional equalization payments.[13]

ONE ISLAND, ONE FIRE BRIGADE

Bourque's vague pronouncement in favour of Island mergers was a signal to his bureaucracy to muse publicly – and unprofessionally – about such things, perhaps by design. The first shot across the bows in Montreal's campaign for One Island One City came from a civil servant. In March 1996 the head of Montreal's fire brigade, Roméo Noël, sent up the trial balloon of merging Montreal's thirty-six fire stations with the twenty-five serving the Island suburbs, all to be under the MUC's control. This would "save money" and afford better fire protection. Just think, Noël said, we would get rid of twenty-nine fire directors on the Island. (He never explained that twenty-nine assistant directors – making more money – would have to be hired to replace them.) He had to reach back to 1972 to find a report that recommended the MUC take over fire services. Both the Pichette Report and the Golden Report for Greater Toronto recommended that they stay with individual municipalities. M. le directeur Noël just happened to mention that Serge Ménard, while public security minister, was in favour of such a project. When the *Journal de Montréal* breathlessly revealed Noël's idea through an exclusive interview,[14] my reaction was headlined, "No Way, Said Westmount, *la riche*." Never missing an opportunity to paint Westmount as the gilt enclave of the anglo rich, the latter term being a pleonasm in Quebec, this newspaper intentionally ignored that I was speaking for all the Island suburbs.

CLAUDE RYAN AND MERGERS

In March 1996 I had invited the then-retired Claude Ryan to come to the Conference of Montreal Suburban Mayors to share with us his thoughts about Ménard, the Montreal Metropolitan Region, and mergers in general. Blunt as always, and even more so in private, he was critical of the Pichette Report, which in his mind was far too quick to embrace big structures and did not establish what should be a minimum size for municipalities, the basic building blocks of any region. In other words, he had expected Pichette to recommend mergers. He went on to say that Outremont was "anachronistic," being surrounded by Montreal. (Out of consideration for his luncheon host – me – he delicately made an elision for Westmount.)

BOUCHARD SPEAKS

In March at one of the biggest Board of Trade luncheons I have ever attended, twelve hundred business types flocked to Hotel Bonaventure to hear Lucien Bouchard. During the meal, Ménard showed Premier Bouchard a 21 March 1996 *Washington Post* article entitled "O Montreal, City of Exodus," which exposed how separatist tension and urban sprawl were devastating Montreal's economy, leading to another anglo exodus. The reporter had followed on the heels – literally, as she interviewed the same people, including me – of a *Maclean's* article about "Anglo Angst." It's one thing to have our dirty laundry displayed to the rest of Canada, but to have the *Washington Post* trumpet "Separatist tension, weak economy, drive Montreal into steep decline" made Ménard and Bouchard wince. During lunch, I chatted with Bouchard, who said there were far too many municipalities in the region, one problem the PQ couldn't blame on the federalists. We did agree that linguistic distortions caused by urban sprawl, as francophones fled to off-Island suburbs, could result in an eventual francophone minority on the Island.

MÉNARD SHOWS OBSTINACY

With his bright eyes, hushed, jerky voice, and unconvincing bursts of laughter, Serge Ménard had a slightly murine appearance and comportment, topped with a slicked-back 1950s hairstyle. He was an honest, intelligent, and decent man but could affect a kind of ersatz bellicosity and stubbornness. Occasionally he could swing the other way to an apologetic mousiness that took all by surprise. I witnessed both sides of his character.

In early March 1996 the MUC was having difficulty in naming someone to the Metropolitan Transport Agency – the AMT. To no one's surprise, the Island of Montreal had the right to only one representative, even though it accounted for over 80 per cent of all mass transit spending in the Montreal Metropolitan Region. Equally to no one's surprise, our nominee had to be approved by the government, in the person of Serge Ménard. With what I thought was impeccable logic, we, the Island suburban mayors, wanted to name the chairman of the MUC Transit Commission to this board. At that time the MUCTC chairman was Yves Ryan, brother of Claude and long-time mayor of Montreal North. Bourque, in one of his obstinate moods, was dragging his feet in giving Montreal's approval to Ryan, and this went on through three consecutive meetings of the MUC executive.* Frustrated, Vera Danyluk went public with the details of the Ryan impasse, as Bourque and I were taking too long to work things out. Bourque finally relented.

In May 1996, Ryan's nomination ran up against another roadblock: Ménard. For some bizarre reason he had got it into his head that, if Ryan was both chairman of the MUCTC and had a seat on the AMT, it would constitute a conflict of interest. He even managed to get an internal legal opinion to this effect, which he adamantly refused to show us. After a number of meetings with Ménard, many letters, and three positive legal opinions later, we were getting nowhere. Ménard continued to refuse Ryan's nomination, even going as far as to say that he would approve my candidacy but not Ryan's. This being a matter of principle, I decided to take legal action. I even had the tepid support of Bourque. Finally, in late November, the Quebec Superior Court ruled that Ménard was completely wrong, saying there was no such conflict of interest and that elected officials were free to sit on any and all such boards, which, after all, were simply structures of the state. The state cannot be divided against itself; it is indivisible. Moreover, it has to be assumed that those who participate in administering the state do so in its interest, not their own.

MÉNARD SHOWS CONTRITION

When, in May 1996, the City of Outremont decided against approving a $525 million plan to build houses and offices in the old Canadian Pacific railyards, out came Ménard's bluster. In the National Assembly he said he would not hesitate to use his powers to stop

---

* While this was going on, another battle was brewing between Bourque and the suburbs. Bourque was quietly getting the letters patent and naming the board of his Montreal International, all without our – his partner's – approval, even though the launching of this organization meant the end of the MUC's Economic Expansion Office. As we shall see, this matter festered for another three years, owing largely to Danyluk's corporate retentiveness.

municipalities like Outremont from blocking regional development: "First, I seek to understand, then I seek to convince, and then I think that I must have the power to intervene." After a ninety-minute meeting with Jerôme Unterberg, mayor of Outremont, Ménard said to reporters, "If Montreal had leaders like that in the past, it would never have become a metropolis."[15] As president of the suburban mayors, I immediately came to Unterberg's defence with a press release deploring Ménard's interference and personal attacks. The next day, I got a contrite phone call at home from Ménard, who said in a wavering voice that he had read my press release, was convinced by its contents, and wanted to apologize without reserve for his actions. Never in my political career have I experienced a minister go that far in admitting a mistake. I was touched and puzzled at the same time.

TRUDEL DUSTS OFF THE MERGER PLAN

When the PQ got back the reins of power in 1994 and Guy Chevrette became the minister of municipal affairs, he said (publicly, at least) he was not in favour of forced mergers. His position hardened with time. In fairly short order after being named as Chevrette's replacement, Minister Rémy Trudel revealed he too was a voluntary merger man. Forced mergers, he said, could have perverse results. He started to use yet another comfy term for mergers: "consolidation." This was the term his boss, Premier Bouchard, had introduced in his inaugural address on 25 March 1996: "In May, the minister will make public a map proposing the merger and consolidation of Quebec municipalities. This map will also describe the incentives and fiscal advantages for the future of these communities."[16] Trudel duly revealed in May that he had a hit list of five hundred municipalities he wanted merged,[17] including Dorval Island and six other unnamed municipalities on the Island of Montreal. Quebec was going to crank up the financial incentives for mergers even further.

Three days later, at the annual meeting of the Union of Quebec Municipalities (UMQ), we heard from Jacques Parizeau, the former premier of Quebec. Parizeau had an endearing habit of suddenly and publicly sticking his nose into his colleagues' affairs like a Jacques-in-the-box. He declared that mergers do not lead to economies of scale and are only for the government's convenience, not the citizens'.[18] Trudel's lame response was that it cost as much per capita to run towns of fewer than five hundred residents as the City of

Montreal. This was true, but his own figures showed that all the municipalities in between these two extremes spent much less.

Next came Trudel's arm-twisting. Whenever a group of franco-phone Quebecers decide to have a secret retreat in order to reach consensus through the alchemy of just being away, they call it a *lac-à-l'Épaule*. When Premier Lesage and his cabinet decided to nation-alize electricity in Quebec in 1962, they came to this decision while sequestering themselves at a fishing camp on a lake by that name, hidden in a nature preserve in the Laurentian woods. Trudel, a man with a ready smile, a pasty pachydermic skin, and combed-back hair, was a hail-fellow-well-met sort of guy who insisted on addressing me using the familiar *tu* while I equally obstinately called him *vous*. He had been the founding rector of the University of Quebec in Abitibi-Témiscamingue, as well as a municipal councillor for five years. Trudel decided to hold a *lac-à-l'Épaule* near Trois-Rivières on Lac Saint-Pierre in May 1996. The two municipal unions were invited.

The purpose of this retreat was – to no one's surprise – to sell us on the necessity of reducing the number of municipalities in Que-bec. Municipal boundaries date from the last century, we were told. I had to refrain from pointing out that so do provincial boundaries, which are far more arbitrary. The sales pitch continued: "consolida-tion" would not only result in economies of scale and better services but would create a new dynamic, whatever that meant. There would be a better sharing of costs. Gone would be the redundancies, lack of planning, and sterile competition among municipalities in urban regions. This patter came directly from the bureaucrats and would serve, word for word, as the pro-merger litany used a few years later by Louise Harel when her turn came to sell mergers.

So began the tradition of invoking platitudes and unsupported assertions to serve as arguments for urban mergers. What Trudel, as the department mouthpiece, did do was make a convincing case for rationalizing rural villages.[19] Of the 1,401 municipalities in Que-bec at that time, two-thirds had fewer than 2,000 residents. And the kicker: these hamlets got handouts from the government to the tune of 19 to 44 per cent of their revenues. In spite of this largesse, some two hundred towns did not even have a fire department. Once again it was clear to any rational being that the "problem" of too many municipalities was a rural, not an urban one.

When he was municipal affairs minister, Guy Chevrette had com-plained of another problem with so many small towns: they wore down his department. His correspondence ran to 38,000 letters, and his department dealt with 480,000 different documents in one year, including 240,000 authorizations permitting various municipalities to borrow money.[20]

In common with everything Trudel and his department did, the merger plan was as complicated as his fobbing off of a $500 million downloading bill a year later. They divided all Quebec municipalities into three groups: the first, 416 rural parishes, villages, and "agglomerations of fewer than 10,000 people," were called on to merge; the second, cities and towns making up the twenty-seven urban agglomerations, were asked for merger "proposals"; the lucky third group was made up of some 728 small towns that were to escape merger completely.[21] While the whole merger plan was voluntary, towns in the first group that did not merge would "live with the financial consequences of their decision and become financially autonomous"[22] – bureaucratese for "we'll cut off your funding."

Whenever it came to mergers, there was an inherent contradiction within the Union of Quebec Municipalities (UMQ): the big municipalities wanted to get even bigger and thus were in favour of forced mergers; the smaller municipalities were against mergers, especially if forced. Gilles Vaillancourt was mayor of Laval and also the president of the UMQ at the time. Shortly after the *lac-à-l'Épaule* gabfest, Trudel announced that the urban agglomerations would have over a year to come up with their merger suggestions. Vaillancourt deplored this delay and pushed for Island mergers. He even sent out a UMQ press release: "The City of Laval," it went boastfully, "would not be as dynamic today if the sixteen municipalities that once comprised it had not merged. We believe that merging certain municipalities will be beneficial for their citizens."[23] As president of the Montreal suburban mayors and board member of the UMQ, I fired off a letter to Vaillancourt, blasting him for his editorializing, and then publicly saying that the Island municipalities were already 35 per cent merged, in that we gave that proportion of our budgets to the MUC for common services. "Everything that was logical to merge has been merged."[24]

MEANWHILE, BACK AT THE MUC

Vera Danyluk was born Vera Mystic in a poor section of east-end Montreal. For the first six years of her life, she spoke only

Ukrainian. She then learned a flawless English and a French that she spoke with only a whisper of an accent. The conflicting air of worldly religiosity that always hung around her like a laic wimple came to her easily: had her father not died when she was fifteen, she said, she probably would have become a nun.[25] She taught in Catholic schools; even her master's degree was in religious philosophy and morals. She had a warm, yet restrained demeanour that, with groomed hair and soignée clothes, made her attractive to all. Her signature and handwritten notes were all in the disciplined, rounded hand taught in the 1950s, which only the teachers seemed to have mastered even then. When she chaired our executive committee meetings, Danyluk had a little bell to call us to order like a scolding schoolmarm. She was known as the mother superior of the MUC. God, she was tough.[26]

This mother superior put a bit of stick about in the MUC and, true to her word, forced the MUC to trim its spending. She also got cracking on turning the MUC into a service corporation. During her first two years there, she trimmed down a clutch of her – mostly political – advisers from sixteen to ten. In September 1995 she prepared a "corporate vision" of the MUC to be approved by the executive committee, saying the MUC was no longer a "regional government" and wanted, above all, to be a slimmed-down "intermunicipal service organization."[27] Then something happened.

Somewhere between then and the spring of 1996, Danyluk had a mild epiphany. The MUC was no longer just a service delivery organization: it should have a political role too – with her as spokesperson. I learned of this sea change when she took me aside on a spring day in 1996.

"Peter, we must have respect for our institutions," she said.

"I suppose," I mumbled. I had no idea where this was going.

"The MUC was given to us to serve as a forum for political discussion."

"You know and I know that the MUC was created overnight in 1969 to bail out Montreal. It was either that or the imposition of One Island One City. A political role means the MUC moves toward becoming a level of government. And creating a level of government was not what you agreed to do when you came here, and certainly not what I nor Bourque agree with."

"Peter, I have evolved in my thinking. I have a political role as well. And I must say, I am getting tired of being treated like a waitress

– not by you, Peter, but by your people and Bourque's people. After all, I am your equal and have the status of an elected official."

"Actually, you don't, Vera. You gave that up to become chairman of the executive committee."

"Well, the MUC lawyers say I do." It was not the last we would hear of this idea.

Then I unintentionally put a little fuel on this fire. After Trudel floated the idea of expanding the MUC's territory to include Laval and the south shore in early May 1996,[28] I took to writing a series of columns in the *Westmount Examiner* about overhauling the MUC. "While nobody denies the need for an Island-wide structure to furnish some common services," I wrote, "the MUC is a rather heavy-handed and sclerotic body that suffers from a structural overburden. It is beset with outgrowths, overlays, and appendages such as public commissions more noted for poor attendance and no media coverage than for any real debate." I then suggested that the MUC transit board be merged with the plethora of other transit organizations cluttering up the Montreal Metropolitan Region.[29] Likewise, economic development, environmental controls, regional planning, and regional parks should be, ah, regionalized. The result would have been a very slimmed-down MUC. One column I headlined "The MUC Unplugged." I'm sure Danyluk took it to be a medical, not a musical, reference.

Next thing I knew, she wrote to me, copying all members of the executive committee, rapping me on the knuckles for giving a "negative vision of our organization" and demotivating MUC employees. At the next executive meeting she called me a loose cannon. The contretemps raised fascinating public governance questions that I laid out in a letter to my colleagues. "Has our society got to the point that we elected officials, in order not to upset our (well-paid) bureaucrats, must not engage in public debate about the size, efficiency, and very existence of our institutions? *Quis custodiet ipsos custodes?* Who will guard the guards themselves? I would think our citizens would be appalled by such a gag order."

By then Danyluk had become an unflagging cheerleader for her concept of the MUC. I suppose this was predictable, as, when you're at the pinnacle of a billion-dollar enterprise, it is hard to be critical of it. Broadly speaking, she was more and more thinking of the MUC as an order of government, with her at its head. I saw it as an inter-municipal service organization that needed pruning before imposing Ménard's Metropolitan Development Commission on top.

Our duelling visions became public in August 1996. During a meeting of the MUC Council, a Montreal opposition-party member put the cat among the pigeons by tabling a motion suggesting the MUC become the forum for debate on matters relating to the Greater Montreal Region. Danyluk rose to support the motion. It was roundly defeated. The fact that Danyluk, a non-elected official appointed by the elected council, would have a differing view from that of the council led the media to talk melodramatically of the MUC's "existential crisis."

The issue was: did we, or did we not, wish to create another level of government? For if the MUC did pronounce on regional issues, it would move towards a de facto level of government, but without the accountability. Should we then have endowed the MUC with the usual trappings of government, universal suffrage and direct taxation? But we already had three levels of government. Did we really wish to create yet another? That was what happened in Toronto. Metro Toronto – their equivalent of the MUC – was politicized and "opened up" to the electorate in 1988, becoming an extra level of government that was soon detested by the population. My theory was that the Toronto megacity project managed to go ahead not just because it merged already large municipalities into an even bigger one but because the process of merger got rid of the hated Metro at the same time.

The Conference of Suburban Mayors felt that a light, indirectly elected structure for the Montreal Metropolitan Region could ensure regional planning and coordination, result in the elimination of most of the gallimaufry of other structures that cluttered up the regional scene, and, most importantly, ensure that the *entire* region paid for regional costs. It would not provide services directly to residents. A pared-down MUC would remain to deliver services on the Island. Montreal also agreed with this idea. So did Ménard, at that point. And so did the Pichette Report. Danyluk did not.

WHO SPOKE FOR THE ISLAND?

Danyluk genuinely felt that the individual cities making up the Montreal Urban Community were secondary to the community itself. I felt *cities* must be the basic building blocks of any regional edifice. People understand and relate to their city. Through their *city*, people should determine what kind of inter-municipal or regional service they want. Bourque spoke for the City of Montreal on regional matters, and other Island mayors spoke through the Conference of Suburban Mayors. Did we really need a third voice?

Who should have spoken for the Island of Montreal? Bourque and Trent, or Danyluk? The political scene, which previously was a diptych, became a triptych, increasing the potential for disputes geometrically. In her enthusiasm, Danyluk had politicized the chairman's role by arguing with us through the media, something her predecessors would never have done: they would have quietly chivvied Bourque and me to arrive at a consensus. Danyluk saw herself as the chair of a board of directors, not as chair of an executive committee whose job it was to execute the wishes of the MUC Council.

By August 1996 she was publicly accusing Bourque and me of questioning her leadership and said she was ready to quit. On hearing this, Ménard got it all wrong, complaining of parochial quarrels and the "never-ending dissention between Montreal and the other members of the MUC."[30] I responded that Bourque and the Island mayors mostly came to agreement. All to no avail: thus was begotten the hardy myth of the "squabbling mayors." At the time I don't think any of us, including Danyluk, appreciated just how this conflict of personalities and convictions would give merger advocates large-calibre ammunition. Not only would One Island One City free the Island from the turbulent mayors and their fiefdoms but it would get rid of the fractious MUC as well.

THE MONTREAL METROPOLITAN DEVELOPMENT COMMISSION

Meanwhile, Ménard brooded as more criticism flowed in his direction about his department being without power or influence. In June 1996 the Liberals had voted against the law that retroactively created his job, but they were a powerless minority. By early September, Ménard had bestirred himself and got busy with his main raison d'être: the creation of the Montreal Metropolitan Development Commission. It was time for a big show at the Palais des congrès, where he formally launched the consultation process in front of five hundred people. By this time the journalist Michel Vastel was calling him the minister of the necropolis.[31] Vastel noted that the area mayors, who had once been burned, were now twice shy after their disillusionment with the setting up of the Metropolitan Transport

Agency (the AMT), a structure totally controlled by the provincial government. A media star when he was minister of public security, Ménard was nearly a spent force, almost an object of derision, both inside and outside cabinet. And his mission was almost impossible. Vastel's take on Ménard was "a doctor at the bedside of a sick man who doesn't want to be looked after."

Despite the welter of criticisms, Ménard soldiered on. It wasn't that his diagnosis was not accurate: in a forty-five-page government document that accompanied his September show,[32] the ills of the region were well laid out, especially the multiplicity of structures that cluttered up the region. The beads in this rosary were now becoming all too familiar: 111 municipalities, 16 counties, one urban community, five Regional Development Councils, 31 school boards, and 20 transit boards. On top of all that, "it was the government itself that divided up the territory into five administrative regions." Unfortunately, in his desire to weld the region together, Ménard had his feet cut out from under him a week before his big show when, according to Henry Aubin,[33] he was instructed by cabinet to eliminate "all references to a single metropolitan region" – even though it was then too late to reprint the document. So much for dealing with Greater Montreal's most important problem.* The score so far was Chevrette (and the regions), 1; Ménard (and Montreal), 0.

Ménard's document went on to pose questions as to the nature of the commission. There were three models presented: (1) a body with only consultative powers; that is, the power merely to recommend to the provincial government; (2) a body with some regulatory powers; it could even deliver certain services; and (3) a body that would be a directly elected level of government.

THE NOVEMBER JAMBOREE

Ménard's much-ballyhooed consultation forum took place in November 1996. This was the last gasp of consultation before his Montreal Metropolitan Development Commission would be enshrined in law. His people managed to elicit eighty-seven briefs, and furthermore

---

* The sacredness of maintaining the Montreal Metropolitan Region chopped up into five bits still obtains today. The congeries of other structures is also still very much with us.

convince seven hundred participants to come to this day-and-a-half jamboree costing $200,000, once again at the Palais des congrès. Actually, I counted only one hundred elected officials, so there were six hundred "other ranks" padding the throng.

The Palais de concrete (as some called it) is a gargantuan grey box straddling the Ville-Marie expressway, trying awkwardly to help cover an irreparable gash cut through Old Montreal. It's a strange place. If you manage to discover the reception area and take the world's longest escalator ride, you are rewarded with hothouse-level sunlight – up until the moment you enter any of the meeting rooms. There natural light is ruthlessly banished. A bit of tinselly tubing is strung up on the ceilings as a decorative afterthought to enliven the unremitting concrete.

At this jamboree, the four blocs – Montreal, the Island suburbs, the south shore, and Laval and the north shore – had already cantoned themselves by advertising their non-negotiable conditions of support for the structure-to-be-born. Montreal insisted on getting a fiscal pact ($100 million a year of pocket money), an easing of labour laws, one administrative region, and regulatory powers for the commission. We, the Island mayors, completely supported Montreal's position, adding that the commission should not deliver services, that the three transit boards should be merged, and that the commission should be exclusively run by municipal politicians. We also insisted that Quebec first clean up the mess of government structures cluttering up the region. In short, we wanted the Pichette Report to be implemented.

In fact, three of the four blocs at this forum were pretty much of one mind. As always, Laval and the north shore wanted nothing to do with any regional structure, being deathly afraid of having to contribute money. For them a regulatory body could impose the sharing of regional costs. But Ménard was not strong enough to build on the three blocs who wanted to create a real, functioning, decision-making body – which is really what he wanted as well. Had he not by then lost a lot of the support of Premier Bouchard and many of his cabinet colleagues, he could have made it happen in spite of the political power of the north shore. This was not to be.

The draft law creating the commission, Bill 92, was duly presented to the Quebec National Assembly on 19 December 1996.[34] The bill created something even worse than just a consultative talk-shop: the commission would be nothing less than the institutionalized trustee-ship of the whole Montreal region by Quebec. I was outraged when I read it. A typical section regarding transport, its plodding legalese somewhat cropped, says it all:

66. The minister of Transport indicates to the Commission the government's policy in transport matters.
67. The Commission develops, in collaboration with the minister of Transport and the Metropolitan Transport Agency [con-trolled by the minister of Transport], a transport plan.
69. The Commission formally adopts the plan.
70. The Commission hands over the plan to the minister of Transport for government approval.
71. The government can approve the plan, with or without modification.[35]

C. Northcote Parkinson could not have come up with a better bureaucratic perpetual motion machine that was totally under the control of Quebec. Journalist Henry Aubin called it "a prescription for paralysis."[36] Even the staff of the commission would, in large part, be on loan from the government. And while thirteen munici-pal officials from the Island of Montreal and another thirteen from off-Island would sit on its council, yet another thirteen would be from "socio-economic" groups, named by the government. *They* would hold the balance of power. The fortieth council member, the president, would be the minister himself. Quebec would choose the two vice-presidents.[37] In short, Ménard's commission was a govern-ment agency with no decision-making powers.

And who would clean up the skein of government structures lit-tering the region's landscape? Why, the very same body, not the gov-ernment. The Liberal critic Liza Frulla got it right: "The minister creates a new structure on top of the two hundred structures that structure the most structured region in Quebec."[38] The sedimentary approach to government structures would continue unchecked.

Ménard was tired. Rumours had already begun to circulate that he wanted out of this detested job come the next cabinet shuffle. He wanted to be minister of justice and dump the whole fractious region in Robert Perreault's lap. As it turned out, he had to wait another ten months.

THE CONTRAST WITH TORONTO

Just before the November forum took place, a bombshell exploded in Ontario. Premier Harris announced without warning that he was going to merge six municipalities in the Toronto urban core, thereby getting rid of Metro – Toronto's version of the MUC. Metro had originally suggested it cover the thirty-municipality Toronto Metropolitan Region. The six central cities had said, "No, let's eliminate Metro instead." The Harris government said a plague on both your houses, we'll get rid of both Metro and the six municipalities and fold them into one big megacity. The shockwaves that began to be felt downstream in Montreal continued for a long time, increasingly energizing the calls over the next few years to do the same thing.

The media were quick to contrast the Ménard approach that layered a government-controlled commission over the Montreal Metropolitan Region while retaining all 107 municipalities with what was happening in Toronto, which was becoming a megacity of 2.4 million people within the larger metropolitan region. Even Ménard waded into the debate: "Toronto is an experiment using the formula 'bigger, better, cheaper.' It has its drawbacks. We are starting to realize that certain municipal functions become more difficult to deliver when they are too far removed from the citizen; you then have to create neighbourhood structures to get closer: that is what is proposed in the Greater Toronto Region. We would be doing the same thing if I had decided to implement the proposition, suggested by some, to integrate 'One Island One City' into the metropolis."[39] This comment about neighbourhood structures was quite prescient, given the *arrondissements* that would be part of the megacity's makeup in 2001. Later, Ménard was even clearer about his opposition to an Island megacity: "To make a big city with more or less two million citizens, that is not the North American trend, nor is it the government's inclination."[40]

THE TRAVAILS OF BOURQUE

In January 1997, out of the blue, Pierre Bourque fired two of his best executive committee members, Pierre Goyer and Sammy Forcillo, the latter who was serving as vice-chair. It seems they had been "disloyal." They also had complained – not without reason – about the incompetence of the chair, Noushig Eloyan. While Goyer was a bit of a free spirit, all were surprised at the firing of Forcillo, liked and respected by just about everybody. While this flap was going on, Bourque was also being personally investigated by the director-general of elections for alleged violations of the electoral law. Other councillors quit Bourque's party. Montreal City Hall was plunged into a crisis. Bourque was forced to delay the annual general meeting of his party, Vision Montreal. And this had followed the ultimate sacrifice for the sinophile Bourque: three weeks before the mess became public, he had cancelled an upcoming Asian trip. He had already dissolved his "committee of wise men," fearing possibly the opprobrium of the business sector.

When Danyluk decided publicly to comment on this crisis, she earned a rebuff from Bourque, who said that her job was to execute what the MUC council decided, and that was it.[41] I agreed with Danyluk, expressing concern that all this was draining Bourque's energies away from the creation of the Montreal Metropolitan Development Commission. Ménard refused to get involved. As it turned out, the director-general of elections found there was "not enough proof" that Bourque was guilty of wrongdoing, leaving enough doubt to ensure that a whiff of impropriety clung to him for a long while. A week later, Justice Danielle Grenier of the Quebec Superior Court ruled that Goyer and Forcillo had to be reinstated: only death or incapacity could shorten their four-year nomination to the executive committee. Interestingly, this judgment forced everyone to realize that a mayor was not a prime minister, that city council was indeed supreme, and that many of the mayor's powers were largely *honorifiques*.

A few days after this crisis, Ménard let slip during an interview what he now thought of Bourque: "I find that it is difficult to work with him. I have a problem to follow his reasoning."[42]

BILL 92 HEARINGS

Ménard, meanwhile, was desultorily nudging his Bill 92, which created the Montreal Metropolitan Development Commission, through the required process that would make it law. The main way station was the parliamentary standing committee, where various groups are invited to parade before the minister, shadow-minister, and an assortment of other parliamentarians. Parliamentary committee hearings take place in a huge, hushed chamber in that wonderful old

Second Empire pile in Quebec, the National Assembly. Opened for business in 1886, it is all very polychrome, with richly tiled floors and pastel walls punctuated with wedding-cake columns. You usually get an hour to try to convince the government to modify a bill before it becomes law, no matter whether you represent one or a million people, no matter how serious or fanciful your presentation. I must have attended dozens of these exercises and can't recall one that resulted in any meaningful change to the various bills under study. About all that happens is that members of the party in power get to snipe at the opposition; then, the favour is returned.

Ménard had got up my nose a week before hearings began by stating that, whatever we said, "his" commission would not be decision-making, that is, would not have regulatory powers. "The metropolitan region is not yet ready to make decisions," as he put it. Liza Frulla, the Liberal shadow-minister, pounced: "Who does he think he is? With only two years' experience in politics plus one year as minister of the métropole ... to say to the whole metropolitan region that they are not ready to make decisions?"[43] I said I was astounded that he had made up his mind before even hearing us and asked why didn't we simply organize a cocktail party in Montreal and have done with it.[44] Bourque, however, totally caved. After all his internal messes, he was in no mood to draw a line or take a stand. Montreal's "non-negotiable" conditions that included a new fiscal pact, one administrative region, and a regulatory body – well, they suddenly became very negotiable.

By the time we got to the parliamentary committee in Quebec, we were all a bit grumpy. I started off by commenting that it was significant we were "discussing the future of the metropolitan region so far from the metropolitan region. Nevertheless, in spite of the minister's comments last week, we have made the trek to Quebec because we want to see the commission be created, but not in its current form."[45] One of the committee members, André Boulerice, responded, "M. Trent, welcome to this foreign city that is Quebec, the capital, the seat of parliament and government."

The mayor of Verdun, Georges Bossé, made it clear that we wanted neither a consultative body nor a metropolitan government nor something that delivered services like the MUC. And if the government did not clear up the "jungle" of structures, we simply could not support the creation of the commission. Ménard said that the commission permitted, for the first time ever in Quebec, local politicians to get involved in some matters that were, up until then, the jurisdictions of the "State of Quebec." He was not totally wrong, but that was the whole point of his government's decentralization policy. In a clumsy attempt to win us over, he revealed that I would be one of the vice-presidents of the commission.

With regard to the commission having to get rid of existing structures by itself, Frulla pointed out that they were not even under Ménard's responsibility as minister, so how could the commission get rid of them? As well as being the most glamorous member of the National Assembly, Frulla did not, as the French say, keep her tongue in her pocket: "The administrative regions come under the minister of regional affairs, M. Chevrette, who said in December 1996 that there was no question of breaking them up. Well, that's a good start! The Regional Development Councils come under the minister of regional development ... The three regional agencies for labour development, they come under the minister of labour, Mme Harel. The five regional boards of health and social services come under the health minister, M. Rochon. The twenty authorities running public transit come under the minister of transport, M. Brassard ... It's all very well to say we'll tidy up the structures, but if that is not even in the remit of the minister who chairs the commission, what can we do?"

Ménard squirmed but said nothing. Then, emboldened, I continued the list. Frulla was singing my song, and I knew the lyrics. "There are sixteen counties and the MUC – they don't come under the minister. There are five regional councils of culture, five regional councils of recreation, five tourist associations, four regional councils for the environment. We also have, just to add a few more, the Metropolitan Transport Agency [the AMT], the three transport boards ... let's say that the total of all this gives about seventy structures, and, if I've got it right, the only one of all these structures that reports to the minister is the AMT."[46]

Thankfully, the whole Quebec City charade lasted only an hour.

Ménard got such a drubbing during the hearings on Bill 92 that, in desperation, he turned to the authors of the Pichette Report for backing. For quite some time, Claude Pichette had shown little enthusiasm for the direction the commission was taking.[47] Then, when they showed up at the last day of the hearings in March 1997, he and his group suddenly embraced all that Ménard was doing. They succeeded in making an about-turn on just about all their recommendations, saying that Ménard's consultative commission with no cleanup of structures was an acceptable compromise.[48] I said that the Pichette Report had "started off the whole metropolitan debate. Why now this diluted position, neither fish nor fowl?"[49] We had based our whole position on the Pichette Report, and here they were negating all their work.

The death knell of the commission started to ring 30 April 1997, with the release of the white paper on local and regional development. Ménard was given the responsibility for the Regional Development Councils for the Island of Montreal and Laval, along with Chevrette's panoply of Local Development Centres. While on the surface it was a victory for Ménard, in fact it was the opposite: Chevrette's uniform regional vision won over Ménard's metropolitan vision. It was, indeed, confirmed that day that the five administrative regions would stay untouched. So even before Bill 92 was adopted 13 June 1997, Ménard's dog was dead, as the French say, given a final blow by Chevrette. A cabinet shuffle allowed Ménard to make a quick exit on August 1997. The new minister of the metropolis was a former Montreal city councillor, Robert Perreault, who was far more interested in the shaky financial situation of the City of Montreal and merging the three transport boards than in giving life to Bill 92. Ménard's pitiful offspring was given the quiet burial of the unloved.

ET IN ARCADIA EGO

The perspicacious reader, as well as forgiving that redundancy, will have realized by now that this book is not just about Quebec's forced municipal mergers; it is about Quebec. Ménard represented the new Quebec, Chevrette the old. Ménard understood urban Quebec, Chevrette championed the rural. There is nothing wrong with Chevrette's nostalgia for Quebec-of-the-regions, as long as that is what Quebec really wants and is prepared to pay the price. However, there is a limit as to how much the outlying regions can sap the economic force generated by the Montreal region before both collapse.

7

A Quebec Divided: Partition and Downloading

A divorce is like an amputation; you survive, but there's less of you.
Margaret Atwood, 1973

We must all hang together, or assuredly we shall all hang separately.
Benjamin Franklin, 1776

The boundaries of most nations were determined by force. Canada, with a separatist political party in its parliament and a Supreme Court reference laying down the conditions for secession, is a model of peaceful give and take, even in the matter of its very existence. But for years the incessant emotive debate on secession was a drain on the whole country. In Quebec this question dominated politics for decades, siphoning off megawatts of brainpower. The energy consumed by the PQ in figuring out how to cajole Quebecers into voting for the New Jerusalem that is a sovereign Quebec and, once done, determining exactly how a postpartum Quebec would be run is not unlike the energy that was spent long ago on theological issues, and, given the referendum result, just as useful. We forget today how much passion and hatred arose over differentiating the doctrine of consubstantiation from the doctrine of transubstantiation, or over whether baptism simply conferred regeneration by washing away original sin or could only work because the baby had to be in a state of something called "prevenient grace." On such issues generations of European polity expended immeasurable time and energy. Likewise, the quest for sovereignty and the incipient theology of its implementation sucked up a lot of intellectual and political energy in the 1990s. This energy reached its feverish peak preparatory to the Second Referendum in October 1995.

NOVEMBER 1996: THE FIRST PARTITIONIST
RESOLUTION ADOPTED

I stayed out of the public debate leading up to the October 1995 referendum, a decision that raised many anglophone eyebrows. As vice-chairman of the MUC and president of the suburban mayors, I felt I had to stay neutral. Besides, had I campaigned for the No, it would have been a godsend for the Yes camp. Of course it would have been far easier to nail my colours to the mast, but that mast could have become a lightning rod for anti-English sentiment, given the resonance that the name Westmount still aroused in francophone Quebec.* The point of the exercise was to win, not for me to sell to the sold in Westmount, no matter how good it might have felt. The referendum was going to be won or lost in the francophone media, not in the *Montreal Gazette*. And the mayor of Westmount denouncing sovereignty in *La Presse* was hardly going to convert voters in Terrebonne. On the other hand, Pierre Bourque and other francophone mayors were put under tremendous pressure to come out for the Yes. To their credit, they did not.

Bourque insisted that I watch the referendum results in his office the night of 30 October 1995. He held court in a high-ceilinged, overly lit room on the second floor of Montreal City Hall. While the windows were tall and elegant and the view magnificent, Bourque had not spent much on decor. When his predecessor, Jean Doré, wanted to differentiate himself from *his* predecessor, Jean Drapeau, he built himself a rather spartan modern office, all white gypsum board and wood trim, carving it out of a large garret on the fourth floor. This work necessitated modifying a window. The window work supposedly cost $300,000 and, along with an adjacent shower with two crystal soap-dishes, became an unfair symbol of extravagance that poor Doré never lived down. His office metamorphosed into a conference room during Bourque's tenure – a conference room with shower.

Bourque had asked me to be with him in case the vote went Yes and he needed help in dealing with apprehended anglophone panic. Most of his people watching the television were rooting for the No.

---

* These feelings came manifestly alive during the demerger debate nine years later.

In spite of Bourque's reputation as a closet sovereignist, I, watching him closely that night, concluded that he genuinely wanted a No result. He certainly was worried about the effect of a Yes victory on Montreal. In the event, the sovereignty option lost by only 49.4 per cent to 50.6 per cent.

The anglophone and federalist populations of Quebec went into a state of shock over the paper-thin referendum result. But for a few votes, Canada could have been lost. To deal with their angst, anglos started clutching at straws. Their chattering classes examined a Kama Sutra of possible constitutional positions, one involving the revival of the idea of federalist parts of Quebec hiving off and joining what remained of Canada in the event of Quebec's accession to sovereignty ("if Canada is divisible, so is Quebec"). This idea crystallized as the partitionist movement. Anyone looking even groggily at the map of Quebec the day after the referendum result could see that the No voters occupied a territory that included all the central and western parts of the Island of Montreal and a contiguous, safe swath that meandered all the way to the Ontario border. If that stretch of land stayed with Canada, salvation for some federalists could be found; or so went the theory of the partitionists.

In December 1995, before the partitionist movement got underway, I had floated the idea of a Montreal regional party to give our region more political oomph.[1] While federalists, sovereignists, and partitionists were waging a nineteenth-century battle over the nature of provincial powers, status, or boundaries, I felt the real issue was the emergence of urban regions as the world's most important economic and political entities. I even said that national boundaries would become Maginot lines in the twenty-first century. Quebec, as well as suffering from sterile anglo-franco friction, was saddled – and is saddled today – with a nostalgic pandering to the regions and an ingrained disdain for Montreal. Chevrette's decentralization plan had been just the latest example of Quebec's tyranny of the rurality.

By autumn 1996, frustrated partitionists who were getting no satisfaction from Ottawa or Quebec turned to the most responsive layer of government and started dragooning local city councils into the battle for the future of Canada. In November 1996, the City of Côte Saint-Luc became the first Montreal Island municipality to adopt a resolution in favour of partition, quickly followed by Hampstead. The master plan was to have all Island municipalities, or at least the central and western ones, adopt such resolutions.[2] If they could then get all the municipal councils between Montreal and the Ontario border to adopt similar resolutions, went their reasoning, then people in this coalesced territory were implicitly stating their desire to remain with Canada in the event of sovereignty. I called this geographical strategy the "freckle theory." If certain key areas did not go along with partition, wouldn't the land bridge to Ontario collapse? And how could city councils pretend to speak for all their citizens?

I was promptly called defeatist and a member of the "lamb lobby." A quote from journalist William Johnson captures the we-will-overcome "angryphone" zeitgeist: "The more councils pass such resolutions, the more unlikely it is that another referendum on secession will ever be held."[3]

So I took an early stand against the partitionist movement: as president of the suburban mayors, I represented municipalities of which, in total, half the residents were francophone. And it was my belief that, when push came to shove, francophones would show a stronger allegiance to Quebec (and to their relatives scattered all over Quebec) than to Canada. Partition was a poor way to convince francophones to vote No in a referendum; in fact, it would have the opposite effect. Tellingly, the francophone media insisted in calling these resolutions "partitionist." The anglophone media had quickly adopted the preferred term of their backers, "unity resolutions," somewhat in the same way that both media had produced a semantic tectonic shift from the label "separatist" to "sovereignist" over the past thirty years.

As for my own municipality, I said that unless our neighbour Montreal unexpectedly voted to remain in Canada if partition were allowed, Westmount would be a Canadian enclave surrounded by a City of Montreal located in the Nation of Quebec – like Berlin in former East Germany. "Would Murray's Restaurant become Checkpoint Charlie? Would we ask Dawson College students riding the metro through town to show their passports?"[4] I also made the point that passing such a resolution would make things worse, considering the threat of amalgamation looming over the twenty-eight Island municipalities; indeed, that was where I was focusing my energies.

In January 1997, the municipal affairs minister Rémy Trudel produced a legal opinion that to no one's surprise declared that "municipalities legally have no competence to take any decision regarding their status within Quebec and Canada." The federal intergovernmental affairs minister Stéphane Dion immediately riposted "the same argument applies to Quebec," pointing out that neither did Quebec have the power to separate just by holding a referendum.[5] Rattling his sovereignist sabre, the provincial intergovernmental affairs minister Jacques Brassard proclaimed "the government will exercise its effective authority over all its territory,"[6] confirming the potential for violence inherent in this explosive issue, just in case anyone had missed it.

In a loose itinerant gang, partitionists went from municipality to municipality, often masquerading as local residents, browbeating a series of city councils into adopting "unity" resolutions. By March 1997, when the City of Dollard-des-Ormeaux was the third municipality to capitulate, the suggested wording had been changed to a simple demand for the right of partition, no longer calling as well for a pre-emptive municipal referendum before the next province-wide referendum. By the time it was Westmount's turn, nine West Island – and majority anglophone – municipalities had adopted such resolutions. They ranged from the aggressively partitionist (petitioning the government of Canada to ensure that their "territory remain part of Canada, irrespective of the result of any future province-wide referendum"[7]) to the mildly partitionist (calling upon the protection, either of the rights of their citizens to "remain in Canada," or of their "continuing presence in Canada"[8]).

To crank up the moxie to confront Westmount City Council, some 650 people came to a rally at Westmount High School on 1 May 1997. A few days later, some of them read my guest editorial in the *Gazette*:

> Adding a bit of fuel to the amalgamation fire is the group making the rounds with their nostrum for our country's ills: the "unity" resolution that supporters insist federalist municipalities must adopt. These resolutions are clearly partitionist, but that has not stopped a number of cities, under concerted pressure, from adopting them. Cities must weigh the very real threat of amalgamation against the very remote possibility that passing such resolutions will make one jot of difference in any future constitutional wrangling. Indeed, Quebec would love to see anglophone cities merged with Montreal. A city that says it will stay with Canada come what may, and then gets wiped off the

municipal map for its pains is hardly going to help the federalist cause.[9]

When 125 militants finally marched past the oaken doors of West-mount City Hall the next Monday night, they were spoiling for a fight. Their leaders insisted we adopt a resolution that began: "Be it resolved that the council of the City of Westmount hereby peti-tion the Government of Canada to ensure that its territory remain part of Canada, and that our citizens remain Canadian, irrespec-tive of the result of any future province-wide referendum." Each and every member of council refused to vote for such a resolution. The audience reaction was white-hot fury. I was asked by one resident to "outline in detail the steps needed to remove you from office." Another said, rather confusedly, "We are being led by shepherds in sheep's clothing and being quietly led to the slaughterhouse." Local gadfly Allen Nutik said I was the only mayor raising the menace of amalgamation in connection with the "unity" resolution campaign. Had I been threatened by the PQ government? Keith Henderson, leader of the Equality Party,* wondered if I had received a direc-tive from Quebec not to pronounce myself on this question. Clearly, few people understood how the partition resolution campaign was a godsend to the likes of Bourque and Chevrette, who had been openly pushing for municipal mergers.

That night we adopted a resolution that was both partition free and content free. Prepared by Councillor (and lawyer) James Wright,[10] it started out: "Whereas the mandate of a Canadian muni-cipality clearly does not encompass constitutional issues or issues of national boundaries ..." It went on to state some anodyne and apple-pie things such as calling upon the federal and provincial govern-ments to "avoid the disruption and division of another provincial referendum which might result in the break-up of Canada." The only other constitutional reference was a blindingly obvious restatement of the results of the October 1995 referendum, "the expressed will of our residents and of the majority of the citizens in the Province of Quebec to remain in a united Canada."

---

* An English-rights pro-federalist party. Keith Henderson, the intelligent, articulate, but splenetic leader of the Equality Party, was heroically trying to keep it alive without any elected representatives in Quebec's National Assembly. He eventually gave up.

So we passed a resolution, but nothing like the one demanded of us. Angry but nonplussed, the crowd, some of whom began calling me a traitor, drifted out. After Westmount and our non-resolution, Pierrefonds, Saint-Laurent and three small towns passed various resolutions, and then that was it. As I predicted, once this movement got to the majority francophone municipalities in the autumn, the "unity" movement hit a brick wall. This was because 61 per cent of francophones living on the Island of Montreal voted for sovereignty in the October 1995 referendum. Partition was unpopular with these people, as well as with a good number of francophones who voted *against* sovereignty. An SOM poll conducted in early September showed only 32 per cent of francophones across Quebec agreed with partition, compared to 58 per cent of non-francophones.[11]

Confronted by a *mobile vulgus* of 250 people in September 1997, the feisty Mayor Michel Leduc of LaSalle adamantly refused for the third and final time to pass a partitionist resolution. He had said during an earlier assault, "We were not elected to decide the boundaries of a country," adding wryly that the crowd, some wrapped in the Canadian flag, did not seem to know the French words to "O Canada."[12] (Lyrics were discreetly handed out for the next try.) After the City of Lachine also turned them down, the serial municipal-resolution leaders declared victory and left the field in haste.

While the PQ government dismissed the partitionist movement as "territorial delirium," the spectre of partition and its inherent constitutional logic in the abstract – in spite of its patent impracticability when applied at the municipal level – clearly had an effect on Quebec's political class. If ever we found ourselves on the brink of separation in the future, most Quebecers had to admit that partition would have to be dealt with in some way or other. But following in the wake of the October 1995 referendum, partition was only of cathartic value to anglophones and was generally regarded with suspicion by francophones. Yes, the partition movement in general, and even the join-the-dots-on-the-map via municipal resolutions campaign, shook up the separatists, but in my view it made no converts to the federalist cause – just the opposite.

Most importantly for our story, the 1997 partitionist movement helped make the PQ converts to Island mergers. I have been told that one of the points used in cabinet a few years later to sell the One Island One City concept was that imposing a megacity would obviate any such upsetting initiatives in the future. Certainly, Bourque used that argument in 1999 and in 2000. If we don't merge, he said, we're going to have partition: "Allow the West Island municipalities another ten years, and it's done.[13] On another occasion he said, "If we don't make Montreal into the heart that beats for everyone, we will wake up the partitionist phenomenon."[14] He was even more explicit when he dismissed the suggestion that the Island of Montreal could be made up of a number of large municipalities, not just one, "How can you think of anchoring Montreal in Quebec society if you leave the West Island alone [as a municipality]? That would only accentuate the partition momentum towards Ontario."[15]

MY PERSONAL PARTITION

In late October 1996, I got a call from Claudia Vaillancourt. Her father, Marc Vaillancourt, the director-general of the Conference of Montreal Suburban Mayors, had given her my number. We set up a lunch at le Piedmontais ostensibly to discuss her future. After a few hours we both silently concluded that her future just might involve me. Over the next little while, it was clear I had to choose between my sterile but comfortable married life and the dizzying passion that I found with Claudia. I had never felt quite that way in my life. After the delirium of being with Claudia, I would sneak back home a few hours before dawn. Two months after that lunch, I was discussing divorce with my wife. For years our marriage had been a dry husk. Becoming mayor had changed me, not necessarily for the good. While I loved the job, I had become somewhat brassy, prideful, and self-absorbed. My wife remained unchanged, retreating quietly and decorously into her own world. In the spring of 1997, after countless bouts of raw bitterness that a concomitant clash of emotions and economics engenders, our divorce was granted. I was launched into the unknown.

TRUDEL'S DOWNLOADING: UNBALLASTING THE SHIP OF STATE

After the October 1995 referendum, the glories that awaited Quebecers through widespread decentralization thanks to sovereignty disappeared as quickly as the signs saying "Vote Yes and it becomes possible." We then had to settle for the very limited decentralization appropriate to a province rather than a country. It didn't take long before this low-grade decentralization metamorphosed into the simple cutting of subsidies. In 1996, Quebec cut some $200 million of funding to municipalities,[16] thereby transferring these amounts to the property taxpayer. Because of the servile position of all municipalities in Canada, subsidy cuts or downloading had become a popular form of passing the tax buck from the province down to the municipalities. It's a sort of forced deputization of the municipalities as provincial tax collectors. Provinces get the credit: municipalities get the blame.

It was not just the fact of subsidy cuts that set Quebec's mayors' teeth on edge: it was also the way it was done. For example, when Quebec decided unilaterally to eliminate the partial rebate that municipalities got on the provincial sales taxes they paid, it was done without warning. Bernard Landry, the finance minister, said the measure would take effect at midnight of the day it was announced. This was, we were told by Municipal Affairs Minister Rémy Trudel, to avoid any of us going out on a spending spree just before the cut took effect. Such was the esteem and trust with which we were held by Quebec. And would the rebate cut mean tax increases? "Quebec property taxes are the lowest in America," piped up Serge Ménard. "We are not talking about a tax; it's the abolition of a privilege. It should not affect the competitiveness of Montreal. The city should simply be more careful in its purchases,"[17] Ménard told us at our annual *colloque des maires*. Some booed and some even left the room. This cut alone cost municipalities $76 million a year, but Landry was just warming up.

It was Landry who brought down the provincial budget of 25 March 1997. Because governments like to make things complex, federal and provincial budgets run from 1 April of one year to 31 March of the next rather than the distressingly simple practice that normal people use of budgeting within a calendar year. Anyway, Landry's budget called for municipalities to "help" Quebec to the tune of $125 million for the first quarter of 1998 – in other words, a "contribution" of $500 million a year starting in 1998.[18]

The PQ had promised the Union of Quebec Municipalities (UMQ) back in 1994 that "it was out of the question that a PQ government would do what the Liberal government did ... in unilaterally transferring some $500 million of its annual expenses onto Quebec municipalities."[19] Yes, right. So the Trudel downloading eerily followed in the same path as the Ryan downloading announced over six years before. Even the initial amount was similar. The subtext of merger was also part of the story.

When Ryan wanted to skim off money from municipalities, he called his program "Towards a New Balance." Trudel called his shakedown "A New Municipal Pact." Two years later, we would have a tome called "Pact 2000." The choice of words suggests what is involved is a coming together of equals. The reality is that Quebec proposes and Quebec disposes. "The municipal participation in the reduction of public spending was fixed at $500 million and will take effect 1 January 1998, and is permanent ... The target of $500 million is not negotiable,"[20] said Minister Trudel. As late as August, even Premier Bouchard said it was "$500 million. Full stop."[21] As we shall see, it was very negotiable and it was not at all permanent.

Half a billion dollars is a lot of money, but for the provincial government it only represented 1 per cent of its budget, yet it was equal to more than 5 per cent of Quebec's total municipal budgets. Bouchard, Landry, and Trudel all said with straight faces that we were to find this money without raising taxes. With Trudel's pro-merger campaign still on, Bouchard had a ready suggestion as to how some of the $500 million could be found. According to the *Montreal Gazette*, "Bouchard said the government's plan to reduce the number of municipalities across Quebec through voluntary mergers will lead to big savings for cities and towns."[22]

While savings through mergers and pooling of resources were supposed somehow to help us find the money, it was admitted that the lion's share would still have to come from salary and wage reductions. A target of 6 per cent of remuneration was suggested: it would get us half of the $500 million. As Trudel and Chevrette[23] (and I) often repeated, municipalities were paying their employees 30 per cent more than the rest of the province's public sector, once benefits and hours worked were factored in.

However, the idea that *we alone* could negotiate a rollback of the remuneration of 78,000 municipal employees was nothing less than a fraud, as we did not have the powers that the province had to decree such things. We were forever being reminded that municipalities were the creatures of the province with only those powers it decided to give us, yet when it came to union contracts, we were on our own, powerless. The government had consistently proven chary of legislating municipal union contracts, preferring to say it was up to the municipalities to negotiate. But they knew and we knew no one can negotiate without the big stick of imposed contracts. Thanks to the way the Quebec Labour Code was interpreted by the courts, we could not even threaten to subcontract to cheaper sources.

This huge disparity between municipal and provincial wages could be traced to the provincial wage rollback in 1982 that cost Parti Québécois premier Réné Lévesque the 1985 election: the problem was that this 20 per cent cut did not apply to the municipal sector. It must be kept in mind that the PQ government was heavily supported by Big Labour and did not want a repeat of 1985, even though, in the spring of 1997, under the threat of a rollback law, it had managed to cut an additional 6 per cent off the overall remuneration of its employees. It was generally thought that it was only fair that municipal employees now did their bit. Unsurprisingly, they saw it differently.

Indeed, it didn't take long for the unions to react to Landry's budget. In less than a week the Canadian Union of Public Employees and the police and firefighters' unions issued a joint press release.[24] "If the government persists in its strategy, the result of which can only be confrontation," it said, "it will find in its path not just one or two unions, but a solid coalition of some 50,000 workers who refuse to be the fall guys." The solution? Trudel should have the guts to do what his colleague Pauline Marois did in forcibly merging 157 school boards into 72, legislation that (according to the unions) resulted in $100 million of savings for the government. They suggested that the 1,400 municipalities should be forcibly merged into 500, disingenuously ignoring all the studies that showed that the larger the municipality, the more it spent per capita – partially because of overpaid unionized employees.

Trudel told us there were a number of ways the remuneration savings could be found: getting rid of minimum staffing levels, allowing pension-fund contribution holidays, or modifying the Labour Code to ease subcontracting, often to companies with non-unionized – and therefore lower-paid – workers. As to the first two suggestions, the labour unions simply boycotted Trudel's negotiating sessions. As to the third, there were more threats: "It will be hell. A war to the bitter end. A call to arms the like of which the government has never seen."[25] Even the president of the MUC police brotherhood predicted "disorder."[26]

By June 1997, things had got to such a state that Premier Lucien Bouchard took over the whole downloading file. The UMQ immediately demanded a special provincial law to roll back municipal labour costs. Bouchard responded, in effect, "A law if necessary, but not necessarily a law." Mario Laframboise, who had replaced Gilles Vaillancourt as president of the UMQ, said that the merger plan, so dear to the heart of the government, was also affected by labour cost considerations. When Premier Mike Harris imposed mergers in Ontario, said Laframboise, he modified their Labour Code to ease subcontracting. And that was not all: "If you have to keep the same number of employees because of minimum staffing levels," he said, "when you merge, everyone will get the best collective agreements." [27]

SCHOOL BUSING

On 20 June 1997 the government made public its proposal as to precisely what things would be cut in order to get the $500 million. It proposed that municipalities would take over school busing without any compensation, saving the government $420 million in subsidies. [28] There would be a minimum and a maximum cost of busing that each of the municipalities would have to bear, based on a percentage of their overall budgets. [29] Half the Montreal Island suburban municipalities found that the minimum kicked in. Why? The answer was simple. On the Island, property taxpayers fund not only public transit deficits but also the cost of reduced fares for students. Less than half of "bused" students on the Island take yellow school buses. In the rest of the province, just about all student busing is by the yellow buses, with Quebec picking up 95 per cent of the tab.

Finally, Quebec had recognized that making the decision to live in the country or the exurbs meant having to pay for at least some of the costs that decision entailed. Although the rural villages would continue to get $125 million a year to pay for their local roads and still got subsidized police services, at least this proposal meant rural taxpayers would partially pay for busing their kids to school, something we on Montreal Island had been doing for years. They would not pay the whole cost because of a limit on tax increases. While taxpayers in towns with fewer than a thousand residents were paying on average the derisory sum $563 a year in property taxes (less than one-quarter of the bill paid by those living in urban municipalities of over 50,000 residents), they would have their tax increase *capped at $77.* [30] It was the larger towns in the regions and the exurbs that really would have been hit with the school-busing bill. In the off-Island exurbs, for example, whether north shore or south shore, the average increase was over 8 per cent – which was still fine with me. They were part of the urban sprawl problem, and up until then they had been unwilling to pay for it.

Before the 1960s most families did not buy a house that was not within walking distance of a school. This served as an effective brake on urban sprawl. With the closing of some neighbourhood schools, and – far more importantly – the increasing reliance on school busing and Mum's taxi, this brake disappeared. In 1961, with a million Quebec students, both rural and urban, attending schools, only 21 per cent were bused; by 1989 there were still a million students, but by then 64 per cent were being bused. On the Island of Montreal, only one-third of students were bused or took mass transit in 1989.* Off-Island, the proportion was two-thirds.[31] While subsidizing school busing in truly rural regions to ensure equal access to education is one thing, to subsidize urban sprawl is something else.

School boards went predictably ballistic with the government's proposal to have most of the $500 million based on municipalities running the provinces 10,000 school buses. "We're talking about a social mission here that should continue to be borne by the state and not by 1,389 municipalities with all the inequalities that that engenders," said the Quebec Federation of School Boards, worried that universal access to education was in danger.[32]

UMQ COUNTERPROPOSES

The UMQ did not share my enthusiasm for using school busing as the way the $500 million should be divvied up, and began frantically working on a counterproposal. As usual with the UMQ, the rural foxes were in charge of the henhouse. At a meeting of the UMQ board on 25 July, we were asked to approve a counterproposal that left school-bus funding as it was; instead the downloading would be simply based on real-estate wealth. We were only told after the vote how much this would cost Montreal Island. Luckily I had made rough calculations during the meeting and warned everybody that

* Only 14 per cent of students in the central school board, the CECM, were transported by school bus or public transit.

we would never accept the idea, as it increased the Island's contribution by two-thirds. The proposal sailed through anyway, because,
of the twenty-seven board members present, twenty were from the
exurbs or the regions: the school-bus proposal was far more expensive for just about every one of the municipalities represented by
these mayors. The fact that the busing proposal at least helped rect-
ify a historic unfairness to Montreal Island taxpayers was of absolutely no concern to them.

The mayors of the six largest central cities, none of whom were at
this UMQ board meeting, reacted with fury at the counterproposal
for the same reasons I had invoked: dividing the bill by real-estate
wealth was uniform treatment, but not equitable treatment, as it left
rural Quebec with its massive subsidies for school busing. (It must
be remembered that Trudel was trying to do two things with his
downloading: slough off $500 million, *plus* come up with a fairer
fiscal system. This was akin to driving a steamroller and fixing a
watch at the same time.)

In September, after this brazen example of self-dealing by the directors of the UMQ, I quit as member of its executive committee.
Georges Bossé, the mayor of Verdun, did likewise. Eventually the
entire Conference of Montreal Suburban Mayors left the UMQ. It
was not just a spur of the moment thing; for years we had felt the
UMQ was rurally dominated. What made it even more infuriating
was that there was another union representing the interests of the
really small municipalities – the UMRCQ.* The UMQ represented the
big, medium, and small towns; the UMRCQ represented the "tiny"
towns, all 1,085 of them, municipalities that on average got one-
quarter of their revenues in the form of government subsidies.[33] The
UMQ represented municipalities that, together, accounted for 87 per
cent of all municipal spending in Quebec; the UMRCQ municipalities
spent the rest. It is a measure of the rural fixation of the Quebec government that they tended to treat the two unions as equals. So we
urban municipalities were doubly diluted, because even within the
UMQ, Montreal Island was treated as just one region out of sixteen.
And each municipality got one vote regardless of size; naturally, this
system favoured the rural municipalities.

---

* Now called the FQM (Fédération québécoise des municipalités).

The UMQ's president, who replaced Gilles Vaillancourt a month after the downloading announcement, was a former notary, Mario Laframboise, the mayor of the village of Notre-Dame-de-la-Paix, a village of barely seven hundred souls. Since his village received nearly one-third of its revenues in the form of government subsidies, it was, in a way, part of the problem. Actually, Laframboise was a rather likeable and intelligent character. He went on to become an MP for the Bloc Québécois. He spoke no English: at UMQ press conferences, I would handle the English media for him. He also had no knowledge of how an urban region such as Montreal actually operated; this proved to be a huge handicap. The six "big-city" mayors – Bourque, L'Allier, and so forth – had their own audiences directly with the municipal affairs minister and Premier Bouchard and so generally bypassed the UMQ.

The government then set up a negotiating table with ten seats to discuss the downloading proposal and counterproposal. Georges Bossé and I were refused a seat because we were no longer with the UMQ delegation. With Bourque not there, there was not one person from the Island of Montreal, which represented a third of Quebec's economy. But the UMRCQ got five out of the ten seats: five hamlets beat out a metropolis. What to do? Bossé and I simply invited ourselves to the table. We piled into his big Chrysler and drove up to Quebec, marching into the room where the meeting was to be held. After waiting an hour with no one showing up – the media had told Trudel of our presence – a flunky came to see us, sheepishly requesting that we see the minister. Trudel was all at sixes and sevens. After hastily checking with the UMQ, he awkwardly declined us a seat at the table in view of their objection. In the event, the table never did come up with a solution, and Trudel imposed a method that was even more penalizing for Montreal Island municipalities.

THE NO CAMPAIGN

The Montreal suburban mayors then launched a massive campaign against Trudel's downloading. We decided our catchword would be "NO" – a little word freighted with meaning in Quebec. The 1995 referendum on sovereignty was still fresh in people's minds, and since the PQ government did not like the word NO – which was the federalist response to the referendum question – it was a way to cock a snook at the PQ government. Huge blue signs went up in each of the twenty-seven Island municipalities: "Our city says NO!" I called them the signs of the cross.

On a sunny Sunday near the end of September 1997, we held a public NO rally at the Verdun auditorium. Some five thousand of our citizens turned up to protest this latest bout of downloading, which, building up since 1992, would have brought the total dumping to a yearly bill of $1.2 billion, *plus* $600 million in increased school taxes. We told the audience that Quebec had essentially not reduced its own budget, yet local governments, with total budgets of $10 billion, were forced to contribute 5 per cent. "Quebec is balancing its budget on the backs of municipal taxpayers," I yelled to the crowd from a stage with fifty huge NO signs as background. Placards saying NO were rhythmically thrust up and down in the audience. Getting a bit too thinkerly for the crowd, I quoted an American jurist, John Marshall, who said in 1819, "The power to tax involves the power to destroy." Quebec's buck-passing I called "taxation by misrepresentation," which got a slightly better reaction. Saint-Leonard Mayor Frank Zampino did much better when he yelled to the crowd, "How do you say NO in Italian?" A puzzled silence. "No!" bellowed Frank.

DIVIDE AND CONQUER

Trudel cleverly sidelined the six central cities by promising them a very low amount of downloading, not to mention, as we shall see, the prospect of giving them their megacities. This left the UMRCQ, UMQ, and us to battle it out. Laval and Longueuil originally trumpeted the UMQ "uniform" approach as eminently fair – that is, until they too demanded the coveted "central city" status and therefore eligibility for preferred treatment. That two classic satellite suburbs could suggest they were central cities in their own right without everyone else being convulsed by giggles is an indication of just how outlandish things had become during the downloading saga. In June 1997, Baie-Comeau, Gatineau, Sept-Îles, Sainte-Foy, Laval, and Longueuil all got in bed with the government once they were designated "central cities" and allowed a discount on their contribution. Self-interest acquaints a town with strange bedfellows.

Then the fight deteriorated into low comedy. Trudel triumphantly declared in early October that he had a deal as to how the $500 million would be shared – well, a deal with the UMRCQ. Well, a deal with the president of the UMRCQ. One small problem: a day later the UMRCQ membership flatly rejected the deal. Wiping pie off his face, the minister had to start again. By then Premier Bouchard had had it.

A MEETING WITH BOUCHARD

In October I was summoned to Quebec City for an emergency meeting with Premier Bouchard. He had taken over the whole downloading mess (once again) from Trudel. Mayors Bossé and Zampino joined me, along with Marc Vaillancourt, the Conference of Montreal Suburban Mayors' director-general. We met in "the Bunker," a kind of annex to the Assemblée nationale. A concrete hulk as ugly as the parliament buildings are beautiful, it is where the *real* decisions are made. We were greeted by two of Bouchard's henchmen, who told us of his "final" offer. We left the Bunker with its concrete coffered ceilings and incongruous pine chair rails and fetched up at the Hilton, another architectural victim of the 1970s mania for exposed concrete. Our meeting at the Hilton was with Bouchard and the UMRCQ. The UMQ had their own meeting, as they had refused to sit in the same room with us. Later that night we four had a private audience with Bouchard.

Bouchard actually thought before responding, a quality quite rare in political circles. During that meeting, my mind wandered for a few seconds as I tried to decide whether Bouchard more resembled a bear, or, because of his thick eyebrows and glowering eyes, a raptor. As suggested by either, he held his interlocutors captive. He knew all about our rally, calling it a "*sortie virulente.*" "You know," he said, "the trouble is, the municipalities you represent don't vote the right way." I replied, "M. Bouchard, you should not further upset 770,000 people. If you think we're anti-PQ now, wait till the tax bills come out." We reminded him of the uniqueness of the Island of Montreal – and how Island municipalities pay for services the rest of Quebec gets free. Just specialized police services and students' fare subsidies cost us over $100 million. I said that any increase in municipal taxes on the Island would work to destroy it, as more and more people fled to lower-taxed suburbs.

We also took issue with Bouchard's new – uniform – formula for divvying up the $500 million, which had now been cut to $375 million in yet another sop to the regions.[34] Each municipality would pay 5.8 per cent of its "compressible" costs – as if costs were some kind of cheap foam rubber cushion. In plain language, it meant that borrowing costs were removed from the calculation – which penalized municipalities like Westmount that had little debt, and favoured heavily indebted municipalities like Laval. The only thing we got from Bouchard was a promise that he would treat us as a separate group from the UMQ.

SOUND AND FURY SIGNIFYING VERY LITTLE

The next year, demonstrating NO means NO, three-quarters of the municipalities in the Conference of Suburban Mayors followed Westmount's lead and challenged the downloading in court, arguing that municipalities cannot tax their citizens and hand some of that money over to the province just for their general revenues; the tax has to be for a specific municipal service. Most importantly, the Canadian constitution prohibits provinces from levying an "indirect tax," which is a tax that is intended to be passed on – in this case, from the province to its municipalities, thence to their taxpayers.

Aware of the dangers of levying an indirect tax and the dangers of getting political heat for municipal tax increases, the government did everything it could to force municipalities to absorb the downloading and therefore not to raise taxes. Using the threat of a law that was adopted in March 1998, most municipalities shaved off 6 per cent of their labour costs. The law specifically and most bizarrely prohibited reducing salary scales: the money had to be found elsewhere. Montreal got their 6 per cent by using such artifices as dipping into pension-fund surpluses, allowing thirty-five-hour work weeks, and guaranteeing their firefighters a minimum of 1,557 job positions. So the endemic overpayment of municipal employees continued; if anything, they became even better treated. The evanescence of the 6 per cent reduction was nowhere better shown than at the MUC. It managed to get a $235 million five-year holiday from contributing to the police pension fund, which boasted a $470 million surplus at the time. Once the holiday was over, the 6 per cent "saving" was no more.

While the $375 million was only to be applied for two or three years until a new "fiscal pact" was arrived at, the permanent legacy of the Trudel Reform was the thirty-five-hour week and minimum staffing levels. We are still stuck with them. So, when the dust settled, municipal employees continued to make 30 per cent too much and Montreal Island taxpayers continued to pay for student busing that elsewhere was paid for by the province.

That Quebec would turn the whole municipal world upside down, waste years of protracted negotiations, drag Premier Bouchard in to the sorry mess, and create permanent enemies all over Quebec in order to extract $375 million for only three years was politically incomprehensible. My account grossly simplifies the complexity of the various scenarios: each involved around twenty-five different factors. It is difficult to describe the monumental waste of time and money involved: each time Trudel came up with a way to split the costs, thousands of municipal bureaucrats spewed out thousands of spreadsheets photocopied thousands of times for the ten thousand elected officials all over Quebec.

Trudel tried originally to dress up the downloading bill as fiscal reform. The way that he originally wanted it to be distributed was fair and would have gone a long way in righting some fiscal wrongs. By the end, it wound up becoming a simple bill.

If it was Trudel's aim to set the municipal world fighting with itself, he succeeded. Rural versus urban, city versus village, suburb versus central city: each succeeding tag team went into the ring, slugging it out as to how the bill would be divided up among them. Many commentators remarked about how stupid the municipalities were in not sticking together, but division was inevitable. Once Trudel bought off the six central cities by promising them a cap of 2.7 per cent of their budgets, he effectively put them on the sidelines, cheering for him. This is why Bourque was so silent on the downloading. He did not want to bite the hand that promised to feed him – or, at least, the hand that promised not to take away too much from him, all the while holding out the promise of his beloved One Island One City. In other words, Bourque had bigger fish to fry.

The downloading fiasco also helped Premier Bouchard to form a very low opinion of municipal leaders. The fratricidal battle that dragged on from April 1997 well into 1998 poisoned the air: relations were strained with both the premier and the minister of municipal affairs. This complex, enervating, futile fight served as a kind of *mise en scène* for the merger battle to follow. And the divide and conquer strategy that worked so well in sticking us with a $375 million bill was employed with great efficiency when the time came to wipe out 212 municipalities across the province. I think it was one of the essential preconditions that allowed the 2001 mergers to take place. Quebec took advantage of these competing interests to ram through the mergers with little comprehensive or cohesive opposition. Indeed, the fractionated municipal world seemed to cry out – to Bouchard – to be merged. Above the cacophony of competing interests, the six "big-city" mayors must have sounded most reasonable.

Looking back, I think I made a mistake in leading the Montreal suburban mayors out of the UMQ, in what was a (justified) fit of pique over its display of egregious self-interest in the downloading saga. As UMQ vice-president, Georges Bossé had been a shoo-in to take over as president. Perhaps we could have reformed it from within and presented much more of a united front against the growing threat of mergers. Certainly, Bossé would not have sought the consolation prize of the presidency of the Conference of Montreal Suburban Mayors when my term was up in January 1998. On the other hand, the NO campaign and the Verdun Rally had galvanized all twenty-seven of the Conference mayors, their city councils, and some of their citizenry: we had never been as united, never as militant, never as politically organized. Quebec saw we were no pushovers. We could not have imagined that four years later our municipalities would disappear.

MARCH 1997:
THE BEGINNINGS OF ONE ISLAND ONE CITY

The *sturm und drang* of the downloading exercise tended to drown out most other things during 1997, but the drumbeat of mergers was never quite out of earshot. The case was consistently being made for rural mergers: rural towns were tied to the government by financial umbilical cords, and these hamlets were deemed too small to provide the range of services the government thought they should provide. The case for *urban* mergers was harder to come by. But slowly one began to hear about the "parasitical" nature of some suburbs and the corollary of "fiscal equity."

While it was hard to identify patterns forming during the municipal turmoil of 1997, I now think that the origins of the megacities in Quebec can be traced to that year, and even to a month in that year. Three events happened in March. First, Guy Chevrette started the ball rolling with public merger musings on the clear lack of fiscal equity on the Island of Montreal. Then the six-city mayors began their own merger campaign on the same theme, starting at the top, in the premier's office. A few days later the downloading was announced – which led, as we have seen, to a permanent splintering of the municipal world in Quebec, thereby creating the perfect conditions for the imposition of mergers.

Some in the media were already on the Montreal merger bandwagon. Even back in November 1996, editorializing crept into what should have been a straight page-one story in *La Presse*: "The City of Montreal has one million people, which makes it the largest municipality in Canada. But it will soon lose this title. The Ontario government has decided to merge the City of Toronto with five other municipalities: the new entity will have 2.2 million people. Halifax will also get bigger. It is a question of a North American trend [*sic*]. In Montreal, we're a long way short of the target. One municipality, Dorval Island, has ... three residents. Senneville: 973. Westmount, the richest city in Canada, is a small island completely surrounded by Montreal, the poorest metropolis in North America."[35] I quote this because I think it reflects the francophone media slant at the time, with its appeal to numerical civic pride and to Island income uniformity.

March 1997 started off quietly enough. Trudel presented the final list of desired rural mergers, announcing that the government dowry would double, and giving rural towns until January 1999 to walk down the aisle, after which date all government aid would dry up. Still, he hastened to add, there would be no forced mergers. Two-thirds of the four hundred-odd targeted municipalities were moving toward merger, according to Trudel; according to another interpretation, only one-quarter were really interested.[36] He then said that those municipalities in the metropolitan regions would know their existential fate only in the autumn. He did let drop that at least the smaller municipalities on the Island of Montreal would be invited to merge, especially Dorval Island with its three inhabitants.*[37] Trying to stir things up, the media asked me for comments. "Get rid

---

* Actually, in the winter there were no inhabitants. Dorval Island is a summer retreat. I often argued with the mayor of Dorval, Peter Yeomans, that the mere existence of this burlesque of a municipality gave our opponents valuable and graphic ammunition for mergers, as it served as a perfect *reductio ad absurdum* argument against small independent municipalities on the Island of Montreal. Yeomans always brushed off my concern, perhaps because he himself had a cottage on Dorval Island.

of the government structures and then we'll talk about mergers,"[38] I snapped.

Gilles Vaillancourt, a few months before stepping down as president of the UMQ, sent out a press release lauding Trudel's list, saying mergers permit "improved fiscal equity, while improving the administrative and financial capacity of the merged municipality."[39] With friends like that, I thought, who needs enemies? And with unsubstantiated claims like those, I thought, who need facts?

FISCAL INEQUITY: A DISEASE THAT ONLY MERGERS CAN CURE

A few days later, things started to heat up. There was a lot of talk of hostilities between Chevrette and Ménard, the former wanting to treat the Montreal region just like all the others. He was not alone. Said the representative for Blainville, "We are sick and tired of being asked to save Montreal. It's not the regions that are going to do that: first of all, you have to sort things out in the centre. Can't the MUC do something for Montreal? There are municipalities on the West Island that are financially well-equipped." A number of these representatives came out for One Island One City "to solve the problem of fiscal inequity among the twenty-nine municipalities on the Island."[40]

That was the signal for Chevrette to pounce. In March 1997 he recentred the debate from one of creating the Montreal Metropolitan Region to one of bailing out the City of Montreal. In effect he was buying the line of the north shore mayors and their provincial representatives that the only problem facing the region was that Montreal was in a mess. (And why was it in a mess? Because the Island suburbs were freeloading off Montreal.) Chevrette waded back into the Island merger debate after a hiatus of fourteen months: this time he was selling not economies of scale but fiscal equity. Solve that problem, he said, before unifying the administrative regions or creating a metropolitan commission. "The biggest problem of Montreal, as the central city," he declared in March 1997, "is the fiscal unfairness that it suffers vis-à-vis the other cities on the Island. When Westmounters pay $1.00 per hundred dollars of evaluation and Montrealers pay $2.17, from my point of view the urgency to act to help Montreal, is to first create fiscal equity."[41] I sent off a press release correcting his numbers: they should have been $1.35 and $1.99 respectively. But the genie was out of the bottle.

Meanwhile, Bourque and his allies were also invoking fiscal equity to justify mergers. The six central-city mayors presented a crucial brief to Premier Bouchard a few days before the provincial budget was tabled with its downloading, part of which was to be funded through the miracle of savings through mergers. But Bourque's gang was not talking about Trudel's voluntary mergers. The central city mayors were playing hardball, pitching the case for *forced* mergers to Bouchard. This marked the beginning of a concerted and continuous campaign for an imposed One Island One City, a campaign that never let up until it happened. Given the significance of the mayors' private brief to Bouchard, I quote an extract:

- Give the metropolitan regions sufficient critical masses, both in order to face the globalization of economic exchange and to ensure the efficient delivery of public services; ...
- Put an end to the waste inherent in the duplication of services and infrastructure and allow a better control of urban sprawl;
- Reduce the fiscal inequalities by assuring a fairer sharing of costs and benefits.

The search for consensus having reached its limit and the government having all the background needed, the State should hit the gas pedal with the consolidation of urban agglomerations ...

- Proceed within one year with the consolidation of the heart of the agglomerations: the Island of Montreal, the Quebec Urban Community, the urban regions of Trois-Rivières, Hull, Sherbrooke and Chicoutimi;
- Make merger studies obligatory, create incentives and support for mergers and impose a deadline for them [to happen].[42]

When the mayors' appeal to Bouchard inevitably dribbled out into the media a few weeks later, Trudel did not take a position for or against. Chevrette had already nailed his colours to the mast. Ménard, on the other hand, stated flatly that he was against One Island One City: "To make a big city with more or less two million citizens, that is not the North American trend, nor is it the government's inclination."[43] He added he did not want a "giant." Unfortunately, because he was fundamentally a fair man, Ménard was the master of mixed messages. So, in spite of this ringing declaration against One Island One City, he had to add that a government study was underway to determine what would happen to Montreal's tax rate if certain municipalities such as Westmount were to merge with it.

I too reacted to Bourque's idea. "The inherent inefficiency of Montreal would be extended over, and suffered by, more citizens,"[44] I said. It would be a "reward for the bad management of the City of Montreal. We'd have a city of 1.8 million badly managed instead of a city of one million badly managed." Besides, I said, we were already 35 per cent merged, in that 35 per cent of our budgets went to the MUC. I then suggested something I had come up with five years earlier: the fission of Montreal, not the fusion of the Island. "Montreal is not manageable. It would possibly be more logical to break up Montreal and create cities of much more interesting sizes."[45] Meanwhile, back in Westmount, I said at our monthly city council meeting, "We have to fight for our very existence."

Bourque, in turn, intoned, "There's a trend around the world to consolidate," an untruth that he never ceased uttering from then on. "We have to work toward a better equity,"[46] he said, cleaving more to the agreed message. "We cannot have disparities such as having the middle classes here, and the less fortunate there. It's far from clear that it's a good thing to keep the well-off cities isolated, unaware of the social problems that surround them."[47]

Out of the toxic soup of the partition movement, the downloading fiasco, the stillborn Montreal Metropolitan Development Commission, and now accusations of Island tax disparities came the solution to all this mess:

Merge!

8

The Seduction of Simplicity:
Turn the MUC into a City?

Politi'cian. n. 1. One versed in the arts of government; one skilled in politicks. 2. A man of artifice; one of deep contrivance.
Samuel Johnson, A Dictionary of the English Language, 1755

It was my birthday, 5 January 1998. I was returning from Christmas holidays in Paris. The airport closed down just after I arrived: the Great Ice Storm had begun. From then until 9 January, some four centimetres (1½ inches) of freezing rain covered the Island of Montreal, and over double that immobilized the south shore. This precipitation does not sound particularly hazardous unless one learns that freezing rain is literally liquid ice; it is water that is supercooled below its freezing point, instantly freezing and coating anything it contacts: electrical wires, pylons, tree branches, roads, and bridges. In the middle of winter, and in a province blessed with so much hydro power that the government once mounted an orgiastic campaign to encourage heating by electricity, an ice storm can spell disaster. Even the circulation pumps for gas-fired or oil-fired heating need electricity.

At first the storm caused innumerable ice-glazed branches to snap off and sever power distribution lines. Then things got serious. High-voltage Hydro-Quebec transmission lines are designed to withstand the weight of only 4.5 centimetres of ice: along the "ring of power" that encircles and feeds Montreal Island, the pylons and power lines were coated with double that. Sagging under the weight and whip-lashed by the wind, one thousand giant pylons crumpled like so many delicate filigreed dominoes.

Most of the Island of Montreal was plunged into the cold and dark. At one point the power to the City of Montreal's water supply plants stopped and, unbelievably, it had no generators. Not only were people told to boil drinking water without the means to do so but the loss of water pressure meant it would have been impossible to fight a major fire.

Because Westmount was the only municipality in the region to have its own electrical distribution system, and because we had a policy of burying many circuits or routinely trimming branches around the remaining power lines, Westmount had few blackouts. That is, up until 9 January at 12:15 PM. I was just about to give a CBC radio interview explaining why Westmount's power was untouched when all the lights went off. Hydro-Quebec could no longer supply our substations. That did not prevent the ineffable Jan Wong to write a big piece published the next day in the *Globe and Mail* sub-headlined, "Montreal's wealthy enclave of Westmount basking in warm glow from electrical power while rest of the city is shivering in darkness."

Westmount had already set up shelters in Victoria Hall and the Shaar Hashomayim Synagogue to sleep three hundred and feed many more. One Westmounter, whose deep freezer understandably wasn't deep freezing anymore, gave the Victoria Hall shelter a huge amount of smoked salmon. Someone rolled out Vic Hall's grand piano, and a classical pianist played (by candlelight, of necessity) while the assembled refugees, mostly from NDG in Montreal, ate their smoked salmon. Some said they did not want to go home. Jan Wong would have been in cliché heaven.

For the first two days the provincial government typically tried to run emergency measures from Quebec City. Then the MUC took over, instituting twice-daily conference calls with the mayors. Nearly ten thousand troops were – eventually – sent into the metropolitan region. The army brass told me that Quebec had a serious plan to evacuate the whole Island; with most bridges closed, I could not image how that was to be done, and why. Confusion reigned supreme.

Commentators as varied as Pierre Bourgault, Lysiane Gagnon, and Jean Lapierre agreed that the City of Montreal performed poorly during the ice storm. The city administration was certainly caught flat-footed: the snow had not even been cleared from an earlier storm, as Montreal often seems to count on solar power to do so. Combined with the ice, this leftover, rock-hard snow made Montreal's roads impassable and actually caused 30 per cent of its snow-removal equipment to break down.

The Island suburbs were quick off the mark in helping citizens, providing firewood, bottled water, shelters, food, and volunteers. The ice storm, in fact, illustrated the difference between the communities that were the suburbs and the bureaucracy that was Montreal. Montreal sent out plaintive press releases pleading for volunteers: in the suburbs, volunteers just showed up at city halls. Thanks partially to them, Westmount could hand-deliver on two occasions a letter from me to every household. That sort of thing was unthinkable in Montreal. In all, Westmount had two hundred volunteers, or the equivalent of ten thousand in Montreal – an impossible number.

There was another lesson, *favourable* to mergers, which related to the ice storm. Of the 199 Quebec municipalities with a population over 5,000, 99 per cent had emergency measures plans in place. Of the 1,173 towns and villages with fewer than five thousand residents, only 27 per cent had operational plans.[1] Once again the merger rhetoric should have been only directed at rural Quebec.

EXIT TRENT

Slowly things got back to a state of normalcy (to use an ugly Americanism). By 22 January, Montreal was navigable enough for me to have a lunch at Le Soubise with Georges Bossé, the mayor of Verdun. I had no idea what he wanted to talk about. I was at the end of my second two-year term as president of the Conference of Montreal Suburban Mayors, and I was going to put my name up for election (likely by acclamation) for a third term. Since the conference began in 1970, only one mayor before me had served more than my four years. When and if my girlfriend, Claudia, returned from Paris where she was doing postgraduate work, and when and if we started living together – or even got married – my plan was to resign as president. I was uncomfortable with the idea of living with the daughter of the conference's director-general while being the latter's boss. The judgment of a man like me, twice as old as his girlfriend and besotted, was hardly – not for the first time in history – of the highest order.

But to return to the restaurant. "I know I promised before Christmas to back you for another term, but I've changed my mind," said Bossé. "I am going to run against you."

I was nonplussed. Finally, I said, "Let me think about it. There is a reason why I would not want a contested election." What raced

through my mind was that, while I was prepared to go on unopposed
and then resign if need be, a contested election was another thing
entirely: while I would likely have won, I would feel I had let everyone down if I quit shortly thereafter because of Claudia. So I called
up Bossé an hour later and told him I would not run. Besides, I had
a very high opinion of him: he was intelligent, very hard-working,
principled, and a francophone from a non-iconic municipality. I was,
however, a little concerned that "bulldog" Bossé perhaps did not
have quite the temperament to keep twenty-seven mayors herded
together – the overarching challenge for any president. Frank
Zampino, for one, told me he had reservations about Bossé. He was
duly acclaimed president 29 January 1998.

On the merger front, things had quietened down. Trudel was
chastened, still smarting from the downloading fiasco. Bourque had
no real champion in Quebec City, although he had been surprised
and chuffed when Mario Dumont, leader of the Action démocratique du Québec* (ADQ) announced that their general council massively voted for One Island One City in November 1997. Aside from
invoking the (by now) standard claims of efficiency and economy,
Dumont baldly stated an untruth: "All major North American cities have simplified their structures by merging."[2] His announcement
was partially neutralized by the Liberal Liza Frulla, whose name was
being bruited about as a possible Montreal mayoralty candidate,
coming out strongly against the idea.

Robert Perreault, once a member of Mayor Jean Doré's party and
chairman of the MUC Transit Corporation, was now the new minister of the métropole. Perreault was far more interested in merging
the three major transit corporations than in merging municipalities. When I met with him in November 1997, he told me he was
not in favour of Island mergers, with the possible exception of the
very small towns. He did not want to allow Montreal's problems to
spread to its neighbours. Unlike his predecessor, he was against merging the Montreal Island fire brigades.

So the One Island One City campaign had, for the moment, turned
into a bit of a phoney war. Had I known that municipal mergers
would virulently recrudesce in a year or so, I might have stayed on as

* A provincial political party that had never formed a government. The ADQ was dissolved in January 2012.

president. (Had I known that my turbulent – mostly intercontinental – love affair, after a hopeless attempt at living together in the summer of 1998, was going to die a slow and wretched death for months thereafter, things equally might have been different.)

DANYLUK REDUPLICATED?

With mergers on the back burner but still on simmer, the main problem looming for the Conference of Montreal Suburban Mayors in late January 1998 was another election: Vera Danyluk's term was up as the chair of the MUC executive committee. Should we renew it for another four years? Tradition had it that Montreal named the chair for two terms of four years each, then likewise the suburban mayors. Danyluk had made it clear to us and to the media that she wanted another term.

The MUC had never had an executive committee chair like Danyluk. From 1986 to 1994 the position had been held by Michel Hamelin, a former Montreal city councillor originally named by Mayor Drapeau. Hamelin's mandate was renewed by Mayor Jean Doré, leader of the party that got rid of Drapeau. As Andrew Sancton has pointed out,[3] the fact that Doré would reconfirm an opponent shows that Montreal did not see the MUC as a politically charged institution. A laconic and contemplative man, Hamelin did a masterful job of shuttle diplomacy between Montreal and the suburbs, keeping the MUC chugging along. He was against an expanded MUC, not wanting, as he said in a rare interview on the subject, to "spread the hegemony of the MUC to other municipalities."[4]

Then along came Danyluk. She was hard working, loved her job, and tried her level best to make employees feel the MUC was a family. She genuinely felt that the MUC needed more recognition for the work it accomplished and that it should be given an independent voice. After four years of her chairmanship, Bourque, Bossé, and I were fed to the back teeth with what we ungraciously saw as her media grandstanding and campaign to enlarge and elect the MUC without either executive committee or council approval. In furthering her conviction that the MUC needed a radical overhaul, she had unwittingly succeeded in creating the myth that the MUC was a wasp's nest (*un nid de chicanes*) of squabbling mayors. That myth has stuck around so long that today it has hardened into "a fact."[5]

The MUC was not a wasp's nest. On the contrary, the suburbs and Montreal managed to resolve most issues: Montreal International, the Metropolitan Transport Agency (the AMT), the approval of the police chief's new approach to policing, the funding of mass transit, the moratorium on greenspace acquisition, or the freezing of property assessments.[6] The same bilaterally placid state of affairs reigned in the MUC Executive Committee. My six years of experience there taught me that the two sides usually worked things out, as a dozen mostly well-intentioned people thrown together will generally do. Even though Danyluk often helped in getting the two sides together, that was not the impression created publicly.

In spite of my annoyance with her – and mindful of her supporters within our ranks – back in early November I got the Conference of Mayors to agree to three conditions for her renewal, the most important of which[7] was that she commit to a reform of the MUC if that were the desire of the MUC council, which was, after all, sovereign. She subsequently brushed off these conditions. I had also met with Bourque to sound him out on the subject of her renewal. By then, Bourque told me, he was dealing directly with Premier Bouchard, not Trudel, on the downloading issue – and presumably on the One Island One City file. Regarding Danyluk, he said he had *"beaucoup de misère avec elle"* – a lot of difficulty with her. Maybe, he said, we could renew her mandate for one year only – which, not coincidentally, would delay the problem until after the next Montreal municipal election.

VERA'S VIEW: ONE ISLAND ONE METROPOLIS

Danyluk gave one of her most impassioned speeches during the 1998 MUC budget presentation in December 1997. She eloquently described how the Montreal Island taxpayers were (and are today) getting stiffed:

> The MUC is structured, financially, as if we were a simple collection of municipalities sharing services for ourselves and among ourselves. This vision is an error, and this error is leading us to a disaster. The MUC is more than a service cooperative in a closed circle. *The MUC is a metropolis* [my italics]. As such, it delivers services directly or indirectly to an ensemble much bigger than its own population. The resulting problem is twofold. On one

hand, the services the MUC delivers are expensive because they stem from its function as a metropolis. On the other hand, these services are only paid for by the Island population. From that comes our current lack of resources to operate properly. But above all, from that comes the unfairness for the taxpayers of the MUC, who find themselves alone in paying for a locomotive that pulls a train with too many passengers not paying their way.

Danyluk went on to explain how the laws that created the MUC envisioned her role as a "mediator," bringing the two partners together to create a community spirit and therefore make "the MUC bigger than the sum of its parts." Her conclusion, after four years in the job, was that the law, while it was supposed to give her post an "undeniable democratic legitimacy," was "too weak" and her function did not have what it needed to "represent vigorously enough the community dynamic." This was her code for the idea that she should be directly elected. "I am convinced that we have to call into question the MUC's structure," she said. "It no longer works. We see it clearly today, and for some time now. It's possible that we will have to go as far as to change the structure. But the final result of any structural modification must be, minimally, to enlarge the circle of municipalities that pay for the metropolitan functions of the MUC."[8]

Four months later, Danyluk continued to plug what she referred to as "One Island One Metropolis," which sounded dangerously close to One Island One City to my ears: "In short, the Island of Montreal is, together, a metropolis; and each of the 29 Cities on the Island is a cog, to varying degrees, of this metropolis. It remains for us to act politically as a metropolis."[9] She meant that Montreal Island was a metropolis mostly in the sense that it provided regional services to a broader population without recompense, but it could be taken in other ways.

MAKE THE MUC A LEVEL OF GOVERNMENT?

Militating for a directly elected MUC executive committee chair and calling for a "One Island One Metropolis" with political muscle played into the hands of the amalgamationists. Everyone knew, except apparently Minister Trudel, that it would have taken someone possessed of far more political capital and gumption than he to force the south shore and especially Laval to become part of the

MUC. Therefore, with no off-Island expansion, there would have been one level of government covering the Island sitting on top of another level of government, the City of Montreal, that paid over half of its costs and had more than half its citizens. The duplication of two levels of parallel structures, tax bills, and voter classes would have quickly led to just one Island-wide level of government. The momentum to "go all the way" would be unstoppable. Besides, people would not have stood for four levels of government. That's what happened in Toronto and what would have happened in Montreal, had not Quebec decided to short-circuit the process by imposing Island-wide mergers.

Danyluk was talking direct election for her job only; she did not at this point publicly espouse complete direct election to the MUC, though that was to come. In 1988, Toronto implemented direct election for the whole council of Metro, their version of the MUC.[10] The arrogance and haughtiness of Metro – symbolized by the construction of a $160-million twenty-seven-storey building to house its bureaucrats and its twenty-eight directly elected councillors and their fifty-six assistants – grated on most Torontonians. After six years of the "improved" Metro, nearly 60 per cent of Torontonians wanted to get rid of it,[11] and so its disappearance was a real selling point for the later Toronto megacity. And the supposedly undemocratic, unelected MUC? Why, 70 per cent of Montrealers, while they had no idea what it did or who ran it,* wanted to keep it.[12]

And it wasn't just Toronto that eased its way to a megacity afterlife. Starting in 1994, all councillors of the Regional Municipality of Ottawa-Carleton were directly elected and local mayors were excluded from it, a change that led to unending and bitter battles between the two tiers of government.[13] At least the megacity of Ottawa, when it was imposed, got rid of that.

---

* In that same poll, only 23 per cent of residents knew Vera Danyluk headed up the MUC, 75 per cent thought the MUC ran fire departments (it didn't), 56–59 per cent thought the MUC maintained streets and provided recreation and library services. My reaction was that this was to be expected and was nothing to worry about: citizens held their mayors and city councillors accountable for both local and regional services and couldn't care less if they got the job done through an intermunicipal service organization. In spite of the dewy-eyed ideal of an "urban community," the MUC never became one. At the time of the forced mergers, no one paraded downtown with signs, "Hands off my MUC!"

With direct election to a regional body, one usually has one councillor who represents fifty thousand or even eighty thousand people. In the case of the Montreal area with its many small municipalities, this would have meant only one representative for, say, Côte Saint-Luc, Hampstead, Montreal West, and Lachine. With time, the pressure for merger, at least for such bundled municipalities, would have been almost irresistible.

And when you create a whole new class of politicians, they have to have most of the money on the Monopoly board. At the time of their becoming megacities, both Metro Toronto and the Regional Municipality Ottawa-Carleton controlled around 70 per cent of both local and regional spending. It was a short hop, skip, and a jump to full merger and 100 per cent.[14]

Political power, like matter, can neither be created nor destroyed. When the MUC was created, its member municipalities (and, to a small extent, the province) lost power. If the MUC had gained even more political power, it would be once again at the expense of its member municipalities. Since the City of Montreal "owned" one-half of the MUC, any power it gave the MUC would not be really lost; however, it would not be the same dynamic for the smaller municipalities. The little power that would have been left would have meant the suburbs would have shrivelled up, eventually to die through irrelevancy.

So a politically supercharged MUC would have inevitably led to One Island One City. I said at the time, "Those who want to endow the MUC with political clout and a higher profile, wish – probably unwittingly – to achieve indirectly what all Montreal mayors have always wanted to do directly: create only one city on the Island. It would be amalgamation by stages."[15] I was not alone in seeing direct election at the MUC as a way station to merger. Professor Luc-Normand Tellier wrote at the time, "The idea of Mayor Drapeau of 'One Island One City' is worth looking at again. The election by universal suffrage of the chairman of the MUC could be the first step in that direction."[16]

Another fan of the transmutation of the MUC to a city via direct election and taxation was the editorialist for Le Devoir, Jean-Robert Sansfaçon. "The Future of the MUC Is a City," he entitled an editorial. Only he stopped short of calling it Montreal: "It's not a question of spreading the hegemony of Montreal to cover the Island, but to create a new Island-wide urban entity. We'll give this city another name if that will suffice to keep quiet those who see Montreal in their coffee. The important thing is the result: a big city supplying all the current MUC services and those of the cities, with full taxation power and run by a mayor and fifty councillors."[17] Why this nomenclatural schizophrenia? Why not just have Montreal annex the other municipalities? The answer could be found in Sansfaçon's earlier editorial: "It's hard to imagine a government forcing the merger of all the Island cities, thereby turning Montreal into one big city with an allophone and anglophone majority."[18]

In her campaign to enhance the MUC, Danyluk had both public and editorial opinion solidly behind her. In a poll conducted in March 1998,[19] 53 per cent of Island residents thought the head of the MUC should be elected by universal suffrage – even though they had no idea what the MUC did. Leaving aside my "slippery-slope" worry, there was another problem with direct election: people would never get out and actually vote. Giving power to the people is fine as long as they are prepared to wield it. Evidence of the people's enthusiasm for direct election to each and every government body can usually be found on pollster's clipboards but rarely in the ballot box. Indeed, regional elections to something like the MUC would have had all the sizzle of school board elections, where a corporal's guard turns out. I suspect that Canadian electors will get out and vote for a maximum of only three levels of government. At the municipal level, we're lucky if we get even a desultory 50 per cent turnout of voters; a regional level sandwiched between the local and provincial levels would have attracted a fraction of that.

THE RÉGIE AND THE DISSIDENT MAYORS

We now return to the renewal of Danyluk's mandate. Thanks to the Christmas holidays, the ice storm, and my stepping down, we had a respite until the end of January. Danyluk's fate would be decided at the next meeting of the MUC council on 18 February 1998.

There was a festering problem inside the Conference of Mayors that had technically nothing to do with Danyluk's renewal but that was the cause of a deep schism going back two years. This was the matter of the Waste Management Board (known by its French title, the Régie), on whose council sat all the mayors of the conference, excepting Yves Ryan of Montreal North. The Régie had signed a contract with Foster Wheeler Ltd to build a $316-million waste-disposal installation involving an incinerator. The Régie had been run, completely out of the public eye, as the personal fiefdom of Michel Leduc, the mayor of LaSalle. Michel was a salty, colourful physician who wore cowboy boots and was never at a loss for a quick quip. In December 1995, fed up with the way the Régie was run, sixteen mayors engineered a putsch led by Bossé, throwing out Leduc and his five-man executive. We then cancelled the contract with Foster Wheeler, who promptly launched a $62-million lawsuit against the Régie.[20] Next thing we knew, the former Régie executive (the "dissident mayors") sided with Foster Wheeler as well as taking a series of legal actions on their own, all of which added an extra million dollars to our legal bills. In a nice touch, Bossé threatened to sue the "dissident mayors" personally. The rancour between the two camps was still deep by the time we got to the problem of Danyluk's mandate. If Bossé wanted her gone, the "dissident mayors" would fight for her. Political decisions are driven by tribalism, not rationalism.

A NON-EXECUTIVE MUC CHAIRMAN?

With our new president, Bossé, the Conference of Mayors had taken a position on 29 January 1998 – nearly three weeks before the vote for or against Danyluk – that Quebec should change the legislation governing the MUC. We decided the chair of the executive committee no longer should be a full-time job, just as was the case with the transit board, and with the MUC before 1982. We recommended that it be chaired alternately for two years by a mayor and by a Montreal councillor.[21] This way, a mayor would not have to give up the mayoralty in order to be chairman of the executive committee. It would also mean that the MUC's director-general, whose mandate would be broadened, could properly run the show rather than having the MUC saddled, in effect, with two directors-general.

I agreed with the suggested change but felt it was far too opportunistic and would look so. I wrote a letter right after the January 29 mayors' meeting when this decision was taken, eighteen for and eight against:

I fear for the Conference. Over the next few weeks, we might see the Conference being torn apart over the Danyluk problem ... Some mayors quickly realized that this change [in Vera's job] had some merit and the timing was good – in that Vera's mandate was up, and the job of MUC director-general was vacant. However, it also dawned on all of them that it was an elegant way of getting rid of Vera without having to deal with the question of her performance, nor, equally, the question of getting one of us to make the ultimate sacrifice in stepping down as mayor in order to become her replacement. So some of the pro-Danyluk camp (including Lasalle Mayor Michel Leduc) went along with this recommendation, in that it would not be seen as a slap on the wrist to Vera. As far as *I'm* concerned, most outsiders, including the media, will view this gambit for what it really is: what lawyers call a "constructive dismissal."

At best, we'll get but lukewarm support from Bourque and Trudel. Vera will cry bloody murder in the media. It will get very messy. And we really don't have a fallback position, since, in my view, we'll never get the majority of mayors to agree to the simple non-reappointment of Vera. So if the constructive dismissal solution does not fly, Vera might still be back for another four-year term. And how can the Conference, especially its brand-new president, stomach the idea of an MUC run by someone who publicly: 1) favours an even stronger MUC, expanding its borders to include Laval and the south shore; 2) wants to turn her position into a directly elected post, thereby creating another level of government, just as Metro Toronto did in 1988; and, 3) refused the Conference's three conditions for her re-appointment? This would be a public humiliation of the Conference. Also, how could Georges Bossé manage a Conference that would be split into two increasingly vociferous factions? It will make the Régie putsch seem like a picnic. And Vera will capitalize on our divisions. She knows first-hand the weaknesses of the Conference.

OUR GOOSE GETS COOKING

Once the news was out, Danyluk's reaction, as I predicted, was swift. "Vera Danyluk, chairman of the MUC, says that Montreal mayor Pierre Bourque and his Westmount counterpart, Peter Trent, are conspiring to get her out of a job,"[22] said one radio station news bulletin. "'They are trying to do indirectly what they don't have the courage to do directly,' said a fuming Danyluk yesterday after learning of a plan to reform the MUC that would effectively leave her out

of a job."[23] And what did the media hear from us? Did we effectively defend the change we recommended? No: instead the mayors
looked like vultures. "I am ready to serve my colleagues," said the
mayor of Dorval, Peter Yeomans, unctuously when he was asked if
he would be a candidate for the position in the event Danyluk was
forced to leave.

As to Bourque, he – sort of – came out against any immediate
change, desiring to wait until the municipal election in November.
Our goose was starting to be cooked. Bourque said he did not have
the energy to devote to re-jigging the MUC: "We have other fish to
fry."[24] By 15 February, he had advised us that he "could not deliver
his people."

While Municipal Affairs Minister Trudel said that such a change
could not and should not be implemented quickly, and that Montreal had to be in agreement with it, he found the proposal interesting, as it permitted the "depoliticization" of the MUC, which in turn
would help him sell the idea of expanding the MUC to Laval and the
south shore.[25]

So the whole "constructive dismissal" tactic evaporated, and we
were faced with a simple renewal of Danyluk's mandate.

The mayors were seen as attacking the saviour of the MUC and
the MUC itself. The media, or at least the editorialists, liked the MUC
and could never understand why the mayors were so obtuse as to be
cool to it, or at least to want to change it. The most frustrating thing
about our long-standing campaign to have the MUC recognized as a
service-delivery organization, not as a level of government, was our
crucial corollary: that a decision-making political body covering the
whole Montreal Metropolitan Region must be set up at the same
time.[26] It was a package deal. We tried to implement the first, but the
implementation of the second was out of our hands.

We handled things terribly during this crisis. We had not made our
case for our vision of the MUC. Danyluk wrapped herself in the cloak
of regionalism and was statesmanlike. The Conference of Mayors,
a group that had always promoted regionalism, came off sounding
parochial, mean, manipulative, and isolationist. What had started
out years before as a battle of ideas had degenerated into an apparent desire for naked vengeance. As well as taking the high road publicly, Danyluk was equally in her element in a bare-knuckles political
brawl. She called in all her many IOUs, including Montreal opposition councillors. She even got the city council of Mount Royal,

where she was once mayor, to adopt a resolution *forcing* the incumbent mayor to vote for her second mandate. She slowly worked on suburban mayors, one by one.

BOURQUE UNDELIVERS

Come 18 February, at the MUC Council meeting that was to decide Danyluk's fate, Bossé tried a face-saving manoeuvre: a one-year extension of her mandate. It nearly worked. When the weighted votes were tallied, the suburban mayors voted 68 per cent for the motion, but Montreal (including Bourque) only voted 48 per cent in favour. With no double majority, the motion did not pass, but only missed by 2 per cent. We then had to vote to approve the four-year renewal. We knew the Montreal opposition councillors would vote for Danyluk, but what about Bourque? We had to wait during four hours of speeches and debates to find out. We couldn't believe it when Bourque and all his party voted to a man and to a woman for Danyluk: 100 per cent of the Montreal vote went for her renewal. Since only 41 per cent of the suburban vote was in favour, the motion did not pass. But it did the next meeting, when sixteen out of twenty-seven suburban mayors voted *for* her.[27]

Even though, months later,[28] these same mayors said their positive vote was simply a question of supporting the tradition of two terms for Danyluk's post and was not an endorsement of her policies, I don't think the Conference of Mayors ever got over this debacle.[29] We were still in a divisive shambles when the campaign for One Island One City really got underway a year later.

While Bourque was not in agreement with Danyluk's views and was fed up with her many public pronouncements, he had decided to get his party to vote for her. Why? As he said, he had bigger fish to fry. Not only did he want to win the November municipal election, he also had his eyes on the One Island One City prize. The longer the acrimonious infighting among the mayors and between them and Danyluk continued, the easier his argument became for putting the whole thing into one big container. I could almost imagine him rubbing his hands during this mess and then going to Quebec, saying "The Island's ungovernable!" One of the huge advantages of One Island One City, Bourque could argue, was that it would get rid of the MUC and its ceaseless internal bickering.

Agnès Gruda, writing in *La Presse* a few days after the six-month drama of Danyluk's mandate renewal was finally over, had a lot to say in an editorial entitled "Big Crisis, Small Victory:"[30]

> The opposition movement that Mrs Danyluk had to face goes well beyond a simple conflict of personalities. What was at stake here were two diametrically opposed visions as to what the MUC should be ... The suburban mayors maneuvered not only to get rid of Mrs Danyluk, but also to change the operation and the role of the MUC, which they wanted to bring back to the more modest size of a simple service co-operative – notably by reducing the political power of its big boss. The chairman, for her part, never stopped in defending her prerogatives and to proclaim from every media platform at what point the MUC must increase its role, speak in the name of the region, debate the big regional issues, and to make its weight felt throughout the whole provincial political scene.
>
> Even if our sympathy goes to Mrs Danyluk and her crusade against parochialism, the suburban mayors had a point: four years ago, when they supported the candidacy of the former mayor of Mount Royal to the head of the MUC, Mrs Danyluk was saying something completely different. At the time, she did not believe in this regional structure at all and she was even committed to tearing it down. One can imagine the surprise of those who had voted for her at the MUC Council, to see her make a 180 degree turn shortly after she took on her new job. If Mrs Danyluk had been elected by universal suffrage, such a flip-flop on a fundamental question would have provoked general indignation and her electors would have accused her of a perversion of democracy.

In spite of Bourque's surprising and essential support for her renewal, by the time he was in the final throes of an election campaign in October 1998, Danyluk stuck to her guns and declared that his "incoherence" and insistence on MUC cost-cutting was imperilling her organization. "The MUC serves only as a budgetary stopgap for Montreal," she said. When Bourque said that "the MUC was of secondary importance," she chided him that his campaign was not focusing on metropolitan issues.[31] Bourque was beside himself with fury at the chutzpah of Danyluk in sticking her nose into a Montreal election campaign.

THE 1998 PROVINCIAL ELECTION

Bourque won the Montreal election. Next came the provincial election. Danyluk was "very tempted" to run in Mount Royal for the Liberals, filling the vacancy left by my friend John Ciaccia. As it turned out, she decided to stay put, feeling rightly that she would have let her supporters down. It was her last chance: the Liberals never came a-calling again.

In the campaign leading up to voting day on 30 November, Jean Charest, the Liberal leader, came out clearly against forced mergers. "I am not of the school of those who make maps of cities, then say: there are this many cities in Quebec, and that many cities in Ontario, and so per capita that makes so much ... therefore, there are too many [here]."[32]

Way back in September 1997, the Liberal Party had given the mandate to their "Policy Commission" to draft a new policy before the next election that would include a "legislative framework formally recognizing municipalities as a responsible local level of government."[33] Then, a month before voting day, out came a letter from the leader himself, enclosing another resolution promising "a reformulation of municipal law giving municipalities real decision-making autonomy" along with "the reestablishment of the principle of voluntary mergers."[34] This hugely important initiative to guarantee municipal autonomy seems to have fallen ever since into a Liberal black hole.

And the PQ? In a milestone interview in *L'Actualité* which came out during the electoral period, Lucien Bouchard rejected the idea of One Island One City, saying that, instead, a cleanup of structures was necessary:

> BOUCHARD: Montreal has a hundred institutional decision-makers. We have to tidy things up there. If we are the next government, we will make it one of our first jobs.
> *L'ACTUALITÉ*: Toronto is going through its third reorganization ... Do we really need so many municipal councils in Montreal?
> BOUCHARD: I don't think that the One Island One City formula is the solution. I think, rather, we need administrative structures

that are more unified and that reflect reality. It's an extremely difficult operation that will require a lot of political courage ... There's a big job to be done, especially fiscally speaking. The state must support Montreal as the metropolis. We also have to take another look at fiscal equity in the Montreal Metropolitan Region and in all of Quebec. As far as Montreal is concerned, I am convinced that the municipal administration has not applied itself to rationalizing budgets.[35]

In everybody's book, Bouchard's statement was interpreted as PQ policy: no One Island One City. Other than that interview, Bouchard and the PQ were pretty close-mouthed with regard to municipal matters during the campaign and even after winning the election. Danyluk chided them: "The government must act quickly at least to show their colours as to what they envisage for the City of Montreal, the Island of Montreal, and the metropolitan region."[36]

DANYLUK PUTS THE BRAKE ON MONTREAL INTERNATIONAL

Everyone had got so used to Danyluk's unauthorized media pronouncements that when she said nothing during the month of February 1999, the press speculated she had been gagged. Some of us on the executive committee did admit publicly that she was called to order for her "untimely and imprudent declarations," especially for her revealing various budget possibilities. By then Bourque and his second-in-command, Jean Fortier, had had it with her. But she was back in business at the end of March 1999 when she came out against integrating the MUC economic expansion office into Bourque's pet project, Montreal International. She got a public dressing-down from Bourque, who told her to shut up.[37] The next day, out came a press release from her office saying she wouldn't shut up. Things were getting downright silly.

In spite, therefore, of the obvious advantage of simplifying and especially regionalizing services, Danyluk dug in her heels and would not let the MUC's twenty-person department be incorporated into Montreal International, saying the latter could "promote" internationally, but not "prospect," thereby guaranteeing confusion in the eyes of foreign investors. By then both the head of the Conference of Mayors, Bossé, and Bourque – the two "shareholders" of the MUC

– were in agreement to incorporate. Not only was Danyluk overtly going against the will of those who bankrolled and controlled the MUC but her attitude was strangely in contradiction with all her earlier pronouncements in favour of creating regional spirit. Finally, by the end of 1999, she had to give way, and the MUC economic expansion office was incorporated into Montreal International.

Writing in *La Presse*, even Alain Dubuc questioned this "fierce opposition that came less from the Island suburban cities than from the chair of the MUC, Mrs Vera Danyluk, who, in this matter, conducted a rearguard action with rare pettiness."[38] But all along Danyluk was convinced that her job was to defend both the MUC staff and the MUC as an institution; furthermore, that she had to ensure that taxpayers' money was under elected control. She was not wrong. But Dubuc had the last word, which he directed at her: "You denounce Montreal International because it is not controlled by elected people. Yet MUC elected officials had accepted to join Montreal International, as well as those from Laval and the south shore. And you, who are not an elected person, you continue to denounce the decision that elected people have taken."[39] Ever since she was appointed chairman of the MUC executive committee, Danyluk had been sensitive to the fact she was no longer an elected person, trying to minimize it by saying she had "the same status of a politician." This vulnerability explained her long-held public position that all regional bodies like the MUC should be run by people elected expressly for that purpose.

THE SEDUCTIVE SIMPLICITY OF ONE ISLAND ONE CITY

I have laid out in detail the friction between Danyluk and the rest of us in order to explain how One Island One City came to be seen as a solution to these interminable harangues. The image of the MUC as a bear-pit even turned off those who might have looked with favour at the MUC's territorial expansion as the alternative to One Island One City. Almost since the MUC's inception, many had said it should have grown geographically, providing its services to Laval and the south shore. But if one were going to let the MUC loose from the confines of the Island of Montreal, why not have it take over the entire Montreal Metropolitan Region, obviating the need for a metropolitan council and getting rid of the thicket of sub-regional structures to boot? It would have forced the whole region into contributing to regional services, would it not?

As well as the insurmountable resistance of the off-Island mayors, there was a fundamental problem with any geographic expansion of the MUC, partial or complete. While public transit and wastewater treatment – two of its three main services – should or could have been metropolized, the MUC police force was already too big and too remote from its clientele.

Politically, a metropolitan police force was unthinkable. The off-Island municipalities were not the least bit interested in incorporating their police into the MUC force, and – for once – it was not a question of salaries, as their cost per police officer sometimes was even higher than the MUC's. Behind this allergic reaction to one big police force lay at least three reasons. To start with, regionalizing the police would mean the off-Island suburbs too would start paying for specialized police services provided by the MUC that everywhere else in Quebec were supplied free by the provincial police. Secondly, the MUC police monopoly came equipped with its own boss, the MUC police "brotherhood": nothing, but nothing, is done without union okay.[40] Thirdly, while it was unlikely, if ever there were a repeat of the 1969 police strike, Laval and the south shore would be helpless victims, not lucky bystanders.

THE BIRTH OF THE MUC

It was a police crisis that launched the MUC into existence. The legislation that gave shape and substance to the MUC and defined its powers was hurriedly cobbled together in less than two months after the illegal seventeen-hour Montreal police strike of 7 October 1969. During the strike, four thousand policemen took to the streets of Montreal, shaking their fists against anyone in authority. Their declared objective was wage parity with Toronto.[41] Once gathered at the Paul Sauvé Arena, they booed and even threatened Lucien Saulnier, Mayor Drapeau's right-hand man. Luckily, the Island suburban municipalities still had their own police forces. The army and the provincial police were also called in. Shops all along Ste-Catherine Street were looted, and a provincial policeman was killed. After a late-night telephone call from Mayor Drapeau to the premier of the day, Jean-Jacques Bertrand, the provincial government promised to come to the aid of the City of Montreal –

financially. Early next morning, it caved in to the police and their salary demands.

This promise to help Montreal took its form in the creation of the MUC. It was nothing less and nothing more than a way to force the suburban municipalities on the Island to bail out the City of Montreal. The pretext was the pooling of services, notably police – and in doing so, hiding the police bad apples in a bigger basket. But the real goal and the real result was a recurring fiscal transfer. There was no consultation, no give and take. The MUC was imposed on the Island on 23 December 1969 less than three months after the police strike. While the off-Island suburbs as usual got away scot free, the MUC did solve the problem of huge disparities in policing throughout the Island. In 1970, for example, Montreal had double the Island suburbs' crime rate and double their policing costs per capita. Mind you, Montreal also paid their constables 20 per cent more.[42]

The MUC was a peculiarly Québécois/Gallic invention inspired by the urban communities of places like Bordeaux and Strasbourg. And, in spite of my many dyspeptic broadsides aimed at it, I always said that the MUC was a far better concept than most of the second-tier municipal structures then operating in the rest of Canada. At least in theory, the member municipalities controlled it. There was no direct election. You voted for a mayor, who in turn voted at the MUC. The focus was on your local municipality, not on some amorphous construct forever remote from a voter.

The main problem with the MUC was its top-heavy structure. It was like an elephant balancing on a three-legged stool. The MUC spent 92 per cent of its budget on only three things: mass transit, police, and wastewater treatment.[43] Now, the MUC Transit Corporation was a stand-alone structure with its own director-general, council, and staff with only a financial umbilical cord to the MUC through which ran the money to cover its deficits. That is not all: the police department had its own director and staff and operated independently of the MUC: so much so that it took the ice storm crisis to make the MUC administration realize that their computers were incompatible with those of the MUC police. So the only major service left was the wastewater treatment plant that pretty much did its own thing. Yet the MUC was stuck with a full-time executive committee chairman in addition to a director-general, all reporting to an eighty-member council with five public commissions that were rarely graced with the public.

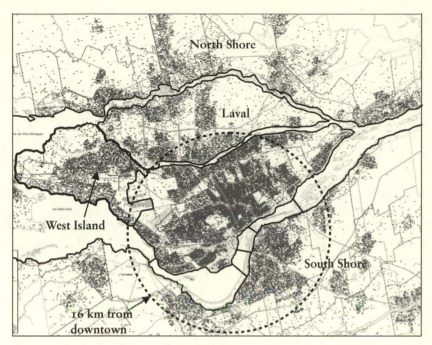

Figure 1 The Montreal Metropolitan Region

THE MUC: SLAVE TO GEOGRAPHY, NOT DEMOGRAPHY

As well as being structurally over-endowed, the MUC suffered from an even more serious problem: its artificial insularity was at odds with demographic realities.

There are five densely habited areas in the Montreal metropolitan region: (1) the south shore, (2) central and eastern Montreal Island, (3) western Laval, (4) the north shore, and (5) the West Island of Montreal. Each is notionally separated from each other by a river or in the case of the West Island, by an airport-cum-industrial area. Unlike the pattern of urban growth in Toronto, which could only expand 180 degrees from its origins owing to Lake Ontario, Montreal, thanks to bridges, could expand 360 degrees. There is no reason in this century or in much of the past one to regard a river as a meaningful barrier to growth. As the crow flies and as cars are driven, the south shore is much closer to downtown Montreal than the West Island. The south shore is also linked to downtown by a metro station and rush-hour bus lanes. The West Island is not. While the south shore and part of Laval is within sixteen kilometres of downtown, after a sixteen-kilometre trip you are just entering the West Island, and it goes on for at least double that distance.

To those who say that bridges, especially traffic-choked bridges, make the south shore in reality more distant, one could argue that the no-man's land comprising Dorval Airport, railroad marshalling yards, and various parks (of the industrial and conventional variety) – that together equal nearly 10 per cent of the entire Island's land area – cuts off most of the West Island just as effectively as the narrow body of water between the south shore and downtown. The statistics bear this out. Even back in 1993, a greater proportion of residents of the south shore and Laval commuted to the City of Montreal than the residents of the municipalities of the West Island, with the exception of Dorval and Pointe-Claire.[44] (And the same percentage of people residing in far-off Repentigny commuted to Montreal as from the close suburb of Lachine.)

In fact, in 1966, three years before the MUC was conceived, the Montreal Metropolitan Region included Laval and fifteen municipalities on the south shore.[45] So it was bizarre, from a planning perspective, to limit the MUC to the perimeter of the Island.[46] This meant that south shore Saint-Lambert, five kilometres from downtown, was excluded from the MUC, but Baie d'Urfé, on the West Island over thirty kilometres away, was included. Topographic shapes won over proximal and demographic realities. Or, more to the point, political realities trumped all others: the MUC was also delimited as a bone-throwing exercise to Mayor Drapeau, allowing him to get one-third of his One Island One City dream via the merger of regional services within the MUC. In 1999, then, we were imprisoned by this faulty decision taken in 1969. Had Laval and the south shore been included in the original MUC, Bourque would never have revived One Island One City. To turn just the Island into the MUC in 1969 made little sense; to turn it into one city thirty years later perpetuated the error.

Let us take a step back and ask what it was we were trying to do. There are four reasons to create regional bodies: (1) to supply regional services such as public transit; (2) to control urban sprawl, car use, and pollution; (3) to promote economic development and tourism; and (4) to redistribute both taxes and central costs – costs such as public housing and cultural venues. Well, it turns out that the last three jobs *must* cover the entire metropolitan region to be fair and effective. The first job of delivering services *could* be metropolitan for mass transit, but would be sub-regional for most other services, such as wastewater treatment and police. So to imagine one body that could do all four was pie-in-the-sky. This is why the Pichette Report suggested giving the services to a bunch of sub-regional agencies, and all the other jobs to a metropolitan council. There was, in my view, no portmanteau solution, as neat as that might have sounded.

The problem was that the MUC was trying to do all four jobs. Controlling urban sprawl, promoting economic development, and redistributing costs should not have been limited to the Island; making the MUC do these three jobs was unfair and ineffective. Expanding the MUC to its closest neighbours would have been a bit better, but still a palliative measure unless it covered the entire metropolitan region, by which time its first job – delivering services – would not work. Certainly to control urban sprawl, just expanding the MUC to the immediate south shore and Laval was like roping in dogies that were no longer straying. Corralling urban sprawl is a prospective, not a retrospective, job. And, moving from a bovine to an equine simile: merging the Island of Montreal was like closing the barn door after the horses had bolted from another barn years ago.

If the MUC doing all four jobs did not work, simply folding the MUC into a megacity, as we said, changed nothing. And if the plan was to have a metropolitan structure to take on the last three jobs, what was the point of the whole megacity sideshow?

Montreal's Disease: Suburban Parasites or Chronic Maladministration?

There is no greater inequality than the equal treatment of unequals.
— Felix Frankfurter, 1949

A great city is not to be confounded with a populous one. Moreover, experience shows that a very populous city can rarely, if ever, be well governed.[1]

— Aristotle, ca. 340 BC

In a Utopian society, ideas would be discussed openly and freely, with opposing arguments getting equal exposure through limpid media. "Utopia," however, etymologically means "nowhere." In the real world of the merger battle, I would have to bombard the media with an incessant barrage of heavy explosives before some shrapnel of argument was picked up by the public. On the fiscal equity issue in particular, our arguments were pretty recondite, and all too often they sounded decidedly self-serving. "One Island One City One Tax Rate" was not just a simple idea; it sounded unassailably logical and fair. I tried to get exposure for our position using the op-ed pages in the newspapers, where some sort of commerce of ideas can take place. But generally, the media traffic in "news," and "news" means reporting on the conflict of personalities, not on the conflict of ideas.

SUBURBAN PARASITES?

We lost the fiscal equity argument, and consequently we lost our municipalities. The Island suburbs were seen as parasitical, living off the City of Montreal in our "fiscal paradises." We supposedly used Montreal when we wanted to and retired to our bedroom communities when we got tired of the noise, the dirt, and the poor.

After March 1997 the campaign for One Island One City never let up until it became a reality; and almost from the outset, its main battle-cry was "fiscal equity." It was March that year when Guy Chevrette publicly complained of gross fiscal unfairness on the Island of Montreal, a theme Bourque and his five "central city" mayors highlighted at the same time in their joint brief to Premier Bouchard. While *La Presse* editorially had been banging away on the fiscal equity drum since at least 1994, other media now enthusiastically joined the band. Jean-Robert Sansfaçon, for example, wrote in *Le Devoir*: "It has become unacceptable that cities of a few tens of thousands in population systematically and systemically sponge off the central cities on which they depend, without contributing their fair share of the costs that are the lot of major centres." He invoked, as examples of such costs, social housing and the Biodome.[2]

La Presse columnist Lysiane Gagnon weighed in with her idea of merging the "élite" enclaves with Montreal, a sort of One Island Thirteen Cities: "Whenever there's a snowstorm, Outremont only has to worry about clearing its little residential streets, but it's the Montreal taxpayers who foot the bill for the clearing of the major arteries that our Outremont friends use morning, noon, and night to get to the office, theatre, or hospital. In Outremont, they are fascinated with charming problems such as what to do with the old Outremont cinema. Montrealers, on the other hand, are stuck with all the weighty problems of a major city – the only one in Quebec – a city that keeps on collecting third-world refugees, while its élites abandon it for the suburbs."[3] (Gagnon's prose got even purpler two years later when she called Montreal suburban enclaves "pockets of intolerable privileges." These "ghettos" did not "contribute to the tax base or the political life of the central city."[4])

In case anyone had missed the point, her colleague, the editorialist Agnès Gruda, wrote in the spring of 1997, "As the six cities have exposed with clarity in their brief ... real fiscal equity comes about by municipal mergers and the disappearance of urban bubbles that profit from all services without paying the price."[5]

The Union of Montreal Island Suburban Municipalities, according to another, later, Sansfaçon editorial, was an organization whose "only goal, let's face it, is to defend their privileges of rich enclaves sitting on the border of the doughnut hole of Montreal."[6]

Fiscal inequity seemed to be the worst thing to happen to Montreal since it burnt itself with the Olympic flame. Was merger indeed the only way to force surrounding communities to pay for costs that Montreal paid alone? Actually, no; as we shall see, the Montreal Metropolitan Community was created just *before* the mergers, and one of its jobs was to have the whole Montreal Metropolitan Region, *not* just the Island suburbs, pay for running social housing and regional structures such as the Biodome.

If one looks beyond the polemics and tries to quantify the central-city costs about which the editorialists got into such a lather, one discovers that the Island suburban spongers were not soaking up very much. Public housing cost the City of Montreal about $12 million, or a paltry 0.6 per cent of its annual budget.[7] Infrastructure that was at least partially used by outsiders, such as the Biodome, Parc des îles, Mount Royal Park, the Planetarium and a host of other things, supposedly cost Montreal $72 million a year[8] – and that's with a lot of lily gilding. Montreal's own studies showed that these attractions were used (very roughly) one-third by Montrealers, one-third by tourists, and one-third by other municipalities in the region. Montreal got tons of tax revenue via a commercial sector that survives on tourism. And, in the very unlikely event that tourists weren't a money-maker, Montreal should have taken the matter up with Quebec, not its neighbours. That left about $24 million to be shared by the rest of the region. And guess what? The Montreal Metropolitan Community soon started to pay Montreal that amount, along with Montreal's social housing costs. Problem solved, without merger.

What about the construction costs of these attractions? In fact, most of the so-called regional infrastructure consisted of (possibly Greek) gifts. For example, in the period 1989–93, of the $442 million invested in cultural or scientific buildings (the Museum of Fine Arts, the McCord Museum, the Biodome, Place des Arts, the Biosphere, assorted museums), the City of Montreal only contributed $24 million, the rest coming from Quebec, Ottawa, or private funding. Surprisingly, five times as much came from private sources as from the City of Montreal.[9]

As for snow removal on main streets, Montreal used its commercial sector as a cash cow; ploughing the streets in order for people to get to their offices and plants was a very small offsetting cost, given that the *total* cost of Montreal's snow removal ran at $55 million a year, or 3 per cent of its budget. Clearing of arterial roads ate up probably less than 1 per cent of the budget.

Talk about much ado about nothing: all those editorial broadsides against the Island suburbs, claiming merger was the only solution to a gross fiscal inequity that bordered on fiscal iniquity were about a piddling sum of money, on the order of $13 million.[10] Compared to the $400 million the Island suburbs were paying – in fact, *over*paying, as we'll see later – to the MUC every year for shared services, this was chicken feed. And, by 2002, had not merger intervened, the Island suburbs were to be contributing nearly $13 million to the Montreal Metropolitan Community (CMM) anyway. And which municipality got just about all of the subsidies from the CMM? Why, Montreal.

RESIDENTIAL TAX BURDENS

The fiscal equity argument was not just about equal sharing of costs, we were told; it had also to do with residents of Montreal being poorer than the residents of the Island suburbs. Montrealers could not or should not carry an equivalent property tax burden. Besides, it was argued somewhat irrelevantly, without Montreal the suburbs would not exist. At the height of the downloading crisis, Bourque blurted out in a TV interview, "Montreal has given everything, its blood ... to the suburbs. Who created the suburbs? They belonged to Montreal. Now we've become poorer because the situation has changed, the middle classes went to the suburbs. They should never forget their origins. If they work, if they have a job, it is because Montreal is there."[11] It was almost a plea to give pocket money to a parent.

There is an urban myth that it's the residents who pay municipal property taxes. In fact, in the former City of Montreal this was simply not true. Montreal residents were heavily subsidized by the commercial sector. The City of Montreal had a huge number of commercial properties, which it had always enthusiastically milked for taxes – not as much as the City of Toronto did, but that's another story. Montreal's 2001 effective commercial tax rate was two-and-a-half times its residential rate.[12]

Residents of the former City of Montreal paid only 40 per cent of all taxes.[13] Who picked up the 60 per cent? Alcan, BCE, Molson, the Bay, the Port of Montreal, the Government of Quebec, to name a few – hardly poor taxpayers. Certainly, Montrealers didn't have quite the *residential* real estate wealth of the suburbs, with their (sometimes) pricey single-family dwellings. But the former City of Montreal had something far more lucrative – a bigger *commercial* tax base that demanded little in terms of service and paid a lot in terms of taxes.*

As my favourite economist, Jacques Parizeau, once said, thousands of suburbanites work downtown, spending money and keeping alive the many commercial establishments. "These buildings, which have a huge taxation value, are not in Outremont or LaSalle."[14]

The dirty little secret of municipal taxation is that the commercial sector is the milch cow of any municipality. And, while Montreal got, overall, more from the commercial sector than the suburbs did, the tax mix in the suburbs ran the gamut from over 80 per cent of taxes coming from the non-residential sector (Montreal East and Dorval) to nearly nothing (Hampstead and Beaconsfield). *This* was fiscal inequality. *This* led to huge differences in tax rates. But did the suburbs want to merge with themselves? Of course not.

WERE, INDEED, MONTREAL'S TAX RATES HIGHER?

Since we have seen that Montreal had no significant extra burden to bear, and since the commercial sector bankrolled the city, is that the end of the fiscal equity problem? No, because those two things still don't deal with Chevrette's complaint that Montreal's tax rate was higher than rates in the Island suburbs. Why was it higher, all other things being equal? First of all, the bureaucratic Montreal administration, a massive debt load, and overpaid employees added a hefty premium to all Montreal property tax bills. But it was more than that. Let's go back to the central cities' mayors' brief to Bouchard, and the nuts and bolts of their fiscal equity argument: "The [1995] global tax rate in Outremont was $1.41, $1.62 in Saint-Laurent, and $1.44 in Brossard, compared to $2.43 in Montreal. On this basis, when differences get to 30 to 40 per cent, how can the citizen of the central city be convinced that fiscal equity exists?"[15]

Since this rhetorical question in the brief amounted to the only island of numbers in a sea of unquantified allegations, and since

---

* According to Montreal's 2000 Financial Report, fully 10 per cent of *all* its taxes came from just twenty buildings.

fiscal equity became the colours under which the urban merger battle was fought and won, I ask the reader to bear with me as I go a little deeper into this claim of "unfair" tax rates on the Island of Montreal. Specifically, we'll examine the frequent claim that Montreal had the highest global tax rate.

First of all, what on earth is the global tax rate? As French Quebecers say, "What does it eat in winter?" According to the Department of Municipal Affairs, to get the global tax rate, you add all the taxes and user-fees in a municipality and divide that number by the total of all property values. They are careful to point out that all taxes *specifically collected from the commercial sector* are to be excluded.[16] In doing the research for this book, I discovered that Montreal included revenue collected from its "water and services tax" in its global tax rate. Why am I bothering to sleuth and record such arcana ten years later? Well, this tax,[17] worth around $160 million a year, was *only* collected from the commercial sector. So it artificially inflated the global tax rate.[18]

Why not just use the plain-vanilla residential tax rate in comparing Montreal with the suburbs? Since most hand-wringing about tax fairness had to do with Montreal residents earning lower incomes than their suburban neighbours, shouldn't we be looking at the *residential* tax burden, unalloyed with the commercial or government sector? Yes. There is one problem: unlike Montreal, the suburbs (Westmount and Dorval excepted) charged residences user-fees for water supply and, in some cases, for garbage removal. The global tax rate incorporates these charges, whereas the bare residential tax rate would not have captured these amounts which ran to hundreds of dollars per house.

Because of false accounting, then, for years Montreal's tax rate was always artificially head and shoulders above those of the suburbs, nourishing the idea that Montrealers paid more in taxes and that the suburbs were *pique-assiettes*. For example, in 1999, Montreal's global tax rate was given as $2.52 – higher than the rate in any of the Island suburban municipalities. Had Montreal reported it correctly without the water and services tax, this rate would have been only $2.14. In fiscal circles, that's a gargantuan difference.[19]

So all this talk about fiscal equity, the only cure for which was merger, was based on an erroneous figure. Although I dispute their logic, the holy grail of fiscal egalitarians was to have similar tax rates in Montreal and the suburbs, or at least not have Montreal's rate the king of the castle, with the suburban dirty rascals all charging lower rates.

With Montreal's true global tax rate at $2.14, how did it compare to its neighbours? It turns out that Côte Saint-Luc, Dollard-des-Ormeaux, Hampstead, LaSalle, Montreal East, Montreal West, Pierrefonds, Sainte-Genevieve, and Verdun all had higher rates.[20] Interestingly, Montreal West, with a rate of $2.43, was a hotbed of anti-merger sentiment, even though their citizens had the most to gain fiscally by joining Montreal.

We all have a tendency to form opinions emotionally and then rationalize and solidify them by selectively capturing a few stray supporting facts fluttering by. It's even worse when the facts aren't true. Everybody, just everybody, knew in their gut that the suburbs were living off Montreal: just look at Montreal's high tax rate! Case closed. I sometimes wonder whether, had Montreal reported its true tax rate, the most powerful argument for merger would have seen the light of day. On such misunderstood details history hangs. Had suburban tax rates been compared fairly with Montreal's, perhaps One Island One City might never have happened. Perhaps.

A LOW TAX RATE DOES NOT A PARASITE MAKE

Even if there were differences in tax rates, so what? As far back as the 1976 Castonguay Report, the government has recognized that tax rate variations are inevitable: "In a given municipality, the level of overall property values determines the property tax rate. For the same basket of services, the higher the total property values, the lower the tax rate. This variation [from municipality to municipality] is in no way unfair, as property taxes, in common with all other municipal taxes, *have absolutely no role in redistributing income among taxpayers*" (my italics).[21] The key was to make sure each municipality was contributing fairly to regional costs, as we shall shortly discuss.

I have often been asked why a house in Montreal, right across the street from an identical one in Westmount, should be saddled with a higher tax rate. It was just another example of tax unfairness, was it not? Actually, no. The assessment in Montreal would likely be lower, thereby lowering the tax bill. Westmount houses command at least a 10–15 per cent premium[22] over identical houses in Montreal because of a lower tax rate and better services. Things tend to balance out – or as much so as you can get in the wacky world of municipal taxation.

TAX RATES BY THEMSELVES AREN'T THE WHOLE STORY

The tax *rate* is only part of the story: the tax bill is a product of the rate times the assessment, plus those residential water and garbage taxes. The municipal world often uses taxes on the single-family dwelling as an indication of residential tax burdens. Because of the higher assessments in many of the Island suburbs, in nearly half of the twenty-six Island municipalities the average homeowner was paying more in taxes than in Montreal – in Westmount, 2.3 times as much.[23]

In fact, lumped all together, the average Island suburban homeowner paid *substantially* more in taxes than the average Montreal homeowner, and, significantly, around double what was being paid off-Island. The real "fiscal unfairness" was therefore either found *among* the Island suburbs, or *between* the whole Island and the off-Island suburbs, none of which contributed to the MUC. What about citizens in general, not just homeowners? The average Island suburbanite was paying nearly one-third more in residential taxes than the average Montrealer.[24] The average Westmounter – adult, child, owner, or tenant* – paid $1,400 in residential property taxes in 2001 compared to $568 for the average Montrealer.[25] And were such higher Island suburban taxes simply funding sumptuous suburban services? Actually, no. In Westmount, for instance, half of the average tax bill – an amount equal to more than the Montrealer's entire bill – went to the MUC to pay for regional services such as police, public transit, and sewage treatment. Looked at another way, Westmount made up 1 per cent of the population of the MUC and paid nearly 3 per cent of its upkeep.

CONTRIBUTING TO REGIONAL SERVICES

Quebec's governing principle going all the way back to the Fiscal Reform of 1980 was that every municipal taxpayer should contribute to municipal costs based on the benefit he or she received.

---

* According to Statistics Canada, half of Westmount's dwellings are rented.

User fees should be employed wherever possible. The redistribution of wealth was not the job of municipalities. Was a Westmounter receiving nearly three times as much MUC services as a Montrealer? Clearly, no. Regional services are mostly consumed per capita, certainly not per dollar of assessment – yet the suburbs paid for their share of MUC services based on property values.

Being a quintessentially personal service, mass transit use has absolutely nothing to do with the value of a taxpayer's property. (Unfortunately, there is a negative correlation.) It's about as relevant as tying transit use to the value of one's furniture or stamp collection. Sewage treatment is likewise a function of population, not assessments. If your house is worth twice as much, you don't put twice as much down your toilets. And police? Breaking-and-entering rates often vary *inversely* with real estate value. Other than protecting against burglaries, police protect people against other people, drugs, and stolen or speeding cars.

Actually, Montrealers consumed even more regional services than their population would have suggested. Just about all the metro system was within the boundaries of the City of Montreal: this was simply a matter of population density and ridership. And 63 per cent of the police in community stations were deployed in Montreal, which had 57 per cent of the Island population. This deployment was three-fifths based on the number of residents and shops, one-fifth based on how much violent crime was committed in a given district.[26] One could argue that the commercial sector in Montreal benefits from a peaceful, crime-free environment that is accessible by metro as much as does Montreal's residential sector. You could also argue that the Island suburbs also benefited from a safe and accessible downtown. That is true, but so was it true for off-Island residents who paid nothing, and pay nothing today, for such advantages.

Regional services are consumed in proportion to the number of people in a municipality, or the population density, or anything else you want to name, but certainly not in proportion to the value of real estate they own. Since no one this side of Margaret Thatcher would suggest a poll tax, the MUC in effect had to charge for regional services based on property values rather than use. What else could they do? Montrealers thus wound up paying for 55 per cent of the MUC's costs while consuming over 65 per cent of its services.

Not only were the suburbs paying for regional services but they were contributing more that they were receiving, with Montreal as the beneficiary. Yet the PQ, with a bevy of editorialists right behind them, never stopped in their brainwashing campaign to convince people that Westmounters and all the other Island suburbanites were parasites living in splendid isolation off all that largesse that others provided.

LOCAL COSTS

So regional costs were paid for by the suburbs – actually, more than paid for. What about Montreal's local costs, things like recreation, parks, street maintenance, garbage collection, and snow removal? Should not suburbanites have helped pay for those too? Suburban-ites, after all, used Montreal's roads and parks, some argued. But proportionally, far more Montrealers used Westmount's roads and parks than the reverse, although Westmount was probably an extreme case.[27] Should Westmounters help pay for snow removal from residential Montreal streets when Montrealers did not contrib-ute to Westmounters' snow removal costs? Of course not. Should Westmounters' pay for Montrealers' telephones or roof repairs?

But others said suburbanites must contribute to Montreal's local costs, because Montreal is and was the home of the poor, the old, the alone, the homeless, and the immigrant. Montreal had the social problems, the suburbs had the barbecues. Of all the arguments in favour of "helping out" Montreal, this was the most poignant and convincing, even though a number of suburbs such as Montreal North and Verdun were not exactly strangers to this kind of social makeup. Professor Andrew Sancton came up with the best response to this argument: "No one wants to promote or defend a system of municipal government that favours the rich and puts undue burdens on the poor. Unlike the situation in Ontario, Quebec municipal-ities have virtually no role in social services and none in relation to income security. Wealthy Montrealers cannot escape paying for social services by moving to a suburb ... The City of Montreal prob-ably bears fewer costs of central-city poverty than almost any other such major central city in North America."[28]

In 1997 the government asked the municipalities in the region to list all the infrastructure, services, and activities that were of a regional nature. Naturally, Montreal threw everything it could think of into its list. Along with the Biodome et al., Montreal listed "home-lessness" and "metropolitan social problems," which together did not even add up to $1 million. They represented 0.04 per cent of Montreal's budget.[29]

There is some indication that indirect demand on services caused by poverty is greater than the direct costs.[30] Many of these indirect costs, however, are regional costs such as policing and mass transit, which, as we have seen, were already subsidized by the Island suburbs.

In no way do I wish to minimize the social problems that the *area* as opposed to the *municipality* of the City of Montreal had to bear. They were real. In 1996, the average household income in the metropolitan region surrounding Montreal was nearly 50 per cent higher than in the City of Montreal itself.[31] This was partially the result of the middle-class francophone exodus from the Island of Montreal; as well, 45 per cent of immigrants to Quebec settled in the city; 75 per cent of Montrealers were tenants.[32] One-quarter of households in Montreal were on welfare. And one-quarter of all Quebec families getting welfare lived in Montreal.[33] Jean Doré, the former mayor of Montreal, used to tell me that the way the regions in Quebec got rid of their poor was to give them a one-way bus ticket to Montreal. The same happened in New York City. However, dealing with this tremendous social rift was not a municipal responsibility.

Succinctly put, then: should the suburbs have subsidized Montreal's local as well as regional costs? My response is that Montreal's commercial sector was already subsidizing the residential tax burden. If that was not enough to provide an acceptable level of local services because of widespread poverty, the province should have funded the difference through the income tax system. And there is, after all, a limit as to how much municipalities can milk their commercial taxpayers before they up and move elsewhere.

If property taxes *are* to be awkwardly and unfairly forced into the role of wealth redistribution even for local services, and if this indeed was the reason for mergers, then why did Laval and the north and south shores escape merger with Montreal?

A TAX BREAK

A short digression on how property taxes operate is now overdue. An American magazine once ran a contest for the most boring headline. "Worthwhile Canadian Initiative" won. "Property Tax Explained" would have been a close second. All Canadians complain about property taxes, like the weather, but know no more about how they work than they do about meteorology. Property taxes are nearly as complicated (and as accurate) as weather forecasting. Besides, it is human nature to avoid understanding unpleasant things. Edmund Burke said it best: "To tax and to please, no more than to love and be wise, is not given to men."

The Assessment Dartboard

Local taxation starts off simply enough: your yearly property tax bill is the product of your municipality's tax rate times the value of your property. In the same way, your yearly income tax bill is the sum of the product of various tax rates times your income. The value of your property is guessed at *in absentia* by the city assessor; your income is precisely as reported by your employer. Now, since the city assessor rarely sees your house, your property value is pretty much pulled out of thin air, although it is influenced by actual sales of supposedly "similar" properties. Especially in neighbourhoods with a variety of housing styles, and in the country, the assessed value can be off by as much as 50 per cent above or below the market value.[34]

So, right off the bat, property taxes are a bit of a crap shoot. If your employer over-assessed your income, you would be enraged at tax time. If it were under-assessed, you would say nothing but think the system stinks. But since no one's property is precisely assessed, *all* property taxpayers are paying either too much or too little – by a long chalk. Someone called it the "assessment dartboard." This is not meant to be a criticism of assessors, whom I have found to be very competent. There are just nowhere near enough of them, and if there were, it would prove prohibitively expensive.

Another quirk of this assessment dartboard is that, in Quebec, all updated assessments are supposed to reflect what a building could have sold for, had it been sold a year and a half prior. This means that, if assessments are in force for three years, a given property is taxed based on an estimated value up to four-and-a-half years old.[35] So the rock-solid foundation upon which Quebec property taxation is based is the selling price you could have got for your property had you sold it up to nearly five years before, in lieu of which you're taxed on a guesstimate arrived at by an assessor, probably sight unseen, this guesstimate essentially being based on houses that did sell in your neighbourhood, along with any improvements you might have made to your property – that is, if you were honest enough to tell the municipality about them. So the darts are hitting your valuation dartboard only though ricochets, and some numbers on the dartboard are up to you to declare. The situation is similar in other provinces and countries.

The dartsman has a thankless job. In my experience, assessors habitually under-assess, no fool they. People who feel their property is undervalued are hardly going to request a formal revision. Now, if all properties were *uniformly* under-assessed, it would make no difference to their tax bill, as the tax rate would be simply set higher. Where things get unfair is when some are under-assessed by much more than others. It happens all the time. If one property is assessed at 45 per cent of its market value, and an identical property is assessed at 90 per cent, the latter owner will pay twice as much in taxes. And all the time he may be secretly congratulating himself on being under-assessed.

Even today it is not unknown for houses to sell for double their assessment, which means the lucky ex-owners were paying half the taxes they should have been paying – assuming, that is, everyone else's assessments were accurate. If it were discovered that even a few people routinely paid income tax on only one-half their income, Canadian taxpayers would indignantly rise up and demand a root-and-branch revision of income tax collection. The degree to which citizens put up with the gross inaccuracies of local property taxes never ceases to amaze me.

What happens when the whole property market changes? If everyone in Canada woke up one golden morning and found their income had doubled, governments would immediately have to cut income tax rates by half. Because in the real world incomes rise more or less in sync with the economy, income tax rates are pretty much constant. Locally, it is another story. Property values can burble along unchanged for a decade, then all of a sudden skyrocket. When this happens, municipalities drop the property tax rate in the same proportion that the values increased. In other words, if values ever suddenly doubled, the tax rate should be halved; otherwise the municipality would be benefiting from undue enrichment. This is why tax rates alone are meaningless, unlike income tax rates. Property assessments alone are likewise meaningless. It is only the product of the two – assessments *and* values – that means anything at all. It's a bit like a seesaw: if you push up on one end, the other must go down, as long as the fulcrum of constant revenue is fixed.

After a period of geyser-like growth from 1981 to 1993, and then the Sargasso Sea of stagnant property assessments from 1993 to 2001,[36] we were back to surging prices from 2001 to 2007 – in common with property values all over the world.[37] It's a terrible way to run a railroad, having such a volatile base for revenues. Right now, 58 per cent of local revenues in Quebec come from taxes based on property values,[38] thankfully down from 70 per cent in 1981. Unfortunately, on the Island of Montreal, taxes in 2005 were still running at 67 per cent of total revenues.[39]

How Should We Pluck the Goose?

How *should* municipalities get the money they need to run their operations? It is generally accepted that there are two ways to tax: based on someone's ability to pay, or on the benefit received (that is, services consumed).

Taxes, at least income taxes, at the provincial and federal level are easy to understand. You're taxed according to your ability to pay, not on how much government services you consume. Are property taxes, too, a measure of someone's ability to pay? The intuitive answer is "yes," as it is assumed that richer people own more expensive houses, and many people thus see property taxes as a kind of a wealth tax. But wealth taxes – in those countries that have them – are usually levied by the central government in conjunction with income taxes, and they apply to all sorts of assets, including jewellery, cars, and boats. Wealth taxes[40] are purely redistributive and have nothing to do with providing services.

Property taxes were around well before sales and income taxes, in the days when property owners were perforce rich – and were the only voters – and such a static tax was easy to collect. Today, the property tax is a hoary appendix that most experts admit does not accurately measure ability to pay. It is the middle class who have most of their capital tied up in their house, not the rich.

The universally accepted way to measure "ability to pay" is income. So if municipal taxes were supposed to reflect ability to pay, then we should simply institute a municipal income tax as permitted in sixteen US states.[41]

What Did Quebec Mean by "Fiscal Equity"?

But that's not the way Quebec sees things: according to the 1980 Fiscal Reform and all subsequent policy statements, you are supposed to pay municipal taxes in Quebec based on the benefit received, *not* on your ability to pay. Income redistribution is the role of "higher" levels of government.

Why is this distinction important? Since "fiscal equity" was touted as the main goal of municipal mergers in Quebec, we need to know precisely what was meant by that term. Luckily, in a recent publication,[42] the government takes the trouble to define municipal fiscal equity as either "horizontal equity" (taxpayers in identical situations should be taxed identically) or "vertical equity" (taxpayers with a greater ability to pay should pay more).

Under the principle of horizontal equity, we read there are two applications: "(1) taxpayers in the same municipality must pay the same amount of taxes when their tax base is the same; and (2) each taxpayer contributes to the cost of services according to the benefits received from them, to the extent possible."

Under the principle of vertical equity, we read that "In the context where the redistribution of wealth is not the role of municipalities, the criterion of vertical equity is irrelevant to municipal taxation."

That's it, then: fiscal equity means paying municipal taxes according to benefits received. And therefore (Quebec said) mergers result in a better adequation between taxes and services consumed. But do they?

Most local taxes in Quebec are charged to taxpayers based on the value of their property, both land and building, and this is supposed to reflect the value of services received. It does not. *There is absolutely no relationship between the value of one's building and the value of services a property owner receives.*[43] If house values go up compared to, say, apartments, they don't suddenly consume more services. Building values decline relentlessly as they age, regardless of fluctuations in municipal services consumed.

In fact, all services are delivered to *people*. Ghost towns cost nothing to run; shantytowns do. Bricks and mortar don't consume services. Buildings don't use roads, take buses, or play tennis on municipal courts. However, if the consumers are more dispersed because they own more land, then the cost of delivering those services to them is increased. So a good case can be made for taxing owners for *some* services based on the size of their land.[44]

If building value were such a fair way to charge for government services, why not pay for highways by charging vehicle owners a tax based on the value of their vehicle? The more expensive the car or truck, the more tax they would pay. The degree to which they *used* the roads would be irrelevant, so vehicle weight, size, or odometer readings would not be a factor in computing that tax. Assessors would visit the car from time to time to determine its market value. A ridiculous idea? Yet that's the way we charge for municipal services: not by measured services consumed but simply by property value. And municipalities can do nothing about it because the province has complete power over how they can and cannot tax.

The Tax Tale of Sainte-Typique

Imagine, if you will, the fictitious Quebec dormitory town of Sainte-Typique,* with 1,000 identical clapboard houses, each owned by a couple with no children. Let's say each house has its land valued at $125,000 and its building valued at $125,000. So the total value of Sainte-Typique's real estate is $250 million. And let's say it cost $5 million to run Sainte-Typique: $2 for every $100 of valuation. Each homeowner, therefore, pays $5,000 in taxes. So far, so good.

Now, let's say exactly half the population of Sainte-Typique gets bitten with Martha Stewart fever and puts granite in their kitchens, marble in their bathrooms, and brick on the outside of their houses. After a visit by the assessor, their houses are declared to be worth $125,000 more. So total Sainte-Typique real estate is now pegged at $312 million. But since it doesn't cost the municipality a cent more to provide services, it can drop the tax rate to $1.60 per $100 of evaluation to get the same $5 million to run the municipality. This means the Martha Stewart fans with $375,000 houses are now saddled with a permanent $1,000 yearly increase in their taxes, and the lucky Philistines with tacky kitchens and bathrooms

---

* Believe it or not, 44 per cent of names of Quebec municipalities begin with Saint or Sainte. When the rather pious Claude Ryan was minister of municipal affairs, he was called the saint of the Saints.

see their taxes drop by $1,000, or 20 per cent. Yet both consume an equal amount of municipal services. So, if my neighbour fixes up his house, my taxes go down. This is how the municipal tax system actively discourages home renovation and rewards home neglect. What if half of Sainte-Typique homeowners decide to double the size of their houses? The result would be the same. They would not use any more municipal services (except possibly for a small theoretical increase in fire protection) but would be stuck with the same 20 per cent increase in taxes.

If half of Sainte-Typique homeowners doubled the size of their *land*, the cost of road, water, sewer infrastructure and their maintenance would be greater. And more buses would have to be laid on to service the same number of people, garbage trucks would have to go further, and the number of fire stations would have to be increased. So the increase in their taxes – through a $125,000 increase in valuation – would at least be somewhat tied to their increase in their consumption of services.

Now what would happen if half of Sainte-Typique houses were homes to four rather than two people? Those dwellings would use more water and give off more wastewater (flushing and bathing twice as much), and their garbage volume would double. They would cause an increase in police numbers, in buses, in the size of the arena and library. But all Typiquois would pay for these things. The more populated households would only pay for half of the cost increase rather than the whole amount. So much for paying according to the benefit received.

But the real aberration (and bonanza) would happen the day Sainte-Typique got commercial or industrial enterprises to locate there. There would be a fairly minor increase in most municipal costs, but, in keeping with standard practice, the commercial tax rate would be something like $5 per $100 of property value. These new corporate citizens with effectively no voting power would heavily subsidize the residential sector. Talk about taxation without representation, and taxation not according to benefit received.

Let's add one more scenario. Go back to the original Sainte-Typique, with the 1,000 homes valued at $125,000 for land and $125,000 for buildings. What if Sainte-Typique merged with Sainte-Atypique, a municipality with 1,000 homes with the same land value, but with buildings worth $375,000? Aside from a possibly greater budget for recreational services demanded by the more pretentious

Atypiquois, the two municipalities would have roughly the same operating costs before the merger, but one would have $250 million of real estate value, and the other $500 million. So before the merger, Sainte-Atypique would have had a tax rate of $1 per $100 of evaluation. After the merger, the tax rate of the new town would be $10 million divided by $750 million, or $1.33 per $100 of evaluation: a one-third tax *increase* for the former residents of Sainte-Atypique and a one-third *reduction* for the former residents of Sainte-Typique. Yet the consumption of services remains the same.

Such are the vagaries of a tax system based on building values, and the reason why mergers do not bring about any sort of fiscal equity – as defined by the Quebec government itself.

What to Do?

Like it or not, we live in a North American context where property taxes are part of the fiscal scene. What we can do is follow US practice and reduce our dependency on property taxes. One-third of local government revenues in the United States are user fees.[45] We could re-institute a municipal sales tax, even a municipal income tax. We can meter water* and garbage.† We can charge for roads and sewers based on a property-owner's land area. Recreational services – the one thing often at least partially covered by user fees – should be charged for. Once we have done this, and perhaps got motorists to pay more for public transit, as they are its greatest beneficiaries, we would have downgraded property taxes to a minor role. The subsidization of the residential by the commercial sector would be eased as well.

---

* Montreal never metered residential water consumption because it's a political hot-button item, especially for tenants, who represent around 70 per cent of their voters. Of course, it's an illogical and anti-ecological policy: residents are metered for natural gas, heating oil, and electricity based on consumption; why not for water? Since 50 per cent of residential consumption is for exterior use, the house-owner would probably foot most of the bill, although a City of Montreal document, *Harmonisation de la fiscalité*, claims apartment dwellers use more water per capita than homeowners.

† In 1993, for fiscal and ecological reasons, I mounted a one-man campaign in favour of user fees for non-recycled garbage, known as pay-as-you-throw. I championed "garbage metering" by weight while appearing as the main guest on the *Droit de parole* TV program, 14 October 1993.

While property taxes are simple on the surface – owners are taxed a percentage of the value of their real estate – they are far from easy to understand in operation. In fact, I am not sure if *anyone* fully understands property taxes and their complex effects. Since the goal of "tax fairness" was behind the creation of the megacities in Quebec, it remains important to understand this rather fiddly subject. During the whole debate on mergers, I got the feeling that the less people knew about property taxes, the stronger they came out in favour of mergers.

While the architects of Fiscal Reform back in 1980 tried to make some sense out of this complex skein of taxation, subsequent ministers have made a hash of their work. In that great, highly decorated fiscal edifice, municipal tax structures are somewhere in the basement. Politicians who would never dare scale the heights of international fiscal theory think nothing of mucking about with local taxation. It must be simple, they reason; after all it *is* only local taxation.

CHRONIC MALADMINISTRATION?

The *Journal de Montréal* once ran a cartoon of Bourque standing knee-deep in shit, holding up a flowery sign that read, "One Island One City," and asking sweetly, "What do the suburban mayors have against it?" Why were the Island suburbs so against One Island One City? Simply put, we did not want to be part of Montreal. To us Montreal represented chronic maladministration. It had an ingrained culture of giantism that had forever fostered a fixation on size, a political party system and public unaccountability, mismanagement and corruption, gross overspending, overpaid employees, and a spiralling debt. Let's examine each of these accusations in turn.

Montreal's Manifest Destiny

Montreal has always been fixated on its size. From 1861 to 1891 the population within the original city limits doubled, but thereafter it started to level out at only 1 per cent per year.[46] What to do? It decided to annex its suburbs, as they were growing by about 6 per cent per year.[47] From 1883 to 1918, Montreal annexed twenty-three suburbs, thereby growing geographically fivefold [48] and demograph-

ically over threefold.[49] The bumper year of 1910 brought in ten former suburban municipalities representing half the acreage collected
during the thirty-five-year annexation spree. The annexation commissioners wrote boastfully, "If the pace continues like this, in a few
years, the City of Montreal will cover the whole Island and perhaps
become the biggest city in North America."[50]

The fattening up of Montreal came at a price: financial indiges-
tion. By 1896, interest payments were consuming 35 per cent of
Montreal's budget.[51] Even though most of the annexations were
voluntary – the targets being in parlous financial shape – Montreal
often promised the municipal equivalent of the moon to sweeten
the deal, as well as taking over the annexees' debt. You want water
mains and sewers? No problem. Streets fixed up? Get rid of toll
gates? Just sign here. Notre Dame de Grâce was a case in point. This
1910 annexation deal with Montreal not only required Montreal to
take over a $1.1 million debt, but committed it to spend $1 million
on streets within three years, plus build three fire and police stations
and a public hall.[52] In all, Montreal's debt ballooned by $28 million
because of annexations.[53] While the province forced Montreal into
making quite a few of them, it was a small price to pay for greatness.

From 1861 to 1941, Montreal managed consistently to corral over
80 per cent of the population of the entire metropolitan region,[54]
thanks to internal growth from 1861 to 1881 and to the 1883–1918
annexations. It became habituated to dominating the regional scene
and throwing its weight around. But by 1951, its population was 73
per cent of that of the metropolitan census region, and by 1956, 69
per cent. By 1960, something was clearly wrong. This was confirmed
in 1961: the Dominion Bureau of Statistics said Montreal was down
to 57 per cent[55] of the region. There had been no annexations since
1918 and, as was happening all over postwar North America, the
suburbs were exploding with growth.

It was time, Montreal figured, for a new injection of suburbs to
bulk up and preserve its relative regional weight and sense of self-
worth. Led by Mayor Jean Drapeau, this time it wanted the whole
thing: One Island One City. When Westmount and others said, "No
thanks," Montreal almost petulantly annexed Rivière-des-Prairies,
Saraguay, and Saint-Michel (Pointe-aux-Trembles was annexed two
decades later). Even though these annexations added about 120,000
citizens,[56] Montreal continued to watch its population drop relative to the region, like a shareholder helplessly witnessing a stock

plummet on the big board: 50 per cent in 1966, 44 per cent in 1971, 35 per cent in 1981,[57] and 31 per cent in 1996.

But the 1960s also saw the strong-arm approach to annexation: the forced merger of fourteen towns and villages on Île Jésus that produced the first "One Island One City," the City of Laval (no temporary structure like the MUC for Laval). The "success" of Laval, even though its creation was strongly resisted, was systematically held up as an example of the virtues of forced mergers. Hold your nose, take your medicine; it will all be worth it. Today Laval is one of the most heavily indebted municipalities in Quebec. A quintessential bedroom community, it has no downtown and is run as a benign suzerainty by Mayor Gilles Vaillancourt. In short, Laval had nothing to teach us about the advisability of merging mature, self-reliant Montreal Island municipalities. It was cobbled together from a collection of small villages, of which only three had even a roads department.

The 1960s ended with the MUC. It was either annexation or the imposition of the MUC – take your poison – according to Dr Robert Lussier, the minister of municipal affairs and "father" of urban communities in Quebec. And so Drapeau did, at least partially, get his dream: the creation of the MUC could be seen as a step toward total merger, in that some services were pooled. You might say it was One Island One-Third City. It just took thirty more years to get to One Island One Whole City.

The Political Party System

City of Montreal and MUC council meetings were both held in the cavernous interior of Montreal's council chamber. Because of the room's size, the chairman's carved throne, and the countless phalanxes of politicians in green leather armchairs, this council chamber resembles more than anything else a parliamentary assembly, and that's precisely the way it operates. This huge box of a room appears to have been designed for the sole purpose of producing echoes. Its builders seemed to favour noise over light, a preference emulated by the partisan beneficiaries of their labours. Mercury-vapour light fixtures gave off a desultory greenish glow so weak that reading glasses were mandatory equipment, even for people like me who were denying advancing age. The media and visitors used to be placed in a gallery twenty feet above the floor. From this eyrie in the gods, they looked down on their politicians in the pits. Even during MUC meetings, the opposition parties of the City of Montreal provided the only debate, which was partisan in the extreme. It wasn't really debate but rather point-scoring. Because of the party system, the "leader of the opposition" did his or her job: oppose.

Like Toronto and most of "English" Canada, the anglophone suburbs (but few francophone ones) had no political parties. In those municipalities, the mayor built consensus rather than imposing it. Since Drapeau, Montreal has been saddled with political parties that made local governing uneven, opaque, and partisan. They have done nothing for electoral turnout or debate: in 1966 less than one-third of voters bestirred themselves to vote, and Drapeau's councillors got 94 per cent of the council seats.[58] Parties led to other distortions: in 1978, Drapeau's party got 96 per cent of the seats with only 55 per cent of the ballots cast.[59]

Unlike mayors Drapeau, Bourque, and Tremblay, Jean Doré led a real party with real policies, as opposed to a political party created around the personality of one man. Although his political appointees were, of necessity, mostly left-wingers with precious little management exposure, they were principled and hardworking and also very bright.

Bourque was the master of the nonce party. People joined, quit, or were thrown out of it with great regularity. It was the political equivalent of Brownian motion. Bourque proved that parties have no place in municipal politics. They were an artificiality introduced by Drapeau to suit his own designs. The instant personal party syndrome results, at least in its first electoral win, in a grab-bag of newly minted councillors, many of whom never expected to get elected. (Former prime minister Brian Mulroney was familiar with that experience.) Back in 1995 I was constantly amazed at the amateurism of Bourque and his claque. I realized that Canadian local governments were gelded and therefore did not attract top-flight people, but this was proof by exaggeration. The first chairman of Bourque's executive committee, Noushig Eloyan, had neither political nor discernable management experience. Then Bourque put Kettly Beauregard in charge of the MUC police (since it was Montreal's turn). He chose her because "she was black and that would look good," he confided, no doubt hoping I would comprehend this political stroke of genius. While charming, Beauregard was out of her depth. Two hours into one MUC executive meeting, it dawned on her she had been trying to follow the *last* meeting's agenda. If average citizens had watched Bourque's circus in action, they would have demanded that Montreal, with its $1.8 billion budget, be put immediately into trusteeship.

Bourque finally managed to get a superb chairman of his executive committee in 1999: Jean Fortier. While not the most diplomatic of people, Fortier was exceedingly competent. It didn't take long, however, for Bourque to find him not nearly pliant enough, and their relationship deteriorated. A disciple of the Drapeau school of mayoring, Bourque was only comfortable with yes-men around him.

Then there is the darker side of party politics. According to Éric Trottier of *La Presse*,[60] writing about Bourque's party and his regime, "Once again, among the most important donors of Vision Montreal in 2001, one finds the contractors who, under the *ancien régime*, got the biggest concrete and asphalt contracts."[61]

Mismanagement and Corruption

One of the most flagrant examples of mismanagement in the City of Montreal was Montreal's Club Med. The "Med" stood for *mise en disponibilité*: employees put on leave of absence. In 1997, 719 city employees were getting paid while the city tried to decide what to do with them.[62] The overall cost of this boondoggle was probably in the neighbourhood of $50 million a year, enough to run the entire City of Westmount.

Louis Roquet, once director-general of the MUC, was lured away by Doré to become the director-general of the City of Montreal. When Bourque replaced Doré as mayor in November 1994, he promptly dumped Roquet, saying Montreal didn't need a director-general.[63] Bourque had all the department heads report to the politicians directly, which meant that he, a former functionary himself, was both political and administrative head of a municipality of one million. In contrast, most municipalities in North America have a director-general, except they call them city managers. Bourque's reshuffling caused the number of departments to double. Yet, to get elected in 1994, he had promised to cut spending by $100 million and to freeze taxes.[64] The opposite happened.

Under increasing pressure from Quebec, Bourque finally re-established the position of director-general. But where to get one? Why, back at the old hunting ground, the MUC. By that time the

MUC had promoted Gérard Divay to DG, so Bourque did a Doré by poaching Divay from the MUC and installing him as DG of Montreal. That too only lasted a couple of years. Divay had the misfortune to take his job seriously and in November 1998 wrote a scathing report on the state of management at Montreal City Hall. He called its organizational vision dysfunctional, archaic, and "profoundly sclerotic." In case the point wasn't clear, he added there was "an absence of strategic planning, ignorance about their clients, a permanently antagonistic labour relations climate, and all employees identified with their union rather than the city." There was "a refusal to compare with others owing to a fear of the result."[65] Bourque dealt with the problem by firing Divay.

The 1999 Bédard Report referred to Montreal's management problems, along with its spending habits. Using its figures, one can calculate that Montreal in 1996 spent 67 per cent more per capita than smaller municipalities (population 5,000 to 100,000). One should remove from this the cost of water supplied to other municipalities ($25 million). And, as we saw, public housing, homelessness, and social problems cost Montreal $13 million per year. Even with these items removed, Montreal spent 64 per cent more than smaller municipalities. This comparison is not really fair as it includes municipalities outside metropolitan areas, but even comparing Montreal's spending with the twenty next-largest municipalities, it was still 28 per cent more.[66] Economies of scales fall from our eyes – or they should.

As far as I can make out, with the exception of Charles Duquette (1924–26), nobody with any high-level business experience has sat in the mayor's chair in Montreal in the last hundred years. While the first fifty years saw generally corrupt Montreal mayors, the last fifty have seen spendthrift or ineffectual mayors. No mayor has ever really cleaned up the Augean stables of an out-of-control bureaucracy and overpaid employees. Especially in the last fifty years, we got lots of "dreams" and "visions" but no rolled-up sleeves. One or two myopic mayors whose field of vision was limited to potholes, garbage-strewn streets, or the number of zeros on municipal bonds would not have gone amiss.

For fifty-five of the hundred years between 1908 and 2008, three mayors ruled over Montreal: Médéric Martin, Camillien Houde, and Jean Drapeau. The populist mayor Médéric Martin, (1914–24, 1926–28) "presided over a thoroughly corrupt and virtually bankrupt city administration."[67] As for "Mr Montreal," Camillien Houde, who served as mayor in spurts for over fifteen years from 1928 to 1954, his Montreal "was noted for its almost totally corrupt city government."[68] Twice during his mayoralty, Montreal was placed in trusteeship. In spite of his huge bulk, Houde wanted to be known as the little guy from the Sainte-Marie neighbourhood (*p'tit gars de Sainte-Marie*); in other words, he was another working-class populist. While Jean Drapeau (1954–57, 1960–86) was not working class, he too was a populist. Completely incorruptible and personally ascetic, Drapeau was flamboyant in his ideas, not in his person – and very authoritarian.

The endemic mismanagement of Montreal created fertile ground for corruption. The former police chief, Jacques Duchesneau, once retired, said, "The gangrene doesn't only affect the politicians, but also the staff, who give out contracts and receive treats." One minister of transport, he said, told him it was common knowledge in his department that the City of Montreal paid 15 per cent too much for its contracts. Suppliers complained they could not sell their products to the city unless they were part of the "clique."[69]

A Culture of Spending and Grandiosity

"The masses need monuments," Drapeau said, and he delivered. In her article "Drapeau the Magnificent," Susan Purcell says the 1976 Montreal Olympic Games cost $1.3 billion, four times its original budget.[70] To that one must add the $1 billion it cost to build the Olympic Stadium,[71] another legacy of Drapeau's spendthrift years. The stadium came in at nearly twenty times the 1972 estimate of $55 million.[72] Thirty years after its construction – and thirty years after it should have been demolished – it needs its third roof, at a cost of at least $300 million. In today's dollars the Olympic spending orgy cost $9 billion, enough to run the megacity of Montreal for two years or to give a property tax holiday to all Montreal Island residents for three years. Since Drapeau left Quebec with the tab, perhaps a more appropriate illustration of the Olympian waste would be to say that avoiding it would have paid for four new superhospitals. Today we can't seem to afford two.

Forty or fifty years ago the Ontario political and social élite worshipped everything British. Quebec atavistically looked a few hundred kilometres further east. Drapeau, in common with most of the

Quebec francophone élite at the time, thought that Paris was the epitome of all that was sophisticated, so that for Quebec to slough off its hick past, all it had to do was slavishly follow whatever was in vogue in France. This colonial cultural inferiority led to his choosing for the Olympic Stadium a Parisian architect who came up with a design totally impractical for our climate and far too rich for our pocketbooks. When French designs are good, they are very, very good, and when they are bad, they are horrid. Montreal is pathetically reduced to telling tourists that the Olympic Stadium has the "world's tallest inclined tower."

This same blind worship for things French led to Drapeau's decision to build metro rolling stock modelled after that in Paris, its narrow wagons no doubt considered wide when its metro was first built in 1900. And what was the latest in metro technology when Drapeau visited Paris in the late 1950s? Why, rubber-tired metro cars, so we had to have some. These cars have three sets of wheels: the main rubber tires, a full set of steel wheels in case of a puncture; and, lastly, horizontally mounted guide wheels to ensure the rubber tires stay on track. This type of running gear condemned the metro forever to run underground, never seeing the light of day even where tunnelling was unnecessary.[73] We were also condemned to pay for blown tires and the capital costs of the steel rails for the steel wheels, the precast concrete rails for the rubber tires, and the steel guide bars for the horizontal guide wheels. To be fair, our metro cars are quieter, can rapidly climb inclines, and have great acceleration and braking – but at what price?

The man who flipped the switch to start the first train going in 1966 was a minister of state for the French Republic, an emissary of Charles de Gaulle. The deliriousness that initially surrounded the Montreal metro is hard to fathom today. In 1967, the minister of transport produced a map of what the metro would look like fifteen years on.[74] It had 270 stations, four times what we have today and equal to the number of stations in the longest metro in the world, London (which, after all, had a hundred-year head start). Of course, in 1967, urban planners were predicting the Montreal Metropolitan Region would have a population of seven million by 2000, the population of London today.

When I first moved to Montreal from drab Toronto in 1968, I loved the style and dash of the metro. Its architecture contrasted with the toilet-tile sameness of the Toronto subway. And on the

Bonaventure expressway, the highway lights embedded in the concrete side barriers a few feet above grade lit up the road surface so elegantly – until one winter's worth of de-icing salt corroded them and they all had to be ripped out. I began to realize that the exuberance of Expo-era Montreal I found so thrilling came with a huge price tag.

Montreal's metro stations, the pride of us all when built, look a bit down-at-the-heel today. Each is uniquely designed, each station having its own style of bench, whether concrete, polymer concrete, fibreglass, or stainless steel. Every station has its own wall and floor tile. This serial architectural smorgasbord does not wear well. The garish 1960s colours, the 1970s sand-blasted concrete, the 1980s flame-treated granite today look pretty dated. And when these one-off benches, tiles, or rubbish bins have to be replaced, they are unsurprisingly no longer manufactured. For example, the company I started, Plastibeton Inc., received contracts to manufacture parts of metro interiors in the 1970s and 1980s. In Villa Maria station, we made the red, orange, and yellow polymer concrete seats and huge decorative wheels. Similar stuff went into the Côte-Ste-Catherine and Plamondon stations. Such limited production runs for each station meant prohibitive costs at the outset and a continuing headache when repairs or replacements became necessary. The practical standardization adopted by most other subway systems would have looked better in the long run and cost a fraction for upkeep.

What is the relevance today of Drapeau's penchant for lavish spending, grandiosity, and a fetish for La France? Except for a few holdouts in the PQ, apron-string Gallomania among French Quebecers is pretty much dead. But buying the vote by giving out bread and staging circuses, or trying to buy Montreal's way to world stature still crop up. The difference is that the Quebec government will not play, refusing to be burned twice. Besides, the province's debt ballooned from 12 per cent of total economic output in 1972 to 52 per cent in 1998.[75] There was simply no money left to bail out Montreal. So today, thankfully, these things are done on a smaller scale. But the FINA swimming championships, the Outgames in 2006, the on-and-off Formula One Grand Prix race, and the continuing myth of the touristy drawing power of the Casino are all examples of Montreal's desperate desire to make the world sit up and take notice, rather than concentrating on the mundane job of making sure the city is well run and preventing, rather than filling, potholes. Clean up our city and its infrastructure, and the world will beat a path to our door. We don't need extravagant gimmicks.

Why have Montrealers put up with such spendthrift city councils? It is partially because of the huge proportion of tenants in Montreal. Tenants do not pay property taxes directly and are unaware of how much their rent is made up of taxes: the average Montreal tenant pays roughly one-fifth the tax bill of the average homeowner. There is thus no incentive for tenants to rein in a mayor's spending extravaganzas. To the contrary, they generally encourage them, as they cost tenants – nominally – nothing. Since businesses paid 60 per cent of all property taxes in Montreal, they, plus the small number of residents who were homeowners, were the ones on the hook.

For the 110 years from 1861 to 1971, the proportion of the dwellings in the City of Montreal that were rented never dropped below 80 per cent. Thirty years later, just before the megacity, this figure had slowly dropped to 72 per cent, and in 2006, in the former city, was at 69 per cent. Montreal still and has always had the highest percentage of tenants of any Canadian city.[76] The explanation for this high rate of tenants is not just that Montrealers are generally poorer: rent is also cheap. You can rent a one-bedroom apartment in the centre of Montreal for $600 a month.[77] As long as rent control keeps rents down, there is little incentive even for better-off residents to buy. As apartment houses are poorly maintained and represent a low rate of return on investment, there is also a depressing effect on property values and hence city revenues.

Tenants tend to move quite a bit, and some are what Lewis Mumford called "urban nomads." Understandably, they take less of an interest in their neighbourhood and rarely get involved in municipal politics. This is not meant as a criticism: I behaved in the same way when I was a tenant in Montreal. It's just that such a high rate of renters is not politically and fiscally healthy.

Labour Costs

Another of Drapeau's legacies, an insidious one at that, was that he allowed the city pension fund to become grossly under-funded. Doré too left Montreal with a costly heritage: the labour lawyer in him gave city workers in 1987 guaranteed minimum staffing levels in their union contracts, meaning that Montreal was stuck with four thousand blue collars whether they needed them or not: it could not subcontract out. While poor Doré was publicly excoriated for buying an $82,000 Fazioli piano and installing a $300,000 window in City Hall, these were peccadilloes compared to his egregious error in labour concessions.

Pierre Bourque's idol was Drapeau. But rather than follow in his mentor's footsteps and mount some extravagant *panem et circenses,* Bourque decided to do what Drapeau never succeeded in doing: create One Island One City. He did manage, however, to give the four-day work week to unionized workers in 1996, so the Drapeau-Doré tradition of irresponsible management continued unalloyed. In fact, Montreal blue-collar workers have called off sick at three times the rate of other employees since they got the four-day work week. One-third of the times, they complained of depression. When work-related accidents were factored in, their absentee rate reached 14 per cent – five or six times that in large private corporations.[78]

In 2000, Montreal employees made roughly 40 per cent more than the rest of the public sector in Quebec ("all in"), and the difference is even greater today. They also make much more than employees in the private sector, as well as having something private-sector employees don't have: job security. Years ago, many justified public-sector job security as a way to give civil servants freedom from being cashiered in the event of a change of political party. Now it's just another perk. How much is it worth? In July 1993, a SOM poll asked unionized employees how much more they would have to be paid in order to give up job security. One-third of them said they would want up to 50 per cent more, one-fifth said over 50 per cent more, and one-half said, in effect, "no way!"

As both mayor and commissioner of finance for the City of Westmount, I managed to freeze Westmount's spending for ten years. That was an 18 per cent reduction after inflation. I did that through getting rid of a layer of management but also by reducing the overall number of employees by 17 per cent. Instead of using highly paid blue collars, we contracted out for things like snow and garbage removal.[79]

Debt

Few would deny that one of the reasons Quebec mandarins were keen on One Island One City was to get the Island suburbs to help shoulder the huge debt load Montreal had accumulated, partially through "borrowing to pay for the groceries" and partially though grandiose monuments. At the end of 1996, the total debt of all municipalities in Quebec was $9.8 billion, or $1,373 per citizen.[80] Montreal's debt was $2.5 billion, or $2,500 per citizen.[81] But that is not all. As revealed in a 1997 government press release, the pension fund deficits of the City of Montreal were staggering, bringing its total indebtedness then to $4.4 billion, or $4,336 per citizen.[82] This number, though not well known, worried Quebec enormously. After all, it was equal to about 7 per cent of the debt of the entire provincial government.

To be fair, Montreal's debt problem was not all to do with misspending. Quebec municipalities fund new infrastructure differently from elsewhere. In Ontario, private developers rather than the municipalities themselves pay for initial infrastructure such as streets. Developers also pay development charges to municipalities to help cover off-site infrastructure costs. Lastly, because Ontario municipalities often resort to pay-as-you-go for capital costs, municipal debt there per capita was only a quarter of that in Quebec.[83]

The suburban allergy to annexation by Montreal was not caused by snobbism, indifference, or miserliness. For us, annexation meant simply sweeping Montreal's problems under a bigger rug.

10

Quebec's Remedy: A Huge New Government or a Huge New City?

One can't be against everything; against mergers, against anything supra-municipal, against reorganization.

The status quo is not an option.

Louise Harel, 1999

Necessity is the plea for every infringement of human freedom.

William Pitt the Younger, 1793

The PQ were re-elected with Lucien Bouchard at their head on 30 November 1998. The heavyweights in cabinet were much the same gang. All those worthies such as Chevrette, Trudel, and Ménard, who had gone through the dolorous downloading exercise or the scuttled Montreal Metropolitan Development Commission saga, were still in cabinet but with different posts. The woman who had been minister of employment and solidarity, Louise Harel, copped both Trudel's and Ménard's old jobs: she became minister of municipal affairs and the métropole. Harel, of course, as member of cabinet and a representative for a Montreal riding, had followed the last few years of municipal shenanigans closely. Now in her mid-fifties, she had seventeen years of experience in the National Assembly.

She was going to do what Chevrette, Trudel, and Ménard had all failed to do: merge municipalities.

Bourque did not meet with the re-elected Bouchard and Harel until early February 1999, when he rode on his One Island One City hobbyhorse in front of them. Ten days later, however, he managed to blot his copybook with the entire PQ establishment when he blurted out at a Jewish Business Network lunch that, like a maturing child, Quebec would outgrow its desire to be independent and seek interdependence. Vice-Premier Bernard Landry soon dressed him down, and another cabinet minister referred to Bourque's comment as "a perfect imbecility." (Bourque was already in the PQ's bad graces for saying six months earlier that a victory for sovereignty in Quebec would weaken Montreal's economy. "It would be a shock," he had said.[1])

MERGER WILL OUT

Then, on 18 March 1999, the government's information colander began dripping all over the place: *La Presse* managed to get what turned out to be accurate leaks from the much-awaited Bédard Report. I speculated at the time that Harel was using the Bédard Report, a report on financial matters, as a stalking-horse to further her own agenda of mergers. In fact, *La Presse* revealed that this report would recommend One Island Three Cities, many mergers off-Island, and a directly elected regional government. The first to react was Vera Danyluk, who was against the merger idea "for the moment" but pushed for her Metropolitan Council (an enlarged, directly elected MUC), which was similar to what the leaked report was recommending. In spite of an order from Bossé to the suburban mayors to keep quiet until a common position could be developed, many spoke to the press, panning the idea of Island mergers, to the surprise of no one. Harel commented on the leak by saying Island mergers "are worth looking at," noting that the reactions to the leak were not all negative.[2] The leak, compounded by delays in printing the 425-page report, proved to be a way for Harel to stick her toe in the anti-merger water to see how warm it was.

She got a reaction soon enough. A few days later, she was the keynote speaker at the annual meeting of the Island suburban mayors, its theme – decided well before the Bédard Report leak – "Building the Metropolis." At the prospect of seeing her, Dorval Mayor Peter Yeomans announced, "I'm planning to eat razor-blades for breakfast," adding that suburban mayors found the idea of forced amalgamations extremely difficult to swallow. He went on to say that we "definitely aren't ready for municipal cleansing."[3] This kind of commentary did nothing to help our cause to be taken seriously by either Harel or the media.

On a cold Friday night in a huge shadowy college auditorium in LaSalle, Harel told us that if local mayors could not agree on something, the government had the responsibility to impose a solution.

"The status quo is not possible,"[4] she said, without telling us why, and not for the last time. She repeated her false mantra that mergers were "a worldwide trend," inviting us to reflect on that "fact." She said that she did not wish to find herself in the position of one of her predecessors, Claude Ryan, who had regretted not studying mergers more closely.

At this annual meeting, we came up with the idea of what we called a Greater Montreal Development Commission, which would be run by local mayors and be very similar to what Pichette had recommended in 1993. The MUC would be a simple service-delivery organization; again, as Pichette recommended. As well as planning and coordinating the region, the commission would administer various equalization funds, including "tax base sharing," whereby the whole region would benefit from disproportionate exurban growth.

WATCH YOUR LANGUAGE!

In those days, merger misery acquainted a man with strange bed-fellows. Whenever mergers were posited, the Island suburban mayors could depend on certain members of the francophone élite to fret – not without reason – about the increase in non-francophones on the Island of Montreal owing to immigration, assimilation, the low francophone birth rate, and (most importantly) the francophone flight to off-Island suburbs. The PQ particularly and francophones generally began to express a concern that One Island One City would ultimately result in a municipality that would be majority non-francophone. A series of major articles in Le Devoir at the end of March 1999[5] extensively quoted demographer Marc Termote, regarded by some, uncharitably, as being a member of the apocalyptic school of French language decline.

"The francophone population of the Island of Montreal has shrunk three times as much as the anglophone population," the first Le Devoir headline ran. Of course, Le Devoir was using absolute numbers, not percentages, but from 1981 to 1996 the number of Island citizens speaking French at home indeed dropped by an astounding 9 per cent, a higher drop than even for English-speakers. Two main forces were at work, Termote said: first, while two-thirds of allophone immigrants continued to speak only their native tongue at home, most of the remaining one-third had switched to English, notably in the Island suburbs. Second, 22,000 "native" francophones

Quebec's Changing Linguistic Landscape, in Percentages

MOTHER TONGUE	Island of Montreal			Montreal Metropolitan Region			Province of Quebec		
	French	English	Other	French	English	Other	French	English	Other
1971	61	24	15	66	22	12	81	13	6
1991	56	19	25	69	15	17	82	9	9
1996	53	19	28	68	14	18	82	9	10
2006	50	18	33	66	13	22	80	8	12
LANGUAGE SPOKEN MOST OFTEN AT HOME									
1971	61	27	11	66	25	9	81	15	5
1991	57	26	17	70	19	11	83	11	6
1996	56	26	19	70	18	12	83	11	6
2006	54	25	21	69	17	13	82	11	8

Source: See note 7

had stopped speaking French at home – again, especially in the Island suburbs where the assimilation rate was three times higher than in the City of Montreal.

Termote was rightly referring to "home language" rather than "mother tongue" francophones in his analysis.[6] The battle between the French and the English language on Montreal Island was being fought in the home, not the cradle, since linguistic losses and gains were largely determined by whichever language immigrants decided to adopt in the home. And when immigrants – most of whom originally spoke neither French nor English – chose to remain on the sidelines and stick with their native tongue, they were counted as allophones, crowding out both the French and the English percentages in a trinary linguistic scorekeeping that was not so long before binary. Termote pointed out that, from 1981 to 1996, the number of allophones on the Island of Montreal had increased by one-half.

Termote predicted that, by 2006, less than 50 per cent of Island residents would be francophone. He was partially right: "mother-tongue" francophones dropped from 53.4 per cent to 49.8 per cent from 1996 to 2006, but "home-language" francophones dropped less: from 55.6 per cent to 54.2 per cent. Clearly more immigrants had begun speaking French than Termote had predicted. To get a better picture of language trends, one has to look at a bigger picture and a longer term.[7]

For the Montreal Metropolitan Region, thanks to the francophone exodus to off-Island suburbs, "mother-tongue" francophones have kept the same proportion of the region's population and, as a home language, French has actually increased.[8] Provincially, there has been little change in the proportion of francophones; in fact, since 1901, they have always represented about 80 per cent of Quebec's population. The proportion of anglophones has plummeted both regionally and provincially, with allophones taking up the demographic space formerly occupied by English speakers.

Even back in 1999 it was clear to me that the traditional obsession with the Island of Montreal rather than a focus on the whole metropolitan region led to a distorted view of things, but for once it was working in our favour so I kept my mouth shut. Especially for the PQ, the linguistic fate of Montreal Island, and Montreal Island alone, was an unassailable touchstone.[9] So when Termote predicted a Montreal Island with francophones in the minority, the political tremors registered immediately in Bouchard's cabinet and were far more effective in cooling francophone ardour for One Island One City than our pitiful mayoral sabre-rattling. That this huge solitaire on offer, this potential jewel in Quebec's municipal crown, could be so linguistically impure as to cut, clarity, colour, and carats did not bear thinking about.

DANYLUK SHARES HER ESCHATOLOGICAL VISION OF THE MUC

Coming all the way out of the public policy closet, Vera Danyluk leaked her personal position on regional governance two weeks before the Bédard Report was officially and finally made public. So we had a leak responding to a leak. "Scuttle the MUC," screamed the front-page-above-the-fold *La Presse* headline on 6 April. The reporter said he had a document signed by Danyluk that would be made public later that week. This document said that she was proposing to wind up the MUC, replacing it with a metropolitan council that would deliver the same services, but would be expanded to include Laval and seven south shore municipalities. I called it "the MUC on steroids." The huge difference would be that politicians sitting on its council would all be directly elected, and it would be financed by direct taxation. It would thus be another level of government with a whole new class of elected official. "At the present time, the electorate never has the chance to have their say on specifically regional matters," Danyluk wrote in an 1,850-word article. "I don't exclude the idea that certain cities would see an interest to merge in order to get better local services at lower cost"[10] – but mergers were secondary. Create the government, she later said, "and then the municipalities might contemplate merging."[11] As we shall see, this became Harel's line of reasoning a month later; the difference was that Harel was talking *forced* mergers.

Warning us (as did Harel) that the lack of a common position on the Island of Montreal could result in the government imposing a solution, Danyluk continued to foster the lack of a common position by sticking to her own. Neither Bourque nor the Island suburbs were in favour of another level of government. On the other hand, Bourque wanted forced mergers, and we did not. Danyluk supported the leaked Bédard Report's regional government, but was against forced mergers. The supposedly bicephalous MUC continued to be tricephalous. Harel must have been delighted with the political charivari that resulted.

As usual, Danyluk made a much bigger media splash than the Island mayors did on unveiling their plan a week before, and she was speaking as a "private citizen" – since she could not speak for the MUC, its "owners" having taken different positions. But she was an unusual "private citizen," with access to MUC letterheads, MUC bureaucrats, and MUC media advisers. Somewhat defensively, she said, "I'm the only official who has a regional mandate, and because of that I have a moral duty to come up with regional solutions."[12] We finally dealt with the problem by having the MUC executive committee, chaired by an uncomfortable Danyluk, adopt a resolution formally advising Harel that the MUC opposed "the creation of a metropolitan structure whose members were elected by universal suffrage."[13] Danyluk's reaction was: "By the very nature of my job, I have the legitimacy to speak, even without a mandate."[14]

MARGINALIZED MAYORS

By 1999, Danyluk had eclipsed the Island mayors in her influence with Harel and her impact on the media. I admit this rankled with most Island mayors, so there was a goodly dose of envy in our attitude towards her. It was not, however, just a question of her undoubted political talent. By ignoring any constraints, she could use her position to give free rein to her colourful and persuasive self. Bourque too, with his stranglehold on his party, was essentially free to say what he wanted, and did – but usually was taken less seriously. Bossé, on the other hand, had to represent twenty-six mayors, all of whom had differing opinions and some of whom (the "dissident mayors") undermined his authority.[15] His public and private pronouncements were of necessity guarded – a deadly handicap.

The suburban mayors, never succeeded in controlling the agenda, even for a few days. And Danyluk's message often struck a resonant chord with one sector or another, academic, editorial, or governmental. Bourque as well slowly attracted powerful people to his side. On the other hand, few in the francophone world supported the Island mayors' position; few, indeed, knew, cared, or understood what it was. Our marginalization and the earlier fractionating of the whole provincial municipal level left us all vulnerable to the threatened mergers. In short, we wielded little power and less influence.

Even though it was like herding cats, I managed to get all the mayors to pull together when I was president of the suburban mayors, but in those days our very existence was not being called into question. In 1999, the only – yet quite persuasive – argument for mergers could be found in this inability of twenty-seven mayors[16] to speak authoritatively and with one voice: in other words, our fragmentation, to use the pro-mergerites' term. But if we were to be accused of being fragmented, it was unfair to claim evidence of it during those extraordinary circumstances. It's hard to play a team sport under a collective death threat: the quality of play is understandably ragged.

The ineffectiveness of the Union of Montreal Island Suburban Municipalities (as we had renamed ourselves) also had a lot to do with the way it operated. Each mayor had a vote regardless of the size of the municipality he (it was usually a he) represented. Senneville (population 900) had the same voting power as Saint-Laurent (75,000). This was all very clubby and federative, but fundamentally undemocratic.[17] Owing to the number of small West Island municipalities, their mayors had disproportionate power whether voting for president or for policy matters. The West Island represented only 29 per cent of our population, yet had 46 per cent of the votes. This was a huge sore point with mayors of municipalities like Saint-Laurent. Moreover, the smaller municipalities tended to have part-time mayors, which meant evening meetings, slow communications, and patchy participation. It's hard to fight a war when one-third of the army is made up of part-time soldiers.

BÉDARD'S BRAVE NEW MUNICIPAL WORLD

What was in the Bédard Report when it finally came out? First, a word about its provenance. In 1997, during the $500-cut-to-$375 million downloading saga, Municipal Affairs Minister Rémy Trudel had realized he could not walk (download) and chew gum (reform municipal financing) at the same time. He, or more to the point, his boss decided to walk first, grabbing the municipalities' money. As formally agreed with the Union of Quebec Municipalities (UMQ) in October 1997, this downloading would only apply for 1998 and 1999 (possibly for 2000); the arrangement would then be replaced with a permanent "fiscal pact." The group given the mandate to come up with this pact was created by cabinet 29 April 1998 and dubbed the National Commission on Local Finances and Taxation. (The PQ had banned the word "provincial" from Quebec's vocabulary; for quite some time now, everything had been "national.") So this commission's job was to do the policy gum-chewing.

The wad produced was prodigious: a 425-page tome finally made public on 20 April 1999, a whole month after the *La Presse* leak. The report went by the pretentious title "Pact 2000." Sometimes when Quebec decides to mess around with municipal finance, they give their goal as seeking a "pact," as if it were all about spitting on one's hands before shaking your buddy's while reciting a secret code, rather than the usual fiat from on high. The last real "pact" was the 1980 Fiscal Reform, where a number of basic principles were agreed to between the two parties. This time the spirit of equal partnership was just not there. The National Commission on Local Finances and Taxation was a creature of the provincial government. Its members, selected by Quebec, were headed up by an economist, Professor Denis Bédard.

In spite of the "finances and taxation" in their title, the commissioners decided to wade into the whole merger question, interpreting their mandate in broad terms. Their analysis of the fiscal side was sophisticated and accurate, if technocratic.[18] They should have stopped there. Their blue-sky musings on political structures were amateurish, as they were in unfamiliar territory. There were neither urban politicians nor urban planners on the commission: the only member who could claim urban political savvy was the eminent historian Jean-Pierre Collin, who served as the commission's vice-president. Other than Bédard and Collin, there was a public-relations executive for a forest-products company, a municipal assessment expert, a tax accountant, the former mayor of Pointe-au-Pic, a municipal director-general, a professor of finance, and a consultant in school bus transport – not the sort of group that should have been pronouncing on urban municipal mergers and structures. But they did. In fact, they were among the first in recent Quebec history openly to recommend *forced* urban mergers.

"The government decision to decree mergers by legislative or other means should be limited to certain situations; for example, the large agglomerations,"[19] the report said. For Montreal and Quebec City, "obligatory mergers" were recommended to arrive at a maximum of twenty municipalities in the Montreal region, and five or six in Quebec City. The Island of Montreal itself would be merged into three or five municipalities. The late Yvon Cyrenne, one of the report's authors and a tax accountant, admitted that "for me, the ideal would be only one city, but I was told that would not be politically feasible."[20]

This tome included pages of coloured maps showing these various merger suggestions like so many butchers' diagrams as to how best to carve up beef.[21] It was as if Harel, who in December 1998 had become the new minister, had instructed the commission to give her a two-for-one: a solution for both the end of downloading and a road map for municipal reorganization.

One would expect a group with the qualifications that the Bédard commissioners had to establish economic principles grounded in logic – and they did not fail. They said, for example, that redistribution of income should be essentially left to higher levels of government, and that property assessment is not an acceptable measure of local services consumed. They even said that taxation based on property values is one of the rare (if imperfect) examples of a wealth tax. And they wheeled out the statistics: large municipalities in Quebec (over 100,000 in population) spend *50 per cent* more per capita than smaller (less than 100,000) ones.[22] One reason for this was that larger municipalities pay their employees 30 per cent more than the rest of the Quebec public sector.[23] They even said that various studies show "that spending per capita increases after merger."[24]

So, one would assume from this, especially considering their fiscal expertise, that Bédard and his co-commissioners would conclude mergers are bad. But no: the report said that the advantages of mergers stem from fiscal equity,[25] a reduction in inefficient intermunicipal competition, and an improved "synergy." But if property assessment is not a measure of services consumed and municipalities are not to be in the wealth redistribution business, the "fiscal equity" argument drops.* And the authors gave no examples of "inefficient intermunicipal competition," nor did they shed light on what was meant by that slippery and then-ubiquitous word "synergy." So these hard-nosed experts, skilled in a quantitative art, resorted to unsubstantiated and unquantifiable assertions outside their ken in order to justify forcing metropolitan areas to endure mergers. They were not the first, and, as we shall see, not the last to make these claims. In another sweeping statement soon to be echoed by others, the Bédard Report concluded "the fragmentation of local municipalities in the agglomerations of Quebec and Montreal make mergers imperative."[26]

As well as suggesting mergers and drawing maps of them, the report also intrepidly ventured to give a detailed description of a supramunicipal structure for the Montreal region. Because, they said, mayors have allegiance to only their local municipalities, they cannot possibly summon up an equivalent allegiance to the whole region.† Ergo, the regional structure should be run by councillors directly elected for that purpose, and the body given direct taxation powers, something Danyluk had been championing for years.[27] This regional government would handle mass transit, planning, economic promotion, public housing, and even possibly school boards and local health clinics (CLSCs).

REACTION TO BÉDARD

Predictably, Harel welcomed the "courage" of the Bédard Report in recommending mergers, saying they were "inevitable." She warned,

---

* Besides, you don't have to merge in order to write a cheque: the MUC was a perfect example of regional cost-sharing among independent cities.

† Using the same logic, since each member of Quebec's National Assembly has only a local electoral base, he or she could not have the province's best interest at heart when voting in that same assembly.

however, that any regional body must be light, and cover all of the Montreal Metropolitan Region.[28] Danyluk was the only other person happy with the report, saying it was important for the government to get moving. As far as regional government was concerned, her idea was very similar, except that she was suggesting a smaller region than the entire metropolitan region.[29] One of the reasons (I assumed) why she was pushing for a smaller region was that even she could not imagine one police force over the entire Montreal Metropolitan Region. Expanding the MUC police to include Laval and seven south shore municipalities, and thereby doubling the size of its territory, was already an incredibly tough sell. Danyluk naturally was completely against the report's idea of breaking up the MUC police by giving each newly merged municipality its own police force.

Bourque came out against the directly elected regional government and, of course, against the idea of One Island Three Cities. He said it would create an anglophone West Island City, and a soulless East Island City. (A month later, he said that wealth would be concentrated in the west and poverty in the centre.[30])

Vice-Premier Bernard Landry, echoing the Bédard Report, "rejected a widespread program of forced mergers. There are fewer municipalities in Quebec than there were, and it's certain there will be fewer in the future; but, overall, excepting very dramatic situations, it's local democracy that will decide." With typical Landry convolution, he added that the situation in Montreal was "more dramatic."[31] So we were seeing a sea change in the province's outlook with regard to municipal mergers. Once viewed as a way to eliminate all the rural hamlets that survived on government handouts, mergers – forced mergers – were now to be directed at urban targets. The next day Harel "refined" Landry's comments by saying that the existence of four hundred village/parish doppelgangers was an archaism that had to be settled soon.

BOURQUE FORMALLY LAUNCHES HIS CAMPAIGN

At a Board of Trade luncheon on 26 May 1999, Bourque finally and formally launched his One Island One City campaign before seven hundred people. "Montreal has a universal destiny that transcends the reality of its immediate environment," he told his audience. "The union of the vital forces of the Island will create a synergistic effect."

One Island One City was a "winning formula."[32] After more than two years of preparation, such mysticisms and clichés were pretty thin gruel for anyone expecting solid arguments for Bourque's cause. He did make the point that 41 per cent of Montreal households lived below the low-income cut-off point, compared to 21 per cent in the rest of the metropolitan region, and that nearly a quarter of the province's social-aid households and one-third of its subsidized housing were found in Montreal, a municipality that accounted for only 14 per cent of Quebec's total population. But he did not explain how merging the suburban municipalities would improve the lot of these families, since their care, as we saw in chapter 7, was a provincial, not a local responsibility. Even subsidized housing cost Montreal only 0.5 per cent of its budget,[33] most of which today is paid by the region.

In a twenty-four-page brochure[34] Bourque had published for his big day and subsequently mailed to 1,100 individuals, one at least could pick out some facts and figures among the poetry. Always a crowd-pleaser, he promised a big reduction in the number of politicians with One Island One City (with no mention of any savings, though). Then out came the hoary old "economies of scale," pegged at a relatively modest $100 million. (Even that sum was contingent on the fantasy of Quebec changing the labour laws to allow for subcontracting and employer lockouts. If that ever happened, the same economies could be made without mergers.) The brochure invoked the very real problem of urban sprawl. But, since their own figures showed that this growth was all occurring *off-Island* for the last twenty-five years, no one explained how one Island city would help reduce it.

We finally got to see Bourque's plan for the region. No new level of government, as expected: the MUC, except for the MUC police, would be expanded to cover the entire Montreal Metropolitan Region accounting for 111 municipalities. This number would be reduced to around ten through mergers.[35]

PROBLEM: NO FINANCIAL ADVANTAGE FOR MONTREALERS

What was downplayed in Bourque's pitch for One Island One City was the question of "fiscal equity for Montreal," that rallying cry going back a number of years that had always led the pack of the arguments in favour of One Island One City. "The biggest problem of Montreal, as the central city," Chevrette had declaimed in March 1997, "is the fiscal unfairness that it suffers vis-à-vis the other cities on the Island." Editorialists, Bourque, provincial politicians, academics – all had bemoaned the sponging suburbs on the Island of Montreal. Why was Bourque now being discreet about fiscal fairness, his slam-dunk argument? It was because his people finally discovered that Montreal would not and could not get any tax relief by swallowing its Island suburbs. It would mean huge tax swings *among the suburbs themselves*, but a paltry (and fictional) 5 per cent reduction in the tax bill of Montrealers. And where did that number come from? Why, from Montreal's own finance department.[36] Worse, their calculations did not take into consideration that, in the event of a merger, each municipality's debt would remain with its former taxpayers. The creation of a megacity, then, would not reduce taxes for residents of the former City of Montreal by getting its purportedly parasitical suburbs to "pay their share." The fiscal equity emperor had no clothes, but nobody was paying attention. After a while, neither was Bourque. Three months later he was back to the old "we have to merge, we have to get everyone to pay for the costs of the city."[37]

When the Municipal Affairs Department got around to running their own numbers six months later, they concluded that Montrealers would see a 0.4 per cent (*point* 4!) reduction in taxes with One Island One City, and that piffling amount was only thanks to a transitional subsidy. Once the subsidy was over, the government was actually predicting an increase in taxes for Montrealers. Montreal's commercial sector would get a bit of a break, *but residential taxes would go up 3 per cent*. The little article in *Le Devoir*[38] that revealed these numbers was completely ignored, yet it knocked out the props from One Island One City's biggest selling point: that it would spread the tax load and give Montrealers some relief.[39]

THE WILY CLOWN

Most of the media – and all the cartoonists – treated Pierre Bourque as a clown. The fans of mergers deplored time and again being stuck with Bourque as chief salesman for One Island One City. "The City of Montreal can try and seem to take this matter seriously by buying full-page ads in newspapers to sell this project, the simple fact that

Mr Bourque makes himself the promoter is enough to make it even more unpopular. There is not even one intelligent suburbanite who does not tremble with dread at the thought of finding himself a subject of Good King Bourque, in a notoriously badly run municipality with this character with zero credibility in charge,"[40] said Lysiane Gagnon in her editorial "A Stillborn Project."

Bourque was universally underestimated in this task: it was certainly true that he hadn't at all the right personality to be a good leader, a good team-builder, and a good mayor. He was a terrible strategist; making the big launch of One Island One City before he had even lined up a few heavyweights to support him publicly was amateurish. But he had other qualities, as anyone who took the trouble to check out his past discovered. His very first job, in 1965, was as chief horticulturist for Expo 67, in charge of seven hundred people. (According to the late Montreal boulevardier Nick auf der Maur, this job was a plum arranged for the twenty-three-year-old by his dad's close friend, Mayor Drapeau.) As long as he was unimpeded by crass things such as budgets, Bourque had an impressive record of creative achievements over thirty years as a Montreal civil servant, running such operations as the botanical gardens. Certainly, he ended that career with quite a triumph: he created the spectacular Biodome.

I had come to realize that Pierre Bourque was a one-time-project guy, not an ongoing management guy. He much preferred creating something to making it run. It had to be his show, though: Bourque suffered no equals, only inferiors. But he got results, which is why I took his One Island One City project seriously. Certainly, the Island mayors were not prepared at all when Bourque officially launched his campaign in May 1999, and we didn't really get moving until the autumn, although we did set up a standing committee on mergers. Most of the mayors were spectators, occasionally taking pot-shots at Bourque in the media, hoping the whole thing would go away. But Bourque had, along with his determination, the immense resources of the City of Montreal and its budget of $2 billion at his disposal. This clown had money.

THE FRIENDS OF WESTMOUNT

For me, the phoney war was over and real war had now been declared. So I got weaving at home in Westmount. To fight One

Island One City, I felt we needed at least two things: facts and influencers. After discussion with members of Westmount City Council, I created an in-house study group headed by senior staff, supplemented by outside experts. They were to research mergers all over North America. I then commissioned an outside firm, Municonsult, to produce a $50,000 study on just what the effect would be of creating One Island One City.

I also started to tap another resource: Westmounters. As I explain in chapter 3, most Westmounters are resolutely middle class, but we were blessed with a sprinkling of highly placed people who had chosen Westmount as their home. We had to exploit whatever armament we had available. I wanted to create a group of *eminences grises* to advise me, to make the right phone calls if necessary, and to ensure, in turn, they understood what was at stake.

Less than a week after Bourque's launch, I started to make the rounds like some brazen sales rep, from office to office of these captains of industry. I saw Laurent Beaudoin, chairman of Bombardier; Peter Blaikie, senior partner at the law firm Heenan, Blaikie; Micheline Charest, co-founder of Cinar films; David Culver, former chairman of Alcan; André and Paul Desmarais, Jr, co-CEOs of Power Corporation; Lamar Durrett, CEO of Air Canada; Yves Fortier, chairman of the law firm Ogilvy, Renault, and former ambassador to the UN; Raymond Garneau, chairman of Industrial Alliance and a former cabinet minister; Stephen Jarislowsky, the biggest pension-fund manager around; Gilles Ouimet, president of Pratt and Whitney; Bernard Shapiro, principal of McGill University; and Paul Tellier, president of CN Rail.

Laurent Beaudoin was very courtly, open, and helpful. He stressed the importance of quantifying the difference between what it cost to run Montreal compared with the rest of the Island municipalities and then giving the results to the Liberals. But he warned me, "Westmount cannot be seen as the only city protesting; in fact, Westmount must not be seen to be leading the opposition to One Island One City." He added he would make some phone calls once the studies were done, but said with a chuckle, "that could hurt our cause." Beaudoin was hardly a PQ supporter.

Raymond Garneau said he was retiring at the end of 1999 and would have to stay fairly quiet until then. He promised to be more active after. When I got to Power Corporation, I was very civilly received. To my complaint that *La Presse* – a Power Corporation subsidiary – had taken an aggressively pro-merger stance, both editorially and in their reportage, André Desmarais responded that they never interfered with *La Presse*'s editorial positions; the only standing orders were that the paper had to be federalist. They then sent me to see the more political John Rae, their executive vice-president and brother of former Ontario premier Bob Rae.

Bernard Shapiro told me that Bourque had already tried to get the four university rectors on board, but he, Shapiro, had been noncommittal. He agreed there were diseconomies of scale with mergers, that they were no solution and that, once done, were irreversible. Yet we had, he said, to find a solution to the problem of Montreal. While he could not offer public support, he would attend meetings. Stephen Jarislowsky, true to form, had "no problem going public." He approved the relatively francophone slant I was taking in the composition of my *eminences grises*, suggesting a bunch more. I came away from our lunch with both the bill and a feeling of strong support.

Interestingly, most of these people when asked did not recommend that I rope in former prime minister and Westmounter Brian Mulroney, which surprised me somewhat at the time. While I had never supported the Conservatives, I had respect for his policies and political acumen, and while he was viscerally disliked in English Canada, he was popular in the arena we were playing in.

I also managed a few phone calls with Gretta Chambers, the chancellor of McGill University. She knew Harel quite well, agreeing with her that the status quo did not work; however, Chambers felt the idea of a whole new level of government was a terrible one. She cautioned me not to give the impression that I was just trying to save our fiefdom. She found the potential linguistic overtones "terrifying."

NON TO ONE ISLAND ONE CITY

I was still making my rounds of the Westmount captains of industry when we were hit with the biggest surprise of the year. On a Monday morning, 14 June, the headlines in *La Presse* blared, "No to the One Island One City Project." Less than three weeks after Bourque's big announcement, Louise Harel was rejecting One Island One City. Instead, she plumped for moving ahead with a directly elected regional government (a "Metropolitan Council") covering the entire region. While she saw merit in Bourque's proposal, she said she did not want to get mired down in an eternal debate. Clearly, the politics of language were on her mind and were the real reason for scotching Bourque's dream. "Is there even one francophone in Montreal who has not dreamt that their city take over the whole Island?" she rather bizarrely asked, as if other linguistic groups were so many domestic animals. "But, at the same time, one has to evaluate the price to pay for discussions. It could take weeks, months, years, of endless debates; not on mass transit, not on subsidized housing, not on economic development or the promotion of Montreal." All of that made a lot of sense. But she ended her thought by divagating to the subject of language again: "It could be the sort of debates that our old demons could bring back to us."[41]

Defending her regional approach, Harel said Toronto had ten years of a directly elected regional government that managed 75 per cent of all municipal budgets before it got around to creating the Toronto megacity. All Toronto had to do at that point was merge the 25 per cent that was left. In other words, she argued, create the regional government first, and merge later: it will be much easier. This reasoning was precisely why I had been against any directly elected body for years.

Then, putting his imprimatur on Harel's statement the next day, Premier Bouchard closed the merger door with a bang. "One Island One City is not in the picture for us," he said laconically. "That's not the angle we are going to take in that dossier."[42] He added, "The problem is much wider than just that of the Island," which constituted the most intelligent sentence ever uttered in the municipal reorganization debate thus far. It was also a reaffirmation of his position taken during the election campaign seven months earlier.

Most pundits speculated that such a bald rejection of One Island One City had to do with PQ fears of megaMontreal becoming a municipality of non-francophones in a decade or so. The other concern had to do with creating the position of megacity mayor, a person who would, in all likelihood, be both Liberal and against sovereignty in any future referendum. In other words, One Island One City was torpedoed for reasons having nothing to do with municipal governance.

Bourque, who was in Holland when Harel and Bouchard dropped their respective bombs, was apoplectic. "At the very least, it's inelegant. I would have thought the premier and Mme Harel would have given me a call. They took advantage of my absence," he pouted at a press conference the moment he got back. And then, revealing a less-than-firm grasp of reality, he said, "They panicked because of the quality of the message we gave and the support we got."[43] In fact, he had garnered no political support at all. And only ten citizens had attended the first night of public consultations in the matter.[44]

I was over the moon: the spectre of One Island One City had flitted away. As for Harel's directly elected government, there was a reasonable chance the regional barons who call the shots in the PQ would never accept its imposition and that Harel would water her wine, putting in the kind of structure we Island mayors and Pichette had been recommending for so many years. I suspected one of the reasons Harel was pushing for this massive governmental overburden was the lobbying from Danyluk, the sole advocate of such a structure to be found in the entire region.

Two months after Harel's and Bouchard's earthshaking declarations, things were not quite so black and white. Harel's new line was that, while the new regional government was the priority, One Island One City could be a second step. She even said it was "premature" to reveal whether she favoured forced mergers or not.[45]

HAREL'S WHITE PAPER: A LEAK LAYS AN EGG

"A government is the only known vessel that leaks from the top," someone once said. In 1999 Quebec's official municipal communications policy seemed to be, "Let's leak it and see what happens." In late August, it was *Le Devoir*'s turn to take a leak. They got a draft copy of Harel's much-awaited white paper on fiscal and structural reform. Front and centre in this hundred-page document was Harel's Montreal Metropolitan Council, which would apply tax-base sharing, development fees, and the sharing of regional costs such as arterial roads, the Biodome, and the deficits of subsidized housing. There would be only one administrative region, and all the counties would disappear. The Montreal Metropolitan Council would not directly deliver services but would subcontract them to other organizations. So far, the contents of the leak were everything we had been asking for. Then came the major problem: Harel was still proposing a directly elected body – in other words, a new level of government. In addition, the territory encompassed only 74 municipalities, not 111. This meant that it would be far less effective in curbing urban sprawl. (This new, truncated region was closer to what Danyluk had been suggesting all along.)

Bossé pounced on the fact that the City of Varennes, in Vice-Premier Bernard Landry's riding, happened to be miraculously excised from the metropolitan council's territory, even though two-thirds of the population of Varennes worked in the metropolitan region. With places such as Saint-Bruno also not counted in, this overt gerry-mandering gave rise to a reporter's observation that the electoral districts of Landry *and* Minister Louise Beaudoin were excluded.[46]

As for the whole idea of a directly elected regional government, only Danyluk was left in the cheering section. The Union of Quebec Municipalities (UMQ) described it as a bureaucratic monster. Bourque deplored Danyluk's choosing it over mass mergers. Mayor Gilles Vaillancourt of Laval said, in effect, let's settle the fiscal problems and forget about the grand structures. As usual, the north shore mayors were beside themselves. "We won't let Mrs Harel demolish the municipal world," said their spokesman, the mayor of Rosemère. With such a metropolitan council, "we'd be left with recreation, snow-removal, and road-cleaning," he said, calling it a "gigantic dis-guised merger." Then he brought out the usual suspects. "Our region is more and more autonomous. The problem is not there. Wealth on the Island of Montreal is badly distributed," he said, giving West-mount as a flagrant example.[47]

The immediate north shore was represented by a half-dozen mem-bers of the National Assembly, all members of the party in power, the PQ. The north shore mayors told their representatives to "sup-port those who had brought them into power," pointedly saying that it seemed that certain representatives on the south shore had more influence, referring to Landry's and Beaudoin's success in snipping off their districts from the Montreal Metropolitan Council's terri-tory. The representatives reacted, all right. "It's not with a new mega-structure that we will win the next referendum of sovereignty," said the representative for Blainville, adding that One Island One City would affect far fewer PQ electoral districts. "The PQ majority is in the regions, not on the Island of Montreal."[48]

Sadly, this frank example of *realpolitik* pretty much summed up what we were up against. Aside from the small town of Montreal East, all twenty-six Island municipalities that would disappear with One Island One City were in Liberal ridings. The PQ held only eight seats on Montreal Island (barely a quarter of the total), but they held four out of five seats in Laval and a total of twenty-eight seats both north and south of Montreal.

François Beaulne, a PQ member on the south shore, was also openly opposing Harel's structure, saying all that was needed was an "equalization fund" for the region. A poll said that 60 per cent of people were against a Metropolitan Council, yet were for mergers. PQ members began demanding a province-wide caucus on the matter. This mass discontent quickly made its way up to the cabinet, where Harel had few allies. The cabinet instructed her to rework her white paper and to include Montreal mergers as a possibility.[49] It was as if the north shore mayors were telling the provincial cabinet what to do.

So the wheels began to come off Harel's proposed directly elected structure. It was something no one wanted, except Danyluk and a goodly brochette of academics. Actually, Harel's approach, while overly academic and technocratic, had the advantage of being logical. But once the PQ caucus realized that its implementation would lose them their seats, politics grabbed Harel's project by the neck and never let go. Since the project owed its existence to the mantra "the status quo is not an option," it could not be killed outright; it had to assume another shape. The degeneration that followed was almost predictable.

OUI-NON TO ONE ISLAND ONE CITY

Harel by now had started to duck and weave, saying that the whole tempest was started by a draft version of the white paper destined for the shredder, a claim no one believed. Everything was now back on the table, including One Island One City – even though the situation was "urgent." The media declared the north shore mayors as winners of the first round. On 22 September, just back from a trip to Japan, Bouchard reversed himself, saying that One Island One City was worth taking a look at.

We were furious at Bouchard's flip-flop. I said, rather boringly, "It's deplorable and very sad the provincial government is considering making a decision that will affect the future of Montrealers for years to come on the basis of partisan Parti Québécois politics." Dorval Mayor Peter Yeomans gave his usual trenchant tropes to the *Gazette*: "The suburban mayors have been too genteel up to now with Mayor Bourque, and he's about to get defeathered. We're preparing for a battle royal. Premier Bouchard has ignited a fire-storm and the mayors are going to launch a frontal attack, because mergers will threaten anglophone institutions, values, and ways of life. We're not going to just sit back and let that happen."[50]

The same day that rant came out, Georges Bossé and I met with Harel, who actually thanked us for our balanced and temperate comments to the media. (Clearly, she didn't read the *Gazette*.) She told us that, whenever it came out, the revised white paper would "assuredly" present merger scenarios on the Island of Montreal but not necessarily for the north or south shore. Much to our consternation, she had forgotten our position on the matter of regional governance. She confirmed that none of the regional scenarios in the white paper would be similar to what we had been suggesting for years, although she did say she was open to incorporating our ideas.

At the end of September came a hint that the government had even found a way around its prime objection to One Island One City, coincidentally throwing a bone to anglophones afraid of their merged municipality losing bilingual status. The spectre of an ultimately non-francophone Island city had always been the biggest drawback of Bourque's dream for the PQ. But now Bernard Landry was talking about the charter of the new city, specifying that it was to be unilingual French, possibly with the added fillip of bilingual districts where anglophone municipalities used to be.

ENTER GUY COULOMBE

While all the politicking about the Metropolitan Council was going on, something was in the works that might have explained Premier Bouchard's new-found interest in One Island One City, and that certainly became the single most important element in Bourque getting his lifelong dream realized. Guy Coulombe agreed to become the director-general of the City of Montreal. We are not talking about any old director-general: this director-general had run both Hydro-Quebec and the provincial police force. He was close friends with Premier Bouchard's intimate counsellors and was held in high regard by Bouchard himself. This was someone whom even the great René Lévesque had admired for his energy and intellect. Coulombe's nick-name was "Mr Fix-It."

At the time, most observers assumed Coulombe's appointment was thrust on Bourque by a government worried about Montreal's out-of-control management mess. I was not so sure. I thought Bourque was telling the truth when he said that the promotion of One Island One City would fall to Coulombe. "It is the most wonderful job to get done at this juncture. Montreal is at a historical turning point."[51]

Bourque knew that he himself was regarded with contempt in Quebec, both on the political and civil service fronts. Getting Coulombe was Bourque's masterstroke; whether he took advantage of Quebec's imposing Coulombe on Montreal, or whether Coulombe simply applied for the job, or whether Bourque actively sought him out, the result was the same. Bourque may have been weird, but he could be foxily weird. He knew that at the end of the day it was the mandarins in Quebec City who made things happen. And Coulombe knew them all by name. While I liked and respected Coulombe, I felt a pinch of worry when I heard the news.

OUR VERY FIRST DEBATE

By the fall of 1999 the media were still not taking Bourque's idea very seriously – mainly because of the messenger, whom they considered some sort of a new-age Don Quixote. The anglo media were almost sniggering at Bourque and anything he came up with. The first "debate" on One Island One City took place at an unprepossessing venue, St George's Church Hall. The regional political options for Montreal had for some time resolved themselves into three, each with its own champion, who now participated in what turned out to be a genteel statement of position. Bourque was there selling One Island One City, Danyluk a new directly elected regional government; I was there plumping for a regional council run by local politicians.

Danyluk said our problems were regional and mergers were secondary; besides, she said, merging every municipality on the Island wouldn't get the Island one more cent of revenue for regional costs. The only solution was a regional government with directly elected politicians, endowed with the power of taxation. Bourque said Montreal was stuck with the poor, the homeless, the contaminated building sites, the arterial roads, and 500,000 visitors per day. Instead of being Montrealers 30 per cent of the way (through contributions to the MUC), the Island suburbs should be 100 per cent Montrealers. After all, he said in his rather dreamy manner, Montreal was the mother of all the suburbs. I said I was stuck between one person who wanted a megastructure and one who wanted a megacity. The main problem facing our region was urban sprawl, and the next – related – one was the financial situation of the City of Montreal. If you have a fiscal problem, I said, solve it with a fiscal solution. "You don't have to merge all corporations in Canada to have a corporation tax." As for a new level of government, I said it was amalgamation by the back door: precisely what happened in Toronto.

The French media accused me of simply wanting the status quo and then stated irrelevantly, "*Westmount veut rester anglais.*" They jumped all over Bourque, too, asking how One Island One City would help urban sprawl. "It would reinforce the heart of the region," said Bourque, weakly. The media also made fun of Bourque for promising to freeze megacity taxes for five years following mergers.[52]

ONE ISLAND ONE FIRE BRIGADE

By now Montreal Fire Chief Alain Michaud had taken up the torch from his predecessor, Roméo Noël, and was selling the merits of one fire brigade covering the whole Island. It would save Montreal $40 million, he said, and cost the suburbs $20 million: a net savings of $20 million on total budgets of $265 million. We the suburbs could very easily restrain our enthusiasm, our attitude partially explained by the spectre of Montreal's fire union, best known for puncturing fire hoses, smashing equipment, and painting fire trucks psychedelic colours. We gave more than adequate fire coverage with some 950 firefighters working out of 27 stations in the Island suburbs: Montreal had 1,557 in their 36 stations.[53] I always felt that talk of such a merger was sending us down the slippery slope to One Island One City. And if there is one municipal service where knowledge of local conditions is paramount, it is firefighting. Since firefighters spend only 2–4 per cent of their time actually fighting fires, fire *prevention* should occupy most of their time, work that equally demands local control.

Public Security Minister Serge Ménard was also pushing for fire department mergers, arguing they would lower Island fire insurance rates which he maintained were higher than in Ontario. He badgered the MUC for a plan. When Danyluk refused (for once I was cheering her on), saying it was a local responsibility, Ménard warned her petulantly, "If we force solutions on you, don't come and complain afterward."[54]

CLAUDE RYAN WEIGHS IN

In early October, Claude Ryan bestirred himself and decided to come out in favour of at least some Island mergers, especially of the "enclaves." Back in 1996 he had told me privately that municipalities such as Westmount and Outremont were "anachronisms" and should be annexed to Montreal; now he decided, for whatever reason, to say it publicly. (I retorted that annexations were themselves anachronisms, but I felt like a snotty schoolboy correcting the revered headmaster.) In common with Claude Picher and Lysiane Gagnon of *La Presse*, Ryan said he was not in favour of going all the way to One Island One City, not at that point. He feared that would lead to "gigantism and a distancing of the politicians vis-à-vis the population."[55] He came out against a metropolitan body with direct election and taxation powers, and therefore against Harel's "fourth order of government." He favoured an enlarged MUC.

MY STUDY CAN BEAT YOUR STUDY

Then we had the warring studies of the financial effect of One Island One City. Montreal seemed to have picked up the trick of leaking documents, as in early September *La Presse* had the scoop on a study done for Montreal. "One Island One City: $100 million in savings," blared the headlines. The only snag to achieving this bonanza, the reader discovered, was that the government would have to adopt laws getting rid of minimum staffing levels and also somehow prevent the highest wages (Montreal's) becoming the standard throughout the Island in a kind of race to the top. The latter phenomenon was, of course, unpreventable in the long term. Some purported savings came through subcontracting, but they could have been had without mergers – if the government had changed the labour law that restricted subcontracting out. The study was honest enough not to claim any economies of scale, but it did ignore *dis*economies of scale. Besides, even if One Island One City could save $100 million a year, that was only 3 per cent of the consolidated spending. As we shall see, Bourque's dream wound up *costing* $400 million more a year.

The makeup of the $100 million a year was revealing. A reduction in the number of firefighters would supposedly save $14 million. The ever-popular promise of reducing the number of politicians from 290 to 61 resulted in a derisory $7 million of savings. Having only one city hall would save another $12 million. Not a thought was given to the poor souls from either ends of the Island who would be forced to drive twenty-five kilometres to attend a city council meeting.

This study was done by the highly reputed consulting firm of SECOR. I gleefully pointed out to *La Presse* that Marcel Côté, the boss of SECOR, had taken a position completely against Montreal Island mergers in January 1998. He had written at the time such mergers were a "refusal to recognize the real problems of Montreal" and would impose the "mediocrity of Montreal's administration" on its suburbs. The poor performance of Montreal, he wrote then, came mostly from that fact it was *too big*.[56] I later learned that Côté, whom I rather liked, was in Europe when his people produced their study and was a little upset by it.

Then out came our own study, which I had commissioned back in July.[57] I de-Westmountized it and dressed it in Union of Montreal Island Suburban Municipalities livery, even getting them to pay for it. I was not really happy with the study, as it was pretty tame in its assumptions. Your study says $100 million savings? Ours says $95 million extra costs. So there. We blacked their white. Montreal's per capita local spending, once spread out over the whole Island, our study said, would result in extra spending of $95 million, mostly owing to the fact Montreal paid their employees more than the suburbs did. Bourque's riposte to this was that per capita spending does not reflect Montreal's spending on the commercial sector (where there is no "capita" – that is, no residents). He had a point, but the same went for the suburbs, although we had a proportionally smaller commercial sector. Besides, the cost of care and feeding of the commercial sector is pretty minimal. Even if one assumed that Bourque was right and the spending on the residential sector was about the same all over the Island, the *quality* of suburban services was head and shoulders above Montreal's, whether it be snow removal, libraries, or (in some cases) public security forces.

And it was not just a question of quality. Small municipalities can offer made-to-order services geared to their local reality. These bespoke services disappear with the one-size-fits-all megacity, as you can't supply different services to residents paying the same taxes. And, when implementing the unavoidable standardization of services, the big City of Montreal would serve as the only yardstick. For example, libraries were open from twenty-four to seventy hours a week all over the Island. With mergers, Montreal's forty-six hours would eventually become the norm, whether people wanted it or not.

I realized that the study Westmount had commissioned on One Island One City, as well as having a media shelf-life of a few days, did little to counteract the Big Myth that mergers were a worldwide trend. I felt we needed something more intellectually solid and over-arching. A book, say. At the beginning of October, I called Andrew Sancton, an acquaintance and an expert in municipal matters. He agreed to write a book, commissioned by Westmount, on the experience elsewhere in regard to municipal amalgamations.

MAYORS FINALLY RETURN FIRE

The Island mayors finally launched a media campaign to counter Bourque's One Island One City blitz in the middle of October 1999, nearly five months after Bourque's launch. There was another problem: it was far from hard-hitting. Our ad agency sold us on more of a "feel-good" campaign, the slogan of which was the forgettable "One Island. Diverse Cities." Full-page ads appeared with pictures of people with lower limbs as tree roots. The cut-lines said things like, "Destroying cities destroys people," "Why lump everyone into the same mould?" Along with radio spots, lapel buttons, polls, and the now-mandatory focus groups, it cost us nearly $300,000, which was the same amount Bourque had spent since May on similar external costs.[58]

Bourque and the mayors weren't alone in spending on promotion, though. Harel had hired National Public Relations to help her sell her regional government. With or without them, she was already cranking up the rhetoric. She took to task certain municipalities acting like "middle-age fortresses, putting up drawbridges and not venturing out except to make incursions into enemy territory."[59]

In November, we released the results of a poll we had commissioned that showed nearly two-thirds of suburban residents did not want merger.

BOURQUE REMAINS BOURQUE

Bourque vaunted his populist roots, which he used to explain his lack of support from the so-called élites. "It's obvious that I am not a politician elected by the élites. I admit it. I was elected against these élites. And they did not help me very much. But they are starting to respect me."[60]

Trying to tease hard facts from Bourque's relatively woolly statements was not always easy. But, in a strange way, you could *sense* what he was saying, and his earnest but inarticulate delivery won people over. And his battery never ran down. Bourque repeated ad nauseam that he wanted to make Montreal big enough to be on the world map and that, as the old song went, "everybody's doin' it, doin' it" (in Eastern Canada, that is). An example of his stream-of-consciousness rhetoric: when asked to explain why he wanted One Island One City, he said during another debate with me: "First, it's the fact that we have to strengthen Montreal. We belong to the world. We want Montreal to become a world city, and we want also to become a model city where there is social justice, social harmony, and economic development. So we have to strengthen the city, give more power to the City of Montreal ... So, globally, we are in a world of, let's say, concentration, world globalization, and our voice should be stronger, and it's good for Canada. This is why a proposal like this, they are doing in Ontario and Nova Scotia. This is the strength of tomorrow – be together ... Next door to us is the City of Ottawa. They will amalgamate a hundred communities into one big city. It's going to be the city of the next century, and they are going to do the same in Hamilton and Sudbury. Toronto is already one great city of 2.4 million."[61] The message was clear: we've got to get on this train.

BIG LABOUR

Then Big Labour threw their lot in with Bourque. The Quebec Federation of Labour (FTQ) said that it was an aberration that enclaves such as Westmount did not have to deal with Montreal's problems such as poverty and heavy traffic and "essentially did not contribute financially except through the MUC."[62] Of course, since the FTQ represented workers and firefighters in 90 per cent of the municipalities, they maintained there would be no savings in remuneration with Island mergers. The advantage of mergers was that "at a psychological level, a big city has much more impact." On the other hand, the FTQ thought Harel's regional government would be a shambles, with only 2 to 3 per cent of the population voting for its directly elected politicians.

RENEWED DOWNLOADING SQUABBLES

Mergers and supra-structures faded from Harel's thoughts when intense bickering on all municipal and provincial fronts broke out in October 1999, lasting right until the end of the year. It hijacked almost everyone's agenda. From the mayor of the smallest hamlet in Quebec to Premier Bouchard, all waged a bloody-minded and self-ish battle as to how the third year of the $375 million[63] downloading bill – payable in 2000 – would be treated. Would we simply have to cut another bunch of cheques, or would the whole amount trans-mogrify itself into a permanent "fiscal pact"? It was as if nobody realized that this was the reason the Bédard Report was commis-sioned in the first place – it was called "Pact 2000," after all. Cer-tainly, this report's cool fiscal analysis and recommendations were thrown aside during the literally dozens of heated negotiating ses-sions between Harel and the two municipal unions. The unions' pos-ition was that the original shakedown was paid to Quebec to help balance the provincial budget; now that was done, it was time to get rid of it. No, said Quebec, the downloading in some form or another is in place *ad vitam aeternam.*[64]

So all the infighting had to do with how this amount should be charged. From which pocket of the taxpayers' trousers would it come? The Union of Quebec Municipalities (UMQ) wanted the Department of Education to dump the financing of school busing on the school boards that would, in turn, have to raise the cap on school taxes to 50 cents per $100 of assessment: a 43 per cent increase.[65] Both the 1980 Fiscal Reform and the 1999 Bédard Report said that schools should not be financed by property taxes; but as usual prin-ciples were irrelevant when trying to fob off the blame for tax hikes onto someone else.

There was a problem, however, in the form of the FQM, the union of Quebec rural towns. The FQM, formerly known as the UMRCQ, insisted that school busing should be given to the counties – who, after all, had precious little else to occupy themselves with – and to urban communities such as the MUC. Economically, the FQM's position made little sense, since municipal employees earned 30 per cent more than the rest of the public sector. The cabinet was div-ided. Finance Minister Bernard Landry and the minister of educa-tion didn't like the UMQ idea. Nor did Guy Chevrette, the minister of transport. Chevrette liked the FQM idea, saying the chronically underused rural school buses could do double duty and take on adult riders. The image of yellow boneshakers carting around the happy denizens of rural Quebec and sometimes sharing their seats with fidgeting eight-year-olds taxed my imagination at least.

The PQ sitting members, at a time when their popularity was at a five-year low, were very cool to the UMQ idea of a 43 per cent school property tax increase, and were, moreover, sceptical that the municipalities would ever give an equivalent tax break from the cancelled downloading bill. When Premier Bouchard said that if the increased school tax option was used, Quebec would pass a law forcing municipalities to drop their taxes *pari passu*, all hell broke loose among an insulted municipal world. When the FQM and the UMQ continued to dig in their heels, a fed-up Bouchard declared that downloading, as is, would apply again for 2000.

Louise Harel put in twenty-three negotiating sessions: the sheer number and variety of the players probably predisposed her to widespread mergers. Trying to get the parties to agree, she said, was "certainly the most difficult thing I have ever done in my political career."[66] A week later the UMQ announced it would attack the downloading in court – something that Westmount and, later, other Island municipalities had already decided to do. Further, the UMQ predicted spitefully that Harel's much-delayed white paper on municipal restructuring would be another "mess." They wanted nothing to do with it.

Right in the middle of this quarrel came a surprising announcement: after years of denying it was their problem, the off-Island suburbs said they would pay their share of Montreal's infrastructure and services from which they benefited, things such as the Biodome and the botanical gardens. It was a breakthrough in getting regional fiscal equity. One off-Island mayor credited Guy Coulombe, Montreal's new director-general, with engineering the breakthrough – not, significantly, Pierre Bourque.[67]

While Harel officially only met with the two other municipal associations during the negotiations for the "Fiscal Pact," we frequently met at her Montreal offices in the Stock Exchange Tower – so-named when Montreal had a stock exchange. Furnished with the usual Quebec government-issue pine furniture, including 1980s chairs with nubby polyester fabric wrapping urethane slabs, and a few ersatz eighteenth-century armoires, these offices of the Department of the Métropole looked as temporary as the department they housed. Because Harel had to be in Quebec most days, we usually met at night. On our side were Georges Bossé, Frank Zampino, Marc Vaillancourt (our director-general), and myself. Harel was usually flanked by the same aides, including André Lavallée, a hulking but genial sleepy-looking man who was a former member of Jean Doré's party and later served on Montreal's executive committee. Harel, a short, handsome woman with a quick, toothy smile, would speak with her trademarked hushed voice, a habit that caused people to pay more attention to her. Her tone could subtly slide into menacing, all without raising her voice. She was always icily polite to me but never friendly, as if to send the message that a representative of working-class *indépendentiste* Hochelaga-Maisonneuve riding could never be chummy with the mayor of Westmount. "You don't win against the government," she told me.

As if to illustrate this premise, she implemented the merger in the Mont Tremblant area, the first forced merger in Quebec since 1982. Here again "fiscal equity" was the justification. Mont Tremblant had ten times the assessment value per capita of neighbouring St Jovite. The only solution? Why, plain old merger. Harel rejected a sharing of revenues or some such fiscal solution. The fact that 96 per cent of Mont Tremblant residents were against it was irrelevant. Merger became the lobotomy that instantly solved incompliant municipal problems. Many of us saw in this a portent of how the PQ government would deal with Montreal when our turn came.

"A FORCED MARRIAGE IS NEVER A GOOD THING"

Premier Bouchard, a principled man at bottom, worried about process as well as product. Intellectually he had trouble sharing Harel's doctrinarism, missionary zeal, and moral imperturbability with which she faced the prospect of imposing mergers. In November 1999 he let his guard down in an interview with a local newspaper in the Saguenay when he blurted, "I don't think the lawmaker should intervene to force municipalities to merge. You know, a forced marriage is never a good thing." Surprisingly, the rough and tough ex-labour leader who had become minister of transport, Guy Chevrette, echoed a similar sentiment: "It's been proven that forced mergers, they don't do anything good. They only create hatred and sterile quarrels."[68] Undoubtedly Chevrette had the dolorous experience of Hauterive and Baie-Comeau in mind: the one forced merger put through by the PQ, it went terribly sour.

11

Walking into a Trap

"Will you walk into my parlour?" said the Spider to the Fly;
'Tis the prettiest little parlour that ever you did spy.
The way into my parlour is up a winding stair,
And I've got many curious things to show when you are there."
"Oh no, no," said the little Fly, "to ask me is in vain,
For whoever goes up your winding stair can ne'er come down again."

Mary Botham Howitt, 1834

The year had started with a big bang: gas explosively escaping from the Y2K balloon the minute 1999 blandly turned into 2000. The belief was so widely and firmly held that technological civilization as we knew it was at risk at that fateful moment that in United States up to $100 billion was spent on this geek chimera. In January 2000 the dot.com bubble, too, was just about to burst. Indeed, there was froth everywhere, froth that was not just created by the computer chip. The mergers and acquisitions craze was also in full swing: according to one estimate, corporate mergers destroyed some $134 billion of shareholder wealth between 1998 and 2001.[1] So the bloom was still very much on that ephemeral rose when Vice-Premier Bernard Landry told a group of business people in Quebec that if mergers of corporations were profitable, that should also be true for municipal mergers. In fact, said he, regional economic development comes about by municipal mergers: "It is not a secret. Our government, as is the case for the majority of governments in the western world, favours municipal mergers."[2] What Landry did keep secret was that his government favoured hostile municipal takeovers, not voluntary municipal mergers. He also didn't mention that, aside from Ontario and Nova Scotia, nowhere else in the world for more than two decades had mass municipal mergers been favoured.

Midnight of 31 December 1999 found me at Westmount City Hall with my faithful director-general, Bruce St. Louis. We were watching in vain for a sighting of the Y2K bug. As I walked home that night, I took stock. Bourque, in his seemingly bumbling way, had managed to get some heavy-hitters in his One Island One City camp: mandarin extraordinaire Guy Coulombe; avowed sovereignist and political heavyweight Mayor L'Allier of Quebec City; the Quebec Federation of Labour; the Grand Old Man Claude Ryan (at least wanting *some* Island mergers); the wunderkind Mario Dumont, leader of the ADQ, giving his third-party okay. As well, *mirabile dictu*, the chattering francophone editorial classes who less than a year ago had spurned Bourque were now actually taking his One Island One City seriously. Even Bouchard had made at least one about-turn.

Whom did we have in our corner? No one, no one at all. The leader of the opposition, Jean Charest, was against forced mergers, but you'd never really have known it. Even Vera Danyluk was as much with Harel as with us. Bourque had beaten us on all fronts. My attempts to corral at least the Westmount "captains of industry" had possibly staved off a small part of the business community from supporting mergers, but I had no idea how long that would hold. We had only one thing on our side: public opinion. Polls said support for One Island One City across the entire Island had plateaued at about 40 per cent ever since Bourque's formal launch in May 1999 and in spite of his energetic promotion of it.

Among those "in the know," though, thanks to incessant repetition, Bourque and Harel had managed to turn the belief that both fiscal equity and economies of scale would naturally flow from mergers into a widely held axiom, even though their own studies showed that proto-Montrealers would get no tax relief with a megacity. The suburbs would not be contributing more to the former Montreal, and the merger would not result in any significant savings.

THE DISUNION OF MONTREAL ISLAND SUBURBAN MUNICIPALITIES

Our side was pathetically weak. And we were playing a game of chess with someone who had all the powerful pieces, who could take as long as she wanted before making a move, and, in fact, who owned the chessboard. There was really no single directing mind on our side, as each piece more or less did what it wanted. On top of that, some chess pieces were removed from the game and others even fought among themselves.

In the past, suburban leaders had often been mayors of the bourgeois municipalities: Westmount, Mount Royal, Outremont, and Beaconsfield. Mount Royal was in the throes of political in-fighting. Its mayor, the very fey Ricardo Hrtschan, had suspended his director-general, whom some say he had designs to replace – abetted by the blue-collar union that had helped him get elected. The director-general was promptly reinstated by the councillors;* Hrtschan then lost an action against his former employer for firing him after discovering he had padded his résumé. The mayor of Outremont, Jérôme Unterberg, was – at the age of thirty-two – looking at a career in the private sector and not really active outside his city. While he sometimes worked himself up into a lather, overall he waged a fairly spiritless war against mergers. And Beaconsfield's unilingual yet affable mayor resolutely focused on local matters.

The strongest suburban mayors on the Island now came from the larger, francophone and "ethnic" municipalities: Saint-Laurent, Saint-Leonard, LaSalle, Montreal North, Verdun, and Anjou. These were also mayors who were full time. But Saint-Laurent and LaSalle were mostly marching to their own drum: they were run by the "dissident mayors" whose fratricidal battle with their fellow mayors went back to 1995. So we were fighting the good fight with a fraction of our forces in the field. It must be said, however, that the West Island presented quite a monolithic and influential bloc, even with few star mayors.

An idea to merge the municipalities of Lachine and LaSalle should have taken the prize for the year's dumbest: it played directly into Bourque's and Harel's hands. After a court exonerated him of electoral fraud, a charge concocted by his own council, the mayor of Lachine, William McCullock, found his council troubles were just beginning. In February, against his will, his councillors in cahoots with the director-general approved a Lachine-LaSalle merger study. "The government wants mergers and will force them on us if they have to. We think it is in the best interests of our residents to do this ourselves," said one Lachine councillor.[3] All this came to the

---

* The director-general then sued Hrtschan for slander and was awarded $173,000 in damages and expenses in February 2001. Hrtschan had been elected to replace Harry Schwartz, who had resigned in 1999 rather than face a legal battle with his council, which had launched an action to remove him from office over expense account improprieties.

apparent surprise of LaSalle Mayor Michel Leduc, who nonetheless was quite enthusiastic about the idea, saying it would lead to savings. According to the *Montreal Gazette*, Bourque was elated with the news, actually laughing out loud when he heard about the proposal. The battle between McCullock and his council and between McCullock and Leduc dragged on all year. The Lachine-LaSalle merger proposal was finally put on hold when it was clearly eclipsed by a much bigger threat.[4]

The straight-shooting mayor of the West Island City of Dollard-des-Ormeaux said he was against One Island One City but in favour of his residential municipality merging with other municipalities with strong commercial or industrial tax bases. He was not necessarily wrong, but his timing could have been better.[5]

Then there was the City of Pierrefonds, whose designs on annexing five of its neighbours became public in November when its council passed a resolution to that effect. Pierrefonds hoped by this stratagem to bulk itself up to a population of 82,000 and thereby avoid being caught in the merger stampede. The mayor persisted in saying he preferred negotiation of a "better deal" for his city to any sort of confrontation.

THE MEDIA ARMS RACE

In January 2000 the mayors met with our media consultants. We changed our theme from the wishy-washy "One Island. Diverse Cities" to "Building Greater Montreal." The message was that with Montreal as a partner, we must build a metropolitan region. Some of us, myself included, felt this was too "nice," and we should be declaring open war on forced mergers. (Dorval Mayor Peter Yeomans warned, "We are sharpening our blades and are ready to go at them [the government] hammer and tongs."[6]) We set up a strategy group: the morning's clippings would be faxed to us by 8 AM, and I and other mayors would have a daily conference call at 8:30 AM to plan our response. This pattern lasted for most of the year and proved very useful.

While research to mount a legal challenge had just started (an initiative funded by Westmount and Mount Royal), there still was no sort of Island-wide media campaign. In early February, Westmount was the first suburban municipality to budget a substantial amount – $250,000 – for its anti-merger campaign, although Anjou had been first out of the blocks in January. By the end of February, blue and white signs started going up in Anjou, Westmount, and the West Island: "One Island One City or any forced merger: no way." Mount Royal then put aside $250,000. Finally, in March, the Union of Montreal Island Suburban Municipalities budgeted $300,000 for a joint campaign.

Naturally, Montreal responded in kind. After spending some $300,000 for twelve months ending April 2000, they said they would spend another $250,000.[7] Mind you, this was in addition to their regular $4 million communications budget and the publicity generated by internal staff. Complaining that the suburban mayors were churning out propaganda and that our figures were wrong, Bourque said, "We are going to re-establish the truth."[8]

POLITICS BY NUMBERS

Our work was cut out for us. That a concept from the days of hula hoops and tailfins had been disinterred and proffered up to us all as still valid, that a four-syllable rhyming jingle (*un île, une ville*) somehow could encapsulate the secret to building the Montreal region, profoundly irritated me as the worst kind of charlatanism. A *La Presse* headline would say it all: "One Island One City: Simple, Clear, and Easy to Understand." While this slogan was simplistic, it was powerful because of its simplicity. It was a great rallying cry that oozed the virtues of unification. The fact it did not reflect the pattern of urban growth and was resolutely nineteenth century in its geography did not remove a scintilla of its appeal. By getting rid of the diverse clutter of twenty-seven municipal councils and the whole MUC apparatus, it looked like a stroke of streamlining genius. Get rid of politicians? Yeah, let's go!

Few stopped to realize that Bourque's idea meant a skeletal local level of government. Instead of 240 councillors in twenty-six councils serving a total of 800,000 suburban citizens, Bourque's plan would have sixty councillors serving 1.8 million citizens. The suburbs would go from an average of ten councillors per 30,000 citizens to only one.[9] There was another problem. Councils of sixty people aren't really councils; they become assemblies, or parliaments, in other words. Assemblies mean political parties, long speeches, grandstanding, and no action. They require executive committees to handle their volume of business and to pre-masticate policy, all of that work carried out in camera and only later rubber-stamped by the public assembly. On the other hand, councils of eight, ten, or even twelve can handle both debate and business – openly.

The problem with a constellation of small councils dotting the Island delivering local services is how to administer Island-wide services. This is why the MUC was necessary. The One Island One City model had the tremendous advantage of being able to handle both local and regional services – at a huge democratic price, as I point out. So the *rock* was one inefficient assembly for all services, and the *hard place* was a bunch of small councils for local services along with an (inefficient) assembly for Island-wide services. But there was a solution, one used rarely in Quebec but commonly in the United States: boards. Instead of a massive assembly such as the MUC, you have a board with a handful of members: one for police, one for mass transit, one for water, and so forth. You will hear more about this later.

MEGACITIES OR MEGASTUCTURES?

Ignis fatuus translates literally as "foolish fire" and loosely as "a misleading or deluding goal." The twin *ignes fatui* of the Quebec municipal world at the beginning of the millennium were megacities and megastructures, both pursued with ardour and conviction by different camps, some overlapping. It was strange that our municipal salvation could be beckoning from two seemingly different directions: either the megacity being sold by Bourque or the new metropolitan level of government being sold by Harel and Danyluk. However, the final result could have been the same. For a municipality like Westmount, an Island megacity meant immediate eradication, whereas a directly elected metropolitan government could lead to Westmount's eventual demise just as the six municipalities in Toronto were merged in 1998 to become a megacity after ten years of sharing such a regional government.

Harel had even confirmed my domino theory: "Toronto had a directly elected metropolitan council since 1988. Ottawa-Carleton, which will soon become a megacity, had a directly elected metropolitan council since 1968; that is, for thirty years. We have to make the one move before the other."[10] An Island megacity now or possibly an even bigger megacity in the future – take your poison. Actually, given a choice, I would have taken the latter. Not only Parkinson's Law about "delay is the deadliest form of denial" would have applied, but Harel would have had to shove this regional government down the throats of the off-Island mayors.

WOULD A METROPOLITAN STRUCTURE MAKE MERGERS UNNECESSARY?

The Island suburban mayors had always been in favour of a light, indirectly elected metropolitan structure as opposed to a fully fledged government. Our hope at the beginning of 2000 was that the birth of such a thing to handle regional planning would, by handing out cheques to the City of Montreal, wipe out the perceived need for One Island One City. No longer could the suburbs be accused of freeloading off Montreal, ever the most persuasive argument proffered up for mass mergers.

Giving birth to this body would not be easy, though. In late December 1999 the government had set up a powerful cabinet committee to manage all municipal reform. Its eight members included Transport Minister Guy Chevrette and Finance Minister Bernard Landry; given the potential linguistic explosiveness of One Island One City, the minister in charge of the French language charter, Louise Beaudoin, was also included. This committee was so notoriously leaky that Chevrette complained openly of a resident "mole." When it was leaked in February that a draft law creating a Montreal metropolitan body would be tabled the moment the National Assembly reconvened on 14 March, the north shore mayors were again up in arms. "It's clear that Quebec wants to have other municipalities pay for the decisions made by the City of Montreal. The problem is on the Island of Montreal and the solution should be found on the Island of Montreal," said their leader, Yvan Deschênes, mayor of the town of Rosemère.[11]

THE METROPOLITAN SKY IS FALLING

Then, in February, Vera Danyluk told Premier Bouchard that time was a-wasting. In a no-holds-barred open letter,[12] she reminded him, as only she could, of his fourteen-month-old electoral promise immediately to put some order in the Montreal Metropolitan Region, a ringing promise that had had a galvanizing effect on her at the time, she said. "Faced with this clear and stimulating signal, I found it necessary to speed up my own thinking in order to embrace a regional vision, even though it meant making a clean break with my former convictions (before being at the MUC, I was the mayor of Mount Royal and a jealous warden of its local prerogatives)." But since the election, nothing concrete had happened. The government, she said, was suffering from the same foot-dragging and the same "fragmentation virus" that had for so many years afflicted the Montreal region. "It's as if the doctor is in as bad shape as the patient ... You have wasted your most precious resource: time," she warned Bouchard. "And that is precisely the resource that the supporters of the status quo or of timorous half-measures have needed to get organized." During these wasted months, she wrote, "You have garnered no support; on the contrary, you have allowed a collection of small forts to be built in our local baronies, more or less openly dedicated to resisting change. We needed blitzkrieg; instead, we are now bogged down in trench warfare. Every day that goes by allows the *status quo* to put down deeper roots."

Then came the direct appeal. Danyluk told Bouchard, "I know you are capable of grabbing the helm. You've done it many times in your career ... Rumour has it that you want to short-circuit these dizzying twists and turns and that you intend to go directly to tabling a draft law. For pity's sake, do it." Bouchard responded by telling her to be patient and something would soon be done. Georges Bossé echoed Danyluk's call for speedy metropolitan action, all the while cautioning against mergers. Bourque, on the other hand, scolded Danyluk, "This is such an important issue that it's not time to disturb them while they are reflecting on this."[13] Translation: "Things are going my way, so keep quiet."

Most municipal leaders, then, on the Island of Montreal were goading Bouchard into taking action – but not the same action.

A few days later, Bourque, while bragging about how much ministerial support he had, publicly suggested two committees be formed, one to negotiate the creation of the Montreal metropolitan body, the other to negotiate One Island One City. To head up both committees as the government agent, Bourque (or, most likely, his director-general, Guy Coulombe) suggested Louis Bernard, a long-time PQ confidant and mandarin. The other members of the committees would be local mayors.[14]

ALL IS REVEALED – OR IS IT?

On 3 March 2000, press communiqués started coming out of Harel's office.

First, the government declared that three "metropolitan commun-ities" would be created for the Montreal, Quebec, and Gatineau regions to replace the three existing "urban communities." So it was goodbye to the Montreal Urban Community that covered Montreal Island and hello to the Montreal Metropolitan Community (CMM) that would cover the entire region. This new structure, like the MUC, would not have direct taxation powers nor be directly elected. It was therefore not a level of government. Unlike the MUC, it *appeared* that the CMM would not deliver services, but it would plan the region's development; most importantly, the CMM would recompense the City of Montreal for regional costs it had been paying that were not already shared by the other municipalities on the Island. It was what we had always wanted, except for one huge lacuna that to me was as obvious as a missing front tooth: what would happen to all the services the MUC currently delivered? I had a sinking feeling that Harel's unspoken premise was that One Island One City was on its way, a move that would automatically make the MUC redundant, as an Island-wide city would take over not just our municipalities but all MUC services. I kept my thoughts to myself. Publicly, I said that the creation of this regional structure to pay for Montreal's pub-lic housing and regional infrastructure would put paid to the main argument for mergers.

Another communiqué said the much-awaited white paper on municipal reorganization would appear sometime between mid-March to mid-April. By the end of June, bills would be tabled in the National Assembly that would give the government the power to decree mergers all over Quebec, with the exception of the three metropolitan regions. The how, which, and why of these mergers would by then already have been revealed in the white paper.

The government also announced that it was naming three commit-tees headed up by three government agents (*mandataires*) for each of the metropolitan regions. All the other members would be local may-ors. Each committee would be responsible for recommending to the government how its metropolitan community would be set up and which mergers should take place within it – exactly as Bourque had suggested. And who was to head up the Montreal committee? Why, it was the very person Bourque (a.k.a. Guy Coulombe) had suggested: Louis Bernard. So Bernard's committee had two jobs; the first was to negotiate how the Montreal Metropolitan Community would work – including how regional costs would be shared. This little bit of work had to be completed by the end of June. He was then to start work on his next, even thornier job. By the end of October, his committee had to make recommendations about mergers in the Montreal region. His mandate was to examine specifically three options: one municipality covering the Island of Montreal; one municipality covering the Island, Laval and Longueuil; and one municipality covering the entire Montreal metropolitan region. And here was the rub: if, in the accomplishment of his work, Bernard could not get the mayors to agree on a common solution, then he was charged with making his own, stand-alone, recommendation to the government.

The whole municipal reorganization – from metropolitan communities to mergers – was going to come into force January 2001.

While Bourque and Danyluk applauded Harel's actions, others were not so kind. Michel Auger, writing in *Le Journal de Montréal*, called it "IKEA" reform: "Harel's reform is like IKEA furniture. When you open the box, you see that everything is there. But you have to put it together yourself, the instructions are in Swedish, and the result is often different than what you saw in the catalogue."[15]

MERGER MANIA

Back in autumn 1999 I had been fed up with the unsubstantiated statements of both Harel and Bourque to the effect that mergers were a worldwide trend and that they led to economies of scale. I had telephoned Andrew Sancton of the University of Western Ontario, a former Quebecer and Rhodes scholar with a doctorate from Oxford University, and an expert on local government. I said, "Andrew, how would you like to write a book about mergers? The City of Westmount would bankroll it, but we would have no control over what direction it took nor what conclusions you drew. How about it?" By October he sent me a proposal,[16] and he soon got to work. While I acted as a sort of hands-off editor, my only contribution was to come up with the book's openly tendentious title: *Merger Mania: The Assault on Local Government*.

On 8 March 2000 we launched the book. This was the *La Presse* reporter's take: "The mayor of Westmount, Peter Trent, spared no expense yesterday. He had invited journalists to Victoria Hall, a handsome greystone edifice built right in the heart of his city, to hear the conclusions of Professor Andrew Sancton, author of a vigorous diatribe against municipal mergers. After the press conference, canapés with shrimp and smoked salmon washed down with wine were served to the thirteen mayors and municipal councillors from the Island of Montreal who took the trouble to be there to support Mr Trent." Actually, smoked salmon sandwiches were served to the journalists at noon, a common practice. And by now I had resigned myself to the terminology: pro-merger studies were plain "studies"; anti-merger studies were "diatribes."

For the benefit of any reader who managed to get beyond the obligatory embroidering of the Westmount caricature – a duty that seemed to be the lot of many francophone print journalists – the rest of the *La Presse* article about *Merger Mania* was fairly accurate. "Sancton's book ... concluded that mergers were out of fashion and, that instead of reducing costs, they increase them. The trend is to small cities. The San Francisco region has 90 municipalities, the Boston region has 282, Atlanta 102, Miami 55 and Montreal 111."[17]

Merger Mania pointed out that no solvent US municipality has been forced to merge with another in almost a hundred years. The most comprehensive single merger in North America since New York in 1898 happened when Laval was created in 1965. The *biggest* merger since New York was that of Toronto in 1998. All indications at the time of writing *Merger Mania* were that the Toronto and Halifax megacities had cost, not saved money.

RCM: NO MEGACITY, THANKS

Contrasted with the impetuosities and improvisations of Pierre Bourque was the substance, thick with thought-out policies, of the RCM – the party of former Montreal mayor Jean Doré, now Montreal's "official opposition." Though they were a bit too left-wing for my taste, and while I never was in favour of municipal parties to begin with, the RCM was a serious and democratic party, unlike Bourque's vapid claque, pompously called Vision Montreal. In March 2000 the RCM came out with a masterful fiscal analysis of the metropolitan region.[18] They concluded, *pace* Bourque and the media, that there was no fiscal unfairness among the municipalities on Montreal Island and that the real problem was that the north and south shore municipalities had tax loads per capita that were less than two-thirds of those on Montreal Island. This report even calculated that municipalities such as Dorval and Westmount were subsidizing other Island municipalities through their payments to the

MUC, to the tune of $600 per capita (Westmount) and $800 per capita (Dorval). Who benefited? The other suburbs such as Montreal North and Pierrefonds, not the City of Montreal itself. This analysis supported my point that the creation of the megacity would only result in a heightened exchange of bills among the suburbs, with no change in the City of Montreal's tax load.

As far as I know, the RCM report had no impact on Louise Harel. The irony of this is that the RCM were made of the same ideological stuff as Harel, and tended to be sovereignists to boot. Yet their carefully worked out analysis got nowhere with her. Perhaps it was because they wrote, "For now, [Harel] proposes new structures and puts off solving the real problems of taxation and urban sprawl. The RCM cannot approve of such a plan. It's the debate on finances that should be the priority. 'One Island One City' and other structural delusions will only have real worth if they bring a solution to the fiscal problem of the Montreal region."

THE SUMMIT ON GREATER MONTREAL

Next, trying desperately to seize the initiative before Harel's white paper came out, the Island suburban mayors organized in March a pompously named Summit on Greater Montreal with Louise Harel as keynote speaker. We billed it as "a forum for all who want to improve the performance and competitiveness of Greater Montreal." We hammered home our vision of metropolitan governance, saying that, if the threat of forced mergers went away, it would be that much easier to get everybody to build the Montreal Metropolitan Region. We sidestepped the problem of the resistance of both the north shore and south shore mayors to the Montreal Metropolitan Community, especially its cost-sharing.[19] In fact, these mayors were boycotting Louis Bernard's committee. Meanwhile, Bernard, who was one of our speakers, cryptically told us there would definitely be mergers "either of municipalities or services." In early April, we met with Harel privately, and she told us point blank that "the public interest requires that mergers cannot just be voluntary."

A RATHER YELLOWED WHITE PAPER

A white paper is a government report that gives proposals on a particular issue. On 23 June 1999 the provincial cabinet had given

Harel the mandate to prepare a white paper on municipal reform, to be released mid-August that year.[20] After its release was delayed innumerable times through autumn of 1999 and spring of 2000, one could have called it a yellowed paper. Cleaving to the now-hallowed tradition of leaking documents, the government made sure that the paper was making its surreptitious rounds well before its formal release date of 25 April. I managed to get a bootlegged copy marked "draft" that was dated 30 March 2000.

By the end of March, Bernard had started meetings of his committee. On 28 March, he had asked the committee for ideas to pass along for incorporation into the white paper. Dutifully, and within three days, the Island suburban mayors prepared a detailed commentary. We had no idea we were wasting our time: the final version of the white paper was unchanged from the 30 March draft copy except for a paragraph about preserving the status of French in Montreal. Clearly, Bernard's committee was being used in an elaborate exercise in pseudo-consultation.

By the time the white paper was released, it was yesterday's news. However, since it was supposed to serve as the philosophical underpinning for Harel's ambitious municipal reform as well as a kind of legislatorial roadmap, we examined every word in this 131-page document, turning them around in the light for hidden meanings. The future of our municipalities literally depended on it.

Starting with a banal title ("Municipal Reorganization: Changing the Way Things Are Done to Serve Citizens Better"), and introduction ("The *status quo* is no longer acceptable. We have to take the road of reinforcing the urban poles throughout the territory of Quebec"), Harel's document proceeded to trot out the shameful statistics of municipal pullulation: 1,100 of the 1,306* municipalities in Quebec mustered only 21 per cent of the total population, and they all had fewer than 5,000 residents each. These micro-municipalities were, moreover, on government life support, getting more than one-third of their revenues in indirect and direct aid. This was a disincentive to merge, as the larger municipalities got much less of this manna, which served as a sort of anti-marital alimony. Or, as Harel herself put it, "The government financed municipalities because they

---

* Down from 1,596 in 1971.

were small, and they stayed small in order to be financed.[21] In stark contrast with rural Quebec, the 31 urban agglomerations, where 290 municipalities thrived, one found 78 per cent of the population, 85 per cent of the jobs, and 90 per cent of value of new construction. So the white paper's own statistics revealed that municipal overabundance was a rural problem.

Next the white paper delved into the "fiscal disparities" in urban agglomerations. It erroneously used the artificially inflated Montreal tax rate to conclude the tax burden for a resident of Montreal was higher than in the suburbs.* It talked of Montreal's "high costs" of public housing, the integration of immigrants, and the homeless, ignoring that they represented only 0.04 per cent of Montreal's budget – once the costs of public housing were removed, as they were slated to be shared by the entire metropolitan region.

Then it came: "Municipal mergers can permit better services to people and at lower cost."[22] The paper gave absolutely nothing to back up this egregious claim, a claim that was especially galling when just about all the academic literature showed the reverse was true. After invoking the need for fiscal equity, for the end to inter-municipal competition, and for the size required to stand out on the world's stage, the authors ploughed on to say that the government would push for mergers in every way possible, especially in Quebec City, Montreal, and Gatineau, "where municipal mergers remain an unavoidable route to improving municipal governance"[23]

To support the thesis that municipal mass mergers were a worldwide trend, the white paper citied the examples of England, Norway, Sweden, Belgium, Germany, and Denmark. But all of those mergers happened between 1950 and 1978 – not a one since. The authors did admit that Greece, Italy, and France had *not* gone that route and that the United States had significantly increased the number of its municipalities in the last forty-five years. What was not said was that the United States, the only non-European example given, was the most appropriate model to compare with geographically and was the country to which Quebec sent 75 per cent of its international exports.

* See chapter 9

The white paper did shed some light on what would happen to the MUC. If One Island One City became the chosen route, MUC services such as the police would be folded into the new megacity. If there were "a very small number" of municipalities on the Island, then those services could be given to an intermunicipal board. Otherwise, police and other services would be administered by a special board of the Montreal Metropolitan Community (CMM) run exclusively by mayors from the Island of Montreal.

The reaction to the document was all over the spectrum. The north shore mayors denounced it as "gross and monstrous" because it would mean very roughly a 5 per cent tax increase for them to share Montreal's regional costs through the CMM. The suggestion that Laval and Longueuil could be merged with the Island of Montreal – a straw man if ever there was one – put Laval mayor Gilles Vaillancourt into an apoplectic rage: "I will resist with unbelievable force any form of merger."[24]

Bourque was "proud" of the white paper and said that it tacitly supported One Island One City. According to the mayor of Montreal North, Yves Ryan, whatever the white paper said, Bourque would say it supported his plan. "He's always happy, no matter what happens. Quebec City could give him a punch in the nose and he would still say it's good for One Island One City."[25] Danyluk approved of it, especially because it meant the birth of the CMM. We also agreed with that aspect.

Bizarrely, Georges Bossé, the leader of the Island suburban mayors, was reported as saying that the white paper meant the end of One Island One City.[26] Here was a government document, approved by the premier, the cabinet, and the whole PQ caucus, baldly stating that in Quebec City, Montreal, and Gatineau, mergers of local municipalities were "unavoidable." The best assessment I could make was that it was certain we were going to get a metropolitan body and a sharing of regional costs; it was equally certain there was going to be quite a lot of forced merging going on. The chances of Westmount escaping it were looking slim.

Instead of launching a blistering attack on the half of the white paper that constituted a rapturous itemization of the many virtues of mergers, the official position that the Island suburban mayors eventually adopted was that we took issue with the one thing in it we did agree with: the CMM. We complained that the CMM in the white paper would have a contradictory and unmanageable mission: to plan for the metropolitan region while concurrently delivering services on the Island of Montreal. We berated Harel for adding yet another structure to be stacked on top of others. "A tower of Babel," we called it.[27] Yet the alternative to this double mission was either yet another structure (the MUC) or One Island One City. We were painting ourselves into a corner.

FRENCH TO THE RESCUE? NOT SO FAST

Bossé was not alone in thinking One Island One City was dead. Michel C. Auger, in *Le Journal de Montréal*, wrote: "It is not difficult to understand that the White Paper on municipal reform sounds the death knell of the One Island One City project. The little paragraph that constitutes the burial of the project is found on page 64 of the white paper: 'It is important to point out that the government wishes that, under no circumstances, the City of Montreal, or any new city that results from a merger with it, would lose its trait of being the largest French-language city in the Americas. Whatever merger scenario is examined, it must not allow for such a thing to happen.'"[28] Auger went on to write that the law allows a municipality to have bilingual status if a majority of its citizens are non-francophone, a situation that would come about sooner or later with One Island One City. This is precisely what the white paper said could not happen. Besides, such a possibility was sure to turn francophones off the whole idea.

As if to make One Island One City less appetizing for anglophones as well, Louise Beaudoin, minister for the French language charter, announced there would be no bilingual districts within One Island One City, and so places such as Westmount would lose their bilingual status.[29] Dorval mayor Peter Yeomans reacted by calling the idea "cleansing from a linguistic standpoint ... This will ignite a firestorm."[30] A few weeks later Beaudoin took things a step further. Mergers would contribute to the "francization" of Montreal Island, she said. "*Fusionner pour mieux franciser*" read the headline in *Le Devoir*.[31] She shied away from the word "assimilation," but that was the subtext.

When Beaudoin realized, in spite of disallowing bilingual districts *within* it, that a bilingual One Island One City was still a possibility under the current law, and that this threatened to kill the whole project, she announced that the language law should be changed. To have bilingual status, she said, a municipality should in future have to have a majority of anglophones, not a majority of non-francophones. And not just any anglophones, but *mother tongue* anglophones, a rarer breed.[32] As this idea took root, the PQ could see that it was the best way to clear the major road block for One Island One City, because while the Island *was* in danger of eventually becoming majority non-francophone, it would never become majority anglophone.

So our main bulwark against Island mergers, a bulwark not at all of our making, could crumble with a simple change of the language law.

WE HEAR FROM RYAN

It wasn't long before Claude Ryan, the former Liberal minister of municipal affairs, decided to comment on the white paper.[33] In a sideswipe at Liberal leader Jean Charest and his belief in voluntary mergers, Ryan said it was time for the government to intervene "with firmness" in the matter of mergers, and the Liberal Party "could not fight, backs to the wall, a rearguard action." However, Ryan continued to believe in forcibly merging only those municipalities that were "veritable enclaves situated right in the heart of a territory that should be that of the City of Montreal." In a surprise comment, he blessed Harel's idea of a Montreal Metropolitan Community (CMM), although he did say the government had done a poor job of clearing up the clutter of structures over which the CMM would be superimposed. He also chided the north shore mayors who insisted on a metropolitan region that did not include them.

HAREL BUYS OFF THE UMQ

Meanwhile, the fiscal pact that was supposed to replace the Trudel downloading was still not sorted out and remained yet another cause of municipal fissiparity. The Union of Quebec Municipalities (UMQ) refused to discuss municipal reform with Harel as long as this matter remained unresolved – to the point it even took Quebec to court over it. After all, for three years, Quebec municipalities had been forced to give $375 million each year to the provincial government to help it balance its budget "temporarily." This amount was supposed to metamorphose into a permanent fiscal pact. The March provincial budget did make the $375 million downloading bill go away, but it unilaterally stripped municipalities of tax revenues of $322 million. The UMQ quite rightly did not regard this insulting and mainly self-annulling bit of financial legerdemain as any sort of an acceptable settlement.

Harel knew she could not push ahead with her reform as long as the fiscal pact was still not accepted by the UMQ, so she did what all governments do – bought her way out of the problem. Harel somehow found $1.5 billion to give to Quebec municipalities over the following five years, thereby making up for their lost revenues. When this unexpected largesse was announced at the annual UMQ meeting at the end of April, a subsequent motion to reject her white paper was itself rejected 258 to 163. So a union that should have defended the right of its members to exist and emphatically reject the pro-merger position of the white paper summarily caved in. Mind you, the UMQ was divided into three camps: mayors of the "central cities," who were rabidly pro-merger, the exurban mayors, who wanted nothing to do with the cost-sharing the metropolitan communities brought, and the suburban and rural mayors, who were simply against forced mergers. Even Premier Bouchard remarked on the UMQ's running up the white flag to the white paper. He said that his government favoured dialogue and mediation before imposing mergers. So it was imposition if necessary but not necessarily imposition.

The UMQ also got a new president in April: Guy Leblanc, the mayor of Trois-Rivières. An affable, athletic, and stocky man, Leblanc was a former notary and a big supporter of mergers. To dilute his "central-city" bias, the UMQ voted in the leader of the north-shore mayors, Yvan Deschênes, as a vice-president. The trouble was, Deschênes was against the CMM but all for One Island One City.

As it turned out, it took nearly six months before municipalities saw the colour of Harel's money, her promised $1.5 billion. The fiscal pact was only signed 10 October 2000, and, by then some $210 million of the money had been redirected, earmarked for what Quebec liked to call "municipal restructuring," or what the rest of us called "mergers." So we, the municipalities, were going to pay for the cost of any mergers imposed on us.

Sixteen Montreal Island suburbs were still contesting the Trudel downloading in court. Finance Minister Bernard Landry made it clear we would not see a cent of this $1.5 billion honey pot unless we dropped our action. We did not. Our government was, in effect, bullying us into submission by – possibly illegally – using such extortion to deny us access to the courts, a freedom guaranteed in any civilized country.[34]

OUR ACHILLES' HEEL EXPOSED

At the parliamentary hearings in late May on the law creating the Montreal Metropolitan Community (CMM),[35] the problem of what to do with MUC services came up more than once. Three solutions presented themselves: give services to an Island megacity to handle, keep a pared-down MUC, or push services up to the CMM. Each had its champion at the hearings.

Bourque said, "One Island One City remains the most logical solution to take over the remaining responsibilities of the MUC: police, mass transit, regional parks ... I must insist that we give the CMM only planning functions and leave to the municipalities the responsibility of delivering services to the public. This new structure is essential, but must be light." He ended his presentation with the usual coda, "Municipal mergers are a strategic solution for development. They are a national and international trend."

Bossé, speaking for the Island suburban mayors an hour later, also said the CMM should be a light structure and not deliver services, at least directly. We pled for keeping a slimmer MUC that would continue to deliver police, mass transit, and other services, as opposed to Bourque's solution of simply having a new megacity do all that: "Our union does not wish and never has wished the abolition as such of the MUC, just as the government has not seen the need to abolish the counties in the metropolitan region, but we do wish to revise it and adapt its powers following the creation of the CMM."

Vera Danyluk took another tack. "For me, there is only one way to do it, and that's to take the MUC and to send everything it does to the CMM." As for the police, "The police department that would continue to serve the Island of Montreal could report to a CMM board that is made up of elected officials coming uniquely from the Island of Montreal"– which is what the white paper had suggested as an option.

Anyone disinterestedly listening to these three positions would have concluded that Bourque's solution for the delivery of Island-wide services was by far the simplest. The delivery of these services became our Achilles' heel. I really don't think we realized how serious a weakness it was. To change metaphors, we were hoist with our own petard. The creation of the CMM, which we had supported for eight years, made the MUC look extraneous, a bit of a lost soul who really did not fit in at the party. Besides, the government had already made it clear that the MUC was no more.[36]

Because the government lacked the political courage to trim the hodgepodge of structures cluttering up the region because of entrenched off-Island resistance from PQ strongholds, the law creating the CMM did not remove even *one* of these structures. So the sixteen counties, twenty mass transit organizations, five administrative regions, and so on all stayed. And yet, in order to avoid One Island One City, here we were fighting a rearguard action to retain yet another structure – the MUC, albeit downsized and in some new disguise. It was one structure too many. We would have done better to have adopted Danyluk's idea.

BOUQUETS FOR VERA

At the end of Danyluk's presentation at the parliamentary hearings on the CMM, one got an idea of the warmth and mutual respect that flourished between her and Harel. Said Danyluk, "In conclusion, I'll repeat what I said when the white paper came out. I saw in it a collection of fundamental ideas that allows us to launch a magnificent leap towards coherence and prosperity. We have a rendezvous with history. Experience shows that this comes to us no more than two or three times in a century. Let's be visionaries. Let's be courageous. It's our duty. Thank you for listening."

Harel said, "Mrs Danyluk, my colleague ... made a comment just now that I endorse. He said to me: 'I adore that woman.' And I take the liberty to tell you that out loud."

"One cannot stop a heart from loving, Mrs Danyluk," piped up André Boulerice, the colleague in question.

Harel continued, "Your courage, your serenity and your capacity to imagine the scope of the future of the whole metropolitan region – gives you a role of inspiration."

This was not the sort of effusion she ever lavished on Bossé, and not even on Bourque. And certainly not on Andrée Boucher, the virulently anti-merger mayor of Sainte-Foy, a suburb of Quebec City. "When she speaks," Harel said once, "I'm under the constant impression that toads, mud, and snakes come out of her mouth"[37] (Mind you, Harel did publicly apologize for that outburst – effusively. And Madame Boucher graciously accepted the apology.)

MERGER BY DECREE

The law[38] creating the Montreal Metropolitan Community (CMM) was adopted June 15. This same day, another law[39] was adopted, a law giving the cabinet (as opposed to the National Assembly) complete discretionary authority to *decree* municipal mergers all over the province. The justification for this plenipotentiary power was, according to the wording of the law, "to favour fiscal equity and to provide citizens with services at lower cost or better services at the same cost." In the past, any forced merger at least had to go through the National Assembly as a special bill. Now the PQ government had arrogated that right, giving themselves a blank cheque to impose wholesale mergers.

THE MONTREAL METROPOLITAN COMMUNITY IS BORN

Meanwhile, the Bernard committee had been beavering away, meeting a dozen times since it was formed. It had made progress on how the Montreal Metropolitan Community (CMM) would function and had not, at this point, got anywhere with the question of mergers. While Bourque had for a year maintained that his municipality paid $209 million yearly for the cost of services and infrastructure that served the metropolitan region, Bernard had managed to whittle this number down to $37 million, restricting it to things like the botanical garden, the Biodome, and the Planetarium.

The CMM would include just over one hundred municipalities and be run by a council of twenty-eight mayors, fourteen from the Island and fourteen off-Island. The mayor of Montreal became chairman *ex officio*, and exercised a "preponderant vote" in the event of a tie. The CMM was responsible for land-use planning, economic development, social housing, metropolitan services and infrastructure, and regional mass transit. Interestingly, the total yearly cost for social housing for the entire metropolitan region, now shared by all municipalities, was only $13 million.

THE MYSTERY OF MUC SERVICES

Louis Bernard was an austere, enigmatic, and cerebral hired hand the PQ brought in for jobs requiring particularly tough negotiation, often those with complex political overtones. Raised in working-class St Henri in a religious family – his brother was a priest and his sister a nun – Bernard earned a doctorate from the London School of Economics. For nearly eight years he was the head of the civil service in René Lévesque's PQ government, all the while an open militant for the PQ party and a staunch sovereignist.[40] So much was Bernard committed to the cause that, much to general surprise, he ran a quixotic campaign to become leader of the PQ in 2005, coming in fourth. Bernard was just one more example of the highly educated and highly sophisticated officers the PQ had for over a generation serving in their political army. The Liberals, with the notable exception of Claude Ryan, were always intellectual bumpkins compared to the PQ in the 1960s to the 1990s. Today, the two parties seem to be on a more or less equal, but much lower, footing.

Bernard was sixty-three when he was named to his eponymous committee, and would receive $154,000 for his efforts.[41] Being a thirty-year friend of Guy Coulombe, the director-general of the City of Montreal, and another former Quebec mandarin and confident of Lucien Bouchard, did not augur well for our side. It was clear Bernard got his orders directly from the premier's office, though his mandate was to make recommendations to Harel. Once his recommendation regarding the CMM was made, he turned to the second and trickiest: the merger issue.

Bernard decided to go about this indirectly by setting up a sub-committee[42] to decide on the future of the MUC. There are two ways of travelling by water: on it or through it. Bernard planed, he did not displace. He sensed that, by innocently asking "What happens to MUC services?" one was really asking the question, "What does the alternative to One Island One City look like?" Our first meeting took place on 1 June at Montreal City Hall, with about a dozen people present, including Bourque and Coulombe. Bernard said that Montreal's position was very clear: the MUC got folded into One Island One City. It was therefore up to the Island suburban mayors to come up with their own approach. "You have to put something on the table," Bernard told us. The next week we did, coming back with our old standby that the MUC be scaled down to an intermunicipal service enterprise. The MUC council would either disappear or be cut back, with few public commissions, the whole thing run by a CEO. Considering the

government had – sort of – said the MUC was history, our suggestion seemed slightly surreal, a quasi-posthumous rearranging of a
body declared dead.

Bernard was clearly not keen on this MUC Lite. He wrote the minutes of our meetings and was not afraid to editorialize: "The proposition seems by its very nature to provoke a democratic deficit in
the collective management of large sums of money ... to distance us
even further from the direct participation by the population that is
currently allowed, using the many public meetings of MUC council
and its commissions."[43] He felt that even the current MUC was not
"democratic" enough: Danyluk's job, for example, should be directly elected. Her long-time crusade to "open up" the MUC had not
been for naught.

We were trapped. A full-blown MUC could not be justified once
another, parallel structure (the CMM) was placed on top, even if it
covered more territory. And, according to Bernard, a slimmed-down
MUC was undemocratic. I took strong exception to that word; after
all, citizens vote for their mayor to handle MUC matters. Over six
years before, the Pichette Report had recommended the same thing
we were suggesting now: indirect election to a slimmed-down MUC
and to a Metropolitan Council.

A WESTMOUNTER MAKES A SOLOMON
OF BERNARD

It turned out that one of my city councillors, Gérard Limoges,
lunched quite regularly with Bernard. Limoges had just retired as
vice-chairman of Ernst & Young Canada. He asked me whether he
should bring up the merger matter with his friend Bernard at their
next lunch and I said, "Why not?" So, on 5 June, Gérard had a
lunch that would change the course of Quebec's municipal history.
On the spur of the moment, Limoges said to Bernard, "Have you
ever thought of *arrondissements*? You know, the way Paris is divided up?" A light went on in Bernard's brain: "Yes!" he must have
thought: "that's the way to square the circle, to have One Island One
City and keep the specificities of the former cities." I don't think
Limoges quite realized what he had done.[44]

Looking back, Lucien Bouchard said of his conversion to the idea
of One Island One City "I was won over this summer when I was
told of the concept of arrondissements ..."[45]

BERNARD DROPS HIS BOMB

After the July holidays, we had our fourth meeting on 3 August. Bernard dropped his bomb:

> I have tried to reconcile your two points of view because I think it's worth it. While what I am about to present to you is the fruit of my personal reflection, you should know that I have already sounded out Premier Lucien Bouchard, Minister Louise Harel, and Guy Coulombe on the matter. My overall aim is to ensure Greater Montreal holds its own on the world scene, and the government I represent is bound and determined to do something concrete. Montreal is more than just the City of Montreal. The heart of the metropolis is not Montreal, it is the whole Island. And I want to create a strong political locus on the Island. The MUC can't do that, it has no political leadership. Besides, the MUC does not function well.
>
> Now, the traditional method for the City of Montreal to grow was to annex contiguous cities. But if it annexed all the cities that are enclaves, and then those that are contiguous such as Verdun and LaSalle, and then the industrial cities such as Anjou and Saint-Laurent (because they should not be alone to exploit their industrial parks); well, you have pretty much merged the whole Island. But such a mass merger would raise animosity, fire, and blood. So I have a compromise for you. *You would make a strategic error if you refuse this compromise.*[46]

Bernard then presented us with his draft working hypothesis. "This hypothesis strives," he had written, "to reconcile the two approaches that have been expressed within the subcommittee – that of maintaining present structures, although in a modified form as advocated by the Union of Montreal Island Suburban Municipalities, and that of One Island One City, advanced by the City of Montreal." He went on to write that his suggestion would give "direct democratic accountability, equitable sharing of the tax burden," all while "it strives to maintain the benefits of political structures that are smaller and closer to residents."[47]

This is what Bernard suggested: the MUC would be replaced by a new city run by a mayor and sixty councillors. In addition to the MUC's existing responsibilities, this new city would handle firefighting, industrial parks, major traffic arteries, and water production and distribution. The existing municipalities (minus eight small ones that would disappear) would retain all their other powers and their status as autonomous municipalities, becoming arrondissements* of the new city with their own local councils. The existing City of Montreal would be divided up into nine arrondissements. The new city would collect all taxes, and the arrondissements would get mostly residential tax revenues. The new city would be born 1 January 2002.

What was Bernard suggesting in plain English? He was suggesting a decentralized One Island One City. In less than a week, *Le Journal de Montréal* had got its hands on Bernard's document and bizarrely billed it as the "dismantling of the City of Montreal."[48] The next day, the *La Presse* headline got it right: "One Island One City, 29 arrondissements." Bourque's public reaction was as positive as the suburban mayors' were negative: Dorval Mayor Peter Yeomans said, "They want to siphon off all our wealth and send it to a city that's in a total mess.† If the government does that, it will find itself facing a mobilization like they've never seen before!" Said Georges Bossé: "By making the suburbs pay for Montreal's sewers, will it make Montreal more efficient? We don't want change just for the sake of change ... No one answers when we ask what is the real problem they want to solve."[49] Danyluk, who was not a member of Bernard's committee, called his idea "interesting and very audacious."[50]

MAYORAL IMMOBILITY

How much more did we need before declaring war? I wondered. One of the few weapons we had to fight mergers was to hold a

---

* Bernard unusually wrote an English version, in which he inserted a "translator's note": "These *arrondissements* are, in fact, Paris-style administrative districts and are being referred to as 'boroughs' by the English media." Since "administrative districts" would have been quite unsellable in English, the government, being far less punctilious than Bernard, from then on liberally translated *arrondissements* as "boroughs," which to the English-speaker (and New Yorker) suggests something of substantial autonomy. Parisian *arrondissements* have no legal status and are financially dependent on an allotment from the city. For a while I insisted on using the French word in my English media interviews but eventually I gave up.

† By then, it had been clear for a long time that the effect of One Island One City would be to share "wealth" among the suburbs. Montreal would *not* get any of the suburb's "wealth."

referendum – not a quick and simple "popular consultation" that could be easily dismissed, but a formal referendum.[51] A referendum was required under the existing annexation law and would be subject to all the requirements set out by law, thereby giving it credibility. The Quebec City area already had had a popular consultation. At least ten municipalities in the Quebec area held them in April and May. Turnout ranged from 20 per cent to 50 per cent. An average of 92 per cent of those who participated rejected merger with Quebec City.[52]

Unfortunately, in June the Montreal north shore mayors debased the referendum coinage. They held what they *called* a referendum for their 475,000 residents but did not follow the lengthy procedures required by law. Even worse, their "referendum" had nothing to do with forced mergers and posed a misleading question.[53] It was their way of rejecting their membership in the CMM, in effect rejecting any contribution to regional costs – estimated to be about $25 per homeowner.[54] While we were threatened with annihilation, they were threatened with cheque-writing.

Since January I had been convinced that an Island-wide suburban referendum was our best tool to underline how undemocratic forced mergers were and to make it hard for Quebec to ignore the expressed will of three-quarters of a million people. It would also serve other purposes: as a didactic mechanism forcing voters to inform themselves, as a rallying event to show Island suburban solidarity and to mobilize citizens already wanting to show their feelings, and as a way of getting media coverage of our position. At the beginning of May, I had managed to get many of the suburban mayors to agree to an October referendum, to be timed with the release of Bernard's report and before any possible merger legislation. By mid-June, the mayors had backslid and resolved into two camps, for and against a joint referendum. I was sickened to realize that some members of the latter group felt mergers were inevitable.

I had had enough. At the end of June, I sent out a three-page letter to all Westmounters ending it by announcing an October referendum in Westmount, appealing for volunteers. Within days, 150 citizens had called our hotline. The final tally ran to 300.

Bossé was furious, saying I had jumped the gun. He allowed his irritation to become public, saying we should wait for Bernard to make his report, scheduled for 30 September, before deciding on referenda. He counselled a more civil approach, avoiding confrontation, "because no one wants to start a war just for the sake of starting a war."[55] By the end of July, Outremont, Mount Royal, Côte Saint-Luc, and Hampstead had joined Westmount in announcing a referendum.

On 31 July, three days before that fateful meeting with Bernard on 3 August, I had a heated discussion with Bossé about his stalling a joint referendum. I felt our Union of Montreal Island Suburban Muncipalities was doing nothing to stop or even slow the forced merger freight train.

"Georges, we both know that to hold a proper referendum requires a long delay. Even if we started the process now, it would be months before we could hold one. You and the Union are doing nothing. As [Hampstead Mayor] Irving Adessky said, 'the natives are restless.'"

"Peter, I am trying to negotiate some sort of a deal with Harel. I want to remove the Montreal region from the list of places that can be merged by decree. I agree if we have it, we all have to have one referendum together, but a poor turnout would weaken my hand with Harel. It might even convince Quebec to go ahead with a straightforward One Island One City. Besides, we need a real and present danger before we have a referendum. You know, to ensure a big turn-out."

I turned on my heel with a Parthian shot, "Georges, by the time the government allows the public to realize there is a real and present danger, it'll be all over."

The next day we reached a compromise. By then Bossé had already got wind of what Bernard was up to. With Bernard openly suggesting wiping out eight of our municipalities and essentially creating One Island One City, Bossé had no choice but to get moving. We decided that on the day of the release of the Bernard Report on 30 September, we would set in motion an Island-wide referendum for 19 November. Meanwhile, groundwork would begin immediately, all coordinated by the Union. This plan was approved by all the mayors on 4 August and publicly announced. I thought the date was very late, but it was worth it to get everybody having a referendum on the same day.

BACK TO BERNARD

While Bernard did not touch the north shore, he had big plans for the south shore. Once his plans to merge eight Montreal south shore municipalities into one megacity leaked out, it created panic. Saying it was better to self-merge than have it imposed, the municipalities floated a number of permutations: two megacities, three megacities, no mergers but one urban community – anything but one megacity, an option supported by only one-quarter of the population.[56] One cabinet minister, Louise Beaudoin, and at least one representative, François Beaulne, both representing south shore municipalities, were against the south shore megacity, opting for an urban community instead.

Meanwhile in Quebec City another government-appointed agent there concluded that no consensus was possible because of the fundamental opposition between the suburbs and the central city. Urban sprawl had been even worse there than in metropolitan Montreal. In forty years the number of municipalities in the Quebec City region had grown by 200 per cent, taking up six times as much land for only 70 per cent population growth. (The equivalent figures for Montreal were 33 percent, three times, and 62 per cent). Just how the recommendation of "two megacities two shores" was going to curb urban sprawl in Quebec City was never explained. But the usual "sterile intermunicipal competition" and "multiplicity of actors" were on parade as arguments for merger.

So megacities were the order of the day all over Quebec – not just on the Island of Montreal.

By suggesting a seemingly reasonable halfway measure between the status quo and One Island One City, Bernard had cleverly kicked out the props supporting our position. The political battle lines were no longer clearly drawn. We looked intransigent if we stayed where we were, and if we negotiated, it was always in the direction of One Island One City. At our eighth meeting on 12 September, Bernard simply said, "Are you people ready to seek a compromise? If not, a solution will be imposed."

Bossé responded, "Once Bourque accepts that the arrondissements have the legal status of municipalities, we can begin to talk."

Bernard said, "You must understand that my proposal should be more easily acceptable to the suburbs than to Montreal. After all, I am proposing the break-up (*fission*) of Montreal into nine arrondissements."

I jumped in: "Give me a break. You are wiping out eight of our cities and emasculating the rest."

A few days after, Bernard said, "The whole political reality of the Island of Montreal revolves around the opposition between

Montreal and the suburbs. Under the system I propose, it wouldn't exist anymore."[57] It all sounded so reasonable.

By the end of September our respective positions were publicly staked out. Bernard, Bourque, and Bossé all agreed that the MUC be replaced by a new city* with a mayor elected at large. Bernard and Bourque wanted around sixty councillors directly elected to the new city's council; Bossé wanted Montreal to be broken up into nine municipalities, and its nine mayors plus the current twenty-six suburban mayors would serve on the new city's council. Bernard, in addition, wanted to create twenty-seven arrondissements that would have the status of municipalities but with reduced powers (stripped of their fire departments, industrial parks, and tax revenue from commercial sectors). Bourque wanted only nine arrondissements that had little or no power, with a yearly allocation of money from the new city.[58] (The writer is not responsible for any headaches this paragraph gives the reader.)

Bourque's position, then, was pure One Island One City. He had not moved a jot. We had moved a lot, all in an attempt to save our skin. We were now in essence suggesting an MUC with direct taxation powers, its head directly elected. Had this been accepted, it would with time have become One Island One City, but our backs were against the wall.

When our position was made public, the francophone media had a field day. "Not only are suburban mayors against mergers, but they want to dismantle Montreal."[59] The editorial opinion was even worse: "a convoluted form of the status quo";[60] "It's crazy ... it takes the effrontery of a triceratops to come up with such a gimmick";[61] "It's just a way to mask the fact that the suburban mayors only want to keep their jobs and their power."[62] And those are just three quotes taken at random. The fission of Montreal, something I had advocated since 1992, was not the best thing to drag out as the alternative to Bernard.

Bourque's plan, on the other hand, got the thumbs up when he made a splashy re-presentation of his plan in front of six hundred people at a Montreal Board of Trade luncheon: "One Island One

---

* We called it "the municipality of the agglomeration," to distinguish it from a city. In the interests of simplicity and mellifluence, I have used the term "new city."

City: Simple, Clear and Easy to Understand," said the *La Presse* headline.[63] Up until then the Board of Trade had taken a mostly negative position on One Island One City, saying it "could not support a slogan" and never would unless major changes were made in labour law, as otherwise costs would skyrocket. They also made it clear they were against forced mergers.[64] When Bourque's friend Normand Legault took over as the president of the Board of Trade in mid-September, their position changed: Legault came out four-square for Bourque's plan.[65]

We then heard from Danyluk, who said both Bourque's and our plan should be tossed in the garbage, but Bernard's plan struck a balance between regional and local interests. It had a "metropolitan vision," she said, a strange term given that Bernard's thrust was to reinforce the Island, not the metropolitan region. Bernard's was in fact a very insular vision. Danyluk also favoured getting rid of the eight small municipalities.[66]

ONE ISLAND, ONE FIRE DEPARTMENT?

In our dozen-odd meetings with Bernard, we rarely got him to back off on something. The one exception was fire protection, which he had centralized in the new city. I had made an impassioned plea for local control over fire departments. While I invoked the spectre of an Island-wide Montreal firefighters' union – a union of over-paid and unruly members best known for intimidating their bosses, sabotaging computers, punching holes in hoses (and fire truck tires), and slapping stickers on fire trucks – my main point was that a fire department should be spending nearly all its time on prevention rather than fighting fires. Both activities require an intimate knowledge of the community: its residents, buildings, and schools. I said there is no service that is more local than fire protection.[67] By 3 October, Bernard had ceded that point to us.

On the elimination of eight of the smallest municipalities that together only represented 2 per cent of the Island's population, Bernard was unshakable. "You weaken your position enormously by trying to protect the eight smallest municipalities from disappearing. There's no place for them. And that's government policy." Even without them, he said, his proposal had become very complicated in order to accommodate our desire for local control. He urged us to support his report, which would in turn "align" Premier Bouchard and force Bourque to support it, too. If we were to rally to his report, he said, we'd have to do it right away. He himself would not defend his report publicly.

I was beginning to think we had been had. We had.

12

Hope and Betrayal: Bernard Proposes, Bouchard Disposes

It is useless for the sheep to pass resolutions in favour of vegetarianism while the wolf remains of a different opinion.

Dean William Ralph Inge, 1919

In politics if you want anything said, ask a man. If you want anything done, ask a woman.

Margaret Thatcher, 1975

After the now-mandatory leaks to the media, the Bernard Report was officially released on 11 October. Bernard did not attempt to establish first principles or give a detailed diagnosis of his municipal patient in his report.[1] What little rationale he did give is worth examination, as it is all we have to go on to try to comprehend his recommendation of major surgery for the entire region. He wrote: "Today's Greater Montreal is no longer made up of a central core and a periphery, the model of metropolitan areas of one or two generations ago. On the contrary, like a lot of modern metropolitan regions, we have a polycentric agglomeration where three major poles of development coexist: a central pole (the Island of Montreal), a northern pole (Laval and the north shore), and a southern pole (the south shore)." To paraphrase crudely: according to Bernard, we had gone from one to three yolks in the Greater Montreal egg.

Now, each pole must develop to the maximum of its capacities, he said, but that was not currently the case. Laval and the north shore had seen the most growth. Why? According to Bernard, it was at least partially thanks to the existence of a strong city, Laval, the product of mergers that allowed it to take over all "of its natural territory." On the other hand, the central and southern poles had languished, suffering from political fragmentation. Bernard was quick to point out that, while this lack of political unity was not "the only or even the principal factor" in explaining the pattern of Montreal's urban development, it was an element. His message was to merge as Laval did in 1965, and regional development would become less lopsided. The corollary to his thesis of Lavalification, then, would be to conclude that, had One Island One City been implemented when Mayor Drapeau started militating for it in the mid-1960s, the Island of Montreal today would have not stagnated, but flourished like Laval. Using the same logic, had the six municipalities in the county of Champlain on the south shore merged in 1965, they would be doing as well as Laval today.*

The facts do not bear Bernard out. During the thirty years after Laval was merged in 1965, it grew by some 70 per cent in population, whereas the six south shore municipalities of Champlain county grew by 100 per cent. Even with the stagnation of the last decade on the south shore, Laval in 2006 had still has not caught up to the former's growth rate.[2] And Laval, with its massive debt, is hardly a shining example of good municipal governance. As Andrew Sancton pointed out, Laval's per capita spending in 1996 was 28 per cent higher than in the six south shore municipalities.[3] By 2003, Laval's per capita spending was 31 per cent higher than the (newly merged) south shore municipalities, and its per capita debt nearly double.[4]

Using Laval, the product of a merger of villages, as a template for the Island of Montreal was unconventional, to be generous. Today, Laval has little sense of community.[†] Only now is Laval planning to give itself an actual downtown, which will resemble a hotted-up mall with a highway running though the middle.

According to Bernard, then, these three poles in the Montreal Metropolitan Region were delimited by their "natural boundaries," and to reinforce these poles, they should be merged into megacities. So for him topography prevailed over demography or established patterns of infrastructure. To Bernard, the skinny half-kilometre wide river that separates Laval from the Island of Montreal was *the*

---

* Bernard recommended that, along with Boucherville and Saint-Bruno, these six south shore cities be merged. Only Saint-Hubert was happy with his report. The mayor of Boucherville called the Bernard Report "a rag."

† Citizens of Laval have the weakest feeling of belonging to their community of any region in Canada (*La Presse*, 21 January 2006).

compartmentalizing feature, almost as if it were as impermeable a barrier as it was a century ago. While all this was not totally devoid of logic, I was not persuaded: certainly not persuaded enough to allow my municipality to be wiped out, sacrificed on the altar of a theory invoked by someone who was, after all, a stranger to the municipal world, in spite of his undoubted intellectual power.[5]

When Bernard turned his attention to Montreal Island, his comments could have been lifted from Danyluk's speaking notes: Bernard wrote that the MUC suffered from a "democratic deficit," since it was not accountable to its taxpayers. To energize Montreal's central pole, the Island needed a "stronger and more united political voice." He also referred to the "interminable conflicts between Montreal and its suburbs" as if they were self-evident.

While the multiplicity of municipalities on the Island had its drawbacks, it had its merits too, he allowed. Bernard recommended turning (most of) them into twenty-seven arrondissements with the same powers and the same status of autonomous municipalities. Arrondissements would keep the responsibility of fire protection – a victory for us. Eight of the smallest suburbs, however, would disappear,[6] and Montreal would be divided up into nine arrondissements, which were called boroughs in English – which they clearly were not. The new city (now unabashedly called the City of Montreal) would have sixty-four directly elected councillors. Including both the local and Island-wide politicians, Bernard was recommending 170 elected officials, down from 290.

He acknowledged that his plan was complicated, but such complications had the advantage of allowing both sides to agree. If, however, the suburbs and Montreal did not rally to his recommendations, these complications "would lose a lot of their raison d'être."

From my point of view, the insurmountable problem with Bernard's report was its fiscal plan. Most of the boroughs' revenue would be an allotment from the central city: they would have extremely limited taxation powers of their own. In fact, when Bernard let Bossé and me see a draft copy of his report before making it public, it sported an appendix that estimated just how much budget the boroughs would actually manage: only 30 per cent of total spending, and 80 per cent of that was the handout from the central city. I was shocked: the boroughs would control only 6 per cent of total municipal spending on the Island. This damning appendix was discreetly removed before anyone else saw it.

In politics, whoever controls the money controls the power. Just ask a school commissioner in Quebec. Ovide Baciu, the mayor of Roxboro, said it best: "If this goes through, the borough mayors will have to practise their royal waves, because that's all they'll be able to do." So, by making the boroughs mancipated by handouts, Bernard had essentially come down on the side of One Island One City, with just enough gewgaws to make it look like a compromise.

Certainly, the way the Bernard Report played in all the media was that it recommended the creation of One Island One City. On occasion, there was a passing reference to boroughs. No media outlet billed the report as a compromise; certainly you didn't read or hear anything like "suburban municipalities preserved as boroughs."[7]

WHO LIKES BERNARD? BOURQUE, BOUCHARD, AND BOSSÉ (SORT OF)

Bourque was quietly pleased with the Bernard Report, although he called it too complicated. Georges Bossé said he was satisfied, although unhappy with the financing of the boroughs: "For us, local services should be taxed locally and the local officials should have total responsibility."[8] He said he hoped "the government would recognize that the project was perfectible" and would be ready to make corrections to it. Danyluk gave it her unconditional support. However, the mayor of Montreal North, Yves Ryan, called it "annexation in slow motion. It's clear: the suburbs have lost the political battle."[9]

Premier Bouchard gave his support to the report the next day, even though he said it had to be simplified. Harel said a government decision would be made by the end of October and that suburban mayors were "playing with fire" if they rejected the report, which, she asserted, gave a lot of power to the boroughs. The government had until 15 November to table merger legislation in order to have it adopted before the end of the year, when the National Assembly would recess until March. Time was running out.

While he did not quite wave the Bernard Report in the air, announcing "I believe it is peace for our time!" Bossé concluded it was a project we could live with, as long as the boroughs got more fiscal autonomy. Two days after it was released, the mayors had a raucous powwow. I said, "For those of you who don't like the project now, wait till you see the legislation. When Bouchard speaks of simplifying, you can be sure it's not to give the boroughs more power." Bossé, to my irritation, had already announced that my idea of a pan-Island referendum on One Island One City was off, as he found it confrontational. He preferred the route of negotiation with Bouchard and Harel. "You can't piss them off and negotiate at the same time," he said. If all his lobbying came a-cropper, he said, Plan B would be "combat."

"But it'll be too late!" I spluttered.

"Peter, all you're saying is, 'No, but.' And all I'm saying is, 'Yes, but.'"

"Georges, there will be no 'but.' The 'but' will never happen. I say the *best* we can expect if we present a united front cheering the Bernard Report is that it becomes law 'as is,' but 'as is' is One Island One City by the back door. You're saying that the *worst* we can expect is the report 'as is.' You're dreaming."

Michel Leduc, the mayor of LaSalle, supported Bossé. The mayor of Saint-Leonard, Frank Zampino, went even further, saying the report was "the best deal we could get" and that time was up, it was no longer "one minute to midnight, but 12:30. We now have to start thinking of taking control of the megacity." The mayor of Outremont said he was happy with the Bernard Report, and so were 80 per cent of his citizens: it was a "reflection of our position" and therefore we mayors could not reject it. As for a referendum, he said, he could not even get a thousand people to turn up. The mayor of Saint-Laurent said we should not refuse Bernard totally.

From then on, our union was split between my camp, who wanted to fight, and Bossé's camp, who wanted to negotiate. Already the mayors of the eight smaller municipalities scheduled to disappear were accusing their confreres of sacrificing them in hopes of getting a bit more for their soon-to-be-ex-municipalities.

An hour later, breaking two days of public silence, I held a press conference. I categorically rejected the Bernard Report,* saying it recommended the fiscal evisceration of our municipalities, turning them into empty husks, a process that would, in a few years, result in one monolithic city. I said, "The power to govern is the power to

---

* Professor Andrew Sancton has come to the intriguing conclusion that, had I accepted the Bernard Report and had its terms been adopted as law with my support, demergers very likely would not have happened. See Sancton, "Les villes anglophones au Québec."

tax."[10] I announced Westmount would hold a formal referendum based on the Bernard proposals and hoped other municipalities would follow suit. Bossé was furious. Five days later, with only a few days' notice, Westmount had a standing-room-only meeting in Victoria Hall where I explained the Bernard Report and why we rejected it. I ended the meeting shouting, "*Ne touchez pas à ma ville!*" and "Let's keep our city a city!" The latter slogan being so lame, at Westmount's next referendum campaign meeting we came up with "Hands off my city!" which, dressed in the yellow-on-black "caution" logo our designer gave it, quickly became the battle cry of the anti-merger forces across the Island.

THE LIBERALS PROMISE TO UNDO MERGERS

The day after that divisive mayors' meeting came what I greeted as a *deus ex machina*. On 14 October, out of the blue at the Liberals' annual congress, Roch Cholette moved an urgent resolution: "It is resolved that, in the eventuality that the PQ government stubbornly forces the merger of Quebec municipalities, a Liberal government would be committed to enacting a law which would ensure the respect of citizens by permitting referenda on whether to cancel these forced mergers, and commits itself to respect the outcome of these votes." Unanimously, the two thousand party faithful there voted for the resolution. Liberal leader Jean Charest, in a later press conference, repeated that his party would act on the pledge to reverse mergers if voted into power.[11]

Surprisingly, this resolution met with little applause from mayors across Quebec. Said LaSalle Mayor Michel Leduc about municipal mergers and the Liberals, "This matter didn't excite them up until now. Then, all of a sudden, whoops! They get interested and tell us they will completely undo things if they get into power. Politically, it's certainly very clever, but I find it pretty whorish." Saint-Leonard Mayor Frank Zampino said, more delicately, the same thing: "There you have a party that decides to make some noise and to have a firmer position on the question of mergers at the very moment when everything is nearly over. Since the issue has been in the public eye for more than a year, we would have wished that M. Charest would have been less quiet all that while."[12] That's what is called biting the hand that did not, but wants to, feed you. I was grateful and – for once – prophetic:[13]

A prominent opponent of Bernard's plan welcomed the Liberals' decision. "I totally support it," Westmount Mayor Peter Trent said. "Once a wrong has been done, you can't turn around and say it's untouchable." Trent agreed the Liberal plan could be cumbersome to implement, particularly in places like the south shore, where individual municipalities would be completely submerged into a single city [Luckily, this was not done]. "When it comes to the issue of practicality, one does question how it would be done. But nothing is impossible," Trent said. He also said the Liberals' idea would be much easier to implement in Montreal, where suburban boroughs would retain their status as autonomous municipalities under Bernard's plan. In those cases, Trent said, holding referendums to undo mergers would be "much more feasible" because boroughs would continue to have separate political structures and budgets for local services, he said. Trent said he believes the Liberals might have stumbled upon a proposal that could galvanize voters in the next provincial election. "It's an excellent strategy," he said. "I think Jean Charest may find this to be a very interesting *cause célèbre*. It would give voters something to sink their teeth into."

A week later, Charest said to me during a telephone conversation that the mayors were "unreliable allies. They bleed themselves in public, and in private do a deal to save themselves."

MORE DELAY. MORE INACTION

In the National Assembly, Liberals made fun of the Bernard Report. Jacques Chagnon played with a Rubik's Cube as a symbol of the report's complexity, asking the premier to explain its "three sorts of boroughs, two tax bills, and three different electoral systems." Bernard warned that the Liberals were "not doing us any favours; the more they said it was complicated, the more the government will be tempted to downgrade borough autonomy." Furthermore, he said, if we had embraced his report with more fervour, we would be negotiating in Premier Bouchard's office by now.

By 20 October, Bossé was still counselling negotiation and delay, with no idea which way the government was leaning. "Until the draft legislation is tabled, we can't really start to mount big demonstrations. We risk having the government telling us that we're jumping the gun." I retorted that in "an ideal world it would be better to wait for the draft legislation, but by then it will be too late," pointing out that, in any case, Premier Bouchard had already said he accepted the main points of the report and the time for negotiations was over.[14]

One mayor who had not laid down his arms was Luis Miranda, the energetic mayor of Anjou. He organized a meeting of anti-merger Quebec mayors in Drummondville. Although we only got representatives from ten Montreal Island municipalities, four south shore municipalities, and six municipalities from Quebec (led by the fire-eating mayor of Sainte-Foy, Andrée Boucher), we formed a common front of some forty municipalities against forced mergers. It was pitifully late.

Bossé finally met with the premier on October 26. He said he felt better after the ninety-minute meeting, but he got nothing concrete. Although he told Bouchard that we were not looking for confrontation, by now he was taking the position that public consultation on the megacity was a must, regardless of what form the legislation took.

HOW THE UNIONS DO IT

Meanwhile, the labour unions were flexing their muscles. While they were in favour of mergers and megacities – which brought them more power – they were unhappy with the law that would freeze collective bargaining during mergers, letting arbitrators impose settlements. They had a practice run when three hundred City of Montreal blue collar workers, led by their president, Jean Lapierre, descended on the PQ's national council in Trois-Rivières in late August. They banged on the door hard enough to split it, while PQ party faithful blocked their entry with chairs. Bouchard's bodyguards, their hands over their pistols, moved to surround the premier. Lapierre told the media that Bouchard would never get "the winning conditions to make a country by crushing his allies."[15]

Then on Halloween night, six hundred blue and white collars, again led by Lapierre, demonstrated outside Louis Bernard's Outremont home, supposedly the first in a series of visits to "government collaborators." Said their leader, "Even if you hide, we're going to find you!" adding, "It's the beginning of the biggest union battle in the history of Quebec!" As for Diane Lemieux, the labour minister responsible for the law, he told her: "The day you run over our body [with the law], we will run over yours in a way that is irreversible."

Given that Lapierre had been sentenced to six months in jail for leading a 1993 riot at Montreal City Hall where rioters forced their way through the front door, these demagogic outbursts were not devoid of piquancy. Lapierre also reminded the PQ that his union was partially responsible for their electoral successes. This little show reminded me of yet another reason why we did not want to merge with Montreal: their union.

The unions can terrorize a government agent without penalty, but we had our knuckles rapped for a mild disturbance in Quebec's cockpit of democracy when fifty mayors from the common front against forced mergers descended on the National Assembly the next day. When we started applauding the Liberal questions and someone actually gave the "thumbs down" sign to Louise Harel, the Speaker threatened us with expulsion. In contrast to the very few meetings the municipalities (other than Montreal) had with Premier Bouchard, the unions had constant access. Henri Massé, the president of the FTQ, the labour group to which Montreal blue and white collar workers belonged, bragged that he met with Bouchard twice a month and had succeeded in modifying the law. Massé was the man who embraced Jean Lapierre just before the latter served his six months in prison.[16]

BOSSÉ IS BETRAYED BY BILL 170

To make the Bernard Report acceptable, Bossé was now insisting on two fundamental changes: that the eight small municipalities must not be forced to merge, and that the megacity have two levels of taxation to permit the boroughs to have tax autonomy.

Then it happened. On 15 November, Harel presented draft legislation, called Bill 170, which (initially) created three megacities in the Montreal, Quebec City, and Gatineau regions. It amounted to 250 pages. Only when we started reading the press release line by line did the extent of its departure from the Bernard Report become sickeningly obvious. The small tax room that Bernard allowed the boroughs, instead of being increased, was eliminated. So the boroughs had no independent financial resources, they were just subdivisions of the megacity. They could not tax. They could not borrow. They had no legal status. They could not even hire. The fire departments, which we had convinced Bernard to keep local, were now yet another responsibility of the megacity. The number of elected officials across the Island dropped from Bernard's 170 to 93. The changes continued to pile up. It was One Island One City, nothing else. "Bourque wins his bet," screamed the headlines.

Bossé was devastated, angry, lost. "The citizens of the Island of Montreal betrayed by their government," his press release read. "An iniquitous project from a hypocritical government." Adjectives flowed out: "fooled," "duped." The whole Bernard exercise, it read, was "an immense diversion."

Even Vera Danyluk was shocked by Bill 170: "They are strictly administrative boroughs. We'll have only one employer. If we want to live a nightmare over the next five years, that's the way to do it."[17] Asked whether she planned to run for the mayor of the megacity, she responded "I can't confirm that at this moment. I'm too angry."[18]

Harel's reaction? "It's the mayors' own fault!" We were the architects of our own misfortune. The Bernard Report, she said, was only going to be implemented if everyone rallied to it. They didn't and so that's that. Had we mayors been more cooperative, the boroughs would not have had their taxation power removed, and generally have been given more power. Besides, she said, the Liberals made fun of the two levels of taxation and other such complexities that were introduced to please both sides.[19]

So Bossé was being punished for the temerity of wanting to improve upon the Bernard Report, and I – presumably – was being punished for rejecting it. But it wasn't the mayors who would pay the price: it was the 1.8 million people living on the Island of Montreal who were condemned in perpetuity to have a system of municipal government imposed upon them that they didn't want, all because of a fit of spite on the part of an omnipotent cabinet minister. And if all those major divagations from Bernard's recommendations had nothing to do with Harel's pique with us, then Bill 170 reflected what the PQ wanted to do all along while they "used the Bernard Report to chloroform suburban mayors by having them think a compromise between Bourque's One Island One City proposal and the status quo was being considered."[20]

We mayors had lost precious months of wrangling when we should have been mobilizing the citizenry *before* any draft legislation. Was that the real purpose of the Bernard Report? Possibly. One thing was for certain: once Bill 170 was tabled in the National Assembly, the PQ knew and we should have known that politically it was next to impossible for the PQ to back down.

Michel Vastel was one of the few francophone commentators who saw things our way – or at least, Bossé's way. In an open letter to Louise Harel, he wrote, "This reform was concocted in the greatest secrecy and behind the back of Louis Bernard, whom you used to put to sleep any opposition ... The ink was scarcely dry on the Bernard Report when your Bill 170 was already written. This scheming left a bitter taste in the mouths of democrats interested in this reform. Your lawyers, in consultation with Guy Coulombe and a few labour union insiders – but not suburban politicians! – had thereby profited from the diversion created by Louis Bernard to devise a brutal reorganization. Worse than that, it is now either 'take it or leave it'! When I asked Pierre Bourque whether one should consider a few changes to Bill 170 to reassure the future borough mayors, he gave an arrogant refusal."[21]

Politically we were outwitted, outgunned, outflanked, and outclassed. As we had felt our fate closing in on us while "negotiating" with Bernard, most mayors had been grasping at straws. Some were almost pleading for their lives. It was not an edifying performance. When we first sat down with Bernard, Bossé was belligerent, demanding that Bernard work from first principles. By the end he was almost meek. As Montreal North Mayor Yves Ryan said about Bossé, "He flies off the handle easily, but he 'de-angers' as quickly as he angers."[22]

The only good thing to happen on 15 November was that, because of what we saw as the government's duplicity, all the Island suburban mayors were now reunited, saying they would fight the megacity to their last breath. Said Bossé, "We've been laughed at enough. People won't accept the bloody mess that the government wants to put us in. Bouchardville will not be built peacefully, that's for sure."[23]

THE FISCAL EQUITY HOAX

Unlike Bernard, who had barely adumbrated the subject, fiscal equity soon reclaimed its status as the overarching reason given for creating the megacity, especially in the November debates in the National Assembly. Louise Harel repeatedly held up Westmount as the Island's parasite-in-chief, claiming its tax rate was half that of Montreal's, yet its "taxpayers benefited from all the services of the City of Montreal." The day before Bill 170 was tabled, she said Westmount's rate was $0.98 and Montreal's, $1.99.[24] I fired off a series of letters asking her what exactly were the Montreal services that Westmount got free, and informing her that Westmount's residential rate was $1.35, not $0.98.[25] But that rate was far from being the whole story. After merger, Montreal's debt remained with its taxpayers. So what was important was to compare were tax rates without debt. I pointed out to Harel that, without debt, Westmount's rate was $1.18 and Montreal's $1.25. So what exactly was the problem? Why merge? My letters were not answered.

The government simulations of the effect of One Island One City on taxes were only made available the day Bill 170 was tabled. They showed the derisory effect the merger would have on the lightening of Montreal's tax burden. Thanks to the creation of the megacity, the average homeowner in the former City of Montreal would see a drop in taxes of 0.6 per cent – *less than one percent, or $19 per homeowner.* In the torrent of information unleashed by the announcement of Bill 170, only *La Presse* reported this crucial figure, but no one seemed to realize that it completely undermined the PQ's main justification for mergers.

By the year 2008, according to the government, half the suburbs would see an increase in taxes because of the merger (the biggest was Westmount's at 24 per cent), and half would see a decrease (the biggest drop was Montreal West at 31 per cent).[26] The effect, then, was a levelling out of tax rates in the suburbs, who didn't want the merger, and no effect on the tax rate of Montreal, the supposed beneficiary and raison d'être of the mergers.[27]

This was not new news. Exactly one year prior, *Le Devoir* revealed that an earlier government study concluded merging all the Montreal Island municipalities would bring a tax *increase* of $73 for the average homeowner of the former City of Montreal, and the former suburban municipalities would experience all the ups and downs.[28]

MERGER SAVINGS WILL CUT TAXES FOR NEARLY EVERYONE

The day after Bill 170 was tabled, *La Presse* published a CROP poll revealing only 39 per cent of Island residents wanted the megacity; but the same poll showed that, if assured that taxes would not increase and services would not be affected, 55 per cent of respondents would be in favour. The same phenomenon applied on the south shore and throughout Quebec.[29] The government was quick to pick up on this: the day the poll appeared, Bouchard promised that the creation of the megacity would lower tax rates for 86.4 per cent of the population.* And that was without any savings. "We know that there will be savings," said Premier Bouchard. "It's impossible that there won't be, from the moment that there will be attrition of personnel, for example, on the Island of Montreal, of 5 per cent per year."[30] According to an official communiqué from Harel's office issued 17 November, "In the much more realistic case where the mergers will create 5 per cent savings, the percentage of the population of the new Montreal entity benefiting from a tax reduction will reach 96.7 per cent." The only municipalities exempted from this manna of tax savings would be Baie d'Urfé, Pointe-Claire, Sainte-Anne-de-Bellevue, Senneville, and Westmount.

The reality would be very different.

While Bouchard and Harel were promising savings from merging, the government knew the opposite was true. The Liberals managed, through the provisions of the access to information law, to get government projections that showed suburban unionized employees would get an extra $108 million if (actually, when) they got the same wages as their colleagues in the City of Montreal. If all the employees in the megacity got the highest remuneration then extant in any of the former municipalities, that would add $205 million dollars to the running of the megacity.[31]

Knowing this, how could Bouchard promise tax cuts? Indeed, how could the PQ government adopt a law imposing mergers when they knew the only beneficiaries would be the already overpaid union members? That the cost of creating the megacity would be hundreds of millions of dollars every year? There is only one word that describes this behaviour and that is: fraud.

---

* The Municipal Affairs Department cranked out this much-ballyhooed, pseudo-precise figure. It was based on their calculation that the merger would just happen to put taxpayers in the former City of Montreal on the winner's side of the ledger – but by a tiny 0.6 per cent reduction in the tax rate, and in five years' time. Leaving aside the question of whether such a derisory amount could be called a "reduction," it would only have taken a small increase in the cost of running the megacity to result in an *increase* in Montreal's tax rate; but that would have presented a problem. Premier Bouchard would then have had to say the creation of the megacity meant tax decreases for only 29 per cent of its population. Sorry, for 28.9 per cent.

FINALLY ON THE WARPATH

Like the British in 1939, realizing they were in no shape to wage war after years of appeasement, we looked around and saw how unprepared we actually were. At least the West Island, Westmount, and Anjou had been girding for a fight for a year or more. For example, on 17 November, little Baie d'Urfé got seven hundred people jammed into a gymnasium on the eve of their referendum. Unfortunately my pan-suburban referendum idea had been delayed so long because of hopes of "honourable compromise" that on 19 November only five municipalities held them and only Westmount had a formal, by-the-book referendum. Turnout rate for all five averaged about 66 per cent, with 97 per cent of voters rejecting the megacity.[32] Many other municipalities had petitions, response cards, lawn signs, and polls. Côte Saint-Luc's poll by Leger Marketing showed 88 per cent were against the megacity, and citizens were much more worried about lower services than higher taxes.

Overall, we calculated that some eighty thousand Montreal Island suburban residents had said "no" to the megacity in the week following 15 November. These numbers could have been doubled, were it not for a complete lack of mobilization in the bigger municipalities: Verdun, Montreal North, LaSalle, Outremont, Pierrefonds – places in which most residents only realized there was a problem once Bill 170 was tabled. In the Quebec City area, mayors also got about eighty thousand saying "No," but over a longer period. On the south shore, some twenty thousand had spoken.

Then came the rallies. The labour unions, experts in such matters, had started their demonstrations almost six months before we finally took to the streets. The West Island hosted a rally at the Fairview Mall on 19 November that pulled in some twelve thousand angry suburbanites brandishing "Hands off my city" placards. Charest, the Liberal leader, gave an impassioned speech, repeating his promise to undo any forced mergers. We saw a re-energized Georges Bossé encouraging people to vote against the PQ's sister party in Ottawa (the Bloc Québécois) in the federal election now eight days away. Charest had also supported this "block the Bloc" strategy, to the surprise of his close adviser, Ronald Poupart, and the head of the Liberal caucus, Jacques Chagnon. (In the event, using the Bloc as a "transmission belt" for suburban anger over impending mergers probably caused the BQ to lose two seats in the Quebec region alone.) Next, we had a rally of five thousand braving the bitter cold on the hill of the National Assembly in Quebec.

Bouchard continued to wear rose-coloured glasses about the mergers. "There are many more people favourable to mergers than those who are against, and the proportion will continue to grow,"[33] he claimed. Three days later, the next poll showed an increase in anti-merger sentiment across Quebec, with 53 per cent against and only 35 per cent in favour, quite a change from 45 per cent against and 41 per cent for reported in the *La Presse* poll a month before. On the Island of Montreal, now 57 per cent were against and only 30 per cent for the mergers.[34] According to *Le Devoir*, who sponsored this Sondagem poll, our campaign was having an effect on public opinion. I think it was the reality of Bill 170 sinking in.

THE PARLIAMENTARY HEARINGS: IT ALL COMES OUT

In some way, the whole merger story came to be encapsulated, with positions clearly staked out, during the parliamentary hearings on Bill 170 in late November. It was as if we were winding up our final arguments before the sentence was handed down, even though we pretty much knew what the sentence would be. In fact, Bill 170 was the stuff and substance of our sentence; in our gut we knew that it would be little changed when the PQ inevitably forced it through the National Assembly, the way all other major merger legislation had been adopted in the past. I quote fairly extensively what Harel, Bossé, and Danyluk said during these hearings, because they were each in a way giving their summation to history. A month later, the latter two had moved on to other things: I suspect they knew the hearings would be their last speech before they gave themselves another role to play.

Harel started off the eight days of parliamentary hearings by enumerating the chaplet of the actions she took that, strung together, culminated in Bill 170: the Bédard Report, the decision to create the Montreal Metropolitan Region, the white paper, and the Bernard Report. It was as if she wanted us to believe they all served as signposts, each successively pointing to the next path forward until the goal of Bill 170 was inescapable. And time was running out to get there, she said. I quote from sections in the National Assembly's verbatim records:

MME HAREL: If it is clear that we must take care to weigh carefully the steps we take in such a matter, it is also essential to act
with celerity in a dossier that has for decades resulted in too
much tergiversation, which led only to immobility. The simple
passage of time proved, again and again, fatal for governments
that preceded us, governments that wound up throwing in the
towel, not having the time to implement such reform ...

This is why I labelled the war to maintain the unchangeable
character of local structures as reactionary, this war that takes
democracy as its battle cry – which it parodies. It's a backward-
looking war that claims the right to decide for those who don't
want to change anything ...

In the last 40 years in Quebec, 16 [forced] merger laws have
been adopted by the National Assembly: there was Laval, Mirabel, Jonquière, Beauport, and many others. Of these, 13 were
adopted by Liberal governments. For a long time, then, legislated
mergers were the rule here in Quebec, as in Ontario, New Brunswick, and Nova Scotia, rather than being the exception. Do I
need to remind you of the famous case of the City of Laval, the
product of the merger on Île Jésus of 14 municipalities, of which
seven fiercely opposed the draft bill of the minister of municipal
affairs at the time, Mr Pierre Laporte? This caused Mr Laporte
to say, and I quote, "It is not the popularity or the unpopularity
of a draft bill that serves as a guide for the government in putting
together legislation, but the common good." The parallel with the
current situation could not be more appropriate ...

The prosperity that we should collectively guarantee for Quebec over the next few years is a direct tributary of our capacity
to establish solidarity in municipal governance as of today. We
have to have strong urban poles in Quebec, able to join the
world club of 318 large urban agglomerations. This is why it is
important, Mr Chairman, that we proceed with the adoption of
Bill 170.[35]

Later that day, Georges Bossé got a crushing weight of resentment off his chest by describing what he saw as the Bernard Report
smokescreen:

M. BOSSÉ: To get right to the point, I would like to set things
straight. It seems that the crucial element in the marketing plan

for Bill 170, because of a lack of good selling points, is a campaign of denigration of the Montreal Island mayors. Since the bill has been tabled, we have become the target of repeated attacks from Madame Harel in a clear attempt to manipulate public opinion and to redirect the legitimate discontent of our citizens away from the government and towards their local elected officials. Madame Harel, I suppose you are proud to have made the headlines with declarations such as, "It's the fault of the mayors!" "The mayors have dug their own grave." "If they had brought a more constructive contribution to the reform, the boroughs would have had more powers and a greater autonomy." Since when has the government based reforms of this importance on the attitude of people? Should not the government seek the welfare of the citizen by being above all personal considerations? And, to make matters worse, on November 20th, in front of the Board of Trade, you added that the suburban mayors opposed the reform with a systematic, even fanatical, obstruction ...

We collaborated in good faith with Mr Bernard, believing he had a clear mandate from the government and, above all, the manoeuvring room necessary. We had no idea that the government would have the attitude of "believe in it, or perish," that a gag order awaited the end of our discussions. All the more so, since the Bernard Report was of very preliminary confection, not supported by any impact or feasibility study, nor any broader consultation nor citizen involvement. And how did the government react to the Bernard Report? By saying, "It's really complicated," it said, "it must be simplified" ...

What is the most important thing? To make things simple, even simplistic, like "One Island One City," or to show a minimum of respect for people, their way of life, their identity, their roots, their local institutions? What is the most important thing? To make things simple, even simplistic, like "One Island One City," or to preserve democracy, the efficiency of 26 local administrations that have stood the test of time? ...

We were betrayed because we were involved in good faith in a process of reform with the government's representative. And the result of all this was to have government chuck the whole thing out. The Bernard Report disappears with the touch of a magic wand. Were we dreaming? Did we get involved with all that for nothing? The coach suddenly turned into a pumpkin. And now

we find ourselves with Bill 170 and the good old "One Island
One City." "It's the triumph of an outdated dream," said Jean-
Claude Marsan ...

MME HAREL: It was not even a week that had gone by after the
Report was released ... when there was a declaration of war, referenda for which the dates had already been planned, and an
opposition that surely swept along with it the Liberal members.
We showed up at the National Assembly the Tuesday that followed the Bernard Report and we get the Liberal spokesperson
making fun of the Report ... The Liberal leader said that the
Bernard Report was the Rubik's Cube of municipal organization.
He added "Mayor Bourque wanted *une île, une ville*, and the PQ
answered, we prefer *une ville*, two bills."

M. BOSSÉ: You will allow me, Mrs Minister, to completely refute
what you are saying ... What we made known in the days following ...was to say that there was a point upon which we wanted
absolutely to be able to continue negotiations. That was local
financing and taxation ... Our propositions – Madame, you
have read them – were very close to the Bernard Report. Much
closer than the position of the City of Montreal, a position that
remained absolutely unchanged from the beginning ...

MME HAREL: Mr Chairman, what I understand, with the multi-
plication of resolutions from the Island municipalities, from the
West Island, is that a lot of them rejected whole sections of the
report and had no intention of rallying ...[36]

So there we had it: a paradox. Bouchard and Harel had made
it clear for months that resistance would be futile and that they
would ignore all public demonstrations against their reform,[37] yet,
strangely, they became ultra-sensitive toward any expression of
rejection of the Bernard Report, using that rejection to justify their
evisceration of it. And what about the north shore mayors? They
even boycotted Bernard's committee, yet Bill 170 left their municipalities pretty much unmerged.
   We were allowed only one hour to present our objections to a law
that would wipe out our twenty-six municipalities with their nearly
800,000 citizens. Only fifty groups and individuals were allowed to

present their case to the government through these hearing, and the PQ had stacked the deck. Each of the south shore municipalities and each of the five municipalities in Gatineau had the right to one hour. And so did the Quebec farmers' union, who explained their taking up time at hearings on the imposition of megacities by saying that the West Island still had some farms!

Right after Bossé came Vera Danyluk, representing the MUC:

MME DANYLUK: For a number of years I have taken it upon myself, at every opportunity, to suggest certain ideas with regard to governing the Island of Montreal, regionally speaking, as I had come to the conclusion that the MUC was not creating the best conditions for regional governance; and to do that, we had to transform the institution root and branch. I even pleaded with the MUC council that it should become the forum for reflecting on this necessary overhaul of regional governance. This pressing appeal was ignored. Happily, in November 1998, the Premier, during the electoral campaign in an interview with *L'Actualité*, formally promised to put a complete municipal reform in place. And so, today, we have before us Bill 170 ...

In the daily running of the MUC, I saw – up close – that our main regional fragmentation came from the political polarization between Montreal and the Island suburbs, and that doesn't even count other passing forms of fragmentation, both within the suburbs themselves, and, sometimes, within the City of Montreal. In short, fragmentation within fragmentation, each mayor or councillor invoking his or her fundamental mandate, a mandate which was essentially local ...

Bill 170, by creating an overall elective structure for the Island, solves this problem of fragmentation and lack of a unified regional vision. Let's hope that it soon affects mentalities ...

Let's keep in mind that, at the beginning, the MUC was basically built from the genetic code of the City of Montreal, transmitted by the many employees and unions of the City who were transplants to the MUC, as well as Montreal services, management tools, and traditions. Then, gradually, over the 30 years of MUC history, we saw a surprising crossbreeding of organizational cultures from the City of Montreal and from the suburbs, from which it picked whatever was best. Louis Bernard, then, saw the MUC as the ideal foundation on which to build the new city ...

By wiping out the cities in order to replace them with boroughs with just about no legal status, simple administrative districts of the megacity, there is a balance that is upset, as Bill 170 abolishes an important distinction between regional governance across the Island and local governance ...

This brings me to the heart of my message; the atrophy of local government will be harmful to the regional governance of the Island. Indeed, I predict without hesitation that the legal anonymity of the boroughs will cause an overflow of local debates into the regional scene, and that, I assure you, will severely handicap the ability of megacity politicians to concentrate on regional affairs ... I know enough of the municipal scene to say that, if things aren't going well within a borough, councillors will say to their electors it's because the megacity doesn't give them enough money.

I was surprised to learn that the MUC borrowed "best practices" from the suburbs. I had never seen evidence of it, the MUC remaining a consummately Montrealist organization. But what surprised me most with Danyluk's speech was her assumption that "political polarization" is bad and must, at all costs, be eliminated. Our political and capitalistic structures are based on some amount of "polarization" and "fragmentation." Be that as it may, Danyluk's years of proselytizing regional power had finally paid off, but even she must have asked herself, "What have I wrought?" when she realized the trade-off the government finally made wiped out local government on the Island of Montreal.

Looked at another way, she got what she was agitating for: direct election to the MUC, but an MUC merged with the City of Montreal and suburbs. For Bill 170 imposed not just a merger of the twenty-seven municipalities on the Island; it imposed a merger of those municipalities *with* the MUC.

MONTREAL'S COMPETITOR, FIVE HUNDRED KILOMETRES TO THE SOUTH

In spite of professing to ignore any attacks on Bill 170, the government nonetheless judged it wise to fund a media campaign selling the necessity of merging. Harel was forever saying Montreal had to bulk up to compete internationally city-to-city, always giving Boston as the best example of what we were up against. I was particularly angered by one big ad the government placed on 25 November in all the major dailies, comparing the number of municipal politicians on Montreal Island with Chicago, Toronto, and Boston. Montreal had twenty-eight mayors and 256 councillors for 1.8 million people; Boston, it said, had only one mayor and thirteen councillors for 0.6 million people. The ad should have read at least one hundred mayors and five hundred councillors for three million Bostonians.[38] I showed a *Boston Globe* reporter a copy of the ad, and when his newspaper subsequently did a major article on the Montreal megacity, this is how it saw things: "Quebec is resorting to disinformation to promote the concept. One advertisement paid by the provincial government has the headline, 'Municipal Mergers: It Just Makes Sense,' along with vital statistics for Boston, seen by Quebecers as an enviable oasis of prosperity. The plain implication of the ad is that Boston is a merged megacity ... Present-day Boston is much closer to Montreal Island as it exists now, a relatively small core municipality bordered by municipalities with strong identities all their own."[39]

THE BIG DECEMBER RALLY

The rallies continued, when, the first Sunday of December, some three thousand citizens of the south shore nearly froze in order to protest Bill 170. A woman we were going to hear from in future, Ginette Durocher of Saint-Bruno, was one of the speakers. The mayor of Longueuil, Claude Gladu, managed to find something else to do that day: "What is the point of waging war when we know the government is determined to go ahead? I took a stand against forced mergers when it was the time to do so."[40]

Then came the mother of all rallies. Thanks to the delay caused by the Bernard negotiations and their chimera of a compromise, the huge rally that we staged on 10 December was almost after the fact. Even the media were billing it as our last chance. Still, it was a magnificent display.

Our rally consisted of seventy thousand citizens marching up University Street, then west and down McGill College Avenue, where the crowd assembled at Ste-Catherine Street before a huge stage. Of course, the media immediately disputed our claim of seventy thousand. A sort of negative auction happens among some journalists because the police nowadays refuse to give crowd estimates. A helicopter crew working for radio station CJAD estimated the crowd as being over sixty thousand. We had four hundred school buses alone to ferry people there, but most came by metro.

Montreal North's mayor Yves Ryan was up first. He gave a barn-burner of a speech. "Good God, I'm happy to be here. I've had it up to here being treated like a petty princeling, and having it said that we mayors were the only people against mergers, being worried about our jobs and our pay." He then addressed Premier Bouchard and his party's obsession with sovereignty: "I read an ad in the newspaper that really bugged me. 'We've been talking about mergers for thirty years.⁴¹ It's time to act.' It seems to me, Mr Premier, that there is another matter you've talked about for thirty years: it's called independence. And you have had two referendums on it – even if you were not very satisfied with the results. Is it possible that we could have just one, on forced mergers?"

I waited my turn under the cavernous makeshift stage. As I grabbed the mike, I looked out and for the first time saw the great press of suburbanites, for many of whom this was their first demonstration. It was packed for two blocks, and McGill College is a very wide boulevard. Above the people, almost independent of them, was a rhythmically bobbing multicoloured forest of signs. Some were handmade, but six thousand had been professionally produced and handed out like muskets to a militia. They said things like: "Mega-merger, mega-city: mega-mistake." "Bill 170: another botched reform." "One Island One City: you can't cure cancer by passing it on."

I'd never given a speech to seventy thousand people.⁴² Mind you, only a tiny fraction – including Jean Charest – actually heard me, in spite of loudspeakers worthy of a rock concert. Because they could not hear, people took their cue from those in front, so the applause rippled away from the stage in a wave all the way down McGill College Avenue in an aural equivalent of body-surfing. I could have recited the alphabet, and, as long as I paused long enough and glowered enough, I would have got a reaction.

I spoke slowly: "According to the *New York Times*, Madame Harel vowed: 'The government will not let itself be dictated to.' Madame Harel, get with the program. In a democracy, *you're* supposed to listen to the people, not the other way around ... Your government says they have consulted. Sure they've consulted. They've consulted with themselves ... They're saying: it takes a referendum to break up a country, but not to destroy a city ... The government doesn't own our cities. We mayors don't own our cities. *You* own your city. It's yours and they are taking away something you own." I ended, adopting my most Churchillian cadence, "I was not elected mayor to preside over the liquidation of my city." It's a good thing so few could actually hear me.

Bossé was the third and last speaker. He started off aggressively enough: "Mr Bouchard: we will never let you demolish our cities ... Never, never, never will we accept such a law." He repeated four times, "Don't assassinate democracy." But then I could not believe my ears: he actually held out an olive branch, which is not something you do at a rally, especially since our stated goal was to scrap Bill 170. He said it is possible that we could approve the megacity if Quebec gave more power to the boroughs. He even said Bill 170 could serve as the basis for discussions. "The Island says 'no' to the status quo ... We will work with you." In a press conference after, he was even more conciliatory. In an interview, LaSalle Mayor Michel Leduc said that we were not saying Bill 170 should be thrown in the wastebasket, just put back on the drawing board.

The next day, Harel, claiming there were only thirty thousand at the rally, said she was only too happy to meet with Bossé with a view to boosting borough power, but under no circumstance would boroughs have the power of taxation. Why not? That would mean "one city, two bills," the very thing Jean Charest and the Liberals had made fun of in the Bernard Report.[43] Public policy, once again, was being influenced by partisan spite.

MEGACITY SUPPORTERS: ARISE AND SIGN!

Knowing he would get a pitiful turnout if he held a rally or a referendum in favour of the megacity, Bourque decided he still had to mount some sort of counteroffensive to the suburbs' campaign. I don't think he was worried that the PQ would not go through with Bill 170; I think he was afraid the bill would be modified to give the boroughs a smidgen of power.

In order to show public support indeed existed for Bill 170, Bourque decided to establish a petition. He told the media on 8 December that he would collect over 100,000 signatures from then until 17 December, just before Bill 170 was scheduled to be adopted. "Anybody can sign a petition," I said, "Nobody's checking who you are. The only real way to test public opinion is through a referendum."[44] And as we shall see, anybody *did* sign the petition; as, especially by the Internet, voting early and often was easy.[45] From the day he announced the petition, the media bugged Bourque daily as to how many had signed to date. The day of the rally, Bourque was particularly defensive; after all, getting on a bus to go to a rally in the freezing cold took far more commitment than signing a petition while shopping or using the Internet. Each day, news items became more and more sarcastic as it became clear Bourque would get nowhere near his 100,000, even though he and his councillors were trolling shopping malls and streets for signatures. The final tally, supposedly, was 50,127 names. As we shall see, even this number was padded, as there were only around 22,000 valid names.

The war of words had its price, though infinitesimal compared to the cost of actually implementing the megacity. Bourque said that Montreal had spent $0.9 million on its One Island One City publicity campaign since summer 1999.[46] The government admitted to spending $1 million on publicizing its pro-merger campaign.[47] On the other hand, the suburban mayors' union spent $1.5 million including the 10 December rally, and its member municipalities spent at least an additional $1 million in publicity, rallies, and referenda. In the Quebec region, the suburbs "squandered" (to use the reporter's term) some $1.5 million in their anti-merger campaign; Quebec City spent another $0.5 million in its pro-merger efforts.[48]

A MEETING WITH BOUCHARD

I was invited, along with five other mayors involved with the common front,[49] to meet with Premier Bouchard and Minister Harel on 14 December. It was a last-ditch effort to seek a delay in the adoption of Bill 170 and to plead for some form of public consultation on the matter. As for me, I made it clear I was not there to negotiate minor changes in the bill, but I wanted to explain to Bouchard face to face why I was opposed to forced mergers.

Bouchard started things off: "You know, there are two basic reasons for merging: efficiency and equity. The first will help Quebec's economy, the second is self-evident. My government has been the only one to have the courage to implement such reform. Former governments were afraid of you mayors." He paused for effect. "For forty years we have nattered on about doing something. Even

Claude Ryan was unsuccessful. It was time to take the bull by the horns, especially since cities are becoming more and more important, needing a better framework in which to flourish." He looked us in the eyes. "Even if this makes us lose the next election, we are going ahead with it."

He continued, "You talk about preserving identity in your fight against us. You know I live in Outremont and I like it; well, Outremont will continue as a borough." Then, looking at me, he said, "Mergers will make anglophones get involved in the larger city." I retorted that the anglophone redoubt of NDG was merged ninety years ago, losing all the advantages of self-government, yet today its residents are no more involved in the "big city" than Westmounters are.

We spent a lot of the time taking issue with Bouchard's contention that mergers were "efficient and equitable." The level of discussion was of a high order, almost cerebral. I got the feeling Bouchard was beginning to be persuaded by at least some of our arguments, but Harel would then interject and he would snap back to a more partisan mood. Of course, we had no idea that in a month's time he would be gone. His subsequent resignation showed his talk was so much bravado. His unwavering support of Harel would result in no cost to him, and his boast of risking the next election on mergers became hollow.

After two hours, we got nowhere. Two days later, Bossé, Saint-Leonard Mayor Zampino, and LaSalle Mayor Leduc met with Harel to try again to get her to delay the adoption of the law, but they had no more success than we did. They were "satisfied with a useless meeting," as a *Le Soleil* headline put it. Harel did tell them we should have "let the small municipalities go," but it was too late to go back to the Bernard recommendations.

BILL 170 BECOMES LAW

With over 350 minor amendments, Bill 170 became law when the PQ invoked closure to ram it through the National Assembly at 2:15 AM, 20 December. The rules of debate were suspended "because of the urgency of the situation." So five megacities were to be created out of sixty-three existing municipalities: Montreal, Longueuil, Gatineau, Quebec City, and Lévis began operation 1 January 2002.[50]

We were as divided in defeat as we were in war. At least four strategies were put forward in the days following Bill 170's adoption, none of them mutually exclusive: challenge Bill 170 in the courts; form a decentralized megacity political party; count on the Liberals' promise to undo the effect of Bill 170; refuse to cooperate with the government committee supervising the transition to a megacity.

Baie d'Urfé, Westmount, and Côte Saint-Luc soon declared in favour of a legal challenge: being bilingually designated municipalities, they could argue that Bill 170 affected them disproportionately, which was, unsurprisingly, the reason Montreal North, LaSalle, and Outremont immediately rejected the idea. They were not designated bilingual municipalities. Besides, said Bossé, a legal fight would drag on too long.

Already some mayors were making public noises about creating a political party within the megacity to "make Bourque pay." Côte Saint-Luc, LaSalle, and Verdun were in this camp. Outremont's mayor said we were already late in setting up a megacity party. I was completely opposed to the idea, which I found opportunistic and self-serving, sending mixed messages about fighting the megacity while ensuring our future in it. Besides, I was still counting on the demerger* promise, whereas Bossé and LaSalle Mayor Leduc had publicly said they "were not at all convinced" the Liberals would undo the mergers.

Mayor Yeomans of Dorval and I said we would not cooperate with the government's transition committee, Bossé said he would. Yeomans said he would lock the doors at Dorval City Hall when they came: "These people represent an occupying force. This is not a case of civil disobedience; this is a case of disobedience with civility."

THE FOG OF WAR

The release of the Bernard Report until the adoption of Bill 170 took only seventy days – seventy days of pure naked political war. It was clear to me that we never should have cooperated with Bernard; the same conclusion applies to his equivalent agents in Quebec City and the Gatineau regions. The government had made it clear that mergers were going to happen: Bernard did not and could not have changed that. Had we orchestrated, as I advocated, an Island-wide

---

* Both *Le Journal de Montréal* and *La Presse* gave birth to this word in French on 21 December 2000, swaddled in quotation marks.

referendum, multiple rallies, and pan-Quebec resistance before November, the presentation of Bill 170 would have cranked up the public into an even greater frenzy. Instead, lulled into thinking a compromise was possible, most mayors and their public were disarmed and unprepared when the law came out, with no possibility to resist – other than a few frozen December rallies and a raft of formal resolutions from city councils.

And even when we finally got around to girding our loins, we sent mixed messages to Bouchard and Harel: at the big December rally, Yves Ryan and I were intransigent, while Bossé was suggesting negotiation, in spite of his being "betrayed." Because our only major demonstration came months too late, we had only two strategies available to us: either go for broke in a fight to scrap Bill 170, or use the demonstration to help negotiate wringing out a few powers for the boroughs. Clearly, Bossé opted for the "concessions" strategy. Since, after all, he was its president, the mayors' union took the route of trying to get the unimprovable improved.

At the end of June 2000, I wrote what turned out to be the first in a series of letters to all Westmounters. I entitled it "The Battle against Annexation: A Report from the Front." During the ensuing six months, amidst the din and confusion, it was hard to see the battle standard or even what was happening. We were rattling sabres while our enemy had a ten-ton bomb. There were diversionary tactics, parleys, and, once, even a full-blown armistice. Some mayors sounded the retreat; some engaged in side skirmishes or attempted side deals. The opposing forces were well armed and well organized, cheered on by the media. Our once-fierce general vacillated, seeking an honourable compromise, feeling that, even though we were no longer owners, being a tenant was better than being a vassal. The people had no idea what was going on until the smoke cleared and they discovered that Bouchard, Bourque, and Harel had won the Island, the south shore, and Quebec. It was a rout.

13

If You Can't Ride Two Horses,
You Shouldn't Be in the Circus

Laws are like sausages. It's better not to see them made.
Otto von Bismarck (probably misattributed)

Politics, *n*. A strife of interests masquerading as a contest of principles. The
conduct of public affairs for private advantage.
Ambrose Bierce, *The Devil's Dictionary*

The state is like the human body. Not all of its functions are dignified.
Anatole France, 1893

In my cynical moments I think that trying to follow a politician's
movements is like trying to make sense of the direction of a stream:
it never goes straight from point A to B; it will zigzag and switch
back on itself. The logic of its seemingly vagarious course can only
be understood when one realizes the stream is condemned constantly to seek an ever-lower level. It moves laterally only where it
can move downward. The gravitational pull of ambition, the motive
force behind all politicians, likewise causes much meandering action.
Unfortunately, a politician is someone in whom ambition and ability
have not always been granted in equal proportions.

OPPORTUNISM KNOCKS

It was the 12 January 2001, eight in the morning. We were at Verdun City Hall, the sleek and impressive municipal home of Georges
Bossé, built in 1958. It was one of the last meetings of the Union of
Montreal Island Suburban Municipalities. Barely a month before,
seventy thousand of our citizens had braved the icy Montreal winter to pledge unconditional support for their respective mayors in

carrying on the battle against the megacity. The air had been thick
with speakers' diatribes against the injustice of Bill 170, with solemn declarations of war against its architects. Now, nearly half of
the twenty-six mayors had shucked off their battledress. They were
in a party mood – that is, a party of the political kind.

The Island suburban mayors were polarized around two leaders
representing two opposite courses of action. Bossé was convinced
the only thing to do was to get involved in megacity politics and
to cooperate with the transition committee whose job it was to get
the megacity up and running and whose members, unfortunately,
reported to Louise Harel. Mayors, above all, had to scrap any idea
of legally contesting Bill 170. Bill 170 was now a law duly adopted,
and we had to move on, Bossé said. Even if the Liberals won the
next provincial election (and they were not credited with much of
a chance), he had no faith in their honouring the demerger pledge.
I was Bossé's polar opposite: I felt we had no mandate from the citizens who elected us to get involved in the megacity. We had promised to fight Bill 170: that meant a court action and no cooperation
with the transition committee. We also had to hold Liberal leader
Jean Charest's feet to the fire to ensure he respected his promise of
demerger. Some mayors clumped around Bossé, some around me,
but most were somewhere between us, constantly shifting under the
two opposite forces of attraction.

Pierre Bourque had just unsurprisingly announced he was running
in the upcoming November municipal election. Led by Bossé, some
mayors were already talking to the media about putting together a
political party to beat Bourque. There was no time to waste, they
said. Bossé and Zampino wanted nothing to do with a legal contestation of Bill 170 because leaving the political scene unoccupied
while waiting for the gears of justice to grind was unthinkable. It
would take "three, five, or even eight years," said Bossé; in the mean-
time, "It would be irresponsible for us to not defend our decentralized vision against Bourque's centralized scheme."[1] Zampino said
the legal process would take "five or ten, or fifteen years," and so be
inapplicable in the event of a win.[2]

It was as if someone had tapped Bossé and Zampino on the shoulder and said, "For you, the war is over." They therefore channelled
whatever was left of their anger – not unmixed with a keen sense of
political survival – towards a "punish Bourque" campaign. I thought
this sink-the-Bismarck approach was short sighted. In fact, a case

could have been made that the re-election of Bourque could have helped the anti-merger cause: his centralized, dictatorial style would have caused people to hate the megacity in earnest and plead for demerger. His re-election would have perhaps done some temporary centralizing harm, but harm that subsequent elections could always remedy. The creation of the megacity itself I saw as being an irreparable and irreversible disaster: that was what we had to focus on. *Urbs longa, vita brevis.*

I wanted nothing to do with a megacity party: "If one organizes a political party to run against Bourque, that sends a message that the fight to save our municipalities is lost,"[3] I said. Some mayors, however, thought they could wage the judicial and political battles at the same time and not look too hypocritical. Dorval Mayor Peter Yeomans said, on announcing he would run for megacity council, "We have no choice. They've left us so little time that we have to play two keyboards at once. The tough part of this election will be to be seen as being positive in a structure the suburbs have been critical of all along."[4] Precisely. Only three weeks earlier Yeomans had said, "We will not have anything to do with this law."[5] This was the very law that created the position that he was now going to seek. By the time we met in Verdun on 12 January, the mayors of Beaconsfield, Dollard-des-Ormeaux, Dorval, Kirkland, Pointe-Claire, and Saint-Laurent had all announced publicly they would get involved in a megacity party, most declaring they would personally run. "I owe it to the people of Kirkland," said its mayor. Within weeks, all six had also publicly agreed to a concomitant legal challenge,[6] soon to be joined by Mayor Robert Libman of Côte Saint-Luc.[7]

LaSalle Mayor Michel Leduc remarked acidly, "I have a lot of trouble understanding intellectually how you can legally contest the size of the rink that was laid out for you, and, at the same time, go and skate on the same rink."[8]

For me, legal action was a bit of a long shot, but not only was it genuine, it would keep the issue alive and warm until the Liberals got in. "We will be holding Mr Charest to his promise, that when – I don't say, 'if' but 'when' – the Liberals get elected in two years' time, Mr Charest would reverse any mergers," I said. "And I say 'when' simply because the autocratic nature of the current government would, I think, make it impossible that a rational population would re-elect them."[9]

The day before our meeting in Verdun, Premier Bouchard had shaken Quebec's political firmament by announcing he was quitting. Less than a month before, I had been sitting across from him, pleading for our municipal lives. Only three weeks before he quit, Bill 170 was rammed through. Not only would Bouchard avoid the political shrapnel the forced mergers would throw into sensitive PQ ridings but it was unlikely the PQ would ever find a leader with the charisma and draw of Bouchard. I used his leave-taking as grist to my demerger mill, as for me it also pointed to a Liberal victory in the next provincial election.[10]

The same day Bouchard announced his retirement, *La Presse* published an op-ed piece by a former Quebec cabinet minister called Gérald Tremblay, who wrote about the huge challenge that Montrealers faced with their impending megacity and in the selection its new mayor. Tremblay had presided over a Montreal commission on public consultation policy in urban planning matters, giving his final report at the end of November 2000. Even though he had no direct municipal experience, Tremblay's article was seen by most as an open declaration of interest in becoming the megacity mayor. "With the adoption of Bill 170 on municipal mergers, we, citizens of Montreal, inherit a rare opportunity to build together a democratic institution adapted to our needs and aspirations," he declared. "The challenge is immense. Can we meet it?" Writing further about Bill 170, Tremblay said, "We must respect this law in the same way we respect all the other laws."[11]

When the mayors met the following day on 12 January in Verdun, I was prepared for the shift in stance from mayors fighting the megacity to mayors seeking to be part of it. Politicians will be politicians. But I was not prepared for the shock of finding out my good friend Marc Vaillancourt, the director-general of our union, was also a defector. He avoided me until I met with Yves Ryan, Bossé, and Zampino, who, a bit nervously, informed me that Vaillancourt was going to be a vice-president of the transition committee charged by Harel to implement the megacity. He had been approached by the government just two days after Bill 170 was adopted and offered $240,000 for ten months' work. Ryan had counselled him to accept it. My jaw dropped. Vaillancourt was the man who had run our organization for ten years and had masterminded the huge anti-merger rally a month before. He was going to implement what he

had fought so passionately against all those years. My shock soon
became fury.[12]

Although I was beginning to think some mayors needed it as a fig
leaf for their voters, at that meeting some eighteen mayors committed their municipalities to start legal action, most in a loose coalition
under a pair of lawyers present at the meeting, Jean Pomminville and
Michel Delorme. To give some structure to our diverse legal actions,
I created the blandly named Joint Legal Action Group. The first of
our thirty-three meetings over the next ten months took place in
Westmount's Victoria Hall on 23 January. My not-so-hidden agenda
encompassed much more than just our legal case: we became a political anti-merger group, of which the first order of business was
to hire a media relations expert.[13] Our *noms de guerre* varied, but
usually came out as the forgettable Coalition of Cities and Citizens
Challenging Bill 170, or something in that vein. For simplicity, I'll
call it the mayors' anti-merger group from here on.

WHO SHOULD RUN FOR MEGACITY MAYOR?

If you have a political party, you have to have a leader – which,
municipally, means someone to run for mayor. At first most of
the West Island mayors backed Georges Bossé, who, according to
LaSalle Mayor Leduc, had "the air of an autoproclaimed candidate." Actually, Bossé had come to see me early in January to tell me
that, since he was too much associated in the public's mind with the
suburbs, he probably could not win the former City of Montreal,
Bourque's fief. Regretfully, he felt that it would most likely take an
outsider to do the job. He had already been in contact with Gérald
Tremblay about running.

Vera Danyluk did not have Bossé's suburban baggage and had a
recent career in running services right across Montreal Island. In the
middle of January she became openly interested in being the mayor
of *la grande ville*. However, Danyluk felt that any political party
formed to run against Bourque should have a proper leadership convention, as opposed to a coronation behind closed doors. Putative
candidate Tremblay soon made it clear he wanted nothing to do
with any sort of leadership race.

But Danyluk, for all her qualifications, had a problem: she had
little public support. Back in October 2000, a SOM *La Presse* poll
revealed that Bourque would have beaten anybody who ran against

him, had there been an election then for the mayor of the mega-city. Leaving aside the very unlikely names of former Premier Pierre-Marc Johnson and Louise Harel, I was the next most popular, even though I had made it clear I did not want the job. Danyluk and Bossé got less than half my support.[14] The *Gazette* came up with similar results in a poll conducted in mid-December 2000.[15] My popularity had nothing to do with my winsome personality and everything to do with my clear anti-merger stance.

At the end of January a confidential poll done by Baromètre[16] concluded that either Tremblay or I could beat Pierre Bourque, and that Bossé or Danyluk clearly "would not make it." When they asked who would be the best person to run the megacity, I got twice as many positive responses as Tremblay from those who were likely to vote. This was probably because at that time only 45 per cent of those polled had heard of Tremblay and 69 per cent had heard of me. The poll was commissioned by the anti-Bourque forces, and I only saw it six months later. It revealed a strong antipathy to Bourque across Montreal Island, a sentiment fuelled by the forced passage of Bill 170 the month before. By March, Bourque was doing much better, but with Tremblay in hot pursuit. Danyluk continued to trail all other candidates. The pollsters by then had taken me off their clipboards.

In spite of the January and March poll results, Danyluk continued to wage an on-and-off campaign for the mayoralty. Finally, in April, she threw in the towel. She would not even get involved with Tremblay and his new party. The fact that Tremblay had already anointed Saint-Leonard Mayor Frank Zampino as his second-in-command perhaps helped her decision. Later she expressed her disappointment: "I wanted to be the first woman mayor of the City of Montreal. I wanted to be the first ethnic mayor since the beginning of the City of Montreal."[17]

Danyluk had the misfortune of being in charge of something nobody knew or understood, the MUC. Had I been a megacity supporter, I would have definitely favoured Danyluk over Tremblay, in spite of all our battles. She had solid experience both locally and regionally. The contempt in which municipal politics is held was no better demonstrated by the fact that the pundits considered Tremblay's lack of municipal experience as an *advantage* in presenting himself as a candidate to run the largest City in Quebec. A mayor who decided to run for the premier of Quebec with no experience in provincial politics would be laughed off the election platform.

THE FINE ART OF FENCE-SITTING

On 27 February, Tremblay announced formally he was running for mayor of the megacity. Mayors fighting the megacity in court such as Mayor Robert Libman of Côte Saint-Luc were front and centre supporting Tremblay.[18] Getting involved in the megacity election was their Plan B, they said, an attitude Tremblay did not seem to find insulting. These mayors were saying that Tremblay's dream, his *grande ville*, was in fact their second choice. He realized that the cognitive dissonance attaching to much of his suburban mayoral support would start to fog up his own message, but he sensed that without this much-advertised ambivalence towards the megacity, he would have never carried the suburbs.

Tremblay probably figured that if you can't ride two horses you shouldn't be in the circus. His position on demerger was another example of extreme accommodation: he would be open to the former suburbs becoming independent if they were not satisfied with the megacity: "If a great majority of citizens in the boroughs say they are not satisfied with the transition, we will hold a referendum. If the result is positive, then [we will] defuse. But it's the citizen who is going to decide – not the Liberal Party or the mayor of Montreal."[19] This kind of talk, necessary to get him many suburban mayors on side, would land him in serious trouble in the future.

By then the Quebec Superior Court had denied our request for a temporary injunction against Bill 170, saying it was best for both parties to argue the full case starting 22 May. This meant that, with the legal case going underground for three months, the megacity would be progressively presented in the media as a fait accompli. This also meant that those mayors anxious to move ahead with political designs on the very megacity they wanted to abort in court would continue to marinate in that paradox for three more months. I was worried, though, that the satisfying, creative energy involved in building a political party could easily eclipse their commitment to our legal case, which was, of course, quintessentially negative. I tried to get the mayors to agree that the best course of action would be to run as independent councillors in the megacity and not go under Tremblay's umbrella. Only the mayor of Pointe-Claire, Bill McMurchie, picked up on this: "Common sense tells me that it is inconsistent to campaign for a candidate seeking political office that I am doing my very best to have abolished via the courts ... In the event there is an election in November 2001, Pointe-Claire citizens need no instructions from me on how to vote."[20]

THE MONTREAL TRANSITION COMMITTEE:
PLANNED COALESCENCE

The term "transition committee" sounds innocuous, even mildly reassuring. One imagines a group of folks sitting around together, smoothing the way from one state of affairs to another. The Montreal Transition Committee's job was to implement Bill 170, getting their marching orders (and paycheques) from Louise Harel. Merging twenty-seven municipalities, creating the 2002 budget, hiring all megacity staff, "harmonizing" some 145 collective agreements representing 22,000 employees,[21] organizing the 4 November elections: those were just some of their responsibilities.[22] The transition committee was supposed to hold monthly meetings in public, something that never happened. Their boss, Harel, just shrugged her shoulders, saying that they had to avoid such "free-for-alls," given the majority of the population were hostile to their work.[23]

The transition committee was made up of a mishmash of university types, business people, former civil servants, and retired politicians who were paid quite handsomely to do their job. Actually, compared to the Ottawa boondoggle, and given the jigsaw they had to fit together, they did their job pretty well. Still, they were hired hands charged with building a bed for other people to sleep in. As Yves Ryan, the mayor of Montreal North, put it later, "Everything is done to assuage fears. We are, until contrary proof is available, witnessing an immense enslavement operation of the boroughs, the whole thing beribboned with promises that might well shrivel up the minute [the chair] Mrs Lefebvre, and her transition team, have disappeared from view in January and the new council will have taken on her unfinished job of knocking heads together ... Imagine, into the bargain, what Mrs Lefebvre calls 'cross-breeding': suburban managers will be chosen in Montreal to inculcate their local culture, while others from Montreal will work in the suburbs to establish the big-city culture. I really worry as to which equilibrium will come about with such a recipe."[24]

And what about the suburban mayors? As well as the antilogy of wanting to get elected to the same megacity one wants to destroy, another litmus test of logic in fighting the merger was the way one approached the transition committee. How can one aid in the implementation of the very law one is contesting? Many mayors called it the treason committee.[25] (It works better in French: the comité de transition became the comité de trahison.) While he somehow felt comfortable with running for megacity council, Mayor Peter Yeomans of Dorval felt that helping the megacity transition committee was tantamount to "taking the road to the abattoir." At first, no mayors contesting Bill 170 in court collaborated with the transition committee. Generally, the civil servants of each contesting municipality were instructed to send up all transition committee requests to their city council, where they just piled up. However, at the end of February, Robert Libman – whose municipality was contesting the law in court – decided to become an advisor to the transition committee. He joined mayors such as Bossé, Bourque, and Zampino, who, of course, were not fighting the megacity in court or elsewhere. Libman said, "I've got to be there to make sure Côte Saint-Luc doesn't get raped. I want to make sure someone's there to make the proper decisions for us."[26] His reasoning was shared by Mayor Paquet of Saint-Laurent and Mayor Unterberg of Outremont, who were also fighting the megacity in court and advising the transition committee.

THE STRANGE CASE OF OUTREMONT

Normally, one would have expected Outremont, which was generally (and not quite accurately) considered Westmount's francophone doppelganger, to have put up a spirited resistance to the mergers and to Bill 170. Jérôme Unterberg, Outremont's mayor at the time, tended to tergiversate on such matters. The cause more than the effect of this could be found in the atypical attitude of his citizens towards merger. Even back in June 2000, when the City of Outremont conducted a Léger & Léger poll, they found a surprisingly low 73 per cent of their citizens rejecting a forced One Island One City; 24 per cent of them actually responded favourably. In most other suburbs the favourable response to One Island One City, *especially if forced*, was infinitesimal. When Outremont held an anti-merger rally in November 2000, barely five hundred people showed up.

Unterberg, who had been the mayor of Outremont since November 1995, was still suffering politically from his municipality's renovation of the Théâtre Outremont, a mess (*Le Devoir* called it

"Vaudeville") that came in well over double its initial budget and four years late.[27] By early January 2001, Unterberg seemingly had become a fan of the megacity, the administration of which he called "the most beautiful political challenge that exists today in Quebec."[28] For him, though, his municipality disappearing meant it was time to move on: he was working on his MBA anyway.

Even when he voted on 22 January 2001 as a member of Outremont City Council against participating in a legal contestation of Bill 170, Unterberg said that if his citizens felt differently, there was time for him and his council to change their minds. Leger & Leger once again was paid to feel the pulse of his citizenry. This poll revealed that 58 per cent were against the forced merger legislation and 37 per cent were in favour; 51 per cent were in favour of contesting it in the courts, 44 per cent against. This lukewarm support was enough to cause Unterberg to shift gears and join our legal challenge in early February 2001. Outremont Councillor Marie Cinq-Mars came to see me, complaining that Unterberg was not fighting the mergers and that she was the only member of council to be active against the megacity.

Why Unterberg's relative pusillanimity and follower-ship? One explanation could be that Outremont served as the hometown of Quebec's political and intellectual élite – who were generally very keen on the megacity. The chair of the transition committee, Monique Lefebvre, lived in Outremont, along with Louis Bernard and a number of PQ cabinet ministers.[29]

SANCTON REDUX

Most mayors saw the situation as binary: win in court or embrace the megacity. I worked hard to change that attitude to a strategy of sniping at the enemy until the Liberal cavalry came over the hill. Our lawyers generally were not keen on our publicly playing up the Liberal demerger promise, though, as it sent a message to the courts that our situation was not so desperate and irremediable that we could possibly be rescued by other means than the hand of justice. Understandably, courts prefer to have difficulties resolved outside their halls. While this made sense, I think this self-gagging hobbled us terribly: it reinforced the myth of the binary choice. It also looked as if we did not believe in the Liberals' promise. While Charest's promise of demerger was popular with the public, even though paradoxically most felt he would not deliver, I had to badger most mayors into taking it seriously.

One element of this broad anti-merger strategy was to harp on the merger mess in Ontario, asking the Quebec public whether they really wanted to slide down the same slope. We set up a series of visiting speakers, starting with Andrew Sancton, who addressed the Canadian Club in early March. Sancton pointed out that in 1996 the consulting firm KPMG said the Toronto merger would save $300 million a year: the reality was far different. "While KPMG assumed all workers would receive the average wage, it forgot the unions. They chose not to accept this assumption." This was one of the reasons the 2001 budget of the megacity of Toronto had a $305 million shortfall. And, warned Sancton, only $47 million of this had to do with the downloading of provincial responsibilities onto Toronto's back. "The prospects for Montreal are bleak," Sancton concluded; "Montreal Island is poised to lose one of its greatest assets: municipalities that provide all kinds of services at different costs. The present system helps keep those costs down. It helps many people feel like they are in control of their lives and their communities."[30]

While the French media covered Sancton's speech, there was nothing in the *Gazette* the next morning, although they sent a photographer and reporter. I called the managing editor to find out what happened. What he said upset me, especially given that his newspaper had been our only media ally in the anti-merger battle. He said, "Peter, the mood on the newsroom floor is that the battle is lost. Besides, they are fed up with the implicit anti-Quebec tone. Nothing Quebec can do seems to be any good. They want more positive stories about Quebec." Then he said, "We don't want to get our readership in a funk. After all, how much of the anglophone exodus in the last few decades was created by the *Gazette* saying 'the sky is falling'? And at one point you have to ask, 'What's good for the Montreal region?'"

THE C.D. HOWE REPORT

The most solid study after Sancton's *Merger Mania* to come out during the whole anti-merger fight was a report from the C.D. Howe Institute by Robert L. Bish.[31] Released 20 March 2001, it was called, without mincing matters: "Local Government Amalgamations: Discredited Nineteenth-Century Ideals Alive in the Twenty-First." Bish contended that municipal mergers were the residue from outdated ideas of centralized control, where competition among municipalities in a given territory was regarded as necessarily a Bad Thing. Bish wrote:

> Some provincial governments are pursuing and imposing the intellectual fashions of the nineteenth century as if those fashions were the embodiment of "common sense." Single governing councils and large organizations are simply incapable of dealing with the diverse range of issues that governments must deal with in urban areas. The diversity of metropolitan areas requires close links to citizens and the ability to handle a wide variety of activities on a small scale. For some activities, on the other hand, the commonality of an entire metropolitan area requires mechanisms capable of integrating local diversity. The current weight of evidence is that *no single organization can accomplish these tasks.* Furthermore, when there is a multiplicity of small municipalities in metropolitan areas, the costs of governance are lower, not higher, and, moreover, the political system is more representative ...
>
> If one has a religious-like faith in large bureaucracies, any system of many governments will appear chaotic – just as markets appeared chaotic to Adam Smith's precursors (and are still difficult for many of us to comprehend).

Bish dismissed the putative savings attendant to mergers. "Most researchers conclude that approximately 80 per cent of local government activities do not possess economies of scale beyond relatively small municipalities with populations of 10,000 to 20,000."[32] As for the argument (often repeated by merger backers in Montreal) that mergers enhance economic growth and planning, thereby improving international competitiveness, Bish said: "Some of the most rapidly growing urban regions in the United States – Silicon Valley, Boston, Dallas, Seattle-King County (home of Microsoft and Boeing) – are also among the most governmentally fragmented areas in the country."

And it's not just a matter of dollars but of democracy. The larger the government, Bish said, the more likely that well-organized groups with special interests dominate meetings. Voter turnout is lower. It becomes more expensive to campaign for office, and donations from these special-interest groups become critical. A single party eventually dominates government.

The C.D. Howe report became our *vade mecum*, our Little Red Book. Westmount got in contact with the institute and agreed to underwrite the cost of a French translation and buy, at cost, a whole sheaf of copies for distribution in Quebec. In June I sent a letter to five hundred Quebec movers and shakers, with a copy of the report and the results of our latest poll, encouraging the recipients to put pressure on the government to scrap Bill 170.

THE POWER OF THE BLUES

One of the incongruities of the French media's enthusiastic advocacy of the megacity was its equally fervid denunciation of labour union tactics and power, which, they freely admitted, would only be turbocharged with the mergers. Headlines warned of the "seizure" of the megacity by the blue collars, and editorials lamented that Louise Harel had "evaded" the whole problem of unions when she "concocted" Bill 170. Harel tried to reassure them, going so far as to claim the reason municipal workers were vastly overpaid compared to the rest of the public sector was owing to "municipal fragmentation," something that was patently untrue, given lower remuneration in smaller municipalities. Using curious circular reasoning, she said that it was "evident" that a merged municipality would be better able to face the "oneness of the unionized world,"[33] when that oneness was created by the megacity in the first place.

Editorialist Michèle Ouimet wrote in *La Presse* about the "chronic incapacity of Montreal to manage its big unions." And about how union leader "Jean Lapierre maintains a detestable union culture" that has known its share of violence. "Will this culture be transposed to the new city?" she asked. "Probably. At this point, nothing indicates the opposite ... Facing these mega-unions, the city is naked, or nearly. It has nothing in its arsenal that would permit it to negotiate with equivalent firepower."[34]

I suppose editorialists such as Ouimet considered the imposition of One Island One City One Union a necessary evil to be borne so that the megacity could see the light of day. Lapierre, the truculent Montreal blue-collar leader, would soon find himself wielding power over 7,000 of his kind from one end of the Island to the other, while a comrade-in-arms would be in charge of 8,500 white-collars. Although it was true that 85 per cent of Montreal Island union locals were already members of the Canadian Union of Public Employees, they were all independent locals. Merger would bring just one single local for each class of employee.

MEANWHILE, ON THE MEGACITY CAMPAIGN TRAIL

Early in the year Pierre Bourque had decided to tour enemy territory, visiting each suburban municipality in a brave attempt to drum up support for himself and the megacity he created. At each whistle stop, he was greeted with a group of protesters from DémocraCité, a grassroots anti-merger group. They formed a "hedge of shame" around him. When he got to Westmount in March, he was supposed to meet a handful of local Westmount grandees in a restaurant on the border of Westmount and Montreal. After his lunch, he was escorted to his limousine by police through a throng of yelling protesters that included former Westmount Mayor May Cutler. Bourque's car zoomed away, running a red light and leaving his bewildered press attaché on the sidewalk. In Baie d'Urfé, he was greeted by two hundred booing people including the town's seventy-two-year-old mayor, Anne Myles, brandishing her sign saying "Hell, no, we won't go!" Only half the local notables who were supposed to meet him showed up. I had to admire Bourque's pluck. I could not possibly imagine Gérald Tremblay being capable of suffering such indignities for his cause.

Faced with the massive groundswell of public support against mergers, in December 2000, Bourque had counter-attacked with the idea of getting 100,000 citizens to sign a petition in favour of the megacity, managing to get only 50,000. Or did he? In March 2001, Marvin Rotrand, an opposition Montreal councillor and gadfly extraordinaire, filed an access-to-information request at Montreal City Hall. Rotrand discovered that, in spite of newspaper and radio ads, a telemarketing blitz, an Internet site, a bunch of students hired to collect signatures in the metro, and a raft of city officials hawking it in shopping centres, far fewer legitimate names were collected. I was on the petition, he discovered, along with many double entries and entries in the same handwriting. Rotrand did all this rummaging around because, as he said, "Bourque's insisting that he had a mass movement of support for mergers influenced the Quebec government."[35] Bourque responded by swearing there were indeed

50,000 legitimate signatures, all counted by civil servants. "We have a way of verifying every name. You can order an audit," he said. So that's what I did. I got forensic accountants from KPMG to examine the petition. They came up with only 22,000 signatures – leaving out Mickey Mouse, Jesus Christ, and Peter Trent, that is. The City of Montreal was so furious that KPMG were told to stop work and stop giving interviews on the project or face a loss of city business.

Editorialist Michel C. Auger commented, "Big discovery: Pierre Bourque's petition was useless. Huh! Of course it was useless! Just as useless as the anti-merger referenda organized by the same mayors that had all the democratic guarantees of an election in North Korea."[36] This was the sort of thing we were up against. Westmount conducted a formal referendum run by a qualified returning officer, using an electoral list and requiring proof of identity, yet Auger equated that with Bourque's manufacturing support and misrepresenting public opinion to the government by a "petition" that was patently a fraud.

I was going after Bourque not to help Tremblay but to further the anti-merger cause. Bourque was the architect, symbol, and personification of the megacity. And, thankfully, most of my efforts were on a higher plane than his petition scam. Since he refused to debate with me, I staged a virtual debate at Victoria Hall on 28 March. I used various statements made by Bourque[37] and countered them, as in this sample:

BOURQUE: *We will have the harmonization of all the collective agreements before the election. When we will arrive at the new city, we won't have any problems with the unions. They were not prepared for that in Ontario.*

TRENT: We'll have One Island One City One Union. One blue-collar union known for smashing down City Hall doors. One firefighters' union best known for punching holes in their hoses. Even if Bill 170 requires a temporary cap on total – rather than individual – wages, while the various unions coalesce, this cap can be easily met through higher salaries and fewer employees (and, ergo, poorer services). And what happens when the initial – capped – collective agreements run out? In a few years, both the cap and the gloves will be off ... After all, what did Toronto discover? That wages quickly climb up to match those paid by the most generous former city. It's the highest common denominator that applies.

BOURQUE: *If you talk to [Mayor] Mel Lastman in Toronto, he'll tell you the citizens are very happy and proud to be part of Toronto as a whole.*

TRENT: Let him speak for himself: "There are no two ways about it, amalgamation has turned out to be a disaster."[38] And "We're not in good shape, we're in bad shape."[39]

BOURQUE: [On imposing mergers without public consultation]: *It is the government's full right to do so according to the Constitution of Canada. It is normal that sometimes people don't understand... It happened at the time of the nationalization of electricity. We had to supply power to everyone in Quebec, so we had to nationalize. Of course there was opposition.*

TRENT: Is it not odd that the government admits that a referendum is required to break up a country but not to wipe out a city? This same PQ government is quite fond of looking to the European Community as a model. Perhaps they are not aware that Europe has a Charter of Local Self-Government, ratified by thirty European countries. Article 5 of this charter states, "Changes in local authority boundaries shall not be made without prior consultation of the local communities concerned, possibly by means of a referendum where this is legally permitted." This same article is incorporated in the draft World Charter of Local Government.

BOURQUE: *It's time to stop urban sprawl – it's time to act. We've been studying all this for forty years; this is not new.*

TRENT: Even you have admitted that the entirety of urban sprawl is occurring *off* the Island of Montreal. So how will the creation of one city on the Island help urban sprawl? In fact, a megacity will exacerbate urban sprawl, as Island residents will decamp to smaller (unmerged) cities off-Island in their search for the kind of communities, low taxes, and responsive local government they once enjoyed. Yes, we have been studying urban structures for forty years, but none of the major studies[40] recommended One Island One City. Many studies – including the Pichette Report – recommended the creation of a structure for the entire greater Montreal region. This body is now in place; it's called the Montreal Metropolitan Community (CMM). As well as attacking urban sprawl, the CMM will also compensate the City of Montreal for much of its regional infrastructure. So what's the problem?

After this detailed disquisition as to why I was fighting the megacity, I tossed off some words about the few Montreal Island mayors who embraced mergers with indecent haste in January and about the mayors who were by then consorting with both the transition committee and with Tremblay. I said they were accessories before the fact. "They feel that they can walk and chew gum at the same time. I'll walk, thank you."[41] And many suburban municipalities were contributing to the mass of 229 civil servants working for the transition committee. For those who thought a boycott was only symbolic, I quoted its president, Monique Lefebvre: "If we had no cooperation from the municipal milieu, it could be mind-boggling, but it's not the case."[42] I went on, "If the mayors had stuck together and refused to collaborate, the transition committee could have never delivered the goods by the end of the year. Most mayors seem to have run up the white flag."

None of my hour of arguments against the megacity found themselves in print, but the media jumped on my uncharitable remarks about my colleagues. *La Presse* ran a picture of me that made me look for all the world as if I was weeping. Editorially, the *Montreal Gazette* came down on the side of the collaborating mayors: "As Côte Saint-Luc Mayor Robert Libman and other pragmatists see it, if the legal challenges fail, they want input on the merger's plumbing ... As well, they don't want to delay creating an island-wide political party. That's very wise." The *Gazette* then scolded me, "When Mr Trent says those mayors who are working with the committee are 'participating in the hanging of their own cities' he seems to be impugning their sense of responsibility."[43] They got that right. Clearly, the *Gazette*, in common with all media and some mayors, saw our predicament as either/or: either we win in court or we have to live with the megacity. Few were talking about, or believed, the Liberal demerger promise. This, I suppose, explained the *Gazette*'s rather indulgent attitude to "pragmatists."

My outburst did not stop the regular meetings of the mayors' anti-merger group that I chaired and for which I was spokesperson. Actually, it had the opposite effect: I managed a mass conversion. A little over a month later we held a press conference[44] saying that, in view of the court hearing that would take place in a few weeks' time, and the "lack of transparency and public accountability of the committee," sixteen municipalities were removing their staff from the transition committee. Even Robert Libman – temporarily – stopped advising the committee, along with the mayor of Saint-Laurent. Libman even stopped working with Tremblay.

When the *Gazette* ran nothing on this boycott story, its president and publisher, Michael Goldbloom got a letter from former Westmount mayor May Cutler: "What, in the name of God, is going on at *The Gazette*?" she wrote. "The fact that 16 suburbs of Montreal are withdrawing help from the transition committee is major news ... Who is deciding what play is given your news stories? Has that person dropped in from Mars and knows nothing of what's been happening here? She ended the letter with, "Am I telling you how to run a newspaper? You're damned well right I am." May, bless her, was a former newspaperwoman and book publisher.[45]

The president of the transition committee, Monique Lefebvre, sent a sharply worded letter to each municipality's director-general: "I strongly deplore the attitude and the position taken by [your municipality], which does not help us in the execution of our mandate." By writing directly to our staff, not only was she bypassing their bosses, the city councils, but she was also encouraging disloyalty. Our staff held tight, however. Lefebvre had already asked for legal opinions about how she could force the three most recalcitrant suburbs, Westmount, Baie d'Urfé, and Senneville, to collaborate with the transition committee.[46]

After the boycott dragged on for six weeks – during which time she had to make do with 120 fewer people to work on the transition to the megacity – Lefebvre started to get really angry. "We are faced with the systematic refusal of seventeen municipalities to collaborate with us. This situation weighs heavily in the organization of staff deployment and early retirements." She pointed her finger at ringleader Trent.[47] To break this logjam, Harel resorted to the time-honoured government method: pass a law. She made the boycott illegal by slipping in a provision in a new law, Bill 29, which was rammed through the National Assembly. Bill 29, which modified Bill

170, required municipalities to provide their employees to the transition committee: yet another example of municipal political eunuchry. I was livid: "As far as I know, all employees of Westmount took on employment with us, not with the province. Bill 170 encouraged employees to be disloyal, Bill 29 requires it."[48] To protect Westmount staff against personal legal action, I reluctantly allowed them to work with the transition committee for the first time since it was set up. They did, but in a most desultory way.

Meanwhile, the megacity campaign was chugging along. By mid-April, Tremblay's party had a name (the Union of the Island of Montreal), a slogan ("Let's live Montreal together"), and the mandatory promise (the new megacity would not bring an increase in taxes nor a reduction in services). Some wags changed the slogan to "Let's leave Montreal together."

Bourque, after his futile forays into the suburbs, was doing the rounds on home turf, furiously selling his megacity, saying it would mean a more equitable sharing of the Island's wealth, that residents of Montreal districts would enjoy the same quality of services as, say, Pointe-Claire: "Some are richer than others. We're going to repair that. We will create more wealth and better spread wealth around. It means more equilibrium and more justice all around."[49] As George Bernard Shaw said, "A government that robs Peter to pay Paul can always depend on the support of Paul." To be fair to Bourque, while he toned down this sort of talk in the suburbs, he still made essentially the same point.

Behind the scenes, Bourque's campaign was a lot seamier. Alfonso Gagliano, the federal minister of public works and the federal Liberals' chief political organizer for Quebec, was allegedly involved in Bourque's campaign. As spokesman for the mayors' anti-merger group, I asked for a meeting with him: what was the federal government doing sticking its nose into local politics and helping the architect of the megacity? Gagliano responded in writing, vehemently denying any involvement by him or by the federal Liberal Party, acknowledging that individual MPs could do as they liked. Yet Benoît Corbeil, the former federal Liberal Party executive director for Quebec, was running for Bourque. Beryl Wajsman, who also did work for the federal Liberal Party, was actively recruiting for Bourque. There was a swarm of federal Liberal advisors, organizers, and employees helping Bourque, something Bourque never denied.[50] Finally, on 22 May, we met with Gagliano. He agreed to send out a directive to all employees of the federal Liberal Party instructing them not to get involved in municipal campaigns. It went out the next day. So when Tony Mignacca, Gagliano's right-hand man, later went to help Bourque, he simply took unpaid leave.

Gagliano went on to become the star of the most celebrated political scandal of recent Canadian history: the federal sponsorship scandal. Benoît Corbeil got a fifteen-month prison sentence for influence peddling and defrauding the federal Liberal Party. Mignacca's name surfaced in connection with another little problem at Lands Canada.

Bourque, in common with most megalomaniacs, was a terrible judge of character. His "big tent" approach attracted many dubious characters, even though he himself was quite politically chaste. He was also too busy looking at the big picture.

CLAUDE RYAN

Of course, the Gagliano episode was really a sideshow, only tangentially affecting my anti-merger campaign. While we wanted to influence the media and captains of industry, we also tried to sway the thinking of the Quebec political intelligentsia. My friend Richard Gervais managed to arrange a meeting with Claude Ryan, the grand old man of Quebec's political establishment, respected by Liberals and the PQ alike. Our first meeting took place in Ryan's modest Outremont apartment one Friday night in late April. There were just the three of us, and we chatted for three hours. In his old cardigan and worn shirt, Ryan clearly lived alone, with the dark, almost funereal atmosphere of his home pierced by the occasional reading lamp. He was extremely gracious and attentive, listening carefully to what I had to say – a rarity, I must say, compared to the media treatment I was then accustomed to. His comments came out in precise staccato bursts. He was impressed with our legal case, which he insisted I describe in detail.

While Ryan continued to believe that "enclaves" such as Westmount should be merged with Montreal, he was very much against one big city. Moving on to the subject of demerger, he said, "You know that Charest's promise will be very hard to put into action. There is a kind of 'law of continuity' in politics, where one government does not undo what a previous government has put into place. That being said, I do not like structures, and the PQ has always been mad about structures." He was very impressed with the C.D. Howe Report, "even though there was only a half-page on Quebec. But even that was very well done." He volunteered that he did not particularly like Gérald Tremblay – "Bossé will run things," he said. He did not think that Bourque was honest, a comment that surprised me. He probably meant intellectually honest, an assessment I would have tended to agree with.

Gervais and I came away elated. While Ryan would not write an opinion piece for us – we were pushing our luck when we asked for that – he did agree to react if asked by the media. We met him again on a Saturday in early June at Westmount City Hall. He promised to take a public position and even write an opinion piece for *La Presse* once we had a Superior Court decision.

MY BRILLIANT PLAN AND THE BOARD OF TRADE FLIP-FLOP

By late April, I devised a plan whereby prominent business people would sign an open letter to Premier Bernard Landry that recommended, because of the Toronto fiasco, a delay in implementing mergers for at least a year. Claude Ryan had commented favourably on the idea when I met with him. In the draft open letter, I laid out the facts as coolly as I could, highlighting the C.D. Howe Report. For two years I was in occasional contact with a group of influential Westmounters, whom I called my *eminences grises*. Probably the most eminent member was Laurent Beaudoin, chairman of Bombardier, an aerospace company with some sixty thousand employees. With my draft letter to Landry in hand, and after getting some input from David Culver (the retired chairman of Alcan), I set up a meeting with Beaudoin. Gracious and concerned as always, he didn't have the time to deal with the details but was quite keen on the idea. He told me to work with his executive vice-president, Yvan Allaire, another Westmounter.

So off I went to talk to Allaire. His first question was, "What's the position of the Board of Trade?" I groaned, although I realized he was right. You can't publish an open letter to the premier signed by the business élite asking to delay Bill 170, when the Board of Trade – which is supposed to represent business opinion[51] – has come down in favour of the megacity. The Board of Trade was going to be a tough nut to crack.

Only a year previous, in May 2000, the Board of Trade's president, Pierre Laferrière, had said: "The Board of Trade is not in favour of forced mergers ...We believe that the elimination of articles 45 and 46 of the Labour Code is an indispensable prerequisite for voluntary mergers." They were even more concerned, Laferrière said, with the whole metropolitan region, where there were too many structures: "111 municipalities, one urban community, 12 counties, three transit boards, 51 economic development agencies, and five administrative regions – it's harmful administrative sedimentation. Montreal cannot continue to struggle in this magma of competing structures."[52]

The Labour Code was not changed, Bill 170 clearly forced mergers, and the region still had its overburden of structures. But by September 2000, the Board of Trade had suddenly become a cheerleader for the megacity. What had happened? The short answer is Normand Legault. According to incoming president Legault, "The status quo is not an option, and I'm really not saying that just as a cliché."[53] Legault, who was also the president of the Grand Prix F-1 of Canada, was chummy with Bourque. On 19 September 2000, Legault came out clearly for the megacity – not Bernard's decentralized megacity but Bourque's centralized megacity – and he dragged the whole Board of Trade with him. "After serious thought," the board backed Bill 170. By April 2001, Legault was touting the Montreal and south shore megacities as "a unique opportunity to design cities that will meet the challenges of the twenty-first century." They would be "models of democracy, efficiency, and vitality."[54] Legault threw his support behind the transition committee. Of course, its president, Monique Lefebvre, happened to be a vice-president of the Board of Trade.

In early May 2001, I called a number of friends who were on the executive of the Board of Trade or past-presidents: they all agreed with the board's former stance and were upset about Legault's engineering this flip-flop. Members were never polled about the change of position. Phil O'Brien, a former president, said to journalist Henry Aubin about the megacity: "For a while, I was behind it. I thought it would produce a better class of politician in Montreal. But now I'm concerned by a big bureaucracy. The board hitched its star last year to the merger, and if the merger turns into a failure, I don't want the board to be hurt."[55] It turned out that Guy Fréchette, who ran Ernst and Young in Quebec, was slated to be the next Board of Trade president. And it also turned out that Gérald Limoges, who used to run the same firm, was a Westmount city councillor. So Limoges got to work on Fréchette, along with writing long letters to a half-dozen members of the board.

By June, Fréchette was back-pedalling – a bit. In a letter to Premier Landry, he reminded him that the Board of Trade's support for mergers was conditional on changes to the Labour Code, and that the government's changes were "insufficient and contravened the sense of our support for mergers." His spokesman then said, "We do not want a municipal merger at any price."[56]

But by that time, faced with the Board of Trade's continuing ambiguity about mergers, Bombardier had pretty much lost interest in my project. I should have worked on the board six months earlier. I chalked another one up to Bourque. In short order, Fréchette was to become a big fan of Harel and of the megacity.

As a footnote to this story, the director of communications of the transition committee, Isabelle Hudon, went from there to the Board of Trade to do the same job. In 2005, Hudon became Board of Trade president, replacing Benoit Labonté, who had been elected the mayor of the downtown borough (called Ville-Marie) of the megacity. Labonté later was disgraced when it was revealed he accepted some hundred thousand dollars in cash to fund his party's leadership campaign – the cash supplied by contractors doing business with the city.

A WORLD CHARTER

As a long shot, I met with Yves Fortier, chairman of the legal firm Ogilvy, Renault, and former ambassador to the UN. Fortier was under the impression that municipal mergers were a worldwide trend, so this myth was alive even at his rarefied intellectual level. He was interested in the C.D. Howe report and how the Toronto merger was going. Since the Council of Europe adopted its Charter of Local Self-Government[57] that disallowed the very thing Bill 170 did (merge municipalities without citizen approval), I asked whether he could find out how close the World Charter of Local Government was to being adopted. He learned that it was going nowhere at the UN, as the charter was in conflict with some nations' constitutions and "its provisions would be binding upon States. It is therefore unlikely that this text will be adopted in the near future, if at all."

As I write these lines, the UN still has not adopted even a watered-down version of the charter, but by 2001 the charter was in force in thirty-three European nations. Today, almost every member state of the Council of Europe is party to the charter, with the notable exception of France.

A DEMONSTRATION OF WEAKNESS

The anti-merger grassroots group DémocraCité was active and organized everywhere. They compensated for the desultoriness and vacillation of most of their municipalities' mayors. Unfortunately, they were convinced, given the polls showing rock-solid support for our cause, that a massive demonstration was just the thing to rally the rather disparate anti-merger forces. Against my better judgment (and that of Richard Gervais, my communications strategy advisor), I gave in and agreed that my mayors' group would fund a demonstration on 11 May. Buses left most of the suburban municipalities full of noisy citizens. City employees came. We had floats: Dorval's allegoric float, "Democracy Quebec-style," consisted of a steamroller flattening out and dismembering chained mannequins covered in blood; a big colour photo of it made the front page of *Le Devoir*. We marched three kilometres under the noon sun to a stage set up outside Premier Landry's office. We then heard Opposition Leader Jean Charest speak. We also heard from Ginette Durocher of Saint-Bruno, who had started an anti-merger coalition right across Quebec. To de-anglicize things, I did not speak.

We had made it clear our demonstration (called Megacity = Megamess) would be nothing like the massive December rally. Well, it wasn't. It was what the French call a wet firecracker, and the English call equivalently a damp squib. According to the media, there were anywhere from 1,000 to 3,500 demonstrators. I think there were probably a few thousand. I looked around and saw a swarm around the stage, and then mostly bare asphalt. It was a huge flop and did us a lot of damage. "Merger: The Contestation Runs out of Steam" read the *La Presse* and *Journal de Montréal* headlines.

HOWARD HUSOCK FROM HARVARD

Having brought in academic experts from Canada such as Andrew Sancton on municipal mergers, we also organized a visit by Howard

Husock from Harvard University to tell us – really, the media – about the US experience, where, over the last half-century, the number of municipalities has actually increased from 16,800 to 19,300. Although mergers "may satisfy the ambitions of politicians and planners everywhere," he said, "citizens prefer small towns." He explained why bigger municipalities cost more to run – aside from increased bureaucracy and union wages, that is. When mergers occur, Husock said, "all the various services and amenities packages of the many individual jurisdictions get put together. No one wants services to be reduced – but, as a matter of political reality, no municipality can provide certain services to only one area. All the jogging enthusiasts who'd previously been outnumbered in Jurisdiction A, suddenly can turn to the new megacity and demand that, because there are great jogging trails in what used to be Jurisdiction B, they, too, deserve such amenities. In other words, rather than be reduced, service provision inevitably rises to meet the many tastes that had previously been separate."

Another problem was the disconnect between the benefits of increased tax revenue and the incentive to create it: "One of the reasons that citizens agree to the permits or zoning changes which allow new businesses to locate in their municipalities is the belief that the benefits they will gain – in employment and municipal taxes – will offset their costs, such as greater congestion. In a megacity, citizens in one small neighbourhood will fear that they are more likely to incur costs than to see benefits – and to employ not-in-my-backyard tactics to stop new construction." Husock went on, "Metropolitan government – a single, far-sighted, expert, benevolent and efficient central administration for urban areas – was to bring order to the chaos of central cities surrounded by their 'crazy quilt' of independent suburbs." The re-emergence of "consolidation" as a solution in the 1960s added to the earlier claims of efficiency two new claims: redistribution of wealth and prevention of urban sprawl. Rather than expanding cities, he said, we should break them up.[58]

FIGHTING FIGURES FROM TORONTO

I continued to bring in Cassandras from Toronto to warn Quebec politicians and media of the megacity mess in Toronto. John Sewell, mayor of Toronto, 1978–80, came in April, and Barbara Hall, the last mayor of pre-merger Toronto, came in May. In April, the City of

Kirkland brought in Michael Prue, former mayor of the Borough of East York, where 81 per cent of votes in a referendum were against mergers. Prue pointed out it was not just a question of escalating costs in Toronto caused by merger; there were many cases of reduced services. Before mergers, the grass in their parks, for example, was mowed eight times a year. Now it was down to four.

We commissioned studies – not that they did much good. The scepticism of the francophone media is evident from this example of *La Presse* coverage of another of our experts who benefited from the supposed "Klondike" of anti-merger studies: "In a highly ambitious exercise, Lionel D. Feldman ... undertook to identify the actual costs of the Toronto merger. What did Mr Feldman conclude? That the Toronto merger 'according to a conservative estimate,' cost $290 million [per year] ...The mayor of Westmount, Peter Trent, chose to appear satisfied with the study and made it known that he was going to pass the hat among the other suburban mayors to share in the $18,000 bill."[59] (Feldman was a Toronto management consultant.)

Yet when the Transition Committee hired Montreal economist Fernand Martin to do precisely the same analysis, his conclusion – released two weeks after the Feldman Study – that the Toronto merger *saved* $136 million a year got wide coverage and was accepted as gospel. Professor Martin did admit, however, that these savings were partly a result of reduced services, and that there were, as well, one-time costs of $275 million to create the megacity in the first place. Financially, "the merger was a total non-event," said Martin, especially when one looked at these numbers in proportion to the Toronto megacity's $6 billion total budget.

Yes, said Martin, the Toronto megacity was spending more in 2001 compared to 1998, but that was the effect of inflation. Martin wrote that, since three-quarters of all municipal activities (police, transit, and so on) had already been merged through Metro Toronto, huge savings were not on offer. Yet that was why Ontario Premier Harris forced the merger in the first place. But the huge lacuna in the Martin study was that it ignored the upcoming costs of harmonizing the remuneration of some fifteen thousand unionized employees.[60] Andrew Sancton brought this up in a riposte to Martin's study. He also pointed out, for example, that Martin used in his study City of Toronto figures, their accuracy now being contested by the province. Sancton went on, "For the Montreal Transition Committee to sponsor a study of which the main aim seems to be to show that

Toronto's amalgamation was not a financial disaster is an indication of how desperate the members are to defend what they are doing."[61]

Martin later made it clear he was not a diehard supporter of the Montreal megacity. "I'm not defending amalgamation, nor proposing it. I haven't studied it seriously enough." He felt that, for example, focusing just on the Island of Montreal was wrong: "One criticism that I did not put in my report, because it wasn't my job, is that you have to eventually go all the way, or do nothing. Because, in both cases, only half of the population is organized into an amalgamated city."[62]

By this time, media attention had already shifted to the courthouse, where we were forced to attack the megacity on linguistic, not economic, grounds.

14

Forced to Play the Language Card

There'll always be a Westmount,
We're twenty thousand strong;
We have more lawyers per square foot
This battle to prolong.

CITIES: THE CONSTITUTIONAL CASTRATI OF CANADA

Back in late spring 1999, I was getting more and more concerned about the possibility of legislated mergers. Politically, we were puny compared with the forces marshalled against us: the City of Montreal, the Government of Quebec, and the entire French print media. And legally? I knew Canadian municipalities were totally subservient to provincial governments, in contrast with the United States where municipalities can only be merged with the approval of their citizens. There must be some legal angle, though. I decided to have a chat with Sylvie DeVito, who was our city attorney and also lived in Westmount. Michel Delorme, her *chum* (a Quebec sobriquet meaning boyfriend), was the head of the municipal law department at Bélanger, Sauvé, where she was also a partner.* So I called Delorme in too.

"Michel," I said, "I know the old cliché about municipalities being the creatures of the province, but there must be *something* we can do if Quebec decides to go the route of Toronto and pass a law forcing mergers."

He said, "Peter, there is absolutely nothing you can do, nothing whatever. Under the Canadian constitution, municipalities are under the total control of the provinces. They don't even have a constitutionally

* Today, they are partners in another sense, and have each been elevated to a judgeship.

guaranteed existence. If a province wanted to, it could get rid of municipalities entirely, and provide all local services itself."

"But doesn't Quebec at least have the obligation to consult citizens? You know, a referendum, or something?"

"Two years ago, when the municipalities in Toronto that were slated to disappear went to court to try to stop the creation of the megacity, the Ontario Superior Court said" – Michel put on his reading glasses and looked at his notes – "ah, yes, here it is: 'Bill 103, which creates the megacity, appeared on the government's legislative agenda with little or no public notice and without any attempt to enter into any meaningful consultation with the inhabitants of Metro Toronto. Such is the prerogative of government and there is no obligation on the government to consult the electorate before it introduces legislation.'"[1]

"What about the Canadian Charter of Rights and Freedoms?" I asked. "Doesn't it limit what a government can do? Everybody and his dog seem to be invoking the Charter these days. And doesn't Quebec have its own charter?"

"The Canadian Charter says that every individual has the right to equal benefit of the law without discrimination. Actually, the Toronto municipalities tried to use the Charter, arguing their citizens would not be getting the 'same quality and quantity of democratic expression when compared to other Ontario municipalities.' Pretty feeble, eh? The Court said, we're sorry, but you people did not provide us any proof of discrimination. And it said, 'the Charter was not intended to alter or limit the legislature's jurisdiction over municipal institutions,' adding no citizens can be 'free from government chutzpah or imperiousness.' So there. The municipalities gave up then and there, although a group of citizens soldiered on, only to lose on appeal and have the Supreme Court refuse to hear their case."

Things looked hopeless on the legal front. It was time to start clutching at straws. These were provided by Ricardo Hrtschan, the maverick mayor of Mount Royal. Hrtschan had taken a former employer to court for wrongful dismissal; the employer accused him of lying about his qualifications, and the whole thing was dragging its messy way through the courts. By chance, Hrtschan had come across a relatively obscure lawyer, Jean Marois, who had come up with this grand legal theory that forced mergers *could* be stopped in the courts.

Marois said the 1998 Supreme Court ruling on the secession of Quebec changed everything. He maintained that citizens' right to local autonomy was an unwritten principle behind the Canadian constitution that had its roots in British common law, Magna Carta, and the 1689 Bill of Rights – all of which could be found in the Supreme Court ruling, but it was a very liberal interpretation on his part. Most of the other mayors had dismissed it all as jiggery-pokery, and, since there was no mayor held in less regard than Hrtschan, poor old Marois was treated as a snake-oil salesman-cum-ambulance-chaser whenever Hrtschan dragged him out to the mayors' various strategy sessions in late 1999.

But then came Montfort.

MINORITY RIGHTS

Montfort Hospital was like any other hospital, one assumed. But it wasn't. Yes, orderlies in white rubber-soled shoes wheeled gurneys about, surgeons in pale green synthetic smocks scrubbed their hands with hexachlorophene-laced soap, and garbled voice announcements echoed in pastel-coloured corridors, the usual hospital atmosphere. Yet the orderlies, surgeons, and announcers all spoke in French – quite the norm in Quebec. But Montfort was in Ontario. This was the Hôpital Montfort; of all the 192 hospitals in Ontario, it was the only francophone university teaching hospital. Montfort was founded near Ottawa in 1953. In those days, every patient, doctor, and nurse was French. By the mid-1990s, Montfort was offering English services, but the training and medical services still remained principally in French. In fact, 20 per cent of its patients were English, but the language of work was French.

In 1996 the Ontario government created a commission to rationalize the delivery of health services in hospitals. In February 1997 this commission recommended Montfort be closed and merged with three other hospitals. Franco-Ontarians rose up in anger, their battle cry, "Close Montfort? Never!" They took the matter to court, and the court agreed with them. "Since the beginning of the seventeenth century," wrote the judges, "francophones have always had a significant presence in the territory that became Ontario ... They lived, worked, sang, studied, loved, fought, suffered, and died in French. However ... they were ravaged by the forces of assimilation by the dominant English language and culture ... Unlike other minorities,

French language and culture – in common with the majority English language and culture – have the right to a specific status by virtue of the Canadian constitution." At the beginning of the twentieth century, the judgment pointed out, 10 per cent of the population of Ontario was francophone; this percentage is now almost cut in half through assimilation.[2]

This judgment, rendered in November 1999 by the Divisional Court of Ontario,[3] declared that the closure of Montfort Hospital was unconstitutional. The judges agreed with the plaintiffs' lawyers that the closure "contravened one of the fundamental structural principles that support the Canadian Constitution, namely, the principle of the protection of minorities." These principles were set down in the Supreme Court's reference in 1998 regarding the secession of Quebec. The Supreme Court had said that the Constitution was "a living tree" – a metaphor that went back to 1930 – founded on four unwritten principles: federalism, democracy, the rule of law, and the protection of minorities. These principles, even though not expressly written, nevertheless could create substantial legal rights. These rights could allow the courts to intervene and impose powerful limits on governmental action if the principles were transgressed.

The Ontario Court judges made the point that Montfort was "a standard-bearer of the francophone minority in Ontario, a symbol of the force and vitality of that community." It was crucial to the protection and preservation of their language and culture. So it was a broader question than simply the provision of francophone medical services or francophone medical training. Their ruling went on to say that "if Montfort were one of a number of francophone hospitals offering similar services and playing the same role, which was the case in an anglophone context for the [closure of] the Lachine Hospital[4] in Montreal, the situation could have been different ... But the Montfort was the only hospital of its type in Ontario." So, if all anglophone hospitals were closed in the Montreal area, one assumes that anglophones would have been able to get the courts to reverse such a mass closure. On reading this judgment, I reflected on the fact that Bill 170 got rid of all the anglophone municipalities in Quebec. Surely the same protection would apply?

If we were to have a chance of fighting legislated mergers, we had to "Montfortize" ourselves. Our enthusiasm was later dampened by both Michel Delorme and Jean Pomminville (a litigator and former mayor of Outremont), who warned us that the situation of francophones in Ontario was much more precarious than that of anglophones in Quebec; and, most importantly, Montfort Hospital was closed by a government administrative decision, while our municipalities were being wiped out by a provincial law. Using the sort of logic that makes the layperson suspicious of the legal system, it seems that these unwritten constitutional principles can invalidate the actions of a government agency but not invalidate a law enacted by a provincial legislature.

We needed high-profile courtroom lawyers, lawyers who could successfully argue anglophone rights without putting off our francophone allies. In July 2000 I put together a team to plead for Westmount: Gérald Tremblay,* Julius Grey, and Jean Marois. (Marois had already been doing legal research for us for six months.) Tremblay, senior partner in McCarthy Tétrault, was a big, affable man with a square jaw, ready smile, and solid handshake. Grey was a friend of mine, as well as a committed socialist, a human-rights activist, a professor, and a scarily brilliant intellectual.

GUY BERTRAND

In the autumn of 2000, lawyer Guy Bertrand was making the rounds in the West Island, selling his services. This gave me great cause for concern, in that we were already walking on political eggs with our argument of a threatened English minority. All we needed was Bertrand, notorious for his grandstanding and incendiary statements, to turn the whole thing into a burlesque. Bertrand was a founding member of the separatist Parti Québécois, unsuccessfully running for them in 1989. After being shabbily treated by the PQ, he had become a committed federalist to the point of fighting the idea of unilateral secession of Quebec in the courts. He was also at that time an ardent partitionist.[5] At the time of writing, he is back being a separatist. Bertrand was literally an "in your face" guy. He had too-perfect teeth, over-black hair, and a suspiciously dark complexion: the *Gazette* referred to him as a tanning salon victim. In spite of

---

* The media (and I, looking at my telephone messages) were always confusing him with Gérald Tremblay, mayoral candidate. Tremblay is the most common name in Quebec, well ahead of Gagnon, Roy, Côté, and Bouchard.

his caricaturally salesman-like appearance, he was very bright and a superb lawyer.

I don't think the West Island mayors – anglophones all – knew just how much the francophone media treated Bertrand as a clown making a living out of tilting at linguistic windmills on behalf of anglos. Even if he had had some major victories in court, just retaining him would reinforce the notion in francophone minds that the people fighting mergers were a bunch of radical anglos. We couldn't look at the legal side alone: to preserve our municipalities, political considerations forced us to keep francophones on side. Bertrand would just turn them off. Our political and legal strategies had to be complementary. In the event, Baie d'Urfé and then Dollard-des-Ormeaux could not resist Bertrand's blandishments and hired him. True to form, the brief he prepared argued, "Bill 170 has as its goal to remove from my clients (residents of Baie d'Urfé) the fundamental right to remain in Canada in the event of a winning referendum on the sovereignty of Quebec." And that was not all: he went on to describe the citizens of Baie d'Urfé (all four thousand of them) as a "people" with the right of "internal autodetermination," whatever that meant. He did, however, get off a good line about the future inferior status of the suburbs, calling the merger "a morganatic marriage."

Not surprisingly, when Baie d'Urfé filed their case against Bill 170, the headline in *Le Soleil* ran, "Guy Bertrand defends the right to partition Quebec."[6] We were not off to a good start.

WESTMOUNT'S WRAITH

My big fear was that Bill 170 would wipe out the City of Westmount at the end of 2001, before our legal challenge against it had run its course. We had to move fast before Quebec started passing laws throttling the ability of municipalities to fund such challenges post-mortem, so to speak. Just over a month after Bill 170 was tabled in the National Assembly on 15 November 2000, we had the letters patent from Ottawa for the Citizens' Association for the Preservation of the City of Westmount. I then got Westmount City Council to approve the transfer of $500,000 to the association. I was careful not to be a director myself, but asked Barrie Birks, Peter Blaikie, and Stephen Jarislowsky to be its officers. These three well-known Westmounters were completely above reproach. The association, then, was a kind of a wraith that would continue to exist after Westmount itself disappeared: it would pursue the legal battle as co-plaintiff; and, in the event we lost, it would then bankroll demerger efforts.

While some other municipalities eventually transferred money to a trust or foundation, their goal was to keep their surpluses for their citizens' use and shelter them from the rapacious megacity – not specifically to carry on the fight. In yet other cases such as Dorval, Kirkland, and Hampstead, municipalities went on a construction spending binge before the merger shut them down.

ROUND 0: OUR COURT DATE IS SET

Both Westmount and Baie d'Urfé launched their legal challenges on 21 December 2000. By the end of the next month, another sixteen municipalities on the Island of Montreal had followed suit. On average, our municipalities were ninety years old, the oldest being Westmount at 127 years. Fourteen of the eighteen municipalities had official bilingual status, which meant, given that our only thread of hope was attached to English minority rights, that the four "French" municipalities were almost going along for the ride. One municipality from the Quebec region, Ancienne Lorette, was also contesting Bill 170 with us.

In spite of the received wisdom that our contestation would take years to drag through the courts, I found the Quebec judicial system can move pretty quickly when it wants to. When our gang of lawyers and the government's gang of lawyers fetched up in front of Judge Danielle Grenier on 19 February 2001, she told them to forget trying for a temporary injunction and go directly to argue the merits of our case. Since the Chief Justice had said he wanted the case to be dealt with quickly, Judge Grenier, brushing off the complaints from the government's lawyers who wanted to stretch things out until the autumn, set 22 May as a date for the trial. She said, "If, for example, this case has to go to appeal, that has to happen before the summer." She also tossed off an interesting remark about our case: "There are some extremely serious matters … uncommon, let's face it."

ROUND I

You would think that on its fourth try, Montreal would get its courthouse right. But no: after the first, built in 1803, burned down in

1844, a second courthouse opened on the same site in 1857. There it still sits, next to Montreal City Hall, a grand affair with lofty ceilings, mosaic floors, ornate iron balustrades, soaring columns, and elaborate millwork. Sadly, it was stripped of its original function in 1974. It now houses city pencil-pushers, and many of its architectural features have been butchered in that cheesy style that only bureaucrats can achieve. An additional courthouse was built right across the street in 1926. Designed by one of Quebec's most brilliant architects, Ernest Cormier, it is a neo-classical delight. Recently restored, Cormier's masterpiece now houses the Court of Appeal, after, perhaps appropriately, serving as a drama school. Both older buildings reek of juridical splendour.

The newest courthouse, which opened in 1971 and shows it, replaced both older buildings. This seventeen-storey slab-sided leviathan is a warren of fluorescent-lit rooms with all the magisterial dignity of government offices in a third-rate country. All the ceilings are claustrophobically low. No natural light penetrates the courtrooms, as if that would inject too much of a distraction. There is no grandeur, no majesty of the law, just grey, grey, grey. This "new" courthouse is completely out of scale and context among the limestone ashlar walls and cobblestone streets of Old Montreal. And for some unknown reason, all three courthouses have been built within writ-throwing distance of each other; it is as if justice in Montreal can only be dispensed from a small patch of legally hallowed ground.

Going to court is a bit like taking the metro or visiting the hospital: all classes of society commingle. Rich businessmen have to go there as well as criminals – or, these days, perhaps that's redundant. Each courtroom is insulated by a set of double glass doors that create a kind of airlock from the corridor. Walking by, you can see but can't hear cases involving things as varied as patent infringements, divorce proceedings, rape charges, and constitutional challenges. Our case was heard in the Jules Deschênes auditorium, the biggest with nearly three hundred seats. The indigo broadloom and upholstery muffle every sound. In this dry, echoless chamber, the future of our beleaguered municipalities would be determined.

Our aim in going to court was to nullify the effect of both Bill 170, which created the megacity of Montreal, and Bill 171, which changed the criterion for a bilingual municipality from a majority having to be non-francophone to a majority having to be mother-tongue anglophone, thereby putting the "allophones" on the French side of the ledger. Westmount came armed with seven arguments, but only the "minority rights" had any real chance of success.

We were going to argue that a modern democracy *can* limit the powers of the legislatures, thanks to the Canadian Charter of Rights and constitutional principles. The declaration that the new megacity of Montreal was officially French speaking had a disproportionate effect on the minority English, and the reorganization of the municipal scene, even if justified, was not important enough to warrant these negative effects.

The municipalities fighting Bill 170 had about twenty lawyers on their side,[7] and the attorney-general of Quebec had about twelve. While listening to this surfeit of legal help, I worked out the cost: twenty lawyers for ten days, ten hours a day, times $250 an hour, equalled half a million dollars. It did give two weeks' employment to about a dozen journalists who were present.

The show began on 22 May 2001. The auditorium was filled with mayors, councillors, and citizens from the nineteen municipalities taking legal action. We had briefed all the citizen groups to refrain from making any comment during the proceedings. The burble of the crowd died down as the judge entered and all rose. Jean Marois led off, a bit tentatively, for Westmount, from 9:30 until 10:45 AM. He embarrassingly dwelt – as he had to do – on the anglo-British argument: Westmount was the torch-bearer for the anglo-British community and symbol of that community's prestige. Such a community needed control of its own institutions to survive, and this community was in precipitous decline. Bill 170 would accelerate this decline. (This, of course, was to make Westmount look as similar as possible to the Montfort Hospital situation.) I started to cringe. I could see the judge was not really sold on this argument. Marois plunged on. The existence of anglophone municipalities, he said, served as a kind of *"pacte de cloisonnement institutionnel,"* a sort of linguistic non-aggression pact tacitly agreed to by all.[8] He went on to describe the times that Montreal tried to annex Westmount, notably in 1910 and 1960. This time around, however, the government's stated goal was to francize* the whole Island. Then Marois changed

---

* Please bear with the neologism "francize." It seems more dignified than "Frenchify" and clearer than "Gallicize."

gears. Westmount was a common-law corporation created under the seal of the lieutenant-governor in 1874. Such a corporation, Marois maintained, could only be dissolved by the founders or their inheritors. The judge did not buy it, but it was unclear to me as to why not.

Next up, from 11:00 to 12:15, was Julius Grey. He just exuded reasonableness and competence with his professorial manner, leaning on his lectern and delivering his exegesis, rarely referring to his notes. He explained that at one point Parliament was indeed sovereign, that it could even abolish the courts if it wanted to. Then the Constitution slowly began to take precedence. The Charter of Rights transformed the Constitution and even put limits on it. "Democracy is no longer just a question of 50 per cent plus," he said. "Paternalism is no longer possible." He went on to say that the Supreme Court has already ruled that the English minority in Quebec needed protection. One did not have to prove that legislators' intent was to infringe on these rights, only that the effect was precisely that. And, he asked the judge, fiscal equity surely could have been achieved by other means than abolishing the municipalities?

Then, at 12:15 Gérald Tremblay got up on his hind legs. At his best before lunch, he was in fine form. As a seasoned litigator, he knew that presentation was everything. He held up his copy of Bill 170 to the judge: "This is Bill 170. Bill 170 has seven annexes, each setting out the charter of the seven new megacities that it creates."

He began reading the first line of each annex. "First annex. Article one. The City of Gatineau is hereby constituted. Blah. Blah," he said. "Next annex. Article one. The City of Longueuil is hereby constituted. Blah, blah."

Speeding up, he read, "The City of Saguenay is hereby constituted. The City of Quebec is hereby constituted. The City of Trois-Rivières is hereby constituted. The City of Sherbrooke is hereby constituted." Then stopping for two beats –

"The City of Montreal is hereby constituted. The City of Montreal is a French-speaking city."

Tremblay stopped, and then squinted quizzically at the judge. "How did *that* get in there, like a piece of hair falling in a bowl of soup?"[9]

Warming to his theme, he went on to say that while the elimination of the anglophone suburbs was not perhaps the main reason for the mergers, these municipalities would get wiped out though "collateral damage." He dismissed the boroughs that replaced our municipalities as "organized trusteeship." By then it was lunchtime, and our little gang from Westmount went across the street for lunch, feeling pumped. At 2:30 PM, Tremblay, a little more subdued than in the morning, went on to say that two of the four unwritten principles of the Constitution that were established by the Supreme Court were the protection of minorities and democratic values. And, following in Marois's footsteps, he said that any reduction in anglophone institutions would increase the possibility of assimilation. It was not just a matter of language, but culture.

It was 3:37 PM already. Next, a parade of lawyers took the stand, starting with Doug Mitchell who was there representing Dyane Adams, the commissioner of official languages. Mitchell had all of seventeen minutes. Late in the day at 4 PM, it was Guy Bertrand's turn. He started off with more of a political than legal position. He said that the cliché that municipalities were creatures of the province was a sophism. They should be creatures of their citizens. He went on about anglo self-determination and how anglos have suffered a drop in Quebec from 20.4 per cent of the population in 1871 to 8.8 per cent in 1996.[10]

The next morning, 23 May, Bertrand got another kick at the can. Bright and early at 9 AM, he made us squirm a bit with his statement that the anglos make up a community that is humiliated and harassed. Then came the headline-making lines: "In some countries when there is a war and bombs start falling, people run to the mountains to escape the bullets. Here, we displace people in another way. People flee from Quebec because ... we treat the English language as a sickness and make anglophones feel they are no longer welcome here."[11] Any anglophones remaining behind in spite of the mergers, according to Bertrand, would be "profoundly humiliated." He was on much more solid ground when he said that the mergers imposed different treatment on different groups, that only 0.7 per cent of the Quebec civil service was anglophone. In a burst of patriotism, he said Bill 170 was anti-Canadian.

During the break after Bertrand had finished, Francine Bastien from our public relations people came rushing over to me, saying that, while we had agreed to keep a low media profile during the trial, we had to react to Bertrand's intemperate words. TV cameras were not hard to find and Bertrand was already in a scrum. After he finished, I gave interviews distancing ourselves from him. I *knew* this would happen, I said to myself.

Journalist Michel David commented sarcastically, "Fortunate-ly, Guy Bertrand is on the lookout. Without him, no one would have discovered that municipal reform was a huge separatist plot intended to systematically wipe out federalist leaders in the next ref-erendum."[12] André Pratte, *La Presse* editorialist, laconically said, "English-speaking Montrealers have to convince their fellow citizens about the validity of their fears. Some would gain by more carefully choosing their words. And their lawyer."

If Westmount was stretching things in pleading its anglo-Britishness, Côte Saint-Luc was much more at ease pleading its Jewishness[13] when its turn came on 25 May. Lawyer Daniel Chénard told the court that Côte Saint-Luc's population was 65 per cent Jewish, its entire city council was Jewish, and nearly one-third of its huge senior popu-lation was made up of Holocaust survivors. Fifty years ago, there were virtually no Jews in Côte Saint-Luc; now there were nearly as many as in the whole City of Montreal. Local government, wrote one expert witness, can help minorities to preserve their cultures, to receive culturally sensitive services, and protect them from prejudice and discrimination. The City of Côte Saint-Luc, for example, takes into account Jewish holidays when dealing with residents.

WHAT IS A QUEBEC ANGLOPHONE?

As this courtroom drama was unfolding, I was involved in my own dramatic effort. We were up to dress rehearsals for a production of *A Man for all Seasons*, which opened the following week. I played the role of King Henry VIII, and Peter Blaikie was Sir Thomas More. It was a play about abuse of power, and the irony was not lost on me. But on the stage, I was the abuser, not the victim. Every morning when I showed up at court to watch the other pantomime continue, I was tired. Acting is much more exhausting than living real life. Blaikie, a founder of Heenan, Blaikie, and a crack litigator himself, each night patiently listened to my recounting the progress of our case. In some vague way, our play illustrated the idea that an anglo community did indeed exist, that this community was threatened by Quebec's efforts to francize the Island.

During some of the more boring pleading in court, I reflected that if there were no Westmounts and no Beaconsfields, could the Que-bec anglo community be quite as sure of its future, diminished as it was by the mass exodus suffered since the PQ first got into power?

The period 1976–81 alone saw a net migration of 106,000 anglophones out of Quebec to the rest of Canada, a 13 per cent drop. Bill 170 was yet another blow. Why should the Montreal anglo culture be suppressed because immigrants were not being francized in great enough numbers to offset dwindling francophone fecundity? And was it not francophones themselves who had decided to decamp to off-Island suburbs, contributing to the de-francization of the Island of Montreal that so worried the PQ? In short, the drop in francophones on the Island was caused by francophones. Anglos became the whipping boys. And rather than obsessing about the Island's linguistic character, why not look at the entire Montreal Metropolitan Region, where French was holding its own?

On the other hand, secure in the comfort of the English-speaking mantle that covers the world, it was easy for anglophones to pooh-pooh the insecurities of Quebec francophones. The unilingual Lafromboises in Vermont telephone directories, the folkloric French in Louisiana, and the slowly dissolving shards of French-speaking Ontario – all serve to concentrate the minds of the six million French Quebecers who desperately maintain political and legal dykes in an attempt to hold back a sea of 20 million anglophone Canadians outside Quebec and (nominally) 300 million anglophone Americans to the south. The drawing power of English for immigrants is incredibly strong: language laws in Quebec over the years have had as one of their primary goals to get immigrants to adopt French. Every five years, Statistics Canada reveals the latest ratios of francophones to anglophones and allophones in Quebec. It is a measure of the understandable anxiety of French-speaking Quebecers that these numerological entrails are still warm when Quebec's high priests of demography start their work, the media standing by for the linguistic augury to come. Is French gaining or regressing?

While it is beyond this book's scope and its author's competence, our court case raised other, allied, linguistic questions. What is an anglophone? Does one acquire this appellation by one's mother tongue, one's first official language spoken,[14] or the language one speaks at home? Do immigrants who have chosen English benefit from whatever rights our laws might bestow on Quebec's anglophone minority, or are they relegated to some linguistic limbo? In other words, is anglophony a tribe, a club, or a label? What about those who speak both French and English, or English and a "non-official" language?

Bill 171, the "sidecar" to Bill 170 (as the *Montreal Gazette* called it), was another circumscription for anglophones, as it presented a more narrow definition of an anglophone. Bill 171 modified Quebec's French Language Charter, confusingly also known as Bill 101 (its debutante title when first presented in the National Assembly in 1977). The Charter allowed bilingual status[15] to municipalities if 50 per cent of their residents spoke a "language other than French." This was rather illogical, as it permitted those residents who spoke neither English nor French to bulk up the English numbers when arriving at the 50 per cent. However, Bill 171 overcompensated: it stipulated that not only must over 50 per cent of a given municipality's residents henceforth be English-speakers for it to get bilingual status but they must be *mother-tongue* English-speakers. Thus, any immigrants who had adopted English were not counted. Some English-rights groups pointed out that radio talk-show host Tommy Schnurmacher would not be considered an anglophone (his mother tongue was Hungarian), nor would journalist William Johnson, whose mother tongue was French.

But let us return to the courthouse.

THE DEFENCE

On 28 May, at 9:00 AM sharp, lawyers for the attorney-general began their defence, starting with Maître Jean-François Jobin. He immediately congratulated our side for "our fertile imagination," saying the Supreme Court of Canada cannot put aside the duly adopted laws of the Quebec legislature. And, furthermore, unwritten principles cannot be used to void another part of the Constitution. "You can't have the Constitution versus the Constitution, unwritten versus written," he said. Then Maître Danielle Allard held forth at length on the history of municipal restructuring in Quebec. After all the studies commissioned by the government, and after the systematic refusal of the elected officials to any change, something had to be done. "The status quo was not an option," she said, unknowingly parroting Louise Harel. "There were too many municipalities," as if this explained everything. She then moved to the present. "Montreal has many more anglophones in NDG than the plaintiff," she said, "So how can Westmount claim to be the anglo standard-bearer?"

The attorney-general argued that Montreal already provided English services. As if on cue, this position immediately got support from someone who volunteered as an unauthorized, out-of-court witness: none other than Premier Bernard Landry. Tossing aside legal protocol that frowns on any comments on a matter before the courts, Landry made front-page headlines in *La Presse*, telling suburban anglophones, "Go see your friends in NDG" – who, he maintained, had never complained of getting served in English because "they get all services in their language in the existing City of Montreal."[16] For good measure, he went on to attack our overall legal position. The next day, continuing the surreal and unheard-of extra-judicial debate, two City of Montreal councillors told *La Presse* that Landry was very badly informed and that English services in Montreal were completely discretionary. A third, Michael Applebaum, had already declared the same thing under oath in an affidavit filed in court by Hampstead.

On 29 May, back came Jobin, saying Bill 170 did not come out of nowhere, it was not a surprise. Quebec, if it wanted, could totally wipe out all municipalities. We were delusional with talk of a plot against the English. Finally, mergers were a political decision, and, as such, not in the court's purview. On 30 May, Maître Benoît Belleau maintained the restructuring had to do with taxes, not language. The only legal obligation for bilingualism to be found in the Constitution related to New Brunswick. The rest of the language provisions of the Constitution related to the courts and education, not municipalities, which were the exclusive responsibility of the provinces. Jobin was back yet again on 1 June, saying that the unwritten principles were there to fill in the voids, for things that were unforeseen by the Constitution. His argument, he said, was an unscaleable wall for the plaintiff. Then came the Montfort Hospital question: Jobin said that the Montfort closure was an administrative decision, while Bill 170 was actual legislation. Unwritten principles cannot overthrow legislation, he said, but perhaps they can overturn simple administrative decisions. Another brick added to the wall, he said. He went on to say that municipalities are there for the whole population, not just for a linguistic group, which was rather a strange thing to say considering Bill 170's declaration that Montreal was a French city. And, he said, Montreal has far more anglo-Britishers than Westmount: ten times as many anglophones live in Montreal as in Westmount.[17] Their culture is not threatened: look at the *Monitor*, a thriving English community newspaper in NDG. And you want to talk about religion? Westmount has only 3 per cent of the Island's Protestants.

By then our public relations strategist, Richard Gervais, was getting discouraged. While the court case had made a huge media splash, all the focus was on language and minority rights, with Bertrand turbocharging that take. What the issue may have gained in legal credibility, he said, it lost in the potential of increased public support among French speaking audiences. The French open-line radio shows were very emotional. The debate on Bill 170 was no longer about the administrative nightmare it would be for all citizens; it was now centred on something affecting only a minority.

OUR REPLY

At noon on 1 June, Tremblay had the right to reply to the attorney-general's case:

> Your Lordship, it's time to set things straight. The attorney-general is trying to convince you of two things: first, that Bill 170 is purely and simply an exercise of the legislature's power over municipalities as set out in the 1867 Constitution; and second, that those extra few words that were slipped in to the law that creates the megacity of Montreal – "Montreal is a French-speaking city" – are only there as a simple legal clarification.
>
> To support the former thesis, Maître Allard took a whole day to tell us about the various commissions that were asked, over the last thirty-eight years, to study the problems of the Island of Montreal. She said something had to be done and the court should not pronounce upon the appropriateness of one solution over another. Two comments: First, even though it is doubtful that the whole history of these studies is even relevant, I cannot refrain from pointing out none of the studies ever recommended One Island One City. And secondly, none of these multitudinous studies ever broached the question of language. And after having said right at the beginning that Bill 170 had nothing to do with language, Maître Belleau spent many hours of court time in order to establish that, yes, the Quebec Legislature has clear power in linguistic matters.
>
> As you know, our contention is that Bill 170 flies in the face of the unwritten structural principles that were established by the Supreme Court of Canada that include, among other things, the protection of minorities and democratic principles. The attorney-

general's response is that unwritten principles cannot override
any written provision of the Constitution. Your Lordship, we
never tried to assert any such thing. Our only point is the following. When evaluating the constitutionality of the exercise of
powers by one of the two levels of government in Canada, one
must take into account these unwritten principles. If they are
not respected, it does not mean that any section of the Constitution is nullified, but that the law in question is nullified. Not
more, not less. *Of course* the Quebec legislature has the power to
legislate on municipal matters. But, in the exercise of this power,
it must respect constitutional principles such as the protection
of minorities and democratic values. And speaking of democratic values: for a number of years, the courts have looked for
guidance by what is done in other countries. For example, the
European Charter of Local Democracy requires a referendum
whenever municipal boundaries are changed.

The attorney-general pleaded that the language question has
nothing to do with this case. I am going to weigh my words carefully. The City of Westmount's position is that there is no hidden
plot. And there is no need to make a connection with the Canadian political situation or Quebec referendums. No, it simply
needs a cold interpretation of the legal wording by people who do
not have this irritating tendency to make selective readings. The
attorney-general forgot to say the Montreal merger is the only
one in the whole history of mergers where the language question
is integrated into the law. You can't say it is just another municipal restructuring. Whether we like it or not, the language question
is central to this merger. Bill 171 – which changed the definition
of a bilingual municipality – was adopted the same time as Bill
170. The attorney-general presented his case for both bills at the
same time. Government policy in this regard is clear, as expressed
by the ex-premier Bouchard, Minister Harel, and Minister Beaudoin. Let me just quote you from a front-page *Le Devoir* article
that appeared a year ago based on an interview with Language
Minister Beaudoin: "Merge in Order to Francize Better," ran the
headline. "The municipal mergers will contribute to the francization of Quebec by the annexation of bilingual cities"[18] went the
text. This is government policy, not anglophone paranoia.

However you look at it, these laws take away something
important from the citizens of Westmount and of the other

anglophone cities. They controlled their own municipality, which operated in English under a provision of the French Language Charter. The anglophone community will lose this acquired right built up over centuries, and be forced to accept in return to become citizens of a megacity legally declared to be French, with the possibility for the megacity, if it feels generous, to offer services in English. Being a bilingual borough will mean nothing, as boroughs are simply administrative divisions of the megacity, with no legal status, dependent on the megacity council for funding and personnel.

Once each of our lawyers had a few minutes of wrap-up, it was all over. After two weeks in a courthouse, I was glad to get out and see some sunshine.

ANGLOS INVISIBLE IN THE MEGACITY'S VISION STATEMENT

These days no self-respecting body can be without a vision statement, and the megacity was no exception. On 4 June, the chair of the Transition Committee, Monique Lefebvre, wrote to all 22,000 employees of the megacity-to-be and revealed to them its vision statement. Unwittingly, she reinforced the position we had been taking in court: anglophones would be invisible in the megacity. Anglos were to be treated as just another member of the "cultural communities," regardless of their special constitutional status and the fact that they were instrumental in founding the City of Montreal, along with many of the suburbs slated for demolition. Certainly anglophones were nowhere to be found in her newly minted vision statement: "[The megacity] is a cosmopolitan city that stands out because of the social harmony it has achieved through the contribution its cultural communities have brought to its identity as a large French-speaking urban centre." There was much more of such platitudinous pap, but no mention of anglophones.

THE OLD STINK OF WESTMOUNT COLONIALISM

A few weeks later, and a week before we learned of the judge's decision, our legal case was the cause of a heated and revealing exchange in the National Assembly that precipitated a storm in the English media. Roch Cholette, the member for Hull, was taunting Harel about the way Bill 170 and bills amending it, such as Bill 29, were rammed through the National Assembly:

M. CHOLETTE: Thank you, Mr Speaker. A bit of history in the world of forced mergers. Last December, Bill 170 was tabled ... 1,066 articles were tabled the fifteenth of December. The *twentieth* of December, Mr Speaker, while invoking closure – that is to say, while the members' right to speak was suspended ... 381 amendments were tabled and adopted in one bundle in less than one hour, in the middle of the night, in a special session of the National Assembly. And *that* modified 30 per cent of the bill, Mr Speaker.

We now find ourselves with citizens who have lost their city, who have lost their feeling of belonging. And, as if that were not enough, the government has the nerve to table Bill 29. Two hundred and fifty amendments, Mr Speaker, that modify a law already amended. Therefore, 50 per cent of the bill was amended in a few months. It's pure improvisation. And we heard yesterday that the government is getting ready to table yet more amendments, most likely imposing a gag, using closure that will once again suspend the right of members to speak.

Mr Speaker, can the minister of municipal affairs climb down from her bulldozer, stop the improvisation, stop the contempt, stop the arrogance, and listen to the citizens?

Harel then explained that Bill 170 was a "framework" bill and that she had often said that detailed bills would follow, fleshing out the original bill and incorporating the various transition committees' recommendations for the megacities that Bill 170 created. Cholette continued to goad her, this time about her lack of openness. Exasperated and cut to the quick, Harel exploded:

MME HAREL: Mr Speaker, it's incredible what they can invent about this municipal reorganization. Mr Speaker, openness? Let's talk about openness. Does the member for Hull not feel uncomfortable being associated with the strategy of ethnic cities like the strategy of Westmount that pleads its anglo-British character, the old stink of colonialism? Is he not uncomfortable?

At this point, Harel glanced over at Premier Landry, fearing she had gone too far. He gave her the thumbs-up. Other PQ members roared with approval. Pierre Paradis, the Liberal house leader, jumped up on a point of order, saying it was an outrage for Harel to discuss a matter that was before the courts, something that as a lawyer she should know. Harel cooled down and continued, this time thumping hard on the fiscal equity drum, reverentially invoking René Lévesque:

> MME HAREL: Mr Speaker, I am going to cite some words that were said within these four walls, in the National Assembly, in 1969, at the very moment there was a bill to create the Montreal Urban Community, and it was René Lévesque who said this: "It seems to me that the metropolitan services that are contemplated in the bill will be the start of a permanent rupture of this artificial mentality that created in the metropolitan region rich ghettos on one hand, and poor ghettos on the other." Mr Speaker, can he also reflect on the fact that it's not very moral to defend the privileges of Westmount as the leader of the Opposition [Jean Charest] did lately? ... Respect is for everyone, including those who do not enjoy fiscal privileges, Mr Speaker. I profoundly believe that, in a compendium of social democracy, under the letter E, it starts with equity. And fiscal equity, that's the essential condition for social equity.[19]

So here we have Harel equating Westmount's pleading its anglo-British character with the "old stink of colonialism." In this outburst, which probably was scripted, the understandable but outdated insecurities of some francophone Quebecers were once again on display. Westmount had not lost any of its iconic power as a symbol to be manipulated by the PQ, but this time we were partially to blame, although the "colonialism" reference was pathetic. If anyone was behaving imperialistically in the forced merger saga, it was Quebec. Interestingly, though, Harel did not equally reprove Côte Saint-Luc for pleading their Jewish character in the court case. True to PQ custom, Harel wore her anglophobia on her sleeve, but anti-Semitism was beyond the pale.

JUDGMENT DAY

It was 28 June 2001 and it was judgment day. By 9:30 AM, most of the eighteen mayors had arrived at the Phillips Square offices of

Gervais, Gagnon, our public relations firm, and were nervously wandering around Gervais's extensive collection of offices and admiring his equally extensive collection of artifacts relating to Quebec political history. Most mayors were sipping coffee and making feeble jokes. I had approved two press releases: one if we won, one if we lost. A press conference was scheduled for 1 PM in a nearby hotel. The judgment was going to be ready at the courthouse at 10 AM. A runner had been sent to collect it. By the time this was done and twenty copies made, it was 10:30. By now we were all assembled in the boardroom. As each of us got our copy, still warm from photocopying, we eagerly rushed to the last page. Unfortunately, that was where the notes were, and it took a few precious minutes to get to the middle where Judge Lagacé had put his decision. We had lost.

As I read the judgment, waves of disappointment crashed over me, as I realized to what extent the judge had sided with the attorney-general. But at least he was sympathetic to our vulnerability as a minority, and at least he sent a rocket to the government for the insensitive way in which the whole thing was handled:

Why did the legislators not submit Bills 170 and 171,* in their current form, to a real debate before they were adopted, and to try at that time to reassure the anglophone minority? Why wait until the court hearing to explain their point of view? And if they really wanted to reassure the anglophone minority about the true goal of municipal restructuring, why did they not keep the current status quo? Why also introduce at the same time and *without any immediate need* an amendment of such a nature as to provoke an additional emotional and useless debate on a question as sensitive as language – a debate much less rational than one on simple municipal restructuring?

It is true that it is not for the court to answer questions that relate to the political domain. That aside, how can it remain insensitive to testimony and to certain slips that reveal a profound anxiety and suspicion on the part of the anglophone minority towards lawmakers who did not give it a proper chance to be heard on the whole matter? Also, in the Court's opinion and

---

* Bill 171 changed the criterion for bilingual status from requiring a given municipality to have a majority of citizens who speak "language other than French" to the much more restrictive "a majority of citizens with English as their mother tongue."

considering the context, both those new linguistic provisions
introduced in Bill 170 ("Montreal is a French-speaking city")
and Bill 171 are useless and only serve to enflame the language
debate in Quebec without advancing the cause of municipal
restructuring on the Island of Montreal. One thing is certain: the
moment chosen for introducing these provisions was ill-timed.

Moreover, how can one assert that the new City of Montreal
will be a "French-speaking" municipality, when the linguistic and
demographic reality shows the contrary? Wanting to believe that
Montreal is a "French-speaking city" does not change the demographic reality and does not help foster social peace with the
anglophone minority ... unless one is trying to insult the minority whose language is not French , as some of the plaintiffs have
argued.

The government's lawyers went on and on pleading that a
municipality has "no sex, no language, no religion," and on that
basis it cannot serve as an instrument to defend or promote certain groups of its citizens. But embedding in Bill 170 the expression "Montreal is a French-speaking city": does it not, above all,
serve the interests of the francophone community? ...

How can one convince the anglophone minority that the "concomitant adoption" of Bills 170 and 171 is not part of a general
policy of francization of the Island of Montreal that aims to mar-
ginalize its presence? The promotion of the French language constitutes a laudable goal, but the method used could not be more
poorly chosen and had the effect of condemning the true reason
behind the restructuring to one of secondary importance. The
result: a legal debate on municipal mergers almost exclusively
based on language.

On his retirement five years later, Judge Lagacé said this was one
of his most difficult rulings. "What made that case difficult was not
so much the legal issues involved, it was the emotional issue because,
as you know, especially in Montreal, some municipalities were losing their powers."[20]

A LEGACY OF CONSTITUTIONAL TYRANNY

As I read the very reasoned arguments of an eminently logical yet
sensitive judge, I started to wonder at the surrealism of the law:

how can we countenance that the words and commas carefully scratched out in copperplate script by the Fathers of Confederation can continue to define the law we use in 2001? "Municipal institutions," which rated only one mention in the Canadian 1867 Constitution, today have evolved into structures that would be completely alien to those worthy men, men who reflected in their document the obsessions of the day such as Catholic or Protestant schooling, but certainly not municipalities. As a hidebound traditionalist, I had a frisson of doubt: how can these long-dead men dare to enslave us, to reach down the decades and clamp their cold hands on today's world? Americans justify having more guns than people cluttering up their country based on a hallowed constitutional amendment that had to do with ensuring an armed militia over two centuries ago. In the same way, Canadian municipalities remain powerless, thanks to a constitution written when they barely existed. It's a wonder our society can function at all, engirdled as it is by this self-imposed ancient straitjacket. It certainly makes Britain's unwritten and evolving constitution look pretty sane, even though forced amalgamations can and did happen there.

Judge Maurice Lagacé said, in effect, that it was not up to him to pronounce on legislation as long as it was within the province's constitutional powers, and that the law in question respected fundamental rights as guaranteed by the Charters of Rights. Thus, the province had the power to create, merge, or abolish municipalities. While Quebec's municipal reform did have some linguistic aspects, and the court could understand the anglos' worries, they were political, not legal, matters. Furthermore, the law was not linguistically discriminatory because it did not affect those anglos in the existing City of Montreal. A place of residence chosen by a minority is not a personal characteristic as defined in the Charter. What about the Constitution? What about Montfort? The judge wrote that the Ontario Court had said that this hospital was necessary for the vitality of the francophone minority in Ontario, but municipalities remain "neutral"; their essential function is not to protect any particular group. Montfort was the only hospital in Ontario offering services in French, whereas anglophones in Quebec can receive bilingual services outside their municipalities, notably in the existing City of Montreal. The evidence did not show any real threat to the provision of such services in the new megacity. So Bill 170 was not in conflict with the Constitution and its unwritten structural principle that protects minorities.

Of course, the media calls began the minute the judgment was given to them at 10:30 AM. We refused to say anything, chewed on a few sandwiches for lunch, and then walked in bunches over to the hotel where I held the press conference. By then everything was anticlimactic for me, almost surreal. Our loss was all over the evening news. The next morning I unrolled the newspapers to see huge pictures of me on the front pages of both the *Montreal Gazette* and *La Presse*. The *Gazette*, as it seemed to have been doing for some time now, ran a rather quirky picture of me with clenched fists, captioned, "Ready for Round 2." In *La Presse* I was staring meditatively into space, palms on my chin in a rather supplicatory pose.

With time, after I had got over what all experts had predicted would be a defeat,[21] I began to feel like a bit of a fraud. We had played the minority rights card, as it was the only one that had even a slim chance of overturning Bill 170. And the judge, an obviously decent man, had taken our expressed fears at face value. He even called it "a legal debate on municipal mergers almost exclusively based on language." But language was always only one of a number of reasons I was fighting Bill 170, even if the threat to the anglophone community was real. Leaving aside the rewarding of Montreal's execrable administration and profligacy by making the city even bigger, the overarching injustice of Bill 170 was the provincial government's abuse of power and the ludicrously weak powers of the third level of government in Canada – all of which had nothing to do with the courts, and even less to do with Justice Lagacé's decision.

On top of that, I felt as if I had used the courts in another way: I knew the chances of winning were almost infinitesimal, but I had adopted the court challenge principally as a strategy to keep the mergers in the public eye. Had we not challenged Bill 170, the whole matter would quickly have become non-news, allowing the Liberals to shelve, ever so quietly, their demerger promise. And then there was the not insignificant matter of the millions of dollars spent on lawyers. I never doubted, however, my fundamental conviction that still burned as strong as ever: forced mergers were wrong. I was not the first person in history to grasp the world of difference between what is wrong and what is illegal. And we were trying to prove that something was unconstitutional, whatever that word really meant. Charles Dickens, when he wasn't writing about the downtrodden, had a thing or two so say about the vagaries of the legal system. He observed that the law "is an edged tool of uncertain application, very expensive in the working, and rather remarkable for its properties of close shaving, than for always shaving the right person."

15

A Fight to the Finish

Men and women come and go; structures remain. One day, I shall return
to anonymity; the reform will have been done, the world will have
changed. For the better; of that, I'm sure.

Louise Harel, March 2001[1]

We have not, as yet, given ourselves a country; but we have given
ourselves a real capital and a real metropolis.

Louise Harel, October 2001[2]

The council chamber in Westmount City Hall was originally a barrel-
vaulted wainscoted affair in the same neo-Tudor style as the outside of the building. In common with most atmospheric, solidly built
buildings, the interior was subjected to the indignities of the 1960s
modernist style when indirectly lit gypsum-board coffered ceilings
were slapped up and rosewood-veneer panels edged in aluminum
were tacked onto the walls. In spite of such typical depredations of
postwar architects, at least the tradition of hanging portraits of former mayors was kept up. In their wing collars, some with chains
of office draped around their necks, mayors going back to 1874
sombrely look down on the frivolities of modern-day council meetings. The one exception to the sobriety and paternalism of the
mayoral portraits is the colourful likeness of Mayor May Cutler,
painted by her son, who made his mother look quite Churchillian in
a Francis Bacon sort of way. Some fragment of history was reinjected
into the chamber in 1983 when John Richard Hyde, a retired judge
and former speaker of the National Assembly and member for Westmount, donated his massive carved oak speaker's chair in which the
mayor has been enthroned ever since. Now the speaker's chair tow-
ered above the eight councillors in Swedish-modern chairs covered
in tufted black nylon, ranged behind modular desks with toffee-
coloured Naugahyde tops.

The council chamber (which seats, in a literal and figurative pinch, one hundred) is the scene of city council meetings, election victory celebrations, civic receptions, and press conferences. On 4 July 2001, six days after our loss in Quebec Superior Court, I held a press conference there. A ragged little plot of variegated microphones had sprung up in front of me, and five TV cameramen in their year-round uniform of beige shorts, T-shirts, and scuffed boots were putting tapes in their cameras while sipping coffee from styrofoam cups. The TV interviewers milled about, immaculately dressed (at least above the waist), contrasting with the radio and print journalists in their jeans. Following Quebec press protocol, I spoke in French first.

I wanted to wait until after the Superior Court decision before making up my mind about getting involved in the megacity or not. If I do, I have two choices: run for megacity mayor, or run as a member of the megacity council. But how could I be a mayor of a city I don't believe in? A megacity that would represent the triumph of bureaucracy over democracy? My overriding mission is to *stop* the megacity, legally, politically, or through demerger. What, then, if I ran for mayor on a demerger platform? It would still be a contradiction to seek to be mayor of a city I want dissolved, to apply for a job I want eliminated. And, alternatively, would I want to be one of seventy-three councillors in a megacity run exclusively by the executive committee? To swear allegiance to the megacity, and to get paid by the megacity? No. Ever since I was twenty-five years old, I have always been my own boss. Whether in business or in serving my city for sixteen years, I have always brought enthusiasm and passion to what I did: it would be impossible to summon up either while working for a job in the megacity, the construction of which requires the demolition of my own much-loved city. I will not lend my name to such an enterprise.

But Westmount cannot completely boycott the megacity if it is created; the "borough" of Westmount would still have to supply a councillor downtown and two local councillors. So we have to ask someone to do what I refuse to do: to wade into the megacity mess and to protect our exposed flank. I want you to know that Karin Marks, a Westmount councillor for ten years, has agreed to boldly go where no Westmounter has gone before. She will run as an independent councillor. Meanwhile, I'll continue the legal battle all the way to the Supreme Court; and, if we fail, I'll put Jean Charest's feet to the fire to ensure he respects his demerger promise. If the megacity is imposed on us, to fight from the outside and to the finish is the only option. When something is wrong, unjust, and iniquitous, you keep on fighting.

Louise Harel was disappointed that I "chose the route of systematic obstruction. In some ways, I have to tell you I almost regret it. I appreciated Mr Trent – obviously, up until this moment."[3]

A LIBERAL PROMISE WITH LEGS

With the chances of winning in court on appeal admittedly fairly slim, we had to shift the emphasis from fighting the implementation of the megacity to having it deconstructed. During 2001 at least, the Liberals stuck tenaciously to their guns with their promise of demerger, in spite of massive broadsides and even ridicule from the press. La Presse editorialist Michèle Ouimet likened demerger to baking a cake and then trying to extract its ingredients. No matter: the Liberals' own polls (and, later, when they won by-elections in the regions) told them they were on to something. Not only were Quebecers upset with the forced nature of the mergers, their anger showed no signs of subsiding: it had legs. During the whole merger saga, the inconvenient truth for the pro-merger forces was that over half the population felt passionately that mergers should not be imposed. Few Quebecers, absent the press, felt passionately in favour of mergers, or at least passionately enough to accept their imposition.

In March, Charest had even promised to put the brakes on the merger process throughout Quebec if an election were held in the summer of 2001 and the Liberals won.[4] By May, he was backing off from that sweeping promise, saying that in some cases mergers were actually a good thing. So the Liberals were back to undoing mergers rather than stopping them. Charest also reminded the public that demergers would not be a matter of a simple referendum: citizens would have to be told beforehand of the consequences of their decision.[5] The media asked an embarrassed Charest how he would vote in Westmount, where he lived. Would he vote to create "holes" in the megacity and turn it into "Gruyere cheese"? He refused to answer, no doubt fundamentally believing in the Holey City.

By June 2001, Landry had come to the conclusion that with the Liberals by now holding a solid 8 per cent lead in the polls (45 per cent versus 37 per cent), his party would probably lose an election if it triggered one within the next twelve months. At least one polling firm reckoned that the impending forced municipal mergers would be the main cause of such a PQ electoral defeat.[6] The PQ thinking was that, by June 2002, the megacities would have been in operation for six months, the mayors who opposed them would be part of them, and the citizens would have calmed down. So Landry decided to batten down the hatches, wait things out, and make sure the mergers were put through with the least amount of hoo-ha and as expeditiously as possible. Obviously any delay in implementing the megacities would allow discontent to continue to fester, possibly until the time the PQ could put off an election no longer. My strategy, of course, was to keep the matter in the public eye to prevent the Liberals from wriggling out of their demerger promise and then to help them win.

In June 2001, Michel David of *Le Soleil* wrote:

At the time of the November 1998 election, 51 per cent of people said they were satisfied with the Bouchard government. His fall in popularity clearly coincided with the beginning of the municipal merger debate in the autumn of 1999 ... The majority (54 per cent) of Quebecers, and one-half of francophones, are opposed to municipal mergers, according to CROP. There are even more (62 per cent) who approve of the idea to annul a merger if the population of the municipality involved say so in a referendum – as the Liberals have proposed. When he took over from Lucien Bouchard, Harel's reform was too advanced for Bernard Landry to cancel the operation, even if he had wanted to. But was it really necessary to carry it out as far as Saguenay-Lac Saint-Jean, where the PQ now finds itself threatened in its own strongholds?[7]

Another poll confirmed this marked resistance to mergers. In June, the group I had created, the Coalition of Cities and Citizens Challenging Bill 170, released the results[8] of an Infras poll we had commissioned. Asked about forced mergers, 40 per cent of residents of the eight future megacities were in favour, 55 per cent against, with women being 31 per cent for and 61 per cent against.* The strongest opposition was found in the Quebec City region, where 32 per cent of their residents were in favour, 65 per cent against. An even greater proportion (77 per cent) of all mega-city residents-to-be thought mergers should be the subject of referendums or be part of an electoral mandate; 66 per cent said that Bill 170 was both undemocratic and rushed. The same proportion also thought that there would be no savings with mergers and that taxes would increase by over 5 per cent. Interestingly, 69 per cent of francophones had no problem with the existing bilingual municipalities keeping that status.

A few weeks later, *La Presse* published yet another poll, confirming the PQ's unpopularity (with 61 per cent of Quebecers dissatisfied with the PQ government). Landry was forced to admit publicly that it had a lot to do with fears people had about mergers. "But when people see that their tax bill will be reduced, their perception will maybe be different."[9] Harel chimed in to the effect that the PQ had to work to change people's perceptions. In other words, the public had it all wrong: what they needed was to be educated.

By the end of August 2001, the Liberals had a 9 per cent lead (39 per cent versus 30 per cent).

AN APPEAL SUDDENLY BECOMES APPEALING

Speaking of polls and of the public's distaste for mergers: *La Presse* commissioned a SOM poll right after the Superior Court's judgment was handed down on 28 June. The results were published 7 July. When pollsters asked residents of the Island of Montreal if the "contesting municipalities should appeal Judge Lagacé's decision," 35 per cent said "no" and 56 per cent said "yes." The most surprising thing was that, in the City of Montreal itself, 37 per cent of respondents said we should not contest the decision, *but 54 per cent said we should contest.*[10] The pollster tried to explain this curious result by

---

* Polls consistently showed females to be more against mergers than males: for every ten males in favour of a megacity, there were roughly only seven females. This was a phenomenon not limited to Quebec; according to a poll published in the *Vancouver Sun* on 16 January 2002, 25 per cent of men were in favour of a Vancouver megacity versus 16 per cent of women. (Overall, 77 per cent were against.) Polling firms put this sexual bias down to females being less adventuresome; I think it had more to do with males considering megacities more macho and impressive.

saying that no one had bothered to explain to people living in the City of Montreal the advantages of the merger. I continued to believe that the explanation was simple: the public does not like things rammed down their throats. Most people were just upset about the forced nature of the mergers. And, for many of them, they didn't care that we had been forced to argue anglophone minority rights in order to quash Bill 170.

The *La Presse* poll was very opportune. I was having a difficult time in convincing most mayors to appeal the judgment. Even though it was a long shot, I always felt we had to go to appeal. Besides, we had to keep the merger issue on the boil; otherwise, demerger would never come about. The evening before the judgment was to be handed down, I had even organized a dinner meeting of most of the mayors fighting Bill 170 and tried to get a consensus that, if we lost, we would all go to appeal. Most were hesitant, and some (the mayors of Kirkland and Côte Saint-Luc) said they would not appeal, the latter saying it was too costly; besides, it was time to move exclusively to the "political arena." By the time the judgment was handed down the next day and I had applied torque to a number of arms, I could put in our press release that a majority wanted to appeal – although for many it was a pro forma gesture, a convenient blind behind which to pursue the political game. Then some mayors (or their councils) started having second thoughts. However, when the poll results in *La Presse* came out a week later, especially a tidbit about 59 per cent of the suburban electors who wanted us to appeal, vacillating mayors vacillated no longer, and a few other mayors had a change of heart and spryly jumped on the appeal bandwagon.

LET THE GAMES BEGIN

The minute the 28 June court judgment came down, a number of Montreal Island suburban mayors felt free to plunge headfirst into the political pool, where Tremblay was only too happy to lead the suburban synchronized swimming team. Tremblay "deplored" the fact the government went ahead with the mergers without consultation, but the legal challenge "had failed" and the political solution must begin, he said. Vera Danyluk echoed the same sentiment. "It's game over. We have to recognize that the whole legal debate is finished and we have to go on to other things. Already this morning people started phoning and asking me what I will be doing. The scramble is on,"[11] she said. After throwing in the towel in April, she now said she was under even more pressure to run as megacity mayor, this time heading up a group of independents.

Eight hours after learning of the judgment, at least a dozen suburban mayors attended a $250-a-plate fundraising dinner for Tremblay's United Island of Montreal party. "ABB" went the battle cry: "Anybody But Bourque." The focus shifted from fighting an unjust law that forced the megacity down our throats to punishing the mayor who came up with the idea in the first place.

Until the judgment, Tremblay's chances of winning had been getting slimmer and slimmer. Even Frank Zampino thought so. Zampino, the mayor of Saint-Leonard, had managed to get Tremblay publicly to guarantee him the second most important job in the megacity: the chairmanship of the executive committee. But Tremblay had to be elected first. Back in the middle of June, Zampino and I had lunch at Da Vinci's. In the past, I always had a good rapport with him, although it got very bruised when he suddenly flipped over to supporting the megacity in January. But at least he wasn't a hypocrite. While brazenly out for himself, he was extremely competent, sage, and cool – not to mention perfectly trilingual. He was very worried that a slew of independent candidates would siphon off votes from Tremblay and allow Bourque to win. And, he said, Tremblay's problem was that, in some places, there were more councillors looking for seats in the megacity than there were seats. Tremblay could offer jobs only to some of them. To add to Tremblay's problems, Michel Prescott, the leader of Mayor Jean Doré's former party, was still sticking around, becoming the spoiler in the mayoral vote. I told Zampino I really didn't care about all that, as battling Bill 170 was far more important than battling Bourque.

The same early July La Presse poll that revealed such massive support for an appeal also showed how badly Tremblay had slipped; and he was now only four months away from the election. In the public's mind, the campaign had not even begun, and Bourque's two uncolourful opponents had stirred up little interest. Tremblay was down to 17 per cent of voting intentions, or half of the support Bourque enjoyed. Mirabile dictu, even in the suburbs, Bourque, the instigator of the hated megacity, was much more popular than Tremblay. Trailing at 9 per cent was Michel Prescott. Then three days after the poll came out, Prescott wisely packed it in and joined Tremblay. That move, along with a flock of suburban mayors recently self-released to play politics, meant that things were soon going to look a lot better for Tremblay.

BOURQUE WAS NOT TREMBLAY

While he had no electoral mandate to create the megacity, and while his maundering arguments for it were hard to follow, you always knew where you stood with Pierre Bourque. And, while he never looked you in the eye, he did not lie. Gérald Tremblay is, to his core, a decent man, but in those days he could waffle, prevaricate, and say what he thought people wanted to hear – as long as they were conversant in MBA, that is. While they hid it under bland exteriors, both men were very emotional, with Bourque sometimes being downright moody.

Both men were parsimonious, were not show-offs, and were careful to avoid confrontation – although Bourque could usually slough off antagonism in his peculiar Zen-like fashion. Physically, Bourque was awkward, shambling around in a suit that always looked as if it were thrown over him, with a tie selected in the dark. Tremblay dressed with refined taste and had a well-bred francophone's studious look. He knew his way around chic Laurier Avenue restaurants and shops in his hometown of Outremont. Bourque's roots were working class, and it showed in his manners and deportment. Socially, you never saw him in the company of a woman, while Tremblay was usually graced with his wife, Suzanne Tailleur. But, in those days, at mixed dinners, Bourque would work the room like a bee pollinating flowers, while Tremblay would shyly remain at one table the whole evening.

Educationally, the two men were a contrast in studies. Bourque had a degree in horticultural engineering. Tremblay was a lawyer, a Harvard MBA, and had taught at university; he was a former cabinet minister and sat on the boards of a dozen corporations. On the face of it, Tremblay was far more sophisticated intellectually, but Bourque had a formidable native intelligence. Bourque was intuitive, a huge asset in a politician. Tremblay had to work everything out deductively from an intellectual framework: he looked distant while he was processing a question. Both men, actually, were wooden on camera, but they looked like game-show hosts compared with Georges Bossé or Frank Zampino. Bossé, who was quite articulate, always looked angry on TV. Zampino, for all his intellectual

horsepower, came across as a funeral director dealing with a death in
his own family. It was surprising that all the important players in the
megacity campaign were so telephobic – except Vera Danyluk, who
was confident and warm with a low voice that drew the viewer in.

TREMBLAY'S FORTUNE CHANGES

Tremblay, in spite of being considered a fairly "big-name" mayoral
candidate among the chattering classes, remained a relative unknown
in the streets. And since he was not going to win Montreal Island
by the sheer force of his personality, his party's ground game was
critical. And that game was not getting off the ground: by mid-July,
only half of the councillors running for his party had been selected.
Bossé, the mayor of Verdun, was Tremblay's political strongman,
deciding who would run where. No public nominating conventions
for him: he formed a secret selection committee, a Star Chamber to
which potential city councillors could send their résumés. And then
the fun (and the waiting) began. As Henry Aubin of the *Montreal
Gazette* put it, "Behind the scenes, this selection process is the stuff
of high drama and low democratic ethics. Abysmally low." The process, for those suburbs that never had political parties, was completely foreign. Before the megacity, in many suburbs, anybody who
felt like it ran for council without any party pre-selection, and the
public decided the winner. To make matters worse, with the megacity, it was the candidate for mayor who stole the show. "To be a
candidate in a municipal party is like being in a mule train. If you're
not the head mule, the scenery never changes," said one independent
candidate, Maurice Séguin.

Something else was also happening behind the scenes: a number
of suburban mayors who were still fighting Bill 170 in court wanted
to get an assurance from Tremblay that he would not stand in the
way of a Liberal government honouring their demerger promise.
Once they had that assurance, mayors such as Bill McMurchie of
Pointe-Claire and Peter Yeomans of Dorval finally climbed on board
Tremblay's train toward the end of July. I had been trying to get such
mayors to run as anti-merger independents (the solution we came
up with in Westmount), but they decided to throw their lot in with
Tremblay. McMurchie, an eminently decent man who felt he had
made the right decision, almost shamefacedly called me to tell me
what it was.

At that point, eight mayors of municipalities still contesting Bill
170 in court were on Tremblay's team. Once again, the media questioned their genuine desire to run the megacity, since they were contesting its creation in court. Tremblay brushed off such niceties: if
these mayors joined his party, "it's because these people believe that
there is a way, if we work together, to make this new city a success."[12] Later, he said that citizens would "be so happy" they would
no longer think about undoing the megacity.[13] This felicity, he maintained, would come about through a decentralization of power to
the boroughs that would recreate them more or less the way they
were before, back when they were independent municipalities. "It
would be a win-win situation because everyone would keep what
they have." One had to wonder what the whole point of the mergers
was if everything could remain as it had been. The end state of any
true process of decentralizing boroughs was individual municipalities: you either have a municipality or you don't. You can't have half
a municipality. No matter: Tremblay made the unpalatable palatable
by selling decentralization.

By early August a *Gazette* SOM poll showed Tremblay was
breathing down Bourque's neck: one-on-one, he had 37 per cent of
voters' intentions, Bourque 41 per cent. Tremblay was as far ahead
in the suburbs as Bourque was ahead of him in the City of Montreal (roughly 50:30 and 30:50).[14] In a three-way race, Tremblay
was toast: Bourque versus Tremblay versus Trent resulted in 36
per cent, 25 per cent, and 22 per cent in voting intentions across
the Island of Montreal, even though I was not even running. A
three-way race with Danyluk gave 39 per cent, 32 per cent, 10
per cent. Interestingly, this poll, done by the same firm that did
the *La Presse* poll three weeks earlier, showed that public support for our legal challenge had actually increased to 58 per cent
– which explained my uncanny popularity with the voters. In
fact, in the suburbs I was ahead of both Tremblay and Bourque in
voters' intentions.

Another SOM poll that *La Presse* conducted a few weeks later
showed, among those who were going to vote, that Bourque and
Tremblay were by then neck and neck; yet bizarrely, people across
the Island of Montreal had more confidence in Trent to run the
megacity than in Tremblay. To be fair, Tremblay was still a relative unknown. Bourque was known by two-thirds of those polled;
Tremblay was only known by one-third.[15]

Worried, Tremblay asked to meet with me to try to get my endorsement and also to get our independent Westmount candidates (for one megacity councillor and two borough councillors) to run under his party's banner. Between late August and early October, we had three meetings. Two were breakfasts in the Ritz-Carlton Hotel garden, a walled oasis in which ducklings disported themselves in a little lattice house while the sun lazily dappled the lawn. (I always wondered about the provenance of the *canard à l'orange* served at the Ritz in late autumn.) Tables and chairs were protected by a huge striped awning. Habitués of the Ritz got the best seating; visiting Americans were usually relegated to the far reaches of what regulars called Siberia. To be known by the Ritz maître d' was almost the social equivalent of being a member of the Mount Royal Club just across the street.

Between bites of scrambled eggs and bacon, I started things off: "To differentiate yourself from Bourque, Gérald, you have to deal more formally and clearly with what the majority of the electorate strongly believes. They believe that the creation of the megacity is a mistake. I know you've said you are against forced mergers, but that's nowhere to be found in your party platform. The same goes for demerger: you have no written, formal position. And what about decentralization? You *say* you are all for decentralization to make the megacity workable, but nowhere do you commit to change the law to give boroughs legal status or the power to tax. With respect, your platform is all pious wishes and feel-good statements – a paean to the wonders of the new city. That's why I and the independent candidates in Westmount can't even think about coming in under your umbrella."

"Peter, it may not be written down, but I agree with most of what you said. The importance is to get elected."

"You'd have a better chance of getting elected with a more honest platform."

"I'm giving you my word of honour that I'll respect the right of cities to demerge. I am a man of my word."

"Even if that were good enough for me, voters would say 'put it in writing.' To put it bluntly, Gérald, unless you formally, publicly promise *not* to dissuade Jean Charest from allowing demergers, unless you formally, publicly acknowledge the weaknesses in Bill 170 and commit to lobby for changes, and unless you formally, publicly denounce the way Bill 170 was adopted, you won't get my endorsement."

At our next meeting, Tremblay suggested some party platform changes to tempt me. All were anodyne, except one that stated his party would respect the right of former municipalities to demerge and would not stand in their way. There was no mention of more borough powers, as it "would confuse voters" before the election. We then talked about the Westmount campaign. Tremblay said, "I'm in a lose-lose situation. If I run candidates in Westmount, I'll get you guys upset ..."

"It would be a declaration of war, Gérald."

"... And if I don't, it'll stand out like a sore thumb."

In the event, Westmount was the only place where Tremblay's party ran no candidates. We did suggest that citizens vote for him as mayor, given the alternative was Bourque. "Even if Mickey Mouse ran against Pierre Bourque, Westmounters would choose Mickey Mouse," I had rather uncharitably said to the media.

For some time, a grassroots anti-merger organization called DémocraCité had sprung up, run by volunteers such as Kell Warshaw, a brilliant web consultant from Montreal West, and Raymond Proulx, a splenetic yet dedicated activist from Outremont. Proulx served as its president. DémocraCité represented citizens of all those municipalities "deserted by their elected officials." In late September they asked me to run as megacity mayor – or, in effect, as non-mayor. "Your mission, Peter," they said to me, in effect, "should you chose to accept it, would be to provide citizens with the referendum that the Quebec government denied us." As Proulx said, I would be "a referendum in a suit." I could then quit, having served the graphic purpose of proving the megacity was not wanted. Since most Montreal Island residents were against the creation of the megacity, they had been effectively disenfranchised: all candidates for the megacity mayoralty promised to make the megacity work. In the end, I refused DémocraCité's request, as my candidacy would simply siphon off votes from Tremblay and result in a Bourque win. Besides, Bourque and Tremblay were each in the process of spending around $2 million to get elected: my chances of winning a month before the election were nil. This vignette reveals the temper of the times and how desperate we all were, ranged as we were against the massed pro-merger forces. But this very short-lived threat sent chills down the necks of the Tremblay people. Zampino and Tremblay phoned me to talk things over. When we met, they were visibly relieved when I told them I was not running.

YOU SAY YOU WANT A RESOLUTION

Meanwhile, on the south shore, Saint-Bruno and Saint-Lambert were hotspots of resistance to the creation of their megacity, the megacity of Longueuil. While his mayor was not much of an urban warrior against mergers, Councillor Sean Finn of Saint-Lambert was preparing the ground for an eventual demerger before it was too late. Finn, whom I used to meet at his Canadian National offices where he was senior vice-president and chief legal officer, was also named tax lawyer of the year in 2000 and eventually went on to became the chairman of the Quebec Chamber of Commerce, while somehow managing to find time to teach tax legislation and policy at the University of Sherbrooke. With his impeccable corporate credentials, he was by a wide margin the most credible anti-merger activist on the south shore, if not in all Quebec.

From Saint-Bruno, soon followed by three other south shore municipalities, came the idea of adopting formal council resolutions calling on the Liberals to honour their demerger promise. Once I checked with the Liberals to ensure that such resolutions would not be seen as a sign we did not trust them, thirteen Montreal Island suburbs passed similar resolutions. Seven of these municipalities were headed up by mayors who were running for megacity council seats under Tremblay's banner, the banner emblazoned with the slogan *Ça va marcher* ("It's going to work"). Incidentally, this uninspired and uninspiring slogan said a lot about the lack of enthusiasm that permeated Tremblay's campaign. I said, "Imagine if, when the United States was created, the Declaration of Independence started off with: 'It's going to work.' That would get a lot of people excited, wouldn't it?"

THE PQ STILL IN TROUBLE

Suddenly, on 28 September Louise Harel formally announced there would be no more forced mergers anywhere in Quebec. (The Ontario government had made the same announcement in February.) By reducing the number of municipalities in Quebec from about 1,400 to a projected 1,050 in January 2002,[16] her goal was more or less achieved, she said, hastening to add that this sudden decision had absolutely *nothing* to do with the fact that there were four provincial by-elections being held in three days' time. Her announcement, made at the Fédération Québécoise des Municipalités convention, was greeted with complete silence. No one clapped. Harel was nonplussed but carried on. The six hundred mayors and councillors present either did not believe her or were just plain angry with her for years of unnecessary upheaval. It did not augur well for the PQ in the by-elections.

These four by-elections happened to coincide with an anti-merger radio campaign I had launched across Quebec. In late September our group of municipalities fighting the mergers in court had paid $115,000 for 1,200 radio spots all over Quebec, with credit going to the Pan-Quebec Coalition of Citizens against Forced Mergers, headed up by an indefatigable woman from Saint-Bruno, Ginette Durocher. (Their slogan was "I Will Remember the Forced Mergers," a play on the Quebec motto "*Je me souviens*.") One of the radio spots, which later won an award, started off with a telephone ringing:

"Hello, I want to place a notice in the obituary column."
"Yes, go ahead."
"The first of January, 2002 ..."
(*Taking notes*) "... One January 2002 ..."
"... Died, ceased to exist, wiped off the map, the following municipalities: Chicoutimi, Grand-Mère, Sainte-Foy, Dorval, Saint-Bruno ..."
"Whoa, whoa! You have a lot of them?"
"Yes. It was an accident. Only the government saw it coming."

When the Liberals snatched two long-time PQ seats in the by-elections and nearly won the other two, the PQ asked the director-general of elections (DGE) to investigate our ads, saying they should have been authorized by the DGE and counted as part of the Liberal election spending. This would not be the last time the DGE investigated me.

One thing was clear to both the PQ and the Liberals: the imposed mergers were still really hurting the PQ, and contrariwise, the demerger promise was helping the Liberals. Another SOM poll in *La Presse* confirmed that the Liberals were still soaring: they had a 10.6 per cent lead over the PQ, at 41.6 per cent versus 31.0 per cent, had there been a general election rather than just four by-elections. When asked whether they were satisfied with the PQ government in regard to mergers, 62 per cent of respondents said no.[17]

ROUND 2 IN THE COURTROOM

While all this was going on, 4 September had seen us back in court
and we were waiting for the results of our appeal of Bill 170. We
were down to fifteen municipalities contesting, three Montreal Island
francophone municipalities having dropped out. Still, twenty-two
lawyers were involved for both parties. This time we had faced three
judges, whose job it was to see if Judge Lagacé had made an error
in law in his judgment of 28 June. We maintained that he had completely ignored our argument that the anglophone community was
in decline, that our municipalities were essential to its survival, and
the threat to anglophone institutions, identity, and language was real
and immediate, not hypothetical. We pointed out that Judge Lagacé
made no reference to the voluminous expert testimony we had filed.
Moreover, not only had he dismissed the many affidavits signed by
mayors, citizens, and historians as "emotional" but thought they
only merited the small endnote he gave them because they were not
legally relevant. The attorney-general's arguments were, on the other
hand, front and centre in the decision. The judge concluded that
there was no proof of a real or a presumed threat of not getting services in English in the megacity of Montreal. "Anglophones have
shown a great capacity to keep their numbers up," he wrote, in clear
contradiction to expert affidavits to the contrary. Richard Bourhis
had written that English speakers in Quebec had dropped from
13 per cent in 1971 to 8.8 per cent in 1996. Jacques Henripin had
pointed out that the emigration rate for anglos from Quebec was
eleven times that of francophones, and that, on the Island of Montreal, anglophones had dropped from 23.8 per cent of the population
in 1971 to 18.9 per cent in 1996.

Judge Lagacé had written that Montfort Hospital was an institution necessary for a continuing francophone minority in Ontario but
that he considered municipalities "neutral" institutions with regard
to language. This was in direct contradiction with Bourhis, who said
"to suggest that government institutions do not reflect the culture
of its majority population is sociological nonsense ... Institutions
do not exist in a cultural vacuum ... Anglophone municipal governments are the only level of government controlled by the anglophone
minority in Quebec."

Lagacé had even said that he was satisfied with the defendant's proof that the existing City of Montreal offers services in a

number of languages, English being one of them. This was contradicted by our witness, Montreal city councillor Michael Applebaum, who wrote, "The megacity of Montreal will be run exactly in the same way as the present City of Montreal and there will be very little room to allow members of the English-speaking community to obtain services in English." And it was not just a matter of getting services in English: it was the awareness that Quebec wanted as a policy to make the megacity more and more French. As the judge said himself, "How can one convince the anglophone minority that the concomitant adoption of Bill 170 and Bill 171 was not part of a general policy of francization on the Island of Montreal with a view to marginalizing them?" In fact, the attorney-general did not contradict my affidavit to the effect that the government did have a goal of the francization of the Island of Montreal. I had quoted a front-page article in *Le Devoir* headlined "*Fusionner pour mieux franciser*" (Merge in order to francize better).[18] In this article, Louise Beaudoin, who, after all, was the minister responsible for the French Language Charter, said that the Island of Montreal must become a strong symbol of the French fact in Quebec. Municipal mergers would help make Quebec more French, in that bilingual municipalities would be annexed [sic] to the larger French entities.

One of our lawyers, Julius Grey, had some interesting comments leading up to the appeal. How can anyone question, he wrote, that Bill 171 is discriminatory, when its expressed intent is to stop a district in Montreal such as NDG from becoming bilingual? And as for the fact that more anglos live in Montreal than in, say, Westmount, so what? Grey pointed out that all anglophones benefit from the presence of McGill University, even those who are attending the Université de Montréal. Grey then asked, "Could a law declare that the megacity is 'Catholic' or 'white'? To pose the question is to answer it. I don't think a judge could hide behind the fact that 'municipalities are creatures of the provinces' or that such a declaration is a 'simple clarification.'"

We presented much of the same testimony as we had done for the first trial. Our lead lawyer, Tremblay, finished off his remarks by saying, "If the courts don't protect anglophones in Quebec, how can they protect francophones in the rest of Canada?"

The attorney-general asserted that the limits on provincial legislatures could only stem from written parts of the constitution. They repeated that a municipality is not an institution to promote the interests of a minority. I suppose, then, that it is seemingly all right for the megacity to promote the interests of a majority? That's what the declaration "Montreal is a French-speaking city" did. One of the appeal judges did ask the defence why this term was not used for any of the other megacities created by Bill 170.

On 16 October we learned that the Quebec Court of Appeal had upheld the lower court's decision. We had lost again. Only the Supreme Court of Canada could stop the contesting municipalities, now down to thirteen, being wiped out by Bill 170 – that is, if the Supremes even agreed to hear our case. By this time many of the mayors were far more interested in getting themselves elected in the megacity election on 4 November.

TREMBLAY WINS THE ELECTION BY PROMISING NOT TO FIGHT DEMERGERS

While we were concentrating on matters legal, Tremblay's momentum in the megacity election continued to grow. One month before the election, he was ahead of Bourque, 39 per cent to 36 per cent.[19] The one single issue that probably sealed Bourque's fate and thus helped Tremblay catapult ahead of him was his inept and protracted negotiation with some squatters occupying a building in late July. His dithering dragged on until October when the police finally evicted them. It made Bourque look weak and incompetent. Unfortunately for him, images of Mayor Giuliani's cool handling of a real crisis after the September 11th attacks on New York were still etched on the public's mind.

Tremblay continued to cozy up to the anti-megacity crowd (all the while saying the megacity was going to be wonderful). His shilly-shallying reached a peak when he promised that, if he were mayor, the megacity would help fund the legal attack on Bill 170. In other words, the megacity would fund the legal attack on itself. After his handlers got to him, he quickly climbed down, but his reputation as a waffler did not suffer.[20]

If the demerger promise was working its wonders for the Liberals and their popularity across the province, it proved to be a poisoned chalice for Tremblay. If he said he would fight any attempt at demerger, it put him closer to Bourque and further away from the 53 per cent of Montreal Island voters who wanted to break up the megacity

– and who were far more likely to get out and vote in the municipal election. On the other hand, the more he said he would step aside and watch his brand-new city broken up, the more he looked insincere, and the more opprobrium was dumped on him by the francophone media.

Essentially, Tremblay's way of grasping the demerger nettle was to lay the blame on the PQ government for imposing mergers and on the Liberals for promising to undo them. It was therefore none of his business, he said. "If the government (of Jean Charest) wants to dismantle the new city, we will respect its decision. We are in a democracy and we will respect any law of a democratically elected government, as we respect the existing law forcing the mergers."[21] He went even further with the editorial board of *Le Devoir*: "I will not even get involved,"[22] he said when asked what he would do in the event of a referendum on demerger. For advocates of the megacity, this abject passivity was appalling. *Le Devoir*'s headline read, "A Mayor Tremblay would not defend his new city." Tremblay did say, however, "There is no one on our team who is stockpiling ammunition for demerger. No one." He seemed to forget the mayors of seven municipalities running for his party who, two months before, had adopted formal council resolutions demanding that the Liberals honour their demerger promise if elected.

As it turned out, Tremblay won the megacity election, and he won it through unadulterated ambiguity. People did not vote *for* him, nor for the megacity; they voted *against* Bourque for being the megacity architect and, not unimportantly, being unable to handle a bunch of media-hungry squatters.

THE PROMISE: THE MONTREAL MEGACITY WILL SAVE $175 MILLION A YEAR

In November 2001, mergers were still hurting the PQ all over Quebec. In an attempt to puncture the Liberal's demerger balloon, Harel made public her department's estimates of the costs of demerger. The downside for the PQ in this strategy was that she had finally to reveal the projected *costs* of the mergers: this was because the government assumed the cost of a demerger would be similar to the cost of the equivalent merger. According to government figures released on 20 November, the creation of the eight megacities would cost

$304 million,[23] with the government picking up only $168 million of it. The eight megacities would have to borrow $136 million to retire staff prematurely – but they didn't have to worry, said Quebec, as they would soon save the cost of the salaries. There was another cost of $24 million to merge medium-sized municipalities, and yet another $48 million to merge rural towns and villages. A grand total of $376 million was to be spent, then, on mergers throughout Quebec. (The final tab was even higher.[24])

Here was the good news, the government said: the creation of the eight megacities was going to save $217 million *a year* in five years' time, an amount equal to 5 per cent of their total budgets: 1 per cent of their budgets would be saved in 2002, another 1 per cent in 2003, yet another 1 per cent in 2004 and so on, until it reached a "cruising speed" of $217 million per year, every year. Just for the megacity of Montreal, there would be yearly savings of $175 million by the end of these five years.[25] If people were stupid enough to demerge, the megacities would miss out on all these fabulous savings. So, said the government, the cost of demergers would not just be a collection of one-time costs but would also have to take into account the missed opportunity to reap these savings. Using just a year's worth of lost savings, the cost of demerging the eight megacities would be, said the government, one-time costs of $214 million[26] plus $217 of foregone savings, for a total of $431 million. But it gets worse: if you factor in what financial people call the present-day value of those savings *ad vitam aeternam*, the cost of demerging, said the government, would be $2 billion.[27]

THE REALITY: THE MONTREAL MEGACITY COSTS AN EXTRA $400 MILLION A YEAR

However, what's sauce for the goose is sauce for the gander. The same reasoning can be used to quantify the cost of mergers, should the creation of the megacities result in extra yearly *costs* rather than yearly *savings*. As it turned out, this is precisely what happened. In the appendix to this book, I calculate the extra costs of the Montreal megacity to be $400 million a year, which means a present-day value of the cost of creating the megacity is over $4 billion.

I didn't have the heart to do a similar analysis for the cost of the other seven megacities.[28]

THE MEGACITY BUDGET AND FISCAL INEQUALITY

In November, the Montreal Transition Committee produced the megacity's first budget. When some details were leaked to *La Presse*, it couldn't wait to revel in the wide disparity between the megacity's allotments to the former suburban municipalities (soon-to-be boroughs) and to those going to the former City of Montreal. The allotments were supposed to pay for local costs, while regional costs were centralized. "Montreal, a City with Two Speeds?" screamed the front-page headline. "The [mega]city's first budget will maintain the fiscal inequity among the boroughs. Is a citizen of Westmount five times better than a citizen of [the Montreal district of] Rosemont?" The article went on to say that Westmount would get a $40 million allotment for a population of 20,000, and the Plateau Mont-Royal (another Montreal district) would get $45 million to service 100,000 residents.[29] The reporter made a glaring error. Westmount, the only place in the Montreal region with an electrical power department, was getting one-half of its allotment just to run its power distribution system. Such matters were mere details: the megacity supporters smelled blood.

"For the first time," said Monique Lefebvre, the president of the Transition Committee, "Montreal Island residents can see the real differences among the boroughs."[30] Editorialist Michèle Ouimet finally had hard numbers to vindicate her crusade for fiscal equity and for the megacity. In an editorial entitled "The Naked Reality," she pointed out that each Westmounter would get $943 in allotment, and each resident of the Montreal borough of Côte-des-Neiges–NDG would get $331. *Quod erat demonstrandum*. "These figures show in black and white just how necessary mergers are to establish a minimum of justice and equity throughout the Island. In the name of what principle can Westmount continue to live in its cozy surroundings while profiting from all the advantages of the big city, all the while not paying its fair share of its expenses?"[31]

I had had enough. "Naked reality," indeed. Unfortunately, the reality was not naked: it was dressed for Canadian winters, swaddled in much accounting bumf. The next day I fired off a press release. The Montreal apples were being compared to the suburbs' oranges. Firstly, the suburban boroughs had been completely independent municipalities before. On the other hand, the newly minted boroughs of the former City of Montreal were fragile and embryonic: they could not survive without the financial and managerial support of the "mother city," where a lot of costs still resided.[32] As an example, the ex-suburban borough allotments included $157 million to cover debt service, whereas the same costs relating to the heavily indebted ex-Montreal boroughs were not included in their allotment. And that was not all. Another $37 million was added to the ex-suburbs' allotment for water supply but not to the ex-Montreal boroughs. These anomalies were corrected in the 2003 budget, but the damage was done and the myth of the coddled ex-suburban boroughs remained very much alive.

But this objection paled beside the fundamental error most observers made in comparing allotments among boroughs. Municipally, you are supposed to pay for what you get, not more, not less. That's government policy. If Westmount residents got three times as much in their allotment for local costs, it was quite simply because *each Westmount resident paid three times as much tax as a resident of the Montreal borough of Côte-des-Neiges–*NDG. And if the boroughs of the former City of Montreal had not inherited its massive dead weight of debt, the denizens of Côte-des-Neiges–NDG would have that much more to spend locally. What were "local costs"? They were things such as maintaining neighbourhood roads, collecting garbage, and providing recreational and library services: in other words, services mostly used by residential taxpayers, not the commercial or governmental taxpayers. If local taxpayers want to give themselves better services and pay for them – a possibility even now in the megacity – what was the problem? Westmount spent $75 per capita on its library every year because that was important for its residents. Outremont spent only $22 per capita on its library – even less, in fact, than Montreal did. As a consequence Outremont taxed its citizens that much less.[33]

But what about the accusation made time and again that Westmounters were living off the central city, that they contributed nothing? The following table shows the opposite: Westmount residents, per capita, contributed five times as much to the megacity for central services as did residents of the typical Montreal borough of Côtes-des-Neiges–NDG.[34]

2002 Residential Tax Load

	Westmount	Côte des Neiges–NDG
Taxes paid by residents	$32 million	$91 million
Number of residents	20,000	163,000
Per Capita		
Residential taxes paid to megacity	$1,600	$557
Share of former city's debt cost	($90)	($116)
Net contribution to megacity costs	$1,510	$441
Allocation from megacity for local services	($943)	($331)
Contribution to central megacity services	$567	$110

But why were such citizens of ex-Montreal getting off so easily? Why were they paying so little in tax? The answer lies with the fact Montrealers were heavily subsidized by the non-residential sector. And that in turn returns to the central question of this book: were mergers necessary in order to establish fiscal equity? The answer is that mergers were not necessary for fiscal equity because Montrealers were not unfairly taxed.

EVERYONE FOR HIMSELF

At the very beginning of 2001, I thought we had all twenty-six Montreal Island suburban mayors on strength to fight the megacity, mayors representing nearly 800,000 citizens. By the middle of January, I discovered that we actually had only eighteen mayors still in the ring, representing around 400,000 citizens. Most mayors of the big suburban municipalities had either decided immediately to throw their lot in with the megacity or to sit things out. At the beginning of November 2001, fully half of the eighteen got elected under Tremblay, who assured the world these now-former mayors were dedicated to building the megacity, not undoing it. Most of the other nine had retired from the field. By the end of the year, there were really only three mayors on strength fighting for demerger.[35] We represented some 30,000 people. The other 770,000 citizens had not changed their minds one whit, but the mayors representing them had. The most pliable of them was Côte Saint-Luc Mayor Robert Libman, who would put on a suit in a phone booth outside the courthouse where he had just made an appearance as the caped Côte Saint-Luc crusader for the cameras, proceeding directly to his other, camera-free day job advising the transition committee, who were busy disassembling his city while building the megacity he publicly called "a bureaucratic monster." A month before the election, Libman said, "I am very much against this forced merger. We are fighting this to the nth degree." A month later, megacity councillor Libman was saying, "The vote doesn't mean that on January 1, with the megacity in place, we're going to undermine the thing. We're not there to do that. If there's a chance to eliminate people's fears, then the resolve to demerge will gradually die away."[36]

Two weeks after the election, a grateful Tremblay made both Libman and Dorval Mayor Peter Yeomans members of the megacity's all-powerful executive committee, at the very moment their disappearing municipalities were contributing funds for our Supreme Court appeal to have the megacity itself quashed. Libman gushed to the *Toronto Star* that his new job was like a "dream come true" and incongruously hoped the Supreme Court "will make suggestions on how to make this important piece of legislation [Bill 170] better ... If we can maintain what we had before in the municipalities, and if we can keep a lid on taxes ... that can be a win-win situation for everyone."[37]

Yeomans said that it was time to start "sharing the wealth" more equitably.[38] One of the few mayors who handled the merger mess with aplomb and dignity was the mayor of Montreal North, Yves Ryan. He would not range himself beside either Tremblay or Bourque. "Both of them are swimming in a huge paradox," Ryan said. "Gérald Tremblay's paradox is to recruit all the merger malcontents [the suburban mayors], at the same time promising to succeed in putting the new city in place. Mayor Bourque's paradox is evident when he says, to please the suburbs, that the new city will be decentralized – yet we have witnessed for years how he has said everything must be centralized in city hall."[39] At seventy-three, after being mayor for thirty-eight years, Ryan finally decided to retire. No more would I make the trek up to his kingdom in Montreal North and consume take-out BBQ chicken for lunch in his office, all washed down with lots of gin while Yves waxed philosophic about the decline in local government.

The new megacity's executive committee was top heavy with ex-suburban mayors, much to the satisfaction of merger supporters, who were pleased as Punch to see such a powerful injection of politicians habituated to running a tight ship and satisfying taxpayers.[40] There was also a goodly dose of anglophones, in spite of a PQ government that, according to Peter Yeomans, "wants to destroy anglophone leadership so there won't be any resistance to the national question in the next referendum." Earlier Yeomans had said, "Bill 170 is going to come back and kick the Parti québécois right in the groin,"[41] It did, in more important ways. Louise Harel was in shock for days after the megacity election: the PQ had expected to be able to deliver the megacity on a platter to Bourque. They had not counted on a Liberal and federalist mayor getting elected. Nor had they counted on the public's anger about forced mergers to continue to resound unabated through Quebec's political ether.

It was not just mayors who had a change of heart after Tremblay won the megacity election. Once the staunchest foes of mergers and a strong supporter of demerger, the *Montreal Gazette* swung its editorial position around to a completely new direction, almost now aligned with that of the francophone media. "A mandate to succeed," the *Gazette* sunnily said of the election results. The suburban (quondam) mayors "have publicly committed to bringing all their efforts to the task of trying to make something work that they originally opposed."[42] As for demerger, the *Gazette* editorially was suddenly cool to what it now called "dismembering" of the megacity, even questioning whether it was "enough to allow a seceding borough to vote, or should the whole city have a say on whether it's dismembered?"[43] Whatever happened, the *Gazette* wrote, the megacity had to be given a chance before even contemplating "secession."

At least one person had not flipped or even adulterated his position – as yet. The day after the megacity election, Jean Charest gave a major television interview on Radio-Canada news, repeating his demerger promise and repeating how it would work. Without Charest's promise, I too would have packed it all in. I was now portrayed as the lonely irredentist. An irredentist is somebody who supports the restoration of a former territory. I had other tags. André Pratte, in a *La Presse* editorial in August, started calling me the *irréductible* mayor of Westmount. Now, *irréductible*, generously translated – and Pratte is a kind man – means implacable, invincible. When journalist Lysiane Gagnon called me the same thing in November, followed by editorialist Michèle Ouimet a month later, they meant "fanatical." When you agree with a stubborn politician, he or she is "principled." If you don't, he or she is "fanatical."

ROUND 3 IN THE COURTROOM

We had our day in the Supreme Court of Canada on 3 December, pleading in front of nine judges clad in scarlet. We asked for a stay of the application of Bill 170, which created the megacity 1 January 2002.[44] The Supremes had to deliberate whether they would even hear our case. "There are two ways to uproot people: by physically moving them from their territory, or by forcibly removing their institutions," said our lawyer Gérald Tremblay. On 7 December the Supreme Court pronounced that they would not hear our case. They gave absolutely no reason, as they are not required to do so. The highest court in the land had let us down. Fifteen minutes later the Ontario Court of Appeal announced it had upheld the Montfort Hospital decision.

I held a rather funereal press conference. It warmed my heart to see there Bill McMurchie, the Pointe-Claire representative on the megacity council. McMurchie not only had the guts to show up, along with two megacity local councillors, but he even bravely reiterated his support for demerger. Louise Harel, of course, was over the moon about our loss. Her beloved reform would go through. The new megamayor Tremblay was elated. His new kingdom was intact.

So it was Government, 3; Political Eunuchs, 0. The legal game was over.

The next thing I knew, a city truck drove up my driveway, unloaded, and set up all my archives in my basement. I cleaned out my desk at city hall, kissed my valiant assistant Marie-José good-bye, pulled my photos off the wall, took the burgundy desk pad embossed with "Mayor," and set up shop in a little room at home. I was given my now-pointless chain of office to keep as a memento, and I carefully stowed it in the back of a closet. With two years to go in my mandate as mayor, I was summarily dis-elected by the provincial government. I was now Westmount's self-described mayor-in-exile.

16

The Poitras Report and a Liberal Victory, or, How Mergers Hijacked the Provincial Election Campaign

So gloriously you stand, dear City!
Government authority is God's gift; yes, the very image of God.
Whoever will not submit to its power must also put aside God ...
> from J.S. Bach, Cantata BWV 119, composed for the
> inauguration of the Leipzig City Council in 1723

We have come a long way from the literally top-down paternalism of nearly three centuries ago. For most Quebec citizens the forced mergers were a throwback to those pre-democratic days; Quebecers deeply resented that the megacities had been imposed through autocratic means, through what the Germans (and Bach's cantata, approvingly) called *die Obrigkeit*, government authority. The PQ government saw mergers as a difficult necessity, and assumed voters would knuckle under once the megacities were formed. It was thought that the populace would soon join the media in circling the intellectual wagons around the Montreal megacity, regarding any suggestion of disassembly through demerger as lèse-majesté. That did not happen, at least for the first year following mergers. The megacity of Montreal remained unpopular;[1] and, during all of 2002 and 2003, half the population supported the Liberals' idea of allowing demergers.

   In fact, quite a number of Montrealers who were in favour of allowing such a demerger vote were personally against "breaking up" the megacity. This generosity and respect for democracy made quite a contrast with the PQ's *Obrigkeit*. This attitude, in fact, was a common phenomenon throughout Quebec; many who were against demerger nevertheless thought the matter should be put to a vote, the very vote they had all been denied.

At the moment the megacity heaved itself into life on 1 January 2002, one could say most citizens' feelings ranged only a half-diapason from repulsion to acquiescence. In Westmount, the mood was unremittingly bleak. The City of Westmount was no more. Westmount City Hall became Westmount Borough Hall, and our three brave councillors technically owed their allegiance to the megacity of Montreal. Since our city hall was occupied territory, I held a public meeting of the now dis-elected council upstairs in the Lodge Room of Victoria Hall in late January. Victoria Hall is a hulking structure of Credit Valley sandstone, built in 1924 in what architect Peter Rose calls the Municipal Armoury style. The Lodge Room was originally fitted out for the Freemasons of Westmount (and their wives, the Daughters of the Nile), and had a domed ceiling, a Juliet balcony, and (at one point) a massive carved throne for the Illustrious Master or whatever he was called. The acoustics make speaking effortless. In this rather mystic space, I spoke about a strategy to make demerger in Quebec a reality:

> Our chances of demerging will dwindle with time; the longer
> we are forced to wait, the more complex the unravelling process
> will become. Once completed, the dissolution of an assortment
> of cities cannot be reversed. And, once completed, the creation
> of a megacity is equally permanent. The process whereby one
> is destroyed to make the other will result ultimately in central-
> ization as a permanent fixture in our municipal landscape. The
> immense centripetal force exerted by the megacity bureaucracy
> will see to it that even the puny powers the boroughs now have
> will slowly evaporate. After all, the borough system was conjured
> up as a sales feature designed to win over the "soft" municipal
> sovereignists.
>
> Most suburban politicians think that, by getting rid of Pierre
> Bourque and putting in Gérald Tremblay, we will avoid the more
> pernicious effects of the megacity. But Tremblay will one day be
> gone; the megacity and its increasingly centralist mentality will
> live on.
>
> Others will say the whole demerger process will be divisive.
> It will open up a can of worms. (This unappetizing metaphor is
> used by those who also don't want to unscramble an omelette.)
> Since when is giving rightful power to people "divisive"? If the
> megacity is so much of a success, why would anyone be afraid

of putting it up for a review by its electors? We know why: the megacity was the wrong diagnosis for our problems. It was created in a frenzy of political hubris and overzealous bureaucratic neatness. If left unchallenged, we are collectively saying that this is acceptable behaviour. We can take small solace in the thought that the Montreal megacity will probably be the last major forced municipal merger in the civilized world.

One of the arguments of merger proponents is that the new megacity will have more political clout in Quebec. The mayor now speaks for 1.8 million people, they say. In a country where cities are subjugated creatures of the province, the bigger the city, the easier it is for the provincial government to wield power over it. Rather than dealing with a few dozen ferrets, the minister of municipal affairs can order around one big docile cow. After all, the Montreal Metropolitan Community speaks for 3.3 million people, but it speaks only in hushed tones; it has a walk-on part, not the principal role that it should have had. Certainly, Tremblay, its president, won't give it the time and effort it deserves.

The rationale for forced mergers in Quebec was "fiscal equity." We'll get fiscal equity, all right. The megacity will cost about $400 million a year more to operate once it reaches cruising speed – and all taxpayers will pay that cost. Not, one imagines, what the fiscal egalitarians had in mind. Instead of each small city delivering those particular services its citizens wanted to pay for, we will have a system where everyone gets the same services, whether they want them or not. Rather than fiscal equity, we'll have fiscal uniformity. And uniformity of services will replace specificity of services. One-size-fits-all trumps made-to-measure.

Our best chance of getting back our autonomy is to convince Jean Charest that the price he'll pay to keep his word, if elected, is that only a few dozen former cities across Quebec will vote to avail themselves of his promise. So we would not be looking at the kind of province-wide upheaval that Harel both fomented and then faced down.

We can't expect many allies in our fight. The francophone media will excoriate us. Even the *Gazette* now wants to give the megacity a chance. The Board of Trade became a cheerleader for amalgamation without even consulting its members.[2] Our only allies will be the people themselves.

THE MOLSON CENTRE MEETING

The day after my speech, I went on a six-week holiday in England. While I was there, an interesting meeting took place in a private box at the Molson Centre (now called the Bell Centre) on 7 February. This meeting was ostensibly organized simply to permit collective enjoyment of the Montreal-Pittsburgh hockey game. All of Mayor Tremblay's and Jean Charest's big guns just happened to be there – in the same box. There were Tremblay's chief of staff, his communications director, and his election campaign manager. Representing Charest were his principal adviser, Pierre Bibeau; the general manager of the Liberal Party, Joël Gauthier;* the chief Liberal fundraiser, Marc Bibeau; and the president of the Liberal Party, Marc-André Blanchard. This serendipitous meeting of sports fans resulted, after a two-week delay for fact-checking, in a front-page *La Presse* article headlined "Charest drops his demerger idea – at least for Montreal, Mayor Tremblay was assured."[3]

> Jean Charest's staff in fact gave this assurance to Gérald Tremblay's top brass ... There is no way Jean Charest will officially commit to holding referendums that could lead to demergers in the former Island municipalities. The staff of the mayor of Montreal, Gérald Tremblay, confided to *La Presse*: "the Liberals won't touch Montreal, or at a minimum, they will make the rules so complicated that what is merged will stay merged." That was the very clear conclusion, we were assured, of a long conversation with, in particular, Pierre Bibeau, principal adviser to Jean Charest ...
>
> To score points against the PQ government, the Liberals had promised to allow the citizens of merged cities to demand referendums to dismantle them. This position, while politically remunerative, becomes more and more difficult to honour, now that mergers have happened. It was felt that to unmake what was made would bring about a veritable political and administrative chaos ...
>
> Gérald Tremblay's staff seemed to be, above all, concerned about the possibility of a strong [Liberal] candidate from the

---

* Joël Gauthier, a lawyer, following the Liberal election victory in 2003, became the boss of the AMT, which runs Montreal region's suburban trains. He was dumped in January 2012, after gross cost overruns on the commuter rail line to Mascouche.

anti-merger mayors who would, in the event of a Liberal win, put constant pressure on Tremblay's administration. They were especially worried by the candidacy of Peter Trent, the mayor of Westmount; but that scenario was quickly ruled out by Pierre Bibeau. The same thing for the former mayor of Mount Royal, Vera Danyluk, who will not be a Liberal candidate, assured Mr Bibeau. "For us, in no way will we touch municipal matters," said Mr Bibeau. "Our policy has been established and we won't change it," he said. "There are clearly more important things at stake right now than the municipal." ... "As time goes by, the mergers will become less and less of an issue; that's what we hope on our side," concluded a Liberal strategist.

When I got back from England, I telephoned Charest, who denied everything. He said Liberal policy was not decided at boxes during hockey games and that, after all, neither he nor Tremblay was there. He was "distressed" by the article, saying it was a Montreal tactic to distract opinion from certain troubles Tremblay was having, and that the Liberal demerger promise would be respected, even on Montreal Island. Charest was careful not to bring up my new status of *candidatus non gratus*, even though I had never taken any steps to become a Liberal candidate, nor had I even trawled for encouragement. I had already got the message that "demergerites need not apply." On the other hand, Monique Jérôme-Forget, a future Liberal minister, kindly called me to say the whole Liberal caucus was upset by the article and that I would be the best candidate they could ever have.

Politics is a madhouse with each inmate yelling something in a language that no one else chooses to understand.

Regardless of Charest's vehement public and private denials,[4] Quebec's political cognoscenti interpreted the Molson Centre meeting as confirmation of a new Liberal policy of backing off from the demerger promise. After all, Charest's representatives who were there made up his "phantom cabinet."[5] The *La Presse* article precipitated a string of comments. The former mayor of Sainte-Foy, Andrée Boucher, a staunch anti-mergerite, felt Charest's demerger promise was out of date: "As time goes by, the more difficult it becomes."[6] The former mayor of Sillery and Liberal member of the National Assembly, Margaret Delisle, said: "In the real world, no one ever really thought we would go back to where we were."[7] Vera Danyluk said demerger was "relatively impossible."[8] And the

Liberal spokesman on the matter, Roch Cholette, said that the cost of reversing the mergers would rise. "We will not be unhappy if no one signs the register [to demerge]" he said.[9] By then Charest felt it was safe to wade back into the debate, announcing that any municipality that demerged would have to shoulder the costs of demerger and that those costs would be revealed before the demerger vote. In other words, the kidnapped would have to pay the ransom.

A ROCKY START

Just before the *La Presse* Molson Centre article came out, Tremblay was mired in the first of a number of minor "scandals." He was pilloried for giving an $850,000 contract to a group he founded and had recently run. Then one problem piled on another, and the media – especially the French media – were not kind to him. He was attacked for giving contracts to people who helped him in his election campaign, for staying on as director and shareholder of some companies that could have dealings with the megacity, for neglecting to mention in a formal declaration his directorship of a $20 million trust, for paying his chief of staff with party funds, and for hiring a key bureaucrat without giving any information to fellow councillors. He also decided to surround himself with a palace guard of sixty-five political advisers, most of whom had worked on his campaign. To be fair, in reporting all these "scandals," the media did not question his integrity, only his judgment. And they did have a point. But I said at the time that, as former suburban municipalities were slowly integrated into the megacity, the population and the media would shift their attention to poor services and away from Tremblay's personal oversights – some of which clearly had to do with his inexperience. Like all big-city mayors, Tremblay would then inevitably resort to a centralized, uniform, command-and-control approach. Which he did. What I did not predict was just how forgiving most people would be. Pierre Bourque never had it so easy.

AN ISLAND HAMLET IS PRIVATIZED AND NEST EGGS ARE BROKEN

A number of other troubles beset Tremblay early on; they were not of his making, but they did involve former suburban mayors who had thrown their lot in with him. One was the matter of Dorval

Island. The pocket municipality of Dorval Island, created in 1915, was a seasonal nano-polis (around 150 residents in summer, none in winter), whose derisory size had constantly undermined our case for retaining small municipalities on the Island of Montreal. Dorval Island even had its own mayor and council. Early in 2002 it was revealed that Peter Yeomans – by now a Montreal executive committee member, the former mayor of Dorval, and a Dorval Island cottage-owner – had, along with all seventy-four other owners, bought all the municipal assets of Dorval Island. The sale was registered three days before the island became part of the megacity. The seventy-five owners forked out all of $25,000 to buy the assets, less than 4 per cent of their value – assets that even included the ferry to get to the island. According to a law adopted in June 2001, any such sale of public assets over $10,000 required the approval of the minister of municipal affairs, but it was back in November 2000 that the Dorval Island council had adopted the resolution accepting the sale. (Individually, they were buyers; collectively, they were sellers.) Inconveniently, no one could get their hands on this resolution in February 2002, as the document was still tucked away on the island ... which was inaccessible until the spring thaw. Years later things were sorted out between Quebec and the rulers of this erstwhile micro-municipality. The result, a sort of condominiumization, probably made sense, but the deal looked pretty shady in the media.

The Dorval Island "scandal" with its rather self-serving council was incorrectly conflated in the media with a different phenomenon: a handful of municipalities that, before their disappearance into the maw of the megacity, had decided – in public – to hive off part of their respective surpluses, salting them away in trusts for the future benefit of their taxpayers. In the case of Baie d'Urfé ($0.65 million), Dollard-des-Ormeaux ($2 million), Sainte-Anne-de-Bellevue ($0.5 million), and Sainte-Geneviève ($0.2 million), money was transferred to a trust months *after* the law expressly forbade such a move. Most of these exercises were redundant, given that the same law stipulated that each borough in the megacity would keep its former city's accumulated surplus, along with, of course, its accumulated debt. On the other hand, most of the towns setting up such nest eggs were faced with a double merger, as they were to be incorporated into much larger boroughs.

These four municipalities eventually had to give all the money back with interest.[10] Their actions, combined with the Dorval Island stunt, did not make for good press. A typical reaction was: "History repeats itself. A privileged class – majority anglophone, very well off – refuses to integrate with ordinary people, often francophones or allophones from the lower or middle classes."[11]

Westmount (for $0.5 million) and Senneville (for $1 million) were the only municipalities to put money aside before the law disallowed it.[12] And Westmount was the only municipality that did it in order to fund the fight against merger and for demerger. For example, Ed Janiszewski, the former mayor of Dollard-des-Ormeaux, said that his $2 million was to supplement cultural and recreational activities and was not a war chest for demerger. This was because he was at the time "very comfortable with the merger plan of Premier Bouchard with its borough-*cum*-cities,"[13] presumably making reference to the Bernard Report.

The new minister of municipal affairs, André Boisclair, was shocked (shocked!) by all these shenanigans: "Quebec citizens were stunned, even angry, to learn that certain municipalities targeted by mergers were involved in transactions that transferred public assets to private interests. You will understand that I share this feeling of indignation expressed by Quebecers, committed as I am to protecting the public's interest and to the main principles that underpinned the municipal reorganization. Let me remind you what they were: first of all, fiscal equity, without which social justice is not possible; quality of services; social solidarity; and the sharing of wealth."[14] Earlier he had said about the megacity, "We created this new city in order to get a better sharing of wealth."[15] This was so much grandstanding, as the minister well knew that no sharing of *past* wealth would happen, as all surpluses (within a trust or outside a trust) were to remain with the taxpayers of the former municipalities and therefore would not be shared. And, as we have seen, the megacity did not result in any sharing of *future* wealth, insofar as the tax burden in the former City of Montreal remained essentially the same.

One thing was clear to me in all this: the government could not touch Westmount's money. As we shall see, had I not decided to put away the half-million dollars in the Citizens' Association for the Preservation of Westmount, I could never have funded the Poitras Report, without which (in my view, at least), demerger probably would never have happened.

THE CLANDESTINE DEMERGER GROUP

In April 2002 I had a lunch with Irving Adessky, who had been mayor of Hampstead for twenty-seven years and who was now dis-elected like me. Adessky was a tough, crusty lawyer who had always given me his support.[16] Back in January 2001, at his suggestion, I had created a group of mayors to fight mergers in the courts as well as the media, a group that was very active until the mergers became reality. Many of those mayors were now ensconced in the megacity.

During this lunch Adessky convinced me to set up a similar group of former mayors and current megacity councillors. He generously offered his firm's conference room for our meetings. We had only one goal: demerger. While I managed to get a number of former may-ors, only a few currently elected people were brave enough to come to our confidential meetings at the beginning. Their boss, Mayor Tremblay, was busy trying to convince the media that all of his team were "building the megacity" and wanted nothing to do with demer-ger. We eventually called ourselves the Association of Elected Offi-cials for Demerger and met thirty times over the next two years, always at Adessky's office.

My maiden speech to kick off our demerger campaign took place in mid-May in Beaconsfield, where barely two hundred demerger faithful (some said one hundred) showed up to hear me. I went to ground until the fall when I spoke in south shore Saint-Lambert. By the end of October, former Saint-Laurent mayor Bernard Paquet had come out for demerger, organizing a rally there of four hun-dred where we both spoke. We formed a kind of anglo-franco team, which helped dilute the Westmounty image I was lumbered with. Paquet, a physician, was a gravelly voiced, no-nonsense politician with a deft populist touch.[17]

THE LIBERALS HIDE A PROMISE AND TREMBLAY
DUMPS A PROMISE

Temporarily trailing the Action démocratique du Québec (ADQ) party in the polls, but ahead of the PQ, and smelling an election in the offing some ten months away, the Liberals rather boldly revealed their campaign program in September 2002. Along with $1 bil-lion a year in personal income tax cuts over five years, a Liberal government would "re-invent the state." Said their press release: "There is a gulf between what Quebecers are: dynamic, imaginative; and what their government is: heavy, tentacular, costly."[18] There was not a word about demerger in the entire document – in fact, in the whole Liberal website. This seemed to confirm the suspicion, which first got currency with the February Molson Centre meeting, that the Liberals were backing off their pledge. Certainly that was *La Presse*'s take, reporting that demergers "were now seemingly on a dead-end track. 'There is not one Liberal who will fight for demerger' a close advisor to Charest confirmed to *La Presse*."[19] And then: "Above all, it's not Jean Charest who will reactivate the political bomb ... Charest has absolutely no intention of campaigning on the matter."[20] By the end of December, Charest was still saying he would permit demerger, but during the next election "there will be no campaign on demerger."[21]

Most commentators were of the opinion that, by relegating demergers to political purgatory, the Liberals had made a wise choice. Mergers and demergers were not on electors' minds, they said. And demerging would be impractical, some said impossible.[22] Michel C. Auger, the respected editorialist of the *Journal de Montréal*, called Charest's demerger promise "the most irresponsible of his career."

When, bizarrely, Pierre Bourque decided to run for the ADQ party, some commentators thought it would hurt the Liberals, as it would remind the electorate of the demerger promise. (As it turned out, Bourque's running was a total flop. He came in third in his own riding.)

In early November 2002, Mayor Tremblay made an announcement. Reneging on a promise made to me, to Bill McMurchie of Pointe-Claire, and to all Montrealers a year before that he "would not even get involved" in defending the megacity against demerger,[23] Tremblay changed his mind, admitting he would now fight demergers. He knew that, had he said that before the election, he would not have been elected, as he needed very heavy suburban support. Announcing his flip-flop, *Le Devoir* said on 2 November 2002, "He admits clearly that he would fight against demerger if such a proposition were in the cards ... '[In the event of a referendum] it is obvious that I will work to show that, beyond the shadow of a doubt, the only solution acceptable for all Montrealers is the new City of Montreal.'" By January 2003, Tremblay was wagging his finger at the three political parties making preparation for an imminent election: "I shall not get involved in any manner in this election campaign, unless there is an attempt to call into question the new City of Montreal."[24]

In one former suburb of Quebec City, and on the south shore of Montreal, there was a small flurry of demergerist activity just before the election. Louise Beaudoin, a PQ minister, publicly stated that the forced mergers would cost her some votes in at least one of the merged former municipalities, Saint-Bruno. She went on to say that the south shore had to be merged: "Only merging Montreal would have created a state within a state and consequently given too much power to that new city."[25]

In polls from October 1997 to spring 2001, the PQ had consistently remained more popular than the Liberals, except for three brief periods, the first one occurring when Charest became Liberal leader in the spring of 1998. Things changed in the spring of 2001, when the Liberals pulled ahead shortly after Bernard Landry took over the PQ. The Liberals remained more popular than the PQ for almost two years thereafter. The ADQ had a brief, fulgurous rise in the summer of 2002 when it beat out both its rivals, but it came down to earth in late December, when all three parties started polling within a few percentage points of each other.[26] This state of affairs continued until early February 2003.

By January 2003, election fever was upon Quebec. Campaign funds were being collected, slogans tried out, candidates chosen, and new membership cards sold. As Shakespeare described the arrangements before a real battle: "From camp to camp, through the foul womb of night, the hum of either army stilly sounds ... the armourers ... give dreadful note of preparation."

THE POITRAS REPORT

One of my handicaps in leading the demerger fight was that, as far as I could determine, a municipal demerger had never really happened before anywhere in the world – except a few very minor cases in, of all places, Quebec. I desperately researched demergers, any demergers, even rural.[27] I found that there might have been some examples of municipal *scissions* or *secessions*[28] outside Quebec, but not of a municipality reconstituting itself subsequent to a merger, and certainly not one of a reparative nature. Even an urban scission would have helped, though. Our great hope that the San Fernando

Valley would break away from Los Angeles was to be dashed when they failed to win a referendum in November 2002, a referendum conducted throughout Los Angeles. (This too was our secret fear: that only one demerger referendum would be conducted throughout the Island of Montreal.) But since the San Fernando Valley had voluntarily merged with Los Angeles back in 1915, it would have not been a reparative demerger following a forced merger; the passage of time tends to turn a potential demerger into a plain scission.

Ironically, then, it seemed only Quebec had ever put through any demergers, and those had to do with four tiny municipalities, only one of which could be called, with some generosity, urban. They took place in the area around Gatineau in 1980 and in 1989 and involved a total of around ten thousand citizens.[29] It was thin gruel, certainly a far cry from demerging the second-largest municipality in Canada, but all we had to go on. I had a selling job to do.

But my biggest difficulty in proselytizing demergers was that most people, while perhaps angry at the forced mergers, thought that demerger was an impossibility: either they thought the Liberals wouldn't deliver on their promise or they thought that demerging was technically impracticable, like "separating the ingredients of a cake already baked," as more than one observer put it.[30] In October, after many desultory attempts to crank up the demerger cause in public, I had a eureka moment – though it was pretty obvious and decidedly late in coming. It occurred to me that what we needed was a substantial report written by a credible person that proved you could indeed "unscramble an omelette," as most of the eggs were yet to be broken. Early in December 2002, Irving Adessky suggested I ask former judge Lawrence Poitras to write the report. By the middle of December, I arranged a lunch with Lawrence Poitras: we hit it off and he was interested, although not keen on dealing with the media. He started work in January once we had agreed on a mandate.

Early in January 2003, I invited three Quebec anti-merger activists to my home. There was Ginette Durocher (from Saint-Bruno, merged with Longueuil; Ginette had formed a coalition of anti-merger groups all over Quebec), Simon Wilson (a restaurateur from Sillery, a municipality merged with Quebec City), and Bertrand Cloutier (from La Baie, a municipality merged to form Saguenay). I told them of my plan and of the report; they were thrilled with the idea, but could contribute little in cash.

In February, I called Kell Warshaw, who had kept the Montreal anti-merger group DémocraCité going. When I told him of the report, he said he thought the whole anti-merger movement had died[31] but that my proposed report was such a good idea it would get him all revved up again. He reactivated their website, and his group (or, really, he) was back in business. This website would become an invaluable tool for us to track demerger activities and all media coverage.

WHAT WAS IN THE REPORT?

In essence, the Poitras Report was all about the feasibility of demergers: their legality, their practicality, and their economic effects. Poitras was responsible for the whole report. It was divided into three sections: the history of mergers in Quebec, a legal "how-to" guide to demerger, and a study on the economic consequences of demerger. Poitras wrote the first section, lawyer Marc Laperrière the second, and professor François Des Rosiers (whom I recruited in January) the third. I provided the framework, the background material, and a sheaf of media clippings and poll results going back six years. Poitras was the former chief justice of the Superior Court of Quebec. At one point in his vast career he had practised municipal law. His name had some resonance in the media owing to another Poitras Report he wrote after being named by the PQ government to become chairman of the Public Inquiry Commission into the Sûreté du Québec from 1996 to 1998. Laperrière, a lawyer with a master's degree in urban planning, once worked for the Union of Quebec Municipalities (UMQ). Des Rosiers, with a PhD from the London School of Economics and a master's degree in urban planning, taught at Laval University and was a property tax expert.

As far back as 1845, wrote Poitras, Quebec law allowed modifications to rural municipalities, but they were always subject to citizen consent. The first Municipal Code in 1870, which governed parishes and villages, required, for any annexation, the approval of two-thirds of the citizens of the annexor and of the annexee. Later, this was changed to approval "by the majority." Up until 1988, the Municipal Code even permitted "demergers," with the same constraints.

As for urban areas, the 1903 Cities and Towns Act permitted annexations – again, always subject to citizen approval. ("Voluntary annexation" carries a whiff of oxymoron, as the word annexation suggests the use of force.) Legislators through the years scrupulously and consistently insisted on citizen approval when changing municipal boundaries, even though, constitutionally, such approval was not required.

The only way the government could (and can today) force a merger was to adopt "special" laws. The Liberal governments, exceptionally from 1965 to 1975, rammed through about twenty such laws. The PQ only tried it once. In fact, it was a PQ government that actually put through the 1980 demerger in Gatineau.

The forced merger creating the City of Laval in 1965 was among the first such exceptions in modern times.* A commission of enquiry prior to the merger came to the conclusion that the existing situation was "absurd and unreasonable," in that the tiny municipalities that dotted the island of what was to become Laval were incapable of offering essential services, faced as they were with a projected doubling of population over the next decade – in fact, only three of them had even a roads department. Another such urgent case was the forced merger in 1971 of a vast rural area to accommodate the gargantuan airport of Mirabel on nearly 100,000 expropriated acres.[32]

Poitras also cited yet another exception: Baie-Comeau was forced by a PQ government to merge with Hauterive with a law adopted in 1982. Opposition to the merger turned violent, with bomb and death threats. This merger created such lasting bitterness that it poisoned the forced merger well for years to come; no party of either stripe wanted to go though such a dolorous experience again.

With these notable exceptions, usually arising from some specific "urgent" condition, Poitras maintained, voluntary mergers had been always the rule in Quebec. But this flew in the face of Harel's claim that *forced* mergers "were the rule here in Quebec, as in Ontario, New Brunswick, and Nova Scotia, rather than being the exception."[33] Who was right? Yes, there were, from 1961 to 1998, the twenty forced mergers – which involved around 100 municipalities.[34] During that same period, however, there were well over 250 *voluntary* mergers involving nearly 600 municipalities. But never

---

* Andrew Sancton in *Merger Mania* referred to Laval as "the most significant legislated municipal merger in North America since New York in 1898." (New York, however, was a voluntary merger.)

prior to 2001 had Quebec resorted exclusively to imposed mergers, and never on such an all-encompassing scale.

The report then moved to the question of demergers and their legal feasibility. The absolute power that a Canadian province has over its municipalities and that permits it to merge them against their will, wrote Poitras, is the same power that allows the province to demerge them. What the province taketh away, it giveth. He suggested the government proceed by adopting enabling legislation (a *loi-cadre*, or framework law) setting out the process for demerger, rather than a whole series of special laws adopted on a case-by-case basis.

Next, Laperrière wrote a demerger how-to guide that showed it was not an impossible task like unbaking a cake, unscrambling an omelette, or putting toothpaste back in a tube.

Then Des Rosiers weighed in. "In actual fact," he wrote, "there exists no study or analysis to date that allows one to justify municipal mergers based on the potential savings that could flow from them ... on the contrary, empirical evidence tends to show mergers result in an increase in the unit costs of local services."[35] He went on to cite the work of Charles Tiebout on the advantages of small municipalities: "Small communities can offer differing packages of services and amenities and we can vote with our feet as to which ones we prefer. Moreover, even when they offer the same sorts of services, they compete as to which can deliver them more efficiently." Far from being "sterile," said Des Rosiers, intermunicipal competition is healthy.

To deal with the "fiscal equity" argument, he worked out an elegant method of equalization payments based on real estate wealth per capita. Next, he calculated the savings inherent in demerger by using the tendency of costs to drift upwards to the highest common denominator in the event of merger. In his most conservative estimate, he calculated that the cost of the Montreal merger would be $200 million per year. (In fact he came up with much higher numbers, which we decided not to include in the report.) Therefore the savings of *demerger* would be the same amount – if all suburban municipalities were demerged. This works out to be $111 per capita, every year.

There was, of course, a one-time cost of demerger. The costs of studies, referendums, and elections Des Rosiers estimated to be about $17 per capita.

A HIDDEN GOAL

My first goal was to come up with a report to prove that demergers were feasible and not costly. But I had begun to realize that there could be a second, even more important goal: to ram the issue of demerger into the election campaign where at least one of the three political parties did not want to hear of it. Only by getting the demerger pledge publicly sanctified during an electoral ordeal by fire would we be assured that it would be a promise that would be honoured – if the Liberals won.[36] Of course, I did not broadcast this second goal, as it suggested that the Liberals were not going to honour their promise.

DROPPING THE BOMB

Through one of his close advisors, I asked if Jean Charest wanted an advanced copy of the Poitras Report. The next day, I got back a clear "no." Charest did not want to be seen to be associated with my initiative, and did not wish to have to dissemble, on the date of its release, that it was the first time he had seen the report. My estimation of Charest went up a notch. The next thing I knew, someone high up in the Liberal Party contacted Poitras and a senior partner of his law firm, trying to get them to delay the release of the report until after the election. The Liberal Party was convinced they would win on the issues of health care and re-inventing government. If their eye was taken off the ball by the now-verboten subject of demergers, they would never win – or so they thought. Poitras told the Liberals that his client was Peter Trent and to take it up with me.

My friend Richard Gervais's firm had long ago agreed to handle the press conference for the report's release, which was originally planned to happen before the election campaign period started. On 12 March, the day the election campaign began, and five days before our target release date of 17 March, Gervais reluctantly called me at Poitras's office to tell me his staff "would revolt" if they were forced to take part in releasing it. They were all convinced it would directly lead to the defeat of the Liberals; and, to their credit, they refused the job for that reason. It must be remembered that all the media commentators shared the same opinion.

I was faced with one of the most difficult decisions of my life. Would the report really sink the Liberals and, not unimportantly,

all our demerger hopes with them? I decided to go ahead: I was
convinced that the Liberals underestimated the intensity of the anti-
merger sentiment right across Quebec, sentiment they could readily exploit.[37] Right after the call from Gervais, I almost ran up the
street to see Jonathan Goldbloom, another media relations expert,
and breathlessly asked if he would handle the press conference. To
my relief, he said yes, saying that on balance it probably would not
hurt the Liberals.

I sent out a media advisory about the report on 14 March, just in
case any one else got cold feet. The three of us – Poitras, Laperrière,
and I – worked at their law firm all day Saturday and Sunday, with
Des Rosiers cranking out his stuff by email as we made major last-
minute revisions. Their bills, amounting to a total of $50,000 for all
their time and costs, were very modest, but everyone had agreed to a
budget back in January and they all believed in the cause.

So, at 11 AM on 17 March at the Delta Hotel, we were assembled:
Réjean Simard, the former mayor of La Baie, Ginette Durocher, the
energetic leader of the pan-Quebec coalition against forced mergers,
Simon Wilson from Quebec, and Poitras. We were only two from
Montreal, and two of the five were – originally – strong PQ supporters. I got Simard to act as host. I spoke a bit, and then Poitras took
over. He did a magnificent job. We had five TV cameras, six radio
stations, and all the major dailies.

THE THIRTY-THREE-DAY ELECTION SPRINT BEGINS

Not unexpectedly, demerger had been a taboo subject when the election campaign kicked off on 12 March. On 15 March, Charest had
refused publicly to sign a demerger pledge that echoed word for word
Liberal policy on the matter. The pledge had been brandished in front
of his nose and before the cameras by a demerger supporter. The
release of the Poitras Report at noon two days later forced Charest
to react to the media. At the time, he was giving a press conference at
a hospital in Loretteville, a municipality that had been merged with
Quebec City in 2002. Charest was trying to talk about his electoral
pet theme, health care. He took the bait. "We will move quickly, in
the first year of our mandate," he said about demergers. "We don't
want to make people wait ... It will probably take enabling legislation."[38] A number of news sources snidely asked whether he "would
support demerger in Westmount, where he lives with his family."

The media clearly linked the release of the Poitras Report with Charest's new volubility on the subject. "The theme of demerger of the new City of Montreal made its appearance in the electoral campaign with the publication of the report."[39] And: "The public announcement of the demergerists yesterday forced the Liberal chief, Jean Charest, campaigning in the Quebec region, to commit more firmly with regard to his old promise."[40]

Then came the commentary. The Poitras Report "threw a huge wrench into the Liberal machinery," wrote Michel David in *Le Devoir* the next day. It would have been "certainly an excellent investment for the PQ ... It seems the Liberal leader's staff doesn't quite know how to react. His campaign is going pretty well. This is not the time to let him get distracted. To attack Maître Poitras, whose professional integrity is difficult to call into question, would get them nowhere."

Michel C. Auger, writing in *Le Journal de Montréal*, was one of many who attacked the messengers: "The demerger partisans are a bit like the pro-life militants or other such ideological groups. Whether they're for you or against you, during an election campaign, the further away they are, the better."[41] *Le Devoir* editorialist Jean-Robert Sansfaçon could not understand the Liberals. Since it was mostly the Island of Montreal anglophones who remained opposed to mergers, he wrote, and they were already going to vote Liberal, why upset all the others, the silent majority who accepted the new order?[42]

As always, *La Presse*'s Lysiane Gagnon had some interesting takes on the Poitras Report. She echoed the general consensus that I had royally goofed by making the report public:

> The question of municipal "demergers" is the big oddity of this campaign. We were expecting it to be the Liberals' Achilles' heel; but, as it turned out, this matter is in the process of becoming a damp squib. Rarely have we seen, at any rate, as many people shoot themselves in the foot: the demergerists themselves, Bernard Landry, and, obviously, the Liberals ...
>
> At the very beginning of the electoral campaign, in publishing the Poitras Report – a report that claims the demerger process could be easy and relatively cheap – former mayors Trent (Westmount) and Simard (La Baie), dragged out into the open a question the Liberals wanted to keep in the dark. In so doing,

they found themselves torpedoing the campaign of the only party that could eventually give them satisfaction! As for political judgment, we have seen better ...

The intervention of the demergerists had other, more underhanded, effects. By bringing this question right into the centre of the campaign, it allowed Bernard Landry to let fly a partisan and murderous little remark – the sort of casual remark designed to associate Jean Charest with the English and with money. During a press conference, M Landry interrupted Minister Marois, who was referring to Sherbrooke as Jean Charest's hometown. "Excuse me, Pauline, he lives in Westmount." * Westmount: the city that still symbolizes the old domination of rich anglophones ...[43]

Gagnon did concede, however, that "in certain francophone ridings where the battle is close, it's not impossible that the anti-mergerists could swing things the other way."

The day after the Poitras Report was made public, the mayors of all the new megacities (except the mayor of Saguenay) hurriedly worked up a joint response. It was to be a clarion call in defence of their megacities, designed to stop in its tracks any renewal of the merger/demerger debate, especially during the quicksand of an election campaign. "One cannot put an egg back in its shell: we want politicians to look towards the future. Whoever wants to lay mines under le Grand Montréal or Quebec City will find some pretty strong de-miners in their way,"[44] said the mayor of Quebec City, Jean-Paul L'Allier – an opponent, I must say, whom I always found to be suave, intelligent, and never at a loss for a colourful image. L'Allier added that the megacity mayors originally had absolutely no intention of getting involved in the election campaign, but faced with the Poitras Report, they had to stop "the whipped cream from rising." Sure enough, the next day out came a press release wherein Tremblay implored provincial politicians not to "engage in a sterile, useless debate that will divide us and leave us even further behind; to engage in a power struggle, when the future is for those who share power."[45]

---

* The PQ never ceased to hammer home that Jean Charest – rather unwisely, perhaps – had moved to Westmount in 1999. The fact that a well-known PQ militant and strategist, who won a Montreal east-end riding in 2003, was a long-time Westmount resident was – to my knowledge – never mentioned in the media.

In spite of the mayors' pleas, and in spite of unremitting media questioning, Charest stood his ground, saying he had no intention of backing off his demerger promise. Bernard Landry, who was (like L'Allier) no slouch when it came to arresting images, said, "The Quebec Liberal Party has made its bed. It's a bed of nails; but it's of their own making, so they'll just have to sleep in it."[46] For all his bluster, Landry was a bit unsure at that point whether demergers would hurt or help the Liberals. Six days after the Poitras Report was made public, the PQ's André Boisclair filed a formal complaint with the director-general of elections alleging that the costs of the report must be accounted for in Liberal election spending, which was, by law, capped. His point was that only the Liberals were promising demergers, and the report was designed to give them legitimacy. Mario Dumont, leader of the ADQ, laughed out loud, mocking the PQ who "seem to imagine that it is an expense that will help the Liberals."[47] The DGE, as requested, immediately launched an inquiry.[48]

Charest, however, recognized that he was on to something. The day after his media grilling on demergers, Léger Marketing's daily tracking poll showed a small bounce in his popularity.[49] However, in the same poll, a paltry 7 per cent of Quebec's population (only some of whom had their municipalities taken away, mind you) said that mergers had an impact on their voting intentions. As we shall see, this was not how people behaved at the ballot box. A few days later, after examining their 13–23 March data, the polling firm CROP said for the first time that a Liberal victory was possible.

Many pundits (before the election results came in) felt that the outbreak of war in Iraq on 19 March saved Charest's bacon by taking his apparent demerger discomfort off the front pages.[50] This was not to be. Try as he might to talk about health care, Charest found demergers remained the most popular topic all over Quebec, at least for the first half of the campaign period.[51]

CHAREST'S OPPORTUNISTIC GAMBIT THAT BECAME POLICY

During the televised leaders' debate on 31 March, Charest pulled off a brilliant manoeuvre to disarm what he – and everybody – saw as the demerger bomb. He brought the subject up himself in his opening remarks, which came after, and contrasted with, Landry's rather wooden introduction. Charest also completely flummoxed Landry by saying he, personally, was in favour of the new megacities, but, crucially, that they had to be legitimized by allowing citizens to vote on them:

> Since the beginning of the campaign, Bernard Landry has done his best to avoid talking about his record and to hide his sovereignty agenda – to such a point he didn't even talk about them in his opening remarks! He will try and do the same thing tonight by speaking to you about, among other things, demergers.
>
> Tonight, let's get things straight. The Quebec Liberal Party is not campaigning *for* demergers. We want to give back to citizens the right to express themselves on the future of their communities. This position, moreover, is precisely the one René Lévesque took in the matter of municipal mergers in 1976.[52] Citizens will regain their right to have a say, and that's what's known as democracy.
>
> I want to make it clear that every citizen must always pay his or her fair share of common expenses. Now, as for me, I hope the new cities succeed; but in my view, it can only happen on the condition that the essential ingredient of democracy is added. As a taxpayer, I have a bias in favour of the success of these new cities."

So Landry was caught completely flatfooted when Charest brandished the very rapier with which Landry hoped to run him through. The word "demerger" did not pass Landry's lips throughout that night's debate. A later poll reported that 54 per cent of those who were watching thought Charest was the most convincing speaker, and only 24 per cent said the same thing about Landry, with ADQ leader Mario Dumont getting 7 per cent.[53] Charest was on a roll.

Those against demergers pounced on Charest's statement "I hope the new cities succeed" as if it counterbalanced or diluted his party's demerger promise. I interpreted it as his statement of personal preference, ("as for me," "as a taxpayer"), not a pledge formally adopted by his party. It got him out of a tight position and was sufficiently ambiguous to please most voters. Unfortunately, as we shall see, this one phrase was the minuscule hook on which most of the future Liberal demerger policy would eventually be hung, and so it did indeed severely compromise their long-held and formal position that they would simply annul the mergers if that was what the citizens wanted.

For two days after the debate, Landry remained gob-smacked by Charest's chutzpah; then he came out even more vociferously against demergers, making them his central theme. With barely ten days to go before the vote, Landry was panicking: he fell back on his stock-in-trade of hyperbole. In spite of his professorial mien and his evident intellectual polish, Landry was an emotional man whose biggest enemy was sometimes his own mouth. Demerger was "purely an antisocial manoeuvre, the victims of which will be the poor," he said. It was a "veritable sociological and institutional time bomb" that would blow up the megacities and "cost two billion dollars." It was "an apprehended catastrophe" that would "logically lead us to an implicit support of the principle of partition."

The mergers, it was almost painfully clear, were hurting the PQ. Landry even got Municipal Affairs Minister André Boisclair to make the "announcement" that a PQ government would not impose any more mergers.[54] No one pointed out that Louise Harel had announced the same thing back in September 2001.

The more Landry talked about demergers, the more people were reminded of their helplessness when his government (and he as second in command) imposed mergers many months before. As one of Quebec's shrewdest commentators, Yves Boisvert of La Presse, put it, "mergers left political wounds. The unhappiness started to create sediment. I am therefore not certain that Mr Landry was well advised to stir up those waters."[55]

The vote on 14 April was almost anticlimactic, especially since the pollsters had called it pretty accurately. The Liberals got about the same number of votes as they did in 1998. The PQ vote dropped by nearly half a million – over a quarter. The PQ vote went partially to the ADQ, but mostly it just stayed home. The final tally: Liberals, 76 seats; PQ, 45 seats; ADQ, 4 seats.

What happened? As far back as early February 2003, ADQ support had started a steady decline that continued right until voting day. Both the PQ and the Liberals were the beneficiaries of the ADQ meltdown. So by the time the starting pistol went off on March 12, the Liberals and the PQ were neck and neck, even though twice as many voters predicted a PQ rather than a Liberal win.[56] In the event, the Liberals continued their upward momentum until the end, with a big bounce after the debate; the PQ peaked in late March and dropped precipitously thereafter.

DID THE POITRAS REPORT RESULT IN A LIBERAL VICTORY?

It wasn't so much that the Liberals won as the PQ lost. And, completely unexpectedly, the election turned on the massive residual anger from forced mergers and its possible palliation by demergers. The Poitras Report thrust these issues onto the central stage of the election campaign, forcing the bashful Liberals to repeat ad nauseam their demerger promise. And none other than Landry said that the PQ lost over twenty seats owing to forced mergers – the difference between a PQ majority and a Liberal one. According to him, the municipal mergers delivered the fatal blow to his government during the April election.[57] The Liberals seemed to agree.[58] Indeed, the Liberal demerger promise reminded the population of just how much they resented the forced mergers and rekindled their desire to penalize the PQ. And having the megacity mayors get up and whine about the demerger pledge had the same effect. It bears repeating that the PQ did not lose the election because of their implementation of mergers but because of their lack of consultation on them.

While the pundits across Quebec repeatedly had said that demerger by election time was no longer an issue, with 58 per cent of the electorate saying they were personally *against* demergers, few in the media mentioned that an equal proportion of voters were in favour of *allowing* demergers, using the very referendums the PQ had originally denied them.[59] This little-known fact says volumes about the well-developed democratic values of average Quebecers – who voted Liberal not because they necessarily wanted demergers but because they believed in the right to have their say.

Two months after the PQ defeat, sitting PQ member Jean-Pierre Charbonneau, a former journalist, long-time speaker of the National Assembly, and former PQ cabinet minister, bitterly emptied his sack (as the French put it) about the effect of the forced mergers on the election results: "A lot of our voters stayed home on election day or decided to penalize us by voting for another party." Why? According to Charbonneau, "You can't rule over people in an authoritarian and autocratic way without there being a reaction ... We had the attitude of people who said, 'This is what is good for you and you'd better support it. In any case, you don't have anything to say about it.'" Charbonneau went on to say it was Bouchard who condemned the PQ in shoving the mergers down citizens' throats: "The government said: 'It's been thirty years that we've talked about it; we have to finish the job.' But we never talked about it in the [1998] electoral campaign and M. Bouchard had said no to Pierre Bourque at the beginning. Suddenly, without knowing why, it became urgent to do it."[60] Charbonneau was speaker when Bill 170 was rammed through, and displayed the intellectual honesty to deplore publicly the way it was done.

The francophone commentators, ferociously against demergers, admitted that Charest, after his election victory, had an unambiguous mandate to get moving with them. Michel David, in *Le Devoir* on 16 April, wrote:

> One thing for sure, Mr Charest can legitimately claim to have got an infinitely clearer mandate than the one sought by the PQ in 1998. During that entire campaign, neither Lucien Bouchard nor any PQ candidate even whispered a single word on the subject of forced mergers. Needless to say, one could not find a line on the matter in their electoral platform. It is undeniable that a number of ridings swung to the Liberal camp Monday night because a lot of electors took advantage of the opportunity to voice their opposition to mergers, if not actually in favour of dismantling municipalities merged in an arbitrary fashion.
>
> This time, one cannot say that it's simply the cause of the anglophones, for which the Liberals would be the servile instrument. The loathing that the mergers arouse in them is certainly real, but it simply adds to their even more bitter hostility to sovereignty.
>
> In Marguerite-d'Youville and Chambly on the south shore, François Beaulne and Louise Beaudoin clearly paid the price of demergers in francophone ridings that the PQ would have held otherwise. Marguerite-d'Youville, above all, was a veritable PQ fortress ... In the Quebec City region, the Liberals fully profited from the anti-merger discontent, whether in Charlesbourg, La Peltrie, or Louis-Hébert.

Using Landry's assessment, there were at least another fifteen PQ ridings lost to the Liberals because of forced mergers. Interestingly, all these twenty-odd ridings were situated outside the Island of Montreal. On average, their voters were 95 per cent francophone, and 55 per cent of them had voted for sovereignty in the 1995 referendum.[61]

Over five years later, the Quebec City region, for one, was still radio-active from the forced mergers.[62] While it was only francophones who tossed out the PQ because of mergers, the media continued to paint the issue as an anglophone *dada*, not a francophone one.

During all the years I've been in business and in politics, the Poitras Report, in concept and in timing, was the one idea I ever came up with that worked pretty much as planned. My luck has not so far been repeated.

17

A Megacity Legitimized by the Indifferent and the Absent

The promise given was a necessity of the past: the word broken is a necessity of the present.

Niccolò Machiavelli

It's Quebec that decides municipal borders, not citizens.

Bernard Landry, 2004

April 2003: winter had finally let go of Montreal. A few receding ice sheets and crusts of snow hung on, blackened with a winter's worth of pollution. The jetsam from the six-month invasion was everywhere: antifreeze bottles, windshield scrapers, dog turd in plastic bags. The seasonal tradition of filling potholes with cold asphalt was busily underway, with five hundred tons used so far. The Canadian Automobile Association alone had recorded thousands of potholes in Montreal streets. Dazed and etiolated, Montrealers shuffled along sandy sidewalks towards any patches of sun they could find. Coroplast signs advertising smiling candidates clung to lamp standards, a reminder of the recent provincial election.

Hope sprang eternal that spring, as we waited for the Liberals to pass the promised law to permit the renaissance of our municipalities.

WHO DECIDES? THOSE WHO VOTE OR THOSE WHO STAY HOME?

Almost before the Liberals had got over their victory party hangover, hot debate had broken out behind the scenes as to the rules governing the demerger referendums in the 212 formerly merged municipalities. This debate continued for over six months, up until the moment the demerger law was adopted. The Liberals turned three important questions over and over in their minds. First, what would be the minimum number of signatures necessary to trigger the referendum process in a given municipality? Second, what should be the minimum voter turnout for a referendum to be considered legitimate? Third, should it take more than a simple majority of Yes votes for demerger to happen?

Early on, Mayor Tremblay's people had been trying to convince Charest's people that a minimum of 25 per cent of potential electors should have to request that a referendum be held, and that a minimum referendum turnout should be set at 50 per cent.[1] The Liberals demurred; they felt that a 25 per cent hurdle would be viewed as an artificial obstacle and wanted a more reasonable 10 per cent. On the other hand, they very much favoured a minimum turnout of 50 per cent, but they soon began to realize it would have the perverse effect of encouraging the anti-demerger forces to stay home in order to keep the turnout low. One Liberal, inspired by a Henry Aubin column in the *Montreal Gazette*, gave the example of a municipality of 100,000 potential voters: even if 49,000 got out and voted Yes for demerger and no one voted No, demerger would not happen – even though every single ballot said Yes. Yet if 25,001 voted Yes and 25,000 voted No, demerger would happen – with only half the ballots in favour.

There was another problem. Voter turnout is calculated by dividing the number of people who actually voted by the number of all potential voters on the list. This is fine as long as voting lists are accurate. They aren't. The lists are full of people who have moved, died, or are ineligible to vote. This is because Quebec voting lists are now compiled by the government based on records such as driver's licences and medicare cards. Unfortunately, not everybody returns these cards like hotel keys when they check out of Quebec. Normally such inaccuracies are irrelevant, as all Quebec referendums and elections in the past were won based on whether more people actually got out and voted for one option or one candidate over those who voted for another: people who stayed home did not count. But, uniquely for the demerger referendums, accuracy counted. For example, even if only 16 per cent of the names on a given voting list were ineligible, a minimum of 60 per cent of the people on the shorter, accurate list would have to get out and vote in order for the official turnout to be 50 per cent of the inflated list.

A minimum turnout rate gave veto power to the indifferent, the ineligible, the absent, or those who had moved (to another municipality or the great voting booth in the sky). Yet, if people don't vote, one can only assume they don't care about the outcome – or are not eligible. In other words, those who decide not to use their right to vote do so in the full knowledge that those who *do* vote will decide in their place. But that's not how the Liberals saw things. For them, those who didn't vote were, by implication, not in favour of demerger. Municipal Affairs Minister Jean-Marc Fournier spoke on the matter of minimum turnout during the parliamentary hearings on the draft demerger law, called Bill 9:

> The bill in its current form does not specify what "significant participation" means. Should we add a minimum turnout rate; and, if so, what rate should be established as a threshold – below which a result of over 50 per cent plus one of valid votes would not be considered a Yes? I have, from time to time, brought up the problem of legitimacy that such a rule would raise. If we did not keep it in the bill, it was because it could encourage those in favour of the new cities to abstain from voting in the referendum in the hopes that the minimum turnout would not be achieved.
>
> On the other hand, not to require a minimum turnout rate has two important drawbacks. First of all, if more that one-half of the population does not get involved in the referendum vote, shouldn't we conclude that the dismantling operation has failed to rally the majority – and, in which case, how can we justify imposing it on them? How could we claim that the illegitimacy of the merger could be corrected by the illegitimacy of the demerger? Secondly, what are the conflicts of legitimacy should the referendum turnout be lower than the election turnout that gave legitimacy to the elected officials of the new [mega]cities?[2]

Fournier's first argument could have been turned around: shouldn't those in favour of keeping an "illegitimate" merger have to prove that *they* were in a majority, rather than the reverse? And his second argument was not swathed in much logic: the elected officials of the megacities knew full well when they were elected that there was a Liberal demerger policy in place. Moreover, it was interesting that Fournier referred to the megacity election conferring legitimacy on elected officials, while calling the megacity itself illegitimate. The megacity politicians were, of course, elected in good faith; but after all, they did participate in an election imposed on citizens who largely wanted no change. People, in voting for megacity politicians because they had no other choice, were definitely not by that act legitimizing the megacity. Besides, in the hierarchy of legitimacies, one would think the need to legitimatize the megacity would trump the one-time election of its first set of politicians, whatever the turnout rate happened to be.

But the debate raged on. The Board of Trade even plumped for a minimum 66 per cent turnout, which made Tremblay look like a real sport with his 50 per cent and would have effectively ensured that no demergers would happen. Most residents of Montreal Island, when polled, agreed with Tremblay and felt that a minimum 50 per cent turnout rate made sense. After all, it was a major decision to demerge.* Few realized that, at the municipal level, a 50 per cent voter turnout rate is quite high, and not only because of inaccurate voting lists. It is also high because tenants – especially younger tenants – just don't get out and vote in the numbers homeowners do.[3] In former municipalities like Saint-Laurent, where 60 per cent of dwellings are rented, getting a 50 per cent turnout is next to impossible. Recent immigrants also are not very active municipal voters.[4] Half of the population of Saint-Laurent, just as an example, is made up of immigrants – the highest proportion on Montreal Island.[5]

Why tenants and recent immigrants by and large don't vote municipally is for someone else to sort out. But for the government, the Board of Trade, the media, and Mayor Tremblay to "save" the megacity by depending on such non-voters was something that appalled me. The endemically low municipal voter turnout (which mergers have made worse) is a stain on our democratic values, a stain that was cynically used to the advantage of all who were against demergers.

In any other place in the world, there would have been a simple way out. If the Liberals absolutely had to underscore the permanent nature of the vote, or ensure that citizens' wishes were completely unambiguous, all they had to do was require the Yes vote be, say, 60 per cent of all ballots cast.[6] But in Quebec this would have been a provocative precedent: for years, sovereignists had been insisting

---

* It is also a major decision for a country to join the European Union. Hungary did it with a 46 per cent turnout rate.

that only a 50 per cent plus one referendum vote was necessary to take Quebec out of Canada. And, as Minister Fournier said himself, how can one create more rigid conditions to leave a megacity than to leave a country?

For nearly six months the Liberals refused a minimum demerger turnout requirement because of the potential for abstention from voting by canny No voters. Then, in November, possibly emboldened by the public's support for such a limitation and equal disenchantment with the demerger bill in general, the Liberals caved. But instead of requiring that the sum of both Yes and No ballots be a minimum of 50 per cent of all potential voters (the 50 per cent turnout rule), they embraced the far more restrictive requirement that the *Yes ballots only* must represent a minimum of 50 per cent of all the potential voters. This was a position, incidentally, held by the megacity mayors and the Union of Quebec Municipalities (UMQ). By the time the demerger bill was finally adopted, the Liberals had whittled the 50 per cent down to a more reasonable 35 per cent. All this new twist did was to deal with Fournier's worry of pro-megacity forces boycotting the referendum process in order to keep the turnout low. It still carried all the unfairness inherent in any minimum turnout rule. Those who didn't care or who weren't there could overturn the decision of those who did actually vote.

It turned out that, in the actual referendum, the requirement that 35 per cent of all potential voters must get out and vote Yes led to the *least* number of municipalities demerging. In fact, I have calculated that either requiring a 50 per cent turnout rate for the sum of Yes and No ballots, or requiring 60 per cent of ballots be Yes regardless of voter turnout, would have resulted in about ten more municipalities demerging. Had normal referendum rules applied, the number of municipalities that demerged would have doubled, and one million people, or 13 per cent of Quebec's population, would have been involved in a demerger. Whether by the minimum turnout hook or the messy voting list crook, the number of demergers was kept to thirty, involving only 6 per cent of Quebec's population.

SENDING THE MEGACITY TO THE DECENTRALIZATION SPA

During all this time, Mayor Tremblay was busy making the megacity more attractive. Probably regretting doing nothing about his

November 2001 election promise to decentralize things, he then realized with the election of the Liberals that decentralization had suddenly become his megacity's salvation: it could be billed as the safe alternative to demerger. So he got weaving: his plan was to re-jig the megacity with a "new organizational model," hoping thereby to firm up the very flaccid ex-suburban support. The megacity opposition party, however, wanted nothing to do with any form of decentralization. They were still faithful to the centralism of Pierre Bourque, their quondam leader who, having abandoned them for the siren call of provincial politics and come a-cropper, would soon be back in his municipal saddle.[7]

The megacity was originally endowed with boroughs, albeit weak ones, in the hopes that such simulacra would mollify the many who missed the real thing. Now, nearly three years later, Tremblay wanted to beef up the same boroughs for the same reason. His lieutenant, Georges Bossé, went out and hired Louis Bernard of the Bernard Report fame. Along with Bernard, the advice of a big consulting firm, and other bits and bobs, Tremblay spent some $600,000 on figuring out how to decentralize the megacity, and that did not count all the megacity employees working on the project. The goal, to use both Minister Fournier's and Tremblay's jargon, was "to develop a policy of voluntary adhesion" to the megacity. (Words such as "demerger" were now *verba non grata*.) By early August 2003, Montreal's executive committee was at an impasse over just how much to decentralize. While most members seemed to agree that allowing boroughs to incorporate as separate legal entities was going too far,[8] Tremblay and his second in command, Frank Zampino, remained holdouts against the popular idea of extending true taxation powers that would permit the self-funding of boroughs. These two finally won their point. They probably understood that any decentralization worth its name must ensure that both spending *and* revenue are decentralized. Since both men were centralists at heart, by not giving boroughs real taxation power, they were only allowing superficial decentralization. The new plan was rammed through party caucus as a fait accompli: take it or leave it.[9]

By mid-August, Tremblay and most of his executive committee publicly presented their "new organizational model" of decentralization. For the public, the most striking suggestion was that borough presidents (a.k.a. megacity councillors) would henceforth be called "borough mayors," with all the rights, honours, and privileges thereto appertaining, the most attractive of which turned out to be the privilege to increase their own emoluments. And all borough mayors[10] – not just the ex-suburban ones – were to be elected at large in their respective boroughs. Editorial praise for Tremblay's decentralization plan in *La Presse* ("Well done!" "A tour de force," "Montreal remains a real city") and *Le Devoir* ("A good compromise") were matched by burbles of delight from Premier Charest and Minister Fournier.

From then on Tremblay constantly worked with a compliant Quebec to turn his decentralization plan into law. He was rewarded with a bill that modified Montreal's charter, a bill that made him "particularly happy"[11] as it was "almost a carbon copy" of his plan.[12] "Tremblay now believes he can beat the demergerites," ran a *Le Devoir* headline. Boroughs were delegated some powers to hire, fire, and negotiate with unions – but everything was subject to rules set by the megacity, which kept exclusivity in setting salaries and hours worked. Boroughs could borrow and tax to augment local services without requiring megacity approval, but just about all of their funding remained in the form of a transfer payment. They also could draft their own budgets, subject to standards set by the megacity. They could sue, but only if the megacity decided such action was in the megacity's interest; after all, the boroughs were not legally incorporated. Of course, the provincial legislation that gave more powers to the boroughs today could be changed just as easily tomorrow, and the boroughs could do nothing about it.

Because Tremblay had refused to do it, I had a rather polite debate with Pierre Bourque at a Canadian Club luncheon in December 2003, during which we both agreed the megacity had not created any savings. Bourque blamed Tremblay and I blamed the megacity. Bourque felt Tremblay's plan was too decentralized; I maintained Tremblay was trying to have his cake and eat it too. "A decentralized megacity is akin to forcing people to marry and then giving them permission to fool around. But they can't go all the way," I said.

Tremblay maintained that his relatively mild decentralization plan would save $225 million a year.[13] He was leading with his chin on that one. If just a bit of decentralization saved that much, a radical decentralization plan – let's call it "demerger" for short – would save a fortune. And this, in a nutshell, was Tremblay's problem, and the problem faced by anybody, even the municipal magician Louis Bernard, who thought it was possible to achieve a truly decentralized megacity that could still be called a megacity. They were trying to square the circle. The more they decentralized, the more it became fuel to the demerger flame, as the end state of any process of decentralization of the megacity was a collection of individual municipalities. After all, if boroughs could be legally incorporated, if they could hire and fire, if they could borrow and tax freely, why, each of them would be a municipality again. And if boroughs can't do any of those things, you can't really call it decentralization. You just call it a city. As Gertrude Stein would have put it, a city is a city is a city.

TREMBLAY'S RAINBOW COALITION LOSES SOME COLOUR

Needless to say, all this internal wrangling about how much to decentralize came at a price. Pointe-Claire's former mayor and current megacity councillor Bill McMurchie was already sitting as an independent – where he sat with Karin Marks, the city councillor for Westmount who up until then had been the lone independent. From the moment of the Liberal victory, various former mayors who were members of Tremblay's party did not hide their partiality to demerger and seemed ripe to go for independence. The former mayor of Anjou, Luis Miranda, declared he wanted his municipality back and that it was too late to fix the megacity: Tremblay had done nothing to decentralize it, he said. Ed Janiszewski, the former mayor of Dollard-des-Ormeaux, while not initially in favour of demerger, was keen on the halfway compromise of the 2000 Bernard Report, a system of "city-boroughs." Bernard's reaction was that it was too late to do that, earning the rejoinder from Janiszewski that Bernard was a *vendu* because he was hired by Montreal.[14]

After various attempts at reconciliation with Tremblay, usually followed by press releases reaffirming their commitment to the megacity, those former mayors who felt increasingly uncomfortable trying to match their pro-demerger electoral promises with Tremblay's increasingly militant anti-demerger stance and feeble decentralization plan quit his party, one by one. The first to go after the Liberal win was the former mayor of Sainte-Anne-de-Bellevue, a jovial, free-thinking rugby-playing Irishman called Bill Tierney. After telling a reporter, "I don't give a shit about the mayor," he was kicked out of the party – to his immense satisfaction – by the very object of his preposition.

By the time Tremblay revealed his new organizational model in mid-August, he made it clear to his remaining pro-demerger councillors that they would have to cleave to the party line or leave. Luis Miranda promptly did the latter. In October, the former mayor of Baie d'Urfé and staunch demergerite Anne Myles trounced Tremblay's hand-picked candidate in a Beaconsfield by-election, attracting 69 per cent of the votes to his 19 per cent. The next renegade to go from Tremblay's party was the councillor for Mount Royal, Suzanne Caron. Then in December, after some tergiversation, the former mayor of Kirkland, John Meaney, left, followed by Ed Janiszewski, the former mayor of Dollard-des-Ormeaux. By the end of 2003, Tremblay's party had lost seven megacity councillors and thirteen borough councillors to the demerger cause, all of whom sat as independents.[15] Tremblay had to engineer a transfusion from Bourque's party to keep his majority on council.

Tremblay himself had long shucked off any pretence of remaining neutral on demergers. He publicly complained that, without a minimum turnout of 50 per cent in demerger referenda, a minority would decide the fate of the megacity.[16] Then the megacity's executive committee spent $300,000 in legal fees in order to investigate possible "legal contestations regarding the demerger bill" and to "defend the integrity" of the megacity.[17] Not only did Tremblay fight against demergers themselves but in September 2003 he also tried to delay the holding of demerger referendums by two years to give the megacities a chance to show their mettle. Rather than having to wrestle demergers to the mat, he understandably preferred to delay the ring being built.

BILL 9: THE LIBERALS BACK OFF ON THEIR PROMISE

Tremblay was just one of our problems. Barely two months after winning the election primarily owing to the demerger promise, the presentation of Bill 9 (the draft law permitting demergers) in mid-June 2003 was the first solid evidence of just how much the Liberals were going to back-pedal on this solemn promise. Municipal Affairs Minister Fournier had steadfastly refused to meet with me, but he met regularly with the megacity mayors. It did not help matters that the same bureaucrats who had written the very law that forced mergers were now trying their best to concoct a demerger law. As for the rest of the Liberal government, their political "centre of gravity" had migrated into the same territory occupied by the megacities.

I never stopped reminding the Liberals that the original wording in their October 2000 resolution committed them to "annul" the forced mergers. During the 2003 election campaign, this pledge had simply been reinforced, albeit with a twist: Charest said he had a favourable bias towards the new cities. Moreover, it was always understood that the demerging municipalities would "pay their fair share" of regional expenses, as they had done, in Montreal at least, through the MUC. Less than ten days before voting day, the term "fair share" got a technocratic makeover and was re-baptized "agglomeration-wide tax," the new term to describe how demerged municipalities would pay for services received from the megacity. There was no mention of the megacities retaining more services than the MUC had administered before the mergers. It was always a question of simply "annulling" the mergers.

My blood pressure doubled on reading Bill 9. It stipulated in black and white that the megacity would retain, as well as all the regional services originally supplied by the old MUC, "fire protection," "municipal court," "garbage elimination," and "arterial roads." There had been no mention of these things sticking to the megacity's ribs in the event of demerger, and certainly we had been provided with no rationale, debate, or consultation on this massive change – this from a political group who tirelessly, and with reason, excoriated their adversaries for not consulting on the forced mergers. What Bill 9 did was to bless and perpetuate the forced mergers as far as these four services went. Any former municipality that demerged would do so minus great hunks of its former responsibilities.

I was reminded of the aphorism that promises are like babies: they are easy to make, hard to deliver. From Bill 9 on, Fournier lectured us there would be no going back to "the old sandboxes," no going back to the "status quo ante," without ever telling us why. He did a marvellous imitation of Louise Harel with her "the status quo is not an option."

WE HEAR FROM LOUIS BERNARD

After his involvement in the creation of the megacity of Montreal, Bernard had become the municipal guru for the PQ, the Liberals, and Mayor Tremblay. Without question the man was brilliant, engagingly self-effacing, honest, and very persuasive. However, he had little experience in matters municipal. Mind you, in that he was on a par with all the other actors involved in the radical reshaping the municipal landscape in Quebec including Louise Harel, and now Minister Fournier. I quote Bernard at length, not just because his reasoning is refreshingly limpid but because he exercised such an influence over Harel and Fournier. Ever the Merlin of the municipal, Bernard held out the possibility of pleasing both sides in a bitter debate. You want one city? You want many cities? Here's how you reconcile the two positions, Bernard said. During the parliamentary hearings for Bill 9, he revealed why he had come up with the borough system:

> Traditionally, a municipality meant local services. When a citizen thinks of his or her municipality, he or she thinks snow and garbage removal, recreation, library, and so forth ... because of this, when we talk of municipal restructuring, the citizen has as a reflex to say: the government wants to reorganize the way local services are delivered. Will it give me better services? Will it cost less? And the citizen judges the result of the municipal reform in regard to its effect on local services ... Now, the recent municipal reform had nothing to do with local services. It's not for local services that we felt municipal reform was necessary. It was because during the twentieth century in Quebec, in common with the rest of the world, a new reality called the large urban agglomeration had developed, and it's that reality that was at the heart of the reform.
>
> The [mega]city of Montreal, which is at the centre of the agglomeration and which represents over one-half its population, was given a double role: to serve as the main motor of the Montreal agglomeration and to ensure leadership within the Montreal Metropolitan Community. This is why the Montreal [mega]city has important strategic functions to fulfill; in particular, the economic, social, and cultural development of the whole Montreal agglomeration. Along with its strategic functions, the [mega]city of Montreal inherited the responsibility for common services that had been delivered by the Montreal Urban Community; that is, police, wastewater treatment, mass transit. Obviously, the [mega]city, as well, kept its traditional mission of delivering local services. The problem, therefore, presented itself: how can we at the

same time enlarge the city, give it new responsibilities, and make
sure it can continue to deliver to its citizens the local services, for
which, intuitively, people feel that local control is important?

When you create only one city, there is a danger of homogen-
ization. Now, we didn't want to encourage that. We wanted to
keep the diversity. And, obviously, in Montreal, there was the
additional problem of linguistic status that we wanted to preserve. How, then, to create a megacity in order to be able to better provide common services in a more democratic way, have
boosted strategic functions, and, at the same time, retain the ability to give people local services that meet their needs?[18]

Bernard went on to explain that the megacity's manifold roles, as
he described them above, were the reason why he had come up with
the borough system to handle local services: boroughs, in fact, with
more autonomy than the law finally gave them. Unfortunately, he
just took for granted – or was told to take for granted – that it was
necessary to "enlarge" the former City of Montreal, which was the
cause of all this role-juggling in the first place.

During this same presentation, Bernard also gave his explanation
of the agglomeration-wide tax:

In an agglomeration like Montreal, the market value, and therefore the tax value, of a property is not created by one or the
other party, but by the agglomeration as such. It's the agglomeration that creates the value of all the properties in an agglomeration. Now, that's very easy to understand. Take all the properties
in Westmount. You don't change them, you keep the same quality
of architecture, materials, site, and so on, and you move them to
a far-away region, you put them in Abitibi, you put them in the
North Shore, you put them in Murdochville – you'll see the value
of those properties drop dramatically. Why? Because they are not
located where they could have value. That, that's the phenomenon of economic rent that was described by Ricardo 200 years
ago. I don't think it's an invention; it's a universal phenomenon.*

---

* If Westmount did not exist, property values of the whole agglomeration would drop
too, probably by a greater amount. Every agglomeration needs and is enriched by the
existence of a well-run residential community close to downtown that caters to both the

So, when we talk about an agglomeration-wide tax, that's what we are trying to say. We are seeking uniform taxation for the entire agglomeration, and that's what we currently have in [the megacity of] Montreal. As we speak, there is a real agglomeration-wide tax because there is only one system of taxation for all the Island of Montreal. And I submit to this committee that, if we allow at one point some municipalities to leave the megacity of Montreal, it must be crystal clear that they continue to contribute in exactly the same way they contribute today; that is to bear their fair share of all the municipal responsibilities of Montreal.

The observant reader may have noticed that Bernard used the term "agglomeration" for the Island in this last quote, and used it for the whole metropolitan region in the first quote. He thereby revealed a big lapse in his reasoning. It should be the whole metropolitan "agglomeration," *Greater Montreal*, that should share regional costs, not just the Island of Montreal. This confusion, this use of bifocals when looking at the Island and looking at the whole region, this insular obsession, was the principal reason for the hash the PQ made of their municipal "reform" and the rehash the Liberals subsequently contributed.

While this was going on, I had just consummated a merger myself. After making the best decision ever made in my life, I, in full dress uniform, married Kathryn Stephenson at a Westmount church on a gloriously sunny afternoon on 6 September. For a while I forgot all about the arcana of municipal restructuring. But immediately on arriving back from our honeymoon, I took part in presenting a seventy-six page brief to the parliamentary hearings on Bill 9, raking the Liberals over the coals for their "partial demergers," pointing out that during the elections they used the word "demerger." Their policy was to "annul" the mergers. Charest said time and time again during the provincial election that municipalities would be allowed to demerge. He never said to "partially demerge."

middle classes and yes, to the small, wealthy element that is essential to a functioning agglomeration. In selling the Montreal region to outside investors, Westmount is one of the secret weapons. Prospective investors look at where they will live before looking at where their office or factory will be located.

By the third week in September 2003, polls showed demerger sentiment was slowly weakening outside Montreal Island. In Quebec City, only half the residents of suburbs that were merged now wanted to demerge. In the megacity of Longueuil on the south shore of Montreal, 56 per cent of those who had been merged wanted the merger to be reversed. On the Island of Montreal, 66 per cent of the suburbs still wanted to demerge and 34 per cent were against.[19]

KEEPING TABS ON MIDDLE-AGED SUBURBAN INSURRECTIONISTS

In October, Quebecers were shocked to learn that the provincial police – the Sûreté du Québec – had launched an investigation into the activities of demergerites. Something called the Department of the Protection of the State, a unit of the SQ, had started the investigation on its own initiative. A detective met with about a dozen people, including Francine Gadbois, the former mayor of Boucherville. The police were worried about "things getting out of hand," they said, and the best way to see what people are up to was to meet with them. The detective asked questions such as "What will you do if demergers don't happen?" Saint-Bruno resident Ginette Durocher, the voluble and gutsy woman who headed up the pan-Quebec demerger group, simply refused to meet with the police. Jacques Chagnon, the minister of public security, called the whole thing "ridiculous" and put a stop to it, saying "the fishing expeditions are over." Apparently, I was the next fish on their list. "All I want is my city back," I said to the media. "Someone stole it from me. I consider that a crime. *That*'s what should be investigated."

COUNCILLORS, CITIZENS GROUPS, AND EX-MAYORS TURN UP THE HEAT

In late October 2003, twenty-three Montreal borough and city councillors – eight of them still members of Tremblay's party – called a press conference in Westmount, militating for complete demerger and for normal referendum rules. This was followed by a rally for the demerger of Saint-Laurent, and then twenty-two Montreal citizen groups sent a letter to Minister Fournier. I organized a press conference in Quebec City with a common front of demerger leaders from across Quebec, representing some thirty-six merged municipalities. We complained that, while Charest had promised to remain neutral during the demerger debate, Fournier, who had still not met with us, was anything but neutral. We said that the PQ's flouting the democratic process by imposing mergers would not be set right by a cooked referendum process with the main purpose of axing the number of demergers.

The day after this press conference, the leader of the Opposition, Bernard Landry, picked up the "annulment" theme I had been bleating on about for months, and said it better than ever I did when he attacked Fournier during the 4 November question period of the National Assembly:

> Yesterday, the former mayor of Westmount, Peter Trent, and the former mayor, Réjean Simard, of La Baie, said that they were expecting a return to the status quo ante. The minister of municipal affairs said a number of times that there was no question of that, but the former mayors replied, "We never heard that from the premier." Could the premier clear up this matter once and for all and say plainly to Peter Trent and to Réjean Simard that they were misled ... ?
>
> You promised the annulment of these mergers. An-nul-ment. Do we need to bring out Latin expressions to make you understand what that particular word means? It means: "is null and void." As we say in law, that means – it never happened. That's what you had promised. And now you're busy deceiving that minority of people who had the temerity to believe in you.

Both Charest and Fournier made the same rejoinder: "We were always very clear. We told them often that there would be no going back to the status quo ante." One small problem – the Liberals never said that until *after* they won the election: all they said before or during the electoral period was that there would be a sharing of common expenses, which they baptized the agglomeration-wide tax. Their saying they always promised only a partial demerger might be called a self-prophesying fulfillment.

The editorialist Michel Auger of *Le Journal de Montréal*, in common with all francophone commentators, was strongly against demerger. Nevertheless, two days after this exchange in the National Assembly, he summed things up neatly regarding the Liberals' sudden switch to only permitting partial demergers, thereby denying full reconstitution of former municipalities:

> This is rich. Today, the Liberals would have us believe that they never promised to reconstitute the former cities that demerge. Pardon?
>
> Tuesday [4 November], in the National Assembly, Premier Charest said he had always proposed a three-fold process: a respect for democracy, an agglomeration-wide tax, and a will to ensure the success of the new cities. It was a great attempt at rewriting history; but before the election, when Mr Charest was talking about three steps, they only had to do with the mechanism for the demerger referendums; that is, the opening the registers, information on the costs of demerger, and the referendums themselves. The problem with the Liberals is that, when one compares their current policy with their former promises, one sees they are playing a double game ...
>
> There was no question, as they are now pretending, that the cities would only recover a part of their former powers and that they would have to leave services such as the fire department or the municipal court to the megacity ... This latest twist, which has nothing to do with the notion of an agglomeration-wide tax, only happened in the autumn, during the parliamentary hearings on Bill 9.

A MEETING WITH CHAREST

A few days later, Bernard Paquet (the former mayor of Saint-Laurent), Francine Gadbois (the former mayor of Boucherville), and I finally met with Jean Charest. The day before, Charest had met with Tremblay and was upset that Tremblay had blabbed to the media about two things: Charest's supposed foot-dragging in turning Tremblay's decentralization plan into law, and the Liberals' proposal of a structure for the Island of Montreal to handle common services in the event of demerger. "I'm fed up," Mayor Tremblay was quoted as saying. We assured Charest we would be well behaved.

While Charest was well briefed, it probably was the first time he had heard at some length as to why demergers made sense – which in itself irritated us and turned our ninety-minute meeting into an uphill climb. We tried to explain what the real problems of the region were, problems that trebling the size of Montreal by merging the former city, the Island suburbs, and the MUC only made worse. We went on about the 40 per cent premium Montreal paid its employees, the plethora of structures in the region, and the success that an urban competitor, the Boston region, was having with its constellation of 282 municipalities.[20]

We then talked referendums. Charest agreed with us that only 10 per cent of the voters needed to sign the register to kick off the referendum for demerger, but asked, "What if only 17 per cent of the eligible voters actually vote in the referendum? We need to be able to void the results in that case." He was not aware of the traditional allergy of tenants to voting municipally, nor of the execrable state of the voting lists, which together completely skewed the turnout rate. He was convinced that a minimum turnout was necessary, and nothing we said could dissuade him.

We did much better when we asked Charest why he and Minister Fournier were always making their "You won't get your old cities back" proclamations. We finally sorted it out. While on Montreal Island we had been paying for common services for over thirty years through the MUC, most other merged municipalities all over Quebec had no such cost-sharing. So, if any of the other municipalities demerged (such as on the south shore of Montreal), they would be stuck with the unpleasant novelty of contributing to regional costs. For us on the Island it would be status quo ante.

Then we got onto the "partial demerger" problem. I asked Charest, "What is the point of keeping things like the courthouses or fire departments merged? In pre-merger Westmount, for example, we had firefighters who belonged to an in-house union, who knew Westmount like the back of their hands, and who spent a lot of their time doing house inspections to prevent fires. We are trading all that in for Montreal firefighters who punched holes in their hoses, sabotaged trucks, and thought nothing of being shifted around to different communities all over the Island." Charest did not provide a satisfactory answer. He did say he would arrange a meeting for me with Minister Fournier. It never happened.

THE PRO-MERGERITES RETURN FIRE

As well as spending $600,000 to investigate decentralization as an alternative to demerger, and another $300,000 in legal fees to "defend the integrity" of the megacity, in November the executive committee went out for bids on $2.25 million of publicity and public relations, supposedly to be used over the next three years. The megacity spokesperson did not deny the spending was to fight demergers. Apparently, "the quantity and the complexity of the challenges the city is faced with require us to go out and get external support for a long period."[21]

What cost nothing was Mayor Tremblay's "Montreal Charter of Rights,"[22] which was designed to "empower citizens to participate more in city affairs." It guaranteed residents access to good-quality drinking water in sufficient quantities, immediate shelter for homeless people upon demand, reduction of noise pollution, and opposition to all forms of discrimination. History is silent as to how many demergerites were converted thanks to this charter.

On 18 November, a group called Coalition Montreal held a splashy press conference. This impressive group, made up of some two hundred academics, artists, business people, labour leaders, and social activists, was organized by Benoit Labonté of the Board of Trade. Alongside the names of hockey hero Jean Béliveau, former premier Lucien Bouchard, Power Corporation's André Desmarais, philosopher Charles Taylor, the rector of the Université de Montréal, and developer Philip O'Brien, I was shocked to see the name of David Culver, the former chairman of Alcan who supported my fight against mergers. I had also been given the impression, at least before the mergers, that Bernard Shapiro (former principal of McGill) and philanthropist and architectural passionara Phyllis Lambert (the daughter of Samuel Bronfman) had been on my side. It seemed that, while they were against mergers, they were now against demergers.

Coalition Montreal's clarion call for the megacity in 350 words was possibly poetic, but offered nothing to sink one's teeth into: "The heart of Montreal beats because Montrealers feel a strong sense of pride and belonging. It is up to us, its citizens, to make of it what we will. Because Montreal is our city ... Since Montreal belongs to all of us, the challenges posed by the creation of a new city give us good reasons to close ranks, roll up our sleeves, and work together. Because we are Montreal, it is up to us to create a city in our own image."[23]

Coalition Montreal promised a powerful campaign to dog us demergerites right until the day of reckoning when the demerger referendums were to be held. Here I was, with Ginette Durocher, alone as the only full-time (and unpaid) demergerites in Quebec, with precious little wherewithal, pitted against the might of the Government of Quebec, the megacity, the media, the unions, and now the deep pockets of Coalition Montreal. To our relief, Coalition Montreal sank without a trace.

Early in December I had lunch with the editorialist of *La Presse*, André Pratte, a cerebral, articulate man for whom I have immense respect. It irritated me that the merger and demerger issues were the only ones on which we seemed to disagree. We got absolutely nowhere: I was surprised how a man of his intellect could wax enthusiastic about the megacity based on unproven assertions and empty appeals to solidarity; he, no doubt, was convinced I just wanted to hang onto the remaining shreds of my power, swaddled in a nostalgia for my "little fiefdom," as he was wont to call it.

BUILDING THE NEW CITY ...
ONE BUREAUCRAT AT A TIME

With the 2004 Montreal megacity budget revealed in late November 2003, the magic wand of mergers was starting to droop. Even the most rabid megacity supporter could see that the 5 per cent savings Premier Bouchard promised would come from merging was so much moonshine. Faced with the threat of demergers, the megacity was not exactly putting its best financial foot forward. In one year, the budgeted costs to run the megacity were scheduled to go up by 5.6 per cent, at a time when inflation in Montreal was oscillating between 2.0 per cent and 2.4 per cent.[24] Administrative costs were up 11.4 per cent. The number of managers and foremen went from 2,086 to 2,233 in two years, and their cost was up an astounding 24 per cent.[25] This budget was a textbook case illustrating the kind of post-merger flab economists had predicted.

Tremblay got busy bureaucratizing his executive committee. He created four new "strategic committees" that co-opted both executive committee members and garden-variety city councillors. The megacity, he said, "now has a new Charter that puts into place the decentralization model as well as greater cohesion and synergy. This is why I created strategic committees, which will encourage teamwork and allow the executive committee to be more efficient while accentuating the interdependence between the different sectors of activity." In case the average Joe had no idea what this meant,

Tremblay explained, "I want to assure Montrealers that these adjustments are a clear demonstration of our desire to put citizens at the heart of our preoccupations."[26]

Thanks to Tremblay's decentralization plan, now given the force of law, it wasn't long before some newly elevated borough mayors and their councils exercised, with some evident relish, their freshly endowed power of legislating the amount of their own pay-cheques, each making "a warm personal gesture by the individual to himself," as J.K. Galbraith put it. In February 2004, the Saint-Leonard borough council gave notice they were increasing borough councillor salaries from $39,000 to $58,000.[27] Frank Zampino, borough mayor of Saint-Leonard and Tremblay's financial czar, thought it was a good idea: "This gives an increased stature to the borough councillors' role and avoids treating them like second-class councillors."[28] Even before decentralization, the megacity had seventy-three councillors who were making a minimum of $58,000 each, while the thirty-one "second-class" borough councillors had been making $39,000. And these were part-time jobs. Compared with Toronto's council of forty-five, Ottawa's twenty-two, and Vancouver's eleven, Montreal's council was not only unworkable because of its size but cost a good sight more.

THE DEMERGER AND ANTI-DEMERGER CAMPAIGNS GET UNDERWAY

The little clandestine demerger group I had set up in 2002 had steadily grown, swollen with the defectors from Tremblay's party. By January 2004 we were out of the closet, coordinating the demerger activities of seventeen former municipalities on the Island of Montreal, plus some on the south shore. I was the spokesperson. Luckily, there was still quite a bit of money left from the half-million dollars Westmount had given the Citizens' Association for the Preservation of Westmount in late 2000. That money paid for things such as studies, leaflets delivered to some 270,000 Montreal Island households, radio spots, and grants to grassroots groups outside Westmount. As for Westmount itself, in January we had set up storefront demerger headquarters with a full-time employee. Bernard Paquet, the former mayor of Saint-Laurent, and I went from place to place like itinerant showmen, giving speeches at dozens of rallies during February, March, and April.

By February 2004, Tremblay had also put his political party on a war footing. A new statute permitted the expulsion of any party member who did not agree with the party's anti-demerger position. Tremblay also declared that his party, rather than the megacity, would fund all the costs of any anti-demerger campaign.[29] Yet the month before, the megacity's executive committee had named the firms[30] who would be paid $2.25 million for public relations and communications work. Ah, said the mayor, this money was not earmarked to *fight demerger*, but to *explain decentralization*. But decentralization was Tremblay's only weapon against demerger, as he readily admitted. "Why demerge?" he asked in a typical speech. "To manage your own affairs? There's no need to demerge for that! The new Charter of Montreal allows the boroughs to have the same powers as before the mergers in terms of local services [*sic*]."[31] One of the megacity's advertisements trumpeted: "Pre-Merger Powers Restored."[32]

So the megacity could spend money selling decentralization as the alternative to demerger, but the boroughs, now supposedly autonomous, could not promote demerger. This was all very logical and legal: the boroughs had no independent legal existence, and you can't have parts of the megacity spending its money trying to break itself up. But it really did not seem fair. This was brought home when the borough of Mount Royal passed a resolution authorizing an expenditure of a modest $20,000 to fund a local demerger group. The director-general of the megacity, on orders from Mayor Tremblay and publicly supported by Minister Fournier, formally instructed the Mount Royal director-general to annul the resolution. After an unsuccessful attempt to get an injunction to reverse this directive, Mount Royal backed down. The episode was an unintended object lesson on the difference between being a supposedly decentralized borough and being an independent municipality. In mid-April 2004, full-page ads appeared in many community newspapers, featuring a letter signed by Tremblay containing the following sentence: "Montreal decision-makers will not impose their vision on local communities, who remain in control of their own destiny."

THWARTED BY PEOPLE WHO CAN'T VOTE

April 2004 saw hundreds of volunteers in the keenest demerger fortresses like Pointe-Claire, Mount Royal, Baie d'Urfé, and Westmount poring over voting lists, trying to purge them of the tens of thousands of names of people who were not eligible to vote. Bizarre examples abounded: three people were listed in one apartment, two of whom were dead; antepenultimate owners were still listed as current owners; fifty people who were renting post-office boxes in one outlet alone were listed as electors; ex-husbands were listed as being reunited with ex-wives; and children were listed who had moved to the United States years before. To get names removed was no small matter: it required showing up at the revision office armed with a death certificate or proof that someone had moved. All the while, the director-general of elections maintained the lists were "very, very reliable" and "the envy of other provinces."[33] When demergerites complained and demanded door-to-door enumerations, Minister Fournier snapped, "Why didn't they say that after the last election? How come for this issue the list is no good and at the last election it was?"[34] We couldn't believe our ears. Fournier of all people knew that, for the first time in Quebec history, a minimum turnout was required; the more the voting lists were inflated, the higher the bar he was setting by requiring that 35 per cent of potential voters must vote for demerger. You might say accurate numbers divided by garbage equals garbage.

In the six days allowed for the first revision – which included Easter – places such as Anjou and Saint-Laurent could not even begin to clean up the lists: it would have required thousands of volunteers. Even with a second revision in June, many errors remained. This is not to say that permanent electoral lists are not a good idea, just that they should be updated by door-to-door enumeration, not by means of an incomprehensible legal flyer addressed to "the occupant." Besides, having real people, as was done in the past, come to your door brings home (literally) the fact an election or a referendum is nigh. One significant cause of the apparently low voter turnout in Quebec elections over the past few decades could very well be owing to terribly inaccurate electoral lists.

TO DEMERGE OR DISMEMBER: THAT IS THE QUESTION

By March, Minister Fournier's office was already saying the referendum question would not use the word "demerger," purportedly because "this word is not in the dictionary. It is not French, and to put it in the law could create a problem in the event of any legal contestation."[35] To his credit, Mayor Tremblay did not agree. He was in favour of a simple, clear question. His suggestion was: "Do you want demerger?" "It's all very well and good to want to find other terms," Tremblay said, "but 'demerger' is the word that creates no confusion and that says in a clear fashion what some people want. In 1989, the word 'proactive' did not exist until I invented it, any more than the words 'industrial clusters' existed before 1991. The word 'demerger' does not exist in the French language, but it's very clear and every one knows what it means."[36]

In April we were spitting angry when we learned that the referendum question, in French, would actually use the term "dismemberment [démembrement] of the megacities" rather than "demerger of the megacities." In either language, the first definition of "dismember" is "to tear the limbs from." In French, the second definition is as tendentious, if less gory: "Divide into parts that which should stay whole." Only a few linguists were aware of its third, very obscure meaning as a technical term from administrative law.[37]

Strangely, the English version of the referendum question used the neutral "de-amalgamation" instead of dismemberment. Westmounters were to be asked, "Are you in favour of the de-amalgamation of Ville de Montréal and the constitution of a municipal entity for the sector of Westmount, in accordance with the Act respecting the consultation of citizens with respect to the territorial reorganization of certain municipalities?" Note that the first image presented is the breaking up of Montreal, something likely to induce guilt. But in French, who could possibly be in favour of *dismembering* the City of Montreal? The word suggested that the Montreal megacity was a whole, living organism that had thrived for years, rather than an artificial construct recently cobbled together by force. Then, instead of talking about the *re*-constitution of the *City* of Westmount, we got "the constitution of a municipal entity," leaving all but the demerger cognoscenti scratching their heads. What on earth was a municipal entity?

We were indeed far from the simple annulment of forced mergers and, in French, close to the most biased referendum question ever posed in Quebec.

DUELLING STUDIES

Back in late March we had been cheered by support from an unexpected quarter. Pierre Fortin, who has been described as "the most influential economist in Quebec," with a "clear sympathy for the PQ" to boot, wrote a one-page article demolishing the pro-merger economic arguments.[38] First of all, he wrote, all empirical evidence shows that after a merger, services cost more and taxes increase simply because service levels and union pay scales rise to the highest common denominator. Moreover, large municipalities are crushed under the weight of their bureaucracies, which are slow to respond to residents' needs. He supported the conclusion of fellow economist (and Poitras Report contributor) François Des Rosiers that the Montreal megacity would cost at least $200 million more a year to run. And as for fiscal equity, Fortin wrote, that could be arranged simply without merger. As for mergers helping economic development, he cited the Boston and San Francisco regions with their hundreds of municipalities. In sum, he wrote, municipal mergers were an economic mirage. Politically, however, they were just the ticket for big-city mayors and unions to increase their power and for the provincial government to simplify their work.

Then, in mid-April 2004, it was my turn to lift the curtain on a study. Knowing that at the end of the month the government was going to release studies on the cost of demerger, I had tried to get someone to do our own studies to counteract the now-obvious government bias against demerger. The government studies were costing $3.5 million, but all we could afford was a more general, economic study that got underway in January. However, since the government studies would only be looking at the short-term financial impact of demergers, it was important to look at their long-term economic effects. The group of well-known economists who produced our report, the Analysis Group, came to similar conclusions to the Poitras Report and Pierre Fortin: the megacity would cost hundreds of millions more a year, and therefore any reborn municipality would at least partially escape the megacity's financial fate. The Analysis Group report estimated that in just two years the megacity had spent $88 million more in wages and benefits – and that was after inflation.[39] "Inflationary salary increases of the megacity create a direct transfer of money from property owners to the employees of the megacity," said Patrick Petit, the lead author. The study calculated that the direct economic impact of the creation of the megacity and its inevitable tax increases could be a possible loss of $2.1 billion in economic activity and a possible loss of real-estate values of $3.7 billion. Any demergers would attenuate these costs.

A week after our report, out came the government studies by SECOR Consulting. The francophone press had a field day of apocalyptic headlines: "$100 Million to 'Dismember' Montreal"; "Cold Shower for the Suburbs"; "Expensive Bill for the Former Cities"; "Demerger Will Be More Catastrophic Than What SECOR Predicts, Says Tremblay"; and "The Real Price of Demergers."[40] Only the Toronto-based *Globe and Mail* ran headlines such as: "Studies Cite Advantages of De-Amalgamation."

SECOR had the unenviable task of trying to figure out the effect of demerger on single-family property tax bills for each former municipality on the Island of Montreal. The government both misrepresented and misunderstood the SECOR report. I discovered they misunderstood the cost of demerging by a factor of seven.[41] While I managed to get the government website corrected, brochures mailed to every household on Montreal Island bore incorrect numbers. Even worse, the government misrepresented as permanent the first-year tax bill increases attendant to demerger, when in fact the difference between leaving and staying would diminish with time. Estimated tax increases were given as ranging up to 28 per cent, with an average of 14 per cent – enough to turn off even some diehard demergerites. What was nowhere to be found in any of the government's publications was that estimated long-term increases averaged only 7 per cent.[42] The calculated tax effect on the former City of Montreal of every former suburb leaving was nil.

Of course, all these numbers had to be taken with a Mount Royal sized grain of salt: we know (as the Poitras Report predicted) that demerging all of Montreal would have saved over $200 million a year, so it made no sense that SECOR predicted it would actually *cost* money – at least for the homeowner.[43] Unfortunately, because the government reneged on its promise to annul the mergers completely and cleanly, quite a few formerly local services were now centralized, and so some of the savings from demerging would vanish. SECOR calculated that centralized services would represent 63 per cent of all costs and that services under local control by a demerged municipality would only represent 37 per cent. Before the merger, in the former suburbs, roughly 38 per cent of the cost of services was centralized under the old MUC and 62 per cent was under local control.[44] This was the cold accounting result of the Liberals' decision to allow only partial demergers.

18

Rebirth for Some, Complexity for All

Human blunders usually do more to shape history than human wickedness.

A.J.P. Taylor, 1961

Agglomerate: verb. 1. Collect into a mass. 2. Accumulate in a disorderly way.

Shorter Oxford English Dictionary

It was now well over two years since my dis-election as mayor and my reinvention as the self-imposed, full-time, pro-bono leader of the demerger movement. In January 2002 I had started off this new job alone, but by now there were dozens of elected officials and thousands of citizens keen to fight the good demerger fight. I, however, was getting a little tired. All my working life I had been involved in creating things; now I was not even trying to *re*create things, I was trying to semi-recreate things. Paradoxically, Mayor Tremblay wanted to get on with the very activity I liked – to create. Of course, I was fiercely opposed to what it was he was creating.

Months after our wedding in September 2003, Kathryn and I finally found a house we liked and moved in together. I joked that most people live together rather than getting married, but we got married rather than live together. This house had not suffered the humiliation of having its back garden be-decked, its ceilings pot-lighted, its bathrooms jacuzzied, its interior brick exposed, its pine woodwork stripped, and its rooms open-concepted. Renovating and restoring this old house in 2004 gave me great pleasure. It was creative, at least. But it was Kath's support that saw me through the rest of that spring.

My decision in 2001 not to run for an elected position in the megacity out of principle started to become a liability. It was not so much that I was personally unaware of what was going on in the megacity but that in the media few remembered or cared as to why I did not run. I was now simply an ex-politician. Or an "activist."

DEMERGER WAS PERMANENT; POWERS CAN CHANGE

One of the arguments for demerger I continually used was that while the piece of legislation that limited the powers of demerged municipalities could be changed, there was only one chance to demerge. In other words, one day, demerged municipalities could have additional powers transferred to them from the agglomeration council that handled regional services; but, come what may, the remaining boroughs would be condemned forever to be part of the megacity – and possibly run the risk of getting docked some of the few powers they had. Of course, Minister Fournier denied that the demerger law would ever change ("turning back the clock is not an option"), but he could only speak for his government, not future governments.[1] I countered that eventually the agglomeration council would have to be changed: "In a modern democratic society, one cannot live with such a contrivance."[2] My nemesis, Louise Harel, happened to agree with me: "The government imposes a direct power of taxation without universal suffrage. [The agglomeration council] is a bastard model that won't last for the very good reason that it will quickly prove to be unmanageable." She went on to call it a "wasp's nest" (*un nid de chicanes*), the same appellation Minister Fournier reserved for the very thing it replaced, the MUC.[3]

While many agreed that the agglomeration councils would have to be revisited, even Bernard Landry said he would not "re-merge" the demerged municipalities. Those who vote to demerge "must live with their decision. We have no intention of reopening this can of worms. We have no intention of re-plunging people into uncertainty."[4]

UNIONS UNSURPRISINGLY AGAINST DEMERGER

After lagging talks that had dragged on for two years within the megacity, intensive labour negotiations in May revealed that the blue collars in former Island suburbs worked, on average, a 38.5-hour, five day week for $19 an hour, and their confreres in the former City of Montreal worked a 35-hour, four-day week for $22 an hour.[5] Total costs with benefits showed the same pattern. According to the Institut de la statistique du Québec, the average City of

Montreal blue collar cost $35.19 an hour "all in" in 2001 – 10 per cent higher, for example, than in the City of Westmount and 11 per cent higher than in the rest of the Montreal region.[6] Using statistics derived from the SECOR report, one can calculate that Montreal paid white and blue collar employees together 12 per cent more than the average paid in the former Island suburbs, and that was after two years of "harmonization."[7]

In the weeks leading up to the demerger referenda, blue collars resorted to their usual obstructive tactics, including hijacking quite a few city trucks and leaving them off in other boroughs, blocking the entrance to the Montreal Casino, and spreading tacks on the road that flattened a few tires. This was just fuel to the demerger flame – blue collar thuggery was no longer just the lot of the former City of Montreal: the megacity meant blue collars right across the Island, 6,200 strong, were represented by the same militant local. Then, the prize for the most unsurprising headline should have gone to the one that blazed out "White Collar Workers Support a United Montreal."[8] Ten thousand white collars opposed demerger, the article said. Why wouldn't they? Merger was an employees' bonanza. Salaries and positions in the former suburbs had been "reclassified" to Montreal's standards, which meant salary increases all around. Suburban employees had been already making roughly 30 per cent more than the rest of the public sector; now, they were happily migrating to the 40 per cent premium that the old City of Montreal paid.

CHAREST VOTES NO TO DEMERGER

Suddenly, after asking his ministers not to pronounce on the matter, Premier Jean Charest announced he was voting No in his hometown of Westmount. He repeated that he hoped the megacities would succeed, but he never explained why – or the reason he had changed his initial anti-merger position. Four of his ministers did go public with a pro-megacity stance, and five brave elected members of his party came out for demergers, but pointedly said they would not vote.

ONLY THE ENGLISH WANT TO DEMERGE?

The lead-up to the referenda began taking on more and more of a French-versus-English complexion. Montreal editorialists had the same insular fixation as politicians; and on the Island of Montreal, most "English" former suburbs wanted to demerge. This gave rise to a genuine worry of a language split, but a few of the worriers were shedding crocodile tears. Diane Lemieux, the PQ shadow minister of municipal affairs, blurted out in late May that francophones, sovereignists in particular, had "rowed like the damned" to create an atmosphere where the two linguistic communities could feel at home. Then, she said, along came the possibility of demerger. "In the east end of Montreal, they'll say, 'Hey, in the west, they don't like us? What don't they like about us? Why don't they want to be with us?'" As usual, Lysiane Gagnon put things in perspective: "Far from feeling, as Mme Lemieux suggests, "victimized" by the threats of demerger, the francophones in the rump-of-Montreal watch the train go by without passion. The passion is in the demergerists' camp, and it speaks French as much as English, it's in Sillery as much as in Westmount, and in Boucherville as much as in Pointe-Claire ... She already predicts that demerger will bring the "rupture" between the two communities! This enthusiasm for catastrophic scenarios is suspect: does Mme Lemieux salivate already at the idea of a new language war that would be grist to the mill for The Cause [sovereignty]?"[9]

In two long op-ed pieces in *La Presse* just before the demerger vote, Pierre Drouilly and Alain-G. Gagnon, professors at UQAM, picked up the "English ghetto" theme in a more sophisticated way. Each article was accompanied by the now-mandatory photos of Westmount. The two professors referred to the holding of demerger referendums as catering to "the domination of the interests of the rich over the collective future":

Thanks to a wave of individualism, the Liberals took advantage of the discontent of the affluent and the frustration of the residents of the established anglophone communities in order to improve their chances for political gain during the April 2003 elections. This short-sighted Liberal position helps undermine the social cohesion that characterizes Quebec since the 1960s, and encourages anglophone Montrealers to be the standard-bearers of Canadian multiculturalism – which is based on the juxtaposition of ethnic groups – rather than creating solidarity with the Quebec intercultural plan which is seen as a major advance in all the liberal democracies that have made as inescapable priorities the management of cultural diversity and the affirmation of citizens.[10]

Drouilly and Gagnon were wrong about the first part. As Don Macpherson pointed out, "The Liberals made the demerger promise in order to take seats from the Parti Québécois in French Quebec, not to hold seats in the West Island that were safely theirs to begin with."[11] But the two professors were embarrassingly right about the correlation between rich communities and high demerger sentiment. They wrote that, on the south shore, the municipalities that were likely to demerge had average family incomes that were anywhere from 26 per cent to 90 per cent higher than that of their central city, Longueuil. In Quebec City, demerger fever was highest in those former municipalities where average family incomes ran from 22 per cent to 115 per cent higher than that of the central city. On the Island of Montreal, municipalities that eventually would demerge had average family incomes that were from 50 per cent to 264 per cent higher than that of their central city, Montreal. It should be kept in mind, though, that average family property tax bills were usually much higher in peripheral cities than in central cities. The authors of the articles also found a high correlation between anglophone presence and demerger sentiment on Montreal Island.

MEDIA BIAS

The media's anti-demerger bias was constantly showing. Columnist Don Macpherson wrote, "Media coverage created the impression that of the 212 former municipalities across the province included in the forced mergers, half were named Westmount. Radio-Canada's reporter was there so often I expected her to take out membership in the lawn bowling club."[12] In the month before the June 20 referendum date, accompanying their various articles on demerger, *Le Devoir* ran nine separate photos of white-haired doddering seniors voting in Westmount. Often, they would manage to squeeze a STOP (rather than an ARRÊT) sign into the photo, which is Quebec code for anglodom. *La Presse* frequently used the word *démembrement* rather than *demerger* to the point that, on the south shore, some demergerists started to say, "*Ce n'est pas un démembrement, c'est le rejet d'une greffe!*" (It's not dismemberment: it's the rejection of a transplant). *La Presse* also ran huge beauty shots of Tremblay in colour, as did the *Montreal Gazette*, when that newspaper, to the surprise of all, came out against demerger.

After having delivered a constant barrage of over fifty editorial broadsides against the mergers over a number of years, the *Gazette* seemed to have lost its way during the demerger period. It was hard to follow. The paper referred to the Liberals' artificial and clearly dissuasive referendum barriers as constituting "ethical bankruptcy." "The whole process stinks," they wrote, going on to castigate Charest for not respecting his promise to undo the mergers completely and Tremblay for rendering "inoperative" his promise not to stand in the way of demergers. They encouraged everybody to sign the registers in order to require referenda be held. Then, three days before the vote, the paper threw up its hands and wrote "voting to demerge would be a mistake" as any demerged suburbs would be "powerless, almost voiceless subordinates of Montreal."[13]

TREMBLAY "WINS" THE TV DEBATES

After months of goading Tremblay into a televised debate, I finally got my wish a few weeks before the referenda. Going to the TV studio for the first debate, I was quite cocky, as it was generally assumed I would beat Tremblay hands down in either language. I got my comeuppance when he bested me, even in English. In that language, I was hectoring, glowering, jerky, intense, and far too technical. McLuhan would have called me "hot." Tremblay was soothing, with only a few excited patches. By the time I did the French debate a week later, I overcompensated, coming off as weak, forbearing, and boring. Tremblay was pumped up and convincing. While I might have spoken with more intellectual rigour, that was irrelevant. The media look for a bare-knuckle boxing match: winners and losers are declared based on which fighter lands the best verbal jabs to a surprised opponent. Truth, accuracy, and politeness go out the window. For weeks after the debates, I felt I had let my side down, as the media glee following my reported discomfiture was unbounded. I quote verbatim from selected parts of the debates.

EXCERPTS FROM THE DEBATE IN ENGLISH

TREMBLAY: Now you are facing a choice and we all have to be clear. The real choice is between a unified yet decentralized

Montreal or what is provided in Bill 9. To vote Yes adds nothing more in terms of local services that you already have. By voting Yes, you will abandon your right to choose the people who will manage two-thirds of your taxes. To vote Yes, you will lose a direct say in the management of your city. Is this what you really want?

TRENT: Well, if we stay in the megacity, all taxes continue to go downtown. We get a handout from the megacity, sort of like an allowance from daddy – if we're good. And they could cut the allowance at any time – by half – and there's nothing we could do about it. With demerger, every dollar of tax we tax locally will be returned to the citizens in the form of services.

TREMBLAY: Our decentralization model gave all the autonomy and all the power necessary to the boroughs to continue to maintain and improve the services, the personal contact with elected councillors, and community life. So power at the local level is in our decentralization model. Now what we're talking about and I'd like to ask you this question – one-third of your taxes will serve these local services. Two-thirds of taxes will go to an agglomeration council. The fundamental question that you have to ask yourselves: would I give my credit card – two-thirds of my credit card – to someone I have no influence over? I can't vote for that person. And that person is going to decide how to spend two-thirds of my taxes.

TRENT: Actually, it's not two-thirds but 59 per cent, but anyway.[14] And when we had the old MUC, 40 per cent of our taxes went to the MUC.[15] So we're going from 40 per cent to 59 per cent. It's not *that* much of an increase, Mr Tremblay. And, after all, a lot of that is a subsidy. Everybody was complaining we weren't contributing enough! ... If we remain as a borough of the megacity, we will have no legal status, no status as an employer, no power of taxation, no local union, and with no property rights. Montreal would continue to own all our assets.

TREMBLAY: I took averages for the boroughs. If you want to talk about Westmount, its 70 per cent versus 40 per cent. It used to be 40 per cent.[16] Twice as much money is going to the agglomeration council.*

---

* He was wrong. Westmount went from 59 per cent to 70 per cent. As I write this, 64 per cent of Westmount's taxes now go to the agglomeration, down from the predicted 70

EXCERPTS FROM THE DEBATE IN FRENCH

TREMBLAY: Three polls showed that 70 per cent of citizens [of the megacity] are satisfied. The boroughs kept the same budgets and even had surpluses ...

TRENT: If everyone were so satisfied with the services, why will there be referenda in twenty-two former cities? Why did you lose eighteen councillors, specifically because of their dissatisfaction? ...

TREMBLAY: The eighteen did work on getting the city decentralized, with the maximum autonomy possible. And that's what we gave them. They *were* satisfied. Then the new government was elected with Bill 9 that gave the possibility of demerger, *now* they want to demerge!

TRENT: Your interest in a decentralized city only arose the moment Charest was elected premier of Quebec ... One third of your team in fact had come to the conclusion that there would be no decentralization in the new city and therefore quit your party – because you had never done anything with regards to decentralization before Bill 9 ...

Can we now talk about unions, Mr Tremblay? We know that in Quebec municipal employees earn 30 per cent more than the rest of the public sector. Now, with the megacity, we have only one union of blue collars for the whole Island of Montreal. At one point, we'll have the four-day work week, not just in the former City of Montreal, but everywhere. Two weeks ago, 450 megacity trucks were hijacked by the blue collars. They blocked the entrance to the Casino. A year ago, the province investigated thirty-three cases of blue collar intimidation.[17] *That's* what we have created with the megacity.

TREMBLAY: Let's talk about blue collars: I think it is a good subject. It's 4 per cent, the difference in remuneration between the blue collars of the former City of Montreal and the blue collars of the former suburban cities. There were even some former suburban cities that paid their blue collars more than the City of Montreal blue collars, notably Westmount. In your city, you paid

---

per cent. It must be kept in mind that all remaining revenues go to fund local services, so the proportion of total revenues – as opposed to total taxes – now going to the agglomeration council is 54 per cent (Westmount), and 50 per cent (all the demerged suburbs).

your blue collars more: $35.25 versus $32.74! Even in Westmount, your rich city, supposedly well-managed, without fat –
you paid your blue collars more![18]

THE UNLOVED MEGACITY

In late May, columnist Lysiane Gagnon had neatly summarized both
the central city apathy to demerger and to the megacity itself:

First lesson: In a democratic society, governments cannot flout
the popular will with impunity. That's what Bouchard's government did with its forced merger law – to the applause of the
whole francophone media, it must be said. The PQ ... paid the
price in last year's elections, and we have seen this week that the
anger has not dissipated, in spite of all the obstacles put in the
way of the demergerists.

Second lesson: Reforms of this magnitude, as necessary as they
might be in the eyes of the élites, must be founded on popular
support. Yet it was already clear from the start that the residents
of the central cities were scarcely interested in the matter, even
though they were going to benefit from the mergers. The polls
at the time revealed that barely half of Montrealers approved
of the merger. The same indifference was showing this year. The
possibility of the dismantlement of Montreal, Quebec, or Longueuil provoked absolutely no reaction in the central cities. In
Montreal, we witnessed the birth of a committee of 200 luminaries coming to the defence of the megacity, but this committee
quickly disappeared from view. One of its members, [Robert]
Lacroix, rector of the Université de Montréal, explained himself the other day by saying the matter was in the hands of the
politicians. He can't be serious. Either that, or it shows that the
expanded Montreal does not deserve to survive, since no one in
civilian society wished to devote the smallest effort to it. In the
end, it turns out that only the megacity mayors are coming to the
defence of their respective fiefs. Yet, it is they who have the least
credibility, since they are fighting to keep their own job ...

Third lesson: Reforms, especially unpopular ones, must bring
something tangible. But the mergers, which led to a deterioration in services in the former suburban municipalities, did not
improve the lot of the residents of the former City of Montreal.

The administration is swollen, people can't find their way between the boroughs and the central city, the residential tax load has not dropped, the blue collars are not more efficient, the streets are even more poorly ploughed of snow than before, and the potholes are even bigger. It's not in asserting abstract advantages such as the one that says a megacity carries more weight internationally (which flies in the face, by the way, of a number of other municipal experiences – Boston, for example) that we overcome the daily frustrations of the voters.[19]

Gagnon went on to say that, in spite of all this, demerger would be "tragic," as the "main advantage" of the merger was to bring to the central city the "traditions of good management and citizen participation" of the former suburbs. With all the profound respect I have for Gagnon, I have to say she was dead wrong on this point. Because it was an annexation rather than a merger, the execrable management, apathetic citizenry, and endemic corruption of the former City of Montreal was being spread throughout the Island, just as some of us had predicted. The former suburban managers I consulted told me that, during the merger process, ex-Montreal, without exception, served as the unique template for megacity structures, organization, and methods.

Meanwhile, as an ambulant uncoverer of apathy, Tremblay ventured forth into the demergerist wilds of the West Island, trying to drum up support for the megacity. He came a-cropper, as did Pierre Bourque back in the days when *he* passed the same stations of the cross while trying to sell the megacity to the same people. In Pierrefonds, Tremblay only mustered an audience of twelve people.

The day before the demerger vote, a few Montrealers staged a much-ballyhooed pro-megacity "love-in" in Westmount Park. This good-natured gathering drew only seventy people, including Tremblay and Bourque. I did not attend, saying my bell-bottoms were at the cleaners. If nothing else, this well-meaning attempt to make the megacity emotionally appealing showed how fruitless such an exercise was. This was in spite of the fact that Tremblay's political party and the anti-demerger side outspent the pro-demerger side by two to one in the pre-referendum period.[20]

Then there were people in the middle. The same day as the "love-in," Vera Danyluk, the former chair of the MUC's executive committee, confessed she had yet to make up her mind how she would vote the next day. Was demerger worth it, with the reduced powers the Liberals allowed? Earlier she had described the agglomeration council as a "lame duck" that would give undue power to Montreal.

THE VOTE RESULTS: MUCH ADO ABOUT NOTHING?

On learning that 92 per cent of Westmount voters had voted Yes in the demerger referendum of 20 June 2004, I climbed on a table in the council chamber of Westmount City Hall to crow, "In spite of the fact the PQ merged us against our will, we got our city back. In spite of the fact that the Liberals tried to stop us from demerging, we got our city back. And in spite of Mayor Tremblay's misinformation, we got our city back!" I thanked the two hundred Westmount volunteers, got down from the table, and after doing some interviews, went home and decided that was it for now.

As it turned out, on the Island of Montreal, fifteen former municipalities got enough votes to demerge. These were the smaller municipalities, with a total population of only 243,000. Had normal referendum criteria applied – 50 per cent plus one of ballots marked Yes for demerger – another seven Montreal Island municipalities would have demerged, including Anjou, LaSalle, Île Bizard, Pierrefonds, and Saint-Laurent, upping the total demerged population to 517,000. Throughout Quebec, had normal rules applied, demergers would have recreated fifty-eight municipalities with a total population of one million people.

Right across Quebec, in the event, only thirty municipalities managed to demerge, and they involved 440,000 citizens.[21] Since the number of citizens affected by the 2001–04 spate of forced mergers was ten times as great, was the whole demerger saga really worth the candle? The answer is yes, for at least two reasons. First of all, demerger was a metropolitan phenomenon: of all the citizens whose municipality demerged, 99 per cent of them lived on the Island of Montreal, on the south shore of Montreal, or in the Quebec City region. Demerged municipalities represented 16 per cent of the total population of these three areas. But above all, these demergers sent a clear message that forced municipal mergers are wrong, and that demergers would be an antidote to be reckoned with in the unlikely event a future provincial government, anywhere in Canada, should get merger fever again.

After losing seven complete boroughs that voted to revert to city status, Mayor Tremblay put up a brave face, calling it a "big victory": "Montreal is stronger than before." He was partially right, although it was far from certain that the large rump of boroughs remaining was uniformly in favour of the megacity. Many probably didn't care either way: they were angrier about the forced nature of the merger than its result. And another thing: the proportion of the megacity's population that was to demerge was only 13 per cent, although the breakaway pieces represented 20 per cent of the taxable assessments. Pierre Bourque was inconsolable. It was close to "indecent" that Tremblay should call the outcome a victory, he said. "It is a huge loss for Montreal." He asked for the Montreal flags to be flown at half-staff.

THE WRONG QUESTION ASKED

The original Liberal resolution regarding the forced mergers, adopted in 2000, called for the *annulation* of the forced mergers; that is, they were supposed to be voided, cancelled, nullified. Even Jean-Marc Fournier, the Liberal minister of municipal affairs, referred to the mergers as "illegitimate." When something is null and void, you go back to square 1. Logically, then, each demerger referendum should have been a substitute for the referendum that never took place at the time of the mergers, and the question should have been: "Do you wish to remain in the megacity?" Had 35 per cent of electors in each former municipality been required to vote *for* the megacity, with anything less meaning automatic demerger, I suspect that most merged municipalities across Quebec would have demerged. I'm even far from sure whether 35 per cent of the voters in the former City of Montreal would have roused themselves to ensure the megacity's survival; certainly, most if not all of the Montreal Island former suburbs would have got insufficient votes to stay in the megacity. In a rational world, this is what would have happened to right a wrong: to shift the burden, requiring the illegitimate to establish its legitimacy. But in a rational world, perhaps, there would have been no forced mergers in the first place.

UNFAIR RULES AND SLOPPY VOTING LISTS
HANDICAPPED THE YES VOTE

The government did not want a simple majority of ballots cast to determine the winner of a given referendum. Because of the apprehended fervour of the demerger voters, the government was afraid that those who voted were not really representative of all citizens – that they would be atypical voters – and so insisted on a significant Yes turnout. For demerger to happen, 35 per cent of all ballots had to be for the Yes. But, in common with many such restrictions dreamed up to ensure "fairness," they can have the opposite result.

Take the former City of Saint-Laurent, where three out of four voted Yes to demerge, with 29 per cent of people on the voting list (riddled with ineligible names) voting to demerge and only 9 per cent voting to stay with the megacity. But because the 35 per cent hurdle was not met, Saint-Laurent did not demerge, even though the wish of those who did vote was unambiguous. With a majority of rented dwellings and a high proportion of recent immigrants, it was very hard for Saint-Laurent to get out the vote. But why did so few megacity supporters vote? Were they so sure the demerger vote would not reach 35 per cent, thereby making their participation unnecessary?[22] Or was their desire to remain in the megacity so weak that it did not make it worth their while to venture forth and express it? The conclusion I drew is that it was patent that a majority of the residents of Saint-Laurent simply wanted to demerge.[23]

The voting lists were a crucial factor in the outcome. Quebec, in common with any democratic state, puts the emphasis on *adding* names to voting lists in order to encourage maximum turnout; *removing* names is not important. Yet by introducing the unheard-of minimum vote rule for the demerger referendum where "purifying" the voting lists was essential, the government, knowingly or unknowingly, handicapped the pro-demerger voters.

Baie d'Urfé had the highest number of corrections, resulting in 11 per cent shrinkage of its voting list. Because of their small population and one hundred eager volunteers, Baie d'Urfé's revision could be used as a benchmark to quantify just how far wrong the other lists were. In fact, it would be a conservative yardstick, as 92 per cent of Baie d'Urfé's dwellings are owned, and homeowners move less frequently than tenants.[24] Unfortunately, most of the larger former municipalities, especially Saint-Laurent, didn't have the volunteers to purge their lists. Using this 11 per cent error rate, at least four other former municipalities would have met the 35 per cent-of-the-list-for-the-Yes criterion and therefore would have demerged.[25] Waxing cynical, a spokesman for the director-general of elections said, "There always was, and there will always be, inaccuracies in the voting lists."[26]

Had the law required that 35 per cent of eligible voters must vote for a given party in order for it to win a Quebec general election, you can be sure the Liberals would have found a way to ensure accurate voting lists. In the 2003 election, only 32 per cent of registered voters actually got out and voted for the Liberal Party.

LINGUISTIC FIRE STOKED BY VOTE

All of the West Island, except for the northern fringe of Pierrefonds, Roxboro, Sainte-Geneviève and Île Bizard, voted strongly enough to demerge, as did the mid-Island former municipalities of Mount Royal, Hampstead, Côte Saint-Luc, Montreal West, and Westmount. The sole community in the east voting in enough numbers to go was Montreal East, which was also the only demerging area on the Island where francophones were in a solid majority, since barely 50 per cent of residents of Mount Royal were francophone and all the other areas ranged from 12 per cent to 39 per cent francophone. The linguistic bias of the demerger vote on the Island unleashed an immediate and visceral reaction from the media. Many francophone editorial hands were wrung and much printer's ink was spilled over the "language fracture," the "digging of a ditch" between the two language groups and the way the English "turned their back" on the megacity and its "plan of integration."[27] All these editorialists chose to ignore the vote on the south shore, where demerger forces blew apart the megacity of Longueuil, and where the francophone component of the demerging municipalities ranged from 55 per cent to 96 per cent.

During the many call-in radio and TV shows I did in French during and after the vote, many callers echoed Lemieux's earlier sentiments. I was told I just wanted "to play on my own English croquet court in Westmount." I was told that Westmounters, the English, and the rich – for most callers, tautological nouns – obviously hated the French and that was why they voted to demerge. Some journalists asked me the same questions, if in slightly less loaded terms.

Meanwhile, Municipal Affairs Minister Fournier reassured the anxious fourth estate that the mass departure of anglo former municipalities from the Montreal megacity would actually "assuage" linguistic tension. "The nascent linguistic tension was born of forced mergers," he said. "It was existent, pre-existent, and we're trying to end it." He had a point. After all, before the mergers, few commentators nattered on about the linguistic divide. It was always geographically there. The demergers allowed many "English" municipalities to go back to their former status (with fewer powers, mind). It was the "French" suburbs that got congealed.

TWO MEGACITY SUPPORTERS STEP DOWN

Both Dorval Mayor Peter Yeomans and Côte Saint-Luc Mayor Robert Libman had waged a campaign to try to prevent demergers, especially in their own boroughs. I had done a number of short TV debates with Libman about the merits of leaving the megacity or not. He was not a persona grata back in his hometown, where people were furious with his volte-face. Nor was Yeomans for that matter. Twelve days after both their boroughs voted to demerge, these two, after consultation with Mayor Tremblay, reluctantly had to step down from their positions as members of the megacity's executive committee, posts they had held since the megacity was imposed in January 2002. "It was a conflict to be on the executive committee and to represent our demerged communities at the same time," said Libman. "It's very hard to walk on both sides of the road at the same time," said Yeomans.

The day after the referendums, Quebec wasted no time in announcing a transition committee for Montreal, which started its work right away. Pierre Lortie was its chairman. Lortie is a Quebec business blueblood: he has been the president of the Montreal Stock Exchange, the president of Provigo, and the president of Bombardier Transport. The committee members all had appropriate backgrounds: three from the provincial government, two from municipal government, four from business, and one from academia.

GETTING THE BLUES ... HOT UNDER THE COLLAR

Meanwhile the blue collars' negotiations that had dragged on since June 2002 came to a head in October 2004 when a binding arbitration decision did exactly what we anti-mergerites said would happen. In order to "harmonize" wages and benefits, the blue collars in the former Montreal Island suburbs got increases in remuneration, along with a reduction in average hours worked from 38.5 to 36 per week. Of course, in order to respect Bill 170, the whole operation had to come out with no overall cost increase for the megacity. This meant the blue collars in the former City of Montreal saw their average wage take a 1 per cent *drop*, and their much-cherished 35-hour week was boosted to 36. They screamed bloody murder, calling the arbitration ruling (which they had themselves asked for) "a hold-up" and "a piece of shit," to use the elegant words of FTQ President Henri Massé. The former president of the blue collars, Jean Lapierre, called the arbitrator, a former union man, a "bastard." The blue collar union appealed the ruling in Quebec Superior Court and lost 22 December 2004.

In actual fact, the extra hour the former City of Montreal blue collars were supposed to work more or less evaporated, as these things tend to do. Their number of days off increased from three to eight, making up 45 of the extra 52 hours. So the four-day week was mostly kept as is, and all they had to do was put in an extra fifteen minutes a day.[28]

THE TRENT *VALE*

Immediately after the June 2004 referenda, I took a sabbatical from media interviews that lasted seven months. Still, everyone assumed I would come back as mayor once Westmount was resurrected as a city in January 2006. But on 31 January 2005, I announced my task had been done: I had wanted my city back, not my job. To return as mayor would have been anti-climactic. It had taken me time to make my decision. "Politics is a drug, and I've gone through seven months of detoxification," I said, adding (and plagiarizing): "A political career is like having an affair. Any fool can start one, but to end it requires considerable skill." I pointed out that it would take many years to repair the damage inflicted on Quebec municipalities by both the PQ and the Liberals. "Rather than an oil painting built up over the years, the municipal landscape has been treated as an Etch-a-sketch." At the end of my press conference, I was careful to say *au revoir*, not *adieu*. I really had no idea what I was going to do, although I did suggest I might write a book, a threat I only started to make good a year later in the absence of any other offers.

That day, I did share some of my feelings on the linguistic side for the first time. At noon on CKAC, I said,

I must tell you that during the time I was leading the fight against mergers and [then] in favour of demergers, the fact I was anglophone and the fact I was from Westmount were two crosses I bore – and two very heavy crosses. It is, after all, very difficult in Quebec for an anglophone to do that sort of thing for all sorts of reasons. And certainly, the stereotype of Westmount that is conveyed is maybe a stereotype that was well deserved forty years ago but no longer exists. It was a battle that was made very difficult: it's a handicap to be an anglophone in that context. Therefore, I hope in the future that I'm replaced by a francophone ... In Quebec, you can't do anything without talking of language. Everything we do is put through the prism of language. And the demergers had a linguistic side that made it more difficult for me as an anglophone to do my job as someone who wanted demerger than had I been francophone. So that's the reality, and I accept it. After all, I have been in Quebec for years and I love Quebec. That is not a flaw; I am just saying that's the reality.

When I made my decision to walk away, it was not as if there had been a power vacuum in Westmount. Karin Marks was very keen and very capable of taking on the job of mayor of the City of Westmount in the November 2005 elections. As borough president, Karin had defended Westmount's interests with vigour, panache, and dedication.

THE MONTREAL DEMERGER TRANSITION COMMITTEE REPORT

In February 2005, Nathalie Normandeau was named minister of municipal affairs. Her qualifications to oversee the reorganization of metropolitan Montreal? For three years she had been the mayor of the village of Maria in the faraway Gaspé region. And the responsibility for "the Regions" was added to her portfolio, lest anyone think that Montreal was even a speck on Quebec's radar screen.

In October 2005 the Montreal Transition Committee made public its interim report, a roadmap for the demerging of fifteen municipalities and the installation of the agglomeration council that handled shared services.[29] The report, which had been gathering dust since March and which had become a source of discomfort – bordering on disavowal – for Minister Normandeau, was very thorough and logical. It managed to cock a snook at the PQ, the Liberals, and, most devastatingly, the megacity. The report took issue with the PQ's claim that the main reason for merging – fiscal equity – could be achieved by simply having the same tax rate all over the Island of Montreal. It made the point that the tax rate in each municipality varied according to three things: the real-estate value per capita, the level of services, and the efficiency in providing those services. "Wilfully ignoring the latter two factors, government policy as embodied in Bill 170, decreed the uniformization of the tax burden," the authors wrote.

Then there was a shot at the Liberals, who had overtly discouraged voters from demerging by requiring that this tax uniformization would be immediate for any former municipality that demerged, while it extended the uniformization process over *twenty years* for any former municipality that remained within the megacity.

But the real shocker was the report's revelation that, from 2001 to 2005, the megacity's spending had increased 21 per cent.[30] Just between 2002 and 2005, spending had increased 16.3 per cent, while inflation had only gone up 6.7 per cent. The report went on to pinpoint a 35 per cent increase in administrative costs from 2002 to 2005, and an increase in remuneration of $133 million, which represented 37 per cent of all cost increases.[31] All these increases were blamed on the merger and the levelling up of salaries and benefits that it (predictably) brought.

The report also calculated what one could call the "reverse dowry" paid by the fifteen divorcing municipalities: $53 million a year. That was the amount of the permanent fiscal transfer that happened during the merger years and that would continue thereafter.[32]

One of the costs of demerger was an ongoing requirement for the agglomeration (and therefore the demerged suburbs) to pay for all new infrastructure that Montreal invested in "downtown," which was defined as a much larger area than just the Central Business District. This contribution, while relatively small, made no sense, as the downtown area constitutes a huge cash cow for the City of Montreal. Besides, even though 7 per cent of commuters to the downtown core come from the demerged cities, the same number come from Laval, and almost double the number come from the south shore – and they are both exempt from paying for "downtown." Montreal Island is one of the few places in the world where suburban cities subsidize downtown; certainly it must be the only instance where only a small piece of suburbia contributes. This obligation remains as a permanent reminder of the myth, so dear to the press and to successive governments, that the Island suburbs were living off the City of Montreal.

The transition committee's report regarded the agglomeration council as a "deliberative organ" of the Montreal megacity; it was not a legal entity and had no employees and no independent financial statements. In other words, it was nothing like the old MUC. The report did recommend a permanent independent "secretariat" to ensure the protection of the minority members (the mayors of the demerged municipalities), who additionally already had the right of appeal to the minister of municipal affairs. The report, honouring a specific provision of Bill 9 that required "rep by pop"[33] recommended an eighty-member council. This council would delegate to the Montreal executive committee the responsibility to prepare its budget and to award its contracts.

Mayor Tremblay, who labelled the report a "demergerite report," strongly disagreed with the transition committee's recommendation that the whole Montreal City Council (sixty-five of them, opposition councillors and all) would join the fifteen representatives of the demerged municipalities on the agglomeration council. To obviate any chance of the suburban minority forming alliances with some opposition Montreal councillors, Tremblay wanted the Montreal mayor to hand-pick the Montreal representatives, who would number fifteen. For me, Tremblay's position was no new news: during the referendum campaign in May 2004, that was precisely the point I kept making: "The megacity mayor will name all the megacity representatives making up the agglomeration council. If we don't leave the megacity, and our borough representative is in the opposition party, we'll have *no* input at all on regional services."

That is exactly what happened when Minister Normandeau sided with Tremblay and ignored the report.[34] As columnist Henry Aubin put it, "No other city north of the Rio Grande gives its mayor as much power as Montreal does today." At least the representatives of the City of Montreal were now required to get a "general direction" from its own council before voting at the agglomeration council.

THE 2005 ELECTION AND THE RENAISSANCE OF THIRTY MUNICIPALITIES

The November 2005 municipal elections were a bit of a lacklustre affair, with Tremblay pitted against Pierre Bourque. Turnout was only 35 per cent, in spite of $4 million spent on the campaign. Potholes and a clean city (which everyone could understand) were big election topics,[35] even though the candidates wanted to contrast their views on decentralization (which nobody could understand). It was a replay of the 2001 election: the autocrat versus the technocrat, the intuitive approach versus the deductive. In the event, Tremblay won handily, and his party won three times the number of seats as Bourque's party. Then, 1 January 2006 marked the actual rebirth of fifteen municipalities on Montreal Island and an equivalent number elsewhere in Quebec. In spite of Tremblay's promise – made while basking in the warm bliss of his electoral triumph – to work with harmony with the now-demerged suburbs, things got downright venomous between them with regard to the agglomeration budget. In February 2006, the "reconstituted cities" accused Montreal of shifting $106 million of local costs to the agglomeration, where Montreal got a 20 per cent discount in that the new municipalities picked up 20 per cent of the tab.

FLIRTING WITH THE ADQ, FIGHTING IN THE AGGLOMERATION

Even though he had been in favour of Quebec sovereignty and mergers and against demergers, ADQ leader Mario Dumont came calling on the demerged suburbs in April 2006 and whispered sibilantly in the West Island mayors' ears. They had just walked out of their latest agglomeration council meeting. Dumont favoured simply getting rid of the council and having the demerged suburbs pay an allotment to the City of Montreal for common services run by independent boards. Finally, after much seduction, mayors of four small demerged Montreal Island towns came out for Dumont in January 2007.[36] The West Island had been "married to the Liberals," as Mayor Bill Tierney put it, "but there has been abuse in this marriage." The *Montreal Gazette* dismissed this initiative as yet more evidence of the same "petulance" that led the forcibly merged municipalities to demerge in the first place.[37] Tensions at the agglomeration council – when the meetings weren't actually boycotted – remained high all during 2006. The demerged suburbs wanted the agglomeration council (1) to be a separate legal entity with its own executive committee; (2) to have all Montreal councillors sit on it; (3) to get rid of the "marching orders" that its members had to get from their respective city councils – which made it a rubber stamp; and (4) to have it bill member municipalities, rather than taxpayers – which would allow municipalities the freedom to set their own tax rates. In short, they wanted the MUC back, without the double-majority voting requirement.

BILL 22 RECENTRALIZED MONTREAL AND DECENTRALIZED DEMERGED MUNICIPALITIES

Starting in January 2007, Charest's Liberals began making public noises about the possibility of giving new taxation powers to the megacity – a parking lot tax, a boosted "welcome" tax, bridge tolls, even the return of the amusement tax. Mayor Tremblay had made the traditional pilgrimage to Quebec, cap and financial projections in hand, the latter which conjured up images of a fiscal chasm opening up right in front of his megacity, stuck as it was with a so-called "structural deficit" of nearly $700 million a year by 2013, even after cutting (on paper) a thousand positions over the next three years.[38]

It was an unconscious repeat performance of Pierre Bourque asking Premier Lucien Bouchard to please, sir, give Montreal a megacity just as Premier Harris had given Toronto a megacity. Gérald Tremblay asked Premier Jean Charest to please give Montreal more taxing powers, just as Toronto got more taxing powers. Montreal merged because that's what Toronto did, and now Montreal needed new taxes, because that's what Toronto got.[39] Nobody had the bad manners to ask what happened to the "economies of scale" and the 5 per cent tax reduction that the creation of the megacity was supposed to bring about. I am not saying such increased taxation powers were not justified, because they most definitely were: Montreal had to and has to reduce its dependency on property taxes. But for Montreal, cost-cutting is always hypothetical and for tomorrow, while its revenue increases are always real and for today. And the more sources of revenue to spread the pain around, the better.

Just five years after the megacity was created, Montreal was admitting it was drowning in red ink. The problems that were supposed to disappear with the mergers had simply got bigger. What was the point of it all? Ah, but few asked that question. At least now Tremblay had something to barter with the demerged municipalities: you support my demand for new tax sources, and I'll allow changes to the agglomeration council. The first step toward reconciliation started with a meeting between the two sides in late February 2007. In June, Tremblay pushed his luck by suggesting the agglomeration council be abolished and that the Montreal City Council be expanded to include the fourteen suburban mayors whenever regional services were debated.

On 21 June 2007, Bill 22 – which modified the agglomeration council and gave new taxation powers to Montreal – was tabled in the National Assembly. But it took a whole year of haggling and posturing on the part of Mayor Tremblay, Municipal Affairs Minister Nathalie Normandeau, and Westmount Mayor Karin Marks before it was actually adopted – with modifications.[40] For example, Bill 22 started off by putting all the Montreal councillors on the agglomeration council, but it ended up with no changes to its number and composition.

Bill 22 did create an agglomeration audit committee and a permanent secretariat that compelled Montreal to provide background information to demerged municipalities. It gave Montreal an extra $34 million a year in aid along with some new fiscal powers such as the parking lot tax and a boosted "welcome" tax. But the bill stopped short of increasing the dedicated mass-transit taxes on gasoline or car registrations, or giving Montreal any portion of the provincial sales tax – 1 per cent of which would have given Montreal $250 million a year of new revenues.

In order to prevent boroughs demerging in 2004, Tremblay had promised that borough powers would not be diluted and that boroughs would have essentially the same powers as a demerged municipality. Four years later, Bill 22 gave Montreal City Council the power to arrogate for itself any responsibility that had previously been attributed to a borough "for a period that it determines." Also, Bill 22 gave the central city more powers over borough land-use planning and made the Montreal mayor the mayor of the downtown borough of Ville-Marie, with Montreal's director-general becoming its director-general.[41] Bill 22 also removed the responsibility for the maintenance of arterial roads from the agglomeration and gave it to Montreal and the demerged municipalities.[42] This was a significant move, as it restored a power to the demerged municipalities. Also, from here on, the demerged municipalities would tax directly for all services, local or regional, and pay the agglomeration an apportionment based on their real-estate wealth, just as they did with the MUC in pre-megacity days. The agglomeration council (in reality, the

City of Montreal) would no longer tax residents of the demerged municipalities.

As some of us had predicted, the difference in autonomy between a Montreal borough and a demerged municipality was becoming greater and greater a scant five years after demerger. To drive the point home, in 2009 the Superior Court ruled that boroughs "were not independent municipalities." The judge overturned a megacity decision that denied a citizen the right to vote on a zoning change in a neighbouring borough. The megacity had originally invoked the borough's exclusive jurisdiction over zoning matters.[43]

CUT THE NUMBER OF BOROUGHS BY HALF?

In March 2009, Tremblay announced that the ongoing cost-cutting program that eliminated a thousand jobs and would supposedly save $300 million was not enough. Another $155 million had to be found. Cosmo Maciocia, a hitherto quiet, staunchly pro-Tremblay executive committee member, suddenly started speculating about cutting the number of boroughs from nineteen to ten to help save money. Each new borough would have a population of about 150,000. It would cut the cost of politicians' emoluments in half, he said. But that was not all. "Boroughs with fewer than twenty thousand citizens, others with six times as many with the same number of administrators: seriously, can we continue to leave it like this? ... nineteen sports and recreation directors, nineteen public works directors, nineteen administrative directors, nineteen human resources directors ... it makes no sense," he said, in his best imitation of Pierre Bourque circa 1999. Tremblay was publicly against Maciocia's idea, "at least for the time being," saying it would only save some $10 million a year.

Others, such as Benoit Labonté (leader of the opposition Vision Montreal party) and a clutch of experts waded in, saying the thing was not to reduce the number of boroughs but to reduce their powers – which had been boosted in an attempt to stop boroughs from demerging in the 2004 referenda. Louise Harel, who had recently quit provincial politics and said she had no intention of running in the upcoming November municipal election, was of the same opinion, styling the current boroughs "baronies": "If we go from nineteen to ten boroughs, but these boroughs remain quasi-municipalities as they are now, we will end up in the worst of situations because we'll have cities ... an Italian city, a Haitian city, an anglophone city, an Arab city – the City of Saint-Laurent – a Jewish city ..."[44] She quickly back-pedalled in the face of public reaction to these remarks. The *Montreal Gazette* pointed out it was she who described the boroughs as "little homelands" when she was setting up the megacity. So seemingly they went from being little homelands to baronies.[45]

So there we had it. The law implacably ruled that boroughs were not "independent municipalities" and we were witnessing an incremental centre-seeking leakage of power, yet the architect of the megacity was insisting the boroughs were nonetheless "quasi-" municipalities. The irony was that, with time, the boroughs were most likely to become the empty shells that Harel seemingly sought and thereby make real the very spectre that drove us to demerge.

19

Scandals, a Swollen Payroll, and an Uncelebrated Tenth Birthday

It is said when a man comes to high office, it makes him worthy of honour and respect. Surely, though, such offices don't have the power of planting virtue in the minds of those who hold them, do they? Or of removing vices?

Boethius, *The Consolation of Philosophy*, 524 AD

The Island of Montreal used to dump its raw sewage straight into the St Lawrence River. A generation ago, the MUC finally took on the very costly job of burying huge sewer interceptors the length of the Island and built a massive wastewater treatment plant to receive the (thankfully) diluted effluent. Since gravity serves as the moving force, sewage can take up to an hour in transit to get to the plant's pumping station one hundred feet below ground. There, what amounts to Brobdingnagian sump pumps move the volume of a swimming pool in one second. In the most nauseous section in the plant, giant screens remove most of the solid items, sad residues of mass human activity. After the screens, the sewage flows out to a field of outdoor sedimentation basins, where the slow natural flocculation is helped along by chemicals. Wheeling gulls scavenge anything they find comestible floating in the basins, spitting out unfiltered bits of plastic onto the aluminium catwalks. Scum is collected on top of the basins, and sludge is pumped to a dewatering station, after which it is incinerated. The whole process is hardly pleasant but vitally necessary.

THE WATER-MANAGEMENT MESS: HALF A BILLION DOLLARS DOWN THE TUBES?

This desperate need to clean up our sewage handling a few decades ago parallels both today's long-overdue need to fix Montreal's potable water system, and, metaphorically at least, the need to clean up the way the megacity went about trying to do it. For the botched water-management contract was indisputably the biggest Montreal municipal story of 2009, the biggest mess of Tremblay's whole career as mayor, and the biggest contract Montreal ever awarded. It was also incontrovertible proof that the megacity, at least at times, is unmanageable – with a web of centralized complexity, with no citizen oversight, with opposition parties scoring points rather than preventing disasters, and with all decisions made in secret by the executive committee.

Unlike many former suburban municipalities, the old City of Montreal did not meter water for most commercial users, let alone domestic users.[1] Not only did Montreal not bill consumers based on consumption but it had no idea how much water was being lost through leaks in the antiquated water distribution system. In 1992 the MUC calculated a 39 per cent loss rate,[2] which helped explain why, then as today, the average water consumption on the Island of Montreal is double that of Toronto. In fact, today, Montreal *leaks* nearly twice the amount of water per capita than the City of Paris actually *consumes*.

To his credit, Mayor Tremblay decided to do something about this lamentable state of affairs. In August 2004, he announced the creation of a water fund that would be financed by a dedicated real-estate tax of $25 million a year (growing to $200 million a year by 2013). He also announced that some thirty thousand new water meters would be installed for commercial users.

Over three years later, the executive committee sent out a press release. It announced "the beginning of the installation of water meters in industrial, commercial, and institutional establishments and the optimization of the potable water distribution system in Montreal. Mayor Tremblay pointed out that it involves an unprecedented investment of $424 million over 25 years."[3]

Then, in a textbook application of Parkinson's Law of Triviality (the time spent on any item of the agenda will be in inverse proportion to the sum involved), six days later Montreal City Council took fifty-three seconds to approve the contract, the biggest the city had ever awarded. *And it was approved unanimously by all political parties, without even one question being asked.* The only opposition came from the demerged municipalities two days later, on the basis that metering water was a local responsibility, and as most of them had water meters anyway, why should they pay twice?

The group chosen to do the work was Génieau, a consortium of Simard-Beaudry Construction, a firm run by one Tony Accurso,[4] and an engineering firm called Dessau. The contract price was $356 million. The only other bidder, a consortium of Catania Construction[5] and SM Consultants, came in at $396 million.[6]

There were other expenses. While the cost for the whole water-management project was given as $424 million, in reality it was $509 million.[7] The thirty thousand new and replacement water meters would start to be installed in 2008, along with something new: six hundred underground chambers for pressure monitoring and (aptly named) water gates for pressure regulation in the water mains – all at a distance. Monitoring could help detect sources of leakage, and the ability to reduce water pressure at night could lessen it. It's a bit like pinching a hose to reduce pressure to lessen a leak. But it's even better just to buy a new hose.

Back in 2004, however, when the executive committee had been told the water meters would cost only $36 million, there had been no talk of pressure-regulation chambers. Since then, the scope had been radically changed and nonetheless approved by the executive committee. Yet very few companies could handle the size and the financing of the revised project. Basic good business practice (if not ethics) would have dictated that the project go back to square one and be broken into smaller pieces. For some reason, that didn't happen.

The Génieau contract was finally signed on 17 March 2008. Frank Zampino, the chairman of Montreal's executive committee, suddenly announced two months later he was leaving in two weeks, only to reappear in January 2009 as senior vice-president and chief financial officer at Dessau, earning $400,000 a year. Dessau, one-half of the Génieau consortium, was the second-largest engineering consulting firm in Quebec, and a company that had been awarded many city contracts over the years.

In early April 2009, Zampino admitted he and his wife had holidayed in the Caribbean in January 2007 and February 2008 on board *Touch*, a 120-foot yacht owned by Tony Accurso, the fellow who ran Simard-Beaudry and therefore one-half of Génieau. When not in use by its owner, *Touch* could be chartered for $60,000 a week. While refusing to make the receipts public, Zampino maintained he had paid his own way.

Shortly after this admission, Tremblay suspended the water-management contract and told the city's auditor-general to study the whole matter. Zampino then quit Dessau, precisely three months after he had been hired.

Montreal's auditor-general made his report public in September 2009. Essentially he said the contract was too rushed, too big, and too dear. The sudden growth of the scope of the project had the effect of "considerably reducing competition," and the project should have been split or even phased in, with the metering first. Consequently, the contract price "seems to us too high." The city should consider a number of possibilities, "including the cancellation of the contract." Tremblay said forthwith he would do just that.[8] Two direct victims of the report were the director-general Claude Léger,[9] who was let go, along with Robert Cassius de Linval, director of corporate services.[10]

LEARNING FROM MONTREAL'S WATER-GATES

For years before the merger, the water supply and most of the distribution system on the Island of Montreal had already been "merged," with the exception of the West Island; Montreal supplied water to fifteen other municipalities and in some cases even maintained the distribution system. Had Montreal decided to upgrade its water management before the mergers, it would have been hard to imagine its suburban clients standing by quietly while Montreal went ahead and spent $509 million on water meters, pressure management, and water gates with no consultation – and the intention of passing on part of the bill.

In 2004, during his campaign to convince boroughs not to demerge, Tremblay declared that the fact that Montreal was finally doing something about its decrepit water distribution system was proof that the megacity was a success. The previous, fragmented, pre-merger situation had allowed such a state of affairs to fester for decades, he said.* Actually, it proved the opposite. It proved that

---

* Mayor Tremblay often made the case that he had to invest heavily in Montreal's water distribution network. This is true. But all politicians exaggerate the burden they inherit, while ignoring the burden their predecessors were stuck with. The massive cost of building the MUC's interceptors and wastewater treatment plant – roughly $2 billion in

what had been for years the largest municipality in Canada had shamefully neglected one of its most basic responsibilities, preferring to spend money on things such as a billion-dollar Olympic stadium. The water system mess was an indictment against municipal bigness, a size swollen by Montreal's monopoly in supplying water to fifteen suburbs. In fact, some of the suburbs were ahead of Montreal, having already installed water meters, even in their residential sectors. And the whole West Island water system made the former City of Montreal's look third world.

When the new Montreal megacity finally did get around to doing something about its dilapidated water distribution system, it resulted in the biggest municipal cock-up in Quebec's history. It was described as a "turnkey" project, but the "n" was superfluous. It was proof that the former City of Montreal did not work (because it had done nothing), and a bigger, bulked-up version was even worse (because it completely made a mess of doing something). The contract was handled in classic Montreal style: it was given gargantuan proportions, it was cooked up behind closed doors, and it smelled of corruption.

Rather than tap into the expertise in the rest of North America, where municipal water distribution was much more advanced, Montreal decided on a "made in Montreal" solution that was unique. There was little expertise even among the hired professional engineers. The whole contract process itself had been contracted out: outside lawyers drafted it, outside engineers wrote the technical specifications, outside accountants and engineers evaluated the bids, and outside experts were to supervise the work. All of it was done by hired hands, a few of whom had sticky fingers. There were no available City of Montreal employees to do these jobs, as they lacked the know-how. Besides, the sudden increase in capital-works spending stretched city staffing to the limit; many experienced administrators had been let go in order to prove the megacity would save money – yet just to administer the virtually unadministrable megacity ate up huge quantities of staff.

The price of the water meter scandal will be high and will be lasting, but not because of the relatively modest cost of breaking the questionable contract. Montreal, afraid of subcontracting out, will

today's dollars – was borne by the taxpayers of the 1980s and '90s. Today, the investment deficit in the potable water system is estimated to be about the same amount.

give blue collars the job of installing the meters as recommended by the auditor-general. The result will be spiralling labour cost increases. The possible inability to avoid collusion and profiteering with outside firms will be replaced with the proven inability to control the wages of the already overpaid Montreal blue-collar workers. So any illegal complicity with contractors will be replaced by a legal complicity with the union monopoly.

And apprehended corruption gave more jobs to generously paid employees in other areas. After a questionable contract with a company providing security to police headquarters – the police themselves being too highly paid for such a job – the blue-collar union made a case for them to take over this responsibility too. Likewise, following a fraud scandal in 2008, the Information Technologies Department reacted by slashing outsourcing. Today, 85 to 90 per cent of its work is now done in-house – provided by employees who earn much more than their private-sector equivalents.[11]

On the other hand, following the water management scandal, Montreal quite rightly boosted the number of engineers working for the city to 250. The City of Laval, however, still depends on outside engineering firms, having only five engineers on staff supervising public works.[12] Estimating, designing, specification-writing, tender documents, and supervision of contracts – all are done by outside private engineering firms. This is a recipe for a repeat of the water management scandal that happened in Montreal.

OTHER SCANDALS RAIN ON TREMBLAY'S ELECTION PARADE

Back in November 2008, *La Presse's* André Noël broke a story of a scandal involving two "paramunicipal" corporations handling some $300 million of city assets: the Montreal Housing and Development Corporation (in French, SHDM) and the Montreal Development Corporation (SDM). Without getting the necessary approval from Quebec, Montreal's executive committee had decided in 2006 to turn the SHDM and the SDM into a single private corporation effective January 2007, in order "to save money." Privatization also meant much less public scrutiny. Soon after, the SHDM sold ninety-four acres of contaminated city land to Catania Construction to build a housing project. Only one other company had been chosen to bid for the land: a company owned by Tony Accurso. The firm hired to supervise the bidding process was a subsidiary of Dessau. The accepted bid was a fraction of the land's assessed value and was conditional on a $16 million subsidy to the purchaser. Montreal's executive committee finally had to modify its rules to approve such extraordinary aid. Frank Zampino, the chairman of the executive committee, quit shortly after. In late 2008, responding to *La Presse*'s revelations, Mayor Tremblay "renationalized" the SHDM, cancelled all its recent transactions, and fired its boss (and Tremblay's former chief of staff), Martial Fillion.

When two auditors' reports presented at the end of April 2009 confirmed that the SHDM had wasted "dozens of millions" of taxpayers' dollars in 2007 and 2008, for Tremblay it was like painfully removing a scab. And police were now investigating.* The auditors also revealed that the director-general of the city, Claude Léger, was aware of the planned land sale in 2007 and did nothing about it.

On 1 May 2009, Tremblay announced he was running for a third term. Less than a month later, Louise Harel let it drop that she was "in reflection" about running for the Montreal mayoralty. She had been bolstered by a poll that revealed she would get 45 per cent of the vote, compared with 26 per cent for Tremblay, now almost mortally weakened by the SHDM and the water-management scandals.

Since the Potemkin political party was de rigueur in Montreal, when Harel announced in early June that she was actually running for the mayoralty, it was as the leader of Vision Montreal. Benoit Labonté had stepped aside to become her second-in-command.[13] My reaction was not kind: "Louise Harel is like the architect who comes to save the building that she herself had badly built."[14]

A flood of further scandals buoyed Harel's mayoral bid.[15]

PRICE-FIXING, BID-RIGGING, AND A LITTLE HIGHWAY ROBBERY

Other scandals shook all of Quebec. A study by Transport Canada had revealed that, per kilometre, highways in Quebec cost 50

---

* In May 2012, after an investigation spanning two and a half years, police arrested Frank Zampino, Martial Fillion, and the president of Catania Construction. They, along with six others connected with the SHDM scandal, were charged with fraud, conspiracy, and breach of trust. The police named Zampino as the ringleader.

per cent more for construction and 40 per cent more for maintenance than the Canadian averages.[16] In September 2009 the new anti-
corruption squad of the Sûreté de Québec started an investigation
into the "fabulous fourteen," a closed club of construction firms that
divvied up highway and City of Montreal contracts among themselves, deciding in turn which one should be the low bidder – at a
price much higher than market. Even a former senior engineer with
the Quebec Department of Transport confirmed this practice, claiming that 3 per cent of the value of contracts went to the mafia.[17] One
contractor maintained that bid-rigging by the "fabulous fourteen"
added 35 per cent to Montreal infrastructure costs.[18] According to
another source, anyone outside the group who tried to bid on City
of Montreal construction contracts wound up in hospital or found
his equipment destroyed.[19]

In spite of the highly charged atmosphere barely a week before the
election, Tremblay decided to meet the editorial staff of *Le Devoir*
and up the ante. The result was a headline worthy of a tabloid: "Is
the mafia at the doors of City Hall? Tremblay fears for his family."[20]
The article went on to say, "Gérald Tremblay maintains that he is not
naïve. When he took power in 2001, he was told by a high-ranking
civil servant about the rumours concerning brown envelopes that
were circulating around City Hall.[21] 'There are a number of contractors that share contracts and territories …' [Regarding threats
and intimidation, Tremblay said,] 'I'm able to take the pressure as an
individual, as mayor of Montreal, but I can't ask my family and my
children to do the same thing.' He recalled that on October 2005,
in the middle of the election campaign, two bombs had been discovered at his cottage in Saint-Hippolyte." Later in the interview, an
exasperated Tremblay blurted out, "There is a limit to what I can do.
I am not a police officer."

The next day, *La Presse* ran an article by André Noël quoting
extracts of telephone conversations that he had managed to obtain.[22]
Noël described an intermediary between Tremblay's party, city
bureaucrats, and firms desirous of getting contracts. This individual was known as "Mr 3 Per Cent," because he allegedly got kick-
backs from contractors equal to that amount of the contract's worth
in order to fund the party, at least up until 2007.[23] Tremblay vehemently denied it. But true or not, the damage was done. Noël also
revealed conversations among Mr 3 Per Cent, Frank Zampino, and
executives of various contractors and engineering firms that proved

they were all in cahoots in the water-management and SHDM scandals. *La Presse* maintained that two water-management "competitors" sailed together on Tony Accurso's yacht. Noël's earlier *La Presse* articles had revealed that the contractors in the SHDM and water-management scandals had connections with the mafia and had been under investigation for tax fraud.

A CODE OF ETHICS TO FIGHT CORRUPTION?

When it came time to react to the plain evidence of corruption at the municipal level, Quebec politicians did what they always did. Got a problem? Legislate it away. There's too much corruption and local politicians don't know their ethics from a hole in the ground? Why, adopt Bill 109: The Municipal Ethics and Good Conduct Act (passed November 2010). Says Bill 109: "The code of ethics and conduct of elected municipal officers must address such issues as conflicts of interest, favouritism, embezzlement, breach of trust and other misconduct, gifts and other benefits." There we are: problem solved.[24]

So rather than addressing the real problem of the megacity itself, Quebec adopted feel-good laws that turned the awarding of municipal contracts into a Byzantine process and required local politicians both to adopt a code of ethics and to take a course in ethics. As well as scaring away decent candidates from running for office in such a culture of distrust, an ethics law just gives ammunition to opposition parties, creating a kind of auction in increasing ethical standards as political parties promise even tighter rules than their opponents, building an ethical edifice only the divine could inhabit. It is a code of political aesthetics, not political ethics. "There are cities that are completely corrupt that boast a magnificent code of ethics," said municipal lawyer Marc-André LeChasseur.[25]

Once again, this reaction was an example of a smaller-city bias. Such laws might have been a way to deal with the alleged corruption that was emerging in Mascouche, Terrebonne, Boisbriand, or Saint-Jérôme, but the approach could do nothing to root out or prevent corruption in the Montreal megacity.

It took the press to uncover just about all the megacity corruption scandals.[26] The megacity reacted, not acted. Were it not for the media whistle-blowing, the water management contract today would be a reality, a waste of $509 million. Just to put this amount into perspective: it equals the total spending of all Quebec municipalities for water distribution infrastructure that year, and 10 per cent of all municipal spending on capital works. It was not only the biggest contract ever for Montreal but most likely in all municipal Quebec. Had Montreal not been merged, it is my contention the contract would never have been blessed.

It took another year or two before the Liberal government really started moving on corruption, other than legislating it away. They created a police anti-corruption squad; the Transport Department got an anti-collusion unit; and, finally, the Liberals most reluctantly agreed to a full commission of inquiry. No one, however, is looking at whether the actual megacity size and structure allows corruption to flourish. There is, let us say, a one-in-fifty chance of outbreaks of corruption in smaller cities but a much higher chance of endemic corruption in very large cities.

This being Quebec, however, there is a linguistic element to the whole sad saga of corruption. Benefiting from years of reflection, one of the most perceptive commentators on the Quebec scene, Alain Dubuc, had this to say: "Our language laws, as essential as they are, have also a perverse effect. One of the biggest causes of the construction scandal is very certainly the cultural homogeneity of Quebec society, protected by its language, which has a tendency to operate in isolation, in a bubble, well protected from outside threats. The construction industry, with its laws, its unique union regime, and its government protection, has developed an inbred business culture. That certainly created a climate that encouraged palsy-walsy relationships, collusion, and public sector complicity."[27]

TREMBLAY WINS AGAIN

In the fall of 2009, Montreal voters were in a sour mood. In the weeks leading up to the November election, the numbers told it all. Across Canada, people were asked whether they felt politically disengaged and powerless. In Vancouver, Calgary, and Toronto, a discouraging one-half of the people said "Yes," but in Montreal it was two-thirds. Just before the Montreal election, 55 per cent of people said they would not even vote; usually most say they will and don't. To admit it is a sign of complete disenchantment. In a clear indictment of the complex governing structure in Montreal, 85 per cent of voters could not even name a candidate running for city councillor.

In another poll, only 15 per cent of people thought the city managed its tax revenues well, while 60 per cent thought the opposite. Some 73 per cent of the electorate said that the scandals would influence their vote in some way. But it would be a mistake to think that scandals had completely supplanted potholes, seemingly the number-one issue in the previous election: 85 per cent of citizens were unhappy with the state of the roads. And, surprisingly, only 4 per cent of respondents said that taxes were their principal preoccupation.

Generally, voting intentions showed that francophones favoured Harel, then Richard Bergeron (a brilliant but slightly eccentric third-party candidate), then Tremblay. For anglophones, it was Tremblay, then Bergeron, and a meagre 10 per cent for Harel. Bergeron was the allophone choice, followed by Tremblay, with Harel trailing again at 10 per cent. On voting day, Tremblay won with 38 per cent of the popular vote, followed by Harel with 33 per cent, and Bergeron with 26 per cent.

Given the stench of scandals surrounding Tremblay, Harel could have been elected mayor had it not been for just any one of the following four things: Bergeron divided the anti-Tremblay voters, Harel was the incarnation of forced mergers,[28] Harel was a committed sovereignist, and Harel's party had its own scandal that came to light two weeks before the election. She had to dump her running mate, Benoit Labonté, when he was caught in a lie about being in contact with Tony Accurso and receiving about a hundred thousand dollars in cash the year before from various firms doing business with the city, including Accurso's. The money apparently went to fund his leadership campaign.

Even had Harel won as mayor, her party would not likely have won a majority of the council seats; consequently, her power would have been severely compromised. The crucial but less broadcast result of the election was that Tremblay's party won a massive 60 per cent of the council seats.

So Montreal, probably for better than for worse, would have another four years of Mayor Tremblay.

I BLUE-BOX MYSELF BACK TO OFFICE

To the surprise of all, including myself, I decided to come back as the recycled mayor of Westmount and got elected by acclamation in October 2009. I came back (not without misgivings), for four reasons. Firstly, Karin Marks, the then-mayor, wanted to step down, but out of duty she felt she could only do it if she had confidence in her replacement. Secondly, in the event of Louise Harel being elected Montreal mayor, I wanted to be around to defend our freedom. Thirdly, I had an idea as to how to gain citizen support for a $37 million proposed recreation centre in Westmount by turning it into probably North America's first underground arena. Lastly, the mayor's chair would serve as a more effective soapbox for the ideas in this book than would the armchair of a long-retired politician.

I returned to find a heightened climate of confrontation in local politics, a climate that contrasted with the days when a referendum revealed that 98 per cent of Westmounters were behind me fighting the mergers. While the retroactive romanticism called nostalgia clouds the identification of trends, I can't help but think that the sort of politician who went into local government thirty years ago is now scarcer. Few will put up with the indignities of office today. The desire to knock politicians down from their admittedly self-made pedestals was always present, but now deadly effective means to do so are readily available thanks to social media. Anyone can create a website, or merchandise rumours and half-baked theories on YouTube. Self-appointed élites try to bring down elected élites, all the while demanding "transparency," today's pressure-group watchword. Complete political transparency is like nudism: it's easier to agree on what it is than on what it achieves. In fact, too much public information creates opacity, not transparency. Besides, what these groups really want is to replace the politician's judgment with their own.

When I came back to Westmount City Hall, I looked quickly around and at first had trouble recognizing it. Four years of merger had subtly infected Westmount; for one thing, salaries and benefits had rocketed up during the merger period to meet Montreal levels.[29] Financially, today's Westmount is not in good shape. I had introduced "pay-as-you-go" – paying cash for all routine capital expenditures – with Westmount's 1994 budget. "Pay-as-you-go" means that today's taxpayers pay for renewing today's infrastructure. But that's not the City of Montreal's way: during the years we were merged with them, they borrowed for everything. In fact, Montreal both pocketed our tax money earmarked for pay-as-you-go *and* stuck us with the debt for the same expenditures on demerging – a bit of larceny that cost Westmount $16 million. We took Montreal to court to get the money back, but to no avail. The court refused to intervene on the grounds that the amount was sanctioned by an order-in-council and courts cannot overturn such government decisions – unless the request is made within thirty days of the decision. Ah, justice is blindfolded but somehow can see a calendar.

When I was forced to leave the mayor's office at the end of 2001, Westmount had an $8 million debt. Partially thanks to Montreal light-fingeredness, when I got back in 2009, debt had grown to $38 million. Operationally, things were no better. The Westmount fire department cost us about $3 million in 2001 to run, or $3.7 million in today's dollars. We are now charged $7.2 million a year for our share of the Island-wide fire department, double what it used to cost us. Had we stayed in the megacity, things would have been no different.

Indeed, in spite of the debt problem, just about all increases in Westmount taxes were caused by the merger, not by the demerger. But that's not how *La Presse* told the story. As if to admonish the disjuncted suburbs that, after all, there was a price to pay to get out of this mess, the myth of the "cost" of demerger was alive and well. I was taken aback one October morning in 2009 with a front-page headline of *La Presse*: "The price to pay for demergers: The secessionists must live with the consequences of their choice."[30] The article, which took up all of pages 2 and 3, described the huge increases from 2001 to 2008 in expenses, taxes, and debt for the demerged cities – increases the writers ascribed to the cost of demerger. Appalled that *La Presse* could get it so wrong, I fired off a letter of correction saying it was the mergers that cost a fortune, not the demergers. *La Presse* compared the change from 2001 to 2008, but demergers occurred in 2006. Most of the increases happened from 2001 to 2006 while everyone was merged.[31] I was doubly appalled when, in spite of repeated calls, no correction was ever made.

THE POWER OF THE UNIONS

The main reason Montreal spending was continuing to spiral upwards was a matter of too many employees who were paid too much. Even in 2011, municipal employees, according to the Institut de la statistique du Québec, were still making 29.2 per cent more than their provincial government counterparts, and for the Montreal megacity the difference was far greater. Aside from a looming pension fund crisis, this state of affairs had a lot to do with union power. It wasn't just the high pay; it was also the number of employees needed to compensate for abysmal output. While it is a cliché to caricature blue collars as lazy and inefficient ("It takes four city workers to fill a hole: one to dig and three to watch"), in 2006, the city actually collected video proof of extreme dilatory behaviour as ten blue collars took ninety hours to fill nine potholes.[32] Shopping, sleeping, and taking long meal breaks on the job were all common practice.

The climate of intimidation, engrained in the system for at least forty years, ensured that the union got what it wanted. Any worker could be threatened when he simply did the job he was supposed to do or refused to participate in union demonstrations. Foremen were intimidated, their cars vandalized. When two thousand blue collars broke through a City Hall door in 1993 with a battering ram, it was almost a metaphor. And all the union president got was a month in prison.[33] The elected officials generally caved in to the union's demands, as nothing concentrates the politician's mind as much as media and angry citizens complaining about the lack of snow removal or garbage pickup. And the blue collars tried to intimidate elected officials as well. On Halloween night in 2003, sixty blue collars demonstrated in front of Mayor Tremblay's house and "decorated" his garden. The street had to be closed off. (The same thing happened to me ten years before – twice. My wife, alone in the house, was taunted through a bullhorn.) In November 2003, hundreds of blue collars demonstrated outside Verdun Borough Mayor Georges Bossé's condominium building. Then a bunch of them managed to enter through the emergency door, get up to his eleventh floor residence, and dump liquid pig manure on his doorstep. A month later the Superior Court issued a ruling that the blue collars could not demonstrate closer than ten metres from a politician's residence, nor in a greater number than fifty. Even then, for one period after the demerger referenda, Mayor Tremblay's house had to be under continuous police surveillance.

Montreal's fire department, for at least a few decades before the mergers, had essentially been run by the firefighters' union. Collective agreements gave the union a say on just about anything, including the colour and number of buttons on their uniforms. Some stations were in the hands of a sort of bikers' gang in blue uniforms. Harassment and intimidation were common. Things did not change with merger, except that the former suburbs were dragged into the mess. During contract negotiations in October 2007, the mega-city resorted to obtaining a court injunction and mounting security guards to get fire chiefs into their offices in twelve different fire stations. The chiefs had been barred by firefighters, some using epoxy, screws, or steel bars on the doors to prevent entry.[34]

Such monkeyshines appeared to pay off. Generous salaries and regular overtime payments propelled many firefighters into the ranks of those making more than $100,000 a year.[35] A ruling handed down at a salary arbitration tribunal[36] in March 2010 sheds more light on just how well paid firefighters are in Montreal, and, by extension, the remuneratory coddling of Montreal municipal employees. This hearing was also interesting in that it featured former premier Bernard Landry appearing as an economic expert for the firefighters' union. Landry averred that, in times of recession, it is necessary that governments give their employees salary increases *higher* than the increase in the cost of living – in order to keep consumption and GDP up. His logic would guarantee that long-term, public sector salaries will continue to ratchet ever upwards, leaving private sector salaries far behind. During cross-examination, Landry had to admit that both in 1982 (when he was in René Lévesque's cabinet) and in 1998 (when he was the minister of finance), the prevailing economic recessions caused his government to cut public-sector salaries by 20 per cent and 6 per cent respectively. The municipal world was spared the first cut, spared itself the second, and has overpaid its employees ever since. Firefighters and police have done very well with their time-honoured method of demanding pay rises based on what other municipalities pay.[37] Thanks to the municipalities selected and the method of computation, the conclusions invariably point to adjustments upwards for the home team.

Robert Lamontagne, the treasurer of the City of Montreal, testified at the tribunal hearing that, in 2008, fire services in his municipality cost $150 per capita, while in the eight other metropolitan regions of Quebec, they cost $77. It cost $105,000 to remunerate each Montreal firefighter in 2008, compared with an average of $81,000 in the other Quebec municipalities. For all Montreal employees, it was $88,000 versus $75,000. Finally, Lamontagne said, it cost $2,317 per capita to run Montreal, versus $1,427 for the other municipalities – a 60 per cent difference.[38]

Big municipalities cost more than small for at least three reasons: bigger bureaucracies, higher salaries, and uniformity of services.[39]

In 2006, the Montreal fire department wanted to hire five hundred more firefighters in order to get a uniform response time for fire calls right across the Island.[40] At first blush, quick and uniform response times seem desirable, even a basic right. If that were so, why not have them the same for the whole region, or even the province? Financially, it is impossible. Response time is partially related to the nearness of the station; this is why there are sixty-six of them on the Island. The more suburban and dispersed the population, the more stations you might need per capita to have the same response times. If so, suburbs should pay extra – which they did, or lived with longer response times. It was their choice.

PENSIONS: A CENTURY OF DISAVOWAL

The most insidious problem affecting overall remuneration remains the cost of Montreal employees' pensions. While this problem dramatically resurfaced after 2008, the underfunding of Montreal pension funds had been going on for nearly one hundred years. Buried in the City of Montreal's 2003 budget documents is a ten-page corporate *mea culpa* of the cavalier manner with which Montreal had always managed its employee pension funds; and how, in January 1966, their deficits (excepting the police pension fund) had been evaluated at $0.7 billion in today's dollars.[41] "These deficits essentially were a result of a generalized and continuous under-funding since 1912. It was soon realized that [even] these deficits were underestimated,"[42] continued this matter-of-fact commentary.

Rather than forcing the city to pay down these massive deficits over time, the province actually allowed Montreal to freeze them and even relieved it of the responsibility of contributing anything at all to pension funds from 1968 to 1970. By 1983, the initial pension fund deficits had reached $2 billion in today's dollars, remaining more or less at the same level until the time of the merger. At that point, along with Montreal's debts, these deficits became part of the tax bill shouldered exclusively by all who own property within the boundaries of the former City of Montreal. They serve as yet another reason why these taxpayers did not "benefit" from the merger.

Today's municipal employees are leaving their jobs earlier and leaving the world later than they used to. Back in 1965, in the former City of Montreal, the average age at retirement was sixty-two with a life expectancy of a further sixteen years; today fifty-five is the average retirement age, with a projected twenty-nine years of pension payments. In 1965 there were over four employees for every retiree. Now there are more retirees than employees. Currently, for every $1 an employee contributes to his or her pension, the City of Montreal contributes roughly $2.50. For a typical Government of Quebec employee, the sharing is one for one.

Let's put some faces on the pension fund problem. Especially since 9/11, we all seem to admire firefighters, but there should be a limit to our material gratitude. The average firefighter in 2012 will cost the City of Montreal $123,000 a year and retire at fifty-two, getting full pension benefits after only twenty-five years of service. And the city pays three-quarters of the cost of firefighters' pension benefits. Is this fair? When you consider that most taxpayers don't even have a company pension, is it fair?[43] When there are 2,800 retired firefighters getting pensions, and only 2,300 actually working, is it fair? And firefighters are not the sole beneficiaries of municipal generosity. Even the average Montreal blue collar costs $92,000 a year "all in."

And it's not just the rank-and-file who are retiring younger yet receiving multiples of what a private-sector pensioner gets.[44] In May 2010, Montreal Police Chief Yvan Delorme retired. Delorme was a good chief, but there is something radically wrong with a system that allows a forty-seven-year-old police chief to retire with a $135,000 indexed pension after only twenty-seven years of service.[45] It was bad enough in 2004, when the Montreal fire chief retired at fifty-two with a pension of around $105,000 a year. The municipal sector does need to pay more for top executives in order to be more competitive, but it should attack the problem directly, rather than using cushy pension benefits to attract new talent.

Along with the stock market meltdown in 2008, these kinds of generous payouts and the provision for future ones explain the dizzying increase in City of Montreal pension costs from $187 million in 2008 to $609 million in 2012. Until Montreal grasps this particular nettle, all other budget-cutting measures are just bromides. But, essentially, only Quebec legislation can deal with these runaway municipal pension costs and the fiscal elephantiasis they engender.

Louis Roquet, Montreal's former director-general, was quite open and categorical about the need to rein in employee benefits, especially pension benefits.[46] He even referred to a "war" in the making. He said that Montreal employee benefits were running at 36 to 38 per cent of base salary, compared to large corporations ("that treat their employees well") where the figure was more like 21 to 23 per cent. Roquet undershot: in 2012, City of Montreal benefits were running at 56 per cent of salary, up from 26 per cent in 2002.[47] If Montreal employees got the same benefits as in large private corporations, the megacity would save around $500 million a year, as the increased cost of pensions continues apace.[48]

The white-collar union was not particularly happy with Roquet's comments, saying that the city should look at management and elected officials' salaries, which, they said, had more than doubled since the mergers – and they were not wrong. As for the blue-collar union, they said they were determined to recuperate the benefits lost by an arbitration decision six years before.

A MEGACITY REPORT CARD

In December 2010, commissioned by *La Presse*,[49] Angus Reid took a poll of residents of the Island suburbs that had demerged, residents of the former suburbs that remained merged, and residents of the former City of Montreal.[50] Only 20 per cent of the demerged residents said the merger was a good thing; 65 per cent said the opposite. Of the residents of the suburbs that remained merged, twice as many said the merger was a bad thing rather than good. Even in the former City of Montreal, more residents said the merger was a bad thing than a good one.[51] To the question "Is the City of Montreal better managed than before the mergers?" roughly 10 per cent of residents right across the Island said yes, with nearly five times as many saying no. When asked if they would vote to reintegrate into the megacity, two-thirds of the residents of the demerged suburbs said no and only 11 per cent said yes.[52] When those residents of former suburbs that remained merged were asked if they would vote to demerge, a slight majority said yes.[53]

On the tenth anniversary of the megacity, *Montreal Gazette*'s Henry Aubin asked people in the Tremblay administration if they could identify achievements over the past decade that could not have been realized without merger.[54] They cited major projects such as the Quartier des Spectacles, new revenue sources, investments in public transit and in infrastructure, and the first-responder service the merged fire department now provides. Aubin points out that all of these things could have been done without merger. As far as the last "achievement" is concerned, Westmount and many other former cities had a first-responder service for years before merger.

CENTRALIZATION AND DILUTION OF BOROUGH AUTONOMY

Starting in late 2010, there was a definite trend in the Montreal megacity to centralization in purchasing, real-estate acquisition and management, and hiring. Even snow removal got "coordinated." This, of course, was in direct contradiction to Tremblay's engagement in 2004, when he was trying to stop boroughs from demerging by promising the same autonomy as the demerged cities would have. I predicted this slow loss of autonomy back in 2004, which I constantly used as a counterargument to his blandishments to get people to stay.

It won't stop there. For example, the auditor-general's report for 2010 noted that boroughs are responsible for the maintenance of structures such as walls, bridges, and tunnels, whereas the central city pays for building new ones. There is therefore no incentive for the boroughs to spend on preventative maintenance, which is the best way to ensure the longevity of capital investments. The pressure will mount for the central city to take over maintenance. Of course, there will be no suggestions going the other way: that the boroughs have complete control of capital spending.

Originally, the boroughs were supposed to be modelled after the fairly lean suburbs, not Montreal. LaSalle, being of some size, was supposed to be taken as the archetype. Instead, the heavy Montreal bureaucratic structure was replicated in nineteen miniature variants. Today, this is one of the reasons why decentralization is far from cheap. Originally, also, there was supposed to be a big equalization fund to be divvied up among the boroughs. This fund remains at $12 million today, so CDN-NDG, the "neediest" of the boroughs, gets an amount barely equal to 2 per cent of its budget.

OUTREMONT *OUTRÉ*

From 2002 on, the borough of Outremont suffered from sopho-moronic shenanigans all the way to criminal behaviour, from the room at its city hall fitted out with a "piano bar" costing $1,000 a month to stock with single-malt scotch and wine, to the mayor billing $2,200 worth of his English lessons to his "political adviser" in order that they be paid by the borough, to fraud on the part of the director-general and the political adviser, to funding the 2005 election with fat wads of cash from local restaurateurs and contractors, to a doubling of the cost of building a community centre. In April 2010, Mayor Harbour, the director-general, and the political adviser were arrested and accused of fraud totalling an amount of $72,000.

Was this an example of why decentralization didn't work? Well, no – aside from the fact that all this happened after the mergers when Outremont had been downgraded to a borough. In a centralized megacity, one has to depend on the print media to uncover things, but even they are not as effective as concerned citizens at the local level. It took investigations by a group of suspicious citizens to drag the mess into public view and then one of the councillors as a whistleblower to start more formal inquiries. Things were slowed down because all the councillors were members of Gérald Tremblay's party, which is yet another reason why political parties at the local level make no sense.

The point about citizen oversight on local councils cannot be made strongly enough. We can attract up to fifty people at a typical council meeting in Westmount, as I am sure Outremont does too. Pro rata to our population, that's the equivalent of an impossible four thousand attending a megacity council meeting. We are in retail, not wholesale democracy.

IS TREMBLAY THE PROBLEM?

So, starting in 2009, the City of Montreal looked more and more like an open bar under the unsuspecting nose of bartender Tremblay. In the past, I never had much regard for Tremblay, as I never forgave him for going back on his word not to interfere with demergers; and while he was dedicated and worked non-stop, his technocratic ratiocination made him less than effective. I must say, however, on seeing him go through hell in the summer of 2009, when one corruption scandal after another was breaking over his head and *La Presse* was telling him not to run again, I really did feel sorry for him. My pity bordered on grudging respect as he ploughed his way on, all the way to the elections. Some speculated that it was his Christian faith that saw him through.

After his near-death experience of the scandals and the November 2009 elections, we saw the emergence of a new Tremblay, a penitent Tremblay, who had learned his lesson. He became far less partisan, for one thing. Not only did he allow two opposition party members into his executive committee (while making himself chairman, it must be said)[55] but he set things in motion to give more clout to the standing committees. Early in 2010, he called for a public budget process involving opposition parties, the first in Montreal's history.[56] Unfortunately, by mid-2011, he had ditched the two opposition councillors and got rid of the new, open budget process. His desire for redemption at least continues with the demerged suburbs; we enjoy a good rapport.

The media made much of Tremblay's unregenerate naïveté. I would rather have an uncorrupt mayor who was naive than a corrupt mayor who was wise in the ways of the world. From the comfort of their keyboards, it was easy for the media to sermonize and call for Tremblay's resignation. In my view, it is unfair to place the blame for the spate of scandals squarely at his feet. Yes, to some extent he was the architect of his own misfortune, but as the megacity is ungovernable, its administrative and political structure is a petri dish in which corruption can breed. The media take on it was that if Montreal had an effective mayor, these scandals would never have happened. Even if that were possible, history shows that Montreal has never had an effective mayor. Why, after Montreal annexed its suburbs, would anything change?

Had the megacity been created by a true merger – the joining of equals – Montreal's penchant for corruption might have been dissipated, or at least diluted. But the megacity was created by annexation: the methods, management, and morality of the old City of Montreal were the norm. Corruption grew from a well-entrenched foundation. Yes, there was evidence of sporadic corruption in some of the former suburban municipalities or current boroughs, but it was not uniform. It did not have Montreal's massive base. The corruption in Saint-Laurent in 2002 had to do with bribes for a zoning change; the scandal later in Outremont was a matter of small-time fraud. The raft of scandals that shook the megacity in 2009, however, were more systemic and had to do with the awarding of contracts made juicier and plumper by the fact of the merger.

And when I blame the megacity, I am not blaming its employees. After all, proportionally, Montreal elected officials have a far sorrier record than Montreal employees do. Of all the politicians elected in the megacity since its inception, roughly 2 per cent are either convicted or accused criminals.[57] This proportion, which I imagine is much higher than what is found in the general population, when applied to City of Montreal employees, would suggest a very improbable four hundred criminals.

As I write this, most apologists for the Montreal megacity have moved away from fingering Tremblay and corruption as the cause of the obvious failure of the megacity, and are now blaming Tremblay and decentralization. Having seen both Bourque and Tremblay in action, I am convinced that Tremblay is the better mayor, and a far less dangerous one at that. Yet no one called the former City of Montreal a failure because of Bourque. If the megacity is so delicate that it can be ruined by one individual, then it is a failure. Likewise, if the megacity needs a man of the stamp of Quebec City's Mayor Labeaume in order for it to be a success, it is equally a failure. To place the megacity mess at the feet of one man is a dangerous simplification. It's not the captain, it's the ship. Yes, as Tremblay's detractors are constantly saying, his attempt at decentralization is part of the megacity's problem of complexity, but for the opposite reasons they give. It's because Tremblay did not go far enough.

That being said, Tremblay's weakness as a mayor is his inability to attract or to retain strong and competent people around him – whether it be a director-general, his executive committee chairman, his key elected officials, his chief of staff, or even his political advisers. You would think he has a revolving door – not an open door – management style. As a boss, Tremblay is a lone wolf. This is a failing he shares with Pierre Bourque. No one individual alone can run the City of Montreal, not even a Jean Drapeau. And it needs consistency; Tremblay is on his fifth director-general since he started as mayor. His choices of executive committee chairs have been questionable at best. However, his backing of Michel Labrecque as chair of the mass transit board was inspired. Competent, enthusiastic, and honest, Labrecque has placed a firm hand on the STM and is seeing it though a kind of renaissance.

Tremblay achieved other things. He caused the city to invest heavily in mass transit and waterworks. He chivvied the region's mayors into adopting a master land-use and development plan, and he got union peace – at a price, mind you. On the other hand, he has done terribly in controlling costs. Even Bixi, a brilliant made-in-Montreal bike-share idea with worldwide appeal, was so mismanaged under the city's aegis that Montreal had to bail it out to the tune of $108 million in loans and guarantees.

Regardless of who happens to be in power, the thing that strikes me is the persistent glaring amateurism of Montreal's political class, and the relative professionalism (not unmixed with lethargy) of the administration.

One further thing: if I have accomplished anything in these last three years as a recycled leader of the Island suburbs, it is to prove that multiple municipalities on the Island of Montreal can get along, as indeed they did before the merger. I could not have achieved this without Gérald Tremblay and his policy, thick with irony, of working cooperatively with his "partners," the Island suburbs. Thanks to this policy, one of the reasons given for the merger – and re-conscripted in the fight to stop demerger – has been proved false. This reason was the supposed inability of the Island suburbs to work with the City of Montreal, a grave malady, it was said, that only merger could cure.

Making Good: Rebuilding Montreal's Local and Regional Government

Facts do not cease to exist because they are ignored.

Aldous Huxley

When I arrived in Quebec in 1968, there was a heady feeling that the province could do anything. Montreal had just been graced with soaring elevated expressways and a lovable metro system with swish blue cars, all built in time for Expo 67. Thanks to Expo, Quebec said to the world, "We have arrived!" The vast territories of James Bay were being harnessed for cheap, plentiful, and clean electrical power, designed by Quebec engineering firms that went on to conquer world markets.

As I write this, Montreal is emerging from a Slough of Despond. Up until very recently, nothing seemed to work or get going. Montrealers even had a name for this malaise: *immobilisme*. For decades, no office buildings were built. It took over five years just to order replacement metro cars. A proposed east-end thoroughfare along Notre-Dame Street has been mired in tergiversations for years. For fifteen years, Montrealers argued about two new superhospitals that are only now being built.

And what has been built was oft-times shoddily done. Pieces of buildings are falling off, and a highway overpass built in 1970 collapsed in 2006, killing five people. In July 2011, great concrete beams suddenly crashed onto the roadway of the forty-year-old Ville-Marie tunnel when some poorly supervised crew was rehabilitating a supporting wall. After less than forty-five years, the gravity-defying swooshes of concrete expressways to downtown Montreal are being desperately patched to prevent them from crumbling. Quebec will have to spend well over $3 billion to re-do only part of it.[1] A third roof costing $300 million is needed for the 1976 Olympic Stadium.

A simple metro extension to Laval ballooned in cost from $179 million to $745 million, and a new commuter train line will cost over $700 million, double the estimate.[2] The pride of Quebec's financial empire and symbol of francophone economic emancipation, the Caisse de dépôt, managed to lose a quarter of its $155 billion in assets in the 2008 market dive – the worst performance of just about any other pension fund manager.

And the megacity that, we were told, would put Montreal on the world map instead has resulted in bloated spending and a string of corruption scandals.

Francophone Quebec has deep unmingled roots, deeper than any found in the rest of North America. Today the people who built the James Bay hydro projects and corporations such as Bombardier, Lavalin, SoftImage, CGI, and Circle du soleil seem dispirited. French Quebec is one huge extended family: a family that quarrels, a family that is inclusive, and a family that knows where it came from. But, right now, it is not a family that knows quite where it is going.

There is no political leadership in Quebec. Ennui and lassitude pervade. Its political class has let Quebec down. Private-sector management in Quebec competes internationally, sharing and learning from international methods. Public-sector management (or governance) is in a compartment of its own, isolated. Since there is more state intervention and control in Quebec than in other places in North America, the effect of its bad political management is more acute.

THE QUIET REVOLUTION

Quebec needs a second Quiet Revolution and a rebirth of the entrepreneurial spirit that created it. Sovereignty, the goal that followed the 1960–70 Quiet Revolution and fired up the creative, intellectual, and much of the political class in Quebec for the past two generations, seems now out of reach and no longer fuels the collective imagination.[3]

During the Quiet Revolution, the Quebec state wrested power from the Catholic Church, especially the responsibility for education and health. It is a Quebec commonplace to say that the state replaced the church. As well as achieving the secularization of social services and the modernization of the state's apparatus, the strong state created by the Quiet Revolution embodied the aspirations of Quebec's francophone élite and populace. Using what is now often referred to as the "Quebec Model," the state was the instrument of gaining economic independence from foreign owners. Public corporations were set up to manage natural resources; the government got into the business of mining, steel, forestry, petroleum, electricity, and asbestos,[4] in addition to bankrolling Quebec entrepreneurs. So this modernization process had strong elements of nationalization, centralization, and big government.

The following, written with knowledge, conviction, and insight by former premier Bernard Landry, explains and celebrates such state intervention:

> Born of the Quiet Revolution, the Quebec Model was conceived to incite and, at the same time, manage the profound changes for which our society had an obvious need at the time. It was especially necessary to get rid of the "colonialism" that still victimized Quebec. This term, which seems strong today, was alas appropriate for those days. It was not for nothing that [Premier] Jean Lesage proclaimed: "Masters in our own house!" We were practically excluded from economic power. There were but a very few directors of Quebec firms. Among them, a miniscule number came from the linguistic majority; and, often, they kept a low profile.
>
> It was our national State – which René Lévesque, when a Liberal minister, described as "the strongest among us" – that was the catalyst for a retaking of power that is now accomplished. At the heart of the process was the nationalization of electricity. From the outset, Hydro-Quebec and the *Caisse de dépôt* became the proof of our managerial ability, which was up until then treated with unbelievable contempt. These achievements of the state had a definite mobilizing effect on the private sector; first as examples, but also by various concrete economic effects in the form of business relationships.
>
> It was mainly the state that resulted in a number of entrepreneurial successes that today make us so proud. Without questioning the intelligence and the courage of those who gave birth to the great capitalism of Quebec, we must realize that most of them profited from the justified benevolence of the public powers. Would Bombardier today be the biggest manufacturer of railway equipment in the world if the City of Montreal had not awarded it, without a call for tenders, the [first] contract to make

metro cars – a field that, one can say without doubt, was not at all the original specialty of the firm?[5]

What helped francophone Quebec achieve economic emancipation may not be the solution to keep it free today. Yet old habits die hard: Quebec gives out over three times per capita the amount in government grants as does Ontario.[6] And it's not just corporate citizens: tuition fees have been frozen at a ridiculously low level in Quebec in the name of accessibility.[7] There are subsidized drug insurance and $7-a-day daycare. If Quebec provided the same level of services to its citizens as Ontario does, it would save $17.5 billion a year. And while it may be a legitimate collective choice, Quebecers don't work as much as others – and not just because of powerful unions. Half the men aged fifty-five to sixty-four in Quebec are employed, compared with two-thirds for the same group in the United States.[8] Quebec's 72,000 civil servants averaged fourteen sick days apiece in 2005 – 40 per cent more than the average civil servant in Canada. Quebecers work, on average, 1,730 hours per year, compared with people in Ontario at 1,820 hours and in the United States at 1,960. All this has a price. Notwithstanding its achievements, the Quebec Model has the downside of ever-increasing debt loads.

In spite of taxing its citizens more than any other place in North America – and a majority of Quebecers don't even pay income taxes – the province still comes up short. Two-thirds of its gross debt in 2009 was made up of the accumulated annual deficits that paid for all these services in the past.[9] Quebec even refuses to increase government-owned Hydro-Québec's electricity rates to levels that are closer to market value, as that extra income would reduce the equalization payments it gets from the richer Canadian provinces.

One of the most respected economists in Quebec, Pierre Fortin, calculates the Quebec provincial public sector debt in 2010 at $173 billion, a number that includes municipal, hospital, and educational system debt. This amount, he writes, is equal to 57 per cent of Quebec's GDP. But, he maintains, it's worse than that: since federal and provincial taxation revenue in Quebec is divided roughly 58 to 42 in favour of the province, that $173 billion debt is supported by only 58 per cent of all taxation revenues. Therefore, the debt is more or less equal to 100 per cent of the revenue base it has access to,[10] making Quebec among the most indebted places in the world.

TYRANNY OF THE RURALITY

Another cause of Quebec's economic malaise is its continuing rural obsession, something the Quiet Revolution did not get rid of. Territorial uniformity is king: all of Quebec is overlaid with ninety-six counties, grouped into seventeen administrative regions. This uniform hierarchy means that the natural homogenous urban region of Montreal is diced up to fit its merciless logic. Rather than a grid, the economic and demographic reality of Quebec is radial, with Montreal as its hub. The Island of Montreal alone produces 35 per cent of Quebec's GDP, and the whole Montreal Metropolitan Region produces 54 per cent.[11] This means that the rest of Quebec – with its vast regions, some eighty counties, and a thousand small cities, towns, and villages – only contributes 46 per cent of the province's GDP.[12] But you would not know it when dealing with Quebec mandarins, for whom the Island of Montreal is just "Region 06."[13]

Trying to shake off his image of being too cozy with the Montreal region (a political no-no in Quebec), Premier Jean Charest made overtures to rural Quebec from the moment he was elected in 2003. His first appointment to the position of municipal affairs minister was Nathalie Normandeau, the former mayor of Maria (population 2,500). While Normandeau gamely struggled to understand Metropolitan Montreal, she was clearly chosen to please the regions. In June 2009, Charest named Laurent Lessard as municipal affairs minister. The former mayor of Thetford Mines (population 25,000) and former minister of agriculture, Lessard is bright, direct, and really does his homework, but he too is somewhat hobbled by his regional background when it comes to Montreal.[14]

The Quebec government refuses to recognize the strategic importance of Montreal. As Alain Dubuc wrote in *La Presse,* "This refusal is based in part on the transposition at the territorial level of a philosophy that consists of wanting to redistribute wealth before it is created. It is also based on obvious anti-urban, and more particularly, anti-Montreal biases."[15] Claude Castonguay, a highly respected former politician who put in place Quebec's health-insurance system, wrote that Quebec ignores Montreal at its peril:

> According to recent data from Statistics Canada, Montreal and its surrounding cities created, during the course of the last year [2006], the entirety of all new employment in Quebec. With

more than 50 per cent of the Quebec population, the Montreal Metropolitan Region produces 70 per cent of Quebec's exports. This performance has an effect of masking the very worrying situation regarding the creation of jobs in the rest of Quebec.

From a fiscal point of view, if statistics on the source of revenues by region were available, a similar picture to that of employment would be revealed. Indeed, since data exist on the amount of public spending in each region, it would be possible to quantify the equalization payments made from Montreal in favour of the regions. Instead of seeing Montreal in a negative light, Quebecers could then better grasp its importance in government revenues and in its ability to redistribute in favour of the regions ...

Quebec continues to see Montreal as a region just like any other ... Election after election, the result is never determined in the metropolis. This explains the fact that it is, for all practical purposes, ignored ... Regional politics take the place of honour in governmental actions and in public debate in Quebec ... In reality, two completely different worlds coexist in Quebec: one is the Montreal Metropolitan Region, and the other one is made up of the other cities and regions. The fact that the capital and the government are situated far away from Montreal definitely does not help in the understanding of the challenges that it faces.[16]

Quebec's negligence of Montreal exacerbates a continuing loss of corporate headquarters.[17] And even within the Montreal Metropolitan Region, Quebec's policies have encouraged urban sprawl – breezily declared a non-issue by the cities circumjacent to Montreal Island – which results in redundant infrastructure investment. Another pernicious effect of urban sprawl is that in a few years French will become the minority language on the Island of Montreal.[18] Quebec cannot afford this linguistic hollowing-out.

Ten years after mergers were imposed, the francophone media and Louise Harel continue to retail the idea that they were a good idea. Look at Quebec City, Trois-Rivières, Saguenay, they say: these megacities have been declared a success by their (hardly unbiased) mayors. Only Montreal is a failure. Once again, the uniformization and reductionism of Quebec's municipal philosophy is at work here, as if Trois-Rivières could be a reasonable template for Montreal, which is saddled with a budget twenty times greater. Even if the medicine were the right one – which I deny – it is not a treatment that could work irrespective of size, degree of heterogeneity, or international influence.

THE QUIET REVOLUTION REDUX?

Rebuilding local and regional governments in Metropolitan Montreal, the right way this time, is a must. Quebec also needs to "decolonize" the Montreal region within the Quebec state. Quebec could show the rest of the world how local and regional government should be organized. This will certainly not happen by catering mostly to the regions. Indeed, some commentators are starting to worry about the power the new regional megacities of Quebec City, Saguenay, Lévis, and Trois-Rivières can wield: "It allows a centralizing mayor to have the means equal to his ambitions."[19] All this can only continue to suck government resources towards the regions. Recently, Jean-Marc Beaudoin of *Le Nouvelliste*, wrote: "Thanks to municipal mergers or because of them, we have seen in a number of Quebec megacities the emergence of omnipotent mayors. Veritable *seigneurs* who control everything in their city; who pay scant attention to protest movements; who make fun of, and walk over, their opposition when there is any left; and who are elected by complete landslides. Mayors who have traction; resolutely populist; with a pile of projects, some sensible, some not; of whom Quebec Mayor Régis Labeaume is only the most flagrant example."[20]

The City of Montreal itself desperately needs to be knocked into shape administratively. While its politicians must avoid thinking that bread and circuses such as the F-1 Grand Prix or a few swimming meets will put Montreal on the map, there is one project that could transform Montreal. Pierre Bourque's idea of Montreal Blue should be revived: we should open up the singular natural richness of a majestic river to Montrealers. The St Lawrence River could be the Mount Royal Park of this century.

In the rest of this chapter, I briefly return to Montreal's overspending, the key internal problem facing the megacity; I also look at two key external problems: urban sprawl and the superfluity of government structures. I then, most presumptuously, suggest solutions.

MEGA-SPENDING WILL CONTINUE IF UNCHECKED

As a species, the skill of homo sapiens to create wonder drugs, supersonic jets, computer chips, and even medieval cathedrals is not often matched by an equal ability to create efficient government structures. Certainly in Quebec the megacity structure just does not work.

The megacity is grossly inefficient. Its yearly report cards, known as financial statements, reveal a mounting malaise of overspending, but the defining moment of the Montreal megacity came nearly six years after its birth when the $0.5 billion water-management contract sailed through city council in less than a minute without objection or discussion. That such a stunningly bad decision could so easily be recommended *and* approved was irrefutable proof that, with its political parties, a lack of citizen oversight, a sixty-four-member council, an all-powerful executive committee, many standing committees, and a massive city administration, the megacity is patently unworkable. In short, the megacity flunked its finals.

By removing externally controlled costs and only tracking the costs affected by merger, I calculate the imposition of the megacity has a price tag of an additional $400 million in yearly spending (see appendix). The main cause of this profligacy is overstaffing and overcompensation of employees. And the demerged suburbs, because of their four-year stint as part of the megacity, have seen their staffing, along with wages, salaries, and benefits, rise almost to Montreal heights.

URBAN SPRAWL

Now on to the megacity's external problems: urban sprawl and the surfeit of structures. Did the megacity do what its supporters predicted and slow the exodus to points off-Island, along with the fiscal inequality that such urban sprawl engenders? The years following the merger showed a one-third *increase* in migration to off-Island suburbs. Not only was the overwhelming majority of this net exodus made up of francophones but nearly 40 per cent of them were in their thirties.[21] Only in 2009 did things start to go back to a pre-merger rate. As the *Montreal Gazette*'s Henry Aubin wrote, "People are voting on the megacity with their feet."[22] If it weren't for new residents coming from outside Quebec, the Island population would have dropped by 150,000 people from 2002 to 2009. In March 2010, Tremblay announced a $48 million "bouquet of measures" in an attempt to stem the tide of young families to off-Island locales.

To its credit, Montreal has always supported public housing. Mind you, off-Island municipalities are only too happy it does. The trouble with Montreal's persistent catering to the home-needy and tenants is that Montreal desperately needs more of the middle classes and small property owners who have massively succumbed to the siren song of the off-Island suburbs. Montreal politicians still don't get it. In February 2010, an opposition city councillor in NDG was elated about a four-hundred unit housing project with a 25 per cent low-cost housing element, up from the required 15 per cent. His party had been calling for this sort of thing "in an effort to halt the flow of families from Montreal to the suburbs."[23] If the long-standing Montreal policy of subsidized housing could have stanched the flow, it would have done so by now. Socially right-minded it might be, but it won't bring back the middle classes.

Ah, but off-Island deniers of urban sprawl claim that Metropolitan Montreal is more densely populated than other such regions in North America and better served by mass transit.[24] Yet between 2006 and 2031, figures produced by the Institut de la statistique du Québec suggest, the Island of Montreal will grow by a meagre 12 per cent in population (19 per cent in households), whereas Metropolitan Montreal will grow by 20 per cent in population (and 29 per cent in households). The north shore (excluding Laval) will grow by 39 per cent, and the south shore (excluding Longueuil) will grow by 32 per cent.[25] The Island of Montreal will lose 500,000 residents, mostly to settle off-Island. If it weren't for a gain of 700,000 new residents from outside Canada, the population of the Island of Montreal would *drop* 26 per cent from 2006 to 2031, according to this study.

The Montreal region's urban sprawl can be expressed in the simplest terms: forty years ago, the Montreal Island population was 1,959,180 and represented 71 per cent of the Census Metropolitan Region. Today it has dropped to 1,886,481, which is only 49 per cent of the whole.

And commuting distances don't improve. In the Montreal Metropolitan Region, the median commuting distance was 8.1 kilometres in 2006. The equivalent distance in Toronto was 9.4, and in Quebec City, 6.9. Fully 40 per cent of Metropolitan Montreal commuters live more than fifteen kilometres from work if their dwelling was built within the past five years and more than ten kilometres if their residence is older.[26]

That the Quebec government encourages urban sprawl is evident. It even allowed the University of Sherbrooke to establish a foothold in Longueuil and Laval University to have a presence in downtown Montreal, as if the four universities in the metropolitan region were not enough and didn't have all the subsidies they could handle. These offshoots drain students away from Montreal universities to courses that are already offered. And the government continues to de-zone the agricultural belt around Montreal. Hubert Meilleur, mayor of Mirabel, the fastest-growing municipality in Canada, said Montreal's exurbs are running out of land for development. Without de-zoning, the exurbs are headed for financial difficulties. "I don't think we have any other choice but to de-zone," Meilleur said.[27]

The government also exclusively funds the new hospitals, schools, and highways that urban sprawl demands. And Montreal Island taxpayers even indirectly subsidize off-Island schools: they pay nearly one-third of all school property taxes in Quebec, while representing only one-quarter of its population. While the highway system, indispensible for urban sprawl, is completely paid for by the government, property taxpayers are the biggest contributor to the operation of public transit on Montreal Island.

Of all the trips using public transit in Quebec, fully 70 per cent take place on the Island of Montreal, with its 760 metro cars and 1,700 buses. Yet government subsidies make up only 9 per cent of Montreal Island mass transit operating revenues. Well, at least it's better than nothing, which is what we had twenty years ago. When in 1991 Claude Ryan left the Montreal Island cities to carry the empty can after he cut all operating subsidies to mass transit, he said, "Don't worry, we'll let you charge more in 'welcome' taxes and commercial taxes, and we'll even give you $30 per car registration to help pay for buses and the metro." Twenty years later, half of that $30 subsidizes suburban trains, which also gobble up half of a 3 cents-per-litre gas tax. Far-flung suburban train services, such as the new one to Mascouche, serving only 11,000 commuters, are the beneficiary of this manna – something that actually encourages urban sprawl.

The Montreal Transit Corporation (STM) hit a high of 383 million trips in 2009. The last time it did so was in 1949. The number of trips bottomed out at 265 million in 1973 and has been climbing ever since. This success did not come cheap, however. Today, the riders of the STM pay half of its costs, so a monthly pass that cost $49 (in today's dollars) in 1990 has ballooned to $75.50 in 2012 – a 50 per cent growth *after inflation*. Montreal Island property taxpayers have been even more squeezed; they fork over roughly $400 million to the STM today, compared with $300 million in the year 2000, and $200 million in 1990 (in today's dollars) – a 100 per cent growth *after inflation*. Property taxes, which started off life as a way to pay for local municipal services, have been turned into a cash cow for mass transit, a strictly regional service. Very regional: since the last metro expansion in 1988, there has been very little mass transit spending on the Island, but billions of dollars have been spent off-Island.

It is true that Mayor Tremblay managed to cajole most of the mayors in the Montreal Metropolitan Community (the CMM) into accepting a metropolitan land-use and development plan (in French, PMAD) in December 2011. But this plan is not as constraining as it first appears. While a modest 40 per cent of new housing is supposed to be so-called transit-oriented development (TOD), three-quarters of that TOD is slated to take place on the Island of Montreal, meaning the rest of the region will be (as always) almost exclusively dependent on transportation by car. Besides, only 38 per cent of all new households in the region are supposed to be built on the Island, whereas its capacity is far greater. Another problem with the plan is that is does not address any of the fiscal unfairness that comes from Montreal Islanders paying for full police services, most school busing, and disproportionate mass transit funding. Lastly, because the plan is applicable to a fixed geography, it cannot stop leapfrogging of development outside its perimeter. Only Quebec can stop that.

APING THE SUBURBS: DOWNTOWN SURBANITY

In the same way that trains have now scrapped their elegant dining cars and needlessly copied airline food service, the city core has unfortunately been shedding its urbanity while aping the suburbs. Montreal's downtown mallification continues apace: department stores have metamorphosed into vertical shopping malls, with stalls for each brand. While there are no acres of asphalt for car parking as in the suburbs, lamp posts, garbage bins, and parking meters make an obstacle course to the downtown pedestrian's progress. Montreal's sidewalks in winter develop a permafrost coating; they are the last surface to be cleared of snow.

Montreal will pull itself up only if it differentiates itself from the suburbs and doesn't try to copy them. It must preserve and enhance its urban sophistication and heritage. Eaton's was a stellar example of what not to do. Eaton's in Montreal was a starchy aunt of a department store, with more style in its architecture than most of its goods on offer. Taking up the entire ninth floor was a breathtaking replica of the high-ceilinged dining room of an ocean liner sailing on Art Deco seas. The city allowed this dowager building to be ignominiously eviscerated by central escalators, its guts ripped out as both an offering to the gods of the Atrium and to accommodate the banal failure of the store that replaced it – at no small cost. In 2004, Eaton's sub-basement was turned into a vast Stygian food court, Canada's largest, seating 1,600 people. Not a ray of natural light penetrates and the oppressively low ceilings, plastic-tray clatter, and conflicting smells make it a 1990s engine room compared to the airy 1930s dining room sitting idle nine floors above.

Outlying residents might move back to a real city, but not to a poor imitation of the suburbs.

STRUCTURAL SPRAWL

Montreal has grown complicated. Currently, if one examines thirteen separate municipal services (water, mass transit, police, recreation, housing, and so on) in the metropolitan region, they are treated at anywhere from two to four levels – borough, city, agglomeration (or county, outside the Island), and the Montreal Metropolitan Community (CMM). Only policing is dealt with at one level. Economic development gets four levels of interference, as does urban planning. Even refuse – today elevated to the status of "residual materials" – gets three. Each borough or city is responsible for refuse collection, the agglomeration is responsible for its disposal, and the CMM is responsible for planning the whole exercise.

The CMM's jurisdiction includes planning at the metropolitan level for economic development, arts and culture promotion, land-use and development (including public transit and the arterial road network), solid waste, air quality, and wastewater. It is also responsible for infrastructure, facilities, services, and activities of a metropolitan nature – including social and affordable housing. Recently, the counties got back land-use planning.

As well as the CMM, we have one Metropolitan Transport Agency (AMT), five administrative regions, seven Conferences of Elected Officials, twelve counties, twenty public transit boards, and thirty development organizations.[28] In February 2004 the OECD produced a devastating report on the Montreal region: if the tangle of structures that handicap the region was not cleaned up, Montreal would suffer economically. The power of the CMM must be boosted, they said, with universal suffrage and delivery of services; the AMT and all economic development efforts must be folded into the CMM.

Now on to solutions. If the Montreal megacity had been a good idea, but one that was done for the wrong reasons, or done in the wrong way, it would make sense to leave it alone. But the megacity was a bad idea that compounded municipal problems rather than solved them. The first step in the remediation of the overlaid governance of the Montreal Metropolitan Region is to admit the megacity was indeed a mistake.

While, *pace* Harel, the status quo before 2002 was definitely an option and a far better one than mergers, even I don't recommend we simply replicate the status quo ante. While the current situation is far worse than what we had, what we did have was not devoid of problems.

The Montreal merger debacle teaches us that urban mergers do not bring savings, fiscal equity, or a solution to urban sprawl. The whole sorry story of the mergers and the downloading of the last twenty years has also taught us that *urban* local and regional governments need more autonomy – existential, fiscal, structural, and operational autonomy – to function properly and, indeed, to attract elected officials of high calibre.

Existential autonomy: Any proposed municipal merger or annexation must be legitimized by the formal acquiescence of the citizens of each individual municipality involved. Quebec should adopt a Charter of Municipal Rights, taking its inspiration from the World Charter of Local Government.

Fiscal autonomy: Urban sprawl should be slowed by local, regional, and provincial fiscal regimes that would require property owners to pay the full cost of their decision to move to the exurbs – in other words, to shoulder the cost of new highways, hospitals, or schools in their area. This could be done though such measures as special school property taxes, development charges paid to Quebec, and a regional sharing of property taxes from new development. Off-Island suburbs should also contribute to metropolitan costs currently assumed by Montreal Island property-owners. Municipalities should employ user-fees intensively, making property taxes a minor component of their revenues. Mass transit should be funded not though property taxes but by increasing the tax on gasoline and car registrations, and by a return to substantial government operating subsidies. After all, highways are not funded through property taxes, and school busing, outside the Island of Montreal, is paid for by Quebec. Lastly, any new responsibilities shifted to municipalities must be accompanied by sufficient and permanent new revenues.

Structural autonomy: Quebec must create a Department of Metropolitan Montreal, with its own minister. The Montreal conurbation should have nothing to do with the Department of Municipal Affairs, Regions, and Land Occupancy and its uniform treatment of Quebec municipalities rural or urban, big and small. Rather than the two full and three partial administrative regions through which all government services are channelled, the Montreal Metropolitan Region should revert to being just one administrative region. All the other government structures cluttering up the region should be dissolved and their budget envelopes given to local or regional governments. Urban municipalities should have the power to structure themselves as they see fit, as decentralized as possible. They should be able to establish the size of their own councils, and subsidies for municipal political parties should cease, although independent candidates should continue to be supported.

Operational autonomy: It must be acknowledged that the biggest problem facing Montreal municipalities is the fact they pay their employees 30–40 per cent more than the rest of the province's public sector. Quebec must devolve onto the Montreal Region some legislative power to fix this longstanding problem, including complete freedom to contract out for blue collar and white collar work to bring the discipline of the marketplace into the equation.

BREAKING UP IS NOT HARD TO DO

In my view, over time Montrealers will have to transfer their admittedly tenuous allegiance to a fiction based on geography (the

Island) to a larger reality based on demography (the region). How many individual municipalities make up this reality is less important, but one megacity containing half the region's population is just too big. Eventually the megacity must be broken up or radically decentralized. The need or desire to break things up presents itself in large municipalities and in large corporations. General Motors did it by maintaining mildly competing standalone marques with their own bodies and engines, aimed at different market segments. Since municipalities are in the service business only, the need to deliver local services with flexibility and autonomy is even more pronounced. Even the army (the ultimate "service" industry) finds it more effective to break up its otherwise monolithic structure. The British and Canadian armies are based on the regimental unit, each different, and each fostering unique traditions, loyalty, and a sense of family.

A single meal at a local restaurant will invariably taste better than the identical meal costing the same served at a thousand-person banquet – plus you get choice. Breaking things up increases the quality and variety of the offering – and, municipally, it decreases the cost. If you are satisfied with uniform services, then you might settle for a centralized municipal system, but the costs will be higher. If you want to be citizen driven and adaptable locally, full decentralization of a city is the answer. Most members of the staff in a large bureaucracy are so far removed from the citizens they are supposed to serve that they forget what they are really there for. Municipalities should be looking at things not from the bureaucrat's perspective but from that of the taxpayers. We have to move to a citizen-as-customer from a citizen-as-consumer mentality.

In private industry, the payment for a service is intimately linked to the delivery and nature of that service. People choose among services based on price versus quality. In local government services, one can only do this, as Charles Tiebout pointed out, by moving to another municipality. With wholesale mergers, this ability is curtailed, and one gets uniform quality at a cost that has nothing to do with the service rendered.

Why not just radically decentralize megacity services? In any municipality, decentralization of local services generally only works if you decentralize both the input and the output: the revenue and the spending. Otherwise the handout from central management will arrive with many conditions and uniform standards attached to it.

You also need a third element: a local political culture. It's like a three-legged stool: you have to decentralize the political, the fiscal, and the administrative elements equally. Political decentralization (the easiest to put in place) matched with centralized taxation and bureaucracy allows the local politicians to shrug their shoulders and say, "I'd like to help you, but my hands are tied. The problem's at the next level." Even with political and administrative decentralization, the local politician is still not really accountable: "We have no money for it. They cut our yearly handout. They needed the money elsewhere. I could raise local fees or taxes, but they'll just cut our handout even more." Once you fully decentralize the political, the fiscal, and the administrative, you run the risk of powerful boroughs warring in the bosom of a single municipality. While to try to avoid friction in politics is Pollyannaish, if you are going to have it, it should at least be between clearly distinct entities. So you come full circle and might as well create a network of smaller municipalities. In other words, the end state of any true decentralization process is a series of small municipalities.

A municipality and its citizens form a pyramidal structure: the greater the population, the greater the distance between the served and the servers: that is, between the council and the citizens. The distance in between is made up of increasing layers of bureaucrats. Provincial and federal governments are far more diffuse. A premier, for example, does not directly run a hospital or a school. The link is much more tenuous. When a bacterium was found in the ventilation system of a hospital, no one called the premier about it. But if the toilets don't work in the arena, or if the snow stays around too long, or if there's a spate of break-ins somewhere, the mayor's office is the first to hear of it – in a smaller municipality. In a megacity, only the lobbyists get to talk to the mayor,[29] while complaints get lost in the system.

After nearly a century of existence essentially in the same physical form, the old City of Montreal never developed cohesiveness, nor did its citizens develop a sense of belonging. It was always a loose collection of wonderful neighbourhoods, run by an indifferent, remote, and expensive bureaucracy. That the architects of the megacity thought that an even bigger city could somehow make Montrealers start to embrace it always surprised me. Bulking up has not made the Montreal megacity any more cohesive – and certainly not more loved – than its predecessor.

RELATIVITY AND CITY SIZE

Whenever the government goes about amalgamating municipalities, its citizens have become conditioned to what they know, and any changes are inevitably compared to the prior condition. If the only municipality a person has known is a large one, there is small likelihood that that person will militate for it to be broken up or care whether it grows. Likewise, citizens of the pre-merger Montreal, while upset by the lack of consultation, did not see much difference once the megacity was imposed and Montreal went from servicing 1.0 million people to 1.8 million. But for citizens of Westmount or the Town of Mount Royal, their municipality suddenly became one hundred times larger.[30] Municipalities delivering local services have a maximum size when it comes to efficiency, and that size is pretty small.[31] In the Toronto amalgamation, where the average population of the pre-merger municipalities had been 400,000, there was more of a change than experienced by the residents of the former City of Montreal, but not nearly as much as for the Montreal Island suburbs. In fact, the *smallest* municipality amalgamated to create the megacity of Toronto was nearly 40 per cent larger than the *biggest* suburban municipality in Montreal. And Toronto had been more "pre-merged" by Metro Toronto.

BLAME MEGACITY WOES ON DECENTRALIZATION?

The decentralization question amounts to this: should the City of Montreal be regarded as a loose federation of boroughs or a unitary city whose core metes out limited power to the boroughs? Is the model one of orbiting planets that get their power and direction from the sun, or is it a constellation of suns?

By November 2007, in trying to explain the evident Montreal megacity mess, Louise Harel had taken to saying that the mergers were a success everywhere in Quebec except Montreal. When she ran for megacity mayor in 2009, she upped the intensity of her message. The megacity, she said, was severely compromised by the 2006 demergers, and even more importantly, by the decentralization – the creation of "quasi-municipalities" – that the Charest government gave to Mayor Tremblay in 2003 in a desperate attempt to seduce electors in former suburbs into voting against regaining their freedom.[32] She cited the "borough mayors" who were, after decentralization, elected by universal suffrage rather than by their peers, even though her own law (Bill 170) allowed direct election for the equivalent positions in the former suburbs. She inveighed against the increased powers of boroughs to negotiate collective agreements, hire and fire staff, borrow, tax, take legal action – again, always failing to mention that these powers were severely circumscribed.

Louis Roquet, Montreal's former director-general, also believed that Montreal is too decentralized, though he would not have gone as far as Harel. With respect, I disagree with him. A much greater decentralization toward a city-like borough would eliminate the biggest albatross Montreal has: its centralized management costing hundreds of millions a year. Roquet wanted to move administrative services upwards; I would move them downwards.

When the apologists for the megacity – the unions, Harel, the media pundits – blamed mounting megacity costs on decentralization and the nineteen "little cities" within the megacity, they forgot that half of the pre-existing condition was made up of full-fledged "little cities"; an arrangement that cost $400 million a year less to run.

Before the mergers, municipal spending on the Island of Montreal (not including an independent body, the transit board) was broken down very roughly as 30 per cent MUC, 30 per cent suburbs, and 40 per cent the former City of Montreal. They all got fused into one unit. Was it the centralization of the MUC and the centralization of the suburbs that caused the explosion of costs, or was it the decentralization within the old City of Montreal? Paradoxically, it could have been all three.

1 The MUC managed to operate with only 3 per cent (about $30 million) of its spending going to administrative costs, as its main services such as police and wastewater treatment were pretty much self-reliant. These services now are saddled with nearly $200 million of administration costs,[33] as, once folded into the megacity, the services got a boosted layer of management dumped on top of them.

2 The suburbs, on becoming boroughs, kept a lot of their existing overheads and got a reinforced layer downtown. As well, the salaries, benefits, and working hours of employees in the former suburbs have now risen to Montreal levels, thanks to the merger; the genie is out of that bottle.

3 Lastly, the former City of Montreal, in a have-cake-and-eat-it mode, created new management structures to deliver local services and kept some of the old structures in the centre city.

MONTREAL: THE COUNCIL AND THE PARTY SYSTEM

In any government organization, bureaucrats flow upstream towards the administrative centre. They are promoted from a job of serving the citizen to one of serving the organization, from the field to the desk, line to staff, and ministration to administration.[34] Bureaucratic forces seek safety: they are both centripetal and self-reinforcing. And the bigger the city, the greater the problem. If the only thing elected officials manage to achieve is to stem this costly centralizing flow, they will have discharged their duty with honour. This rarely happens, especially in a megacity like Montreal.

Unlike a private corporation where most members of the board of directors know how a company is run and can (in theory) ask pointed questions of top management, few municipal elected officials in Montreal have ever run an organization. From behind a blind of bluster and bluff, most politicians lob softball questions to municipal administrators, who are not unhappy with this state of affairs. Spending, therefore, continues apace.

Lysiane Gagnon of *La Presse* wondered about the generally low calibre of Montreal municipal politicians and concluded it had nothing to do with remuneration:[35] "The salary of the garden-variety city councillor is $49,000, to which is added a non-taxable amount of $15,000, and this is for a job that should not be full-time. It's more than what the average community college professor makes for a whole academic year!" At an income-tax rate of 40 per cent, that's the equivalent of $74,000 a year, not much less than the $99,000 that the forty-four full-time Toronto city councillors make.

Aside from a handful of superb exceptions, most local elected officials have had greatness thrust upon them. Some wind up with a fawning clutch of press attachés, political advisers, *chefs de cabinet* – let alone an army of ego-stroking bureaucrats at their beck and call. I've seen how politics can cause a number of thoroughly decent and idealistic people to go through a personality metamorphosis. The problem is compounded by salaries that can range up to $150,000 a year with extra posts – in some cases, a multiple of the amount they had earned on civvy street. It all can go to their heads. And, at worse, it can create the suspicion that political decisions are made based on ensuring this comfy state of affairs continues.

One problem is council size. The City of Montreal's large councils are a product of history, as it absorbed smaller municipalities, attempting to keep the same number of representatives. The sixty-four member Montreal City Council (the biggest in North America) should be reduced to nineteen. The typical size of an urban US city council is twelve.[36] The executive committee should be eliminated. The Montreal executive committee was originally created by referendum in 1921 to check the power of the mayor; however, Mayor Jean Drapeau and his Civic Party gained control of it in the 1960s. Ever since, the mayor (usually) only names members of his party to the executive committee; if the mayor's party has a majority of council seats, there is no substantive public debate. Everything is decided in camera.[37] At least when reasonably sized councils meet in private, they represent all the electorate, not just the wards that happened to vote for councillors who were later appointed to the executive committee.

It is not the number of municipal councils that count, it is not even the number of councillors that count, it is the number of councillors *on each council* that count. Councils over a certain size get unwieldy, necessitating a "super-council" (an executive committee), where the rump of the council is turned into a useless underclass. Without such a tiered structure, the permutations of interactions become astronomical. If you are going to have a council, whether for a municipality serving a thousand citizens or millions, there are maxima and minima in their size to be efficient. A council of three becomes either a chummy or a fratricidal triumvirate – and not a council. A council of sixty-four becomes a parliament, which is perhaps the best way to run a province or a country, but a terrible way to run a service-delivery organization such as a city. In other words, a hockey team of three can't do the job; and a hockey team of sixty-four doesn't know – or care – where the puck is.

Municipal governments have two different roles: they are in the service-delivery business (transport, security, recreation, and so on), but they also have a crucial social role (managing the built environment, land-use planning, and economic development). Large, parliamentary-type councils are the worst kind of structures to administer the first role, and they are usually unimaginative and partisan in fulfilling the second.

Large councils, in common with parliaments, have to rely on political parties to deal with the inherent inefficiencies of size. The introduction of parties to Quebec municipal politics was a bad legacy from Jean Drapeau. Members will vote according to the party line, not according to what their consciences dictate. And it's hard to keep opposition parties going. Just ask Louise Harel, who lost her best councillor, Pierre Lampron, early in 2012. Lampron got tired of waiting in the wings. Party power congregates around whatever happens to be the incumbent party, which can dole out plum and remunerative postings for elected officials. Also, as a consolation prize for defeated candidates, the party in power can always find jobs within the administration.

Municipal political parties must go: they often attract mediocre rank-and-file councillors, people who would permit themselves to serve as worker ants and become a claque for the winning party's clique – the executive committee. As journalist Henry Aubin has calculated, Tremblay's party spending in the 2005 election worked out to $11.19 per voter, compared with the Liberals' $4.45 in the 2007 provincial race. The need to raise this mass of money creates many IOUs with suppliers and contractors. Total spending of all parties in the 2009 municipal election was $3.2 million.[38] As well, a party's ongoing funding is based on its share of the votes in the last election, which also works against new and opposition parties.

Mergers brought political parties, and big parties at that, to many areas that never had them before. In future there is a real danger that provincial parties will invade the municipal world: Montreal's size and the merging of election dates now make it worth their while.

The megacity was created by provincial government bureaucrats and parliamentarians who know nothing of municipal operations and governance. With its overpopulated council, muscular executive committee, and warring political parties, the megacity of Montreal has possibly one of the most undemocratic systems of municipal government in North America. To add to the problem, the mayor has control over naming members to the agglomeration council that delivers regional services.

COUNCILS OR SINGLE-PURPOSE BOARDS?

Regardless of the future of the Montreal megacity, the agglomeration council is a structure whose only success to date has been to convince its partners of the need to scrap it.

The Montreal Island Agglomeration Council should be replaced by three special-purpose boards delivering regional services. Luckily, there already is a Montreal Mass Transit Board for the Island in place. There should also be a Montreal Water Management Board for potable water production and wastewater treatment. Lastly, the police and fire protection[39] should be gathered up in a Montreal Public Security Services Board. Rather than the existing tri-level political structure comprising a council, standing committees, and an executive committee, we would have just three distinct boards.

Administratively, both the megacity chief of police and fire chief currently report to the director-general, and politically to the public security standing committee of the agglomeration council. However, since the Montreal Police Department has its own human resources, public relations, and legal divisions,[40] it would not be a big step to make it completely autonomous, reporting to an independent board similar to the Toronto Metropolitan Police Board. The Montreal Fire Department likewise has its own public relations division of fourteen people and a human resources division of fifty-one. (Naturally, the City of Montreal has its own public relations and human resources division for good measure.)

The activities of these three boards equal roughly 90 per cent of all current agglomeration council spending. The remaining 10 per cent would be easily parcelled out. Management of the municipal court, refuse, and public housing should return as local responsibilities, while the coordination of refuse and the financing of public housing would remain with the CMM. Property assessments, economic development, regional parks, and the funding of cultural activities could all fall within the jurisdiction of the CMM. Then there would be nothing left of the agglomeration council.

THE GOVERNMENT CONGLOMERATE

In the business world over the last fifty years, conglomerates have gone in and out of fashion. There is some logic to the idea of creating a corporation that's a conglomerate: when its stake in one industry is suffering a downturn in the economic cycle, its investment in a different, ideally complementary industry could pick up the slack in cash flow. In the 1970s, the SCM Corporation made typewriters, paints, foods, and vacuum cleaners. More recently, BCE Corporation was in telephones, a trust company, pipelines, real estate, and newspapers. Accountants and strategic planners loved the concept. The trouble is, it's hard to get a CEO who is passionate and knowledgeable about each and every business in that kind of corporate smorgasbord.

Whatever its possible or improbable merits in business, the conglomerate rationale makes no sense in government – but that is what regional governments tend to be: government conglomerates. In the case of Montreal Island, the agglomeration council provides such unrelated services as police, mass transit, sewerage, water,[41] and law courts. This is equivalent to one company providing all the telephony, electricity, natural gas, alarm systems, and newspapers to all the households on Montreal Island and sending out one yearly lump-sum bill to local municipalities. Intuitively this makes no sense. Government conglomerates can work on a small scale (as in the case of smaller local governments) but are unwieldy when they get big. Trying to keep all those disparate services under one roof makes for unfocused and uninterested management and staff. You also get duplication in the form of a massive administrative structure on top of the collection of the individual services.

Even the most centralist of thinkers accepts that certain services requiring a lot of personal contact or adaptability should be delivered locally by local municipalities. Recreation, snow removal, and zoning are examples of such local services, although I would add fire protection and neighbourhood policing (I fight a rearguard action on those two). On the other hand, services high in uniformity such as water supply, sewage treatment, and mass transit can or must be delivered regionally. But does it really make sense to have each and every regional service lumped together under the same big-tent parliamentary council? And for the same territory? And, while we are at it, charged out based on property values?

A whole grab-bag of unrelated services, artificially circumscribed by an allotted geographic area, has been the model in Quebec, loosely based on the French "urban community" structures. The idea at the time was to create a sense of regional belonging, a "we-feeling." This warm and fuzzy goal was never even remotely achieved: after thirty years, the MUC remained an artificial construct unknown to citizens – although infinitely more efficient than the megacity that replaced it.

Why not *divorce regional service delivery from geography*? This way, a given service, run by a board, can be delivered over whatever geographic area that makes sense. While local taxes need to be tied to local services that vary according to local needs, charges for generally uniform regional services can be spread over a wide area. A bill can be sent to each local municipality based on the service's true cost and be a "fee," not a "tax." Redistributive taxation, equalization payments, revenue sharing, and development charges can then take place at the metropolitan level, which is only fair. This would be done by the CMM, along with land-use planning and controlling urban sprawl and pollution, all of which activities *must* be metropolitan. So a typical local municipality would get service fees from a variety of boards for regional services and also have to pay one metropolitan tax bill from the CMM. The service fees would be based on consumption, and the regional tax would be based (at this stage) principally on property taxes. Citizens would actually know how much services cost and how much redistribution was taking place, if at all.

THE GROWTH IN REGIONAL SERVICES

Over the past fifty years, the urban municipal world in Quebec has shifted slowly from being a provider of solely local services to one that, more and more, furnishes regional services. In 1960 the old City of Montreal provided only two quasi-regional services: potable water and buses. True regional services came about in 1966 with the arrival of the highly structuring metro and the later realization that we could no longer dump our excreta directly into the St Lawrence. These sorts of things were quintessentially geographic and obviously could not be handled locally.

This regionalizing tendency has led to the belief in some quarters that most municipal services should become regional and therefore centralized. The average citizen would probably not agree with this near-trivialization of local services but would prefer the default setting to be local; certainly, the forced regionalization of services such as policing was not popular. The provincial government opportunistically regionalized Montreal Island policing when it could not stare down the police brotherhood, but there was no real logic to it, except for specialized services.

As regions grew geographically, they bumped up against the ceiling of jealously guarded provincial responsibilities. This is why regional bodies in the past sucked power from below, not above. The regionalization should continue, but this time it could take some powers from the province: urban expressways, commuter trains, and some environmental matters come to mind. The planning of such things could remain provincial, but the construction and operating job could devolve to the regional.[42] There is a limit, however. Andrew Sancton, in his *The Limits of Boundaries*, concludes that city-regions simply cannot be self-governing and that the province or state should contine to deliver many regional services and certainly do the strategic planning.

The drawback of small, urban municipalities, goes the theory, is that they cater to an electorate exclusively interested in local matters.[43] Well, the Montreal megacity is no different. Few questions asked at Montreal megacity council meetings are regional in nature: they are mostly either to do with city or even borough operations. One can harangue, lecture, or shame local electors, but it won't get them suddenly interested in regional matters – at least, not yet. Citizens stayed away from the old MUC in droves, and today show even less interest in the agglomeration council or in the CMM, where getting more than a corporal's guard of questioners happens as often as visits from angels. Merger, therefore, changed nothing.

Island suburban citizens, by voting for demerger, rejected the regional influence that was theirs by being subsumed into a megacity and instead opted for local control. That's the price they willingly paid. Is it the inevitable price to be paid to have a small city? Can one have and eat one's slice of the local/regional power pie? It is possible. A number of small-city mayors do manage to transcend their local base and concern themselves with the greater, regional good. And there is absolutely no evidence that the hoary old solution of direct election to a body running regional services would result in greater citizen interest. I am not enamoured with the idea of two levels of politicians; it creates confusion and even greater voter apathy. The same way that a city councillor, while elected by a small portion of the city, has to take into account the interests of the whole city, a mayor, while elected by the residents of only one city, can juggle the interests of the entire region. Similarly, a member of a provincial or federal riding has to take into account the larger interests of the province or country. It can be done.

SUMMARY

Back in 2003, the OECD produced a necessarily rather sketchy study on the Montreal megacity at that point.[44] They concluded their analysis with "skepticism that amalgamation will be able to achieve the desired efficiency and equity goals and maintain public satisfaction ... The amalgamation process substantially reduced citizen access to city representatives in other cities." Overall, they wrote, "We find it difficult to imagine a satisfied public in Montreal in the following years." They also recommended, almost with a note of desperation, "The municipal government must 'sell' amalgamation to the people. Not only should a public relations campaign occur before amalgamation but also it should be ongoing, and continue for five or ten years after."

The present web of structures is untenable. We know it costs hundreds of millions more than the former structures that served us reasonably well. The temptation will be to centralize the current megacity of Montreal. It won't save money and will poorly serve its citizens. The only right thing to do is to boost the power of the borough administrations, get rid of the central bureaucracy, and slowly move towards something approximating individual municipalities. Since Montreal cannot exist under such a constant threat of disaggregation, going all the way in the short term would not only be extremely unlikely but unwise.

Such a change would take incredible political courage, of a stamp we have not seen of late. But if a Quebec government screwed up enough courage to merge 212 municipalities against the will of the people, surely a future government can find the strength to admit a past mistake and go in the other direction – this time with popular support? I live in hope.

But things go deeper than that. The reason for Montreal's continued decline is not the merger-demerger serial fiascos – although they did not help – but Quebec's long-standing fixation on its regions and the unrelenting, pernicious, and wilful neglect of its only metropolitan region. The solution lies not with Montreal but with Quebec.

The Montreal Megacity by Numbers: Performance versus Promise

In the gush of material, mostly dithyrambic, that issued forth about just how much the megacity would change things once in place, there was precious little in the way of hard numbers. Yet most people would agree that of all the reasons, overt or covert, for imposing the megacity, the principal ones were economic: "fiscal equity" was in the lead, followed by "economies of scale." In the initial section of this appendix, I attempt an appraisal of the first four years of the "pure" megacity, comparing the estimated figures given out in support of creating it with figures that reflect what actually happened.

THE PERIOD 2001 TO 2005

Let us begin with overall spending growth from 2001 to 2005 and then deal with the tax side of things during the same period. By the fourth year of the merger, the cost of running the megacity was up by a very sizable $473 million, or $278 million after inflation.[1]

The $473 million was arrived at after removing those costs that had nothing to do with the merger, such as contributions to public transit and interest charges (the prime rate dropped by half during the period). This number bears witness to the spread of Montreal's malady of financial incontinence throughout the Island of Montreal. The increase was in stark contrast to the assertions of Premier Bouchard and Louise Harel, who had promised $175 million of savings through the miracle of merger. Indeed, during 2001, the megacity budgeteers seem to have been issued with rose-coloured glasses. The 2002 budget had sunnily predicted $65 million of savings just in the first year of the megacity's operation,[2] thanks in part to reductions in political payroll, professional fees, and the number of managers, not to mention the seemingly obvious "elimination of vacant positions." The entire $65 million was to be saved through the "consolidation" of the former MUC, suburbs, and City of Montreal, which was going to lead to a "lightening of the administrative structure."

Some lightening: of the $473 million spending increase from 2001 to 2005, most of it went to salaries, benefits, and professional fees. In a Montreal Transition Committee internal document,[3] the number of managers and white collars was supposed to drop by more than one thousand, and the overall number of employees (or "person-years," to use management-speak) was supposed to drop by seventeen hundred. Instead, the number of managers, foremen, professionals, and white collars increased by over four hundred, just from 2002 to 2005.[4] Apparently this influx of brainpower was not enough to keep the megacity chugging along: the amount spent on professional fees increased by one-third in the three years following the megacity's creation.[5] The number of employees who actually delivered services – blue collars, police officers, and firefighters – dropped slightly during this period. But they weren't ignored in their pay-cheques. From 2002 and 2005, the 22,500 megacity employees got raises in salary and benefits that were on average 2.5 times the inflation rate.[6] What were all these highly paid people doing? Was there a sudden increase in service demand? No: the population of Montreal Island remained virtually unchanged during the period.[7] Suddenly, were there better services? No study or poll has indicated that services had improved – on the contrary.

All of this, sadly, was predicted by megacity detractors. For us, it was like being forced to watch an accident we said would happen. Meanwhile, Mayor Tremblay was putting on a brave (and a straight) face when he continued to promise that the megacity would save $175 million after five years – the same $175 million that Harel had promised.[8]

WHERE TO HIDE $473 MILLION

Why, if the cost of actually running the megacity exploded between 2001 and 2005, did tax bills not go through homeowners' roofs, setting off alarm bells no one could ignore? Well, first of all, the post-megacity period just happened to be one of declining interest rates. The Canadian prime rate fell by half from 2001 to 2005. This directly led to a saving of $82 million[9] on borrowing costs, savings that came out of the blue and had absolutely nothing to do with the merger. This windfall sopped up a bit of the megacity overspending once overall expenditures were totted up. More help came from erstwhile tightwads: revenue from government transfers and "in lieu of taxes" went up by $160 million. But there was still a lot of money missing.

So taxes just had to go up. The megacity resorted to the time-honoured method of going easy on the residential (and voting) taxpayer by hitting businesses, their favoured tax patsies. But the reported increases were pretty feeble: between 2001 and 2005, according to the megacity, taxes in the commercial sectors went up about 7 per cent. Residentially, taxes went up by a paltry 1.5 per cent, mostly to fund desperately needed work on the water system. These modest increases, well below the inflation rate, guaranteed that the immediate post-merger period was one of voter tranquillity, mixed with a growing relief that the merger was not so bad after all.[10]

There was only one problem with this idyllic tax picture: it was untrue. Taxes actually increased by $337 million between 2001 and 2005, three times more than the claimed derisory increases would generate and 5 per cent greater than the inflation rate.[11]

What extraterrestrial paid the missing few hundred million dollars in taxes? It turns out that those increases of 7 per cent and 1.5 per cent only referred to the "tax load" on properties listed on the previous year's assessment roll. All changes and additions were not included. Over this period, new construction amounted to roughly $6 billion in taxable value, generating new taxes the megacity conveniently left out of the calculations of increases. That's what accounted for all the missing money.

For 2001 ushered in a four-year bonanza in the value of building permits across the Island of Montreal, reaching a high of $2.5 billion in 2004, up from $1.5 billion in 2000.[12] Residential building permits almost trebled in value during the same period. Yet there was no influx of people to fill the nearly thirty thousand dwellings added between 2000 and 2004: the long-established trend of fewer and fewer residents per dwelling simply continued.* In sum, all this building activity brought in tons of tax revenue (including an increase in revenues from the "welcome tax" of $35 million between 2001

---

* This is a pan-Canadian phenomenon. From 1971 to 2006, the Canadian population grew by half, while the number of dwellings more than doubled.

and 2005). However, because the population – and therefore service demand – did not materially change, the income went straight to the bottom line and helped camouflage the surge in spending.

So more than enough revenues were found to stuff the huge spending hole. They were used to fund greater spending in the delivery of the same services to the same number of people. This trend continued after demerger. The 2009 Montreal megacity budget, for example, trumpeted the fact that Montreal continued the "freeze on tax loads for a fourth consecutive year." Montreal taxpayers should keep that in mind next time the new deck they built onto their house jacks up their assessment and their tax bill. The deck (and the municipal taxes that go with it) will vanish into an accountant's never-never land when it comes to calculating the change in tax loads in the city that year. According to Montreal's logic, their house taxes are still frozen: it's just that their new deck attracted new tax.

But, you might argue, the megacity is right in only reporting tax increases for existing buildings that did not undergo modification. After all, a company can quite accurately say they have had no price increases, even if their sales have increased owing to new customers. But here's the problem: in the case of the megacity, the "sales" increased, but the number of customers did not, nor did the quality or quantity of services received. In my book, that's a price increase. But that's the perniciousness of the property tax system, which charges buildings for services rendered to people. But, you might say, did not these new buildings take up space and require new services? That would be true if we were talking about new municipal infrastructure, but most of the land built upon was already serviced and therefore already being taxed.

FISCAL EQUITY: ONE ISLAND ONE RATE, OR PAYING ONE'S FAIR SHARE?

We now move on to "fiscal equity," *the* justification for imposing the megacity. For advocates of the megacity, starting with Premier Bouchard and Louise Harel and ending with the media, it was an article of faith that fiscal equity was simply a matter of achieving a uniform property tax rate for the entire Island of Montreal. It is crucial to understand that there was already a uniform rate for regional services such as police, mass transit, and wastewater treatment.

What the rate uniformitarians were after was a uniform local rate as well. This uniformity, it was felt, would force the suburban taxpayer to cough up more, thereby lowering the tax bill paid by the taxpayers of the former City of Montreal for their local services. This did not happen.

A uniform rate sounds eminently sensible and fair. What was wrong with it? There are uniform income tax rates, after all. The trouble is, income taxes have nothing to do with your consumption of government services. Municipally, your tax bill is supposed to reflect your consumption of services. Now, a uniform rate multiplied by your water consumption, your garbage (de)consumption, your use of roads, and so on would be logical. But your property tax rate is not multiplied by your consumption of anything: it is multiplied by your property's value. And your property's value has absolutely nothing to do with your consumption. Properties don't consume; people do.

For decades, the Quebec Department of Municipal Affairs has been trying to get municipalities to replace local property taxes with user fees, which actually reflect the cost of services consumed. What is the difference between property taxes and user fees for local services? The property tax system is a bit like having your neighbourhood garage fill your gas tank or repair your car whenever you want, keeping no record of it. At the end of the year, you get a bill that is simply x per cent of your car's estimated value. When you protest to the garage that this is unfair, you are told, "What do you mean, unfair? All my customers get charged exactly the same percentage." Fundamentally, it was building on this egregious logic that drove Bouchard and Harel to impose megacities all over Quebec. But standardization of an insane system does not make it saner. In fact, to go back to our garage illustration, the megacity goal was to force all the garages on the Island of Montreal to charge the same percentage for local services. At least the pre-merger system could be tweaked locally with different percentages that reflected the overall consumption in each community.[13]

It seemed that the concept of a uniform tax rate was so hydrophobic it could not survive the short trip off-Island to resolve real inequalities within a region (off-Island freeloaders who don't pay full freight) or between the Montreal region and the outlying regions (where local policing is often subsidized and school busing is free).

HOUSES: SAME TAX RATE AS APARTMENTS, BUT FIVE TIMES THE TAXES

Another example of real fiscal inequality is the taxation gap between houses and apartments. In the same way that the commercial sector massively subsidizes the residential sector, Montreal homeowners massively subsidize apartment dwellers. They do it differently, though. Houses and apartments are taxed at uniform – or similar – rates.[14] However, because of rent control and other factors, the values of apartment buildings have plummeted over the last few decades, to the point that in 2001 the average assessment of a dwelling in an apartment building on the Island of Montreal was only $28,000, compared to $170,000 for a house.[15] Because of a uniform tax rate, this five-fold assessment differential went straight to the tax bill.

But don't homeowners use far more services than apartment dwellers? Not really. Take water: apartment dwellers supposedly use more water per capita than people living in houses.[16] The only justification for taxing the resident of a single-family dwelling more than an apartment dweller has to do with the compactness of apartment blocks: this compactness makes the delivery of some municipal services much cheaper. Otherwise, the rest of municipal services are consumed per capita. It turns out that transport of all kinds makes up 36 per cent of a municipality's costs. So one could justify such a premium for single-family dwellings, but instead the average Montreal house is stuck with this burden of nearly five times the tax load of a typical apartment. Because there are more residents in a typical house than in an apartment, the former each pay on average $1,000 per year in property taxes, while the latter each pay $370.[17]

A condominium high-rise looks much like an apartment house and consumes a similar amount of municipal services. The only real difference is that the residents of the former own their dwellings and the residents of the latter don't. Yet when it comes to paying the city for services, taxes on dwellings in condominium high-rises are three to four times higher than on their rented cousins. But the rock-solid principle of municipal taxation in Quebec is that one is taxed according to the benefit received. Why should ownership have anything to do with the consumption of services? It doesn't.

So, in order to have apartments pay taxes that are closer to the cost of providing them with services, why not raise the tax rate on apartment houses to, say, the going commercial rate? After all, their owners are operating a business. Here's the rub: the owners would simply pass the increase on to their tenants, and the vast majority of low-income earners are tenants. According to the Institut de recherche et d'informations socio-économiques, only when household income gets to be over $50,000 do tenants pay housing costs that are in the same proportion to their income as those of homeowners. And the older they are, the more they pay a punishing proportion of their income in rent. Many tenants thus could not possibly afford to pay taxes in line with the property-owners' burden – and commensurate with their consumption of services. In 2006, nearly two out of five Montreal tenant households (and nearly half of Westmount tenant households) spent more than 30 per cent of their income in rent, while only one in five of owner households were in the same predicament. But it is not the role, nor is it within the capability, of municipal government to tax according to one's ability to pay. In fact, Quebec recognizes that principle with a property tax refund[18] for people filing income tax returns "whose property taxes are too high in relation to their income." In 2008, this refund could reach $588 per dwelling. If tenants shouldered their fair share of property taxes, the property-tax refund would have to be radically revised upwards.

TAXONOMY: A WATER TAX THAT WAS NOT A WATER TAX

Throughout the decade prior to 2001, the overall residential tax rate in the former City of Montreal was roughly 13 per cent higher than those in the Island suburbs taken together. However, because Montreal apartment dwellers were not pulling their weight, by 2001 residential taxes paid per capita were 19 per cent lower than in the suburbs. On the other hand, the commercial tax rate was 34 per cent higher in Montreal. Overall, in 2001, taxes per capita in the former City of Montreal were only slightly higher than in the Island suburbs.[19]

Yet when Louise Harel talked of fiscal equity, she did not talk about a mere 13 per cent difference in the tax rate between the former City of Montreal and the Island suburbs (and she certainly never breathed a word about lower residential taxes per capita in Montreal). Her figures were far more dramatic. As explained in chapter 9, the official tax rates compared Montreal apples with suburban oranges: Montreal's "global tax rate" was artificially inflated by its "water and services tax." This levy should not have been included in the global tax rate for two reasons: it was not tied to water consumption,[20] and it was levied on the commercial sector only – in fact, in exactly the same manner as the business tax,[21] which was excluded from the calculation for the global tax rate. In 2001, the former City of Montreal collected $173 million from the "water and services" tax out of a total of $1,378 million of taxes collected overall. It was not a minor tax.

Because of this artifice, Montreal's official global tax rate managed throughout the 1990s to be consistently 33 per cent higher than the Island suburbs' rates collectively. Had Montreal's rate been reported fairly – that is, without the bogus "water and services" tax – the difference would have been 13 per cent, which is not exactly a Boston Tea Party difference. And, most importantly, the actual taxes per capita were almost identical.

SUBURBAN SPECIAL

Why bother with the "global tax rate" at all? Why not just compare residential "general" rates? As we saw in chapter 9, nearly all suburban municipalities had a raft of "special" taxes in addition to their general rate. These were mostly user fees for water and garbage, and "local improvement" taxes. Together they added 15 per cent to the residential general rate.* In contrast, Montreal's "special" residential taxes added only 1 per cent. In the years just before the merger, owing to these special taxes,[22] at least eight suburbs had overall residential tax rates higher than Montreal's.

REASSESSMENT

Things changed a bit in 2001. New assessments announced in autumn of 2000 caused the 2001 suburban rates to drop, creating a bigger spread with Montreal – well after the decision to impose the megacity but not too late to use it to bolster the arguments for it.[23] In fact, it was just before the government passed the merger

---

* The City of Laval in 2001 added 33 per cent in special taxes to its general rate.

legislation that assessments were revised: the former City of Montreal saw its taxable values drop by over $2 billion (about 5 per cent) while the suburban values stayed put. Single-family dwellings generally increased in assessed value in the suburbs while remaining frozen in Montreal. Many suburbs lowered their tax rates on houses; some used surplus cash to lower tax rates even more, not wishing to leave money around for the megacity to pocket. So, in 2001, only three suburban municipalities had tax rates higher than Montreal's.

Why the difference in rates? It had nothing to do with suburban parasitical behaviour and much to do with the composition of a municipality's real estate. Overall, the suburbs were residentially richer and commercially poorer than Montreal. Take Hampstead, Montreal West, and Beaconsfield: those municipalities had little or no commercial sector to milk for taxes. Yet the residents of these municipalities were obviously prepared to pay a higher tax rate than their commercially rich neighbours for the quality of life their municipality gave them. Many other municipalities, over time, had managed to acquire a commercial base to serve as a cash cow. A modest example is Westmount. Without its commercial sector, its tax rate would have been similar to that of Beaconsfield, Hampstead, or Kirkland. At the other extreme from the "bedroom communities" were municipalities like Dorval, Montreal East, and Saint-Laurent, where the commercial sector paid multiples of the amount of taxes borne by the residents. The former City of Montreal was no slouch either, with the commercial sector contributing the lion's share of taxes; as an added bonus, Montreal collected 81 per cent of all "in lieu of taxes" paid by federal and provincial governments on the Island of Montreal.

Let's look at just one illustration of the joy that commercial buildings brought to a municipality where overall commercial tax rates were 2.5 times the residential rates. In 2001, one building alone (albeit the biggest in town), Place Ville Marie, brought in $20 million in tax revenue[24] to the City of Montreal, with very little demand on municipal services aside from transport. That same year it would have taken nearly 7,500 single-family houses in Montreal to contribute the same amount in taxes, with a huge demand in services.

WHAT HAPPENED TO TAX RATES AFTER THE MERGER

When merging the tax rates followed, as night the day, the merger of municipalities, the goal was in the fullness of time to have only one tax rate – once the debt charges were removed.[25] In 2003, including debt charges, Montreal was below the target tax rate by only 3 per cent. By 2005, even this small difference had been wiped out.[26]

The merger, coupled with assessment changes, did bring about a reduction in the disparity of tax rates among the former suburbs, even though they had been quite satisfied with the way things were before the merger. For example, throughout the 1990s, the municipality with the highest tax rate, Verdun, consistently taxed at double the rate of Senneville, the municipality with the lowest rate.[27]

TAX BURDENS? MUCH ADO ABOUT NOTHING

Let's now move away from tax rates to look at changes in overall tax burdens following the merger. Four years after the megacity's creation, it had brought essentially no change to the proportion of total taxes paid by taxpayers (of all stripes) in the former City of Montreal compared to taxes in the Island suburbs.[28]

To tease out in more detail the winners and losers from the operation of the Montreal merger is far from easy, as not only was there a slow merging of tax rates subsequent to the creation of the megacity, and not only did the municipal politicians decide to shift taxes onto the commercial sector, but assessment increases in 2001 and 2004 varied greatly among the former suburbs and the former City of Montreal. It's like trying to determine the winners and losers when many traffic streams merge: the identity of each vehicle does not change, and a truck is still a truck and a car is still a car, but their official weight classification or speed measurement changes, all subject to new, uniform, speed limits.

One thing is clear. As Figure 1 demonstrates, residential taxes per capita in the former City of Montreal did indeed drop, but the same thing happened in the suburbs. In both cases, homeowners' tax breaks were funded by the commercial sector. Had this shift not occurred, there would have been no relief for the Montreal residential taxpayer.

But all this came as no surprise to the PQ government. In documents prepared on 15 November 2000, given to Louise Harel, and widely distributed the day Bill 170 was tabled, the government's own experts had calculated that the megacity would bring no change to the tax bill of homeowners in the former City of Montreal. Half the suburban municipalities would see increases, half would see decreases.[29]

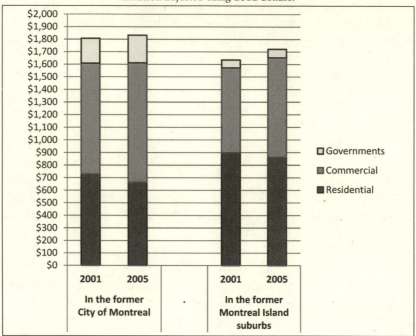

Figure 1: Tax hikes to businesses helped fund megacity overspending and subsidized the homeowner.

MONTREAL COULDN'T DROP ITS DEBT CHARGE OVERBOARD

At the end of the day (and at the beginning of the megacity), the main reason for the difference between the tax burdens in the former City of Montreal and its suburbs was one four-letter word: debt. Montreal, with 84 cents on every two dollars of tax billed residentially, had the highest amount of debt service buried in its tax rate of any municipality on the Island of Montreal. In the suburban municipalities, debt charges ran from one cent (in bucolic Senneville) to 83 cents (in highly industrialized Montreal East). This was why Montreal had an overall tax rate higher than most of the suburbs. But the law required that existing debt had to remain with the taxpayers in the former municipality subsequent to merger and not be a kind of negative dowry brought to the forced marriage. This was why, when all the taxes on the Island were slowly to move to one uniform rate after merger, it was one rate only after old debt was removed. Former Montrealers were to be stuck with their debt like old gum to their shoes. They were not supposed to scrape it off, but it seems they did manage to offload quite a bit.[30]

THE PERIOD 2001 TO 2012

The last year that the megacity covered the whole of Montreal Island was 2005, before demerger chipped away at its size; but as the megacity continued to provide Island regional services, its share of all Montreal Island municipal spending only dropped from 100 per cent to 92 per cent. This is why the longer period of 2001–12 is still relevant; besides, since the merger legislation had a built-in brake on wage increases in the first round of collective agreements, pent-up wage rises showed up years after the merger.

From 2001 to 2008, the Island of Montreal's spending performance was even worse than from 2001 to 2005, with an increase of $509 million after inflation over the period. While the latter number is my own calculation, it is comparable to figures found in one of the most incisive reports written in the last few decades about the Montreal Region.[31] It was commissioned by the Montreal Board of Trade, a quondam cheerleader for the megacity.

In presenting the 2009 budget, Mayor Tremblay was quick to point out that the tax burden on the average single-family dwelling had been frozen since 2002. Had taxes kept up with the 16 per cent inflation, he said, it would have cost the average owner almost $500 more in 2009. When he talked about this "tax freeze," it was just for the residential (and voting) taxpayer, as from 2002 to 2008 all property taxes (including those paid by government) grew by $627 million, which is $305 million after inflation.[32]

The motive behind this residential tax freeze, according to the Board of Trade report, was that the megacity "wanted to allow its citizens from 2002 on to benefit from the expected fruits of the unification of the Island and to assure a more competitive fiscal regime." The authors continued: "Let us not forget that the mergers were supposed to lead to substantial economies of scale that were supposed to translate into a reduction in the tax burden and thus render Montreal more competitive with the suburbs."[33] What this little nugget of a comment was quite delicately saying is that Montreal, in spite of mounting evidence of diseconomies of scale, wanted voters to think that all was going well and according to plan, that the megacity was a success, and the promised tax relief had actually happened. This little hoax was paid for by the non-residential sector. The kindest thing one can say is that perhaps this "stabilization" of the tax paid by homeowners in Montreal was an attempt to slow the tide of people seeking cheaper houses off-Island. The report goes on to show how a residential property with an average assessment in the territory of former City of Montreal paid $3,695 of taxes in 2002 and the same amount in 2008. Meanwhile, in Laval, the average residential bill went from $2,376 to $3,094, and in Longueuil from $1,940 to $2,335.

From 2001 to 2012, overall operational spending (without interest charges) rose by $1.7 billion, or 70 per cent. This rate of growth was three times the Montreal inflation rate of 23 per cent for the period. The $1.7 billion is made up of a $0.2 billion increase in the contribution to mass transit, a $0.5 billion increase in spending for goods and services, and a $1.0 billion increase in salaries and benefits. Since the mass transit contribution went to a corporation that was independent of the megacity and did not undergo any change, I focus here on the other two expense categories. However, one may well ask how much of the increased contribution for mass transit funded improved services and how much simply was eaten up to boost salaries and benefits. One thing is certain: two-thirds of the increased non-transit spending of $1.5 billion went to salaries and benefits.

Beyond 2008, it becomes increasingly difficult to quantify the spending increases that the creation of the megacity engendered, as massive pension cost increases starting in 2009* should be removed from any reckoning, as they could not fairly be ascribed to merger. This is what Figure 2 does.

Figure 2 tracks the aggregate spending of all Island of Montreal cities for the period 2001–12, adjusted for both population (that is, demand) and inflation. A distinction is made between those costs affected by the merger and those subjected to purely external forces.[34] The trend of total spending is relentlessly upward after a

---

* At over $0.6 billion, the yearly cost of pension benefits in 2012 for the City of Montreal alone is over three times the 2008 amount.

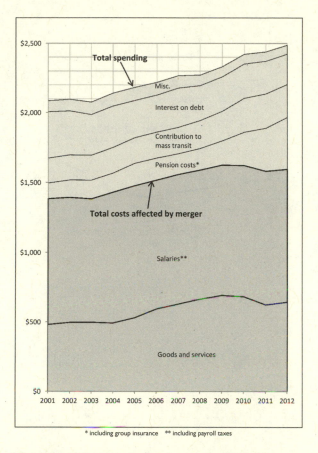

Figure 2 Spending growth after the merger, all Montreal Island cities, per capita spending, inflation adjusted using 2012 dollars.

two-year plateau.[35] However, costs affected by the merger peaked in 2009. Now, was the 2001–09 rise owing to the merger, or were costs already spiralling upwards? As it turns out, the opposite had been happening. Figure 3 looks at this bigger picture: Island spending before merger, after merger, and after demerger. The lead-up period before the merger is important, as it was a period of spending cuts. But pre-merger cuts were achieved by reducing the number of employees from 26,000 to 22,000, while post-merger spending was made up of increases in both remuneration and the number of employees from 22,000 to 23,500.[36] In a nutshell, what Mayor

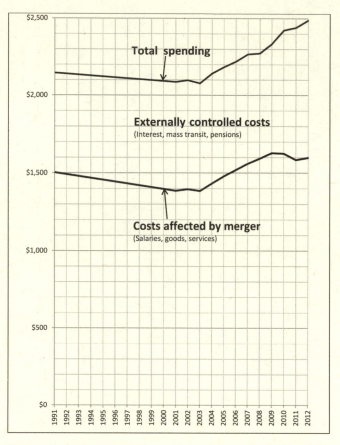

Figure 3 Spending growth before and after the merger, all Montreal Island cities, per capita spending, inflation adjusted using 2012 dollars.

Bourque and Vera Danyluk had achieved in reducing costs, the megacity put back on – and much more.[37]

Of the four thousand positions cut from 1991 to 2001, some came out of bureaucratic flab, but some undoubtedly resulted in service reductions. It is very unlikely that any of the fifteen-hundred person increase from 2001 to 2012 resulted in service improvement, but that is always a tricky thing to measure. However, the number of police officers can serve as a proxy for service levels rendered when it comes to public security. Even with more spending on salaries and benefits between 2001 and 2012, public security service levels actually dropped slightly.

Number of Montreal Island Uniformed Police Officers per 1,000 Residents, 1991–2012[38]

1991	2001	2012
2.49	2.33	2.27

For all departments, increases in employee remuneration went to boost both employee pay-packets and the number of bureaucrats. After inflation, the average total remuneration rose by 28 per cent from 2001 and 2012 and by 43 per cent between 1991 and 2012:[39]

Increase in Cost of Salaries and Benefits: Average Montreal Island Municipal Employee (inflation-adjusted using 2012 dollars)[40]

1991	2001	2012
$74,400	$83,000	$106,500

CONCLUSION

Even to come up with an approximation of the cost of the megacity requires stripping off extraneous layers, like peeling an onion. All costs that were not under the control of the megacity have to be removed: interest costs, inflation, mass transit costs (controlled by a separate corporation that was not merged), health and welfare costs (a responsibility delegated from Quebec), and fringe benefits after 2008. Once these opaque and lightly attached layers are removed from the onion, a more pellucid (and lachrymatory) interior is revealed.

Looking at Figure 3, we can see that, after 2001, these core costs increased from $1,385 per capita in today's dollars and (so far) have stabilized at $1,600 after 2008. Had the megacity not been imposed, we have no reason to think that the costs of delivering municipal services across the Island of Montreal would not have remained at their 2001 levels, since both inflation and population have been factored into these figures. Instead, we have a sudden rise in costs of $215 per capita following merger. With an Island population of 1,886,000, this means the imposition of the megacity cost $400 million a year in today's money.

Some will say that part of this $400 million increase had to do with the cost of the post-2006 decentralization. As I explain elsewhere, I remain very much in doubt about that. One thing is for sure: before the megacity and its boroughs were imposed, we had a better (and manifestly cheaper) way to achieve decentralization through individual cities.

The ratchet effect will ensure that megacity overspending will be repeated year after year, building up to a number in the billions, dwarfing even the gross cost overruns of other government projects of the time such as the metro extension to Laval. At least the metro gave the region something of value, not a recurring liability. The megacity is a cost that keeps on costing. Likewise, the megacity's failure to deliver the advertised "fiscal equity" to the supposedly beleaguered City of Montreal taxpayer is equally permanent. Besides, rather than making some pay more and others pay less in taxes, the megacity spending explosion ensured that everybody paid more – a lot more.

Notes

1 These mergers affected 4.3 million citizens, or 60 per cent of Quebec's population at the time. Of these 4.3 million citizens, 3.6 million saw their municipality disappear on the same date: 1 January 2002. The 212 municipalities that were merged (nineteen of them parishes) became forty-two new entities.

2 The thirty demerged municipalities had a total population of 440,000. Had normal referendum rules been used, demergers would have recreated fifty municipalities with a total population of one million.

3 The increased costs of operating the megacities dwarfed even the massive cost of setting them up in the first place. Just the costs of merging Toronto, Ottawa, Montreal, and Longueuil amounted to at least $700 million. Adding the rest of Ontario and Quebec mergers, total merging costs were over $1 billion. As we shall see, the added cost of running the Montreal megacity alone is $400 million a year. For all the merged municipalities in Canada, an estimate of extra operating costs of $1 billion per year is defensible.

4 Cited in an editorial in *The Economist*, 5 February 2005. In Canada, things were a little different, at least for the banks. In 1996, Canadian Prime Minister Jean Chrétien, Finance Minister Paul Martin, and the federal Competition Bureau refused to allow four of the biggest Canadian banks to merge into two in order to compete better with US banks. Perhaps it was not just coincidental that Canadian banks were the least affected by the meltdown of international banks in 2008 and 2009, which resulted in four Canadian banks being counted among the top ten largest banks in North America.

According to Bloomberg (13 August 2010, http://www.bloomberg.
com/), more recent corporate mergers have fared no better. "Companies
struck $10 trillion of deals during the last merger binge [2005 to 2008],
even after more than a decade of research showing deals often don't pay
off for the buyers."

5 It is true that Denmark went through a second wave of amalgamations,
   but they were in 2007. (New Zealand is in the process of forcibly merging
   some municipalities, but that is today, not ten years ago when the "worldwide trend" claim was made.)

6 Britain gets only about a 25 per cent local electoral turnout, compared
   with around 65 per cent for most other European nations. See *The Economist*, 4 May 2002. Part of this voter lethargy may have something to
   do with financial indentured servitude: British local councils get three-
   quarters of their funding from central government grants. Considering
   the linguistic overtones that coloured the Quebec merger battle, there is
   a soupçon of irony that France had the greatest number of municipalities
   per capita (65 per 100,000 people); while Britain, at 1 per 100,000, had
   the lowest.

7 Andrew Tobias, foreword to Mackay, *Extraordinary Popular Delusions
   and the Madness of Crowds*, xiii.

8 I personally lived through at least four separate suggestions for regional
   governance: the Montreal Metropolitan Council (1993), the Montreal
   Metropolitan Round Table (1994), the Montreal Metropolitan Development Commission (1997), and the Montreal Metropolitan Community
   (2000) – in French, the CMM. The last one actually saw the light of day,
   though only one out of ten Montrealers today would even be aware of its
   existence.

9 The parallels were interesting: (1) In the early 1990s, Quebec planners were worried about urban sprawl and the lack of metropolitan fiscal equity. The Liberal government in Quebec, after commissioning the
   Pichette Report that recommended an upper-tier metropolitan council for
   Montreal, lost the election to the PQ in 1994. The PQ's strong electoral
   base (the so-called 450 area, after the telephone area code) that engirded
   the Island of Montreal, wanted nothing to do with being governed by such
   a thing. And they represented nearly one-half of the population of the
   metropolitan region. (2) In the early 1990s, Ontario planners were worried about urban sprawl and the lack of metropolitan fiscal equity. The
   NDP government in Ontario, after commissioning the Golden Report –
   inspired by the Pichette Report – that recommended an upper-tier metropolitan Council for Toronto, lost the election to the Progressive-

Conservatives in 1995. The PC's strong electoral base (the so-called 905 area after the telephone area code) that engirded the six municipalities of Metro Toronto wanted nothing to do with being governed by such a thing. And they represented nearly one-half of the population of the metropolitan region. (3) The PCs in Ontario forcibly turned Metro Toronto into a megacity that was born 1 January 1998, saying it would reduce "waste and duplication." The PQ in Quebec, after installing a very-weak upper-tier government, forcibly turned the Island of Montreal into a megacity that was born 1 January 2002, saying it would reduce "waste and duplication."

10 *Policy Options* 20, no. 9 (November 1999): 54–8.

11 Certainly the architect of mergers, Louise Harel, claimed fiscal equity as *the* driving force behind mergers. She wrote in the *Montreal Gazette* of 2 September 2009 that "the ultimate goal of the 2002 municipal mergers was to establish fiscal equity for all Montrealers."

12 After a period of adjustment. That part of the rate relating to debt and pension fund deficits was not uniformized, as debts remained with each former municipality.

13 For municipalities with a population over 25,000. In 2011, the difference was still 29.2 per cent (Government of Quebec, l'Institut de la statistique du Québec, *Rémunération des salariés: État et évolution comparés*, 2011.) Of course, this gap is nothing like the sickening unfairness created by the rapaciousness of the top hundred Canadian private-sector CEOs, who made over 250 times the earnings of their workers in 2007. On the other hand, big-city mayors rarely make more than four times the earnings of their blue-collars, and they put in easily twice the number of hours – without the job security.

14 Arvida was named after *Arthur Vining Davis*, the first head of the Alumium Company of Canada.

15 *Montreal Gazette*, 17 November 2000.

16 *Le Soleil*, 24 November 2000.

17 According to the Institut de la statistique de Québec, from 2001 to 2008, the "core" of the metropolitan region – the Island of Montreal, Laval, and the immediate south shore – grew by 5 per cent, and the rest of the region, where barely eight municipalities disappeared, by 22 per cent.

18 See City of Montreal, *Portraits démographiques: La dynamique migratoire de l'agglomération de Montréal*, January 2011. In 2001–02, there was a net loss to off-Island suburbs of 18,112. By 2009–10, it had reached 22,489.

19 *La Presse*, 23 December 2000.

20 As we shall see in chapter 5, forty municipalities were wiped out in the greater Montreal region in the period 1992–2002, yet some forty new government-imposed structures were added.

21 *La Presse*, 27 April 1999. In fact, this article reveals Montreal police were earning 3 per cent *more* than their counterparts in Toronto; and, based on GNP per capita, Quebec had a "capacity to pay" that was 22 per cent lower than Ontario. In 2002, according the Montreal Metropolitan Community, the GDP per capita of the Toronto metropolitan area was $36,002, while Montreal came in at $29,129. It is interesting that police and firefighters in Quebec get pay parity with Ontario, but doctors, nurses, and teachers do not.

22 "Les anglais avaient raison." *La Presse*, 4 and 6 June 2007.

23 In many Montreal boroughs the elector today is faced with a dizzying assortment of people to vote for municipally: the mayor of Montreal, a city councillor, a borough mayor (who also sits as a city councillor), and a borough councillor. Before the megacity, voters simply voted for a mayor and a local councillor. While this worked for the small suburban municipalities, for the former City of Montreal the old arrangement meant that everything was centralized at Montreal City Hall.

24 Seventy-four members from 2002 to 2006.

25 It is the same today. In June 2009, the outgoing minister of municipal affairs, who in a prior life was the mayor of Maria (population: 2,500), was replaced by Laurent Lessard, former minister of agriculture and the former mayor of Thetford Mines (population: 25,000). Actually, Lessard, in spite of this handicap, has been one of the best municipal affairs ministers for a long time.

26 See http://www.bdso.gouv.qc.ca/pls/ken/Ken263_Liste_Total.p_tratr_reslt?p_iden_tran=REPERQY4XKS42-131591916944W71`&p_modi_url=0703094902&p_id_rapp=1855.

27 See http://www.bdso.gouv.qc.ca/pls/ken/Ken263_Liste_Total.p_tratr_reslt?p_iden_tran=REPERQY4XKS42-131591916944W71`&p_modi_url=0703094629&p_id_rapp=916.

28 Sometimes these ridings parked their vote with Quebec's third party, the Action démocratique du Québec. This is what happened in the 2007 Quebec election, when, with only three exceptions, in all the ridings surrounding the Island of Montreal – the north shore and the south shore – the ADQ was voters' first or second choice.

29 Government of Quebec, *La réorganisation municipale: Changer les façons de faire pour mieux servir les citoyens* (Harel's White Paper), 2000, 129.

30 Population 10,000 to 100,000.

31 Collin and Léveillée, in collaboration with Rivard and Robertson, *Municipal Organization in Canada* (Groupe de recherche sur l'innovation municipale 2003). This report points out that Quebec only reduced its number of municipalities from 1,433 in 1996 to 1,147 in 2003, a 20 per cent drop. (According to Andrew Sancton, in roughly the same period, 1995 to 2002, Ontario reduced its number of municipalities from 815 to 447, a 45 per cent drop. See http://www.aqdc.qc.ca/colloque_2001_04_20/A.Sancton.htm.) Professor Collin had said earlier (*Le Devoir*, 6 March 2002): "The big agglomerations, that's spectacular, but not necessarily efficient. There are still 800 municipalities with fewer than 2,500 people."

32 Lysiane Gagnon, *La Presse*, 18 November 2000. When it came to the "parasite" argument, Franco Nuovo, writing in the *Journal de Montréal*, 6 December 2000, was also typical of the francophone press: "Westmount, located five minutes from downtown and profiting from all the services of Montreal, does not participate in the public funding of services that its residents use everyday." As this book reveals, taxes in Westmount went up 50 per cent after the merger, but Montreal did not really benefit. The money went mostly to other former suburbs or to pay for the increased spending of the megacity.

33 Gagnon, in *La Presse*, 30 April 2009, wrote about Tremblay as "a deaf, dumb and blind man who didn't see the [possibly criminal] scheming that was hatching right under his nose ... Tremblay does nothing, but at least he does nothing wrong." By then it was clear that her main argument for the megacity (that "the quality of its politicians will inevitably be improved") had not been borne out. In fact, she now writes that it is the exodus of the middle classes to Laval and the south shore that deprives the megacity of a pool of citizens who "could enhance the quality of our elected officials." Tremblay remains, she writes, "naïve, easily influenced, timorous."

34 Landry, "Montréal, l'espoir!" (June 2007). Since nearly 90 per cent of francophones feel that on the Island of Montreal the French language is threatened, the underlying integrationist goal is linguistic in nature.

35 *Montreal Gazette*, 13 April 2005.

36 This dark suspicion was given added weight by those who felt that mergers were also sold as a way to eliminate the threat that independent "anglo" municipalities would militate to remain with Canada in the event of the separation of Quebec. That mergers would eliminate the possibility of partition was a powerful argument, one that I was told was invoked in the PQ cabinet and elsewhere. See chapter 7.

37 In 2001 there were 99,470 residents of the former City of Montreal who spoke only English at home, yet there were 193,350 such anglophones living in the Island suburbs. On the other hand, there were 549,180 former City of Montreal residents who spoke only French at home, double the 280,945 francophones living in the Island suburbs – all of which disappeared with the merger. One gets similar ratios using single-response mother-tongue statistics. (Figures from L'Institut de la statistique du Québec.) To those who would argue that the former City of Montreal disappeared too, one can simply respond that, for the average Montrealer, the merger threatened nothing: neither services nor taxes would be affected. It was, as I have pointed out, an annexation *by* Montreal, not a merger *with* Montreal. Even the banal commercial logo of the pre-2002 City of Montreal became the logo of the new, bigger municipality.

38 According to a 2 July 2004 article in *Le Devoir* by professors Pierre Drouilly and Alain Gagnon, both of UQAM. Using an average family income index of 100 given by Statistics Canada for Quebec in 2001, Westmount rated 328; Hampstead, 263; Senneville, 253; Mount Royal, 239; Beaconsfield, 208; Montreal West, 205; Saint-Lambert, 187; and Baie d'Urfé, 183. The other two former municipalities in the top ten were Outremont (192) and Sillery (191), both of which did not demerge.

But there was some compensation to Montreal. The Montreal Transition Committee report in 2005 calculated what one could call the "reverse dowry" paid by fifteen divorcing municipalities on the Island. This amount was $53 million a year, being the amount of the permanent fiscal transfer that happened during the merger years and that would continue thereafter.

39 Polls conducted over a year and a half after the megacity was imposed showed a strong linguistic divide when it came to demergers. In the former Montreal Island suburbs, 50 per cent of francophones were in favour of demerger, as opposed to 77 per cent of non-francophones, according to a SOM poll conducted in September 2003. A few weeks later, an Impact research poll done for the borough of Verdun found that 51 per cent of anglo Verdunois were in favour of demerging and only 20 per cent of francophone Verdunois.

40 For the first time ever, Bill 124, adopted in June 2000, gave the cabinet (in reality, the minister of municipal affairs) the power to impose mergers anywhere in Quebec if they would result in "greater fiscal equity" and "services at lower cost or better services at the same cost." By a legal fiction, the cabinet could by decree impose a merger "as if the municipalities had made the request themselves." In effect, the National Assembly (the

legislature) had given the cabinet (the government) a blank cheque with Bill 124.

41 *Le Devoir*, 28 September 2002.

42 For me, Quebec demergers were, in reality, de-annexations. This is why, for the purposes of this book, a demerger is defined as being the act of reconstituting a previously merged municipality within its original boundaries. Quebec's Office de la langue français is more generous, as it defines demerger as the creation of "two or more municipalities from a municipality previously created by merger." However, even the loosest definition – the breaking off of a piece, or pieces, of a previously merged municipality – would, to my knowledge, only add one more instance of demerger: the rural area of Headingly, which seceded in 1992 from the Winnipeg megacity after being part of it for twenty years.

43 Débats de l'assemblée nationale, 10 May 1979. In 1982, Lévesque momentarily lost his sense of democracy when his government put through the only merger the PQ ever imposed – that is, until Louise Harel came on the scene.

44 *Le Soleil*, 28 November 2008.

45 *Le Devoir*, 17 April 2010.

46 For municipalities with a population over 20,000. See http://www.mamrot.gouv.qc.ca/pub/observatoire_municipal/etudes_donnees_statistiques/muni_stat_2004_no_1.pdf. One exception was Laval, as for years voters there had a Hobson's choice of one party, one mayor. Gilles Vaillancourt has been the mayor of Laval since 1989. In 2005, voter turnout there was only 29 per cent.

47 Throughout the 1970s, 1980s, and 1990s, Montreal's turnout had averaged 48 per cent.

48 *Montreal Gazette*, 4 November 2009. Later, in *La Presse*, Harel claimed she needed at least a 42 per cent turnout to win. She was defeated by the boroughs of Montreal that eight years before had been independent municipalities and whose citizens voted massively for her competitor, Gérald Tremblay.

49 Government of Quebec, *Données sociodémographiques en bref*, vol. 8, no. 3, June 2004. Statistics Canada gives the median family net worth in Ontario as 66 per cent higher than in Quebec, and the average net worth as 42 per cent higher. See http://www40.statcan.ca/l01/cst01/famil99a.htm. And it's not just a question of assets: 2002 average Ontario family incomes were 30 per cent higher, according to *Données sociodémographiques en bref*. There are, in addition, proportionally more high-income earners in Ontario than in Quebec. In 2003, there were 70 per

cent more returns per 1,000 tax-filers in which declared incomes were over $75,000, according to the Canada Customs and Revenue Agency.

50 In 2006, local debt per capita in Quebec was $1,940. In the rest of Canada it varied from a high of $1,306 to a *negative* (that is, a surplus) of $799. Ontario, for example, had a surplus of $202 per head. See Claude Picher, *La Presse*, 29 November 2008. One of the reasons for the higher debt in Quebec is that Quebec municipalities generally fund the cost of new infrastructure for land development, whereas elsewhere in Canada the developers foot the bill and pass it on to owners in the form of higher prices.

51 *Les Affaires*, 3 May 1997.

52 Subsequently, Tremblay either denied making this promise or conceded it only lasted one day. But it was well documented over a long period of time. See note 22, chapter 15.

53 In 2004, Tremblay denied lobbying for a minimum turnout rate. But on 18 June 2003, he said to *La Presse*, "With an unrestricted turnout rate, we would be allowing a minority of people to decide on the fate of the metropolis. It's totally unacceptable." He wrote op-ed pieces in *La Presse* and *Le Devoir* saying the same thing. The CBC reported Tremblay as saying, "The Liberal bill is totally irresponsible. They are making demergers too easy by not setting a minimum level for voter turnout in referendums."

54 I base this conclusion on the fact that, in the municipalities that did finally demerge from the megacity, taken together, a phenomenal eight votes went to Tremblay for every one that went to Pierre Bourque. (In Beaconsfield, Côte Saint-Luc, Pointe-Claire, and Westmount, it was twelve to one.) Had all these municipalities voted even two to one in favour of Tremblay over Bourque (as did the rest of the suburban voters), Tremblay would have lost 24,000 votes and therefore lost the election to Bourque. (Bourque lost the election by only 16,000 votes, as Tremblay polled 32,000 more votes.) It's an interesting fact that *all* the boroughs that voted more than four to one for Tremblay over Bourque wound up demerged, and they were the *only* ones to demerge. Every other borough voted three to one or less for Tremblay – and they all stayed with the megacity.

55 *La Presse*, 21 November 2000. The first part was paraphrasing a 1974 speech of a former Liberal minister of municipal affairs, Dr Victor Goldbloom.

56 Actually, mergers just shifted the "sterile" competition among many smaller units to "sterile" competition among fewer larger units such as Montreal, Laval, and Longueuil.

CHAPTER TWO

1 My first, and by no means last, experience with redevelopment. It would be a mistake to imagine that "scientific" urban redevelopment under the hands of town planners was just a postwar phenomenon: it was in vogue well before the Second World War and was even given voice during the war itself. "Building science is advancing so rapidly that we have no right to build for a thousand years ... a house should be regarded as permanent only for about thirty years and then should be replaced by an up-to-date one ... For the good of the community, private interests must be subordinated to public ones." So said Donald Gibson, city architect of Coventry in December 1940, three weeks after German bombs had virtually wiped out Coventry's medieval city centre. Gibson – successfully – plumped for a clean-slate, ahistorical approach for the redevelopment of his city.

2 Government of Quebec, Ministère de la culture et des communications, *Le Français langue commune* (March 1996).

3 Government of Canada, *Royal Commission on Bilingualism and Biculturalism*.

4 That the church handicapped French-Canadians in regard to public library service is certain. Only in 1917 did the City of Montreal open a municipal public library, thirty-three years after the Toronto Public Library was opened, and eighteen years after the City of Westmount built its library (the first public library in Quebec). The church and its list of prohibited books (including works of Balzac, Flaubert, Descartes, and Rousseau) had a lot to do with the rarity of libraries in Quebec. In 1901, Montreal turned down a Carnegie grant to build a library because the church did not approve of the grant's condition that the library's books be available to all.

The longstanding francophone lack of interest in libraries had little to do with money. Before Outremont's new library was built (and Westmount's library expanded) in the mid-1990s, the Westmount, Town of Mount Royal, Côte Saint-Luc and Pointe-Claire libraries had, on average, over seven times as much floor area as the former library found in the back of Outremont City Hall. It was just not a priority.

5 *Royal Commission on Bilingualism and Biculturalism*, vol. 3.

6 *La Presse*, 17 March 2005.

7 *Allocation du premier ministre, M. Bernard Landry, Symposium sur la société québécoise et les Autochtones*, 26 March 2002.

8 *Montreal Gazette*, 17 June 2003. Bourgault wasn't entirely anglophobic. Writing in the *Journal de Montréal* in August 1997, Bourgault, who did not know me, actually suggested I should become the next mayor of

Montreal: "I like this man. I like this mayor. Intelligent, competent, level-headed, with a quiet strength and a pleasing sense of humour." He went on to say, "Trent would not leave the verdant slopes of Westmount for the infernal politics of Montreal, but one can dream, can't one?"

9 Only a quarter of allophones who arrived in Quebec before 1961 became French-speaking, compared with three-quarters of those who arrived after 2001.

10 As an example, according to the Fraser Institute, in 2007 the Quebec government gave $6 billion (more than four times per capita the amount Ontario gave) in subsidies to business.

11 According to Jay Bryan, writing in the *Montreal Gazette*, 19 October 2006, Quebec has 127 public-sector workers per 100,000 residents; Ontario has 113.

12 Government of Quebec, *La Présence syndicale au Québec*, 7. Also, see Claude Picher in *La Presse* 12 March 2009. In France, surprisingly, the workforce is only 8–9 per cent unionized. See *The Economist*, 26 July 2008 and 31 October 2009.

13 About 57 per cent of Quebec's construction sector is unionized, versus 22 per cent in the rest of Canada. See: Government of Quebec, *La Présence syndicale au Québec*, 21.

14 A 2002 Quebec government edict refers to the Quebec flag as "the national emblem."

15 *Montreal Gazette*, 29 April 2004.

16 *La Presse*, 15 February 2004.

17 Ibid., 30 June 2005.

18 Scowen, *Time to Say Goodbye*.

19 *La Presse*, 28 April 2007.

20 Ibid., 9 October 1996. Robert Bourassa was a former premier of Quebec who, posthumously, became toponomastically unlucky. A few years ago, Mayor Tremblay wanted to change the name of Park Avenue to honour him but, faced with a storm of protest, backed down.

21 The other five are David Azrieli, Robert Miller, Lino Saputo, Charles Bronfman, and Stephen Jarislowsky (as tabulated by *Forbes Magazine* 2010).

22 The Quebec Community Groups Network and Léger Marketing insisted in 2010 that anglophones actually earn less than francophones in Quebec. Demographer Charles Castonguay disputed that conclusion in *Le Devoir*, 3 August 2010.

23 *La Presse*, 2 April 2007.

24 Ibid., 30 June 2005.

25 A Léger Marketing poll conducted in May 2009 discovered that two-thirds of francophones felt that "There is too much English spoken in Quebec."

26 Fear is one thing. Dislike of the English language is another. The theme of a book published in Quebec in 2009 with the title *Anglaid* ("Uglyeng-lish") was that English was "a language irremediably destined for imperialism and ethnocentrism." See Michel Brûlé, *Anglaid*. It is hard to imagine the equivalent book being published about French (although one francophone wag suggested the title *Frenshit*).

27 Dufour, *Les Québécois et l'anglais*. Paradoxically, those anglophones sympathetic to the francophone cause in the 1990s (such as I) were dismissed as "members of the lamb lobby" by their more militant linguistic brethren.

28 In a *La Presse* editorial of February 2008.

29 The gulf between francophone and anglophone attitudes towards ethnics was neatly illustrated during the 2007 provincial election campaign. André Boisclair, one of the least racist politicians in Quebec, was running as leader of the PQ and made a passing reference to Asians, using the term "slanted eyes." Francophone commentators were genuinely baffled by the firestorm of anglo reaction. Pierre Foglia, writing in *La Presse* on 17 March 2007, insisted that it was not a pejorative term in French, going as far to say it was yet another example of anglophone contempt for francophones. In English Canada, where tolerance of visible minorities has become somewhat of a fine art, people were aghast that Boisclair did not step down. Interestingly, over ten years earlier Boisclair was one of the few *péquistes* to renounce anglophobia, pleading age: "The people who talked about the big damn English [unilingual salesclerk] at Eaton's are not part of my generation. I was not there for 'McGill *français*.' I wasn't there when they had the riots in Saint-Leonard" (*Montreal Gazette*, 13 January 1996).

30 *La Presse*, 4 October 2005.

31 Ibid., 7 October 2005. This idea seems to have been something of an obsession with Landry. When he was premier, he even talked in the National Assembly about how the SAQ had created an "interesting movement" away from the consumption of hard liquor "inherited from our British and Scottish influences." See *Débats de l'assemblée nationale*, 10:30 AM, 20 June 2001.

32 *La Presse*, 8 October 2005.

33 *La Presse*, 29 September 2003.

34 Ibid., 27 October 2003.

35 Ibid., 29 and 30 October 2003.

36 Ibid., 28 October 2003.

37 Ibid., 5 November 2003.
38 André Pratte, *Aux pays des merveilles*, 49.

CHAPTER THREE

1 The information in this and the next two sections came from a number
of sources, including my own files. Some dates, addresses, and figures
were slightly contradictory. Principal among the outside sources were
Hélène Saly, *Old Westmount*; Aline Gubbay and Sally Hooff, *Montreal's
Little Mountain*; City of Westmount, *Westmount: A Heritage to Preserve*;
Elizabeth Ida Hanson, *A Jewel in a Park*; Aline Gubbay, *A View of Their
Own*; and the Government of Quebec, Direction générale du patrimoine,
Maison Braemar, November 1981.

2 In 1881, residents of Côte St Antoine were about 90 per cent of British
origin and those of Notre Dame de Grâce West were about 80 per cent of
French origin. These proportions held for at least 20 years.

3 Using 2006 borders (Institut de la statistique de Québec, *Données socio-
démocratiques en bref*, February 2008). The population of all of Quebec
in 1911 was two million.

4 Linteau, *Histoire de Montréal depuis la Confédération*, 259. Also see
http://www2.ville.montreal.qc.ca/archives/democratie/democratie_fr/expo/
maires/payette/index.shtm.

5 I worked out the relationships in this paragraph from http://trenholm.
org.

6 Trenholme was a good negotiator. The annexation deal with Montreal
not only required Montreal to take over a $1.145 million debt, but they
were committed to spend $1.0 million on streets within three years, build
three fire and police stations and a public hall, and abolish toll gates. See
City Council of Montreal, *Commission for the Study of the Metropolitan
Problems of Montreal. General and Final Report*, January 1955.

7 This financial tit-for-tat resurfaced in 1921, three years after Montreal
was forced to annex the City of Maisonneuve and absorb its huge $9 mil-
lion debt.

8 Letter to the City of Westmount from the Chief Herald of Canada, 14
September 1990.

9 The word "worship" does *not* mean "adoration": it is a holdover from
an archaic meaning of "worthiness," or, literally, "worth-ship." When
Spenser wrote of the Red Cross Knight wanting "to win worship," he
meant to gain honour or renown. This is why the Canadian and British

use of "Your Worship" is semantically equivalent to the American "Your Honor."

10 van Nus, *Montreal Metropolis, 1880–1930*, 64.

11 Ibid., 63–4.

12 MacKay, *The Square Mile*, 192.

13 *Montreal Gazette*, 30 June 1962.

14 Marsan, *Montreal in Evolution*, 332. See also *Urbanité* (the official organ of the Ordre des urbanistes du Québec), November 2003, 61. Both sources refer to *Horizon 2000*, a document worked on by City of Montreal planners from 1963 to 1967.

15 Udy, *The Death and Life of de Maisonneuve Blvd.*

16 Council of the City of Westmount, *Minutes of Proceedings of the General Committee of the City of Westmount*, 16 January 1961.

17 Council of the City of Westmount, *Westmount Letter*, May 1961.

18 City of Montreal, *Annuaire statistique des ménages et des logements de la Ville de Montréal*, 2003. This document used 2001 statistics. Since the number of Westmount owned dwellings increased from 4,095 to 4,375 between 2001 and 2006, I adjusted the proportions accordingly.

19 An excellent history of the whole project is Laureen Sweeney's *Polishing the Jewel*.

20 I got involved with most aspects of the library project, especially the design and construction, even going to Ogilvy's to pick out the armchairs. While I chose the architect, Peter Rose, we had a stormy five-year relationship. He probably dismissed me as belonging to the Prince Charles School of Architecture. When it was all finished, he told me, "This became your project, Peter. Not mine."

21 Paquin and van der Plancke, *Nomination de la ville de Westmount*, 26.

22 Memo to Westmount City Council from the Office of the Secretary-Treasurer of the City of Westmount, 8 February 1956.

23 This was a radical change, as in the 1991 census leaflet we were told that "Ethnic or cultural origin refers to the ethnic 'roots' or ancestral background of the population, and should not be confused with citizenship or nationality."

24 *La Presse*, 12 September 1993.

25 Since 2006, Statistics Canada now routinely reports median income figures, not average income figures.

26 From Statistics Canada. The investment and self-employment income earned by all Westmounters amounts to nearly 10 per cent of what the entire Island of Montreal collectively earns in these categories. See http://www.craarc.gc.ca/agency/stats/gb04/pst/locsts/pdf/ls04hd5-e.pdf.

CHAPTER FOUR

1 The material for these three paragraphs was taken from Jacques Parizeau, *Le Rapport de la Commission d'étude sur les municipalités.*

2 City of Montreal, *Document de réflexion déposé par la Ville de Montréal devant le Groupe de travail sur Montréal et sa région* (1992). Unlike in Canada, many municipalities also levy income taxes, gasoline taxes, and "sin taxes" on things like cigarettes and alcohol.

3 Government of Quebec, Comité Québec-municipalités, *La revalorisation du pouvoir municipal: bilan et suivi de la nouvelle fiscalité* (1982).

4 This is still invoked today as policy. See Government of Quebec, Ministère des Affaires municipales, *La fiscalité des organismes municipaux au Québec* (2004), 7. In an earlier document put out by the same government department in 1995, *Répertoire des expériences de tarification*, 11, in view of taxpayer mobility, taxing according to capacity to pay would send the taxpayer to another municipality. Again, it plumps for taxing according to benefit received.

5 Municipal assessments also grew by a factor of five between 1981 and 2006. The government was too clever by half, as had they kept the full school tax, they would be pulling in about $5 billion a year today, double what they get from one-quarter of today's sales tax revenues. Whether they could have got away with financing schools principally from property taxes is another matter.

6 Now that only one-half of capital gains is taxed, I feel it's about time we got rid of the exemption for people's residences, as long as any capital gains are reduced by inflation and improvements. Economists argue that the homeowner already enjoys "implied rent." If the exemption were cancelled, the black market in home renovation would shrivel up and die: contractors could no longer avoid sales and income taxes by accepting cash because owners would need receipts. Likewise, the common practice of renovating without building permits would be stopped cold.

7 In 2007, school board voter turnout was 7.8 per cent across Quebec (7.1 per cent for francophone boards). On Montreal Island, turnout was 5.6 per cent (francophone boards varied from 3.4 to 5.0 per cent). In a desperate attempt to boost school-board election turnout, in early 2010 the Quebec Federation of School Boards lobbied the government to hold simultaneous elections with the municipal sector in 2013. This move would almost guarantee less media coverage and great confusion (especially where there are both English and French school boards). In the long-ago past, school boards were truly local and often covered the same territories as the local

municipality. The subsequent decimation of school boards has resulted in sprawling boards that range over many municipalities, rarely sharing common borders. This makes simultaneous elections difficult. But the real problem is one of using the walking wounded to carry the stretchers of the nearly expired. As it is, municipal election turnout is around 45 per cent – and dropping. School board election turnout is 7.8 per cent – and dropping.

8   M.-C. Prémont, "La fiscalité locale au Québec."

9   In July 1998, the change from confessional school boards to linguistic ones was accompanied by this reduction from 158 to 72. See Jean-Pierre Collin's article "La réforme de l'organisation du secteur municipal au Québec." Today, the seventy-two school boards in Quebec, with a budget of nearly $10 billion, spend $561 million in administration (*Le Soleil*, 13 May 2010). At first blush this ratio looks good, until one realizes that it does not include the costs of administering Quebec's Education Department and that boards are often just transfer agents for this funding. Even the school boards admit that the mergers in the late 1990s did not bring about the anticipated $100 million in savings.

10 From 1974 to 1981, the assessment of single-family dwellings went up by 146 per cent across the Island of Montreal: for apartments, the equivalent rise was 51 per cent. The commercial sector went up even less. See Government of Quebec, Comité Québec-municipalités, *La revalorisation du pouvoir municipal*.

11 This was not and is not a peculiarly Westmount problem. In 2001, across the Island of Montreal, homeowners were paying nearly five times the tax bill paid by apartment dwellers.

12 In 1983, municipal taxes on the average single-family dwelling in Westmount reached $9,000 in today's dollars. The next year, they dropped to $7,500, after which they remained in a channel from about $7,200 to about $8,200 until the 2002 merger, when they started to climb. In 2011, they were at $11,300 (all figures in 2011 dollars).

13 Quoted in a beautifully written article on Quebec municipal taxation by Pierre J. Hamel, "Le 'Pacte fiscal' entre le gouvernement du Québec et les municipalités."

14 Government of Quebec, Department of Municipal Affairs, *Partage des Responsabilités Québec-municipalités: Vers un Nouvel Équilibre*, 14 December 1990.

15 In 1992. See Lachance, *Analyse du fardeau fiscal relatif en impôts fonciers et taxes municipales entre le Québec et l'Ontario*, 31. Another source calculates the difference in "capacity to pay" between Quebec and Ontario

(as opposed to their principal cities) in 1997 as 21.6 per cent. See Government of Quebec, *Pacte 2000*, 338.

16 Ibid., 13 and 33. In Toronto, for example, the commercial tax rate was more than quadruple the residential rate. In Montreal, a commercial rate of double the residential rate was more the norm (figures for 1995). Today, in both Toronto and Montreal, commercial property tax rates are around 4.2 times the residential rates.

17 Ibid., 2 and 28.

18 The original amount was made up of $220.7 million of operating grants and $45.5 million for major repairs. Later, the first number was increased to $249.1.

19 Lachance, *Analyse du fardeau fiscal*, 11.

20 Claude Ryan, *Comments to the Quebec National Assembly during the Debate on Bill 145*, 19 June 1991. See http://www.assnat.qc.ca/archives/Archives-34leg1se/fra/publications/debats/journal/CH/910619.htm. Thanks to the SQ's (and their union's) longstanding campaign to absorb them, today there are only thirty-three municipal police forces left in Quebec. Of the 5,345 uniformed members of the SQ in 2009, 1,463 were former municipal police officers. It goes without saying that they have better salaries and benefits. The current law stipulates that municipalities of a population less than 50,000 can avail themselves of SQ services rather than have their own police department; now, the SQ union wants to raise that bar to 100,000. Since the SQ is paid for by all Quebecers, and since the SQ only charges 53 per cent of the true cost of providing local police service, this is yet another example of the Quebec government subsidizing rural Quebec. In 2009, this subsidy was worth $235 million, according to the Montreal police brotherhood.

21 *Le Devoir*, 7 March 1991.

22 Government of Quebec, Ministère des Affaires municipales, *Bilan de l'impact financier du réaménagement du partage des responsabilités Québec-municipalités de 1992*. This report concludes that the Ryan Reform created a municipal budgetary deficit of $281.3 million. However, because the authors could not estimate the effect of the elimination of government subsidies for public transit major repairs, they simply left that item out. Originally, the government estimates were $45.5 million for such a cut. In addition, the $281.3 million does not include increases in the welcome tax of $44 million. And, since compensation grants of $43.5 million were only temporary, they also have to be added back. On the other hand, increased payments by the federal government of $46.8 million, offset by assorted decreased grants by Quebec, reduce the global

amount by $35.2 million. This is how I get the final figure of $379.1 million.

23 Government of Quebec, Ministère des Affaires municipales, *Repenser les relations avec les municipalités* (2004). This study completely ignores the surtax, the increased welcome tax, and the fact that $45.5 million of transit subsidy cuts were left out of the 1992 report.

24 Government of Quebec, Cabinet Meeting of 26 February 1992, decision no. 92–050.

25 Claude Ryan, memo to cabinet, 13 February 1992 (my collection).

26 *Montreal Gazette*, 3 April 1992.

27 On 8 October 1992.

28 *Montreal Gazette*, 15 January 1993.

29 *Pour Montréal et sa Région, un appel au dépassement*, transcribed by Jean Larose, s.o., of Riopel, Daigneault, Gagnon, Larose & Ass., 5 March 1993.

30 Ibid.

31 Even Tremblay's 2005 Montreal budget was labelled "evolutionary and dynamic." He gets full marks for consistency.

32 *Le Devoir* and *La Presse*, 2 April 1993.

33 Ninety-one municipalities merged into thirty-nine. See Marc-Urbain Proulx, *Les territoires du Québec at la décentralisation gouvernementale*, 28.

34 Minutes of the National Assembly, 8 December 1969.

35 From 1972 to 1988, 220 municipalities merged into 106. See Petrelli, *Scénarios de réforme des institutions locales et régionales au Québec*, 7.

36 René Lévesque, *Pointe de Mire*, 3 July 1971.

37 Government of Quebec, Ministère des Affaires municipales, *Le regroupement de municipalités* (1993).

38 *Urba*, October 1994. This article counted as forced mergers all twenty-four "special laws" adopted by the National Assembly during the period. At least four of them (Chomedey, Alma, Vaudreuil, and Rouyn-Noranda) were voluntary.

39 The net reduction in the number of municipalities was 195. See Proulx, *Les territoires du Québec at la décentralisation gouvernementale*, 28.

40 Parizeau Report.

41 Ralph Mercier, *La Presse*, 2 April 1993; Ulric Blackburn, *Urba*, October 1994.

42 Claude Ryan, "Québec et le monde municipal: Bilan et perspectives," speech delivered at the 73rd annual congress of the UMQ, 7 May 1994. Ten years later Ryan was to recall, "I said to the municipalities, Montreal

in particular, that they had some soul-searching to do; and, while I did not wish to impose anything on them, sooner or later, if they did nothing themselves, there would be worse" (*Le Soleil*, 20 June 2003).

43 *La Presse*, 30 May 1994.

44 Ibid., 10 May 1994.

CHAPTER FIVE

1 *La Presse*, 20 February 1992; *Le Devoir*, 20 February 1992; *Town of Mount Royal Post*, 2 April 1992.

2 *Montreal Gazette*, 11 March 1992.

3 Recently, the agglomeration of Longueuil, with its population of 406,000, has been pushing to become a single administrative region, like Laval. It realizes the handicap it has by being part of the vast Montérégie region.

4 Because it was an advisory body, Ryan was not concerned with demographic weight, so there were seven from the Island, seven from the south shore, and seven from the north shore.

5 Government of Quebec, *Les orientations du gouvernement en matière d'aménagement du territoire* (1994). Marc Levine in *La CUM et la région métropolitaine*, 111, says that from 1980 to 1998 Quebec spent $238 million to build forty-two schools off-Island, while thirty-one Island schools were closed.

6 In the 1990s, 75 per cent of all immigrants to Quebec came to the Island of Montreal.

7 Government of Quebec, Florent Gagné, secretary and deputy minister, *Compte rendu de la table de concertation du Montréal Métropolitain*, 20 May and 13 June 1994.

8 Jean Doré, *Présentation du mémoire de la ville de Montréal au Groupe du travail sur Montréal et sa région*.

9 By 1997 there were seventeen administrative regions.

10 *La Presse*, 15 October 1994.

11 Conseil régionale de développement de l'Île de Montréal, *Plan stratégique, 2000–2005, Bilan des réalisations et interventions.* 24 September 1999.

12 I supported Montreal Mayor Pierre Bourque when he, fed up with the special interest groups, decided to become one himself and force the RDCIM to give $1 million each to the Tourist Board and to Montreal International, both of which promoted the Montreal Metropolitan Region abroad.

13 Conseil régionale de développement de l'Île de Montréal, *Notes de présentation du budget*, 199–7. This document also revealed that the total

administrative overheads for all RDCs across Quebec were running at $10 million a year.

14 The Montreal CRÉ's fuzzy, feel-good, and all-encompassing goals, if taken seriously, would daunt even the Quebec and Canadian governments, if not the United Nations. The following is taken from *Conférence régionale des élus de Montréal: Bilan des réalisations, 2008–2009*, published in 2010 (my collection): "Develop human capital by success in schools and education for all ages. Promote scientific culture in the public at large. Attract, retain, and recognize the value of talents, experience, and expertise. Invest in innovation and creativity while maximizing their impact. Stimulate the growth of entrepreneurship, notably the social economy. Support our centres of excellence and our emerging sectors on the word's stage ... Coordinate the actors in social development. Support family services. Turn a healthy diet and guaranteed food supply into urban concerns. Further the socioeconomic integration of immigrants ... Put in place a cluster of clean technologies. Increase environmental improvements and the reduction in greenhouse gasses. Promote urban landscapes. Develop a strategy for water. Support cultural development ... Support turnover, male-female parity, and diversity in decision-making bodies. Encourage networking and speaking out." In the CRÉ's Five-Year Plan for 2005–10, one finds such head-scratching goals as: "Publicize social economy organizations and encourage the practice of solidarity in purchasing."

15 Not any more, at least not since Serge Ménard accused Vaillancourt in 2010 of offering him $10,000 in cash during the 1993 provincial election campaign. Vaillancourt denied it, but subsequently dropped a threatened lawsuit against Ménard. I believe Ménard. A police investigation was launched. Vaillancourt was forced to step down from the board of Hydro-Quebec, but refused to leave the board of the UMQ – which precipitated my own resignation in protest.

16 Vaillancourt, "Présentation du mémoire de la Ville de Laval devant le Groupe de travail sur Montréal et sa région" (1993).

17 *Montreal Gazette* and *Le Devoir*, 26 November 1994; *Le Devoir*, 18 December 1994.

18 It is Statistics Canada that defines a census agglomeration (what Quebec was calling a "central city" or an "urban agglomeration") as having an urban core population of at least 10,000.

19 *Le Devoir*, 26 September 1995.

20 *Les Affaires*, 26 August 1995.

21 In 2010 the gasoline tax rate was increased to three cents and the one-cent per $100 of assessment contribution was cancelled.

22 Government of Quebec communiqué, "L'Agence métropolitain de transport: Une réalité dès le premier janvier 1996," 15 December 1995.

23 Raymond Chabot Martin Paré, Comptables agrées, *Montréal International, États financiers au 30 septembre 1997*, 4 December 1997.

24 Quoted in Conference of Montreal Suburban Mayors, *L'organisation du soutien au développement économique dans la région métropolitain de Montréal*, 8 December 1997 (my collection).

25 As we shall see, the responsibility for the RDCIM, along with the Local Development Centres on the Island of Montreal and of Laval, was finally removed from Chevrette and given to Ménard on 30 April 1997.

26 *La Presse*, 12 June 1996.

27 As quoted in a *Le Devoir* editorial, 5 May 1997.

28 Government of Quebec, *Politique de soutien au développement local et régional* (1997), 2.

29 Government of Quebec, *Décentralisation: Un choix de société* (1995).

30 Jacques Desbiens in *Fusions municipales et économies d'échelle* gives the 1995 US figure as 3,200.

31 Ibid., 82–5.

32 Today there are nine CLDs on the Island of Montreal, to which one should add six CDECs, two SODECs, and one RESO, for a total of eighteen members of this general species, without counting the Service d'aide aux jeunes entrepreneurs (SAJE). In addition, there is a kind of commercial-artery sub-species called Sociétés de développement commercial (SDC), of which there are fifteen in Montreal alone.

33 *La Presse*, 31 October 1997.

34 Ibid., 7 October 1997.

35 "Note d'information du ministre responsable du développement des régions: Pour une action gouvernementale résolument locale et régionale," Quebec, 23 January 1997.

36 The economic development corporations (CDEs) were mostly replaced with the CLDs.

37 Government of Quebec, *Politique de soutien au développement local et régional* (1997).

38 This enumeration of structures excludes things like the Waste Management Board or the Conference (later the Union) of Montreal Suburban Mayors, as they were something the mayors decided to establish on their own. Being non-government structures, they have not survived. What has survived and what was not enumerated are the twenty-nine community councils (*tables locales de concertation en developpement social*, or *tables de quartier*, for short) on the Island of Montreal, with a total of eighty

employees. These councils are made up of community, institutional, political groups. They are engaged in community development.

39 Sometimes, inflated titles disguise a chopped-up region. The Greater
Montreal Convention and Tourist Bureau, in spite of its name, only worries about the Island of Montreal.

40 Enumerated in City of Laval, *Mémoire de la ville de Laval [au] Forum de
consultation sur une commission de développement de la métropole* (1996).

CHAPTER SIX

1 "Mega" was not an exaggeration: the new City of Halifax took up 10 per
cent of Nova Scotia's total land area.

2 Claude Ryan, "Québec et le monde municipal: Bilan et perspectives,"
speech delivered at the 73rd annual congress of the UMQ, 7 May 1994.

3 *La Presse*, 9 December 1995.

4 Ibid., 29 December 1995.

5 Guy Chevrette, form letter to all mayors, 18 January 1996.

6 Union of Quebec Municipalities, *Questionnaire de l'UMQ sur les orientations des parties politiques*, 23 August 1994, 8.

7 *Le Devoir*, 27 January 1996.

8 *La Presse*, 31 January 1996.

9 *Le Devoir*, 31 January 1996.

10 *Montreal Gazette*, 1 February 1996.

11 *Montreal Gazette*, 8 February 1996.

12 *Le Journal de Montréal*, 14 February 1996.

13 *La Presse*, 6 March 1996.

14 *Le Journal de Montréal*, 11 March 1996.

15 *La Presse*, 14 May 1996.

16 http://www.premier.gouv.qc.ca/salle-de-presse/discours/1996/mars/1996-
03-25.shtm.

17 *Montreal Gazette*, 2 May 1996.

18 *La Presse, Le Soleil*, 5 May 1996.

19 Government of Quebec, *Table Quebec Municipalités*, 23 and 24 May
1996 (my collection).

20 *La Presse*, 20 January 1996.

21 Three-quarters of the towns in the latter group had populations less than
fifteen hundred.

22 Government of Quebec, *Muni-express*, April 1997.

23 Union of Quebec Municipalities, communiqué, 30 May 1996.

24 *Le Devoir*, 31 May 1996.

25 Most of this material came from an interview by Nathalie Petrowski writing in *La Presse*, 29 December 1995.

26 After a sudden and rare illness, Vera Danyluk died in October 2010.

27 Communauté urbaine de Montréal, Demande d'autorisation au comité exécutif, 12 September 1995 (my collection).

28 *La Presse*, 20 April 1996.

29 Merging transit boards has its dangers. As Lawrence Solomon has written, "Public transit as one large monopoly, if intelligently run, will always be preferable to many small monopolies. If unintelligently run, one large monopoly spells doom, as did Toronto's Transit Commission after a previous amalgamation: its densely populated, highly profitable City of Toronto routes were plundered to service unprofitable suburban routes, leading to the entire system's virtual collapse." See http://www.urban-renaissance.org/urbanren/index.cfm?DSP=content&ContentID=507.

30 *Le Devoir*, 23 August 1996.

31 Michel Vastel, *L'Actualité*, 15 October 1996.

32 Government of Quebec, *Vers une commission de développement de la métropole: Document de consultation* (1996).

33 Henry Aubin, *Montreal Gazette*, 24 September 1996.

34 Following the forum, Ménard had announced that his commission would be consultative only, but it would become decision-making in five years' time, at which point there would be direct elections. Even then, it would only deal with economic promotion, transport, and land-use planning. By the time it was presented as Bill 92, all references to the Cinderella-like transformation to a body elected by universal suffrage were gone.

35 Assemblée nationale du Québec, *Projet de loi no. 92*, Éditeur official du Québec, 1996.

36 *Montreal Gazette*, 7 January 1997.

37 In the law as adopted, the council named the vice-presidents

38 *La Presse*, 19 December 1996.

39 Serge Ménard, *Notes pour l'allocution du ministre d'État à la métropole (...) Chambre de commerce du Montréal métropolitain*, 21 January 1997 (my collection).

40 *Le Devoir*, 5 April 1997.

41 *La Presse*, 15 January 1997.

42 Ibid., 2 February 1997.

43 Ibid., 27 February 1997.

44 Ibid.

45 Assemblée nationale du Québec, transcript of the Commission permanente de l'aménagement et des équipements, 10:08 AM, 5 March 1997.

See http://www.assnat.qc.ca/archives/archives-35leg2se/fra/Publications/
debats/journal/cae/970305.htm.

46 Ibid., 10:40–10:45 AM. Had I known then the number of Local Development Centres and Local Employment Centres that Chevrette was to create
in the Montreal Metropolitan Region, my total would have been 120, not
seventy structures.

47 *Les Affaires*, 5 October 1996.

48 The former members of the Task Force on Greater Montreal, *Permettre à
la métropole de réaliser tout son potentiel*, February 1997.

49 *La Presse*, 20 March 1997.

CHAPTER SEVEN

1 Henry Aubin, *Montreal Gazette*, 26 December 1995.

2 Actually, as far back as July 1994, McGill law professor Stephen Scott
and his Coalition for Canadian Unity had tried unsuccessfully to get
municipalities to adopt resolutions to ensure "Canadian territorial integrity" that declared "that this municipality will not accept ... any unilateral declaration of independence." From "Recommended Text of a Municipal Council Resolution," dated 1 July 1994 (personal communication to
author).

3 William Johnson, *Montreal Gazette*, 8 November 1996.

4 *Westmount Examiner*, 24 April 1997.

5 *Montreal Gazette*, 2 January 1997.

6 Ibid., 30 January 1997.

7 Dollard-des-Ormeaux, Beaconsfield, Kirkland.

8 Montreal West, Pointe-Claire, Dorval, Town of Mount Royal.

9 Peter Trent, *Montreal Gazette*, 4 May 1997.

10 Jim Wright, the most decent man I ever met, was killed in a freak accident
in 2007.

11 *La Presse*, 15 September 1997.

12 *Montreal Gazette*, 15 July 1997; *La Presse*, 16 July 1997.

13 Quoted by Michel Vastel in *Le Droit*, 13 September 1999.

14 As quoted in *L'Actualité*, 1 November 1999, 8.

15 *Les Affaires*, 6 May 2000.

16 Since 1979, Quebec municipalities, instead of getting property taxes from
utilities (telephone, gas, and electricity), got a small percentage of the sales
of these companies. In 1996, Quebec cut this revenue stream by $50 mil-
lion, along with: $10 million cuts in library grants, a new $18 million
contribution to the Metropolitan Transport Agency, an increase of $46

million in fees for the provincial police (the SQ) and their training college, and the elimination of the sales tax rebate worth $76 million.

17 *Le Devoir*, 29 November 1996.

18 While the $500 million took everyone by surprise, it was, in fact, anticipated in a document leaked to the Canadian Press in 22 March 1994 – precisely three years before this downloading, and three years after Ryan's 1991 downloading of about the same amount. Florent Gagné, deputy minister of municipal affairs at the time and the chief architect of the Ryan Reform, had prepared a document for Quebec's (Liberal) cabinet that recommended another $500 million of downloading would be advisable by 1997. And that's precisely what happened. Gagné even got the year right. It would seem that, for the Department of Municipal Affairs, $500 million has some kind of talismanic value. This also shows how the bureaucrats, regardless of the party in power, make the same suggestions, be they to do with downloading or with mergers.

19 Union of Quebec Municipalities, *Questionnaire de l'UMQ sur les orientations des parties politiques*, 5

20 Rémy Trudel, *Un nouveau pacte municipal*, Assises annuelles de l'UMQ, 25 April 1997 (my collection).

21 *Le Devoir*, 23 August 1997.

22 *Montreal Gazette*, 27 March 1997.

23 Well over a year before the downloading, when he was minister of municipal affairs, Guy Chevrette, while pointing out that the government had managed to roll back their employees' wages in 1982, dismissively said, "The municipalities, who didn't take the same initiative, now pay their employees 27 to 32 per cent more than our employees. It's up to them to make an effort" (*La Presse*, 24 November 1995). In fact, the PQ government actually helped augment this gap. When the Liberals were in power, municipalities were allowed to freeze employees' salaries for two years and cut benefits by 1 per cent. On assuming power, the PQ government forced the municipalities to give the 1 per cent back.

24 Coalition québécoise du secteur municipal, Communiqué de presse, 1 April 1997 (my collection).

25 *Le Devoir*, 30 May 1997.

26 *La Presse*, 11 June 1997.

27 Ibid., 10 June 1997.

28 A miscellany of other things, positive and negative, included compensation to the MUC for its specialized police services that were paid for by the government in the rest of the province.

29 The six "central cities" would benefit from a ceiling of 3 per cent of their budgets; for all the other municipalities, there would be a floor of 3.5 per cent and a ceiling of 9 per cent.

30 Press release, Government of Quebec, Department of Municipal Affairs, 20 June 1997

31 Cited in Government of Quebec, *Problématique des villes-centres* (1994), 40. By the school year 1995–96, according to the minister of transport, only 27 per cent of Montreal Island students used buses or mass transit, compared with 62 per cent throughout Quebec.

32 Press release, Quebec Federation of School Boards, 21 August 1997. Nobody seemed to want to opt for the obvious solution: why not have the Department of Transport continue to oversee yellow school bus transport and bill the municipalities accordingly? Later, the government said it would be the ninety-six counties that would run the buses. At least it would give them something to do.

33 *Le Devoir*, 10 October 1997.

34 Even though the $500 million was cut to $375 million, Montreal Island still paid the same, with the rest of Quebec getting a whopping $125 million break.

35 *La Presse*, 8 November 1996.

36 *Le Devoir*, 8 March 1997.

37 *Montreal Gazette*, 8 March 1997.

38 *La Presse*, 8 March 1997.

39 Union of Quebec Municipalities, press release, 7 March 1997.

40 *La Presse*, 11 March 1997.

41 Ibid., 12 March 1997, and *Montreal Gazette*, 12 March 1997. *Le Devoir* of 24 April 1997 published an op-ed piece that I wrote as a rebuttal to Chevrette: "In 1996, the Montreal Island suburbs contributed more than $400 million to the MUC and received approximately $300 million in services. The balance, $100 million," went to help the City of Montreal.

42 Central Cities of the Metropolitan Regions of Quebec, *Mémoire au premier ministre du Québec Monsieur Lucien Bouchard, notes de présentation*, March 1997. My collection.

43 *Le Devoir*, 5 April 1997. Ménard did, however, favour merging Island fire departments; in my book this was the slippery slope to full merger. Ménard also felt there were too many little municipalities off-Island. Six months earlier, impressed by how Laval, Longueuil, Montreal, and the Island suburbs had worked together to build Montreal International, Ménard had mused about mergers outside that core area. See *La Presse*, 18 September 1996.

44 *Le Devoir*, 8 April 1997.
45 *La Presse*, 12 April 1997.
46 *Montreal Gazette*, 10 April 1997.
47 *Le Devoir*, 12 April 1997.

CHAPTER EIGHT

1 *La Presse*, 8 January 1999.
2 Ibid., 17 November 1997.
3 Sancton, *La Réorganisation du gouvernement local au Canada depuis 1975*, 33.
4 *Le Devoir*, 24 February 1993.
5 Some years later (*Le Soleil*, 24 November 2000), Premier Lucien Bouchard would say that, both in Quebec City and in Montreal, the mayors who made up the urban communities were always at each others' throats: "The Quebec Urban Community is at loggerheads, it's a shambles. In Montreal, the MUC never worked. It caused squabbles and conflict." Some years after *that*, the Liberal minister of municipal affairs, Jean-Marc Fournier, was the one to call it a wasp's nest, based on hearsay alone. Michèle Ouimet, in an editorial in *La Presse* 24 April 2004, wrote, "Everyone criticized the MUC. With reason. It was a wasp's nest where the suburbs systematically opposed Montreal." Mayor Tremblay and Benoit Labonté (president of the Montreal Board of Trade at the time) both wrote about "the paralysis that accompanied its double majority system" and how "with the system of a required double majority, the MUC found itself too often paralysed" (letters to *Montreal Gazette*, 22 September 2004, and to *Le Devoir*, 24 September 2004, respectively). None had any personal experience with the MUC; they all repeated what others had said before them in a bad game of Telephone.
6 Dissention between the suburbs and Montreal was pretty rare – unless the subject of the Cavendish Boulevard extension came up, and that little conundrum, even as I write, is still not resolved. In fact, since 1998 the City of Côte Saint-Luc has agreed to the extension, and the whole matter is stuck in the apparatus of the Montreal megacity.
7 Another condition was a request going back to 1995 to permit the director-general of the Conference of Mayors, Marc Vaillancourt, to be present at MUC executive committee meetings, something Danyluk had adamantly refused up until then, saying that meetings must be behind closed doors. The other condition was that the MUC director-general's position, vacant since October, would not be filled without council's prior

approval, something she was required to do anyway. (Vaillancourt was not a disinterested party in helping formulate the latter condition; he was keen on becoming the next director-general of the MUC.)

8 Danyluk, "Notes pour une allocution ... lors de la présentation aux membres du Conseil du budget 1998 de la CUM," 10 December 1997 (my collection). This was the first (and likely only) time Danyluk made territorial expansion a precondition of giving the MUC more powers.

9 Vera Danyluk, "Les iniquités fiscales sur l'Île de Montréal, un problème fondamentalement politique," delivered 21 March 1998, in Bélanger et al., *La CUM et la région métropolitaine*, 166.

10 Well, it was not *total* direct election as in the Ottawa case: the six local mayors sat on the Metro Toronto council along with the twenty-eight directly elected councillors.

11 Louise Quesnel, "La métropole comme espace politique," in Bélanger et al., *La CUM et la région métropolitaine*, 129.

12 Claude Masson, "La CUM et l'opinion publique," in Bélanger et al., *La CUM et la région métropolitaine*, 61.

13 Sancton, *Merger Mania*, 143. Ottawa directly elected the chair of its regional government in 1991 before electing all of its council in 1994.

14 As Andrew Sancton has pointed out to me, the 70 per cent figure was inflated, as a lot of this spending was for welfare and policing, the former controlled by the province, and the latter controlled by powerful police commissions that did not report to the regional councils. Still, the 70 per cent was not *locally* controlled.

15 Trent, guest editorial in *Montreal Gazette*, 5 April 1998. Also, in the *Westmount Examiner*, 4 December 1997, I wrote: "If we regard the MUC as a service co-operative, there will be little pressure to get rid of it through Island amalgamations. On the other hand, if the hegemony of the MUC continues to grow, aided by talk of an MUC fire brigade, the Island would be that much closer to becoming just one megacity."

16 Luc-Norman Tellier, "L'agglomération montréalaise à la croisée des chemins: Région en tutelle, 'mégaville' ou Ville-État?," in Bélanger et al., *La CUM et la région métropolitaine*, 109.

17 Jean-Robert Sansfaçon, editorial in *Le Devoir*, 17 April 1998. See also Bélanger et al., *La CUM et la région métropolitaine*, 132.

18 Jean-Robert Sansfaçon, editorial in *Le Devoir*, 3 November 1997.

19 Masson, "La CUM et l'opinion publique," in Bélanger et al., *La CUM et la région métropolitaine*, 60.

20 After some three hundred days of hearings, a judgment was rendered in October 2008. Foster Wheeler was awarded $20.3 million, including

interest and costs. In October 2011, the Court of Appeal reduced the award to $2.2 million.

21 I was ineligible as I had just stepped down from the MUC executive committee to sit on the transit board. I came back only later that year.

22 CJAD Radio, 7:33 AM, 4 February 1998 (my collection).

23 *Montreal Gazette*, 4 February 1998. Because of the atrocious timing and the klutzy way it was handled, the recommendation to change the status of the MUC executive committee chair looked as if it came out of nowhere (we had considered it for years), which in turn reinforced the idea it was just a sleazy way to rid us of a problem. Interestingly, it was Danyluk herself as president of the Conference of Mayors who wrote to Municipal Affairs Minister Claude Ryan on 23 September 1993, asking for a change in the law to permit the chairman of the MUC executive committee to remain a mayor.

24 *Le Devoir*, 6 February 1998; *La Presse*, 6 February 1998.

25 *La Presse*, 7 February 1998. Trudel's interest in our idea was an indirect admission that a *more* politicized MUC (with direct election of its chairman or council) would have made its geographic expansion that much more difficult.

26 This was the recommendation of the Pichette Task Force and, incidentally, the recommendation to the Task Force by the Conference of Mayors when Danyluk was president.

27 The MUC rules for voting for the chairman gave the candidate two kicks at the can; at the second go-round, only a simple majority of two-thirds was required. To no one's surprise, at the MUC Council meeting on April 15, Danyluk won with 78 per cent of the vote. Had the "dissident mayors" (i.e., those who had been bounced off the Régie executive) not supported her, she would have got just under two-thirds of the overall vote and consequently her mandate would not have been renewed.

28 Georges Bossé and Marc-André Vaillancourt, *Rapport Synthèse des entrevues individuelles réalisées auprès des membres de la* CMBM *Juin-Juillet 1998*, October 1998, 23 (my collection).

29 This internecine fight even spilled over to the MUC executive later that year and the next when there were two attempts – one successful – to bounce "dissident mayors" off that body.

30 *La Presse*, 18 April 1998.

31 *Le Devoir*, 28 October 1998.

32 *La Presse*, 21 November 1998.

33 Included in a letter to all Quebec mayors sent by shadow minister Margaret Delisle, 30 January 1998.

34 Included in a letter to all Quebec mayors sent by Jean Charest, 2 November 1998.

35 *L'Actualité*, 15 November 1998. The interview would have been given weeks before this date.

36 *Le Devoir*, 9 December 1998.

37 *La Presse*, 31 March 1999.

38 Alain Dubuc, editorial in *La Presse*, 20 December 1999.

39 Alain Dubuc, *"répliques"* in *La Presse*, 22 December 1999.

40 Even when it came to expanding the MUC police force. The former president of the MUC police brotherhood and the then-president of the Fédération des policiers du Québec, Yves Prud'Homme, was categorically against the expansion of the MUC police force, although his replacement at the MUC, Alain Simoneau, was not necessarily against it.

41 Sancton, *Governing Canada's City-Regions*, 83.

42 Montreal Urban Community, *Rapport du Conseil de sécurité publique, préparé sous la Présidence de M. le Juge Jacques Coderre*. Before the MUC merged police forces, Westmount spent slightly more per capita than Montreal for its police department. Interestingly, 2 per cent of Montreal's 3,817 policemen were anglophone in 1970, versus 80 per cent of Westmount's policemen. In 1970, Westmount had seventy-eight police of all ranks (including seven detectives), all of whom served a population of 32,500. By the year 2000, 20,000 Westmounters and 13,000 neighbouring residents were together served by thirty-one patrollers. Police services in 2000 cost Westmount about $10 million through their MUC payments.

43 Montreal Urban Community, *2000 Financial Report*. I pro-rated administrative costs. Of the remaining 8 per cent, 2 per cent went to the assessment department, 2 per cent to parks, and 1 per cent to the arts.

44 Deloitte & Touche, *Impacts des navetteurs sur les finances municipales*, 12.

45 Government of Quebec, Ministère des Affaires municipales et de la métropole, *Problématique de la région métropolitaine de Montréal* (1999).

46 As if to repair this lacuna, back in January 1972 Maurice Tessier, who replaced the "father of the MUC," Dr Robert Lussier, as municipal affairs minister, became the first in a long line of people to suggest that the MUC include Laval and the south shore (Benjamin, *La Communauté urbaine de Montréal*, 76).

CHAPTER NINE

1 Aristotle was, of course, referring to city states.

2 *Le Devoir*, 11 April 1997.

3 *La Presse*, 15 April 1997.

4 Ibid., 3 April 1999. A resident of Westmount, Jean Hudon, wrote an excellent op-ed piece countering Gagnon's comments in *La Presse*, 12 April 1999.

5 Ibid., 30 April 1997.

6 *Le Devoir*, 17 December 1998.

7 City of Montreal, 1999 Budget, adopted 17 December 1999.

8 Government of Quebec, *Pacte 2000*, 185.

9 City of Montreal. *Montréal, ville d'affaires* (1993). In fairness, it should be noted that two-thirds of the private funding was directed at only two projects: the Canadian Centre for Architecture and the McCord Museum.

10 First, assuming the $24 million of infrastructure costs were shared by all suburbs in the region in proportion to their "fiscal potential," and given that the Island suburbs' "fiscal potential" was 40 per cent of all regional suburbs, this meant that the Island suburbs would have borne $10 million of these costs. Second, assuming the $12 million of social housing costs were shared by the entire region *including* Montreal, this would add another $3 million to the Island suburbs' bill, as they only represented 28 per cent of the region's "fiscal potential."

11 CFCF-TV interview, *Pulse News*, 19 September 1997.

12 See City of Montreal's *Fiscalité municipale* (2002), 11.

13 This figure includes "in lieu of" taxes. See City of Montreal, *Budget 2001*, 51. In 2008, even after absorbing many residentially rich suburbs, the megacity still got only 43 per cent of its tax revenue from the residential sector (my collection). Interestingly, Harry Kitchen, in the November 2000 issue of the C.D. Howe Institute's *Commentary*, refers to a KMPG study that concluded that residential properties in Vancouver paid 40 per cent of the taxes and consumed 71 per cent of the services, whereas the non-residential properties paid 60 per cent of all property taxes and consumed 29 per cent of services ("Municipal Finance in a New Fiscal Environment," 10). In the report by the City of Vancouver (Property Tax Policy Review Commission) we learn that, in 2006, residential properties paid 45 per cent of the taxes, consumed 76 per cent of the services, and represented 83 per cent of the assessment base; whereas the non-residential properties represented 17 per cent of the assessment base, paid 55 per cent of all property taxes yet consumed 24 per cent of services. According to another source, residential taxpayers in Toronto pay only 35 per cent of the taxes, yet own 70 per cent of the assessment base.

14 *Les Affaires*, 3 May 1997.

15 Central Cities of the Metropolitan Regions of Quebec, *Mémoire au premier ministre du Québec Monsieur Lucien Bouchard, Notes de présentation*, March 1997, 5 (my collection), refers to 1995 rates (also quoted in *La Presse*, 12 April 1997). En passant, for this brief to list only those municipalities that just happened to have very low tax rates was tendentious, although I was surprised they did not cite Chevrette's favourite whipping boy, Westmount.

16 Government of Quebec, *La Réorganisation municipale* (2000), 32.

17 I intentionally call it a tax, not a user fee, as it was based on a percentage of a building's rental value. It's significant that revenues Montreal got from it were around three times the cost of producing the water.

18 Why did Montreal inflate its global tax rate? One reason could be that property taxes (called "in lieu of taxes") paid by Quebec and Canada were tied to the global tax rate. So the higher it was, the more money Montreal got.

19 The given global tax rate was $2.5197; removing the water and service tax results in $2.1351: $1,075,189,800 in "admissible" taxes divided by $42,672,184,825 in equalized taxable value = $2.5197 per $100. Removing $164,115,300 of water and services tax: $911,074,500 in taxes divided by $42,672,184,825 in equalized taxable value = $2.1351 per $100.

20 The global tax rates were as reported in Government of Quebec, *Pacte 2000* (the Bédard Report), 181. This report made the same mistake everyone else made: it assumed the reported global tax rate for Montreal ($2.5197) was correct and used it to (mis-)calculate the taxes on a single-family dwelling in Montreal.

21 Government of Quebec, Ministère des Affaires municipales, *L'Urbanization au Québec* (Castonguay Report), 269.

22 As calculated by Andy Dodge, real-estate evaluator, in his affidavit filed in court during our legal challenge against Bill 170.

23 For 2001: Government of Quebec, Ministère des Affaires municipales, Direction des politiques fiscales et économiques, *Comparaison: Taux de taxation et compte de taxes moyen d'une résidence unifamiliale*. See also City of Montreal, *Budget 2002*, 31. For 1999, see *La Presse* 22 January 2000. The same results for 1999 can be calculated using the 1999 tax rates in *Pacte 2000* (the Bédard Report) multiplied by the average single-family dwelling assessment per municipality, reported in a very interesting study of the projected effects of Island mergers written by Gilles Champagne, CMA of the City of Verdun, titled *Analyse des statistiques provenants des previsions budgétaires 1999, villes de la* CUM.

24 In 1999, residential taxes in the suburbs amounted to $575 million for 770,000 people. In Montreal in 1999, $590 million of taxes came from the residential sector with 1,037,000 people. (Champagne, *Analyse des statistiques provenants des previsions budgétaires 1999, villes de la* CUM).

25 Montreal taxed $603 million from the residential sector with a population of 1,061,000. Westmount taxed $28 million from the residential sector with a population of 20,000. (Both amounts came from each municipality's respective 2001 budgets.)

26 MUC Police Department, *La répartition des effectifs dans les postes de quartier en 2000,* 2.

27 In 2003, just during rush hour (6 AM to 9 AM), Westmount's daytime population increased by 17,046 people: 4,938 to work, 9,700 to study, 830 to shop, and 1,578 for recreation. Only 12,035 Westmounters, in turn, left Westmount: 3,792 to work, 3,020 to study, 2,935 to shop, and 2,288 for recreation. City of Montreal, *Profil sociodémographique: Westmount,* 22, 23. November 2010. According to Statistics Canada, in 2006 there were 66 per cent more jobs in Westmount than workers living there.

28 Sancton, *Merger Mania,* 164.

29 Government of Quebec, Ministère des Affaires municipales, *Le relevé des interventions municipales à caractère supralocal (1997) de la Communauté urbaine de Montréal et de la région.*

30 The work of Janet Rothenberg Pack in this regard is referred to in Government of Quebec, *Pacte 2000,* 177.

31 Ibid., 185.

32 Government of Quebec, *La réorganisation municipale: changer les façons de faire pour mieux servir les citoyens* (Harel's White Paper, 2000), 39.

33 Things have not really changed. In 2009, 42 per cent of all welfare recipients in Quebec lived on the Island of Montreal, which has 24 per cent of Quebec's population.

34 Houses in Westmount, for example: in 2007, Westmount houses sold at prices ranging from 59 per cent to 236 per cent of their assessments. In July 2009, PQ leader Pauline Marois and her husband put up for sale their 12,000 square-foot house, nestled on 1.7 million square feet of land on Île Bizard. The asking price was $8 million. The assessment? $2.8 million.

35 It is true that assessments are updated each year by multiplying them by what is called the "comparative factor," thereby bringing them closer to market value. The trouble is, there is only one factor per municipality. Therefore the unfairness among properties in a given municipality are

systematically perpetuated until the next revision – which is usually once every three years, but is sometimes prolonged.

36 Predicting the future by extrapolating from the past is always dangerous. Because of this stagnation of property values from 1993 to 2001, the Conference Board of Canada in May 2003 predicted they would continue to be sluggish just at the moment they started to take off (assessments always lag the market by a few years). Their prediction for 2006 assessments was that they would grow an anemic 10 per cent over the 2001 value. In the event, they were over 60 per cent higher. Oops.

37 A number of sources tracking residential prices in both Canada and Quebec noted essentially no increase from 1988 to 2000 and a doubling of prices from 2000 to 2007. In the Montreal region, the Greater Montreal Real Estate Board has calculated the median selling price of a single-family dwelling has nearly doubled from 2002 to 2009. Meanwhile, according to the City of Montreal's Assessment Department, the total real-estate assessment on the Island of Montreal has grown from $41.3 billion ($80 billion in 2010 dollars) in 1983 to $195.8 billion in 2010.

   One solution to the problem of fluctuating assessments that smooths out both the municipality's revenue base and the individual's property tax bill is Nova Scotia's Cap Assessment Programme, which, since 2008, has limited residential assessment increases to the inflation rate, with the exception of additions or renovations to the property. Unfortunately, the law of unintended consequences applies and the rich tend to be favoured over the poor in such a scheme.

38 Actually, "property taxes," by provincial definition, include more than just taxes based solely on the value of property; they also include taxes charged to a property-owner for certain services such as water supply and garbage removal. It seems to me that the latter charges are eminently sensible and are in perfect accord with Fiscal Reform and the principle of user fees. It is value-based property taxes that are so arbitrary, having nothing to do with services rendered.

39 See Government of Quebec, *Comité de transition de l'agglomération de Montréal, 2ième rapport d'étape*, 20 October 2005. "Taxes" include "in-lieu of taxes."

40 A cynic would say that all taxes have to do with wealth: you can tax people on their accumulated wealth (wealth taxes), you can tax people as they accumulate wealth (income taxes), and you can tax people as they disaccumulate wealth (sales taxes, gift taxes, and death duties).

41 Slack, *Easing the Fiscal Restraints*.

42 Government of Quebec, *Le financement et la fiscalité des organismes municipaux au Québec* (August 2009), 3.

43 In fact, as the authors of *Pacte 2000* point out, thanks to things like burglar alarms and swimming pools, which are found in more expensive houses, the reverse could be true. See Government of Quebec, *Pacte 2000*, 79.

44 A serious case has been made since Henry George first made it in 1879 that *only* land should be taxed. Property taxes on buildings discourage renovation and improvement. And the value of buildings decays, while the value of land appreciates as communities grow and prosper around it, through no effort on the part of the landowner. So, for land (as opposed to buildings), being taxed based on its value can reflect the benefit received, insofar as enhanced services can increase its value.

45 From the US Census Bureau, as quoted in Government of Quebec, *Pacte 2000*, 72.

46 1891–1911. Paul-André Linteau, *Histoire de Montréal depuis la Confédération*, 76, 188.

47 1881–1901; ibid., 85.

48 van Nus, *Montreal Metropolis*, 59–60. Interestingly, Toronto went though the same annexation phase between 1883 to 1914, annexing some eighteen villages; things then quietened down until well after World War II. See Isin and Wolfson, *The Making of the Toronto Megacity*.

49 Linteau, *Histoire de Montréal depuis la Confédération*, 160, 352.

50 Government of Quebec, Ministère des Affaires municipales, *Municipalité* (special edition, 1984), 6.

51 Linteau, *Histoire de Montréal depuis la Confédération*, 160.

52 City of Montreal, *Commission for the Study of the Metropolitan Problems of Montreal, General and Final Report* (1955).

53 Magnusson and Sancton, *City Politics in Canada*, 65.

54 http://faculty.marianopolis.edu/c.belanger/quebechistory/stats/pop61-21.htm; http://faculty.marianopolis.edu/c.belanger/quebechistory/stats/pop31-96.htm.

55 These three percentages come from Paul-André Linteau, *Histoire de Montréal depuis la Confédération*, 314, 460.

56 As calculated by Ronald Poupart, *Notes pour une allocution au Colloque 1993 des Maires du Grand Montréal*, 27 November 1993 (my collection).

57 These three percentages come from Paul-André Linteau, *Histoire de Montréal depuis la Confédération*, 460.

58 Magnusson and Sancton, *City Politics in Canada*, 71.

59 *La Presse*, 3 December 1999.

60 Ibid., 2 April 2002.

61 Eight years later, when Harel was running for the job of Montreal megacity mayor under Bourque's old banner (Vision Montreal), her second-
in-command, Benoit Labonté, had to bow out of the race when it was
revealed that, to fund his party's leadership aspirations the year before, he
had accepted hundreds of thousands of dollars in cash from contractors
doing business with the city. The miasma of bid-rigging and other sleaze
that surfaced during the 2009 Montreal election campaign had a lot to do
with the financing of the party system.

62 *Montreal Gazette*, 1 October 1997. In 1999 there were 517. By 2003,
according to *La Presse* of 23 July 2003, there were still 505 on Club Med,
costing the city some $36 million annually. The auditor general's report
for 2004 came up with 524.

63 Roquet came back as director-general of the megacity in 2009. Born in
1942, Roquet has an MBA from the HEC (École des hautes études commer-
ciales de Montréal) and a doctorate in administration from Harvard. He
was a vice-president of Steinberg, whence he became the director-general of
the Montreal Urban Community in 1990, and then DG of the former City
of Montreal in 1994.

64 *Le Devoir*, 20 June 1994.

65 Ibid., 7 January 1999.

66 Government of Quebec, *Pacte 2000* (Bédard Report), 41. *Les regroupements municipaux sur l'île de Montréal*, a study done by Municonsult in
1999, estimated Montreal spent 16 per cent more than the Island suburbs per capita, once all costs of a regional nature were removed. These
regional costs were based on a list put together by Montreal and were
taken at face value.

67 Sancton, *Governing the Island of Montreal*, 30.

68 Ibid., 32.

69 The entire 2009 Montreal megacity municipal election centred on the
megacity's rampant corruption and Mayor Gérald Tremblay's inability so far to clean things up. Tremblay got re-elected anyway by a cynical
electorate. Duchesneau, in February 2010, headed up a provincial anti-
collusion unit investigating the construction industry. He was let go in
October 2011, because he was doing too good a job – and for being far
too frank for his boss's taste.

70 Susan Purcell, quoted in Allan Levine, *Your Worship,* 173.

71 http://www.rio.gouv.qc.ca/pub/parc/statistiques.jsp#8. In November 2006,
the debt of $1.5 billion (in 1976 dollars) for all Olympic installations was
finally paid off.

72 Robert Prévost, *Montréal, a History*.

73 It costs around $160 million/km to tunnel. Some say, though, that rubber tires can be used outside in Nordic climes if the rails are heated, or if the trains run inside a glass tube.

74 *La Presse*, 14 October, 2006.

75 Ibid., 24 March 2006.

76 Metropolitan Montreal (as opposed to the City of Montreal) has a tenancy rate of about 50 per cent, which is the highest in North America, with the exception of New York and Los Angeles.

77 Even as late as 2009, according to Canada Mortgage and Housing Corporation, the average rent of a *two*-bedroom apartment in Greater Montreal was $669, compared to $1,096 in Toronto.

78 *La Presse*, 28 March 2001.

79 Robert Bish, in "Local Government Amalgamations," cited one Canadian study that showed waste collection cost $42.29 per household when done by city crews and $28.02 by private-sector crews.

80 Government of Quebec, *Pacte 2000*, 334.

81 City of Montreal, *Budget 1999*, E-34 and E-35.

82 Government of Quebec, Department of the Métropole, 28 November 1997. Similar figures may be found in the document produced by the City of Montreal, *Mémoire de la Ville de Montréal* (1996), 9. See also City of Montreal (megacity), *Budget 2003*, Cahier d'information complémentaire, 50.

83 Government of Quebec, *Pacte 2000*, 334. Serviced land in Quebec should therefore be generally cheaper yet more highly taxed than in Ontario, where developers pay for infrastructure and consequently sell land at a higher price. One would expect, then, Quebec property tax rates to be higher owing to two factors: lower land assessments and the debt financing of infrastructure costs.

CHAPTER TEN

1 *Le Devoir*, 10 September 1998.

2 *La Presse*, 24 March 1999.

3 *Montreal Gazette*, 25 March 1999.

4 *La Presse*, 27 March 1999.

5 *Le Devoir*, 29 March 1999, 30 March 1999, and 3 April 1999.

6 After all, "assimilation" is defined as the process of adopting a home language that is different from one's mother tongue. That home language becomes the mother tongue of the next generation. You might say, for

immigrants, the "home language" chicken comes before the "mother tongue" egg. The opposite was true when it came to the francophone flight to the off-Island suburbs and low francophone birth rates. These latter two trends have led to what has been called the "defrancophonization" (reduction of mother tongue francophones) of the Island. This defrancophonization could lead to the "defrancization" (decline of French as the common language of the Island). See Marc Levine, *Usage du français*, 366–78.

7   The source for the 1971 statistics was http://www.spl.gouv.qc.ca/publications/statistiques/tableau.html. For the 1991 statistics, see Michel Paillé, *Diagnostic démographique de l'état de la francisation au Québec*, 29 November 2007. For the 1996 and 2006 statistics, the source was http://www12.statcan.ca/english/census06/analysis/language/index.cfm. These statistics don't always match those given by Termote, owing to his way of allocating multiple responses. At one time, Statistics Canada simply asked respondents to choose among French, English, or Other as best describing their mother tongue or home language. Starting in 1983, Statistics Canada decided to complicate things by allowing such combinations as "English and French," "French and a non-official language," "English and a non-official language," "French, English and a non official language," and just to be sure, "Two or more non-official languages." This change gave rise to interminable debates as to how such multiple responses should be allocated when inevitably having to simplify data or to make historical comparisons. Statistics Canada treats the "English and French" category, for example, by allocating responses one-half to French and one-half to English. This table reflects Statistics Canada's method. Termote allocated multiple responses one-quarter to French, one-quarter to English, and one-half to Other.

8   Metropolitan Montreal increased in geographic size by 60 per cent from 1971 to 2006, and the off-Island population grew by 130 per cent. This territorial expansion sopped up more and more rural areas once almost exclusively French, thereby compounding the effect of the francophone flight to these same exurbs. In other words, there might have been a drop in the proportion of francophones living within the original 1971 metropolitan limits over those thirty-five years. This same phenomenon exaggerates the rate of anglophone decline in the metropolitan region.

9   Even a year later, the minister responsible for language matters, Louise Beaudoin, said that after schooling and working in French, the third most important symbol of the French fact in Quebec was the Island of Montreal (*Le Devoir*, 17 May 2000).

10 *La Presse*, 7 April 1999. Even the Bédard Report agreed there were no economies of scale in merging.

11 *Le Devoir*, 15 May 1999.

12 *Montreal Gazette*, 8 April 1999.

13 Montreal Urban Community, *Extrait du procès-verbal d'une séance du comité exécutif tenue le 27 mai 1999*.

14 *Le Devoir*, 1 June 1999.

15 *La Presse* 9 February 1999. As if to reinforce the image of the squabbling mayors within the Union of Suburban Municipalities, later, in August 1999, Bossé asked Harel to name a conciliator to mediate the internecine battle with the "dissident mayors," now numbering five, in the $60 million Régie lawsuit. These same mayors, along with the mayor of Outremont, had already rejoined the Union of Quebec Municipalities (UMQ) in spite of an Island mayors' boycott against the UMQ arising out of the downloading crisis.

16 It went from twenty-seven to twenty-six with the (voluntary) merger of Ville Saint-Pierre (population 4,700) and Lachine (population 34,200), finally approved in late November and effective 1 January 2000.

17 In 1995, I managed to get the mayors to change the voting rules to the effect that the accord of mayors representing at least 50 per cent of the population was required for any decision relating to the MUC. Of course, at the MUC, there was no question of one mayor, one vote: our vote was carefully weighted according to the population we represented.

18 Commission vice-president Jean-Pierre Collin later admitted that none of their fiscal recommendations were ever really heeded by the government. See his article "La réforme de l'organisation du secteur municipal au Québec."

19 Government of Quebec, *Pacte 2000* (Bédard Report), 266.

20 *La Presse*, 7 April 1999.

21 These maps were inspired by those contained in a long report prepared for the commission by Robert Petrelli in *Scénarios de réforme des institutions locales et régionales au Québec*, 28 January 1999. Petrelli came up with an interesting third option that was rejected: One Island, Eleven Cities.

22 Government of Quebec, *Pacte 2000* (Bédard Report), 37.

23 Ibid., 337.

24 Ibid., 266.

25 *Pacte 2000*, 180–1, used the erroneous figure of $2.52 as the global tax rate for the City of Montreal, which was 21 per cent higher than all the other Island municipalities (plus nine off-Island). The actual figure, as pointed out in chapter 7, was $2.14. Had the authors used the right figure, it might have changed their conclusions.

26 Ibid., 275.

27 I was in favour of a regional authority – but not an elected one, which I called "a fourth level of government." "Once you start on that route, you're on the road to amalgamation," I said, giving the example of Toronto (*National Post*, 21 April, 1999).

28 Harel, "Notes pour une allocation devant les membres de l'assemblée générale du CRDÎM," 23 April 1999 (my collection).

29 Montreal Urban Community, *Tour de l'Île* newsletter, 29 April 1999.

30 *La Presse*, 27 May 1999.

31 Ibid., 7 May 1999.

32 Bourque, "Montréal: Notre avenir commun. Notes pour une allocation du maire de Montréal à la Chambre de commerce de Montréal métropolitain," 26 May 1999 (my collection).

33 $9.6 million in a 1999 budget of $1.821 billion. City of Montreal, *Une île, une ville*, 7 and 12.

34 Ibid.

35 Ibid., 22

36 City of Montreal, *Montréalités* 18, no. 4 (June 1999): 7. This study was also reported in *Le Devoir*, 2 June 1999. In chapter 9, I explained why merger would not reduce Montreal's tax rate. In the study used in these two 1999 articles, the One Island One City scenario resulted in a projected 20 per cent drop in taxes for Montreal West and Pierrefonds, on one hand; and a 72 per cent increase for Senneville, a 54 per cent increase for Baie d'Urfé, and a 41 per cent increase for Westmount, on the other. The other municipalities came in between these extremes. The Montreal tax rate went down from $1.98 to $1.89, a 5 per cent drop. However, since their taxpayers would be stuck with Montreal's huge debt – which this calculation did not factor in – the real impact would have been zero, or even a tax increase.

37 *Montreal Gazette*, 22 August 1999.

38 *Le Devoir*, 18 November 1999. The government study calculated the debt borne by residents of the former Montreal would be $0.77 per $100 of assessment. Added to an estimated general rate of $1.27 for One Island One City, it gave a Montreal rate of $2.04, 3 per cent higher than the 1999 rate.

39 An article in *La Presse* of 18 December was the last word on the tax front for 1999. It was headlined "The project 'One Island One City' would end fiscal unfairness, according to a study." The article quoted UQAM professor Serge Gosselin (who became Bourque's chief of staff three months later) as saying that merger would reduce the tax rate in Montreal by the same 5

per cent as the earlier City of Montreal study. However, his study too failed to take into account the debt that proto-Montrealers would be stuck with.

40 Gagnon, *La Presse*, 29 May 1999. Jean-Robert Sansfaçon wrote an almost identical attack in *Le Devoir*, 30 August 1999.

41 *La Presse*, 14 June 1999.

42 Ibid., 15 June 1999. Significantly, *Le Soleil* wrote the same day, "M. Bouchard considers that Mayor Bourque's project does not really correct fiscal inequality."

43 *Le Devoir*, 16 June 1999.

44 *Montreal Gazette*, 2 June 1999.

45 Ibid., 11 August 1999.

46 *Le Devoir*, 27 August 1999.

47 Ibid., 31 August 1999.

48 *La Presse*, 14 September 1999.

49 Ibid.

50 *Montreal Gazette*, 23 September 1999.

51 *Le Devoir*, 16 September 1999.

52 "For the next five years, 90 per cent of the 1.8 million citizens will see absolutely no tax increase. We can promise that. The opportunities to make savings are so great that it allows me to make this promise" (Pierre Bourque in *Montreal Inc* magazine, October/November 1999).

53 The fact that the City of Montreal had 62 per cent of the firefighters is explained by the fire loss records that show that Montreal suffered 66 per cent of all property damage from fires on the Island of Montreal.

54 *La Presse*, 30 September 1999.

55 Claude Ryan, "Le rapport Bédard et l'avenir de la région métropolitaine de Montréal," speech given to la Chambre de commerce et d'industrie Thérèse-De Blainville, 7 October 1999. Also, *La Presse*, 8 October 1999. Some years later, Ryan said, "I always had reservations about 'One Island One City.' To have the same mayor from Pointe-aux-Trembles to Sainte-Anne-de-Bellevue, I always found that to be a little monstrous" (*Le Soleil*, 20 June 2003).

56 *La Presse*, 5 September 1999, 30 January 1998.

57 Municonsult, *Les regroupements municipaux sur l'île de Montréal*.

58 *La Presse*, 21 September 1999.

59 *Le Devoir*, 18 November 1999.

60 *L'Actualité*, 15 December 1999. This would have been from an interview in November.

61 From a transcript by Caisse, Chartier, of a CJAD radio debate, 2 December 1999. I had ordered the transcript because *La Presse* had claimed that

I called Bourque a dictator during this debate; in fact, I was only quoting Phyllis Lambert – which this transcript clearly confirmed.

62 *La Presse*, 11 December 1999.

63 Contemporary reports refer to $375 million, then to $356 million, and sometimes even to $321 million for the actual amount of Trudel's downloading. From the original $375 million, the government decided to give back $54 million to the six central cities; hence, the government claimed the downloading was only $321 million. However, to ease their self-created financial pain, the government unilaterally appropriated $35 million of the municipalities' telecommunications, gas, and electricity tax: that explains the $356 million figure. Some, treating the government's decision to subsidize the six municipalities as a separate transaction, even argued the downloading was $410 million. For the benefit of readers who, with reason, will have trouble following all this governmental fiscal prestidigitation, I have used the figure of $375 million throughout this book.

64 *Le Soleil*, 15 October 1999.

65 Because of its high assessments, the Island of Montreal would have been hit very hard if the cap on the school property tax rate had been increased from 35 cents to 50 cents. Already local taxpayers paid 23 per cent of the school boards' costs on the Island, compared with 14 per cent in the rest of Quebec.

66 *Le Devoir*, 10 December 1999.

67 Ibid. 19 November 1999.

68 Both quotes from *Le Journal des débats* of the National Assembly, 2 May 2000. The first was published in *Le Réveil*, a weekly paper in Jonquière (now Saguenay), 14 November 1999.

CHAPTER ELEVEN

1 *The Economist*, 5 February 2005, 9. Columnist Jay Bryan, writing in the *Montreal Gazette*, 12 December 2000, cited a KPMG study that showed, among the major corporate mergers in the late 1990s, fewer than 20 per cent created new value for shareholders.

2 *La Presse*, 31 March 2000.

3 *Montreal Gazette*, 16 February 2000.

4 In February 2000, McCullock filed a $3 million defamation suit against his city and its councillors, then in January 2001 asked the court to rescind the city's budget and remove nine councillors from office. The city, in turn, started court proceedings against him. McCullock resigned in May 2001. Unlike his waffling council, and like Mount Royal Mayor Hrtschan,

McCullock never wavered in his conviction that One Island One City was a bad idea. Both mayors were sidelined by their never-ending problems with their councils.

5 *Montreal Gazette*, 17 August 2000.
6 Ibid., 6 January 2000.
7 LCN–TV, 17 April 2000.
8 *La Presse*, 22 March, 2000.
9 City of Montreal, *Une île, une ville*, 17.
10 *La Presse*, 27 August 1999. Ottawa-Carleton got a two-tier municipal system in 1969 (not 1968). As of 1994, all regional councillors in Ottawa-Carleton were directly elected to serve only at the higher level, and local mayors were excluded from the regional council. See Sancton, *Merger Mania*, 142–3.
11 *La Presse*, 9 February, 2000.
12 Published as an op-ed piece in *La Presse*, 18 February 2000. Danyluk had clearly changed writers: the style of this letter bordered on the poetic.
13 *Montreal Gazette*, 19 February 2000.
14 *La Presse*, 24 February 2000. On 10 January 2000, Bourque had written to Harel, starting off with comments on the "fiscal pact," then moving on to his real purpose, merger: "The conclusion of the recent negotiations between the Union of Quebec Municipalities and the Government of Quebec was, you will agree, a big disappointment for all the parties involved. This failure once again underscores the enormous difficulty, if not the impossibility, to reform the municipal reality with formulas that take into account the specific interests of 1348 municipalities and 96 counties." Bourque's letter went on to say that Montreal had been happy to contribute nearly $100 million in downloading over the past two years, but hoped it would stop in 2000, or at least 2001. Bourque then brought up merger. To combat the effects of thirty years of neglect of, and exodus from, Montreal, it was urgent to put an end to years of debate, he wrote. He proposed tripartite negotiations among the government, the City of Montreal, and its suburbs to put in place One Island One City. In fact, two groups would be formed: one to make a proposition for the Montreal Island merger, another to do the same for a Metropolitan Council.
15 Michel C. Auger, *Le Journal de Montréal*, 7 March 2000.
16 "I propose to write a document for the City of Westmount describing, analyzing, and assessing the extent to which municipal amalgamations have been used, successfully and unsuccessfully, as a policy device in advanced liberal democracies to enhance the fiscal, social, and economic well-being of city-regions, also known as 'metropolitan areas,'" Sancton

wrote. This "relatively short book" would be written "for the intelligent layperson."

17 *La Presse*, 9 March 2000.

18 Rassemblement des Citoyens et des Citoyennes de Montréal, *Équité fiscale et nouvelles ressources pour Montréal et sa région.*

19 Ads started to appear in north shore newspapers in April 2000: "Cheques for Montreal and bills for us: do you agree to pay in your next tax bill part of more than $270 million of the costs of Montreal's supposedly regional infrastructure? Enough is enough. Harel's reform goes too far!" Then followed a list of things: the Botanical Gardens, Insectarium, Biodome, and Planetarium ($38.5 million), various arenas ($18.9 million), large parks ($14.7 million), traffic arteries ($45 million), and so on.

20 *La Presse*, 23 June 1999.

21 Quoted in *Municipalité* magazine, June-July 2000.

22 Government of Quebec, *La réorganisation municipale* (Harel's White Paper), 59

23 Ibid.

24 *La Presse*, 26 April 2000.

25 *Montreal Gazette*, 26 April 2000.

26 *Le Journal de Montréal*, 26 April 2000.

27 Union of Montreal Island Suburban Municipalities, press communiqué, "The metropolitan community must be created, but not any which way, nor at any price," 3 May 2000.

28 *Le Journal de Montréal*, 1 May 2000. Using the same reasoning, Michel David, writing in the *Gazette*, 5 May 2000, said Bourque's "One Island One City proposal is toast."

29 *La Presse*, 5 May 2000.

30 *Montreal Gazette*, 6 May 2000.

31 *Le Devoir*, 17 May 2000.

32 Gagnon, *La Presse*, 11 May 2000. See also *La Presse*, 17 May 2000.

33 *La Presse*, 17 May 2000.

34 While the matter is only tangentially related to mergers, the reader might be interested in how our legal contestation ended up. The sixteen municipalities had, after all, paid about $100 million to Quebec over three years, or 10 per cent of the total amount of downloading collected.

Our main argument was that, under the Canadian Constitution, provinces do not have the power to impose "indirect taxes." An indirect tax (the concept goes back to John Stuart Mill) is any tax levied with the "expectation and intention" that the recipient will pass the tax on to a third party. This interdiction came about to prevent Province A taxing one of its taxpayers who could pass the tax on to a resident of Province B who did not benefit from nor vote for the services provided by Province A. Justice Allan Hilton's judgment, when it finally came down on 11 December 2001, said that "nothing indicates that the lawmaker had any intention that each municipality transfer the [downloading] contribution to municipal taxpayers. Obviously, a given municipality had the possibility to transfer the amount, but a number did not do it." Quoting another judge, he said, "What is required to constitute an indirect tax is the passing on of the tax itself in a recognizable form, not in its recovery by more or less circuitous operation of economic forces." In this matter, Judge Hilton wrote, there was no "recognizable form" of the tax to the municipal taxpayer: it was therefore not an indirect tax.

Since the judgment had come four days after the Supreme Court had pronounced on the forced mergers, it was anticlimactic. We did not appeal, as our municipalities were a few weeks away from disappearing. I have to note, however, at least Westmount and Beaconsfield had put on each taxpayer's bill a specific amount representing their share of the downloading bill. Still, we did not pass on the whole bill; we managed to absorb most of it – temporarily.

35 Quebec National Assembly, *Débats de la Commission de l'aménagement du territoire*, 26 May 2000. See http://www.assnat.qc.ca/archives/archives-36leg1se/fra/Publications/debats/journal/cat/000526.htm.

36 Looking back, I think that our insistence on the CMM being a planning body that did not provide services, a position we had held since before Pichette, was a mistake. When there was no threat of amalgamation, this made sense. But, by requiring the MUC to continue to survive after the CMM was created (in order to deliver Island services), it meant there would be two regional bodies. We argued, almost desperately, that nobody was suggesting the counties should disappear: why not view the MUC as a big county?

37 "Quand elle parle, j'ai l'impression que c'est des crapauds, pis de la boue, pis des couleuvres sortent de sa bouche tout le temps" (*Le Devoir*, 19 May 2000).

38 Bill 134.

39 Bill 124.

40 Bernard's background details come from his formal resumé and an article by Michèle Ouimet in *La Presse*, 18 March 2000.

41 *Le Journal de Québec*, 20 February 2001.

42 Members of the subcommittee were: Pierre Bourque and three Montreal councillors, Verdun Mayor Georges Bossé, Montreal North Mayor Yves

Ryan, Saint-Leonard Mayor Frank Zampino, and the author, mayor of Westmount. Two civil servants were there: Guy Coulombe of the City of Montreal and Marc Vaillancourt of the Union of Montreal Island Suburban Municipalities.

43 *Compte rendu de la 2e réunion du sous-comité sur la succession de la* CUM, 8 June 2000 (my collection).

44 Linda Gyulai, in the *Montreal Gazette*, 16 September 2000, wrote: "Bernard won't say who made that suggestion [about arrondissements], other than to say the person is a municipal politician he knows personally – by implication, a suburban mayor."

45 *L'Actualité*, January 2001.

46 An almost word-for-word reconstruction from my personal notes (my italics).

47 Louis Bernard, three-page untitled document marked, "Draft for discussion," undated.

48 *Le Journal de Montréal*, 9 August 2000.

49 *La Presse*, 10 August 2000.

50 Ibid., 11 August 2000.

51 The director-general of elections confirmed to me that a popular consultation (or plebiscite) should elicit a "For" or "Against" answer; whereas a referendum must elicit a "Yes" or "No" answer.

52 *Le Soleil*, 15 and 23 May 2000. In February the Montreal suburb of Côte Saint-Luc had a mail-in card survey that garnered a 10 per cent response rate and with 96 per cent voting against merger with Montreal.

53 "Louise Harel, Minister for Quebec Municipal Affairs and the Montreal Region, has proposed merging [*sic*] the municipalities on Montreal Island, Laval, the north shore and the south shore to create the Montreal Metropolitan Community (CMM). Consequently, all taxpayers will be required to pay an additional amount of money on their annual tax bills. Are you in favour of Minister Harel's plan which would force the town of ... to join the CMM?" In the event, the vote was 97 per cent "No" with an average 38 per cent turnout.

54 *La Presse*, 16 June 2000.

55 *Montreal Gazette*, 5 July 2000.

56 *La Presse*, 28 September 2000.

57 *Montreal Gazette*, 16 September 2000.

58 In all three plans, the new city would have full taxation powers and take over all the MUC's responsibilities, plus arterial roads. In Bernard's plan, all water filtration plants would be run by the new city; in our plan, only Montreal's plants would be taken over. Moreover, in our plan, specialized

fire services would be centralized in the new city, and fire department mutual aid would be mandatory across the Island.

59 *La Presse*, 19 September 2000.

60 "Une forme alambiquée de statu quo." *See* Mario Roy, *La Presse*, 20 September 2000.

61 "C'est loufoque ... Ça prend un front de tricératops pour balancer une semblable patente." See Yves Boivert, *La Presse*, 20 September 2000.

62 "Ce n'est qu'un moyen de masquer le fait que les maires de banlieue ne veulent que conserver leurs jobs et leurs pouvoirs actuels." See Michel Auger, *Journal de Montréal*, 21 September 2000.

63 *La Presse*, 20 September 2000.

64 See the Board of Trade's newsletter "Monde des affaires au centre-ville" for April 2000, *La Presse*, 8 February 2000, and *Les Affaires*, 10 May 2000.

65 *La Presse*, 20 September 2000.

66 Ibid., 2 October 2000.

67 Montreal maintained that they served as an "insurance policy" for the suburbs and that Montreal fire trucks regularly passed in front of suburban fire halls to get to a fire, and vice versa. The solution to those problems was mandatory mutual aid, which existed in the suburbs and which Montreal had always refused, plumping instead for one Island, one fire department.

CHAPTER TWELVE

1 Louis Bernard, *Regroupements municipaux dans la région métropolitaine de Montréal*. Columnist Henry Aubin called the Bernard Report "one civil servant's monastic exercise."

2 This may have something to do with the large areas of land that are zoned agricultural in Laval.

3 Andrew Sancton, *Merger Mania*, 55. In 2001, the finance department of the City of Longueuil, just before the merger of the eight south shore municipalities to form the megacity of Longueuil, calculated their aggregated taxes per capita were 25 per cent lower than Laval. And the aggregated debt per capita in the eight municipalities was nearly one-half that of Laval (*Le Journal de Montréal*, 16–18 February 2001).

4 Laval, with a population of 354,773, budgeted 2003 spending at $516 million a year and had a debt of $701 million. The newly merged Longueuil, with a population of 386,229, budgeted 2003 spending at $398 million a year, with a debt of $429 million. See http://www.mamr.gouv. qc.ca/cgi-bin/co1affipf2003.pl, and http://www.mamr.gouv.qc.ca/cgi-bin/ co1affipf2003.pl.

5 Bernard was far from being the first person to advance the idea of polycentrism as a way of looking at the Montreal region, of course. But there were and are many variants. Certainly, the region's *economic* poles were different and more numerous than Bernard's. Given in order of importance, they were: downtown Montreal, Saint-Laurent–Dorval, Anjou, Laval, and the south shore.

6 "Already, the existence of boroughs of less than 20,000 residents complicates the proposed structure and adds to the complexity of the system. To try to build an integrated structure starting with units of 1,000, 3,000, or 6,000 residents is impossible" (Bernard, *Regroupements municipaux dans la région métropolitaine de Montréal*, 20).

7 Except, curiously, Éric Desrosiers, writing in *Le Devoir*, who called the report "The victory of the suburbs."

8 *Le Devoir*, 12 October 2000.

9 *La Presse*, 12 October 2000.

10 *Le Devoir* and *La Presse*, 14 October 2000.

11 *Le Soleil* and *La Presse*, 16 October 2000. According to Roch Cholette a few years later, he did not produce the resolution like a rabbit from a hat. He had already run it by veteran member Jacques Chagnon and even Charest's chief of staff. See Denis Lessard's column in *La Presse*, 29 March 2003.

12 *La Presse*, 17 October 2000.

13 *Montreal Gazette*, 17 October 2000. *La Presse*, the same day, said I welcomed the resolution "with joy." Regarding the Liberals, I said, "In allowing municipalities to go back over forced mergers, they are being logical. And I support them."

14 *Le Devoir*, 20 October 2000.

15 *Le Journal de Montréal*, 28 August 2000.

16 Yves Boisvert, *La Presse*, 20 December 2000.

17 *La Presse*, 16 November 2000.

18 *Montreal Gazette*, 16 November 2000.

19 *Le Devoir*, 18 November 2000.

20 Peter Trent, quoted in the *Montreal Gazette*, 15 November 2000.

21 Michel Vastel, *Le Soleil*, 8 December, 2000.

22 *L'Actualité*, 1 December, 2000.

23 *Le Devoir*, 16 November 2000.

24 Quebec National Assembly, *Proceedings of Debates*, 2 PM, 14 November 2000.

25 A new assessment roll in 2001 did cause Westmount's tax rate to drop more than Montreal's, although by less than the government's estimate.

26 Government of Quebec, Ministère des Affaires municipales et de la Métropole, Direction des politiques fiscales et économiques. *Comparaison: taux de taxation et compte de taxes moyen d'une résidence unifamiliale* (2000). The following were the government's calculated effects of One Island One City on the tax bill of the average single-family dwelling in each of the Island municipalities: Anjou, +0.9%; Baie d'Urfé, +21.3%; Beaconsfield, –14.4%; Côte Saint-Luc, –4.9%; Dollard-des-Ormeaux, –13.6%; Dorval, +4.7%; Hampstead, –26.9%; Kirkland, +8.6%; Lachine, –5.8%; LaSalle, –16.2%; Île Bizard, +3.5%; Montreal, –0.6%; Montreal East, +0.8%; Montreal North, –29.3%; Montreal West, –30.9%; Mount Royal, +8.2%; Outremont, –10.2%; Pierrefonds, –9.7%; Pointe-Claire, +20.4%; Roxboro, –19.1%; Sainte-Anne-de-Bellevue, +19.0%; Sainte-Geneviève, –8.3%; Saint-Laurent, +5.9%; Saint-Leonard –14.1%; Senneville, +21.1%; Verdun, –21.1%; Westmount, +24.3% (figures reported in *La Presse*, 17 November 2000).

27 I brought this matter up at the parliamentary hearings on Bill 170: "Yet if we examine the government's financial projections – and I'm not talking about the projections where there are savings of 5 per cent, because we all know there are no savings – the strange thing is, that is for Montrealers, the tax bill does not change. So why are we doing all this? It's an exchange of tax bills among the suburbs. In Hampstead, they'll see a drop in taxes. Montreal West: a drop in taxes. Westmount? An increase. *But Montreal does not change.* If we are seeking fiscal equity, it seems to me that Montreal should find itself the beneficiary ... I find it aberrant that we are doing all this, we are turning everything upside down to get fiscal equity ... yet, at least for Montrealers, it will make no difference to their tax bill" (Assemblée nationale du Québec, *Débats de la Commission de l'aménagement du territoire*, 4 pm, 28 November 2000). See http://www.assnat.qc.ca/archives/archives-36leg1se/fra/Publications/debats/journal/cat/001128.htm

28 *Le Devoir*, 18 November 1999.

29 *La Presse*, 16 November 2000. According to this poll, conducted a few weeks before Bill 170 was tabled, 41 per cent of all Quebecers were in favour of mergers, and 45 per cent were against. However, if mergers didn't bring tax increases or a drop in services, then 61 per cent were in favour, and 33 per cent against. Clearly, people thought mergers brought tax increases or service deterioration.

30 *Le Devoir*, 17 November 2000. The 5 per cent seems to have been pulled out of thin air. The government's own Bédard Report concluded there were no savings in merging; on the contrary (Government of Quebec,

Pacte 2000, 266). Even the study SECOR did for Pierre Bourque in 1999 could only come up with a very optimistic 3 per cent, and that had many (mostly unfulfilled) conditions attached. In fact, a director of SECOR wrote an op-ed piece in *La Presse*, 30 November 2000, saying, in effect, that these estimated savings were now below 2 per cent, and even that would not happen because the government had not changed the unequal balance of power between the unions and the city, a precondition for any possible savings on merging.

31 *La Presse*, 23 December 2000.

32 Westmount's question, which was formulated around the Bernard Report, read, "The provincial government is planning to make the City of Westmount into a district of the proposed Island-wide City of Montreal. Are you in favour?" The voter turnout was 63.4 per cent, 98.1 per cent of them voting "No."

33 *La Presse*, 22 November 2000.

34 *Le Devoir*, 25 November 2000. This poll was taken 17–23 November. Another poll taken 13–20 December showed 53.2 per cent of Island residents were against the megacity and 29.3 per cent were in favour (*Montreal Gazette*, 16 November 2000).

35 Quebec National Assembly, *Débats de la Commission de l'aménagement du territoire*, 10–10:30 AM, 28 November 2000. Contradicting Minister Harel's assertion, the Poitras Report of 2003 said that voluntary mergers were the rule in Quebec, not forced.

36 Quebec National Assembly, *Débats de la Commission de l'aménagement du territoire*, 3 pm, 28 November 2000.

37 "A government that listens to demonstrators does nothing. It's the status quo, it's sclerosis and paralysis," said Bouchard (*La Presse*, 22 November 2000).

38 These figures come from an ad paid by Côte Saint-Luc correcting the government's ads. In fact the Greater Boston Region has some 282 municipalities, according to Sancton in *Merger Mania*.

39 Colin Nickerson, *Boston Globe*, 4 December 2000.

40 *La Presse*, 5 December 2000.

41 Little of the talk and few, if any, of government reports recommended One Island One City. Writing reports on the municipal condition in Quebec is something of a cottage industry. Generally, each and every recommendation is scrupulously ignored, but it does give superannuated politicians, underemployed academics, and cast-off bureaucrats something to do. Then, when something really "has to be done," Quebec never dusts off studies. It's always the quick fix. In 1969, it was the MUC. In 2000, it was mergers à go-go.

42 Considering my handicap of being a Westmount anglophone who reinforced the francophone media's take that this was an anglo movement, Georges Bossé called me a few days before and suggested I should not speak. My response to him was quick and unprintable.

43 *Le Devoir*, 12 December 2000.

44 *Montreal Gazette*, 8 December 2000.

45 On 10 December, Mike Boone of the *Montreal Gazette* signed the on-line petition as John Lennon of 1 Penny Lane in the municipality of Strawberry Fields, Elvis Presley of Lonely Street in the municipality of Graceland, Hans Offmycity in Kirkland, plus Moe D'Lawn, O. Howard Hertz, Anita Drink, Justin Hale, George Stayontopothis, and 102 others. In each case, he got the acknowledgment "the City of Montreal thanks you for your support." On December 12, Bourque claimed 14,000 signatories to date, saying he was "particularly proud of the level of participation on the Internet."

46 *Le Devoir*, 8 December 2000.

47 *Le Journal de Québec*, 20 February 2001.

48 *Le Soleil*, 21 January 2001. The City of Westmount alone spent $300,000 in public relations in 2000, plus $183,000 to conduct a referendum.

49 Three from the Quebec region (Sainte-Foy Mayor Andrée Boucher, Beauport Mayor Jacques Langlois, Charlesbourg Mayor Ralph Mercier), with Saint-Lambert Mayor Guy Boissy from the south shore and Anjou Mayor Luis Miranda.

50 The adoption of Bill 170 marked the end of the autumn session of the National Assembly. Premier Bouchard said of the merger bill on the day it was adopted, "We have done it with the visor up, straightforwardly, with the complete solidarity of our parliamentary team. I said it and I'll repeat it: this legislation will count among the major reforms put forward by the various PQ governments." He was referring to three other pieces of legislation adopted in the past: car insurance reform, agricultural zoning, and the Charter of the French Language.

CHAPTER THIRTEEN

1 *Le Devoir*, 10 January 2001.

2 *La Presse*, 11 January 2001.

3 *Montreal Gazette*, 9 January 2001.

4 Ibid.

5 Ibid., 20 December 2000.

6 *Montreal Gazette West Island Edition*, 4 and 11 January 2001.

7 "Mayor Robert Libman sees no contradiction in attacking the law in court, all the while putting in place a political party that will elect seats in the new City of Montreal. Though he is confident of winning the case, he prefers to plan for a solution in case of failure" (*La Presse*, 27 January 2001).

8 Ibid., 11 January 2001.

9 *Westmount Examiner*, 11 January 2001.

10 *La Presse*, 12 January 2001.

11 Ibid., 11 January 2001.

12 As president and vice-presidents of the Union, Bossé, Zampino, and Ryan had already approved the cancellation of Vaillancourt's contract. It was no skin off their noses: Bossé and Zampino were exclusively going the political route, and Ryan was going to retire. I got the lawyers who had taken an action against Bill 170 on our behalf to write to Harel complaining about Vaillancourt's appointment, on the ground that he had been party to prior confidential discussions of our legal strategy. Less than a month before this meeting, Vaillancourt had received a legal opinion from two of our lawyers, outlining mostly the weaknesses of our court challenge to Bill 170. We were taking to court the very government he would now be working for. Nothing happened.

13 We chose my old friend Richard Gervais. The City of Westmount was using Jonathan Goldbloom for media relations, which sometimes made for interesting differences of opinion.

14 *La Presse*, 16 October 2000.

15 *Montreal Gazette*, 28 December 2000.

16 *Sondage sur le potentiel de cinq candidats possibles à la mairie de Montréal 2001*, les Sondages Baromètre Inc., February 2001. In this study, 504 people were polled on the Island of Montreal from 28 to 31 January. This document was sent to the author by Vera Danyluk, 24 July 2001.

17 *Montreal Gazette*, 13 June 2001.

18 Aside from Côte Saint-Luc, there were mayors from Beaconsfield, Dollard-des-Ormeaux, Kirkland, Roxboro, St-Anne-de-Bellevue.

19 *The Suburban*, 28 February 2001.

20 Bill McMurchie, "Pointe-Claire Mayor Comments on Public Participation in the Political Process," 5 March 2001 (my collection).

21 The end state of this process was to be one blue-collar union of about 7,000 members, one white-collar union with about 8,500 members, one police brotherhood, one firefighters' union, and another dozen or so other, smaller unions. Overall, 145 unions were to be folded into about 15. Over 80 per cent of the union membership was controlled by the Canadian

Union of Public Employees (CUPE). The blue- and white-collar unions would regain the right to strike in July 2002.

22 At first the committee wanted to rid the megacity of multiple instances of the same street name: for example, five Victorias, six Saint Josephs, and five Cardinals. There were 1,500 such names out of a total of 7,500 streets. After much deliberation, and owing to the unpopularity of the merger itself, things were left alone. (I had pointed out that London had some sixteen Victoria Roads, and Londoners seem to muddle through.) The question, for other transition committees, of the name of their new megacity could not be solved the same way. On the south shore, the name of Longueuil was imposed by Quebec after bitter debate. Columnist Yves Boisvert, tongue-in-cheek, held a write-in contest. While Longueuil won, Outrepont (Across-the-Bridge) came in second. Wal-Mart-on-the-River came just after Champlain, and just before Laval South. Bungalopolis, Bouchardville, and Harel Beach had hundreds of votes. In naming the Outaouais megacity, there were some linguistic overtones as Gatineau won over Hull (it was, however, the more populous municipality), and Aylmer and Buckingham disappeared as municipalities. But the bitterest debate happened in the Lac-Saint-Jean region, where the evocative, long-standing names of Chicoutimi and Jonquière were scrapped in favour of Saguenay.

23 *Le Devoir*, 3 April 2001.

24 *La Presse*, 27 September 2001.

25 Many were surprised when Sam Elkas, a former mayor of Kirkland and a former provincial Liberal cabinet minister, decided to join the transition committee. He was hesitant to join, he said, but "allowed himself to be convinced" by some suburban mayors. In fact, Harel had great difficulty in finding anglophone members for the transition committee. Just about all the leading lights of the anglophone community turned her down, and I could name quite a few. While this seems to reinforce the notion the anti-merger movement was anglophone, it must be remembered francophones were in the minority in the Island suburbs slated to disappear. For the south shore megacity, it was another linguistic dynamic.

26 *The Suburban*, 28 February 2001.

27 Outremont seems to have a knack for bringing in projects at double their budget: in 2009, the Intergenerational Community Centre came in at $11.4 million instead of the budgeted $6.6 million. In the latter case, a police investigation was started by the Sûreté du Québec.

28 *La Presse*, 12 January 2001

29 Outremont's unenthusiastic battle against mergers evolved into an even less enthusiastic penchant for demergers. In May 2004, only 2.6 per cent

of its electors even bothered to sign the registers to trigger a demerger referendum, or one-quarter of the 10 per cent minimum required. *Le Devoir* (26 May 2004) called it "the Outremont mystery."

30 Sancton, speaking notes, "Toronto's Megacity: Will Montreal Make the Same Mistake?" 5 March 2001.

31 Robert L. Bish was professor emeritus, School of Public Administration and Department of Economics at the University of Victoria, and formerly co-director of its Local Government Institute. Professor Bish had researched and published on local government since 1967.

32 Jacques Desbiens, in *Fusions municipales et économies d'échelle*, calculates this population threshold is only two thousand, in Quebec.

33 *La Presse*, 13 March 2001.

34 Ibid., 28 March 2001.

35 *Montreal Gazette*, 14 March 2001. Pierre Bourque himself said (ibid., 8 March 2000), "I have to tell the government I'm not alone in supporting this."

36 *Journal de Montréal*, 5 April 2001.

37 I am indebted to Martin Barry and Wayne Larson of the *Westmount Examiner*, who got these quotes in an interview with Bourque.

38 *Montreal Gazette*, 15 February 2001. In this article, the *Gazette* wrote that Mel Lastman told the premier of Ontario, Mike Harris, to keep his hands off Toronto because "everything he has touched has turned to crap." When asked how he could have any sort of a dialogue with Harris after that comment, Lastman said, "I shouldn't have said crap. I should have said shit."

39 *Toronto Star*, 1 February 2001.

40 Hanigan (Government of Quebec, 1973) said it was preferable to merge only those Montreal Island municipalities with very small populations, bringing the total from 29 to 19 municipalities; Castonguay (1976) recommended essentially the same mergers as Hanigan; Parizeau (1986) counselled against mergers, Johnson (1991) did not mention them, Pichette (1993) did not recommend them, at least as a first step; and Bédard (1999) recommended either three or five, but not one municipality.

41 According to *The Suburban*, 14 February 2001, "Bourque heaped scorn on fellow members of the mayors' committee advising the Transition Committee ... Bourque wondered why mayors against mergers would consult with the committee charged with preparing the megacity they oppose. 'You can't be part of something and against it at the same time.'" For once I agreed with Pierre Bourque.

42 *Montreal Gazette*, 9 March 2001.

43 Editorial, ibid., 3 April 2001. When Michèle Ouimet of *La Presse* wrote an editorial back in 20 February saying that Outremont's mayor Jérôme Unterberg was "hard to follow," because he was both in court against Bill 170 and served as an advisor to the transition committee, Unterberg responded with the same *Gazette* logic: "One has to be pragmatic, and we can't know what will be the decision of the court ... A policy of standing there with folded arms would turn out to be disastrous."

44 Press release, "14 Municipalities Are Withdrawing Their Employees' Services from the Montreal Transition Committee," 8 May 2001. Shortly thereafter, two more municipalities joined the boycott.

45 A month later Cutler wrote a more formal, four-page letter to Goldbloom about the sketchy *Gazette* coverage. During the month of May, after rattling the tin cup around Westmount, she funded a whole series of small, punchily written ads in *Le Devoir*, about the Halifax, Toronto, and Ottawa merger experiences and the fate awaiting Montreal.

46 *La Presse*, 9 May 2001, *Le Devoir*, 12 May 2001.

47 *La Presse*, 19 June 2001.

48 *The Suburban*, 27 June 2001.

49 *Montreal Gazette*, 5 May 2001.

50 He counted on the federal Liberal Party "to sell the One Island One City plan west of Saint-Laurent Boulevard when the provincial Liberal machine was against me," he later said to *Le Devoir*, 26 February 2002. According to Henry Aubin (*Montreal Gazette*, 19 October 2001), the president of Bourque's party was Bernard Synnott, past campaign manager for federal Liberal minister Martin Cauchon. Bourque's co-campaign managers, Sergio Gentile and Jean-François Thibault, were veterans of Liberal campaigns. Two local Liberal MPs, Nick Discepola and Raymond Lavigne, were helping Bourque.

51 The Montreal Metropolitan Board of Trade, the product of the merger of the francophone Chambre de commerce and the anglophone Board of Trade in 1992, was generally run by presidents of medium-sized companies, vice presidents of large companies, entrepreneurs, and partners in legal and accounting firms. The CEOs of large multinationals (like Bombardier) generally were not directly involved. Because, at that time, presidents of the Board of Trade had day jobs, they are only in that office for one year, policy continuity devolving onto the general manager, who was in fact a pro-merger man at the time.

52 Pierre Laferrière, "Le Monde des affaires au centre-ville," 1 April 2000 (my collection). A month later, he repeated his opposition to forced mergers in *Les Affaires*, 10 May 2000. In the same article, the Canadian

Federation of Independent Business and the Conseil du patronat du Quebec were cool to mergers and cold to One Island One City. In June 1999, the former president of the Board of Trade, David McAusland, said the board supported only voluntary mergers, and on the condition that the Labour Code would be changed. The creation of a metropolitan body was more important, he said.

53 *Montreal Gazette*, 15 September 2000.

54 *Montreal Business Journal*, April 2001. When Harel was presenting Bill 170 in the National Assembly on 13 December 2000, she made a point of quoting Legault and underlining his support.

55 *Montreal Gazette*, 22 June 2001.

56 *La Presse*, 15 June 2001.

57 First drawn up in 1985. By 2001 the charter was in force in thirty-three nations and had become a prerequisite for all new member states in the Council of Europe.

58 Notes from a speech given at the Omni Hotel, Montreal, by Howard Husock, director, Case Studies, John F. Kennedy School of Government, Harvard University, "Why Bigger Local Government Isn't More Efficient: The Case for Breaking up Cities," 18 May 2001.

59 *La Presse*, 12 June 2001. The same dismissive tone coloured the media's reaction to another of my initiatives when we funded a four-page report by the Montreal Economic Institute against mergers that came out in September. It was one of the few anti-merger reports produced in Quebec. *La Presse* covered the report with barely two inches of type, headlined, "Another Economic Study against Mergers."

60 Fernand Martin, *Impact budgétaire de la création en 1998 de la nouvelle ville de Toronto*. See also Yves Boisvert, *La Presse*, 27 June 2001; *Le Devoir* and *Montreal Gazette*, 27 June 2001, as well as Henry Aubin's *Montreal Gazette* column, 6 July 2001.

61 *Montreal Gazette*, 17 July 2001.

62 Quoted in *Policy Options*, September 2001.

CHAPTER FOURTEEN

1 Quoted from the 24 July 1997 judgment of Justice Borins in East York (Borough) v. Ontario (Attorney-General). The judge also wrote: "There was no evidence that before it introduced Bill 103 for first reading on December 17 1996, the government conducted any study directed specifically to the need to restructure Metro Toronto ... Bill 103 came as a surprise to most inhabitants of the municipalities, as the restructuring of

Metro Toronto and the mode of its governance were not included specifically in the government's election platform."

2 During the same period, the percentage of anglophones in Quebec had also dropped by half – through migration. While the number of francophones in Ontario is a respectable 85 per cent of the number of anglophones found in Quebec *by mother tongue*, franco-Ontarians only muster 25 per cent of the number of Quebec anglophones when tallying the language spoken at home. This is sad evidence of assimilation.

3 Ruling by Justices Carnwath, Blair, and Charbonneau, 29 November 1999.

4 The reference to the closing of the Lachine Hospital is interesting. In 1995, Minister Jean Rochon, in another of those sweeping reforms that the PQ is partial to, announced that a number of hospitals in the Montreal area would be wiped out. The grand theory behind the closures was called *le virage ambulatoire*, designed "to avoid hospitalization or significantly reduce hospital stays." These mass closures were almost a dry run for wiping out 212 municipalities six years later: we were told they were going to "improve services" and "save $190 million dollars a year" on the Island of Montreal alone. Again, like the municipal mergers, they affected anglophones disproportionately, as the closures included three anglophone hospitals: the Reddy Memorial, the Lachine General, and the Queen Elizabeth. Part of the anglophone community rose up in arms. I was in that part: we went by bus to Quebec City to demonstrate our unhappiness in the legislature, presenting a 125,000-signature petition against the closure of the Queen Elizabeth. I suspect those in the medical community who were planning the anglophone megahospital were not unhappy about the closures, as it meant more grist to their particular mill. Whatever the case, the Queen Elizabeth Hospital Foundation took legal action and was represented by Julius Grey. The foundation claimed, among other things, linguistic discrimination. The Quebec Superior Court ruled, in 1996, that institutions cannot claim discrimination, only individuals, and that the closures were done in an effort to improve efficiency according to objective criteria. The court said, moreover, that Quebec government had no constitutional obligation to provide services in "a language other than French," which did surprise me. Significantly, this judgment was rendered before the landmark Supreme Court reference of 1998.

5 As president of Citizens for a Democratic Nation, Guy Bertrand had published a partitionist booklet called *The Canada Insurance Plan* in 1999.

6 *Le Soleil*, 21 December 2000. Already, in *La Presse* of 17 November, Bertrand had said this about the reasons for Baie d'Urfé's legal challenge: "Eventually, it's the right to stay in Canada that will be lost."

7 The legal lineup of just the senior barristers: Westmount (represented by
   Gérald Tremblay, Julius Grey, and Jean Marois); Baie D'Urfé and Dollard-
   des-Ormeaux (Guy Bertrand); Anjou, Beaconsfield, Dorval, Île Bizard,
   Kirkland, Montreal East, Montreal West, Mount Royal, Outremont,
   Pointe-Claire, Sainte-Anne-de-Belleville, and Senneville (Jean Pomminville
   and Michel Delorme); Côte Saint-Luc (Daniel Chénard); Hampstead
   (Ronald Caza – the Ontario lawyer who acted for the plaintiffs in the
   Montfort Hospital case); Saint-Laurent (Jacques Richard). One Quebec-
   area municipality was included in the proceedings: Ancienne Lorette
   (Roger Pothier), as well as the Commissioner of Official Languages of
   Canada (represented by Doug Mitchell) on behalf of Westmount.

8 We had filed reams of expert testimony with the court describing the tacit
   agreement that had developed between the French and the English on the
   Island of Montreal, testimony that called it a "cohabitation of cultures"
   that led to "ethnic compartmentalization." One expert even maintained
   that the proliferation of municipalities that were either majority French or
   English had helped to contain language tensions in the 1960s.

9 Interestingly, Quebec's Charter of the French Language starts off in a similar manner: "French is the official language of Quebec."

10 Actually, the anglophone high water mark was in the mid-1800s, when
    they made up 25 per cent of the population.

11 *La Presse* and *Montreal Gazette,* 24 May 2001.

12 Michel David, *Le Soleil*, 24 May 2001. Chapleau, *La Presse*'s cartoonist,
    adopted the habit of drawing Bertrand with a bulbous red-rubber clown's
    nose held on with an elastic band. Chapleau's and Michel David's humor-
    ous reaction can be contrasted with that of Gilles Proulx, Quebec's radio
    "shock-jock" extraordinaire, who called Bertrand "Mephistopheles in a
    gown, an hysterical lawyer, liar, manipulator, mental case, and fanatic"
    who should not be left at large. Bertrand sued Proulx for defamation (*La
    Presse*, 9 August 2001).

13 Few could fail to notice the sizeable proportion of Jewish people in the
    anti-merger movement, especially among the more vocal element. This
    should not be surprising; if any group was sensitive to the issues that
    forced mergers raised, it was the Jews.

14 The descriptor First Official Language Spoken (or FOLS, known as PLOP in
    French) was introduced by Statistics Canada for the 1986 census. FOLS is
    an algorithmic confection derived from three census questions about know-
    ledge of the official languages, the mother tongue, and home language.

15 Having a bilingual status allowed a municipality to produce bills, bro-
    chures, correspondence, and administrative documents in both English

and French. Council meetings could also be conducted bilingually, although in practice Westmount ran council meetings in English. All correspondence with the government or corporate citizens had to be in French.

16 *La Presse,* 29 May 2001. NDG councillor Marvin Rotrand was already on record that English language services were "hit-and-miss" there and that his citizens often felt that service in their language was "an afterthought" (*Montreal Gazette,* 6 May 2000).

17 It must be kept in mind that, according to Statistics Canada data for 1996 or for 2001, only 11 per cent of the former City of Montreal's population was mother-tongue anglophone, the other Island municipalities were 27 per cent anglophone, the West Island was 43 per cent anglophone, and Westmount was 60 per cent anglophone.

18 *Le Devoir,* 17 May 2000. Minister Beaudoin's comments came two months after a report on the problem of francization of Quebec, *Les défis de la langue française à Montréal et au Québec au XXIe siècle: constats et enjeux,* a report that was adopted by cabinet and made public 14 March 2000.

19 This exchange was based primarily on *Débats de l'Assemblée nationale,* 10:30 AM, 20 June 2001, along with two press reports: *Le Soleil,* 21 June 2001, and the *Montreal Gazette,* 21 June 2001.

20 Quoted in Kathryn Leger's column, *Montreal Gazette,* 24 November 2006.

21 Most academic experts were not sanguine about our winning our case. André Braen, a University of Ottawa law professor, saw little in common between the Montfort case and ours (*Le Devoir,* 10 January 2001). University of Montreal law professor Jean Hétu and Laval University law professor Henri Brun also did not think we had a good case (*Le Devoir,* 25 May 2001).

CHAPTER FIFTEEN

1 Quoted in an interview by Georges-Hébert Germain, *Le Devoir,* 3 March 2001.
2 Quoted in *Le Devoir,* 1 November 2001.
3 *La Presse,* 5 July 2001.
4 *Le Soleil,* 12 March 2001.
5 Ibid., 5 May 2001.
6 Ibid., 8 June 2001.
7 Ibid., 16 June 2001.

8 *Rapport sur les fusions municipales: Les perceptions des électeurs des nouvelles grandes villes créées par la loi 170 et de certaines villes que le gouvernement projette de fusionner*, Infreas Inc., June 2001 (poll conducted 22–28 May)

9 *La Presse*, 24 June 2001.

10 Ibid., 7 July 2001.

11 *Montreal Gazette*, 29 June 2001.

12 *Le Devoir*, 27 July 2001.

13 *La Presse*, 17 August 2001.

14 *Montreal Gazette*, 2 August 2001.

15 *La Presse*, 25 August 2001.

16 This came about through the imposition of eight new megacities, of twelve new smaller municipalities that were also the product of merger, and of 240 mergers of rural villages which had begun under Trudel in 1996. According to the Municipal Affairs Department, in its *Rapport annuel de gestion 2001–2002*, there were 1,113 municipalities in March 2003, and 67 per cent had a population of 2,000 or less.

17 *La Presse*, 13 October 2001; 25 per cent said they were "not satisfied," and 37 per cent were "not at all satisfied" in the matter of municipal mergers. This was the worst score out of six areas of government responsibility.

18 *Le Devoir*, 17 May 2000.

19 *La Presse*, 6 October 2001. The same SOM poll showed continued support for our legal challenge to Bill 170 (52 per cent vs 38 per cent) and for demerger (53 per cent versus 40 per cent).

20 *Le Devoir*, 17 October 2001.

21 *La Presse*, 22 October 2001. In the *Gazette* 22 September 2001, Tremblay said, "We won't try to reverse the mergers. But if a democratically elected government decides to, we will honour that decision."

22 *Le Devoir*, 23 October 2001. When Tremblay had met with the *Gazette* editorial board on 12 October 2001 – as reported in their editorial the next day – he had made the same statement: that he would not stand in the way of demergers. He was also quoted saying something similar in *La Presse*, 27 October 2001. Lysiane Gagnon in *La Presse* and Bernard Descôteax in *Le Devoir*, both writing in November 2001, commented on Tremblay's promise to remain neutral in any demerger debate. Earlier, Tremblay had been even more extreme. According to *The Suburban*, 28 February 2001, Tremblay would not wait for the Liberal Party to hold a demerger referendum: "If a great majority of citizens in the boroughs are not satisfied with the transition, we will hold a referendum," he said. Even

as late as 10 April 2002, he reiterated the non-interference pledge in *The Suburban*: "Tremblay said while he would prefer citizens be happy in the megacity, he would not stand in the way of a demerger. 'I believe in democracy. The same way that I went along with the forced mergers, it's not my decision. It's a decision that the newly elected Quebec government would have to make.'"

Two years after making the promise Tremblay began to deny it. Speaking to *The Suburban*, 22 October 2003, Tremblay said. "I didn't make that promise. I made a statement that did not fully represent what I meant." Somewhat confusingly, he then went on to say he regretted the statement as soon as he had made it. He also emphatically denied saying something similar to me 24 August 2001 during a breakfast meeting and earlier to Mayor Bill McMurchie in order to get him to run with Tremblay's party. Then Tremblay started to wobble. The *Montreal Gazette* of 28 April 2004 reported, "The mayor conceded he had once stated that he would remain neutral during public consultations on demerger, only to change his views the next day." Tremblay finally came clean when Pointe-Claire Mayor Bill McMurchie confronted him in person. Tremblay said that, while he did promise to stay out of the debate, the demerger bill changed all that. "Bill 9 leaves residents with less than they have now. That is why I couldn't stay out of the debate" (*The Chronicle*, 12 May 2004).

23 The $304 million was made up of $33 million for transition costs, $22 million for running the elections, $100 million to put in place the megacities, $136 million for early-retirement severance pay, and $13 million for miscellaneous items. See http://communiques.gouv.qc.ca/gouvqc/communiques/GPQF/Novembre2001/20/c9154.html. This website gives the costs for Montreal; the costs for the seven other municipalities can be found at similar website addresses. See also Radio-Canada and *La Presse* reports for that day.

24 It is not an easy task to uncover just what was the total cost of implementing mergers in Quebec. According to the Ministère des Affaires municipales in *Rapport annuel de gestion 2001–2002*, some $150 million was borrowed to finance early retirements (not $136 million). And, under the Programme d'infrastructures Québec-municipalités, some additional $80 million went into "work required to modify municipal infrastructures following mergers," for the five biggest megacities alone. I think a conservative estimate would peg the cost of implementing the mergers at over $500 million.

25 By a strange coincidence, $175 million was precisely the one-time estimated cost of implementing the megacity of Montreal (Montreal

Transition Committee, *Présentation du cadre budgétaire de la nouvelle ville de 2002 à 2006*, 19 April 2001).

26 This was the government's cost of $168 million, plus, principally, $20 million for the holding of demerger referendums and $22 million for new elections.

27 *La Presse*, 10 November and 21 November 2001.

28 In 2006, Mayor Andrée Boucher of Quebec City estimated the mergers cost Quebec City $200 million on an overall budget of $800 million. Two-thirds of the increase, she said, was due to wages and benefits. See argent. canoe.com/chroniques/notreargent/archives_2006/1... argent.canoe.com/ chroniques/notreargent/archives_2006/12.html.

29 *La Presse*, 15 November 2001.

30 Ibid., 20 November 2001.

31 Ibid., 21 November 2001. Even as late as 2006, Michèle Ouimet wrote, "Spending per resident remains the best indicator, even if imperfect, to check whether the boroughs are treated equitably." This was after Alan DeSousa, borough mayor of Saint-Laurent and a chartered accountant, had pointed out to her that spending per capita was not an appropriate guide: for the downtown core, Saint-Laurent, or Dorval, a lot of local spending had to do with supplying services to non-residents. See *La Presse*, 16 October 2006.

32 Even as late as 2004, the costs of a number of local services in the former City of Montreal were still centralized. See SECOR Conseil, *Étude sur les conséquences et les coûts*, 6n.

33 Association les bibliothèques publiques du Québec, *La réorganisation municipale*, 1 December 2000.

34 See City of Montreal, *Budget 2002*, 22 and 39. The 2002 residential assessment for Westmount was $2.491 billion with a tax rate of $1.2873. The 2002 residential assessment for CDN-NDG was $4.564 billion and the effective tax rate was $1.99. The 2002 tax rate to cover debt service costs for Westmount was $0.0718 and for Montreal, $0.4156. For the purposes of this comparison, it is assumed that all the other taxes raised in the two boroughs (such as commercial and governmental tax revenues) went to fund the central city, paying for things such as police and fire protection, mass transit, and wastewater treatment.

   The allotments per capita of $943 and $331 came from the Transition Committee's budget, *Nouvelle Ville de Montréal: Budget 2002*, 36. They had in turn been derived from the basic allotments but had been adjusted by the Transition Committee in an effort to put all the allotments on an equal footing. Unfortunately, everywhere else in the budget the allotments for the ex-suburbs included debt costs and their cost of buy-ing water from Montreal; yet the equivalent allotments for the ex-City of Montreal were free of such costs. Unfortunately, when the newly elected megacity council adopted their own budget in December 2001, they used the same unadjusted allotment figures as the Transition Committee: the ex-suburban boroughs were still inflated with debt and water costs, while the ex-Montreal borough were just the bare bones.

35 The mayors of Baie d'Urfé, Hampstead, and Westmount. Given the unilin-gualism of the other two, I remained the only spokesperson for the demer-ger camp. The mayor of the Town of Mount Royal was still at war with his council, and the mayors of Montreal West and Senneville were more or less inactive, having full-time jobs elsewhere. The rest had simply gone on to other things.

36 *Montreal Gazette*, 10 November 2001.

37 Quoted by Martin Patriquin, *Toronto Star*, 22 November 2001.

38 Quoted in the *Montreal Gazette*, editorial of 7 November 2001. Barely a year before, Yeomans had declared, "They want to siphon off all our wealth and send it to a city that's in a total mess." (Yeomans was seem-ingly unaware that the only "wealth" that would be shared was among the ex-suburbs. None would go to the former City of Montreal.)

39 *La Presse*, 2 August 2001.

40 Today, all these agents of change have gone, thanks to demergers (Yeomans, Libman) or simply being fed up (Bossé). By 2008, Zampino, the last of the original suburban mayors, also left Montreal's executive com-mittee for somewhat different reasons.

41 *Montreal Gazette*, 23 August 2001.

42 Ibid., 6 November 2001. Given the "love-hate" statements regarding the megacity made by most West Island mayors running for the megacity council, and given their clear support for demerger and their fighting the megacity in court, it was arguable whether these politicians had any sort of mandate to make the megacity work. Certainly, that was not the senti-ment of those who voted for them.

43 Ibid., 12 November 2001. To justify their logic, the *Gazette* editorial asked, "After all, could Quebec leave Canada in a legal and amicable fashion without the rest of Canada agreeing to the divorce?" This was not the first time someone raised the question of having the entire Island of Montreal vote on any demerger; or, indeed, ratify the whole merger. Often, the same metaphor was used, but it's not really apt. Firstly, the ter-ritory of Quebec had become part of Canada voluntarily, whereas our municipalities were forced into the megacity. Secondly, no one was sug-

gesting that all the provinces of Canada could vote on allowing only Quebec's secession. Thirdly, as the Supreme Court had ruled, the rest of Canada could not prevent Quebec from seceding after a clear indication of wanting to leave. Fourthly, although Montreal merged *de jure* with its suburbs to form a new megacity, *de facto* Montreal simply annexed its suburbs. You can't give the annexor a veto in undoing a forced annexation; otherwise, you are not allowing a wrong to be righted. The principle behind the Liberal promise of demerger was that, as long as regional costs were shared fairly, citizens of a given municipality should be able to decide which city they lived in, not the government, nor the citizens of another city.

44   Some of our main arguments before the Supreme Court were: (1) None of the government studies in the last thirty years ever recommended One Island One City nor the elimination of all anglophone municipalities. Justice Lagacé's conclusion that "the principle of democracy has therefore been respected" was based on a false premise. (2) The goal of wiping out anglophone institutions was clear. As Minister Beaudoin said, "*Fusionner pour mieux franciser.*" (3) Forced mergers are no longer permitted in Europe. (4) Justice Lagacé accepted the defendant's idea that public political institutions such as municipalities are culturally neutral. As our expert witness wrote, "To suggest that government institutions do not reflect the culture of its majority population is sociological nonsense." (5) According to Justice Lagacé, "there is no proof of a real or presumed threat of not receiving [English] services in the future City of Montreal." This was countered by one of our witnesses, Councillor Michael Applebaum, who wrote, "I am satisfied that the new megacity of Montreal will be run exactly in the same way as the present City of Montreal and there will be very little room to allow members of the English-speaking community to obtain services in English." (6) Justice Lagacé wrote, "Anglophones have shown a great capacity to keep their numbers up." This was patently not true, as all our expert witnesses proved. (7) The boroughs that replace our municipalities are empty shells. The boroughs cannot hire, borrow, or tax. They do not even have legal status.

CHAPTER SIXTEEN

1   From mid-1999 until the creation of the Montreal megacity in January 2002, support for the megacity had varied right across the Island from about 30 per cent to about 45 per cent, ending up at 35 per cent (with 52 per cent against). After the merger, support was stuck at about 35 per

cent until 2003, when it slowly began to rise, getting to 45 per cent only near the end of 2003. In all of 2002 and 2003, as many people supported *allowing* a demerger vote as were against the idea. Those who said they would actually *vote* for demerger started dropping in numbers in 2003. (Data synthesized from the results of about twenty different polls conducted over the period 1999 to 2003.)

2 The Board of Trade had maintained that their support of mergers was conditional on labour code changes to control the power of the unions – which of course never happened. Around the time I made this speech, Guy Fréchette, the president of the Board of Trade, sent out a press release congratulating Harel: "Thanks to her vision, her tenacity, and her courage, we were witness to the birth of the new City of Montreal on January 1, a strong, unified city that can play a leading role on the national and international scene."

3 *La Presse*, 23 February 2002.

4 Charest wrote to *La Presse* editorialist André Pratte on 28 February, excoriating him for accusing the Liberal Party of saying one thing in private and another in public. Charest complained that Pratte's accusation arose from the Molson Centre article, which was "based on anonymous sources." Pratte replied that the article was supported by solid sources and contained no errors, and that he made the accusation following a number of conversations he had had over the last months with Charest's aides and members of his caucus. "There is absolutely no doubt in my mind," Pratte wrote, "about the fact that, in private, their position is very different from the one you hold publicly." Lysiane Gagnon wrote shortly afterwards that for several months Charest's aides had been telling francophone journalists off the record that, at the appropriate time, the Liberals would extricate themselves from their demerger promise.

5 Even two years later, Pierre Bibeau, Marc Bibeau, and Marc-André Blanchard were being referred to as part of Charest's "phantom cabinet" whose members "have a much bigger influence than cabinet ministers on government policy and on the office of the premier." See the transcript of Radio-Canada's broadcast of 26 April 2004.

6 *Le Soleil*, 25 February 2002.

7 Ibid., 25 February 2002.

8 *Montreal Gazette*, 26 February 2002.

9 Ibid.

10 This went on elsewhere in Quebec: Saint-Lambert ($0.7 million), L'Esterel ($2.4 million in land), and Val Bélair ($0.75 million), and Ivry-sur-le-Lac ($0.05 million) all put money aside. But all this salting away of money

was at least for the benefit of taxpayers. The Lachine City Council, on the other hand, one month before Lachine was to disappear into the mega-city, inexplicably decided to be nice only to its retiring fifty-seven-year-old director-general. As well as a $400,000 severance payment (double his annual remuneration including benefits), he got a cool $2.4 million dumped into his pension fund. And the council took pains that both little gifts would remain out of the public's eye. It was not even approved by the Transition Committee, a fact that the current City of Montreal is invoking in a lawsuit in an attempt to claw back from the former director-general some $1.3 million. (The remuneration of the director-general of Lachine was for years the stuff of legend. In 1997, his salary was $10,000 higher than that of the premier of Quebec.)

11 Letter to the editor, *La Presse*, 5 March 2002.

12 In the event, a Superior Court judgment in 2004 ordered Senneville to reimburse the City of Montreal the $1 million.

13 *Le Devoir*, 30 March 2002. In a related matter, Dollard-des-Ormeaux also liquidated $8 million of surplus to reduce their 2001 tax rate, thereby giving their citizens back some of their money before the merger happened. This helped explain a 15 per cent tax increase in 2002.

14 Press conference by Minister André Boisclair, 28 March 2002.

15 *La Presse*, 20 March 2002.

16 Irving Adessky died in September 2010.

17 Bernard Paquet, following a long heart operation, died in April 2005.

18 Press release, Quebec Liberal Party, 12 September 2002.

19 *La Presse*, 13 September 2002.

20 Ibid., 17 September 2002.

21 *Le Devoir*, 30 December 2002.

22 J.-Jacques Samson, writing in *Le Soleil*, 6 January 2003, was typical: "Demergers are as impossible as separating the ingredients of a cake once baked." Using another domestic image, Sampson also wrote, "The costs of undoing the knitting will soon discourage the most ardent adversaries of mergers."

23 *Le Devoir*, 23 October 2001. In 2003, Tremblay confusingly both denied and regretted making this promise. But similar statements were recorded in *La Presse*, 27 October 2001, and made to *Montreal Gazette* editorial board, 12 October 2001. For more details, see note 22, chapter 13.

24 Gérald Tremblay, op-ed piece in *La Presse*, 11 January 2003.

25 *Le Journal de Saint-Bruno*, 4 March 2003.

26 This comes from a summary in *La Presse*, 13 March 2003, of about fifty separate CROP polls.

27 The rural area of Headingly (population 1,600) had separated from the Unicity of Winnipeg twenty years after that megacity's creation, but this was not a demerger in that the area in question did not match that of a reconstituted former municipality. (There had possibly been a demerger in the Belgian city of Antwerp after liberation, reversing a forced merger during the Nazi occupation – an example that was hardly germane.) So I had to scrub a planned chapter in the Poitras Report that was headed "Demergers outside Quebec" because it would have been blank.

28 Technically, "secession" (from the Latin, "to withdraw") is the act of removing oneself from membership in an alliance, a federal union, or an association – none of which describes a city, even a merged city. "Scission" (from the Latin, "to split") means to split off from a body. The reader will forgive me when I use the two interchangeably in this book, especially since "scission" comes unprovided with an equivalent verb. ("Separation," in Canada, is not a word one is tempted to employ for the municipal level.)

29 In 1980 (the bill was adopted in 1979), the town of what would become Masson-Angers was demerged from the town of Buckingham near Ottawa, along with the municipalities of L'Ange-Gardien and Notre-Dame-de-la-Salette. All three had been forcibly merged with Buckingham in 1975 by the Liberals. Total population of the three municipalities was about 7,000. The only other "true" Quebec demerger occurred when the rural village of Cantley (population 3,500) demerged from Gatineau in 1989. I have ignored the case of the municipality of Côte-Nord-du-Golfe-du-Saint-Laurent, created in 1963, which was only partially "demerged" (in the case of Blanc-Sablon) but mostly underwent voluntary scission (St-Augustin, Bonne-Espérance, Gros-Mécatina) from 1990 to 1994. Besides, the writer considered these changes in a vast (6,000 km²), sparsely populated territory as irrelevant to the purpose at hand.

30 One of the reasons for the impression that demerger was impossible happened to be lexicological in nature: the roots of most words for merger, even the word "merger" itself, came from an imagery of blending liquids, giving us words such as "fuse," or "amalgamate." One cannot really un-blend, and this is why there was no word for what we wanted to do. Even the neologism "demerger," which is in the *Oxford Dictionary*, refers to the undoing of a merger of *two* entities. I always felt that the creation of the megacity was an example of annexation; the word "de-annexation" would have conveyed a facility of undoing much better than "demerger."

31 There was no grassroots support for demerger by the winter of 2002. Few thought it would ever happen. When the Westmount Municipal Association offered me the presidency of their organization, I said I would do it

only if the WMA focused exclusively on demerger. They demurred, feeling the WMA had to concentrate on defending Westmounters' interests inside the megacity. This was the prevailing mood in all the former cities: municipal elected officials were focusing their energies on sorting out how the megacity would run.

32 Mirabel Airport (or what's left of it) now only sits on a mere six thousand acres, the rest of the land having been sold off over the years.

33 Quebec National Assembly, *Débats de la Commission de l'aménagement du territoire*, 10:00–10:30 AM, 28 November 2000.

34 Most sources give the number of "special" laws merging Quebec municipalities from 1961 to 1985 as being twenty-four. But not all those special laws actually forced mergers. At least four of these laws – those relating to Chomedey (1961), Alma (1962), Vaudreuil (1963), and Rouyn-Noranda (1985) – called for either a referendum to approve the merger or the respective council's approval. (Île-Maligne in the Alma merger did not go along with it, but the other municipalities in that merger did.) These four laws were the only special laws adopted before 1965 or after 1982.

35 François Des Rosiers, writing in Poitras, *La Défusion municipale au Québec*.

36 For example, in 1994 the PQ had promised, a few months before that election, that they would reverse the Ryan reform. Nothing, of course, happened once they got elected. It is promises made *during* an election that count.

37 I had no poll results to guide me at the time. In June, two months after voting day, CROP came up with the following results as reported in *L'Actualité*, 1 October 2003: 39 per cent of Quebecers were in favour of municipal mergers, 44 per cent were against; 41 per cent of Quebecers were in favour of a law permitting demergers, 47 per cent were against.

38 As reported by *Canadian Press* on Canoë website at 5:27 PM, 17 March 2003. The Poitras Report had recommended exactly the same thing: that the National Assembly adopt enabling legislation; that is, a general law to permit demergers.

39 This was Radio Canada's take the next day. *Canadian Press* (on Canoë at 5:27 PM, 17 March) said that Charest "elaborated on this controversial question for the first time since the beginning of the electoral campaign." *Le Journal de Montréal* and *Montreal Gazette* said it was "the first time [ever]" that he elaborated that much on the subject, especially enshrining the demerger process in law.

40 *Le Devoir*, 18 March 2003. J.-Jacques Samson wrote in *Le Soleil*, 19 March: "Jean Charest had been on the defensive regarding municipal

demergers these past few weeks. The release of the report ... allows him to now to hold his head high. Right to the end of the campaign, he will be able to fall back on a theoretically independent report ... Demergers, with which his party is associated, can no longer be dismissed as a completely crazy and financially unrealistic adventure. This is why the Liberal chief immediately followed suit, in Quebec, in endorsing one of the recommendations of the Poitras Report without any further delay; that is, as a first step, the adoption a general law to give structure to the process of backtracking." Lest the reader think Samson approved of the Poitras Report, let me add one further quote: "Above all, it's a political manoeuvre that is all part of a settling of accounts led by merger adversaries against the PQ government."

41 *Le Journal de Montréal*, 19 March 2003.

42 *Le Devoir*, 20 March, 2003. This sentiment was not confined to the francophone media. Sean Gordon, in the *Montreal Gazette* of the same day ("A Sore Point for Some, a Dead Issue for Most") wrote, "The promise to undo forced municipal amalgamations no longer garners the type of attention it did only two years ago, but the hopes of the small pockets of hard-core opposition have been fanned by the Liberal leader's words. Analysts say that by feeding these hopes – which reside primarily in Montreal's anglo suburbs – Charest might be wasting his best chance to make up ground on PQ leader Bernard Landry, who polls suggest is holding and even widening his lead among francophones. 'This issue is a loser for him,' said Guy Lachapelle, a political science professor at Concordia University. 'I don't understand why he would want to talk about it at all ... francophones don't want to hear about old squabbles. Once you've lost, you've lost. The fight has happened and it's over.' Though you can still spot the occasional "Hands off my city" and "Je me souviendrai" sign in parts of suburbia, a recent poll by Léger Marketing found most people don't care to revisit the issue. Fifty-six percent of respondents said they're not interested in demergers, and a majority was skeptical of Charest's commitment of actually carrying out the plan."

43 *La Presse*, 9 April 2003.

44 Ibid., 19 March 2003.

45 Tremblay, who had pledged to remain neutral during any demerger debate, had not consulted his party before the mayoral coalition went public. Tremblay's initiative led directly to Pointe-Claire "borough president" Bill McMurchie and his two "borough councillors" quitting Tremblay's party, accusing him of deceiving them with his earlier pledge of non-intervention in order to get them to run for his party.

46 *La Presse*, 20 March 2003.

47 Ibid., 24 March 2003.

48 The director-general of elections sent a retired police officer all over Quebec to interview anybody who had – even notionally – funded the Poitras Report. He filled out reams of transcripts in longhand and collected a boxful of receipts. A year after the election, both the Citizens' Association for the Preservation of the City of Westmount, which essentially paid for the costs of the Poitras Report, and the writer (as its accomplice) were fined for the offence – not of producing the report itself but for holding the press conference where it was made public. We were fined because the report "disapproved of" acts done by the PQ. This was not, in fact, true. The PQ as a *party* never had mergers in their program: it was the PQ-led *government* that imposed mergers without an electoral mandate. We decided to fight the two charges. Eventually, faced with a potential mountain of legal fees on one hand, and the bottomless pockets of government on the other, we settled out of court. The DGE dropped the charge against me, and the association paid its fine.

49 *Montreal Gazette*, 21 March. The proportion of Quebecers who thought Charest would make the best premier went from 27 per cent to 30 per cent. Landry remained steady at 35 per cent.

50 Don Macpherson, in his *Gazette* column of 22 March 2003, entitled "Fortunately for Charest, the Sound of Bombs Drowned out the Talk of Demergers," wrote, "If Landry looked like the main beneficiary of the war, he was not the only one in the Quebec campaign. The war also came to the rescue of Jean Charest at a time when he was on the defensive over municipal demergers and cut short discussion on that subject. It's hard to understand what the demerger movement hoped to accomplish by reviving the issue during the election campaign with the publication of a feasibility report on how the forced mergers of former suburbs with their core cities might be undone. But raising the demerger issue in the campaign was going to hurt the only party in favour of demergers, rather than help it."

51 *Le Devoir*, 29 March 2003

52 He was referring to the demerger of Buckingham, Quebec. Lévesque, the leader of the PQ, was elected in 1976 and demerged Buckingham in 1979.

53 *La Presse*, 11 April 2003.

54 Reported on the CBC, 4 April 2003.

55 *La Presse*, 15 April 2003.

56 Press release, Léger Marketing, 15 March 2003.

57 As reported on Radio-Canada, 1 October 2003. In the *Gazette*, 2 December 2003, Don Macpherson wrote, "If there was one issue that decided the

election alone, it was the mergers; Landry has said the PQ lost 20 franco-phone seats because of them, the difference between a PQ majority and the Liberal one. Finally, in *La Presse* 4 April 2007, Bernard Landry wrote, "In 2003, the PQ, with a satisfaction rating of over 50 per cent, lost the election essentially because of the municipal mergers: we're talking about the loss of more than 20 ridings."

58 The new Liberal minister of municipal affairs, Jean-Marc Fournier, said that, thanks to the PQ and to the megacity mayors, the demerger pledge took on such an importance that it became an election issue that led to gains in "most if not all" the places where forced mergers took place. See the minutes of the Quebec Parliamentary Commission for Territorial Planning, 3 July 2003. See http://www.assnat.qc.ca/archives/travaux.htm.

59 *La Presse*, 11 April 2003, reported the 58 per cent figure from a CROP poll, with only 28 per cent in favour of demerger. However, according to SOM poll results broadcast on Radio-Canada on 26 March 2003, while 60 per cent did not want to demerge, 62 per cent "wished that residents of the former cities could pronounce themselves by referendum on the demergers."

60 *La Presse*, 14 June 2003.

61 In the next general election in 2007 the Liberals hung on to only a couple of these ridings: most of their voters took a flutter with the ADQ. After another ADQ meltdown in the 2008 election, the PQ started to see only a minority of these ridings creep back to their fold.

62 I am referring to the interview PQ leader Pauline Marois gave to *Le Soleil*, 28 November 2008.

CHAPTER SEVENTEEN

1 *La Presse*, 14 May 2003. In September, the mayor of Longueuil and the Union of Quebec Municipalities also insisted on 25 per cent of voters having to sign the registers that would set in motion the referendums; rather than giving people five days to sign, they said only one day was enough.

2 From the transcript of the introductory remarks made by Municipal Affairs Minister Fournier at the first of a series of parliamentary hearings on Bill 9 on 9 September 2003.

3 This is not just a Canadian phenomenon. In the United States, where homeowners move on average every nine years and tenants every two, 69 per cent of the former voted compared with 44 per cent of the latter. See *The Economist*, 18 April 2009, 78. In long-established communities like Westmount, older tenants vote more because, in many cases, they

have lived there many years and were perhaps themselves homeowners at one point. Another contributor to both low voter turnouts in Quebec and inaccurate voting lists is that, from 1999 onwards, a Quebecer could have moved to a municipality one day and voted the next – and, naturally, rarely did. Previously, a municipal voter had to live in the community for at least twelve months before being eligible to vote.

4 Myer Siemiatycki, in *The Municipal Franchise and Social Inclusion in Toronto: Policy and Practice*, October 2006, writes: "Neighbourhoods with the lowest voter turnout are characterized by: large number of immigrants, visible minorities and non-citizens, many residents without English as a mother tongue, many residents living in high-rise apartments, and many low-income households."

5 According to Statistics Canada, in 2006, 53.2 per cent of the residents of Saint-Laurent had a mother tongue other than French or English. Only Saint-Leonard had a greater proportion at 57.2 per cent.

6 While around the world a simple 50 per cent majority is the norm for approving referendum questions, there have been cases of a 60 per cent "supermajority" requirement. Even some provinces in Canada have on occasion required 60 per cent to ratify constitutional amendments or electoral reform. But from Newfoundland joining to Quebec leaving, from prohibition to conscription, Canada has usually stuck to the 50 per cent requirement. Rarely, if ever, has there been a minimum *turnout* requirement, even with some referendums drawing less than half the registered voters.

7 At the time it was considered a huge coup for Mario Dumont to get Pierre Bourque to run in the provincial election for his party, the ADQ. Bernard Landry, who desperately wanted to recruit Bourque himself, was beside himself with anger about this perceived snub: he saw it as almost traitorous that the *concepteur* of the megacity would not want to join the party that made it happen. (Bourque had been active in the PQ, but some decades before.) It did not take too long for Dumont and Bourque to become like two scorpions in a bottle, forcing the latter to maunder around the province doing very little of anything. In the event, both Dumont and Bourque flamed out; and Bourque slunk back to his jilted municipal party.

8 Pointe-Claire's Bill McMurchie had a good explanation in the *Montreal Gazette* of 6 August 2003 as to why conferring legal status on boroughs was important: "Anything short of that will be subject to amendment by the next [mega]city administration or even this administration." One only need look at Montreal's police department, which had alternated between major centralization and decentralization projects with nearly every

change in police chief over the years, McMurchie said. Reform, he said, "is cyclic. It's like El Niño."

9 Suzanne Caron, the Mount Royal borough mayor, wrote about this period, saying it was the lack of debate and the weak decentralization that caused her to quit Tremblay's party. See her op-ed piece in *Le Devoir* 18 June 2004.

10 The term was not new, even on this side of the Atlantic. Louis Bernard, in his October 2000 report, *Regroupements municipaux dans la région métropolitaine de Montréal: recommandations du mandataire*, talked of "municipal councillors who fill the role of borough mayor." I, rather ungenerously, called them "mayorettes."

11 This bill was called Bill 33. Curiously, Harel, five years later, said to *La Presse* (17 February 2009), "The modification of the charter transformed the [mega]city into a federation of quasi-cities. And Gérald Tremblay resigned himself to this modification." In fact, the Tremblay Plan (as Minister Fournier himself called it) was adopted holus-bolus as Bill 33, much to Tremblay's pleasure. See "Tremblay Gets What He Wanted," *Le Devoir* 13 November 2003, "Quebec Goes Ahead with the Tremblay Plan," *La Presse* 14 November, and "Tremblay All Smiles over 2-Tier City," *Montreal Gazette*, 14 November 2003. Harel's comment about Bill 33 is interesting. Back in 2000, she had said she was ready to implement the original Bernard Report, which recommended a more decentralized megacity than Bill 33, but since the mayors did not rally to it, she went for the very mildly decentralized city that Bill 170 created in 2002.

12 *La Presse* 14 November.

13 Montreal City Hall's press release, 15 August 2003 and the document "Montreal: Une ville à réussir ensemble" adopted by Montreal City Council 4 September 2003 (my collection).

14 By 22 October, Janiszewski had started to rethink things; on radio station cjad, he was quoted as saying he would "openly start campaigning for demergers" within Tremblay's party and that "Tremblay was breaking an election promise by not supporting demerger." Janiszewski has always been almost obsessively concerned about doing the right thing.

15 Six of the seven city councillors quit (or were thrown out of) his party. The seventh, Anne Myles, replaced the late Roy Kemp, a member of Tremblay's party. Twelve of the thirteen borough councillors quit his party. The other replaced a member of Tremblay's party who died. Tremblay also lost a city councillor, Jeremy Searle, from the former City of Montreal, but not to demerger. Finally, two members of Tremblay's party, Irving Grundman and René Dussault, were thrown out because of corruption charges laid against them.

16 Tremblay's complaint was in the form of an open letter to Minister
    Fournier, and in various comments given to *La Presse*, *Le Devoir*, *Le Jour-
    nal de Montréal*, and the *Montreal Gazette*, all 18 June 2003. On CBC on
    the same date, Tremblay was quoted as saying "the Liberals' bill is totally
    irresponsible. They are making demergers too easy by not setting a min-
    imum level for voter turnout." In a letter to the *Gazette*, 23 April 2004,
    Tremblay denied everything, writing that it was "completely erroneous to
    state" that he lobbied for a minimum turnout.

17 *La Presse* and *Le Devoir*, 10 July 2003.

18 From the transcript of the parliamentary hearings for Bill 9, 11 September
    2003.

19 SOM polls taken 17–28 September 2003.

20 It also might have something to do with the 34 per cent of Bostonians
    over the age of twenty-five with a university degree compared with Mont-
    real's 20 per cent – the lowest rate of just about any North American
    metropolitan region.

21 *La Presse*, 5 November 2003.

22 *Montreal Gazette*, 11 December 2003.

23 Ibid., 20 November 2003. In their embryonic form, Coalition Montreal
    did publish an op-ed piece back in June (*La Presse*, 11 June 2003) that
    shed some light on their pro-megacity position. Unfortunately, there was
    little of substance and a lot of unsubstantiated assertions ("for too long,
    territorial divisions and parochialism have seriously slowed down the
    development of Montreal"). They continually confused Montreal Island
    with the metropolitan region, which is twice as large. For example, the
    authors said that it was necessary that "all the residents of the Island con-
    tribute their fair share of projects, facilities, and other responsibilities of a
    metropolitan nature," but they then incongruously admitted the metropol-
    itan region included Laval, the north shore, and the south shore. And they
    invoked "international competition" as a raison d'être for the megacity
    but said this competition was among *metropolitan regions*. And, of course,
    they named Boston as one of Montreal's competitors, without mentioning
    that the Boston region has 282 different municipalities and does very well
    without a megacity.

24 The actual audited 2003–04 operating cost increase for megacity Mont-
    real was only 2.8 per cent. But the 2004–05 increase was 5.7 per cent,
    compared with an inflation rate of 2.2 per cent.

25 *La Presse*, 9 January 2004. See City of Montreal's *Budget 2002*, 291, and
    Budget 2004, 151.

26 City of Montreal press release, 26 January 2004.

27 These amounts include a tax-free allowance of $13,000 for which no
   receipts are needed – the tax-free feature alone is worth roughly an additional $4,000. After a deafening uproar, Saint-Leonard finally paid their
   borough councillors "only" $49,000.

28 *La Presse*, 23 February 2004.

29 The total amount Tremblay's party spent to fight demerger in 2004 turned
   out to be $800,000, according to their financial statements. Roughly half
   of the party's revenues came from the megacity in the form of an allotment (see the *Montreal Gazette*, 2 April 2005). Tremblay's party advanced
   $395,000 to the No committees during the actual 20 June 2004 referendum
   campaign, which amount was reimbursed (presumably by Quebec). This
   $395,000 advance contrasts with the $142,000 the Yes side spent during
   the referendum period. (Confusingly, the director-general of elections maintained that the No side spent $612,000 and the Yes side spent $387,000.)

30 According to *Montreal Gazette* columnist Henry Aubin, the megacity
   communications chief (who served as a senior party worker in Tremblay's
   election campaign) told him one hundred megacity staff were involved in
   communications, not counting support personnel, in addition to these outside contractors.

31 From Tremblay's closing speech to his party's convention, as reported in
   The Suburban, 25 February 2004.

32 *Le Messager LaSalle*, 25 January 2004. This was clearly not true: the
   boroughs were not given back legal status, control over local funding,
   or ownership of their facilities – all of which would be recuperated by a
   demerged municipality.

33 The last door-to-door enumeration, where two people went door-to door
   collecting eligible voters' names, had been conducted in 1995. Since then
   the lists had been updated by means of drivers' licences, medicare cards,
   and information from the Public Curator and Immigration Canada.

34 *Montreal Gazette*, 17 April 2004.

35 *Le Droit*, 19 March 2004.

36 *Le Journal de Montréal*, 30 March 2004. Actually, the word "proactive"
   in its current meaning has been used in English since 1946 and in Quebec
   French since at least 1983. "Industrial clusters" has been used in Quebec
   in French and in English since at least 1980.

37 The Department of Municipal Affairs must have been burning the midnight oil to come up with that definition of "dismember." As the Rom-
   ans would have put it, *redolet lucernum*: it smelled of the lamp. Actually,
   it smelled of bias. The linguist Marie-Éva de Villiers said about the choice
   of the word *démembrement* (dismemberment), "It could have a dissuasive

effect on voters. It makes you think of a dissection! ... You can't say it's wrong, but it's certainly not a standard meaning. It's a technical term from administrative law" (*La Presse* 22 April 2004). Guy Bertrand, the linguistic ayatollah of Radio-Canada, was quoted as saying that *démembrement* is rarely used in municipal matters and not all dictionaries accept that use; furthermore, he said the word *défusion* (demerger) was perfectly acceptable. Benoît Melançon, professor of literature at the Université de Montréal, said the use of *démembrement* was clearly "tendentious and has a strong smell of partiality," noting that even the Office de la langue française approved the use of *défusion*. Noëlle Guilloton of the Office said the use of *démembrement* suggests there was a whole that existed beforehand. *Défusion*, in other words, was a more accurate term (*Le Devoir*, 23 April 2004). Minister Fournier did not agree with any of these expert opinions. For him, *démembrement* was "more precise legally" and *défusion* "was not a French word."

38 *L'Actualité*, 1 April 2004.

39 Analysis Group, *Les Défusions municipales au-delà de leurs aspects comptables: une perspective économique à long terme*.

40 All headlines were for 22 April 2004: "100 millions pour 'démembrer' Montréal"; "Douche froide pour la banlieue"; "Note salée pour les anciennes villes"; "La défusion sera plus catastrophique que ce que prédit Secor, dit Tremblay"; and "Le vrai prix des défusions."

41 *La Presse*, 14 May 2004. The predicted demerger cost for the whole Island of Montreal all of a sudden went from $100 million to $60 million, thanks to my correction.

42 This is a weighted average. The government gave the tax increases resulting from a demerger in 2004, when the real demerger date was already set for 2006. Because of a progressive uniformization of tax rates within the megacity, the tax bills of many of the former suburbs were to increase in those two years, thereby reducing the difference between staying and going. SECOR admitted that the government, by using 2004 rather than 2006 as a demerger date, had artificially increased the "cost" of demerger (*Montreal Gazette*, 19 June 2004).

The government did something else to dissuade people from demerging. It did not allow any demerged municipality the advantage of a yearly cap to ease sudden tax increases – a cap for which they were eligible if they stayed – so the full brunt of paying for agglomerated services hit right away. This is why the long-term effect of demerging was much less than the immediate. Lastly, the government figures inexplicably did not include the effect of debt on the tax bill of a demerged municipality.

43 Using figures on page 38 of the SECOR study, one can readily calculate that the average employee of the former City of Montreal delivering local services earned 12 per cent more than the equivalent in the former suburbs – and that was after two years of integration. Therefore, any former city not demerging would see their employee cost rising to those of the former City of Montreal.

44 With the former City of Montreal included, the breakdown was roughly 31 per cent central and 69 per cent local. (These costs do not include interest charges.)

CHAPTER EIGHTEEN

1 Bizarrely, in *Le Devoir*, 22 May 2004, Fournier said the law that governed the division of powers between the agglomeration council and the municipalities (Bill 9) would not be modified by Charest's government, nor by "future governments."

2 *Le Devoir*, 18 May 2004.

3 Ibid., 19 June 2004

4 Ibid., 18 June 2004

5 See *La Presse*, 3 and 4 May 2004; *Montreal Gazette*, 3 May 2004; *Le Devoir*, 3 May 2004.

6 Government of Quebec, l'Institut de la statistique du Québec. *Enquête sur la rémunération globale.*

7 Calculated from borough by borough remuneration data provided in SECOR Conseil, *Étude sur les conséquences et les coûts éventuels de la reconstitution des anciennes muncipalités*, 38.

8 *La Presse*, 1 June 2004.

9 Ibid., 20 May 2004.

10 Ibid., 17 June 2004.

11 *Montreal Gazette*, 26 June 2004.

12 Ibid., 22 June 2004.

13 Editorial, *Montreal Gazette*, 17 June 2004.

14 The number given in the government's report was 59 per cent. See SECOR Conseil, *Étude sur les conséquences et les coûts éventuels de la reconstitution des anciennes municipalités*, 74.

15 The 2001 audited financial statements found tabulated on the Department of Municipal Affairs' website give the total apportionments paid by the suburbs to the MUC as $376.8 million, to which one should add the amount paid to the City of Montreal for water (the supply of which is now an agglomeration responsibility) $21.9 million, for a total of $398.7

million of shared costs. On total tax revenues of $989.7 million, that's 40 per cent.

16 The 2001 audited financial statements give the total apportionment paid by Westmount to the MUC as $21.6 million and the amount paid to the City of Montreal for water as $1.8 million, for a total of $23.4 million, which, on total tax revenues of $39.8 million, gives 59 per cent. The 70 per cent number comes from the SECOR report.

17 Not to mention the 300–400 blue collars who created a massive downtown traffic jam during three hours with 150 city vehicles in September 2003. It affected 35,000 people. On 17 September 2007, the union lost a class action suit taken against them and were forced to donate $1.16 million to charity. In September 2010 the union was also condemned to pay $2 million in punitive damages in a class action suit to do with their illegal strike during a December 2004 ice storm that turned sidewalks into ice rinks.

18 This accusation was described by most commentators as Tremblay's "KO punch." I didn't feel it that way at the time; in fact, the tape of the debate shows me shaking my head vigorously at that assertion. I knew that Westmount paid its blue collars less. A press release the next day correcting Tremblay's figures did nothing to change the media's verdict. According to the Institut de la statistique du Québec's *Enquête sur la rémunération globale,* updated 4 February 2005, the "global remuneration" for the average City of Montreal blue collar worker was $35.19 per hour in 2001; for Westmount, it was $32.15.

I can trace my decision to get out of politics in January 2005 at least partially to my debates with Tremblay – not because I was disappointed that I had "lost," because, morally, I was far from sure that that was the case. No, it was because I finally realized that politics has nothing to do with telling the truth and doing the right thing. The media treat it as a show. Political debates today are not too far removed from spectacles in ancient Rome. The media are out for blood, no matter how it is caused. That Tremblay used incorrect figures concerned the media not one whit. He scored a KO. End of story. A further illustration: three years later during the 2007 provincial elections, Boisclair, Dumont, and Charest put on a debate. To me it was clear that Charest kept his cool and presented good arguments and rebuttals. Dumont was all over the place. And then out of the blue Dumont produced a 2004 internal government memo that he maintained warned the Charest government of the poor state of a Laval highway overpass that finally did collapse in 2006, killing five people. "You have hidden that from Quebecers," Dumont accused Charest, proud of his self-described "atomic bomb." As it turned out, the memo in question was warning of a problem that had nothing to do with the collapse and, later on in the same document, said that no intervention was needed. But the damage was done. Charest was destabilized. Who won the debate according to both the media and the polls? Dumont, of course. The fact that he clearly misrepresented the contents of the memo seemed to be perfectly acceptable, along with the fact that he brandished the memo in front of the cameras in violation of the agreed-on rules of debate. All's fair in political love and war.

19 *La Presse*, 22 May 2004.

20 *Montreal Gazette*, 13 June 2004.

21 For every seven Quebec municipalities merged, there were referenda in three of them, with only one of them actually demerging.

22 I think this unlikely. Interestingly, in rural Quebec, the No sometimes won, not by the failure of the Yes to get 35 per cent but by outvoting the Yes. In nine villages, the No vote was over 35 per cent; in each case, the No beat the Yes.

23 It would have taken only one-third of non-voters to be in favour of demerger to bring the pro-demerger camp up to 50 per cent of all residents on the Saint-Laurent voting list.

24 In many cases, corporations were added to the voting lists, which inflated them even more, frustrating attempts to reach 35 per cent of Yes votes. Corporate officers generally do not vote.

25 Île Bizard, Masson-Angers, Roxboro, and Sillery. Roxboro missed by 74 ballots. Île Bizard, with 33.7 per cent voting Yes, missed demerging by only 133 ballots. The Île Bizard demerger committee took the director-general of elections (DGE) to court, accusing their board of revision of an unjustified refusal to eliminate over 400 clearly ineligible names on the voters' list. In May 2008, the Quebec Superior Court agreed, and annulled the Île Bizard referendum results but did not declare a demerger win, saying that was a political matter. Interestingly, the DGE did testify there is a plus-or-minus 5 per cent error on any permanent electoral list. In my experience, it is more like 10–15 per cent. Subsequently, the Quebec Court of Appeal reversed the lower court's decision and the Supreme Court of Canada refused to hear the case.

26 *La Presse*, 16 July 2004.

27 As Henry Aubin pointed out, homeowners were also disproportionately represented among the municipalities that demerged: no one talked of a "homeownership split." (In fact, the Jewish population voted disproportionably in favour of demerger: no one talked of an "ethnic" split, or a "religious" split.)

28 *La Presse*, 3 December 2004.

29 Government of Quebec, *Comité de transition de l'agglomération de Montréal, 2ième rapport d'étape*, 20 October 2005.

30 In the appendix I present my own calculations that remove mass transit and other expenses that had nothing to do with the creation of the megacity. I still got the same 21 per cent increase from 2001 to 2005: well over double the rate of inflation. The transition committee's document also calculated that, for purely local costs (i.e., no mass transit, police, and wastewater treatment costs) the increase was $411 million, or 22.4 per cent – two and a half times the rate of inflation.

31 This 37 per cent is based on internal cost increases only; I have removed mass transit cost increases, as they were not part of the megacity's operations.

32 It must be kept in mind that much of this amount did not ease former Montrealers' tax burden; quite a bit of it helped lower taxes in former suburbs that decided to remain in the megacity.

33 Bill 9 was the basis on which people had voted to demerge or to stay in the megacity.

34 The final report – see Government of Quebec, *Comité de transition de l'agglomération de Montréal, Rapport d'activités* – came out 21 December 2005, after eighteen months of work. It contained stinging rebukes directed at both the City of Montreal and the Quebec Department of Municipal Affairs for their lack of cooperation in the committee's work. Regarding the government's penchant for centralization and uniformization, the authors said that places such as Boston, Atlanta, and Seattle prove that heterogeneous metropolitan regions work better; besides, it's attitudes, not the particular architecture of municipal structures that count. One thing is for sure: you don't mobilize societies by "diktats and excommunication." Contrasting the Anglo-Saxon tradition (so well described by de Tocqueville), which values the intimate connection of people to their community, to the French centralist view of the state, the authors wrote in their conclusion that regrettably the Department of Municipal Affairs espoused the latter with an evangelical drive that precluded any other consideration: "It's the raison d'être of the state that takes precedence and which does not put up with the decentralization that gives real power to local communities. The demerger referenda came and upset this vision of how things should be. Democracy won a round, but Jacobin attitudes are well implanted. The reconstitution of municipalities whose sizes vary a lot among themselves and particularly in relation to the central municipality offends their Cartesian reflex." This was not your usual milquetoast government-commissioned report.

35 A year later, at least one commentator was getting tired of Tremblay's pot-hole promises that seemed to be just as empty (and unfilled) as the potholes themselves. Wrote James Minnie in the *Montreal Gazette*, "Stop announ-cing pothole campaigns and street-cleaning programs as if they were Nobel Prizes. You're not doing us a favour by keeping the streets clean – you're only doing your job." In late January 2007, the number-one campaign issue, cleanliness, blew up in Tremblay's face when Charles Lapointe, the intelligent, sophisticated, and dedicated head of Tourisme Montréal, com-plained in a Board of Trade speech that the Montreal was ugly, unkempt, graffiti-ridden, and just plain dirty. The board's president, Isabelle Hudon, taking careful aim at the messenger, accused Lapointe of "auto-flagella-tion." Mayor Tremblay, who stormed out of the room, next day essentially called for Lapointe to resign: "Toute vérité n'est pas bonne à dire en pub-lic." (Not all truths should be said in public.) The two finally made up.

36 In the lead-up to the March 2007 elections, the ADQ, the PQ, and the Lib-erals were each polling 30 per cent of the decided voters.

37 The *Montreal Gazette* had already expressed their "hard cheese" line in an earlier editorial 4 March 2006: "We have only limited sympathy for the demerged municipalities, whose voters acted in imprudent anger rather than in cold self-interest when they chose in the referendums of June 2004 to 'take back' their cities. The rules of the demerger game meant in fact they were taking back only the empty shell of self-government ... The sub-urbanites brought their current problems upon themselves. They were warned the Liberal government of Quebec had imposed ridiculous rules for demerger, and an undemocratic structure for the aftermath. They knew the game was fixed, but they were so angry they dealt themselves in all the same. Now they are complaining they have lost." The message being that, for the *Montreal Gazette*, the unfair agglomeration situation would obtain unchanged forever and therefore all the forcibly merged municipal-ities should have stayed merged. History has proven the *Gazette* wrong. The agglomeration council has evolved and will continue to evolve, albeit slowly. And having complete local control of tax revenues for local servi-ces – which the demerged municipalities have – is just a fading memory for the former municipalities that remained in the megacity. In fact, they have seen their powers reduced.

38 Of these 1,000 positions, 250 were in the management ranks. Expected savings were to be around $300 million. This cost-cutting plan was put in effect for 2007, 2008, and 2009. See City of Montreal (Montreal Transition Committee), *Pour relancer la Métropole,* 31 January 2007 (revised February 2007).

39 It was not really pointed out that the new Toronto taxation powers were capped at $50 million, a fraction of Toronto's overall revenues. Also, in order to get these new revenues, Toronto had to cut its own spending by some $150 million.

40 It was on 12 June 2008 that Montreal, the Island suburbs, and Minister Normandeau all agreed to a pact, the terms of which would be enshrined in the final version of Bill 22.

41 Not long after Bill 22 was tabled, Tremblay personally started taking over certain responsibilities of the Ville-Marie borough, which included downtown Montreal. The mayor of Ville-Marie, Benoit Labonté, took great umbrage at these initiatives, resigning from both Montreal's executive committee and Tremblay's party. Tremblay had created an instant adversary – or, really, he had merely exposed one. In November 2007, after getting rid of the man, Tremblay made it clear he wanted to get rid of the job: he said the mayor of Montreal should also be the mayor of the Ville-Marie borough. This was nothing new: Tremblay had said the same thing back in 2003; Labonté had recommended it (only when he was in his previous job of president of the Board of Trade, mind you); and even Louis Bernard had suggested it in his 2000 report. It was generally accepted that keeping downtown as an independent borough was dysfunctional and even potentially dangerous if ever its mayor were in the opposition party.

42 In addition, certain Montreal buildings and activities that the agglomeration had been funding were repatriated to become the exclusive responsibility of the City of Montreal.

43 *La Presse*, 1 August 2009.

44 *Montreal Gazette*, 11 March 2009.

45 Actually, the 2000 Bernard Report recommended even more borough powers than Tremblay had put through later. The only reason Harel did not agree to the Bernard proposals was that we mayors (especially the writer) did not accept them, wanting no merger at all. "It's the mayors' fault," she had said when explaining why the Bernard proposals were not turned into law in late 2000.

CHAPTER NINETEEN

1 Even though Montreal charged some fifteen suburbs for bulk water based on estimated consumption, a number of those municipalities installed meters just to avoid being overcharged by Montreal. As for residential consumption, a recent poll revealed that 54 per cent of Montreal citizens are in favour of metered water. Today, alone in North America, Montreal

charges the demerged suburbs for water based on property values, not consumption – which is ecologically and economically as absurd as unmetered electricity or natural gas.

2 In a series of articles on 9 and 10 October 2003, *Le Devoir* posited that part of this "loss" was, in fact, the practice of "pirating" cold water for use in commercial refrigerators and freezers and even in residential air conditioners. A small tube containing the hot refrigerant from a refrigerator is placed within a coil where tap water is allowed to run continuously. The cooling of the refrigerant is absolutely free, as no electricity is involved. And, of course, the water used is "free," not being metered. *Le Devoir* claimed that many restaurants and *depanneurs* (convenience stores) have such devices. A half-inch pipe running continuously would use up 26,000 cubic metres of water per year.

3 Press release, 21 November 2007. Just about all the investment, in fact, was immediate, not over twenty-five years. Originally the contract called for monthly payments over twenty-five years, but it mysteriously got changed somewhere along the way. The $424 million did not include $71 million of subsidies, nor $14 million to the engineering company overseeing the bidding process.

4 According to *La Presse*, 22 April 2009, the FTQ Solidarity Fund was an investor in Simard-Beaudry. In fact, they had invested some $300 million over the years in various businesses run by Accurso. The FTQ is a labour union, the Quebec Workers' Federation.

5 According to Montreal's auditor-general, out of twenty-one different companies that were awarded public works contracts by the City of Montreal from 2006 to 2009, fully 20 per cent of their value went to Catania, and 16 per cent to Simard-Beaudry and Louisbourg Construction (also controlled by Tony Accurso). In the borough of Verdun, twenty-six such contracts were awarded during the same period, and all twenty-six went to Catania. In the borough of Anjou, five such contracts were awarded, and all five went to Louisbourg Construction.

6 *La Presse* later maintained (23 October 2009) that both the president of Group SM and the vice-president of Dessau holidayed together on Accurso's yacht.

7 The $424 was made up of $312 million ($107 million for the meters, $205 million for the 600 chambers), plus $44 million of sales taxes and $68 million of "incidental expenses," such as the command centre and new municipal staff. But these numbers do not include $71 million for subsidies, nor $14 million to BPR for the engineering consulting work that started in 2005. There was no allowance for contingencies either.

8   Cancelling the Génieau contract finally cost some $11 million.

9   Léger had replaced Robert Abdallah, who had resigned in May 2006. In November 2008, Abdallah fetched up as the president of Gastier, a project management and construction firm owned by Simard-Beaudry. Gastier had done work for the city to do with the Génieau contract. Yves Provost, an assistant director-general, also quit the megacity, joining the engineering firm BPR in December 2007, three months before the Génieau contract was signed. Montreal had outsourced to BPR the job of writing specifications and assessing the bids for the Génieau contract. BPR and Dessau had been partners in a number of consortia.

10 There were some heroes. Réjean Lévesque, who until recently was in charge of the megacity's water system and used to run the MUC's wastewater operation, blew the whistle within the hearing of top management, who chose to ignore him. And Lévesque was not alone.

11 *Montreal Gazette*, 27 June 2011.

12 *Le Devoir*, 26 October 2010.

13 Quebec municipal parties are all fabricated around the personality of whoever is currently vying to be mayor. They come and go, and even can be adopted. Louise Harel needed a party as a vehicle to enter the Montreal mayoralty race, and so she just took over Pierre Bourque's old party, which had temporarily been the instrument to further the mayoral ambitions of Benoit Labonté. The fact that this party was notorious for flouting Quebec's electoral law did not seem to bother Harel: it did come with some money in the kitty and a collection apparatus.

14 *La Presse*, 4 June 2009.

15 On 16 June 2009, *La Presse* reported that the Sûreté du Quebec, at Tremblay's request, was conducting its sixth investigation regarding the City of Montreal. The first was in Saint-Laurent (the Catania Group for bribes, the director-general for a trip to Italy, and the two councillors, Irving Grundman and René Dussault, for corruption). The second investigation was in Outremont: the awarding to Dessau of a contract for the intergenerational community centre. The third was a fraud in the City of Montreal's information systems department (*infra*). The fourth was the SHDM scandal. The fifth was the water-management scandal. The sixth had to do with the president of the company redoing the City Hall roof who claimed that the mafia demanded he give $40,000 to two Montreal city councillors if he wanted to continue the work. Five out of the six investigations were still ongoing. Then, on 26 August, *La Presse* reported about a manager in Montreal's public works who resigned after it became known that he and his wife went off on a junket to Italy with a contractor

who dealt frequently with the city. On 9 September, police arrested the former section head of Montreal's information systems, a man who had been fired one year before regarding an $8 million fraud. Even though it is quite normal in a workforce of over twenty thousand to have such problems, the publicity did not help Tremblay's cause.

The headlines didn't stop. On 17 September, *La Presse* disclosed that Tremblay's vice-chairman of the executive committee, André Lavallée, had been involved with the FLQ at the age of nineteen. In 1971 he was caught in a police sting operation when he participated in a robbery of bingo money from a church basement. Lavallée, by far the most competent, respected, and dedicated of Tremblay's team, was devastated. His mistake, of course, was not making the incident public when he first started in municipal politics in 1986, or at the very least, not telling his boss about it. The timing for Tremblay could not have been worse, but he stood by Lavallée. The next day *La Presse* reported that Tremblay's party was being investigated for illegal campaign financing. On 20 October came another *La Presse* story about Montreal's auditor-general investigating an $80 million telephone contract awarded to Telus in 2008.

16 *La Presse*, 25–28 September 2007.

17 *Globe and Mail* and *La Presse*, 16 October 2009.

18 *Montreal Gazette*, 16 October 2009.

19 *La Presse*, 14 and 21 September 2009.

20 *Le Devoir*, 22 October 2009. *Maclean's* magazine (9 November 2009) took its cue from this article and emblazoned its cover with yellow bands screaming out: "Montreal is a corrupt, crumbling, mob-ridden disgrace. What was once Canada's most glamorous city is now a disaster … Even the mayor fears for his safety."

21 In *Le Devoir* the next day, Jean Fortier, the chairman of the executive committee at the time of Pierre Bourque, confirmed that the "brown envelopes" were around in his day, just before Tremblay took over.

22 *La Presse*, 23 October 2009.

23 Linda Gyulai of the *Montreal Gazette* in 2005 reported that, of the 302 companies whose executives or directors gave money to Tremblay's party over the previous four years, 284 got contracts from the megacity.

24 Later on, Bill 15: An Anti-Corruption Act, was passed on June 2011. It was designed "to prevent and to fight corruption." Then there was Bill 35, passed on December 2011: "An Act to prevent, combat and punish certain fraudulent practices in the construction industry and make other amendments to the Building Act."

25 *La Presse*, 15 July 2009.

26 When *Maclean's* magazine came out in September 2010 with a cover story on Quebec, "The Most Corrupt Province in Canada," *Montreal Gazette* columnist Henry Aubin quite rightly rushed to Quebec's defence by writing that the headline should have read: "The Province with the Most Journalistic Success in Unearthing Corruption." In other words, the Quebec press could easily have been doing a better job of sleuthing out instances of corruption than was going on in the rest of Canada. It did not follow that Quebec was "the most corrupt province."

27 *La Presse*, 9 March 2012.

28 In some ways Tremblay won the 2009 election the same way he won the 2001 election. Then, a good number of people could not bring themselves to vote for Pierre Bourque, the father of the megacity; this time, some people just could not vote for Harel, the mother of megacity. The anger against forced mergers had a long half-life.

29 There were some things left untouched. In 2009, Montreal's auditor-general discovered the number and amount of car allowances in boroughs originating in the former City of Montreal were four times those paid in the former suburban boroughs.

30 *La Presse*, 14 October 2009.

31 For the average single-family dwelling in Westmount, for example, property taxes went from $6,185 in 2001 to $9,682 in 2006, a 57 per cent increase before inflation. The 2008 figure was $10,083, a 4 per cent increase from 2006. Clearly, being merged into the megacity cost the Westmount taxpayer, not demerging. And that 57 per cent cost of merger had not exactly been unpredicted. In my last letter as mayor to Westmount citizens dated December 2001, I wrote, "Your taxes will increase by 50 per cent over the next five years or so."

32 *La Presse*, 21 January 2008.

33 Michèle Ouimet's two comprehensive articles about the climate of violence among blue collars appeared in *La Presse* on 22 and 23 January 2008.

34 Ouimet wrote two articles about this climate of violence among firefighters (*La Presse*, 28 and 29 April 2008).

35 According to the Montreal auditor-general's report of 2007, 202 of the 772 employees making more than $100,000 worked for the fire department, and most were unionized fire captains. The overtime cost alone was $19.3 million.

36 Government of Canada, *Tribunal d'arbitrage de différend Ville de Montréal et l'Association des pompiers de Montréal* (1 March 2010).

37 During the hearing, the firefighters union maintained that their 2006 overall remuneration was $45.33 per hour, while their Toronto counterparts

got $55.06. Not so fast, said the City of Montreal representatives: we calculate it as $46.48 for Montreal and $46.23 for Toronto. One thing was clear: it costs a lot more to keep up with the Joneses in Toronto, where the 2008 GDP per resident was 21 per cent higher than Montreal and the 2005 median family income was 34 per cent higher. In 2012, the average cost of Montreal firefighters' remuneration is $123,428 – but that does include the cost of pension benefits to retired firefighters.

38 Unlike their fire brethren, Montreal police make roughly the same as police in other Quebec municipalities. In June 2010, another arbitration tribunal (Government of Canada, *Tribunal d'arbitrage de différend Ville de Montréal et la fraternité des policiers et policières de Montréal Inc.*) awarded the Montreal police a permanent 1.5 per cent "metropolitan premium" by virtue of their more difficult and dangerous responsibilities (such as street gangs and terrorism) compared to the rest of Quebec. In July 2012, this premium will climb to 3 per cent. Average global remuneration of police in 2007 was $85,720 in Montreal and $84,661 for the median of sixteen other Quebec police forces. In 2012, the average cost of Montreal police remuneration is $138,168 each – but that does include the cost of pension benefits to retired police.

39 For example, firefighters who worked in Baie d'Urfé had no training in fighting fires in high-rises, as Baie d'Urfé had none.

40 Part of this increase was owing to the provincial government's fire-safety risk coverage plan that dictated fire safety standards throughout Quebec – the cost, of course, to be picked up by the municipal taxpayer.

41 Complementary Information Booklet, p. 48, City of Montreal Budget, 2003.

42 Ibid.

43 According to the *Globe and Mail* of 12 May 2011, 80 per cent of public-sector employees in Canada have a workplace pension plan, and only 25 per cent of private-sector employees do. Kevin Gaudet of the Canadian Taxpayer Foundation has described (*Montreal Gazette*, 16 April 2010) a "growing pension divide in Canada. On one side of the divide are those who enjoy generous pensions. On the other side are those who pay for them." Gaudet maintains that two-thirds of Canadians have no pension plan at all.

44 Things aren't much better in the United States, where only 21 per cent of private workers enjoy a defined-benefit pension, whereas 84 per cent of state and local workers do. See *The Economist*, 12 December 2009. According to *The Economist* of 13 February 2010, in the United States, per hour worked, state and local government workers enjoy 34 per cent

higher wages and 70 per cent more benefits than their private-sector counterparts.

45 A year before, Delorme's pension credit was boosted by $400,000 in order to persuade him to stay another three years. He was making $194,000 a year.

46 *Le Devoir*, 26 May 2010.

47 City of Montreal, *Budget 2012*, 115.

48 Back in 2009, the city treasurer had calculated that pension costs alone would jump from $259 million in 2009 to $467 in 2012. See Government of Canada, *Tribunal d'arbitrage de différend Ville de Montréal et l'Association des pompiers de Montréal* (1 March 2010). Costs, in fact, reached $609 million in 2012.

49 In November 2011, to commemorate rather than celebrate the tenth anniversary of the megacity, *La Presse* asked Angus Reid to conduct a similar poll. This poll was much less significant, as the demerged suburbs were excluded and no differentiation was made between the merged former suburbs and the old City of Montreal. In this poll, an equal number of megacity residents said that merger was a good or a bad thing. With the exception of Gatineau, all other Quebec megacities said that their merger was a good thing – but, illogically, none said services had clearly improved since merger; most said they had less control over their decisions and had less for their money. Perhaps resignation had set in.

50 The 18–34 age group, who made up nearly 30 per cent of the respondents, were only 9–25 at the time of the merger and obviously not taxpayers then; indeed, many would not be in a position to judge differences before and after merger. This group was systematically more favourable to the merger and, by their own admission, the group least affected by it. In the same vein, had the poll differentiated between owners and tenants, the results for the former would have been even more negative to merger.

51 Overall and across the Island, the only group in which more residents said the merger was a good thing rather than a bad thing were members belonging to the 18–34 age group. Only 17 per cent of the 34–54 year-olds said merger was a good thing; 59 per cent said it was bad. In the 55–plus group, the numbers were 26 per cent and 65 per cent respectively.

52 If the 18–34 age group is removed, 80 per cent would vote no and 6 per cent vote yes.

53 If the 18–34 age group is removed, nearly twice as many would vote to leave as to stay.

54 *Montreal Gazette*, 5 January 2012.

55 So Tremblay was the mayor of Montreal, chairman of Montreal's exec-
    utive committee, president of the Montreal Metropolitan Commun-
    ity, mayor of the borough of Ville-Marie, and president of the Montreal
    Agglomeration Council.

    Tremblay was not alone in his "big tent" openness. Caroline St-Hilaire,
    who had been a Bloc québécois MP for thirteen years, won the November
    2009 election as mayor of the megacity of Longueuil, but her party won
    only eleven of the twenty-six seats. Mayor St-Hilaire, a month after being
    elected, decided to extend an olive branch to her demerged municipalities,
    inviting the mayors of Brossard and Boucherville to sit on Longueuil's exec-
    utive committee for matters relating to the agglomeration. Unlike the Mont-
    real agglomeration, where the demerged municipalities represent only 13
    per cent of the population and pay 19 per cent of the costs, the demerged
    municipalities in the Longueuil agglomeration make up 40 per cent of the
    population and pay more than 50 per cent of its cost. For nearly three
    years, the demerged municipalities of Brossard, Saint-Hubert, and Saint-
    Bruno had boycotted the agglomeration council meetings, complaining of
    runaway expenses and the "despotism" of the central city, Longueuil.
56 I was a member of this committee and in June came up with budget prin-
    ciples and 2011 spending guidelines that were unanimously adopted.
57 Irving Grundman, René Dussault, Stéphane Harbour, and Frank Zampino.

CONCLUSION

1 According to the Quebec Department of Transport, of all the highway
   structures built in the last one hundred years on the Island of Montreal,
   61 per cent were built in the 1960s and an additional 31 per cent in the
   1970s, for a total of 92 per cent for the two decades.
2 In mass transit matters, the PQ did not stand alone in mastering the fine
   art of budgetary understatement with their Laval metro extension. The
   AMT's commuter train to Mascouche, which is 51 km long and will have
   11,000 riders a day, had an original price ticket of $300 million in 2006.
   By January 2012, it was up to $715 million. The cost of ensuring that the
   bi-modal (electric and diesel) engines can go through the Mount Royal
   tunnel safely is still unknown.
3 Only 14 per cent of Quebecers now believe that Quebec will become
   independent within thirty years. Support for it remains at 40 per cent,
   however, because only 15 per cent feel that the French language is more
   secure than it was thirty years ago. Still, 77 per cent of Quebecers want a
   moratorium on constitutional debates.

4 SOQUEM, SIDBEC, REXFOR, SOQUIP, Hydro-Québec, and SNA, respectively.

5 *Magazine Forces*, spring 2007. One is obliged to point out that this same favouritism towards a native son (now very much grown) still operates today, without the noble justification that Landry evoked. In 2006 the Liberal government forced the Montreal Transit Corporation to award a contract for 342 metro cars to Bombardier without a call for tenders. The cars were to replace the initial order placed in 1965 that Landry was writing about. The Liberal member for the region where the cars would be manufactured was behind this violation of free trade. In 2008, Alstom, another manufacturer, successfully sued to have its piece of this inflated pie, forming a consortium with Bombardier. In 2010, a third company, CAF, equally successfully sued for the whole order (now at up to 1,053 cars) to be put to public tender. Meanwhile the metro still has no replacement cars. This strong-arming also exquisitely combined inveterate pandering to the regions, the patent lack of punch of the mayor of Montreal – the very thing mergers were supposed to create – and good old-fashioned crass politicking.

6 In Quebec, $6 billion, versus $3 billion in Ontario in 2007. See *La Presse*, 28 November 2009.

7 What this long-standing policy does is compromise the quality of education by chronic underfunding. When McGill University raised its tuition fees for MBA students from a derisory $3,672 to $29,500 (which would still be a North American bargain), the education minister in Quebec decided to fine McGill $2 million and claw back the fees, having said, "Our responsibility is to ensure that the quality of education is comparable throughout Quebec. It's one of my values and is something we'll continue to defend." A flabbergasted Alain Dubuc, writing in *La Presse*, put the minister's indignation down to a reflex of "egalitarianism, against a background of poorly understood social democracy and beautiful bureaucratic logic. It's so much simpler and clearer when everybody is the same." In another column he wrote, "This value that the minister wants to defend is … the logic of everyone the same. As we well know, it is also one of the lowest common denominator. When one equalizes, it's invariably by going lower." If one replaces the word "education" with the words "local government" in this little story, one can see the similarities to the race to the bottom in Quebec municipal services by dragging them down in the name of egalitarianism and accessibility.

8 Marcel Boyer, *La performance économique du Québec*. The rate of people still working after age sixty-five is 40 per cent higher in Ontario. From sixty to sixty-four, 39.7 per cent are still working in Quebec versus 51.4

per cent in Ontario. From sixty-five to sixty-nine, the ratio is 15.9 per cent (Quebec) versus 22.4 per cent (Ontario). See *La Presse*, 13 January 2010.

9   *La Presse*, 27 February 2010.

10 Ibid., 25 June 2010. Looked at another way, the total Quebec provincial debt was $163 billion in 2009. If one adds Quebec's share of the federal debt ($123 billion), the total debt was equal to 94 per cent of GDP, just behind Iceland at 96.3 per cent and Greece at 102.6 per cent (*La Presse*, 27 February 2010). By 2012, total provincial debt had reached $184 billion, and that does not include pension fund deficits of $29 billion.

11 Government of Quebec, Institut de la statistique du Québec, 2007. If one removes the GDP contributed by public administration, the Montreal Census Metropolitan Region contributed 55 per cent of Quebec's GDP in 2007. (According to Claude Picher of *La Presse*, 16 June 2007, the Montreal metropolitan region accounts for 60 per cent of Quebec's GDP – and climbing.) The Montreal CMR in 2011, according to Statistics Canada, represented 48.4 per cent of Quebec's population.

12 Up until May 2012, the City of Montreal was not even a member of the Union of Quebec Municipalities (the UMQ). Montreal left, along with Longueuil, in November 2004, saying the UMQ "can no longer adequately defend its interests and those of the smaller municipalities at the same time." Bereft of the economic locomotive of Quebec, the UMQ was reduced to being a union of the rest of the province, forced to celebrate the "solidarity of the rural and the urban." The UMQ's president very optimistically maintains that rural Quebec represents 30 per cent of Quebec's GDP. (The UMQ must include many regional cities in that calculation. The Institut de la statistique du Québec gives the GDP produced outside the six Census Metropolitan Regions of Saguenay, Quebec, Sherbrooke, Trois-Rivières, Montreal, and Gatineau as being 26 per cent of the province's total GDP – and that residual territory includes many regional cities such as Drummondville, St Jérôme, and Granby.) During the UMQ's ninety years of existence, the mayors of all sorts of cities, towns, and villages have served as UMQ president, but never the mayor of Montreal. There were forty-five members of the UMQ's Administrative Council, with only twenty-one seats assigned to the "big cities," which, as we have noted, did not include Montreal. "Big cities" are municipalities with a population over 100,000.

13 The current City of Montreal has the same population as the *total* of the next six most populous municipalities in Quebec, which together would have to occupy over eight times Montreal's land area to arrive at that population.

14 Lessard was also named, for five months, minister of agriculture, fisheries, and food in September 2010. Minister Lessard, while worrying about pig and fish farms, had to squeeze in a little time for the Montreal metropolitan region where more than 50 per cent of the province's GDP is produced. Six months later, federal minister Christian Paradis, responsible for the Montreal region in federal cabinet and another native of Thetford Mines, warned against his political opponents' "metropolitan obsession."

15 *La Presse*, 7 February 2007.

16 Ibid., 8 and 9 February 2007.

17 According to the Fraser Institute, Montreal had 19 per cent of Canada's corporate headquarters in 1990; by 2008, the proportion was down to 15 per cent. Calgary was the big winner over the 1990–2008 period, going from 9 per cent to 16 per cent, for the first time taking over second place from Montreal. *The Economist*, 20 March 2010, reported that of the twenty biggest companies in Canada, ten are in Toronto and six in Calgary.

18 According to demographer Marc Termote, quoted in *Le Devoir*, 8 April 2010, mother-tongue French will drop from 50 per cent to 43 per cent by 2016, and home-language French will drop from 54 per cent to 43 per cent in 2031.

19 Serge Belley of ENAP, as quoted in *La Presse*, 15 May 2010.

20 "Tremblay ne fait pas tendence," *La Presse*, 26 November 2011.

21 See http://www.bdso.gouv.qc.ca/pls/ken/p_afch_tabl_clie?p_no_client_cie=FR&p_param_id_raprt=1506.

22 *Montreal Gazette*, 23 March 2010.

23 Ibid., 10 February 2010.

24 Metropolitan Montreal is more densely populated only because of the Island. In fact, at 5,000 residents per square kilometre, Westmount is the most densely populated municipality in the region. The City of Montreal weighs in at about 4,400 and Montreal Island at about 3,800. The six largest municipalities in Quebec (aside from Montreal) average out at only 540 residents per square kilometre. So, compared with the rest of Quebec, Montreal Island is indeed very densely populated. But the smaller cities in Quebec should not be the yardstick. The City of Toronto has a similar population density to the City of Montreal, for example.

25 Montreal Metropolitan Community, *Perspective Grand Montréal*, May 2010. The municipalities that had population growth from 2006 to 2011 that was over 18 per cent were places like Mirabel, L'Assomption, Mascouche, Vaudreuil, Oka – all far away from the Island of Montreal.

26 Ibid., October 2009. Only one-third of Montreal's labour force does not drive to work. Average commuting times (both ways), according to the

Toronto Board of Trade, are eighty minutes in Toronto and seventy-six minutes in Montreal – yet fifty-seven minutes in Boston.

27 *Montreal Gazette*, 13 February 2008.

28 CLDS and CDECS and the like. There are also thirty-six CLES (Local Employment Centres) in the region.

29 In 2009, megacity executive committee member Luis Miranda was responsible for a huge dossier: economic development (and the social economy). Almost as a throwaway responsibility, he was also in charge of "services to citizens." Now, it is true that the boroughs are supposedly responsible for local services, but still: only one of a dozen members of the megacity's executive committee had, as almost as an afterthought, the job of "services to citizens." In a nutshell, that is what is wrong with the megacity. When it comes to delivery of what the city is there to do, the buck should start and stop with the mayor.

30 The merged municipalities on Montreal's south shore experienced a less dramatic difference in size, but some were forced to contribute for the first time to regional services, which greatly affected their tax bills. Saint-Bruno, for example, had not been preconditioned by an urban community providing regional services.

31 Howard Chernick (2001) has found for most local government services, including police, fire, and garbage collection, "minimum costs per capita are reached at a low level of population – around 20,000 – and remain constant until about 250,000, and then begin to increase." Robert L. Bish maintains that "beyond populations of 160,000, no economies of scale have been found for any service" in amalgamated cities. Both quotes may be found in Askin et al., *Assessing Montreal's Amalgamation*, 18n.

32 In 2000, Harel, through her representative Louis Bernard, did exactly the same thing as Tremblay did in 2003 and for exactly the same reason, to rally the obstinate municipalities such as Westmount into willingly embracing the megacity. Had the Bernard Report been incorporated into Bill 170, it would have given a similar degree of decentralization to that in Tremblay's plan – in some respects, even more. When I led a number of mayors to reject the Bernard Report, Harel went ahead with a more centralized megacity, blaming its centralization on the likes of me, still, however, praising the idea of boroughs, which she called "little homelands."

33 City of Montreal, 2010 Budget. Once handled by the MUC, they are now under the agglomeration council's responsibility. Some services such as firefighting and water supply have been added since the MUC days, but most such services are self-sufficient and need little or no additional administration.

34 C. Northcote Parkinson noted that in 1914 the Royal Navy (the world's largest navy at the time) had sixty-two capital ships and 146,000 officers and men. By 1928, the navy had only twenty capital ships and 100,000 officers and men – but the number of admiralty officials had increased from 2,000 to 3,569 during the period. "A magnificent navy on land," someone called it. It got worse: admiralty staff grew to 8,118 by 1935 and to 33,788 by 1954, by which time the Royal Navy was a shadow of its former self.

35 *La Presse*, 21 May 2009. There is the opposite problem for city administrators. One of the many reasons that megacities are inefficient has to do with top-level remuneration. In the private sector, the larger the company, the more the CEO gets – mind you, to a fault. In large corporations, CEOs are obscenely overpaid; the CEO of the Royal Bank and the CEO of CN not long ago each got $22 million in just one year. And in 2010, the top 100 executives in Canada made an average of $8.4 million, 189 times the average wage. But at least there is recognition that larger companies are more complex to run and require the best managers. In the public sector, this pattern only holds very weakly. The chief administrative officer of a city with a $4 billion budget will make possibly twice the salary of a CAO in charge of a $40 million budget. The CEO of a corporation with sales of $4 billion can earn twenty times whatever the CEO of a smaller corporation gets. While this difference is unjustifiable – few managers are worth twenty times another – many are worth more than double what another makes. This is not an apologia for the excesses of the private sector; it is a plea for fairer management remuneration all around.

36 The following is a list of various US and Canadian municipalities, their population in millions, and the number of city councillors: Houston (1.9), 14; Phoenix (1.3), 9; Philadelphia (1.5), 17; San Diego (1.2), 8; Dallas (1.2), 14; San Francisco (0.78), 11; Boston (0.6), 13; Edmonton (1.0), 13; Toronto (2.5), 44.

37 When Montreal had four experimental public meetings of the executive committee in 2004, only a handful of people showed up.

38 The take was down a bit over previous elections, thanks to the climate of scandal that caused donors to be more circumspect. The care and feeding of a municipal party is more than just what is spent at election time: in total, the three Montreal municipal parties managed to go through $5 million for the 2009 year, nearly two-thirds of it from the public purse.

39 In my world, the fire department would revert to individual municipalities.

40 In Montreal the relationship between the mayor and the police chief is very different from that in the rest of North America, especially in the

United States. Mayor Tremblay rarely meets with the police chief, whereas, for example, I was told that the mayor of Boston called his chief every morning at dawn.

41 Potable water is technically a product, but its supply is treated as a service by its users.

42 Commuter trains used to be run by the Montreal Island's mass transit board, rather than by the current government-dominated AMT.

43 Over the past two years, of the roughly five hundred questions that citizens have posed to me as Westmount's mayor during public question period, only one or two had to do with truly regional matters. Even questions about policing – a regional service – had to do with local traffic. Citizens' letters, emails, and phone calls were no less local. Yet regional costs make up 64 per cent of Westmount's property tax bills – or 54 per cent of total revenues. It's as if citizens regard regional costs as something beyond their ken and control.

44 Askin et al., *Assessing Montreal's Amalgamation*.

APPENDIX

1 In 2001, aggregate budgeted spending of all Island municipalities, including the MUC, amounted to $3,061 million; in 2005, the megacity budgeted $3,552 million (and spent $3,513 million). Once interest, mass transit, health and welfare, and Hydro Westmount costs are removed from each number, the difference between them becomes $473 million. The Montreal inflation rate from 2001 to 2005 was 8.9 per cent.

The following comments are for accounting cognoscenti only: (a) The 2001 figure came from the consolidated 2001 budget numbers found in the megacity's 2002 budget document. No consolidated – Montreal, suburbs, and the MUC – 2001 financial statements are available. Besides, the nearly thirty 2001 individual financial statements were loaded down with winding-up expenses. (b) Some may feel I have failed to remove extraordinary spending increases in water distribution and garbage collection during the period. My rejoinder is that, first, there were some services for which increases were below inflation; second, the point was to show a propensity for massive spending increases, regardless of who paid the bills; and third, the water supply improvement generally went to the capital account, except for $35 million of consulting fees in 2005. (c) I removed the contribution to the Montreal Transit Corporation as it was not under the megacity's bureaucratic control, did not change in size, and did not suffer from diseconomies of scale. (d) The one-time costs of actually setting up the megacity had been taken from surplus.

2 See the City of Montreal, Montreal Transition Committee, *Nouvelle Ville de Montréal: Budget 2002*, which (p. 26) gives more details regarding the $65 million savings, including $4 million to be saved through the unification of the fire departments and $11.5 million to be saved by eliminating "pay-as-you-go" financing for capital projects. In other words, by borrowing and therefore spreading capital costs over many years, short-term savings were projected. Ultimately the Montreal practice of borrowing for everything just added to interest costs and put the city deeper in debt. Of course it cost much more in the long run. This document also claims (p. 59) a reduction in executives from 365 to 250, cutting payroll for this group by 20 per cent.

3 Comité de transition de Montréal, *Présentation du cadre budgétaire de la nouvelle ville de 2002 à 2006*, 19 April 2001.

4 See City of Montreal, *Budget 2002, Cahier d'information économique et budgétaire*, 60, and *Budget 2005*, 148.

5 In 2005, $35 million of the fees was earmarked for consultants to advise the city on what to do about water-management. But, again, this kind of thing was part of the megacity problem. With such an extraordinary growth in administration, could not someone do the work in-house? This liberal use of outside professionals was part of the scandal that broke in 2009 regarding the $356 million water-management contract.

6 See City of Montreal, *Budget 2002, Cahier d'information économique et budgétaire*, 60, and *Budget 2005*, 148.

7 According to the City of Montreal in *Portraits démographiques: La dynamique migratoire de l'agglomération de Montréal*, citing numbers from the Institut de la statistique du Québec, Montreal Island's population grew 1.1 per cent between 2001 and 2005. Even this very mild increase in population would not immediately result in an increased demand on services.

8 *Le Devoir*, 29 November 2002. Tremblay averred this on the occasion of the tabling of the 2003 budget.

9 This number is the sum of four numbers buried within the City of Montreal's *Budget 2002, Budget 2003, Budget 2004*, and *Budget 2005*, 47, 54, 147, and 101 respectively. Mind you, interest on city investments diminished too, but that was on the revenue side.

10 In the City of Montreal's *Budget 2005*, 21, we can read the following: "The owners of residential properties, on average, have not undergone any tax increase between 2002 and 2005, excluding the agreed effort to improve the water system."

11 The actual numbers give an even bigger increase. The number I used is the revised one that adds $26.7 million of revenue to the budgeted 2001

tax take of those municipalities (including, curiously, Montreal) who were naughty enough to grab a bunch of surplus lying around in their last year of existence to reduce their tax bill as a kind of going-out-of-business present to their taxpayers. They did not trust the megacity with this cash.

12 See City of Montreal, *Budget 2009* (p. 9 of the annex).

13 Trent's First Law of Municipal Taxation states (tongue only slightly in cheek), "The smaller the geographic area, the greater the tendency of property taxes to reflect the actual consumption of local services."

14 Montreal and a few other municipalities introduced slightly higher rates for apartments in 2001. They had and have a very long way to go to achieve any sort of fiscal equivalency.

15 City of Montreal, *Harmonisation de la fiscalité*, 5.

16 Ibid., 21. I find this hard to believe.

17 This is using the Statistics Canada figure of 2.9 persons per dwelling for Montreal houses and 1.6 for apartments, the latter being a conservative number as it refers to apartment buildings over five storeys rather than for apartment buildings with over five *units* – which is the basis for the tax information.

18 This refund, introduced in 1978, currently costs Quebec some $235 million a year.

19 The residential tax rate was obtained by removing the "water and services tax" from the calculation of the official global rate 1990 to 2000. The per capita numbers and the commercial tax rate refer to the year 2001 and were derived from the City of Montreal's *Fiscalité municipale: Compétitivité sur le plan régional et stratégie*.

20 Technically, a tiny fraction of this tax was actually related to consumption, which was measured by the three thousand water meters Montreal had installed for industrial users. These metered taxpayers paid a tariff that was only triggered in excess of "normal consumption." In the 1990s this tariff raised only $1–2 million dollars a year, rising to $3.6 million in 1999 – some 2 per cent of the overall "water and services" tax that year. As for residential taxpayers, they paid nothing for water: in 1987, Mayor Jean Doré abolished the $60 per-dwelling water tax that had been introduced in 1983, which in turn had replaced a previous water tax based on real estate value. The $60 figure represented roughly 20 per cent of the actual cost of supplying water to each dwelling.

21 The business tax was charged at the rate of 12.99 per cent of rental value, and the "water and services tax" was charged at 8.89 per cent.

22 In fact, once debt was removed, the majority of Montreal suburban municipalities had residential tax rates higher than Montreal's, at least in 1999

and 2000. In the event of merger, debt remained with the taxpayers of the former municipalities; therefore, the free-of-debt rate was much more telling.

23 Montreal's official global rate in 2001 was 43 per cent higher than the overall suburban rate, or 21 per cent once the "water and services" tax was removed. What is interesting is that in the City of Montreal, *Fiscalité municipale*, the overall 2001 residential rate in Montreal is calculated to be only 15 per cent higher than in the suburbs.

24 See City of Montreal, *Rapport financier annuel 2001*, 64.

25 After a number of decades, even these old debts would be paid off, and there would be only one tax rate including debt.

26 In fact, in the SECOR Conseil report *Étude sur les conséquences et les coûts éventuels de la reconstitution des anciennes municipalités*, the authors calculate that Montrealers would actually save money if the megacity were dissolved in 2006.

27 In 2001, with revised property assessments, Verdun still had the highest rate, but Westmount took over the lowest spot, with a rate half that of Verdun's. By 2008, however, while Montreal West had the highest tax rate, it was only 56 per cent greater than the municipality with the lowest, Baie d'Urfé.

28 In 2000, taxpayers (both homeowners and businesses) in the former City of Montreal paid 58 per cent of the $2.4 billion of property taxes collected on the Island of Montreal, with suburban taxpayers paying the remaining 42 per cent. By 2005, Montreal's share had dropped slightly to 56 per cent of all Island property taxes, which had reached $2.7 billion by then. However, even this small drop had nothing to do with the merger. It was simply a direct result of a reduction in the former Montrealers' relative share of total Montreal Island taxable real estate values from 52 per cent in 2000 to 50 per cent in 2005. All figures were calculated from the financial statements (as posted on the Department of Municipal Affairs website) of the individual Island municipalities in 2000 and of the megacity in 2005.

29 The November 2000 simulations were not a flash in the pan. Even back in October 1999, the Department of Municipal Affairs had done a study (published in *La Presse*, 22 January 2000), showing a 6.5 per cent increase in taxes for the owner of the average former City of Montreal single-family dwelling subsequent to merger, or $185 per house. Montreal came out worse than nineteen out of the twenty-six suburban municipalities.

30 The government's number-crunchers in November 2000 had calculated that $0.84 of Montreal's $2.19 residential tax rate was simply servicing

the city's debts and pension plan deficits. By law, these amounts remained with the taxpayers of the former City of Montreal subsequent to merger. Mysteriously, this amount was cut in half by the time the megacity was actually born. An earlier government study (published in *La Presse*, 22 January 2000) used $0.77 out of a residential tax rate of $2.03 for debt. The differences between the two studies came about owing to the new real estate assessments in 2001. The earlier study used the old assessments, the later study the new.

31 See Marcel Côté et al., *Une métropole à la hauteur de nos aspirations*. Total megacity spending is given as $4,047 million for the year 2002 (74). Deducting the costs of mass transit ($767m), interest ($491m), and capital works ($381m), health and welfare ($103m), and Hydro Westmount, it nets out at $2,286 million. Inflation is given as 12.6 per cent (77), or $288 million. So the net 2002 operational spending in 2008 dollars is $2,574 million. For the year 2008, total spending on the Island of Montreal is given as $5,580 million. Deducting the costs of mass transit ($1,153m), interest ($472m), capital works ($760m), health and welfare ($109m), and Hydro Westmount, one gets a net 2008 operational spending of $3,063 million. The increased spending is therefore $489 million after inflation. My own calculations for 2001 (not 2002) to 2008 give a $509 million increase after inflation.

32 See ibid., 77.

33 Ibid., 75

34 Budgeted numbers rather than actual results were used, as, starting in 2007, the financial statements incorporated the operations of "subsidiaries" such as the mass transit board, and therefore the reported results cannot be compared to prior years. Health and welfare costs are included in miscellaneous spending; before 2000 they were negligible, and after that date they were a delegated responsibility from Quebec. Hydro Westmount costs make up the rest of miscellaneous spending. I would like to thank Luc Ménard, CA, who verified my numbers used in this graph.

35 This plateau needs explaining. For the years 2001–03, the budgeted spending increase was 4.9 per cent, which was not far off the inflation rate increase of 4.5 per cent for the two years combined. The megacity was on its best spending behaviour – on paper. However, the actual results came in – very unusually – over budget. This revealed a strong upward pressure on costs, which became evident in the 2004 and 2005 budgets with their combined spending increases of 10.6 per cent versus a 4.2 per cent inflation increase. Overall, the first four years gave a 16.0 per cent spending increase versus inflation at 8.9 per cent.

36 The number of employees is in person-years and came from Champagne, *Analyse des statistiques provenants des prévisions budgétaires 1991, villes de la* CUM, City of Verdun (my collection); the 1991 and 2001 MUC budgets; the 1991, 2001, and 2012 Montreal budgets; and the Department of Municipal Affairs website (2012). Headcounts do not include employees working for the "*sécurité du revenu*" department and the mass transit corporation, nor are any elected officials included.

37 Bourque and Danyluk did have some help in their determination to cut overall costs. Both the MUC and the former City of Montreal took pension fund contribution "holidays" starting in 1999 to comply with Quebec's edict to cut remuneration costs by 6 per cent (without touching salaries) in order to pay for the province's $375 million downloading bill. These holidays, which continued well into the 2000s, reduced pension costs by some $83 million a year by the year 2002: the police pension contribution holiday saved some $39 million in 2001 alone.

38 Numbers from the 1991 and 2001 MUC budgets and the City of Montreal 2012 budget. Population figures used were 1,775,871; 1,812,723; and 1,886,481, respectively. It is true that the number of "civilian" Police Department employees increased after the merger – as a way to supplement the proportionately diminished number of uniformed police officers – bringing the total ratio closer to the 2001 figure. In theory, it meant more cops on the beat and fewer cops filling in forms. I remain sceptical of whether the desired effect was achieved; most likely, it simply means more people are doing paperwork than before. All counts are "person-years," not simply "positions." Today's effective numbers have to be reduced by the 100–130 on pregnancy leave – the price of progress. The 1991 and 2001 numbers include the uniformed security guards in the metro who were absorbed into the police in 2007, and the 2012 numbers include a detachment of thirty-five at Trudeau airport.

39 The 2012 figure is swollen by pension fund contributions, about a third of which funds retirees' benefits as opposed to those of current employees.

40 From Champagne, *Analyse des statistiques provenants des prévisions budgétaires 1991, villes de la* CUM, City of Verdun; MUC budgets for 1991 and 2001; City of Montreal, *Budget 2002*; and the 2012 budgets of Montreal Island cities. With the help of economist Jean-Pierre Aubry, *La Presse*, 19 January 2011, calculated the average overall employee remuneration for the City of Montreal (not Montreal Island) as $100,805. The City of Quebec weighed in at $77,834, and the Government of Quebec at $62,739.

Bibliography

Many of the sources referred to in the notes have not been published in the formal sense, and others have never been published. These materials include speeches, press communiqués, committee and cabinet minutes, orders-in-council, internal government reports, letters, periodicals, pamphlets, newspaper articles, TV and radio transcripts, and other such materials. They are in the author's possession but not necessarily generally available, and so do not appear in this bibliography.

Askin, Molly, Daniel Leopold, Shin Changho, and Wang Yang. *Assessing Montreal's Amalgamation: A Canadian Case Study Approach*. Organization for Economic Co-operation and Development 2003.

Association les bibliothèques publiques du Québec. *La réorganisation municipale: Des enjeux de taille pour le réseau des bibliothèques publiques du Québec*. 1 December 2000. See http://www.bibliothequespubliquesduquebec.ca/archives/memoireFusion2006.pdf.

Aubin, Henry. *Who's Afraid of Demergers?* Montreal: Véhicule Press 2004.

Aubry, Jean-Pierre. *Un meilleur suivi des règles de gouvernance par nos gouvernements pour une meilleure gestion des municipalités*. Assises de l'Union des municipalités du Québec, 13 May 2010.

Bélanger, Yves, Robert Comeau, François Desrochers, and Céline Métivier, eds. *La CUM et la région métropolitaine*. Québec: Presses de l'Université du Québec 1998.

Benjamin, Jacques. *La Communauté urbaine de Montréal: Une réforme ratée*. Montreal: Les éditions de l'aurore 1975.

Bernard, Louis. *Regroupements municipaux dans la région métropolitaine de Montréal: Recommandations du mandataire*. Montreal, 11 October 2000. http://www.mamrot.gouv.qc.ca/pub/organisation_municipale/historique/reorganisation_loi170/rap_mand_ber.pdf.

Bish, Robert L. "Local Government Amalgamations: Discredited
    Nineteenth-Century Ideals Alive in the Twenty-First." *Commentary*
    (C.D. Howe Institute) 150 (March 2001).

Bouchard, Pierre. "Espaces urbains et coexistence des langues: Montreal."
    Terminogramme 93/94 (Summer 2000).

Boyer, Marcel. *La performance économique du Québec: Constats et
    defis*. Montreal, February 2001. See http://www.cirano.qc.ca/pdf/
    publication/2001RB-01.pdf.

Boyne, George. "Population Size and Economies of Scale in Local Govern-
    ment." *Policy and Politics* 23, no. 3 (1995): 213–22.

Brûlé, Michel. *Anglaid*. Montreal: Michel Brûlé 2009.

Champagne, Gilles. *Analyse des statistiques provenants des prévisions
    budgétaires 1991, villes de la* CUM, City of Verdun. n.d.

– *Analyse des statistiques provenants des prévisions budgétaires 1999,
    villes de la* CUM. City of Verdun, 7 July 2000.

City of Laval. *Mémoire de la ville de Laval [au] Forum de consultation sur
    une commission de développement de la métropole.* 5 November 1996.

City of Montreal. *Annuaire statistique de l'agglomération de Montréal.* 2007.

– *Annuaire statistique des ménages et des logements de la Ville de
    Montréal.* 2003.

– *Budget 1999.* Adopted 17 December 1998.

– *Budget 2000.* Presented 19 November 1999.

– *Budget 2001.* Adopted 18 December 2000.

– *Budget 2002.* Adopted 18 December 2001.

– *Budget 2003.* Approved 28 November 2002.

– *Budget 2004.* Approved 17 December 2003.

– *Budget 2005.* Adopted 14 December 2004.

– *Budget 2006.* Approved 20 January 2006.

– *Budget 2007.* Adopted 18 December 2006.

– *Budget 2008.* Adopted 12 December 2007.

– *Budget 2009.* Adopted 11 December 2008.

– *Budget 2010.* Adopted 13 January 2010.

– *Budget 2011.* Adopted 15 December 2010.

– *Budget 2012.* Adopted 13 December 2011.

– *Commission for the Study of the Metropolitan Problems of Montreal,
    General and Final Report.* January 1955.

– *Document de réflexion déposé par la Ville de Montréal devant le
    Groupe de travail sur Montréal et sa région.* 6 November 1992.

– *Fiscalité municipale: Compétitivité sur le plan régional et stratégie.* Sec-
    retariat of the Sommet de Montréal 2002, 23 April 2002.

– *Harmonisation de la fiscalité*. Secretariat of the Sommet de Montréal 2002, 23 April 2002.
– *Mémoire de la Ville de Montréal présenté à la Commission sur la fiscalité et le financement des services publics*. September 1996.
– *Montréal, ville d'affaires*. April 1993.
– *Montréalités* 18, no. 4 (June 1999).
– *Portraits démographiques: La dynamique migratoire de l'agglomération de Montréal*. November 2009.
– *Portraits démographiques: La dynamique migratoire de l'agglomération de Montréal*. January 2011.
– "Présentation du cadre budgétaire de la nouvelle ville de 2002 à 2006." 19 April 2001.
– *Profil sociodémographique: Westmount*. November 2010. http://ville. montreal.qc.ca/pls/portal/docs/PAGE/MTL_STATS_FR/MEDIA/ DOCUMENTS/PSD_WESTMOUNT.PDF.
– *Pour relancer la Métropole: Des solutions nouvelles et durables*. 31 January 2007 (revised February 2007).
– *Rapport des activités 2009: Service de sécurité incendie de Montréal*. April 2010.
– *Rapport du vérificateur général au conseil municipal de Montréal sur les aliénations d'immeubles de la société d'habitation et de développement de Montréal (SHDM) du 1er janvier 2007 au 24 november 2008*. 27 April 2009.
– *Rapport du vérificateur général au conseil municipal et au conseil d'agglomération sur la vérification de l'ensemble du processus d'acquisition et d'installation de compteurs d'eau dans les ICI ainsi que de l'optimisation de l'ensemble du réseau d'eau de l'agglomération de Montréal*. 21 September 2009.
– *Rapport du vérificateur général au conseil municipal et au conseil d'agglomération pour l'exercice terminé le 31 décembre 2009*. 17 May 2010.
– *Rapport financier annuel 2000*. 30 March 2001.
– *Rapport financier annuel 2001*. 28 March 2002.
– *Rapport financier annuel 2002*. 16 June 2003.
– *Rapport financier annuel 2003*. 31 March 2004.
– *Rapport financier annuel 2004*. 24 March 2005.
– *Rapport financier annuel 2005*. 31 March 2006.
– *Une île, une ville: Pour une métropole dynamique*. 26 May 1999.
City of Montreal, Montreal Transition Committee. *Nouvelle Ville de Montréal: Budget 2002*. Presented November 2001.

City of Quebec. *Deux villes, une communauté: Pour une capitale unifiée, prospère et dynamique*. March 2000.

City of Vancouver. Property Tax Policy Review Commission. Final Report. September 2007.

City of Westmount. *Westmount: A Heritage to Preserve*. Westmount, 1991.

Coalition pour un Québec des régions. *Montréal dans la perspective d'un Québec décentralisé*. October 2008.

Collin, Jean-Pierre. "La gestion métropolitaine et les relations ville-banlieue à Montréal, depuis 1830." INRS-Urbanisation, Culture et Société, 2001.

– *Municipal Organization in Canada*. September 2003.

– "La réforme de l'organisation du secteur municipal au Québec: La fin ou le début d'un cycle?" *Organisations et territoires* (August 2002).

Conference of Montreal Suburban Mayors. *L'organisation du soutien au développement économique dans la région métropolitain de Montréal*. 29 August 1996.

Conseil régionale de développement de l'Île de Montréal. *Notes de présentation du budget 1996–97*. 22 March 1996.

– *Plan stratégique 2000–2005, Bilan des réalisations et interventions*. 24 September 1999.

Côté, Marcel, Claude Séguin, André Boisclair, André Delisle, Gilles Godbout, and Diane Wilhelmy. *Une métropole à la hauteur de nos aspirations: Rapport réalisé par le groupe du travail sur les enjeux de gouvernance et de fiscalité de Montréal*. March 2010.

Cox, Wendell. *Local and Regional Governance in the Toronto Area: A Review of Alternatives*. 10 January 1997. http://www.publicpurpose. com/tor-demo.htm.

de Tocqueville, Alexis. *Democracy in America*. Vol. 1. 1835: reprint, London: Folio Society 2002.

Deloitte & Touche Consulting Group. *Impacts des navetteurs sur les finances municipales*. Montreal: January 1998.

Derksen, Wim. *Municipal Amalgamation and the Doubtful Relation between Size and Performance*. Local Government Studies, November/December 1998.

Desbiens, Jacques. *Fusions municipales et économies d'échelle: Mythes et réalités*. Le groupe Jacques Desbiens 1999.

Doré, Jean. "Présentation du mémoire de la ville de Montréal au Groupe du travail sur Montréal et sa région." Montreal, 11 March 1993.

Dufour, Christian. *Les Québécois et l'anglais: Le retour du mouton*. Montreal: Les Éditeurs réunis 2008.

Goldsmith, Stephen. *The Twenty-First Century City*. Lanham: Rowman & Littlefield 1999.

Government of Canada. *Royal Commission on Bilingualism and Biculturalism*. Ottawa: Queen's Printer 1965.

– *Tribunal d'arbitrage de différend [Dispute arbitration tribunal]. Sentence arbitrale partielle. Ville de Montreal et l'Association des pompiers de Montréal*. 1 March 2010.

–*Tribunal d'arbitrage de différend … Ville de Montréal et la fraternité des policiers et policières de Montréal Inc*. 21 June 2010.

Government of Quebec, Assemblée nationale du Québec. *Débats de l'assemblée nationale*. http://www.assnat.qc.ca/archives/travaux.htm

– *Les orientations du gouvernement en matière d'aménagement du territoire*. 1994.

– *Décentralisation: Un choix de société*. 1995.

– *Pacte 2000: Rapport de la Commission nationale sur les finances et la fiscalité locales* (Bédard Report). Quebec: Les publications du Québec, April 1999.

– *Politique de soutien au développement local et régional*. April 1997.

– *Problématique des villes-centres*. 8 December 1994.

– *Projet de loi no. 92*, Éditeur official du Québec 1996.

– *La réorganisation municipale: Changer les façons de faire pour mieux servir les citoyens* (Harel's white paper). April 2000.

–*Vers une commission de développement de la métropole: Document de consultation*. 1996.

Government of Quebec, Comité de transition de l'agglomération de Montréal. *2ième rapport d'étape*. 20 October 2005.

– *Rapport d'activités*. 21 December 2005.

Government of Quebec, Comité Québec-municipalités. *La revalorisation du pouvoir municipal: Bilan et suivi de la nouvelle fiscalité*. 20 October 1982.

Government of Quebec, Department of Municipal Affairs. *Report of the Study Committee on the Montreal Urban Community* (Hanigan Report). 30 May 1973.

Government of Quebec, Direction générale du patrimoine. *Maison Braemar*. November 1981.

Government of Quebec, l'Institut de la statistique du Québec. *Enquête sur la rémunération globale: Municipalités locales de 10 000 et plus de population 2001*. Updated 4 February 2005.

– *Rémunération des salariés: État et evolution comparés*, 2010. Fourth quarter, 2010.

Government of Quebec, l'Office québécois de la langue français. *Caractéristiques linguistiques de la population du Québec*. May 2005.

– *Rapport sur l'évolution de la situation linguistique au Québec 2002–2007*. March 2008.

Government of Quebec, Ministère de la Culture et des communications. *Le Français langue commune: Enjeu de la société québécoise*. Rapport du comité interministériel sur la situation de la langue française. March 1996.

Government of Quebec, Ministère des Affaires municipales. *Bilan de l'impact financier du réaménagement du partage des responsabilités Québec-municipalités de 1992*. Presented to the Table Quebec Municipalités, 5 May 1995.

– *La fiscalité des organismes municipaux au Québec*. November 2004.

– *Le financement et la fiscalité des organismes municipaux au Québec*. August 2009.

– *Municipalité* (special edition). 1984.

– *Muni-express*. April 1997.

– *Partage des responsabilités Québec-municipalités: Vers un nouvel équilibre*. 14 December 1990.

– *Rapport annuel de gestion 2001–2002*. October 2002.

– *Rapport annuel de gestion 2002–2003*. October 2003.

– *Repenser les relations avec les municipalités*. 9 December 2004.

– *Le regroupement des municipalités: Un choix judicieux*. 1993.

– *Répertoire des expériences de tarification*. 1995.

– *Le relevé des interventions municipales à caractère supralocal (1997) de la Communauté urbaine de Montréal et de la région*. (Also known as *Les inventaires des équipements, infrastructures, services, et activités à caractère supralocal des régions métropolitains de recensement*). 15 September 1997.

L'urbanisation au Québec. (Castonguay Report). 13 February 1976.

Government of Quebec, Ministère des Affaires municipales et de la métropole. *Cadre d'aménagement et orientations gouvernementales pour la région métropolitaine de Montréal*. June 2001.

Problématique de la région métropolitaine de Montréal: Présentation au Comité des priorités. 30 March 1999.

Government of Quebec, Ministère des Affaires municipales et des régions. *Les territoires du Québec et la décentralisation gouvernementale*. 2005.

Government of Quebec, Ministère des Affaires municipales, Direction des politiques fiscales et économiques. *Comparaison: Taux de taxation et compte de taxes moyen d'une résidence unifamiliale. Valeurs 2001,*

*pacte fiscal, sans économies de regroupement et plafonnement à 5%
annuellement dans des cas de hausses de taxes.* 15 November 2000.

Government of Quebec, Travail Québec. *La présence syndicale au Québec
en 2010.* April 2011.

Gubbay, Aline. *A View of Their Own.* Montreal: Price-Patterson 1998.

Gubbay, Aline, and Sally Hooff. *Montreal's Little Mountain.* Westmount:
Trillium Books 1979.

Hamel, Pierre J. "Le 'Pacte fiscal' entre le gouvernement du Québec et les
municipalités: La raison du plus fort est toujours la meilleure." *Organisations et territoires* (Autumn 2002).

Hanson, Elizabeth Ida. *A Jewel in a Park.* Montreal: Véhicule Press 1997.

Horak, Martin. "Governance Reform from Below: Multilevel Politics and
the "New Deal" Campaign in Toronto, Canada." Global Dialogue Series, No. 4. Nairobi: UN-Habitat 2008.

Husock, Howard. "Why Bigger Local Government Isn't More Efficient:
The Case for Breaking up Cities." Speech given at the Omni Hotel,
Montreal, 18 May 2001. http://www.iedm.org/30500-lets-break-up-the-
big-cities?print=yes.

Isin, Engin F., and Joanne Wolfson. "The Making of the Toronto Megacity:
An Introduction." Working paper, Urban Studies Programme, York University, 1999.

Kitchen, Harry. "Municipal Finance in a New Fiscal Environment." *Commentary* (C.D. Howe Institute) 147 (November 2000).

Kushner, Joseph. "The Effect of Urban Growth on Municipal Taxes." *Canadian Public Administration* 35, no. 1 (1993): 94–102.

Kushner, Joseph, Isidore Masse, Thomas Peters, and Lewis Soroka. "The
Determinants of Municipal Expenditures in Ontario." *Canadian Tax
Journal* 44, no. 2 (1996).

Lachance, Renaud. *Analyse du fardeau fiscal relatif en impôts fonciers et
taxes municipales entre le Québec et l'Ontario.* Montreal, 21 July 1997.

Landry, Bernard. "Montréal, l'espoir!" *Forces.* Distributed in *La Presse*, 19
June 2007.

– *Symposium sur la société québécoise et les Autochtones.* Quebec, 26
March 2002.

Langelier, Richard. *Le cadre juridique applicable au processus de défusion
des villes québécoises ayant fait récemment l'objet d'une fusion forcée.*
2001.

Lévesque, René. *Pointe de Mire* (magazine), 3 July 1971.

Levine, Allan, ed. *Your Worship: The Lives of Eight of Canada's Most
Unforgettable Mayors.* Toronto: James Lorimer 1989.

Levine, Marc V. *La reconquête de Montréal*. Montreal: VLB editeur 1997.

– "Usage du français, langue commune." In *Le français au Québec: 400 ans de vie*, edited by Hélène Duval, Pierre Georgeault, and Michel Plourde, 366–78. Québec: Éditeur officiel du Québec 2000.

Linteau, Paul-André. *Histoire de Montréal depuis la Confédération*. Montreal: Boréal 2000.

Mackay, Charles. *Extraordinary Popular Delusions and the Madness of Crowds*. Foreword by Andrew Tobias. 1841; reprint, New York: Harmony Books 1980.

MacKay, Donald. *The Square Mile: Merchant Princes of Montreal*. Vancouver: Douglas & McIntyre 1987.

Magnusson, Warren, and Andrew Sancton. *City Politics in Canada*. Toronto: University of Toronto Press 1985.

Marsan, Jean-Claude. *Montreal in Evolution*. Montreal: McGill-Queen's University Press 1981.

Martin, Fernand. "Impact budgétaire de la création en 1998 de la nouvelle ville de Toronto." Montreal: Comité de transition de Montréal 2001.

Montreal Metropolitan Community. *Perspective Grand Montréal*. October 2009.

– *Perspective Grand Montréal*. May 2010.

Montreal Urban Community. *Rapport du Conseil de sécurité publique, préparé sous la Présidence de M. le Juge Jacques Coderre*. 26 August 1970.

– *Extrait du procès-verbal d'une séance du comité exécutif tenue le 27 mai 1999*.

– *2000 Financial Report*. Audited 15 March 2001.

Montreal Urban Community, Police Department. *La répartition des effectifs dans les postes de quartier en 2000*. 20 April 2000.

Municonsult. *Les regroupements municipaux sur l'île de Montréal*. Montreal: Union des Municipalités de Banlieue sur l'Île de Montréal (commissioned by the City of Westmount), October 1999.

Paillé, Michel. *Diagnostic démographique de l'état de la francisation au Québec*. Montréal: Commission de consultation sur les pratiques d'accommodement reliées aux différences culturelles, 2007.

Paquin, Daniel J., and Jean-François van der Plancke. *Nomination de la ville de Westmount: Quartier historique d'importance nationale à la Commission des Lieux et Monuments Historiques du Canada*. Ottawa: June 2000.

Parizeau, Jacques, chairman. *Rapport de la Commission d'étude sur les municipalités*. Montreal: Union des municipalités du Québec November 1986.

Peddle, Francis K. *Cities and Greed*. Ottawa: Canadian Research Committee on Taxation 1994.

Petit, Patrick; Marc VanAudenrode, Pierre-Yves Crémieux, and Philip Merrigan (of the Analysis Group). *Les Défusions municipales au-delà de leurs aspects comptables: Une perspective économique à long terme*. Montreal, 14 April 2004.

Petrelli, Robert. *Scénarios de réforme des institutions locales et régionales au Québec*. Prepared for la Commission nationale sur les finances et la fiscalité locales, 28 January 1999.

Plunkett, Thomas J. *Urban Canada and Its Government: A Study of Municipal Organization*. Toronto: Macmillan 1968.

Poitras, Lawrence A. *La défusion municipale au Québec*. Montreal, 17 March 2003.

Pratte, André. *Aux pays des merveilles*. Montreal: VLB éditeur 2006.

Prémont, M.-C. "La fiscalité locale au Québec: De la cohabitation au refuge fiscal." *McGill Law Journal* 46 (2001).

Prévost, Robert. *Montréal, a History*. Toronto: McClelland & Stewart 1993.

Proulx, Marc-Urbain. *Les territoires du Québec at la décentralisation gouvernementale*. 2005. See http://crdt.uqar.ca/documents/CRDT%20-%20 Rapport%20MAMR%20-%20Territoires%20et%20d%E9 centralisation.pdf.

Rassemblement des Citoyens et des Citoyennes de Montréal. *Équité fiscale et nouvelles ressources pour Montréal et sa région*. March 2000.

Raymond Chabot Martin Paré, Comptables agrées. *Montréal International, États financiers au 30 septembre 1997*. 4 December 1997.

Saly, Hélène. *Old Westmount*. Westmount: Westmount High School 1967.

Sancton, Andrew. *Governing Canada's City-Regions*. Montreal: Institute for Research on Public Policy 1994.

– *Governing the Island of Montreal: Language Differences and Metropolitan Mitics*. Berkeley: University of California Press 1985.

– *The Limits of Boundaries*. Kingston and Montreal: McGill-Queen's University Press 2008.

– *Merger Mania: The Assault on Local Government*. Kingston and Montreal: McGill-Queen's University Press 2000.

– "Municipal Mergers and Demergers in Quebec and Ontario." Colloque sur les réalisations du gouvernement Charest." 9–10 December 2005.

– *La Réorganisation du gouvernement local au Canada depuis 1975*. Toronto: ICURR Press 1991.

- "Les villes anglophones au Québec: Does It Matter That They Have Almost Disappeared?" *Recherches sociographiques* 45 (2004): 441–56.

Scowen, Reed. *Time to Say Goodbye: Building a Better Canada without Quebec.* Rev. ed. Toronto: McClelland & Stewart 2007.

Schnobb, Philippe. *Faire-part pour mariages forcés.* Lanctôt éditeur 2001.

SECOR Conseil. *Étude sur les conséquences et les coûts éventuels de la reconstitution des anciennes municipalités.* March 2004.

Siemiatycki, Myer. "The Municipal Franchise and Social Inclusion in Toronto: Policy and Practice." Inclusive Cities Canada, October 2006. http://www.inclusivecities.ca.

Slack, Enid. *Easing the Fiscal Restraints: New Revenue Tools in the City of Toronto Act.* 21 February 2005. http://www.rotman.utoronto.ca/iib/ITP0507.pdf.

Sweeney, Laureen. *Polishing the Jewel.* Westmount: City of Westmount 1995.

Udy, John. *The Death and Life of de Maisonneuve Blvd.* Canadian Institute of Planners, October 1976.

Union of Quebec Municipalities. "Questionnaire de l'UMQ sur les orientations des parties politiques." 7 July 1994.

Vaillancourt, Gilles. "Présentation du mémoire de la Ville de Laval devant le Groupe de travail sur Montréal et sa région." Laval, 25 March 1993.

van Nus, Walter. *Montreal Metropolis, 1880–1930*, edited by Isabelle Gournay and France Vanlaethem. Toronto: Stoddart 1998.

Index

Accurso, Tony, 475, 478, 481, 483
Action démocratique du Québec
(ADQ), 468. *See also* Dumont,
Mario
Adams, Dyane, 359
Adessky, Irving, 407, 410
agglomeration council: demerged
cities boycott, list demands,
468–9; Harel, Trent say cannot
last, 450; Montreal accused
of shifting costs to, 468; more
powers of which will devolve on
demerged cities, 450; changes to
(Bill 22), 469–70; proportion of
property taxes go to, 455; transition committee's recommendations, 467
Allard, Danielle, 362, 364
Allaire, Yvan, 342
Alliance Quebec, 41
amalgamation. *See* mergers
AMT (Agence métropolitaine de
transport): beginnings, 124;
Island nominee refused, 140–1
Analysis Group Report, 447
anglophone. *See* language/culture;
mergers: linguistic integration
Anjou. *See* Miranda, Luis

annexation. *See* mergers
Applebaum, Michael, 363, 389,
601n44
Arvida, 9
assessments. *See* mergers: fiscal
equity
Association of Elected Officials
for Demerger, 407, 443. *See also*
demergers: referendums
Atkinson, Gordon, 42
Aubin, Henry, 149, 151, 343, 382,
425, 467, 503, 516
Auf der Maur, Nick, 247
Auger, Michel C., 336, 408, 416,
438–9

Baciu, Ovide, 298
Baie-Comeau, 172, 263, 412
Baie d'Urfé (Baie-D'Urfé on 2006
reconstitution), 51, 308, 354,
405, 461; Bourque visits, 335.
See also Myles, Anne
Bastien, Francine, 359
Beaconsfield, 51
Beaudoin, Jean-Marc, 502
Beaudoin, Laurent, 248, 342
Beaudoin, Louise: admits will lose
votes, seat, owing to mergers,

Dorval, City of. *See* Yeomans, Peter

Dorval Island, 177n, 404–5

downloading: amount, 22, 172, 261, 579n63; announced, 165; Bédard Report, 241–3; central-city preferred treatment, 172; challenged in court, 174, 262; definition, 96; divide and conquer, 172–3; first wave under Liberals, 97–100; Harel eliminates, to get UMQ to be pro-merger, 280–2; mayors' legal challenge, 581n34; NO campaign, 171–2; paid by real estate value, 169; paid by remuneration roll-back, 166–8; paid by school busing bill, 168–9; Pierre Bourque's attitude, 580n14; Quebec renounces, 91; second wave under PQ, 165–76; third year, 261–2; waste of energy, 175–6. *See also* mergers: fiscal equity, Ryan Reform

Drapeau, Jean, 40, 138, 158, 185, 199, 202, 225, 228–9

Drouilly, Pierre, 452–3

Dubuc, Alain, 198, 482, 500, 627n7

Duchesneau, Jacques, 112, 113, 228

Dumont, Mario, 184, 418, 468

Duquette, Charles, 227

Durocher, Ginette, 315, 345, 387, 410, 415, 437, 441

Durrett, Lamar, 248

Eloyan, Noushig, 152, 225

Equality Party, 41, 162

Erickson, Arthur, 65

ethics. *See* corruption

Felardeau, Pierre, 48

Feldman Report, 347

Ferland, Roger, 114

Fillion, Martial, 479, 479n

Finn, Sean, 386

fire department: Bernard suggests Island-wide, 293, 303; merge all Island brigades under MUC, 139, 256

fiscal equity. *See* mergers: fiscal equity

Forcillo, Sammy, 152–3

Fortier, Jean, 197, 226, 622n21

Fortier, Yves, 248, 344

Fortin, Pierre, 447

Foster Wheeler Ltd. *See* Waste Management Board

Fournier, Jean-Marc, 608n58; agglomeration powers immutable, 450; execrable voting lists, 445; minimum turnout for demergers, 426–8; only partial demergers, 432–3

Fox, Francis, 126

FQM (Fédération Québécoise des Municipalités), 170

Francoeur, Jacques, 64

francophone. *See* language/culture

Fraser, Graham, 77

Fréchette, Guy, 343–4

Frulla, Liza, 151, 155, 184

Gadbois, Francine, 437

Gagliano, Alfonso, 340–1

Gagnon, Alain-G., 452–3

Gagnon, Lysiane: anglos in Quebec cabinet, 42; demerger and language, 452; low calibre of Montreal politicians, 14, 514; megacity apathy about demergers, 457–8; Poitras Report, 416